A PROJECT OF THE

Mesorah Heritage Foundation

BOARD OF TRUSTEES

RABBI DAVID FEINSTEIN
Rosh HaYeshivah, Mesivtha Tifereth Jerusalem

ABRAHAM BIDERMAN

JOEL L. FLEISHMAN
First Sr. Vice President, Duke University

JUDAH I. SEPTIMUS, ESQ., C.P.A.
President, Atlantic Land Title & Abstract, Ltd.

JAMES S. TISCH
President, Loews Corp.

RABBI NOSSON SCHERMAN
General Editor, Artscroll Series

RABBI MEIR ZLOTOWITZ
Chairman

INTERNATIONAL BOARD OF GOVERNORS

JAY SCHOTTENSTEIN *(Columbus, OH)*
Chairman

STEVEN ADELSBERG	STEPHEN SAVITSKY
RABBI RAPHAEL B. BUTLER	FRED SCHULMAN
YOSEF DAVIS *(Chicago)*	ELLIOT SCHWARTZ
REUVEN D. DESSLER *(Cleveland)*	HERBERT E. SEIF *(Englewood, N.J.)*
BENJAMIN C. FISHOFF	BERNARD SHAFRAN
HOWARD TZVI FRIEDMAN *(Baltimore)*	NATHAN B. SILBERMAN
MICHAEL GROSS, MBE *(London/Herzlia)*	SOLI SPIRA *(Jerusalem/Antwerp)*
SHIMMIE HORN	ALAN STAHLER
LESTER KLAUS	A. JOSEPH STERN *(Edison, N.J.)*
EZRA MARCOS *(Genève)*	MOSHE TALANSKY
RABBI MEYER H. MAY *(Los Angeles)*	ELLIOT TANNENBAUM
ANDREW J. NEFF	SOL TEICHMAN *(Encino, CA)*
BARRY M. RAY *(Chicago)*	JAY TEPPER
KALMAN RENOV	THOMAS J. TISCH
ZVI RYZMAN *(Los Angeles)*	GARY H. TORGOW *(Detroit)*
ELLIS A. SAFDEYE	STEVEN WEISZ
A. GEORGE SAKS	HIRSCH WOLF

TWERSKI on CHUMASH

RABBI ABRAHAM J. TWERSKI, M.D.

© *Copyright 2003 by* Shaar Press
First edition – First impression / November 2003

Cover: *Torah breastplate, courtesy Tiferes Stam, Brooklyn, NY;* **design:** *by Eli Kroen*

ALL RIGHTS RESERVED

No part of this book may be reproduced **in any form,** *photocopy, electronic media, or otherwise — even FOR PERSONAL, STUDY GROUP, OR CLASSROOM USE — without* **written** *permission from the copyright holder, except by a reviewer who wishes to quote brief passages in connection with a review written for inclusion in magazines or newspapers.*

THE RIGHTS OF THE COPYRIGHT HOLDER WILL BE STRICTLY ENFORCED.

Published by SHAAR PRESS
and Distributed by MESORAH PUBLICATIONS, LTD.
4401 Second Avenue / Brooklyn, N.Y 11232 / (718) 921-9000 / www.artscroll.com

Distributed in Israel by SIFRIATI / A. GITLER
6 Hayarkon Street / Bnei Brak 51127 / Israel

Distributed in Europe by LEHMANNS
Unit E, Viking Industrial Park, Rolling Mill Road / Jarrow, Tyne and Wear, NE32 3DP / England

Distributed in Australia and New Zealand by GOLDS WORLD OF JUDAICA
3-13 William Street / Balaclava, Melbourne 3183, Victoria / Australia

Distributed in South Africa by KOLLEL BOOKSHOP
Shop 8A Norwood Hypermarket/ Norwood 2196 / Johannesburg, South Africa

ISBN: 1-57819-391-5

Printed in the United States of America by Noble Book Press
Custom bound by Sefercraft, Inc. / 4401 Second Avenue / Brooklyn N.Y. 11232

Table of Contents

Introduction to Chumash	9

ספר בראשית — Bereishis/Genesis

Introduction to Bereishis/Genesis	14
Bereishis / בראשית	15
Noach / נח	28
Lech Lecha / לך לך	37
Vayeira / וירא	43
Chayei Sarah / חיי שרה	51
Toldos / תולדות	58
Vayeitzei / ויצא	63
Vayishlach / וישלח	70
Vayeishev / וישב	76
Mikeitz / מקץ	85
Vayigash / ויגש	93
Vayechi / ויחי	101

ספר שמות — Shemos/Exodus

Introduction to Shemos/Exodus	111
Shemos / שמות	112
Va'eira / וארא	120
Bo / בא	129
Beshalach / בשלח	136
Yisro / יתרו	145
Mishpatim / משפטים	152
Terumah / תרומה	159
Tetzaveh / תצוה	166
Ki Sisa / כי תשא	174
Vayakhel-Pekudei / ויקהל־פקודי	183

ספר ויקרא — Vayikra/Leviticus

Introduction to Vayikra/Leviticus	191
Vayikra / ויקרא	192
Tzav / צו	199
Shemini / שמיני	206
Tazria-Metzora / תזריע־מצורע	213
Acharei Mos / אחרי מות	224
Kedoshim / קדושים	233

Emor / אמור	243
Behar / בהר	252
Bechukosai / בחקתי	259

ספר במדבר — Bamidbar/Numbers

Introduction to Bamidbar/Numbers	267
Bamidbar / במדבר	268
Nasso / נשא	279
Beha'aloscha / בהעלותך	293
Shelach / שלח	306
Korach / קרח	316
Chukas / חקת	323
Balak / בלק	328
Pinchas / פינחס	336
Mattos / מטות	341
Masei / מסעי	348

ספר דברים — Devarim/Deuteronomy

Introduction to Devarim/Deuteronomy	355
Devarim / דברים	356
Va'eschanan / ואתחנן	366
Eikev / עקב	379
Re'eh / ראה	387
Shoftim / שופטים	395
Ki Seitzei / כי תצא	402
Ki Savo / כי תבוא	414
Nitzavim / נצבים	423
Vayeilech / וילך	431
Haazinu / האזינו	436
VeZos HaBerachah / וזאת הברכה	443

Introduction to Chumash

דְּרָכֶיהָ דַרְכֵי־נֹעַם וְכָל־נְתִיבוֹתֶיהָ שָׁלוֹם

"Its ways are pleasant ways, and all its paths are peace" (Proverbs 3:17)

At the beginning of Bereishis/Genesis, Rashi comments that if the sole purpose of the Torah was to instruct us regarding the mitzvos, the entire book of Genesis was unnecessary, and the Torah should have begun with the first mitzvah in Shemos/Exodus.

Although we may not understand the reason for the individual mitzvos, the Midrash says that as a whole, the mitzvos were given to enable us to refine our character (*Vayikra Rabbah* 13:3). Aside from the refinement of character that results from the performance of mitzvos, there is also a wealth of instruction on *middos* (character traits) that is contained in the narratives in the Torah. In addition, we are fortunate that Torah scholars throughout the ages have shown us in what ways the performance of mitzvos helps us develop proper *middos*.

The Talmud states that God wished to benefit the Children of Israel, therefore He gave them an abundance of mitzvos (*Makkos* 23b). We can understand the greatness of this benefit from the following quote.

"Had the Torah not been given to us, we would have been obligated to learn proper *middos* from the observation of nature. For example, we would have been obligated to learn property rights and the prohibition of theft from the observation of ants. (If an ant has left a piece of grain, no other ant will take it.) We would have been obligated to learn fidelity from the observation of doves, who are monogamous" (*Eruvin* 100b). If we had failed to learn proper *middos* from the observation of nature, we would have been held culpable.

We might ask, if not for Torah, why would we have been held responsible for learning proper *middos* from ants and doves? Perhaps we would have adopted negative traits, such as rapaciousness from tigers and promiscuity from dogs.

The answer lies in a verse: "God created man just" (*Ecclesiastes* 7:29). It is innate within human intellect to know what is or is not proper.

It is obvious that the human intellect is far superior to that of all other living things. All creatures operate by innate instinct, which leads them to act in a way that satisfies their bodily drives. Animals do not abstract. They do not write masterpieces of literature, compose symphonies, paint pictures, record history or invent computers. Human intellect has the capacity to do all these things and so much more.

But to what end? If all that was expected of man was to satisfy bodily drives, to be rapacious and promiscuous, why was he given this superior intellect? Animals are far better at satisfying bodily drives than is man. Furthermore, it is the human intellect that is responsible for much of human suffering. Animals may be anxious when they fear they will be attacked, but they do not have the many anxieties that plague mankind. Animals do not have to worry that their company may be downsized and they may lose their livelihood. They do not have to worry about stock market fluctuations. They do not have to worry that their children may become addicted to drugs. These and the countless other anxieties people experience are the result of the superior human intellect. Man could not have been given this intellect in order to achieve contentment in life. The superior intellect actually defeats this goal.

Even the unaided human intellect should have come to the right conclusion: Man has a purpose in existence other than self-gratification. Once this was realized, the intellect would lead one to adopt those traits observed in nature that are not primarily self-gratifying. We would, therefore, have been responsible to learn proper *middos* from observing nature, and we would have been held culpable for dereliction in doing so.

Inasmuch as God wished to benefit us, he greatly simplified things for us. By giving us the Torah and mitzvos, He spoon-fed us the ability to develop proper *middos*. Yet, even with this great gift, the cunning of the *yetzer hara* is so powerful that it can render us oblivious to the teachings of Torah. God, therefore, gave us a second great gift: Torah scholars who pinpoint the teachings of *middos* contained in the Torah. The great works of Torah ethics from the time of the Talmud to our own era elucidate these Torah teachings.

The primacy of *middos* is evident in the writings of R' Chaim Vital, the principle disciple of the Ari z"l. "One must exercise even greater caution in the avoidance of bad *middos* than in the fulfillment of the positive and prohibitive mitzvos, because if one possesses good *middos*, he will easily fulfill all the mitzvos" (*Shaarei Kedushah* 1:2). Rabbeinu Yonah, on the Mishnah (*Avos* 3:21), "If there is no *derech eretz* there is no Torah" comments: One must first prepare himself with *middos*, for in this way Torah can rest upon him, because Torah will not rest upon a body which does not possess good *middos* (cited in *Michtav MeEliyahu* vol. 4 p. 245).

The Midrash says that the Torah was given as "black fire written upon white fire" (*Tanchuma, Bereishis* 1). We may understand the "black fire" to be the manifest instructions written in ink, and the "white fire" to be what is contained between the lines. Our Torah scholars, with their brilliant insights, have made the white fire legible for us. It is here that we find the *middos*.

From the teachings I have absorbed in my lifetime, both from my studies and from my teachers, I have gathered some valuable Torah teachings. These are but a tiny fragment of the wisdom contained in the Torah. In the letter to his son, Ramban recommends that after studying Torah, he should see in what way he can apply what he has learned. Hopefully, the lessons of *middos* will enable us to do this.

Wherever possible, I have listed the source of the material presented. However, there are many things I learned whose sources I do not recall. In addition, I have tried to demonstrate some of the psychological insights found in Torah. As the Talmud says, "Review it (the Torah) and review it, for everything is in it" (*Ethics of the Fathers* 5:26).

This is hardly a definitive work. Rather, I hope it will whet the appetite so that people will increase their study of Torah works to discover the great wealth to be mined in this Divine gift.

ספר
בראשית
BEREISHIS/GENESIS

Introduction to Bereishis/Genesis

The prophet refers to the Book of Bereishis/Genesis as *sefer hayashar*, the Book of the Upright (*II Samuel* 1:18). Rashi explains that this title was chosen because it contains the life-stories of the patriarchs Abraham, Isaac and Jacob, whom the Torah refers to as "the upright" (*Numbers* 23:10).

Solomon says, "This I did find: God has made man simple, but they sought many intrigues" (*Ecclesiastes* 7:29). The natural state of man is "simple," i.e., straightforward and just. Man forfeits his innate state of simplicity when he complicates matters.

Ramban cites the sin of Adam and Eve eating of the "Tree of Knowledge of Good and Bad," i.e., whose fruits enabled one to distinguish between good and bad. Ramban asks, how can it be that by defying the Divine commandment they acquired the ability to distinguish between good and bad? It would seem that the sin should have caused a decline in their character rather than an improvement. He answers that prior to the sin, man was guided by instinct. Animals intuitively avoid poisonous foods and things that are harmful to them. Instinctive guides are far more efficient than intellectual guides. Had man not sinned, there would not have been any need for intellectual discernment between good and bad, because bad would have been intuitively avoided. Intellectual knowledge of what is bad is far less reliable. People regularly do things that they think are good because the intellect is fallible, whereas instinct is not fallible. The sin of Adam and Eve resulted in a descent rather than an elevation.

If bad could have been avoided intuitively, man could have used his enormous intellectual powers to perfect himself to a near-angelic state. "You have withheld but little from the Divine" (*Psalms* 8:6). This was nascent man. Loss of the instinctual avoidance of bad caused man to fall back on the relatively unreliable intellectual discernment between good and bad. This is the "many intrigues" to which Solomon refers. Man deviates from the simple and just path in life because his intellect is so vulnerable to self-deception.

The lives of the patriarchs show us how to approach the status of man which God desired in creating man "in the likeness of God" (*Genesis* 5:1). The patriarchs are the *yesharim* who give the Book of Genesis the appellation *sefer hayashar*, the Book of the Upright.

The words of the Torah are concise. Both by transmission of the Oral Law and by derivation from the words of the text, we can learn how to be *yashar* from the lives of the patriarchs and the events in Genesis.

פרשת בראשית ‎ೀ
Parashas Bereishis

בְּרֵאשִׁית בָּרָא אֱלֹקִים אֵת הַשָּׁמַיִם וְאֵת הָאָרֶץ
In the beginning of God's creating the heavens and the earth (1:1)

Toward a Meaningful Life

Most people have many things on their minds: the family's health, the job, finances and sundry other concerns. If they were asked, "Have you given much thought to the purpose of your existence? What do you really hope to achieve with your life?" I dare say that many people will say that they have not spent much time on such reflection. Yet, even if not in their conscious thinking, the existential question is in their subconscious thought.

Very few people are so fortunate as to weather a lifetime without periods of distress. We can accept suffering when we know it has a purpose. We will accept the discomfort of dental or medical procedures because we know that they restore or preserve our health. We will spend long hours in study to acquire a professional degree, and we tolerate the inconveniences of the workplace because we wish to earn a livelihood.

In every person's life there is some suffering which does not lead to an apparent goal: illness, accidents, deprivation, problems in children's lives, to name just a few. These may be difficult to tolerate under any circumstances. If we can conceptualize that somehow everything fits into a master design, we can accept them as being purposeful in a way which we cannot understand. If, however, there is no purpose for existence, suffering becomes intolerable. In a purposeless world the creed, "Eat, drink and be merry for tomorrow we die," is reasonable.

If the world was not created, but just "happened" as a result of some chance accident of primordial matter or energy, there cannot be an ultimate purpose to life. There can be many intermediate goals. We fill the automobile tank with gasoline for the purpose of driving and we shovel the snow in order to have access to our homes, but these are not the ultimate goals in life.

If the world was created, the Creator had a purpose in creating it. This purpose may be unknowable to anyone except Him. However, if there is reason for the world's existence, we can begin to postulate a reason for our existence.

Even the most perfect belief in God may not enable us to understand the purpose of suffering. The Talmud says that Moses asked God why the righteous suffer, and God responded that this is the one thing that no one inhabiting a mortal body can understand (*Berachos* 7a). But with faith, one can more easily accept that suffering is not without purpose.

People who have never been religious often turn to God in a time of distress. The belief that there is a master design to the universe and that their suffering is not meaningless provides a modicum of comfort.

No one escapes the existential question. Of course, if a person feels purposeless in life, one may at least temporarily escape the discomfort of a meaningless existence by engaging in any of many activities that will, at least temporarily, distract one from reflecting on the meaninglessness of life. However, the question continues to haunt one, and there are people who have spent their lives in futile attempt to escape the existential question.

Torah, which is a guide to living, therefore begins with an answer to the existential question. *God created the world and all that is in it.* There is a reason for the existence of the world, albeit incomprehensible to us. With the faith that the world was created for a purpose, we can probe and investigate what our role in the world may be.

בְּרֵאשִׁית בָּרָא אֱלֹקִים אֵת הַשָּׁמַיִם וְאֵת הָאָרֶץ ...
וַיְבָרֶךְ אֱלֹקִים אֶת־יוֹם הַשְּׁבִיעִי וַיְקַדֵּשׁ אֹתוֹ כִּי בוֹ שָׁבַת
מִכָּל־מְלַאכְתּוֹ אֲשֶׁר־בָּרָא אֱלֹקִים לַעֲשׂוֹת

In the beginning of God's creating the heavens and the earth (1:1) *... God blessed the seventh day and sanctified it because on it He abstained from all His work which God created to make* (2:3)

Truth Is Godliness

These two verses encompass all of Creation. The opening three words end in the letters *taf, aleph, mem*, which spell *emes* (truth), and the closing three words end in *aleph, mem, taf*, which again spell *emes*. R' Simchah Bunim of P'shis'che cites the Talmudic statement, "The seal of God is *emes*," and comments, "It is customary for an author to place his name in the opening of his book. God placed His Name, *emes*, in the opening chapter of the Torah. *Emes* thus envelops all of creation, a testimony to God as the Creator."

Divrei Shaul notes that all traits can be a matter of degree. There can be greater beauty and lesser beauty, greater wisdom and lesser wisdom, greater strength and lesser strength, etc. Only one trait cannot be more or less: truth. There is no such thing as greater truth and lesser truth. Something is either true or it is not true.

God is identified with truth. Just as truth can never be altered, because altered truth is no longer truth, there can be no change in God (*Malachi* 2:6).

The Talmud says that *emes* is broad-based, consisting of the first letter of the alphabet, *aleph*, the middle letter, *mem*, and the last letter, *taf* (*Shabbos* 55a). Truth, therefore, has stability and durability. Falsehood, on the other hand, is the Hebrew *sheker*, consisting of three letters near the end of the alphabet. *Sheker* is top-heavy, and cannot endure.

To the extent that a person lives with truth is the extent one identifies with God. Any falsehood distances a person from God.

בְּרֵאשִׁית בָּרָא אֱלֹקִים אֵת הַשָּׁמַיִם וְאֵת הָאָרֶץ וְהָאָרֶץ הָיְתָה תֹהוּ וָבֹהוּ

***In the beginning of God's creating the heavens and the earth,
the earth was barren and empty*** (1:1-2)

Spiritual vs. Mundane

R' Mendel of Kotzk said, "If a person knows that God created the heavens and the earth, then he will realize that all earthly things are barren and empty."

In *Ecclesiastes*, Solomon repeatedly negates everything mundane. "Futility of futilities; all is futile" (1:2). The Talmud says that Solomon immediately qualifies this statement by saying, "What gain does man have for all his labor which he toils beneath the sun?" (1:3). Everything *beneath the sun*, i.e., of an earthly nature, is futile. Only that which is *above the sun*, i.e., celestial and spiritual, is of real and enduring value.

The Talmud says that Moses gave us 613 mitzvos. David condensed these into 10 principles: "Who may dwell on Your holy mountain? One who walks in moral integrity, practices righteousness and speaks the truth from his heart. Who bears no slander upon his tongue, does not do evil to his fellow, nor tolerates an aspersion cast upon his neighbor. In whose eyes that which is blameworthy is despised, and who honors those who fear God. He will not change a vow that is to his own harm. He does not put out his money for usury, nor takes a bribe against an innocent man — he who acts by these principles will not falter forever" (*Psalm* 15).

Isaiah condensed them to six principles: "One who walks with righteousness and speaks with truthfulness, spurns extortionate profit, shakes his hands from graft, seals his ears from hearing bloodshed and shuts his eyes from seeing evil" (*Isaiah* 33:15). Michah condensed them to three principles: "What does God ask of you? But to do justice, love kindness and to walk humbly before God" (*Micah* 3:6). Habakkuk condensed them to a single principle: "A righteous person shall live through his faith" (*Habakkuk* 2:4).

Neither David, nor Isaiah, nor Michah nor Habakkuk negated a single mitzvah of the 613 given by Moses. Rather, they sought to group them under several principles. Habakkuk ultimately concluded that if a person had sincere faith in God, this would subsume all the mitzvos of the Torah.

In the final analysis, a philosophy of life is based on one of two attitudes. Either the world was created by God, which means that there is a specific purpose for its existence and that man was created to achieve a particular goal with his life, or that the world is the result of a happenstance, unplanned occurrence, in which case there is no ultimate purpose to anything, as was noted in the opening article.

Habakkuk's statement is that sincere faith in God as the Creator of the universe will result in the realization that contentment is not the goal of man. Animals with lesser intellect are far more content than man. They do not have the anxiety and worry that man's sophisticated mind can generate. Clearly, the human intellect and man's ability to develop high levels of spirituality testify that he was created to achieve lofty spiritual goals.

Experience confirms the statement of R' Shneur Zalman in *Tanya*, that mundane and spiritual drives are polar opposites. A truly spiritually motivated person is not indulgent, and partakes of earthly things only to the extent necessary for survival.

Earthly things can become a distraction. If it were possible to exist without dependence on earthly things, that would be preferable. In themselves, apart from being necessary for survival, earthly things have no value whatsoever.

This is the meaning of R' Mendel of Kotzk's comment on the opening verse of the Torah, "In the beginning, God created the heavens and the earth. And the earth was barren and desolate." R' Mendel said, "If a person knows that God created the heavens and the earth, then he will realize that all earthly things are barren and empty." To the extent that a person partakes of worldly goods and pleasures beyond that necessary for survival, to that degree his absolute faith in Divine creation of the universe is lacking.

The very first verses of the Torah convey Solomon's concept: Everything *beneath the sun*, i.e., of an earthly nature, is futile. Only that which is *above the sun*, i.e., celestial and spiritual, is of real and enduring value.

Is it within the capacity of a human being to negate everything mundane? The Torah does not ask the impossible of us. Developing this level of spirituality is difficult, but not impossible. But even if we do not attain it, it is important to understand what the ultimate goal of a human being should be.

The Beauty of Light

וַיֹּאמֶר אֱלֹקִים יְהִי־אוֹר וַיְהִי־אוֹר

God said, "Let there be light," and there was light (1:3)

There was a 96-year-old resident of a nursing home who had not spoken a single word for over a year. No amount of cajoling could get her to speak. It was assumed she was suffering from senile dementia.

One of the volunteers, a young girl of 14, was assigned to sit with this woman. The old woman looked out the window, totally ignoring the young woman's efforts to engage her in conversation or in an activity. Nothing could distract her from looking out the window.

After an hour, the young woman had just about had it. She arose to leave, but couldn't help asking, "What are you looking at?"

The "demented" old lady looked at her and smiled, "Why, at the light, my child."

We, whose mental faculties are intact, probably never look at the light. It is with the help of the light that we can see things, and we focus our attention on the many things we see, but not on the light itself.

Isn't that strange? In the story of creation, Scripture states, "And God said, 'Let there be light,' and there was light. And God saw the light *that it was good*." Stop and think for a moment. According to the account of creation, the light was the first thing created. There were no trees, no grass, no animals, no birds. *There was nothing to see by the light*, yet God saw that light was good. There must be something intrinsically good about light, even if it has no practical application.

I had never thought about this until I heard about the old woman's remark.

Perhaps her mental condition was such that she could not focus on anything. All she saw was the light, and she felt that it was worth looking at.

We often think of wisdom as a kind of light. We speak of wise people as being "enlightened," and we may say that a person had a "bright" idea. Indeed, Solomon says, "A commandment (mitzvah) is a lamp, and Torah is light" (*Proverbs* 6:23).

I think that many people do not value wisdom unless it has some practical application. They think that knowledge is of value only if it is useful. But the determination of what is morally right or wrong, good or evil, requires wisdom. True, the conclusions may not necessarily have a practical application. Perhaps this has contributed to an abduction of thinking about moral and ethical issues.

We are told that in Gan-Eden (Paradise) the righteous will be rewarded by basking in the glow of the *Shechinah* (Divine Presence). I do not know how many things there are to "see" in Gan-Eden. The ultimate delight will be in the perception of the light itself.

We are too often distracted by the application of light to think of it as having value all its own. Maybe there is something we can learn from a 96-year-old "demented" woman.

וַיֹּאמֶר אֱלֹקִים נַעֲשֶׂה אָדָם
And God said, "Let us make Man" (1:26)

All or None

Rashi states that God's statement "Let *us* make Man" indicates that God held counsel with the angels on the creation of man. God does not need anyone's opinion. He held counsel with the angels as a teaching to man that even the wisest person should seek the counsel of others, even those of lesser wisdom.

The Midrash elaborates on the proceedings of this counsel. Angels representing human traits disagreed about the creation of man. The angels of *chesed* (kindness) and *tzedek* (justice) were in favor of the creation of man, because man can be kind and just. The angel of *shalom* (peace) opposed man's creation "because man constantly feuds." The angel of *emes* (truth) also opposed man's creation "because man is thoroughly false." God then cast the angel of *emes* down to earth and created man (*Bereishis Rabbah* 8).

Many of the commentaries ask, why did God cast the angel of *emes* down to earth rather than the angel of *shalom*, who likewise had opposed man's creation?

The author of *Mashal U'Melitzah* gives a brilliant answer. The argument of the angel of *shalom* was not wholly correct. Man may indeed feud, but it is wrong to say that he *constantly* feuds. Many people have lived tranquil lives and have not clashed with other people. Although his statement was wrong, the angel of *shalom* was not self-contradictory. The angel of *emes*, on the other hand, said that man is *thoroughly* false. This statement, too, is incorrect. Whereas man may lie, he may also be truthful. It is an exaggeration to say that man is *thoroughly* false. By exaggerating, the angel of *emes* overstepped the boundaries of truth, and in doing so, was self-contradictory. An exaggeration of a truth is no longer true. This is why the angel of *emes* was cast down. In his zeal for truth, he opposed the creation of man. But this zeal caused him to make a false statement, and he could no longer function as the angel of *emes*.

This is an important teaching. Truth cannot be compromised. An act which is 95 percent benevolent and has only a tiny undesirable effect may be an act of *chesed*. Truth is like a hermetic seal, which is rendered non-functional by a pinpoint opening. There is no such thing as a partial truth or even something which is 99 percent true. Something is either wholly true or it is not true at all.

We must be cautious in our pursuit of truth. If we overstep the boundaries of truth, even for good reasons, we are championing truth with false means. That cannot succeed.

וַיְכַל אֱלֹקִים בַּיּוֹם הַשְּׁבִיעִי מְלַאכְתּוֹ אֲשֶׁר עָשָׂה

"By the seventh day, God completed His Work which He had done" (2:2)

The Creation of the Shabbos Spirit

Inasmuch as creation was completed by the end of the sixth day, why does the Torah say that God completed His work on the *seventh* day? Rashi explains that the world was incomplete because it lacked *menuchah* (rest), and when Shabbos came, *menuchah* completed creation. In other words, it was the absence of more creation which occurred on Shabbos that completed the work of creation.

This explanation is valid only if we understand *menuchah* to be a passive phenomenon, an absence of creation. However, there is reason to assert that the *menuchah* of Shabbos is more than just passive. In the Shabbos afternoon service we refer to the *menuchah* of Shabbos as a "*menuchah* of love and magnanimity, of truth and faith, of peace and serenity and tranquility and security." These are positive characteristics with which the *menuchah* of Shabbos was endowed. The verse states that "on the seventh day God rested and *vayinafash*, He was refreshed" (*Exodus* 31:17). Obviously, God was not exhausted and in need of a day of rest to be refreshed. Sforno explains that *vayinafash* refers to *nefesh* (spirit), and it means that "God endowed Shabbos with an extra degree of spirituality." If so, then there *was* a creation on Shabbos: the creation of an extra degree of spirituality. How does this comply with the prohibition of all work on Shabbos, which God observed as an example for His children to emulate?

Perhaps the answer lies in the fact that the unique *menuchah* and *nefesh* of Shabbos are its very essence. The Talmud says that "the wicked are considered to be dead even while they live" (*Berachos* 18b). Although they are physiologically alive, they are alive in body only, but in absence of any spirituality, they are alive as animals, not as humans. The uniquely human feature, the spirit, is what makes man distinct from other living things. Without spirituality, a person *as a human being* is considered to be lifeless.

Rashi says that the world lacked *menuchah*. Without spiritual *menuchah*, the world would be as lifeless as a person without a spirit. Inasmuch as the world required this *menuchah* in order to be considered a living world, it was in a state of *pekuach nefesh*, of its very life being endangered. Under such circumstances, it is permitted and indeed mandatory to do everything necessary on Shabbos to preserve life.

Rashi's explanation may be that there was indeed a creation on the seventh day, the creation of *menuchah*. But God did not violate the prohibition of work on

Shabbos, because this was a case of *pekuach nefesh*, and it was necessary to create the spiritual *menuchah* to preserve the life of the world.

We indeed observe Shabbos by a total abstinence from all work. But we must remember that without the spiritual *menuchah*, Shabbos is grossly lacking. Just as man has both body and spirit, so does Shabbos. The halachos governing restriction of work on Shabbos are the body of Shabbos; the spiritual *menuchah* is its *neshamah*.

וַיְבָרֶךְ אֱלֹקִים אֶת־יוֹם הַשְּׁבִיעִי וַיְקַדֵּשׁ אֹתוֹ

God blessed the seventh day and sanctified it (2:3)

The Sanctity of Shabbos

It is noteworthy that Psalm 92, "A song for the day of Shabbos" does not have a single reference to Shabbos. In what way, then, is it a Shabbos psalm?

The Midrash states that when Adam sinned, he was to be punished by death: "For on the day that you eat of it, you shall surely die" (*Genesis* 2:16). Inasmuch as Adam's sin took place late on Friday, his death would have occurred on Shabbos. The Shabbos day came before God and pleaded, "Master of the Universe! During the six days of creation, no living thing perished. Is the first death in the world to occur on my day? Is this how I am sanctified? Is this how I am blessed?" This plea resulted in God commuting the death sentence. When Adam saw that he was saved by the intervention of Shabbos, he wished to sing its praises. Shabbos responded, "I am not the one to be praised. You and I together shall praise God." Thus, Psalm 92 is not a praise of Shabbos, but a song in which Shabbos praises God for the wonders of His creation (*Yalkut Shimoni*).

R' Avraham Pam points out that it is forbidden to cause any distress to another person during the entire week. However, if one does so on Shabbos, it is a grievous sin, because it violates the sanctity and blessedness of the day.

The candles of Shabbos are intended to bring the light of *shalom bayis* (domestic tranquility) into the home. The traditional greeting is *Shabbos shalom.* Is it not tragic that family disagreements often occur on Shabbos? Is it not paradoxical that arguments in shul may erupt on Shabbos? Will this not cause Shabbos to complain before God, "Is this how I am sanctified? Is this how I am blessed?"

The Talmud relates that there were two neighbors who consistently quarreled before Shabbos. R' Meir intervened and reconciled the two. The voice of Satan was then heard, "Woe is me! R' Meir has expelled me from these homes. I was so pleased here" (*Gittin* 52a).

Why did Satan choose Friday afternoon to incite quarrels? Because when people are pressured to prepare for Shabbos and hurry with last minute details, they are likely to be very impatient and more readily irritated. It is a triumph for Satan when he can convert the day of peace to a day of strife.

Observant Jews are careful not to do any forbidden act on Shabbos. We should be equally cautious to speak softly on Shabbos, to be more tolerant and to make Shabbos a day on which we concentrate on prayer and Torah study. Let us not cause Shabbos to complain, "Is this how I am sanctified? Is this how I am blessed?" (*Atarah LeMelech* p. 5).

BEREISHIS / GENESIS: Bereishis

עַל־כֵּן יַעֲזָב־אִישׁ אֶת־אָבִיו וְאֶת־אִמּוֹ וְדָבַק בְּאִשְׁתּוֹ וְהָיוּ לְבָשָׂר אֶחָד

*Therefore a man shall leave his father and his mother
and cling to his wife and they shall become one flesh* (2:24)

The Torah Concept of Marriage

The very first mitzvah in the Torah is for a person to marry and have a family. It is certainly admirable to do a mitzvah in the finest way. Some people spend hours choosing an *esrog* for the mitzvah on Succos. Special care is taken to have the best matzoh on Passover and *tefillin* that meet the most stringent specifications.

What about the mitzvah of marriage? The Torah makes it clear that husband and wife should not be two people, each having a separate goal. Rather, "They shall become one flesh." It is possible that in married life one spouse says or does something that displeases the other. How often is such an incident followed by anger and retaliation? If a person sustains a wound on his arm, does he punish the arm for causing him pain? If one is hurt by a spouse and responds with an angry and usually hurtful remark, is that not a flagrant violation of the Torah commandment that "they shall become one flesh?"

Many relationships are built on a love that is self-love rather than a true love for the other person. A young man falls in love with a young woman because he feels she can satisfy his emotional needs, and vice versa. Even when there is no passion, such as marriages that are arranged as a *shidduch* with little communication before the wedding, each partner may come with his or her own agenda.

The formula for marriage is stated in halachah, "To respect her more than one respects oneself, and to love her as one loves oneself" (*Rambam, Hilchos Ishus*).

> *R' Aryeh Levin was consulted by a young man for guidance in marriage. R' Levin showed him a copy of a letter which the Chazon Ish had written.*
>
> > *It is a mitzvah in the Torah, "he shall gladden his wife whom he has married" (Deuteronomy 24:5). How does a husband gladden his wife? It is the nature of a woman to take pleasure in finding favor in the eyes of her husband. Therefore, the husband should strive to achieve a closeness with his wife by demonstrating his affection and in heartfelt, soothing conversation. It is obligatory on the husband to relate to his wife with dignity and respect. The respect should blend with the affection and closeness, so that there are no barriers between them. When he leaves he should tell his wife where he is going, and when he returns he should tell her where he has been and what he did, as well as similar "little things," pleasant things that are supportive and can gladden her heart, the goal of which is to strengthen the bond between them.*
>
> *R' Levin stated that he achieved this unity in his marriage. One time, when his wife was ill, R' Levin said to the doctor, "Our foot hurts."*
>
> *R' Levin added that the kabbalist, R' Naftali Katz, repeatedly used words of endearment in his will: "my beloved, my dearest, my most precious." This kabbalist stated that they had made a pact with each other that they should not survive each other, and that when one dies, the other should*

pray for death. In his will he recanted this pact, stating that his wife should live the years allotted to her by God.

R' Levin added, "If a holy and saintly person could write this in his will, that teaches us how pure and holy their relationship was."

R' Yitzchak Silberstein points out that the show of chivalry does not necessarily constitute respect and consideration. Husbands who appear to respect their wives in social settings may nevertheless be abusive in their private lives.

R' Silberstein cites a remarkable statement by R' Chaim Vital, that a person's character traits are measured *only* according to his behavior toward his wife. "If a person does acts of kindness to others — lending them money, visiting the sick, consoling the bereaved, bringing cheer to newlyweds — yet, if he is irritable and inconsiderate toward his wife, none of his merits will stand in his favor on his Judgment Day" (*Aleinu Leshabe'ach* vol. 1 p. 206).

Koheles Yitzchok cites the verse, "The man called his wife's name Eve, because she had become the mother of all the living" (*Genesis* 3:20), and points out that the Torah puts this verse immediately following God's sharp reprimand and punishment of Adam for eating from the Tree of Knowledge: "Accursed is the ground because of you, etc." He says that the approximation of these verses is to point out Adam's reaction.

By giving Adam the forbidden fruit, Eve unleashed the Angel of Death and brought an eternal curse to mankind. Undoubtedly, Adam's reaction upon hearing his severe punishment from God must have been an intense feeling of anger toward Eve. However, this anger never came to be expressed. Rather, he consoled her with his statement that she was to be the mother of mankind.

We can imagine what the average husband's reaction would be if he found that his wife's behavior had brought down a severe curse upon him. But not so with Adam, whom the Talmud says was a great *chassid*, a pious person who was magnanimous and forgiving (*Eruvin* 18b). By approximating these verses, the Torah teaches us how a husband must be able to restrain his anger even when it is justified.

Our great *tzaddikim* were as meticulous in observing the mitzvah of "they shall become one flesh" as they were of all other mitzvos. We would do well to learn from their example.

כִּי יֹדֵעַ אֱלֹקִים כִּי בְּיוֹם אֲכָלְכֶם מִמֶּנּוּ
וְנִפְקְחוּ עֵינֵיכֶם וִהְיִיתֶם כֵּאלֹקִים יֹדְעֵי טוֹב וָרָע

"For God knows that on the day you eat of it your eyes will be opened and you will be like God, knowing good and bad" (3:5)

The Human Limitation

R' Zusia of Anipole asked his brother, R' Elimelech of Lizhensk, "Melech, we are told that in Adam were contained all the neshamos of all human beings to come. That means that you and I were there, too. How did we ever allow him to transgress God's commandment and eat from the Tree of Knowledge?"

R' Elimelech answered, "I'll tell you, my brother. The Serpent, the embodiment of Satan, had told Adam that if he would eat from the Tree, he *would be as wise as God. Had Adam not eaten, he and all mankind after him until the end of time would have thought, 'If only I had eaten from the Tree, I could have been as wise as God.' I decided that to have the delusion that it is possible for a mortal to be as wise as God is far more serious than to commit the sin of eating the forbidden fruit, so I let him do it."*

The Midrash says that God took Adam through the Garden of Eden and said, "Look at all the beauty I created, and it was all for you. Take care that you do not ruin my world" (*Koheles Rabbah* 9). By transgressing the Divine commandment, Adam brought ruin to the world. Yet, R' Elimelech said that the destruction that would result from man's thinking that it was possible for him to be as wise as God would be far worse than the ruin resulting from his sin.

Unfortunately, people have had the delusion that not only are they as wise as God, but that they can even outsmart Him. People who seek to increase their wealth by methods that the Torah forbids are trying to outsmart God.

R' Elimelech was right. The harm that has resulted from people thinking themselves to be infinitely wise is greater than that resulting from a single sin. It is an attitude of omniscience and arrogance, of failure to defer to the authority of Torah.

Adam was spared this pitfall when he ate from the Tree of Knowledge and then discovered how limited his wisdom was. Today, the enormous scientific advances that man has made has not prevented man from making the fatal mistake of thinking himself as wise as God.

וַיֹּאמֶר ה׳ אֱלֹקִים אֶל־הַנָּחָשׁ כִּי עָשִׂיתָ זֹּאת אָרוּר אַתָּה מִכָּל־הַבְּהֵמָה וּמִכֹּל חַיַּת הַשָּׂדֶה . . . וְעָפָר תֹּאכַל כָּל־יְמֵי חַיֶּיךָ

And Hashem God said to the serpent, "Because you have done this, accursed are you beyond all the cattle and beyond all beasts of the field ... and dust shall you eat all the days of your life" (3:14)

A Relationship with God

"What kind of curse is this?" R' Yitzchok of Vorki asked. "If it can eat dust, then a snake will never be without food."

R' Yitzchok explained that that precisely is the curse. All other living things look to God for their food. Even beasts turn to God for their sustenance. "The young lions roar after prey and to seek their food from God" (*Psalms* 104:21). "Who thus gives the beast its food, to the young ravens that after which they cry" (ibid. 147:9). To the serpent God said, "You are so repugnant to Me that I never wish to hear from you. I created you, so I must provide your food. It will be ubiquitous dust, so that you should never have to call upon Me." The curse of the serpent was that he lost his relationship with God.

One of the chassidic masters said, "I feel sorry for the wealthy. They may be so secure with their wealth that they think they don't have to turn to God. Most people are sorry for the poor, and do not realize that precisely because they must pray for their food, they are the most fortunate."

If only we realized how precious our relationship with God is, and that we are privileged to call upon Him many times each day!

כִּי־עָפָר אַתָּה וְאֶל־עָפָר תָּשׁוּב
"For you are dust, and to dust shall you return" (3:19)

The Eternity of the Neshamah (Soul)

This verse states the mortality of man. However, it should be remembered that it was only the *body* of man that was formed from dust. Man's *neshamah* (soul) is the breath of God: "And Hashem formed the man of dust from the ground, and He blew into his nostrils the soul of life" (*Genesis* 2:7). Just as the body returns to its origin of dust, the *neshamah* returns to its origin in God. Only the body is mortal. The *neshamah* is eternal.

Man's uniqueness is not in his body, which is quite similar to the bodies of animals. Man's distinction is his *neshamah*, which sets him apart qualitatively from other living things. Is it not both ironic and tragic that most people care a great deal for their body, that which is animal-like, and relatively little for their *neshamah*, which is really the essence of man?

There appears to be a natural drive to immortalize oneself. People of means affix their names to buildings that will outlast them. They may be commemorated by huge, lavish monuments. But buildings may be razed, and monuments crumble with time. The Talmud says, "We do not make monuments for *tzaddikim*. Their words are their memoriam" (*Jerusalem Talmud, Shekalim* 2:5). The words of *tzaddikim* are Torah teachings, and just as Torah is eternal, the words of *tzaddikim* are eternal.

The way we live is an indication of the strength of our belief.

As was noted earlier, the Talmud says that Moses gave us 613 mitzvos which the prophet Habakkuk said could be encompassed by the single principle, "A righteous person shall live through his faith" (*Habakkuk* 2:4). If we truly believe that we were created with a Divine *neshamah* which is temporarily housed within a physical body, we would spend the lion's share of our day caring for the *neshamah* rather than for the temporary receptacle in which it is contained.

> *Graf Petotski was the son of a nobleman, and his conversion to Judaism was a threat to the Church, which condemned him to death if he did not recant. Petotsky fled and lived incognito in a little village, where he spent his time studying Torah. The villagers knew his secret, but of course would not disclose his whereabouts.*
>
> *There was a young boy in the village who often harassed him, and Petotski pleaded with him to desist. The young boy told his father that Petotski had shouted at him, and to retaliate, the father revealed Petotski's identity to the Church. Petotski was taken into custody and was told that if he did not recant he would be burned at the stake.*
>
> *Petotski refused to recant and the cruel execution was about to be carried out, with Petotski's reciting the Shema with his last breath.*
>
> *The executioner, seeing that Petotski was unperturbed by his imminent death, said, "You are no doubt thinking that when you get up to heaven you will bring down the wrath of God on us."*
>
> *"Not at all," Petotski said. "When I was a child, I had little clay soldiers with which I played. One young boy was jealous of me and broke my soldiers. I cried to my father and asked him to punish the boy. When my*

BEREISHIS / GENESIS: Bereishis [25]

father ignored me, I thought, 'Wait until I grow up and become the local feudal lord. I will then punish this boy.'

"When I grew up and did have the power to punish him, I was mature enough to realize how foolish it was to make an issue of something as insignificant as a few little clay soldiers, and I did nothing to punish the man who had broken them when he was a child.

"When I get to heaven and realize the insignificance of this puny little body that you are about to destroy, do you think I will make an issue of it?"

We should not have to wait until we get to heaven to realize the insignificance of the body and the primacy of the *neshamah*. We can achieve this awareness by a true faith in God and Creation.

וַיְגָרֶשׁ אֶת־הָאָדָם וַיַּשְׁכֵּן מִקֶּדֶם לְגַן־עֵדֶן אֶת־הַכְּרֻבִים
וְאֵת לַהַט הַחֶרֶב הַמִּתְהַפֶּכֶת לִשְׁמֹר אֶת־דֶּרֶךְ עֵץ הַחַיִּים

Having driven out the man, He stationed at the east of the Garden of Eden the Cherubim and the flame of the ever-turning sword, to guard the way to the Tree of Life (3:24)

Angelic or Otherwise?

Rashi explains that the Cherubim were "destructive angels." The only other time we find the term "Cherubim" in the Pentateuch is in relationship to the cover of the Holy Ark: "You shall make two Cherubim of gold" (*Exodus* 25:18). There Rashi explains that the Cherubim were in the image of infants. How strange that the same term should be used in such polar opposite connotations.

R' Yaakov Kamenetsky comments that when a child is raised with Torah, symbolized by the Holy Ark, he can be angelic. In the absence of Torah, the child can grow up with destructive behavior.

However, we must recognize that some children of Torah-observant families, children who have been given a Torah education, may nevertheless behave destructively. Is this to be seen as a failure of Torah?

In the instructions for fashioning the cover of the Holy Ark, the Torah says that the Cherubim were to be of one piece with the cover, i.e., they were not to be fashioned separately and then attached to the cover. Rather, they had to be hammered out of one piece of gold, to be an integral part of the cover.

Torah observance can be of two kinds, which may be externally indistinguishable but are different in essence. A person may be an individual for himself who complies with the commandments of Torah. He may indeed perform all the mitzvos and observe all restrictions. However, he has his own agenda. His goal in life is to succeed, to have as much wealth as he can amass, to achieve recognition and/or to live as comfortably as possible.

Whereas this person may be in complete compliance with halachah, he may be lacking in *middos* (appropriate character traits). When things stand in the way of his personal goals, he may be inconsiderate of others, pushing them out of his way. He may react with rage when his personal wishes are frustrated. He may harbor resentment toward people who have offended him.

I have extensive contact with youngsters who have drifted away from Judaism. Many have fallen into the use of drugs. A common feature among them is their antipathy toward Yiddishkeit. They describe the religion that they observed either at home or in school or both as being rituals devoid of *middos*.

A person whose life is totally directed toward fulfillment of every aspect of Torah has no personal agenda. His only desire in life is to do what God wants of him as revealed in the Torah. His behavior is governed not only by halachah, but also by the works on *middos*, such as *Mesillas Yesharim* (*Path of the Just*) and *Orchos Tzaddikim* (*Ways of the Righteous*). Children who are raised from infancy in an environment of love, consideration, sensitivity, absolute honesty, selflessness and all the other fine *middos* that our ethical works describe are unlikely to develop negative feelings toward Yiddishkeit.

The Cherubim who are angel-like are those who are one with Torah. If they are separate from Torah and just attached to it, they may be far less than angelic.

וְאִם לֹא תֵיטִיב לַפֶּתַח חַטָּאת רֹבֵץ וְאֵלֶיךָ תְּשׁוּקָתוֹ

But if you do not improve yourself, sin rests at the door; its desire is toward you (4:7)

The Seduction of the Yetzer Hara

Just what is meant by "sin rests at the door?"

The Maggid of Dubnow explains that a beggar who asks for alms usually stands at the door awaiting whatever will be given. Not so when a person is requesting a significant sum. He asks to come into the house to present his case. If his request is for a huge sum of money, he will ask to meet the prospective donor in his office.

The *yetzer hara* does not begin by making huge demands, to eat *tereifah* or to violate the Shabbos. It knows that there is no chance that a Torah observant person will yield to these. The Talmud states that the *yetzer hara* begins with suggesting minor deviations that may seem almost insignificant, such as dropping a traditional custom or harboring a grudge against someone or saying something uncomplimentary about another person. Once it has succeeded in this, it has a foothold from which it may operate to entice a person to ever-more serious transgressions.

The *yetzer hara*, like a beggar asking for just a pittance, stands at the door. He wants just a little something, anything you may be willing to give him. In contrast to someone asking for alms, to whom you should be most courteous, you should not even carry on a conversation with the *yetzer hara*. It is exceedingly sly and can delude you. When the *yetzer hara* asks for even the slightest deviation from Yiddishkeit, slam the door shut in its face. "Its desire is toward you." It wants all of you.

פרשת נח
Parashas Noach

The Great Deluge

This portion of the Torah narrates the episode of the flood that destroyed a wholly corrupt and sinful generation. The Midrash states that for 120 years, Noah was engaged in building the Ark, and he warned people that unless they abandoned their corrupt behavior they would be destroyed. When the flood came, only Noah and his family were saved. God said to Noah, "Come to the Ark, you and all your household, for it is you that I have seen to be righteous before Me in this generation" (*Genesis* 7:1). How is it that over a period of 120 years not one individual took Noah seriously?

The Midrash states that the sin that resulted in the annihilation of that generation was theft. But it was a unique kind of theft. They stole things that were worth less than a *perutah*, a small amount of a few cents. The halachah is that theft of less than a *perutah* is not remediable by court. Their reasoning was that inasmuch as a court does not recognize this as theft, it is not forbidden. In their distorted logic, this generation legitimized theft.

The Alter (Elder) of Kelm commented on the verse, "God saw the earth and behold, it was corrupted" (ibid. 6:12), that God was the only One who saw that the people were corrupt. All humans had made peace with the corrupt behavior as being legitimate.

Legalizing wrong also occurred in the Biblical cities of Sodom and Gomorrah, whose laws, according to the Midrash, legitimized every abomination. This is why these cities had to be destroyed, and even the patriarch Abraham's fervent pleas to spare the cities were futile. If a person is able to discover that what he did was wrong, it is possible that he may amend his ways. Once an improper act is legalized, there is no chance of *teshuvah* (repentance). A person will not repent for what he thinks was permissible and proper.

After the flood, God said that the rainbow would be a sign that He would never again destroy the world population. In a virtuous generation, the rainbow would not have to appear. There would be no need for our being assured that there would not be another flood. The appearance of the rainbow is essentially a statement that only by virtue of God's promise are we spared the fate of the generation of the deluge. But why? Granted that our generation is far from perfect, it is certainly not hopelessly corrupt.

At least, not yet. But there are ominous signs that we may be heading in that direction.

There is an ever-increasing attitude that if an undesirable behavior is uncontrollable, it should be legalized. Gambling has been widely legalized, and there is considerable pressure and sympathy for the legalization of drugs. Several decades ago, abortion was a crime. Today it is not only legal but publicly funded. When the first physician-assisted suicide came to light, there was a cry of outrage. Two state legislatures have already legalized physician-assisted suicide and more are certain to follow suit. Each year laws are introduced to legalize euthanasia. They are still being defeated, but the margin of the majority is steadily decreasing.

It may be only a matter of time before we sink into a legalized depravity. The rainbow is indeed reassuring, but we should understand its message.

וַיֹּאמֶר אֱלֹקִים לְנֹחַ קֵץ כָּל־בָּשָׂר בָּא לְפָנַי
כִּי־מָלְאָה הָאָרֶץ חָמָס מִפְּנֵיהֶם

*God said to Noah, "The end of all flesh has come before Me,
for the earth is filled with robbery through them"* (6:13)

The Cry of the Aggrieved

Rashi states that although the generation of the deluge were idolaters and immoral, their doom was sealed only because of robbery.

There are numerous references throughout Torah literature regarding God's intolerance of people who inflict suffering on others. The Torah says, "You shall not cause pain to any widow or orphan" (*Exodus* 22:21). Rashi comments that it is forbidden to cause pain to anyone. The reason the Torah mentions the widow and the orphan is because they are generally defenseless against an abuser.

Solomon says, "God seeks (to rescue) the persecuted" (*Ecclesiastes* 3:15). The Midrash states that even if a *tzaddik* is persecuting a *rasha* (wicked person), God will come to the defense of the *rasha*.

R' Zev Soloveitchik of Brisk explains that while idolatry and immorality are grievous sins, there is no persecutor and no persecuted. These are sins committed with consent. Robbery, however, has a victim, and God will punish an abuser more swiftly than any other sinful person (*MeShulchan Govoha* vol. 1 p. 44).

How tragic that our society tends to blame the victim! I have personally seen a number of instances where a woman had to leave her home because her husband was abusive. *She* was the displaced person, not he. The community still prefers to believe the myth that Jewish husbands do not abuse their wives. Some rabbis refuse to believe the woman's account of abuse, especially if the husband is a pillar of the congregation and is highly esteemed. Why, he could never be an abuser! The woman must be fantasizing! I wrote the book *The Shame Borne in Silence* in the hope of calling the attention of the community to this problem, which is in fact present among Jews.

Women who are victims of abuse need the support of the community, not their scorn and contempt. Yet, some abused women have been shunned and ostracized by the community. Their accounts are heartrending. Perhaps it is the cries of the aggrieved who do not find consideration or support, but to the contrary, are scorned and isolated, that invoke the wrath of God.

The suffering of Jews appears to be endless. Some people attribute this to failure to observe the Torah. But just what violation of Torah is apt to evoke the worst consequences? R' Soloveitchik says that causing pain, especially to defenseless people, may be the reason for the Divine wrath.

Let us not turn a deaf ear to the plight of victims. If we are more receptive to their cries, God will be more receptive to ours.

וַיָּבֹא נֹחַ וּבָנָיו וְאִשְׁתּוֹ וּנְשֵׁי־בָנָיו אִתּוֹ אֶל־הַתֵּבָה מִפְּנֵי מֵי הַמַּבּוּל

Noah with his sons, his wife and his sons' wives with him, went into the Ark because of the waters of the flood (7:7)

Rashi comments on the phrase, "because of the waters of the flood," that Noah did not enter the Ark until the rising waters of the flood forced him to do so. Why? Because Noah was of diminished faith. He believed yet did not believe that there would be a flood.

The Torah commentaries struggle with Rashi's statement. The Torah describes Noah as being "a perfect *tzaddik*." How can a perfect *tzaddik* be lacking in faith? Furthermore, just what is meant by, "He believed yet did not believe?" This statement appears to be an internal contradiction.

The Steipler Gaon provides us with an important psychological insight. Knowledge of something can be of two types: There can be an *intellectual* knowledge and an *emotional* knowledge. For example, a person may have a desire for something, and is told to avoid going after it because there is excessive radiation in that area and the exposure is dangerous. If his desire for the object is intense, he may risk the exposure. However, if the object is in a building that is aflame, even an intense desire will not make him risk his life. Why the difference? Because a person does not *see* radiation. One can *understand* that radiation can be dangerous and even lethal, but this is an *intellectual* awareness, which can be overcome by an intense desire. The danger of fire, however, is grasped *emotionally*, and is strong enough to override temptation.

Rashi is not critical of Noah, who was indeed a perfect *tzaddik* and had a complete intellectual faith in the word of God that there would be a flood. Rashi does not say that Noah was *lacking* in faith. Indeed, his faith was complete, but was of a lesser quality because it was only intellectual. This is what is meant by the phrase, "He believed yet did not believe." Noah believed intellectually, but not emotionally. Perhaps Noah was simply incapable of having an emotional awareness, and this limitation was not his fault.

The Steipler Gaon's explanation is of great practical value. I see this regularly in my work treating alcoholics, who typically do not accept treatment to stop their destructive drinking until they hit rock-bottom, i.e., until they experience a severe crisis which forces them to acknowledge their problem. In my book, *Substance Abusing High Achievers*, I cite cases of people of the highest intellect who *know* that their drinking is destructive, yet are unable to stop. One physician who was the director of a treatment center for alcoholics and who regularly saw the ruination caused by alcohol was himself a heavy drinker. His intellectual awareness of the dangers of drinking was not enough to make him stop.

Billions of dollars have been spent to prevent young people from using drugs. None of the many prevention programs has proven effective. This is because regardless of how much we impress youngsters with the dangers of drugs, they achieve only an intellectual awareness, which is not sufficient to overcome the emotional desire to get "high."

Distraught parents whose child wishes to intermarry desperately try to discourage this move in every possible way. They have the rabbi talk to their child and they may take him or her to a psychologist. Rarely are these efforts successful. The child may *understand* why he should not intermarry, but this intellectual knowledge does not change his mind.

What can be done to prevent young people from self-destructive behavior? Unfortunately, very often nothing can be done. Parents agonize over their powerlessness to prevent their child from harming himself. They can only hope and pray that the child will come to his senses, and this may occur only when the child eventually experiences the harmful consequences of his actions.

Even Noah, "a perfect *tzaddik*," believed yet did not believe.

בַּעֲבוּר הָאָדָם כִּי יֵצֶר לֵב הָאָדָם רַע מִנְּעֻרָיו

Since the imagery of a man's heart (yetzer) is evil from his youth (8:21)

The Yetzer Hara (Evil Inclination)

A person comes into the world with physical drives, and more of these develop as a person grows. The physical drives *per se* are not evil, but the *yetzer hara* directs them to gratification by improper means.

Our ethical works describe the *yetzer hara* as being wily, seductive and deceptive. As a rule, the *yetzer hara* does not tell a person to do something that is patently wrong. Rather, it deludes a person to think that what is wrong is right and what is bad is good. Given the human mind's ingenuity in rationalizing, the *yetzer hara* can present temptations in a manner that that person may be defenseless to resist. The only safeguard is to be on constant alert for the *yetzer hara's* deceptiveness.

> A chassid asked R' Yisroel of Rizhin for a guideline to avoid sin. R' Yisroel told him that a tightrope walker maintains his delicate balance by leaning slightly toward the side opposite to which he feels himself pulled. If he did not do this, he would fall to his death.
>
> "Most of our urges derive from the yetzer hara," R' Yisroel said. "Therefore, when you feel yourself drawn to do something, lean a bit toward the other side and think why you should perhaps not do it. This way, you are more likely to discover reasons why you should not give in to the urge."
>
> One of the Chassidic masters cited the verse, "Protect my soul, for I am a chassid" (pious person; Psalms 86:2). "Why," he asked, "does a pious person need extra protection?"
>
> "It is because," he said, "when a person has an urge to do something and he is unsure whether it is permissible or prohibited, he can consult the Shulchan Aruch (Code of Law) and see whether this particular act is permissible or not. However, a pious person goes beyond the minimal requirements of the Shulchan Aruch and wishes to do things which are not

BEREISHIS / GENESIS: Noach

addressed therein. This gives the yetzer hara an opportunity to deceive him and present a sin as a mitzvah. A pious person, therefore, requires extra protection from the yetzer hara.

"How does the yetzer hara accomplish this? It tells one, 'That person is a sinner. It is a mitzvah to humiliate him and speak defamatorily about him.' Or, 'That person is dishonest. It is a mitzvah to deprive him of his ill-begotten money.'"

R' Shneur Zalman says that although the yetzer hara incites a person to do wrong, it really wishes that the person would not listen to it. He cites a parable given by the Zohar, of a king who wished to test the mettle of his son, the prince, to see whether he was morally upright. To achieve his goal, the king engaged someone to seduce the prince to act improperly. That person did as he was instructed to do, because that was his job, but he really hoped that the prince would not yield to his entreaties.

R' Shneur Zalman says that this is equally true of the yetzer hara. God created it and assigned it the task of seducing a person to sin. The yetzer hara must do its best to fulfill its charge, but in reality hopes that a person will resist it. Therefore, if a person resists the yetzer hara, it is actually pleased that it was defeated.

The Baal Shem Tov gave another parable. A king wished to see whether his subjects were loyal to him. He, therefore, engaged a person to try to persuade people to disobey the king's laws. Some people were gullible and yielded, while others argued with him. The truly wise person said, "How is it possible that a king who is so powerful would tolerate someone inciting people to defy him? It can only be that this is the king's way of testing our loyalty. Therefore, there is no purpose in arguing with him. I'll just ignore him."

"That is the proper approach to the yetzer hara," the Baal Shem Tov said. "Obviously, Almighty God could do away with it. God allows it to function to test our loyalty. If we try to argue with it, it may present cogent arguments why we should not observe the Torah, and we may be vulnerable to yielding to its logic. The only safe approach is to say to the yetzer hara, 'I know what you're up to. Go away and don't bother me.'"

But the *yetzer hara* is very powerful and cunning. Only serious study of *mussar* and *chassidus* and guidance by a Torah authority can defend us against its wile.

וְאַךְ אֶת־דִּמְכֶם לְנַפְשֹׁתֵיכֶם אֶדְרֹשׁ

"However, your blood which belongs to your souls I will demand" (9:5)

Preservation of Life and Health

We regularly refer to Torah as *Toras Chaim*, a Torah of life. With the exception of the three cardinal sins—idolatry, adultery and murder—the concern for life overrides all the other positive and prohibitive mitzvos. It is well known that when there is a danger to life, *pekuach nefesh*, it is not only permissible to violate the Sabbath but it is obligatory to do so. Furthermore, to save a life, no attempt should be made to have the necessary work done by a non-Jew or a child, because this may result in dangerous delay.

The respect for life and health is primary in Torah. During an outbreak of cholera when fasting posed a threat to life, Rabbi Yisroel of Salant ordered people to eat and drink on Yom Kippur. Because he was concerned that some people might be hesitant to do so, he publicly ate on that Yom Kippur.

The Talmud derives the prohibition of self-injury from the above verse, "Your blood which belongs to your souls I will demand" (*Genesis* 9:5), and states that this applies to any self-injury even if it is not life-threatening (*Bava Kamma* 91b).

It is, therefore, halachically incumbent upon every person to preserve one's health, and particularly to avoid doing anything that jeopardizes one's health.

It is utterly incomprehensible how people who are dedicated to observance of Torah can be grossly negligent of their health. Years ago, when the toxic effects of smoking were not known, people welcomed the relaxing effect of smoking. Today it has been established beyond the shadow of doubt that smoking is toxic, and is a leading cause of lung cancer, emphysema and heart disease. Research has also implicated smoking in several other diseases. Furthermore, smoking in the presence of others is injurious to them. It is clear that given our present knowledge, smoking should be halachically forbidden as inflicting damage to one's body.

Unfortunately, many people find it very difficult to break the smoking habit. However, this difficulty cannot justify continuing the self-injury. One is obligated to do everything necessary to avoid harming oneself in this way.

Recent research has confirmed the deleterious effects of obesity, which, by putting an excessive demand on the heart, contributes to heart disease and high blood pressure. Obesity is also a factor in the adult-onset form of diabetes. Totally aside from cosmetic considerations, avoiding obesity is necessary to comply with the halachic requirement of protecting one's health. Diet fads have repeatedly resulted in rapid weight loss which is most often followed by rapid weight gain. Maintaining proper weight requires considerable effort and dedication. Just as we put great effort into observance of all other Torah mitzvos, we should invest similar effort in protecting our health.

Needless to say, use of drugs and excessive drinking, which are deleterious to health, constitute a violation of halachah.

A proper Torah *hashkafah* (perspective) requires diligent care of one's body as well as one's soul.

נֹחַ . . . וַיִּטַּע כָּרֶם וַיֵּשְׁתְּ מִן־הַיַּיִן וַיִּשְׁכָּר וַיִּתְגַּל בְּתוֹךְ אָהֳלֹה

Noah planted a vineyard. He drank of the wine and became drunk (9:20-21)

When the World Changes

How is it that Noah, whom the Torah describes as "a perfect *tzaddik*," should be intemperate and drink to intoxication?

The *Sfas Emes* says that prior to the flood, Noah knew how much he could drink without becoming intoxicated, and he drank that same quantity now. What he did not take into consideration was that there had been a major upheaval. The world's population had been destroyed, and this was no longer the same world as before the flood. Pre-deluge guidelines were no longer valid. New guidelines had to be established.

I frequently urge young people who are about to be married or who are already newlyweds to become educated in child rearing. Some counter with, "Why do we need parenting classes now? Our parents and grandparents raised their children without parenting classes."

True, but today's world is not the same as just several decades ago. When I was a child, a child who grew up in the street had a good chance of becoming a decent human being. The street was not contaminated as it is now. There were no drug pushers at every street corner. There was no explicit indecency on billboards and in news magazines, and there was no television that brought violence and immoral behavior into the home. In my school days, being sent to the principal's office was dreaded. Today it is the principal who fears the students. Rampant school killings by disgruntled students was unimaginable then. Today the school may not be a safe place.

Just several decades ago, people knew how to wait. It took three days to go from New York to Los Angeles. Today people lose patience with a plane trip that takes five hours! There were no fast food outlets on every block, and it took over an hour for a potato to bake. Today one eats on the run, and a potato is microwaved in six minutes (and does not taste as good). The point is that the miracles of technology have resulted in our losing our tolerance for delay.

Technology has also given us unprecedented comforts. No one today would tolerate the sweltering heat as I did as a child. Computers and a huge assortment of appliances have eliminated much mental and manual labor, and television commercials are constantly telling us that we should not deprive ourselves of anything that can ease our daily living. Today's youngsters grow up in a world that promises many instant pleasures, and if they do not feel they have had their share of it, they are frustrated. One way to get instant pleasure is by the use of drugs, and they are not at all hesitant to avail themselves of them.

Raising decent children today means battling the toxic street and a hedonistic culture. We cannot afford to rely on our innate parenting skills, nor is it enough to raise our children the way we were raised. It is a different world. Noah did not realize this and he became intoxicated with alcohol. If we do not realize that the world is changed, our children may become intoxicated with alcohol or drugs. We need all the help we can get to parent our children properly.

The *Sfas Emes'* comment is not just an explanation of what happened to Noah. It is an invaluable teaching which we should apply in our daily lives.

וַיְהִי כָל־הָאָרֶץ שָׂפָה אֶחָת וּדְבָרִים אֲחָדִים . . . וַיֹּאמְרוּ אִישׁ אֶל־רֵעֵהוּ . . .
הָבָה נִבְנֶה־לָּנוּ עִיר וּמִגְדָּל וְרֹאשׁוֹ בַשָּׁמַיִם וְנַעֲשֶׂה־לָּנוּ שֵׁם

The whole earth was of one language and of one common purpose.
They said to one another, "Come, let us build us a city, and a tower
with its top in the heavens, and let us make a name for ourselves" (11:1-4)

The Merit of Unity — R' Yisroel of Kozhnitz cited the Talmud, "Jealousy, lust and pursuit of glory remove a person from the world" (*Ethics of the Fathers* 4:28). These three traits were present in the early history of man. Cain slew Abel because of envy, the generation of the deluge was destroyed because of unbridled lust and the generation of the Tower of Babel was in pursuit of acclaim. However, the generation of the Tower of Babel was only dispersed but not severely punished.

The Midrash states that because the generation of the deluge were thieves and, therefore, there was no unity among them, they were destroyed. But because the generation of the Tower of Babel "were of one mind" and were united, they were merely dispersed and allowed to survive and flourish. Rebbe says, "This teaches the importance of peace and unity: Even if the Israelites were idolatrous but united, God says, 'I cannot punish them because they live in peace and unity' " (*Bereishis Rabbah* 38:6).

Jews have suffered unspeakable suffering since our exile from the Holy Land. We have the assurance of the Talmud that if we would be united, we would be spared all our suffering. Yet, in spite of repeated expulsions, the massacres of the Crusades and the pogroms, and the horrors of the Holocaust, we still fail to do the one thing that would save us: unite. We should not let the differences between us fragment us.

In my work treating alcoholics, I see people who are behaving self-destructively, and who are told by everyone that drinking is destroying them. Even after suffering disastrous consequences, they persist in their self-destructive behavior. They continue this until they reach a rock-bottom, an experience which finally convinces them that they must stop drinking.

Throughout history we have sustained severe persecution. Something as horrific as the Holocaust should have been our "rock-bottom" and made us overcome our divisiveness. If the Holocaust was not enough to make us unite, I shudder to think of what it will take to bring us to our senses. I can only hope that just as our salvation in Egypt came at a time when we were not deserving, merciful God will save us even though we may not be deserving.

Each, in our own way, can hasten the redemption by forging a unity with our fellow Jews.

וַיֹּאמְרוּ אִישׁ אֶל־רֵעֵהוּ הָבָה נִלְבְּנָה לְבֵנִים וְנִשְׂרְפָה לִשְׂרֵפָה וַתְּהִי לָהֶם הַלְּבֵנָה לְאָבֶן . . . וַיֹּאמְרוּ הָבָה נִבְנֶה־לָּנוּ עִיר וּמִגְדָּל וְרֹאשׁוֹ בַשָּׁמַיִם וְנַעֲשֶׂה־לָּנוּ שֵׁם

They said one to another, "Come let us make bricks and burn them in fire." And the brick served them as stone. And they said, "Come, let us build us a city, and a tower with its top in the heavens, and let us make a name for ourselves" (11:3-4)

Delusion of Omnipotence

R' Yosef Chaim Sonnenfeld pointed out that the order of the verses seems to be reversed. It would appear that first they had the desire to build the city and tower, and after that they sought the building materials. Why does the Torah reverse the order?

R' Sonnenfeld makes a cogent point, to which we can bear testimony. The Midrash says that the intent of building a tall tower was to ascend to the heavens and do battle with God. R' Elya Meir Bloch says that they could not possibly have been so foolish as to think they could find God in the sky and do battle with him. Rather, what they sought was to break loose from *hashgachah* (Divine providence). The "battle" they proposed was to rebel against the authority of God.

R' Sonnenfeld says that they would never have had this arrogance *had they not become grandiose and exaggerated their own power.* As long as they were dependent on naturally occurring stone for a building material, they would not have had the audacity to wish to escape Divine providence. It was only after they had advanced and fashioned building material of their own that they felt they could be independent of God. That is when they decided to rebel against Divine authority (*Lekach Tov, Bereishis* p. 54).

This strikes a familiar chord. The twentieth century witnessed an unprecedented advance of science and technology. X-rays, sonograms, MRI and laboratory tests enabled doctors to determine the cause of a disease. Antibiotics, wonder drugs and new surgical techniques saved lives that had heretofore been doomed. Travel and communications were revolutionized. Microwaves and instant foods reduced the labor of food preparations. Air conditioning relieved the discomfort of torrid heat, and the development of nuclear energy put an unimaginable source of power in man's hands. These dramatic achievements led some people to believe that man was indeed omnipotent, and thus the era of "God is dead" came to be, ushering in a drastic lessening of the influence of religion. Man felt that he was now so powerful that he no longer had a need for God.

The advances of science and technology are indeed most welcome and we are their fortunate beneficiaries, but this should not cause us to develop a delusion of omnipotence.

Moses was aware of this danger, and before the Israelites entered Canaan he said, "You may say in your heart, 'My strength and the might of my hand made me all this wealth.' You shall remember that it was God Who gives you strength to make wealth" (*Deuteronomy* 8:17-18).

The Tower of Babel was four thousand years ago, the entry into Canaan over three thousand years ago, and the "God is dead" era was in our own time. We should indeed use the genius of the human mind to improve man's conditions, but we should not allow it to lead to a delusion of omnipotence.

It is reported that one of the astronauts was asked, "Did you see God when you were up in the sky?" He responded, "No, but when I returned to earth and my wife delivered a perfectly formed baby, that is when I saw God."

We can see God everywhere, unless we close our eyes and minds and refuse to see or think.

פרשת לך לך
Parashas Lech Lecha

וַיֹּאמֶר ה׳ אֶל־אַבְרָם לֶךְ־לְךָ מֵאַרְצְךָ
וּמִמּוֹלַדְתְּךָ וּמִבֵּית אָבִיךָ אֶל־הָאָרֶץ אֲשֶׁר אַרְאֶךָּ

*God said to Abram, "Go for yourself from your land,
from your relatives and from your father's house,
to the land that I will show you"* (12:1)

The Management of Emotions

Rashi states that God did not tell Abraham which land was his destination in order to increase his reward. I.e., God emphasized his leaving his roots by specifying "from your land, from your relatives and from our father's house" to endear his place of origin to him so that his leaving it to fulfill the Divine will would earn him greater reward, as the Talmud says, "The reward is commensurate with the difficulty involved" (*Ethics of the Fathers* 5:26). Rashi says this is also the reason why, when God commanded Abraham to bring Isaac as an offering, He said, "Take your son, your only son, whom you love—Isaac." This was to intensify Abraham's love for Isaac.

R' Henoch Lebovitz cites the Midrash that says that when Abraham put Isaac on the altar, Abraham wept profusely (*Yalkut Shimoni, Vayeira* 101). Although Abraham arose early in the day and was most diligent to carry out the Divine command joyously, he nevertheless felt pain that he was going to lose his beloved son.

The Alter (Elder) of Slobodka asked, why did Abraham not use his enormous powers of self-mastery to suppress his feelings for Isaac? He answered that it is not the Divine wish that a person be *devoid* of natural emotions, but rather that one must overcome them in order to fulfill the Divine will (*Chidushei HaLev, Bereishis* p. 45).

> *My great-grandfather, Zeide R' Motele of Hornosteipel, had a library which contained rare manuscripts. When this library was destroyed by fire, he was in deep anguish. Subsequently, he said to his chassidim, "The Talmud says that one must praise God for the bad that one experiences as well as for the good (Berachos 54a). If I had come into a fortune, you no doubt would have asked to celebrate with a L'Chaim. You should do so now as well." One of the chassidim asked, "Then why were you in such obvious anguish?" Zeide R' Motele replied, "When God causes a person to experience adversity, one must feel the pain associated with it. God does not wish us to be devoid of normal emotions. It is just that after one has felt the pain, one must have faith that everything that God does is for an ultimate good."*

R' Yisroel of Salant said that there are indeed some character traits, such as arrogance, that one should extirpate. Many other character traits do not have to be eliminated, but rather redirected into constructive channels.

When reading about the greatness of *tzaddikim,* some people say that they cannot seek to emulate them, because they were spiritual angels rather than mere mortals like us. It is important to know that our *tzaddikim* were extraordinarily great human beings, but they never lost their humanity. God sought to intensify Abraham's love for Isaac, and Abraham wept at the very moment that he was joyous that he would fulfill the Divine command.

God does not ask us to abandon our humanity and emotions, but to dignify them by being masters over our emotions rather than subject to them.

וַיְהִי רָעָב בָּאָרֶץ וַיֵּרֶד אַבְרָם מִצְרַיְמָה לָגוּר שָׁם כִּי־כָבֵד הָרָעָב בָּאָרֶץ

There was a famine in the land, and Abram descended to Egypt to sojourn there, for the famine was severe in the land (12:10)

Distortion of Judgment by Personal Interest

Torah means teaching, and this is so vital that Torah spares no one in order to deliver a message.

R' Yehudah Leib Chasman, a prominent *mussar* authority (*Ohr Yahel*) cites these astounding words of Ramban: "You should know that our father Abraham sinned by leaving the land to which God had directed him because of famine. He should have trusted that God would save him from death due to famine. It was because of this that his descendants had to be in exile in Egypt."

Think of it! Abraham, whose trust in God was so perfect that he withstood 10 formidable trials, including being asked to sacrifice his beloved Isaac, and Ramban views him as lacking trust in God!

What this teaches us, says R' Chasman, is that even the greatest of the great must recognize that his judgment may be affected due to personal interest. Suppose that two litigants came to the patriarch Abraham in a dispute over a paltry sum of money. If the patriarch had even the slightest personal interest that would favor one of the litigants, he would be disqualified to hear their case. Is it even imaginable that someone of the enormous spiritual stature of Abraham would rule improperly because he favors one of the litigants? Nevertheless, the Torah says that a judge who has a personal interest in the case *will be blinded*, and will not be able to render a just decision. Inasmuch as the Torah says this, no one is exempt, not even the holiest of the holy.

We make numerous decisions every day, and each decision is essentially a judgment. Some decisions are rather minor, but others require weighing pros and cons and some may involved ethical issues. If Ramban says that even Abraham's judgment could be affected by personal interest, how much more so are we vulnerable to being biased by the outcome we would prefer.

What can we do to avoid the pitfall of distorted judgment? First, we must be acutely aware of our vulnerability. Second, we should study the ethical works to be better prepared to recognize our likelihood of bias. And third, we should engage a disinterested, objective person, a mentor or a devoted friend, whom we may consult about decisions that are of greater import.

וַיְהִי־רִיב בֵּין רֹעֵי מִקְנֵה־אַבְרָם וּבֵין רֹעֵי מִקְנֵה־לוֹט וְהַכְּנַעֲנִי וְהַפְּרִזִּי
אָז יֹשֵׁב בָּאָרֶץ: וַיֹּאמֶר אַבְרָם אֶל־לוֹט אַל־נָא תְהִי מְרִיבָה בֵּינִי וּבֵינֶךָ

There was quarreling between the herdsmen of Abram's livestock and the herdsmen of Lot's livestock—and the Canaanite and the Perizzite were then dwelling in the land. So Abram said to Lot, "Please let there be no strife between me and you" (13:7-8)

Why Can We Not Live in Harmony?

Beginning with the Five Books of Moses to the most recent writings of *mussar*, we are repeatedly adjured to avoid internecine strife and divisiveness. We are promised unlimited blessings and success if only we are united. Alas! Satan continues to plague us with the worst curse that can befall us, as he sows divisiveness and pits one Jew against another.

In the above verse, the Torah tells us that the quarrel between Abram's and Lot's herdsmen occurred at a time when "the Canaanite and the Perizzite were then dwelling in the land." Abram's plea to Lot was, "Please let there be no strife between me and you." Abram was saying, "Here are two different nations, the Canaanite and the Perizzite, living side by side in peace. Why do we, who are blood relatives, have to quibble and live in dissension?"

Abraham's plea continues to reverberate in our ears throughout our history. We Jews are children of one ancestor, why must we be at odds?

We can give various reasons for our disagreements. I firmly believe that these are nothing but rationalizations. I believe that our archenemy, Satan, sows the poisonous seeds of disaccord. He causes us to be divisive and to separate from each other. This is the basis of our fragmentation. Inasmuch as senseless divisiveness would be intolerable to rational people, we ingeniously formulate rationalizations to just why we cannot live in harmony. Rationalizations are logical-sounding reasons that serve as excuses, but they are not the true reason. The Canaanites and the Perizzites had their differences, but Satan did not bother to sow dissension among them, so they lived in peace. When we justify our divisiveness, we are handing Satan his greatest triumph.

When the Chafetz Chaim learned that there was dissension among the staff of his yeshivah, he said, "I will close down ninety yeshivahs rather than allow one iota of dissension."

We can easily find more reasons why we should be together than why we should be apart. But we can find them only if we so desire.

וַיִּשְׁמַע אַבְרָם כִּי נִשְׁבָּה אָחִיו וַיָּרֶק אֶת־חֲנִיכָיו יְלִידֵי בֵיתוֹ . . . וַיִּרְדֹּף עַד־דָּן

When Abram heard that his kinsman was taken captive, he armed his disciples who had been born in his house and he pursued them as far as Dan (14:14)

Pitfalls of Distorted Judgment

Tosafos say that Abraham "armed" his disciples by giving them gold so that their attention should not be diverted from rescuing people to amassing booty (*Chullin* 47b).

R' Henoch Lebovitz asks, inasmuch as these were Abraham's disciples,

BEREISHIS / GENESIS: Lech Lecha [39]

spiritual people who were undoubtedly loyal to his teachings, how could they be suspected of being derelict in saving lives because they wanted to enrich themselves with booty? Furthermore, they did not set out to garner the spoils of war, but to save Lot. How could they lose sight of their goal? He answers that even spiritual people, in moments of stress such as battle, may lose their sense of values; it is conceivable that they might be attracted to the booty, even at the risk of neglecting lives.

The Midrash states that some members of the Levite family of Kehot, whose assignment was to carry the Menorah, the Shulchan (Table of the Showbread) and the Holy Ark, died because they did not show proper respect for the Holy Ark. When the Sanctuary was to be moved, each one wanted to have the privilege of carrying the Holy Ark, and they began to squabble over this.

In the heat of the argument, they lost sight of the fact that they were in the presence of the Holy Ark, and their irreverent behavior resulted in their death (*Bamidbar Rabbah* 5:1). Although these Levites were highly spiritual and were competing over the sacred privilege of carrying the Holy Ark, they were nevertheless diverted from their goal by petty competition.

This teaches us how conscientious we must be to concentrate on our goal and not be diverted. The Midrash states that Abraham's disciples would have been diverted from their goal of saving lives. The Levites were diverted from the holiness of the very holy object they strove to carry.

One Erev Yom Kippur, R' Yisroel of Salant was accompanied by a Torah scholar on the way to shul. The scholar was so preoccupied with the solemnity of Yom Kippur that when R' Yisroel asked him the time, he did not respond. R' Yisroel was critical of this.

The goal of Yom Kippur is to refine our *middos* (character traits). To be so preoccupied with Yom Kippur that one does not respond to another person indicates that one has lost sight of the goal because of preoccupation with the means.

If asked what their goal in life is, many people would answer, "To do the will of God." Yet, our involvement in the tasks of daily living may divert us from being cognizant of our goal. We have seen that even highly spiritual people were vulnerable to losing sight of the goal. How cautious we must be!

וּמַלְכִּי־צֶדֶק מֶלֶךְ שָׁלֵם הוֹצִיא לֶחֶם וָיָיִן וְהוּא כֹהֵן לְקֵל עֶלְיוֹן

Malchizedek, king of Salem, brought out bread and wine;
he was a priest of God the Most High (14:18)

To Learn from Everyone

King David says, "From all those who have taught me, I have learned wisdom" (*Psalms* 119:99). Every year, when the portion of *Lech Lecha* was read, my father would repeat this story.

The chassidic master, R' Meir of Premishlan, once met with the great Torah scholar, R' Shlomo Kluger. The two conversed for several hours. Before leaving, R' Meir cited the above verse in Genesis and interpreted it in his unique way.

ספר בראשית: פרשת לך לך

> "The Talmud says that Malchizedek was Shem, the son of Noah (Nedarim 32). Shem had an academy of Torah study, the academy of Shem and Eber, where they studied the Divine teachings transmitted by Adam. The Midrash says that the patriarch Jacob studied at this academy for fourteen years. Shem was thus a great Torah scholar.
>
> "The patriarch Abraham was known for his extraordinary service of God, as exemplified by his unparalleled hachnasas orchim (hospitality to wayfarers).
>
> "When these two tzaddikim met, each tried to glean something from the other. Abraham sought to acquire Torah teachings from Shem, and Shem tried to learn about the mitzvah of hachnasas orchim from Abraham.
>
> "This is what the Torah tells us. 'Malchizedek, king of Salem, took forth bread and wine;' i.e., Malchizedek learned from Abraham the mitzvah of providing bread and wine for sojourners, to fulfill the mitzvah of hachnasas orchim. 'And he, Abraham, took from him, from Malchizedek, the teaching of being a priest to the Most High, of serving God through Torah.'"

Why did my father repeat this every year? He knew that I had heard this interpretation several times. It could only be because he wished to impress me with the importance of always being teachable, ready to learn something from every person.

וְהֶאֱמִן בַּה' וַיַּחְשְׁבֶהָ לוֹ צְדָקָה
And he trusted in God, and God reckoned it to him as righteousness (15:6)

Development of Faith

The Torah tells us that God considered the patriarch Abraham's faith to be meritorious. But let us reflect a moment. If God spoke to any of us, would we not have an unshakeable faith? In what way is Abraham praiseworthy for believing in God with Whom he communicated directly?

This question is also asked about Moses. How could Moses fulfill the mitzvah of having faith in God when he was in direct contact with him? We do not have faith that there is a moon or that two plus two equals four. That which we see or understand does not require an act of faith.

The answer was given by R' Mordechai of Lechovitz, who cited the Talmud that on a person's Judgment Day he will be asked, "Did you transact in faith?" (*Shabbos* 31a). This is usually understood as asking whether one transacted business honestly. R' Mordechai said that it has an additional meaning. When a person transacts in business, he negotiates and tries in every way to maximize his profit. He does not settle for a meager gain. This is what one will be asked on Judgment Day: "Did you *transact* in faith?" i.e., did you do everything possible to maximize your faith, or did you just accept whatever you were given?

Abraham and Moses *transacted* in faith. They, of course, *knew* there was a God. They did not have to have faith in His existence. But they tried to strengthen their faith by coming to an ever greater knowledge of God, and believing even that which they could not see about God.

Some people take their faith in God for granted. Of course they believe that

BEREISHIS / GENESIS: Lech Lecha

there is a God. But they may not have gone beyond that to try to know more and more about God. We have great works available to us to increase our faith and broaden our concept of God. If we fail to do so, we will have no answer on Judgment Day when we are asked, "Did you seek to improve the quality of your faith? Did you *transact* in faith?"

וַיֹּאמֶר לָהּ מַלְאַךְ ה' הִנָּךְ הָרָה וְיֹלַדְתְּ בֵּן וְקָרָאת שְׁמוֹ יִשְׁמָעֵאל כִּי־שָׁמַע ה' אֶל־עָנְיֵךְ: וְהוּא יִהְיֶה פֶּרֶא אָדָם יָדוֹ בַכֹּל וְיַד כֹּל בּוֹ וְעַל־פְּנֵי כָל־אֶחָיו יִשְׁכֹּן

An angel of God said to her, "Behold you will conceive, and give birth to a son; you shall name him Ishmael, for God has heard your prayer. And he shall be an untamed brigand of a man; his hand against everyone and everyone's hand against him" (16:11-12)

The Fulfillment of a Prophecy

The prophecy about Ishmael, progenitor of the Arabs, has unfortunately come true. The accurate translation of the angel's words is, "He will be a wild-ass of a man."

Many years ago, the Chafetz Chaim said that the words of the Torah are immutable. "The descendants of Ishmael will always be untamed. Even if the nations of the world try to civilize them, it will be in futility. Ishmael is untamable. If he will be a lawyer, he will be a wild lawyer. If he will be a professor, he will be a wild professor. His wildness will never be overcome." After saying these comments, the Chafetz Chaim said, "Woe! Who knows what Ishmael will do to our people in the end of days!"

There is a further prophecy in the remarkable interpretation of Onkeles, written 2,000 years ago. For the Hebrew "his hand against everyone and everyone's hand against him," Onkeles interprets as, "He will be dependent on other nations and other nations will be dependent on him." This was written eons before there was a need for oil and before it was known that oil is found in Arab lands. There was no logical reason to assume that other nations would be dependent on Ishmael. The Hebrew does not in any way lend itself to this interpretation, and it can be only the Divine spirit of prophecy that enabled Onkeles to make this interpretation.

Another prediction was made by R' Yaakov Baal HaTurim some 800 years ago. The last verse in *Chayei Sarah* (*Genesis* 25:18) refers to the descendants of Ishmael, and in stating where they dwelt, the Torah uses the expression, "over all his brothers he fell." The very next verse is, "These are the offspring of Issac, son of Abraham." The Baal HaTurim comments on the approximation of these two verses: "In the end of days, when the descendants of Ishmael will fall, there will be the rise of the descendant of David, from the offspring of Isaac."

How clear these prophecies are!

פרשת וירא ‎‎
Parashas Vayeira

וַיֵּרָא אֵלָיו ה'‎ . . . וַיִּשָּׂא עֵינָיו וַיַּרְא וְהִנֵּה שְׁלֹשָׁה אֲנָשִׁים נִצָּבִים עָלָיו . . .
וַיָּרָץ לִקְרָאתָם . . . וְאֶקְחָה פַת־לֶחֶם וְסַעֲדוּ לִבְּכֶם

God appeared to him (Abraham) . . . He lifted his eyes and saw: And behold! Three men were standing over him . . . so he ran toward them . . . "I will fetch a morsel of bread that you may sustain yourselves" (18:1-5)

Worship and Kindness; Oneself and Others

The episode of the patriarch Abraham's hospitality toward the three men who were angels in human form is regularly cited as indicative of his *hachnasas orchim* (hospitality to wayfarers). Inasmuch as Abraham was at that time in communion with the *Shechinah* (Divine Spirit) that visited him, yet left to welcome the travelers, the Talmud derives the principle that *hachnasas orchim* takes precedence over communion with God (*Shabbos* 127a).

My mother would regularly quote R' Yisroel of Salant's statement that the trouble with the world is that people are most concerned about their own *guf* (body) and another person's *neshamah*. We tend to pay more attention to satisfying our own physical needs, but as far as others are concerned, we seek to improve their spiritual rather than physical welfare. The patriarch Abraham set the proper priority: to care for the physical welfare of others.

There are few things indeed that would divert us from pursuing our own physical needs. We should also not be diverted from other people's needs.

> *R' Shneur Zalman, author of Tanya, lived above the apartment of his son, R' Dov Ber, the Mittler Rebbe. One time, R' Shneur Zalman heard an infant crying, and when he came down, he saw R' Dov Ber so profoundly engrossed in his Torah study that he was oblivious to the baby crying. R' Shneur Zalman reprimanded his son. As important as Torah study is, it should not render you oblivious to the cry of a child.*

> *The Gaon of Vilna was studying Torah in his succah and was unaware that a man had entered. After standing there a while unnoticed, the man left. He later asked the Gaon why he had ignored him. The Gaon apologized profusely, explaining that the man had entered so quietly that he had not noticed his entrance. He begged the man's forgiveness and blessed him that he should live to age 100.*

At age 98, the man became sick but refused the care of a doctor. "I know I will be well," he said. "The Gaon promised me that I would live to 100." And so it was.

Nothing, even intense spiritual involvement, should make one oblivious to the needs of others.

וַיִּשָּׂא עֵינָיו וַיַּרְא וְהִנֵּה שְׁלֹשָׁה אֲנָשִׁים נִצָּבִים עָלָיו . . . וַיִּקַּח חֶמְאָה וְחָלָב וּבֶן־הַבָּקָר אֲשֶׁר עָשָׂה וַיִּתֵּן לִפְנֵיהֶם וְהוּא עֹמֵד עֲלֵיהֶם תַּחַת הָעֵץ וַיֹּאכֵלוּ

He lifted his eyes and saw: And behold! Three men were standing over him ... He took cream and milk and the calf which he had prepared and placed these before them; he stood over them beneath the tree and they ate (18:2-8)

Greater than Angels

R' Yehoshua of Belz said that a human being has the ability to surpass angels in spirituality. While angels are indeed emissaries of God, they do not have any mitzvos. A mitzvah is not only a Divine commandment, but the word "mitzvah" also means "bond." Performance of a mitzvah binds man to God. This is something which even angels cannot achieve.

Initially, when the angels visited Abraham, their spiritual status was greater than his, hence they "were standing *over* him," i.e., superior to him. After Abraham had served them and fulfilled the mitzvah of *hachnasas orchim*, "*he* stood over them." By virtue of the mitzvah he had surpassed them in spirituality.

My cousin, the late R' Noah Rabinowitz, related the following story:

His father was a fine Talmudic scholar, and as a young man, excelled in halachah. He approached R' Chaim Soloveitchik of Brisk and asked to be tested for semichah (ordination). R' Chaim asked, "Do you already have a semichah?" R' Noah produced a semichah he had received from a noted halachic authority. R' Chaim read the semichah and said, "This is rather pareve," meaning that it did not describe R' Noah's scholarship as being exceptional. R' Noah commented, "What could you expect? After all, he is a misnaged (opponent of chassidim) and I am a chassid."

"And what do you think I am?" R' Chaim asked.

"You are partially a chassid," R' Noah said.

"What makes you think so?" R' Chaim asked.

"Because the Torah does not say of Abraham that 'he stood above them,' but rather uses the present tense, 'he stands above them.'"

R' Chaim became very excited. "You know that story? Then relate it to the people here."

R' Noah said, "R' Yoseph Dov, R' Chaim's father, was a son-in-law of a chassid of R' Moshe of Kobrin. When R' Chaim was an infant, R' Yoseph Dov lived with his father-in-law, and R' Chaim became very ill. The doctor said he had no treatment for him. At that time, R' Moshe of Kobrin was a house guest of R' Yoseph Dov's father-in-law, and the latter asked R' Moshe for a blessing that the child should recover.

"R' Moshe asked to be taken to the child's room, and standing beside the

crib he said, 'The Torah says that when Abraham served the angels, "he stands over them and they ate." It would have been more appropriate to say "he stood over them." Why does the Torah use the present tense?'

"R' Moshe continued, 'The Torah means to tell us that the mitzvah of hachnasas orchim was so dear to Abraham, that whenever one of descendants fulfills that mitzvah, Abraham comes down from Gan Eden to stand with him. Inasmuch as by my being here you are fulfilling the mitzvah of hachnasas orchim, the patriarch Abraham is certainly with us.

"'The Midrash says that Abraham wore a pearl around his neck, and that if a sick person looked at the pearl, he would be healed. So the child will look at Abraham's pearl and will have a refuah shleimah (complete recovery).'"

R' Noah continued, "Inasmuch as you recovered due to a berachah (blessing) from a chassidic Rebbe, you are partially a chassid."

R' Chaim then gave R' Noah an exhaustive test, and gave him semichah.

כִּי יְדַעְתִּיו לְמַעַן אֲשֶׁר יְצַוֶּה אֶת־בָּנָיו וְאֶת־בֵּיתוֹ אַחֲרָיו וְשָׁמְרוּ דֶּרֶךְ ה'
לַעֲשׂוֹת צְדָקָה וּמִשְׁפָּט לְמַעַן הָבִיא ה' עַל־אַבְרָהָם אֵת אֲשֶׁר־דִּבֶּר עָלָיו

For I have loved him (Abraham), because he commands his children and his household after him that they keep the way of God, doing charity and justice (18:19)

Virtue Lies in the Process

I have recourse to this verse in counseling parents when their child deviates from Yiddishkeit or becomes addicted to drugs. In addition to the parents' agony over their child's self-destructive behavior, they invariably feel guilty for having failed as parents.

To be sure, it is possible that parents may make errors in raising their children. Most parents try to do their best, but they may not realize that what they may think is best for the child may not be good enough. Parents are apt to raise their children the way they were raised, but the fact is that today's world is radically different than the world of just one generation earlier. We are living in an age of unprecedented challenges in raising our children. The street is flooded with immorality and violence, and children are lured to indulge in physical pleasures. Along with the defiance of authority that prevails in society has come defiance of parents. We cannot rely on intuition and traditional methods of *chinuch* (training). It is most important that parents receive teaching and guidance in child-rearing, to maximize the likelihood of their children adhering to Yiddishkeit. We must seek ways in which to help children withstand the onslaught of modern society. Ideally, counseling for parenting should begin before the first child is born.

But even when parents employ the best techniques in child rearing, there is no guarantee of outcome. We may not know all the reasons why some children deviate, and the parents may not be at fault. When parents have had good guidance and have been devoted to their children, there is no reason for them to carry guilt. Parents can only do what they can. They have no control of outcome.

In our prayers we invoke the merits of the patriarchs Abraham, Isaac and Jacob. Abraham's son, Ishmael, deviated from his father's ways. Only one of Abraham's sons, Isaac, followed in his ways. Yet, we refer to God as the God of Abraham. Isaac had two sons. Jacob was a *tzaddik,* whereas Esau was a rogue. Yet we pray to the God of Isaac.

God tells us why He loved Abraham: "Because he commands his children and his household after him that they keep the way of God, doing charity and justice." Abraham was a great *tzaddik* who did his utmost to transmit the way of God to his children. That only Isaac followed in his footsteps does not detract from Abraham's greatness.

Again, we must do our utmost to learn how we can best raise children in this age of social decadence. But if a child, Heaven forbid, deviates from Yiddishkeit in spite of good parenting, parents should not wallow in guilt. They have control only of the *process* of child rearing, not the *outcome.*

וַיֹּאמֶר הִנֶּה נָּא־אֲדֹנַי סוּרוּ נָא אֶל־בֵּית עַבְדְּכֶם וְלִינוּ וְרַחֲצוּ רַגְלֵיכֶם וְהִשְׁכַּמְתֶּם וַהֲלַכְתֶּם לְדַרְכְּכֶם . . . וַיַּעַשׂ לָהֶם מִשְׁתֶּה וּמַצּוֹת אָפָה וַיֹּאכֵלוּ

He (Lot) said, "Behold now, my lords; turn about, please, to your servant's house; spend the night and wash your feet, then wake up early and go your way"...
He made a feast for them and baked matzos, and they ate (19:2-3)

The Impact of Modeling

Many books have been written about parenting. There is universal agreement that the single greatest influence on children is their parents' behavior. All other techniques parents may employ are not nearly as effective as what they themselves do. Parental behavior is deeply engrained in children.

The Torah teaches us this in the character of Lot. Lot was a rogue who rejected Abraham, saying, "I want neither Abram nor his God" (*Rashi, Genesis* 13:11). Lot chose to live in the corrupt city of Sodom, fully aware of their decadence (ibid. 13:13). He married a woman of Sodom, who turned into a pillar of salt as punishment because when Lot asked her to give his guests salt, she said, "Are you trying to bring this wicked trait of hospitality to us?" (Midrash). According to the Midrash, giving food and shelter to wayfarers was punishable by death in Sodom. Yet this depraved scoundrel, Lot, risked his life to take in guests, and indeed aroused the entire populace against him. He put himself in even greater danger when he defied the populace and sought to protect his guests. This seems to be incongruous with his degenerate character.

R' Meir Rubman (*Zichron Meir*) says that having been exposed to his Uncle Abraham in his youth and having witnessed the overwhelming dedication which Abraham had to *hachnasas orchim* made an indelible impression on Lot. There is every reason to believe that Lot assimilated to his environment, and indeed, he was spared from the destruction of Sodom solely because he was Abraham's nephew (*Rashi, Genesis* 19:17). In spite of his depravity, he could not extirpate this particular trait, to the point of risking his life to be hospitable to guests.

This is a convincing example of the power of early imprinting. It is commonplace that children who were victims of parental abuse may swear that they will never be harsh to their children, yet they often repeat the very abuse they despised. This may seem to defy logic. However, the early imprinting of a behavior may overwhelm logic.

There is only one effective method to teach children proper behavior, and that is for the parents to practice it themselves.

וַיַּשְׁכֵּם אַבְרָהָם בַּבֹּקֶר אֶל־הַמָּקוֹם אֲשֶׁר־עָמַד שָׁם

Abraham arose early in the morning to the place where he had stood before God (19:27)

Creating a Holy Site

The Talmud states that a person who establishes a place for his prayer is considered a disciple of Abraham, a pious and humble person (*Berachos* 6b). Talmud commentaries have struggled with this statement. It is clear that there are many people who occupy the same seat in shul day after day and year after year, yet they may not be deserving of being called "pious and humble, disciples of Abraham."

The Talmud derives its principle from the verse cited above, that Abraham returned to pray in the same place where he had previously prayed. But if the Talmud is referring to a geographic place for prayer, it could have referred to an earlier verse: "He (Abraham) proceeded on his journeys to the site of the altar which he had erected there at first; and there Abram invoked God by Name" (*Genesis* 13:2-3).

Occupying the same place is not what the Talmud means. Establishing a place for prayer means imbuing a place with holiness, because a sacred place is most propitious for prayers to be accepted (*Berachos* 6a).

We are taught that the trait of vanity is so repulsive that God says, "I and a vain person cannot dwell together" (*Eruvin* 15b). On the other hand, humility invites the Divine Presence, as the prophet says, "I am with the contrite and those of lowly spirit" (*Isaiah* 57:15).

When Abraham prayed for Sodom to be spared, he said, "I desire to speak to my God although I am but dust and ash" (*Genesis* 18:27). The Talmud cites this as Abraham's profound expression of self-effacement. This humility invited the Divine Presence, and this place became sanctified. When Abraham wished to pray again, he returned to the sanctified place. Inasmuch as there is no reference to an expression of humility at the site of the altar mentioned in *Genesis* 13:3, the Talmud does not cite this as its source.

This is what the Talmud means. If a person can, by his behavior and refined *middos* (character traits) invite the Divine Presence and sanctify the place where he prays, he is indeed pious and humble, a disciple of Abraham.

To sanctify a place of prayer is a great spiritual achievement. If we cannot accomplish this, at the very least we should not make the place of prayer uninviting to the Divine presence. Carrying on conversation during the services is an affront, a flagrant disrespect of God. If we wish our prayers to be heard, we should do our utmost to make God desirous of resting His Presence in the place where we pray.

> וַיִּכְלוּ הַמַּיִם מִן־הַחֵמֶת וַתַּשְׁלֵךְ אֶת־הַיֶּלֶד תַּחַת אַחַד הַשִּׂיחִם:
> וַתֵּלֶךְ וַתֵּשֶׁב לָהּ מִנֶּגֶד הַרְחֵק . . . כִּי אָמְרָה אַל־אֶרְאֶה בְּמוֹת הַיָּלֶד
>
> *When the water in the skin was consumed, she cast the lad beneath one of the trees. She went and sat herself down at a distance... for she said, "Let me not see the death of the child"* (21:15-16)

Is Parental Love Always Unselfish?

This episode of Hagar and Ishmael arouses some very distressing feelings. As R' Samson Raphael Hirsch says:

"Hagar's whole behavior is extremely characteristic and reveals the shortcoming, the imperfection, of the Hamitic character. A Jewish mother would not have forsaken her child, even if all she could do would be to try to pacify him, even if it were only to soothe him for the millionth part of a second. To go away, just because 'one cannot bear to see the misery' is not sympathetic feeling for another but is the cruel egoism of a human nature which is still crude. In truly humane people, the feelings of duty master the strongest emotions, make one forget one's own painful feelings and give helpful assistance even if one can do no more than provide the comfort of one's caring presence."

One aspect of parental love is self-love, because our children are extensions of ourselves. Hirsch makes an extremely important point when he says, "The feelings of duty master the strongest emotions, make one forget one's own painful feelings." In addition to loving children, parents have a duty to them. Children did not ask to be brought into the world, and parents have an obligation to provide the child with the means to achieve success and happiness. While we cannot give our children happiness, we are duty-bound to do whatever we can to enable them to find happiness.

It is often stated that one of the "inalienable rights of man" is the *pursuit of happiness.* Modern western civilization seems to have interpreted this to mean pursuit of *pleasure,* as though pleasure and happiness were synonymous. There are many ways in which we can give our children pleasure, by giving them age-appropriate things. But *happiness* consists of *spiritual* fulfillment as well as fulfillment of one's basic physical needs. By providing children with a proper Torah education and modeling spirituality for them, parents can give their children the ingredients from which they can fashion happiness.

Sometimes parents may object to their child's choice of a spouse because it is indeed a poor choice, but the child's passion blinds him to what the parents discern. But there are also instances when the child's choice is in fact good, and the parents object because they feel that the other family is beneath them or follow traditions that differ from theirs. Parents must be careful not to put their needs above those of their child.

Some young people unfortunately behave in a self-destructive manner. Typical of this is the youngster who uses drugs. Distraught parents want to help their child. However, I have seen cases where the parents did not do their utmost to help their child, because to do so would expose that there is a problem in the family that would reflect negatively on them. In order for a youngster to have the maximum benefit from drug treatment it is crucial that parents participate in a parent-support group. Yet some parents have refused such participation for fear that this may reveal that they have a drug-addicted child. Too many cases of drug use go untreated because parents do not wish to confront the problem.

I believe that parents have every right to protect their reputation. However, when this conflicts with what is best for the child, "the feelings of duty *should* master the strongest emotions, and *should* make one set aside one's own painful feelings."

The Torah is a guide book rather than a history book. The episode of Hagar and Ishmael is not merely a narrative but rather a lesson to be taken to heart.

וַיֹּאמֶר קַח־נָא אֶת־בִּנְךָ אֶת־יְחִידְךָ אֲשֶׁר־אָהַבְתָּ
אֶת־יִצְחָק וְלֶךְ־לְךָ אֶל־אֶרֶץ הַמֹּרִיָּה וְהַעֲלֵהוּ שָׁם לְעֹלָה

He [God] said, "Please take your son, your only one, whom you love — Isaac — and go to the land of Moriah; bring him up there as an offering (22:2)

Harnessing the Yetzer Hara

The Talmud says that when the Torah says one must serve God with all of one's heart, it means with the *yetzer hara* (evil inclination) as well as the *yetzer tov* (good inclination). Many explanations have been offered as to how one can put the *yetzer hara* to the service of God.

The *akeidah*, Abraham's readiness to sacrifice Isaac to God as an offering, is cited as the ultimate test and proof of Abraham's devotion to God. I was asked, how did Abraham know that the voice he heard commanding him to sacrifice Isaac was in fact the voice of God? Why did Abraham not consider the possibility that he was hallucinating, and that this was an auditory hallucination? The Talmud says that Abraham was able to fulfill all the mitzvos of the Torah long before Sinai because his devotion to God was so complete that he intuitively knew what God desired. The Torah is vehement in denouncing human sacrifice (*Deuteronomy* 12:31). In his condemnation of idolatry, Abraham certainly condemned this practice. Inasmuch as Abraham knew that human sacrifice is an abomination to God, why did he not consider the possibility that the voice he heard was not the voice of God but rather an auditory hallucination?

The answer to this is provided by the Midrash. It is likely that Abraham weighed both possibilities, and was awaiting a sign for the truth. The Midrash says that Satan confronted him, in the guise of an old, wise man. "Where are you going?" he asked.

Abraham responded, "To pray."

"Then why are you carrying wood, fire and a knife?" Satan asked.

"Perhaps I will have an opportunity to make an offering," Abraham said.

Satan then said, "Old man, don't you think I was present when God told you to sacrifice your son?" Abraham then knew that what he had heard was indeed the voice of God.

Satan then tried every trick to discourage Abraham. "Have you taken leave of your senses? Are you going to slaughter the son that you had at age 100? You will deeply regret this tomorrow." But nothing he did could stop Abraham (*Tanchuma, Vayeira*).

The point is that Satan defeated his purpose by confirming for Abraham that it was a Divine commandment that he had heard. Any possible vestige of doubt as to

BEREISHIS / GENESIS: Vayeira

the authenticity of the command was removed. It was Satan (the *yetzer hara*) that enabled the mitzvah.

The works of *mussar* teach us the wiles of the *yetzer hara*. By knowing these, we may be able to distinguish right from wrong.

Satan gave Abraham a number of logical reasons why it would be wrong to sacrifice Isaac. Each of these elicited the response from Abraham, "For that reason I *will* bring the sacrifice." The teaching of the Midrash is that when we begin to find reasons why *not* to do a mitzvah, that should encourage us to do it.

In the episode of Joseph and the wife of Potiphar (*Genesis* 39:7-13), the Midrash states that her intent was to carry out the Divine plan, because she had astrological evidence that she was destined to have progeny from Joseph. This was indeed true, because Joseph subsequently married her daughter (*Genesis* 41:45; *Bereishis Rabbah* 85:3). She certainly used this argument in her seduction. Inasmuch as this was true, how did Joseph know that it was not the Divine will?

The answer is in the verse, "And so it was—just as she coaxed Joseph day after day" (*Genesis* 39:10). It was this persistence that enabled Joseph to know it was not the Divine will. The *yetzer tov* does not *nudge* (pester). The *yetzer tov* gives a person an instruction once. The *yetzer hara* does not give up, but repeatedly urges a person. If we find ourselves repeatedly urged to do something, this should raise our suspicion that it may not be proper, and we should then ask for guidance from a competent Torah authority.

We can thus fulfill the Talmudic requirement to serve God with the *yetzer hara*. By identifying the *yetzer hara's* tactics, we can avoid transgressing God's will.

פרשת חיי שרה
Parashas Chayei Sarah

וַיָּבֹא אַבְרָהָם לִסְפֹּד לְשָׂרָה וְלִבְכֹּתָהּ
Abraham came to eulogize Sarah and to bewail her (23:2)

Mastery over Emotion

The Hebrew word for "bewail" in the Torah is written with a diminutive letter *kaf*. The implication is that Abraham did not cry much over Sarah's death. Commentaries struggle with the question, how is it possible that Abraham did not grieve over Sarah's demise?

I have repeatedly said that it is not enough to know the Torah laws. We must know how to live spiritually as well as halachically. Our greatest source of teaching us how to live is in the lives of our *tzaddikim*, our great men and women who lived true Torah lives. We are fortunate in having a number of biographies that can serve as spiritual guidelines. In *Not Just Stories* I tried to convey episodes in the lives of our *tzaddikim* from which we can learn proper behavior.

Some people raise the objection that the lives of *tzaddikim*, as presented to us, are of limited help. "They are described as angels, not as human beings. We cannot be expected to emulate angels."

This is not a valid criticism, and may be nothing more than a rationalization, an excuse why not to make the effort to refine our *middos*.

We are extremely fortunate in having contact with people who knew the Chafetz Chaim. My first Talmud teacher studied under the great sage. The Chafetz Chaim was a real person, not a myth. The stories told of his extraordinary *middos* are true. This holds true for many *tzaddikim* who were and are our contemporaries.

I was privileged to have personal contact with the Steipler Gaon. He, too, was a real person. Yes, angelic in character, but a flesh and blood human being.

The Steipler Gaon was a brother-in-law to the Chazon Ish, for whom he had enormous reverence. The two brothers-in-law shared a common dwelling for some time. When the Chazon Ish died on Friday night, people were surprised that the Steipler Gaon showed no emotion, and his behavior on that Shabbos was as though nothing significant had occurred. The moment the last word of the *havdallah* ritual closing the Shabbos was uttered, the Steipler Gaon burst into uncontrollable weeping, to the point of fainting. Because halachah forbids mourning on Shabbos, the Steipler Gaon had controlled himself all Shabbos long. The pain he felt at the death of the Chazon Ish was severe, but inasmuch as he was not *permitted* to feel grief on Shabbos, he did not feel it.

Is it superhuman to have such control over one's emotions? Not at all. It is within every person's capacity, but it does require great effort, which most people do not expend.

There were eyewitnesses who reported that when the Chaftez Chaim's son died, he said, "Master of the Universe! The love that I can no longer give to my son, I will give to You." Superhuman? No. Just human greatness.

How does this explain the patriarch Abraham limiting his mourning over Sarah's death? R' Yaakov Neiman (*Darkei Mussar*) explains:

The Talmud says that Abraham observed all of the Torah long before it was given at Sinai. The Midrash states that the *akeidah* (offering of Isaac) occurred on what would be our Yom Kippur, which Abraham observed. As the Torah says, the distance to Moriah was a three day journey. The three day journey home brought Abraham to Hebron on the day before Succos. There was only one day on which Abraham was permitted to grieve for his wife, because one may not mourn on the Succos festival. With the advent of Succos, the patriarch was master over his emotion, and curtailed his grief.

One might say, "But Abraham lived thousands of years ago. We cannot expect to have mastery over our emotions like the Biblical personalities."

The Chafetz Chaim and the Steipler Gaon lived in our own time. Mastery over one's emotions is not impossible. It just requires concerted effort in spiritual development.

וְאַבְרָהָם זָקֵן בָּא בַּיָּמִים וַה' בֵּרַךְ אֶת־אַבְרָהָם בַּכֹּל

Abraham was old, came along with the days, and God blessed Abraham with everything (24:1)

The True Blessing: No Regrets

The translation often given for this verse, "Abraham was old, well on in years," misses the point. Having said that Abraham was old, the phrase "well on in years" is redundant and tells us nothing. "Came along with the days" is a rather unusual expression and calls for explanation.

We can only experience the present. We may reflect on the past and think about the future, but the feelings we have about the past or about the future can only be felt in the present. Feelings in the present can be overwhelming. If one has a severe toothache or headache, one is totally occupied with the distress of the present. At the moment of severe pain, little else matters. Getting relief from the pain is at that point in time perhaps the most important thing in a person's life.

The days of our youth and those of the prime of our lives are indeed important. We are generally so occupied with the present that we may give little thought to the feelings we may have toward the close of our lives. Yet when those days arrive, the feelings we will then have are every bit as pleasant or distressful as those of our younger years.

The feeling of powerlessness is most distressing. We are powerless to change the past. If we look back on our lives and realize the errors we have made, whether errors of commission or omission, the discomfort can be most distressful.

Every day of our later years is of the same 24-hour duration as those of our younger years. We will all reach days in which, unless we render ourselves oblivious of the past, we will reflect on our lives. Those days can be pleasant or unpleasant. The suffering of the days of our later years is no less distressing than that of our earlier years.

Both as a rabbi and as a physician, I have had many opportunities to be with people toward the end of their lives. If their minds are alert, they often reflect on the past, and many people express profound regret. If only they could turn back the clock! If only they could have a chance to relive their lives and avoid the mistakes they had made. Alas! What was done cannot be undone.

In all my experiences I have never heard anyone say, "My one regret is that I did not spend more time at the office." People may rationalize spending much time at work in order to advance themselves and earn more, purportedly to give their families a better life. Why, then, do so many people regret this? Because when they confront the moment of truth, they are aware of how relatively insignificant those things are that a person can acquire with more money, and how precious is the time spent bonding with their loved ones. They could have had a much more meaningful relationship with their children and grandchildren, which they foolishly sacrificed in the pursuit of economic success.

When we reflect on the past, there are days we wish we could eliminate. We may think of days in which we had hurt someone or of days when we dissipated time foolishly. If only we could erase those days! The pain of these remembrances and the powerlessness to eradicate those days can be exquisite.

The patriarch Abraham grew old, and he "came along with the days." There was not a single day that Abraham regretted. There was not a single day that he wished he could eliminate. "And God blessed Abraham with everything." There can be no greater blessing than looking back on our lives and thinking that if we had the ability to relive our lives, we would spend every day exactly as we did.

"Abraham died at a good old age, mature and content" (*Genesis* 25:8). What a blessing to look back upon one's life and be content!

וְאַשְׁבִּיעֲךָ בַּה׳ . . . אֲשֶׁר לֹא־תִקַּח אִשָּׁה לִבְנִי מִבְּנוֹת הַכְּנַעֲנִי . . .
כִּי אֶל־אַרְצִי וְאֶל־מוֹלַדְתִּי תֵּלֵךְ וְלָקַחְתָּ אִשָּׁה לִבְנִי לְיִצְחָק

I will have you swear by God . . . that you not take a wife for my son from the daughters of the Canaanites . . . Rather to my land and to my kindred shall you go and take a wife for my son, for Isaac (24:3-4)

Intellect vs. Middos (Character Traits)

Granted that Abraham disapproved of the Canaanites, but why were his kindred so much better? Abraham's family were all idolaters, and from what we know of Laban, he was a conniving scoundrel. Why were they preferable to Canaanites?

The *Ksav Sofer* states a psychological truth. A person with faulty intellectual concepts and erroneous beliefs may be reeducated to correct his thinking. However, a person who was raised in an environment where bad *middos* were imprinted on him is unlikely to undergo change, even with intensive education. Abraham's kindred were indeed idolaters, but Abraham believed that under his tutelage a young woman's erroneous beliefs could be corrected. A Canaanite woman who was exposed to corrupt *middos* in her childhood was hardly likely to reform with education.

As a result of my work with drug addicts, I can attest to the failure of education in deterring people from using drugs. With the billions of dollars spent over the past 30 years on educating people about drugs, what we have achieved is the most knowledgeable generation of drug addicts in history, but we have not made a dent in the prevalence of drug use.

By means of Abraham's statement, the Torah is teaching us a crucial principle of *chinuch* (training). If you intend your children to grow up to be honest, moral and decent people, you must practice *honesty, morality and decency* in your home. Do not expose your children to bad *middos*. Know who their friends are, and do not allow them to form attachments to peers with bad *middos*. Be aware that the television is a purveyor of the worst *middos* of which a human being is capable. If you think that by explaining to your children how abominable the violence and immorality on television is you can prevent its impact on them, you are in serious error.

Children can be educated in reading, writing and arithmetic. They can even be educated in philosophy. Character traits are absorbed from their environment: home, school and friends.

וַיְהִי כַּאֲשֶׁר כִּלּוּ הַגְּמַלִּים לִשְׁתּוֹת וַיִּקַּח הָאִישׁ נֶזֶם זָהָב . . .
וּשְׁנֵי צְמִידִים עַל־יָדֶיהָ . . . וַיֹּאמֶר בַּת־מִי אַתְּ

*And it was, when the camels had finished drinking,
the man (Eliezer) took a golden nose ring . . . and [placed] two bracelets
on her arms . . . And he said, "Whose daughter are you?"* (24:22-23)

Coping with Personal Interest

Rashi says that Eliezer gave the gifts to Rebecca before he inquired whose daughter she was because he had perfect faith that Abraham's merit would insure that this young woman was the one destined to be Isaac's wife. The Alter (Elder) of Novaradok asked, "If Eliezer was so sure that Abraham's merit guaranteed the success of his mission, why did he feel it necessary to pray to God, 'Do kindness with my master Abraham?'"

The Alter, therefore, adds an insight which can be a lesson for us. The Midrash says that Eliezer had hopes that Isaac would marry his daughter. Eliezer was loyal to Abraham and was afraid that his desire to have Isaac marry his daughter might affect him so that he might unwittingly thwart the *shidduch* with Abraham's kin. Aware of this vulnerability, Eliezer took measures to assure that he would not undermine his mission. This is why he prayed intensely that God help him carry out his mission and not be deterred by his personal interest.

As soon as Eliezer saw that Rebecca had offered to water the camels, which he had indicated as a sign that she was the wife destined for Isaac, he quickly gave her the gifts. Had she not become Isaac's wife, he would have had to pay Abraham for having given such precious gifts to the wrong person. He now had additional motivation for completing his mission successfully.

This is why, the Alter said, when Eliezer was served food in Rebecca's house, he declined to eat until he had spoken his piece (*Genesis* 24:33). Eliezer hastened to finalize his mission, knowing that any delay would present an opportunity for him to have second thoughts.

In this way, the Torah teaches us an important lesson. We should try to be aware of our personal interests and how they might distort our judgment. Once we are aware of them, we should act in a manner that decreases the possibility of our being misled by our personal interests.

Virtually every time we choose something or make a decision, there may be personal interests which could influence us to choose or decide in a way that would please us most rather than what is the most correct thing to do. We should be aware of this and take measures to enable us do what is right.

וַיִּקַּח אֶת־רִבְקָה וַתְּהִי־לוֹ לְאִשָּׁה וַיֶּאֱהָבֶהָ

He (Isaac) married Rebecca, she became his wife, and he loved her (24:67)

Love: the Basis for Marriage?

Too often we may read a verse in the Torah without pausing to analyze its full meaning. Is it not noteworthy that the Torah points out the sequence, she became his wife and *then* he loved her?

Western civilization is awash in love. The media bombards us with love via every possible modality: verbal, graphic and lyrical. Is it not strange that with all the emphasis on love, the divorce rate is an alarming 40 percent?

What passes for "love" in western civilization is either blind passion, or at best, self-love. Neither of these are a basis for an enduring relationship. Passion dissipates fairly soon and self-love may be rather easily frustrated.

The dynamics of a couple "falling in love" is something like this: The young man sees in this young woman a person who he feels can satisfy *his* emotional needs, and she sees in this young man someone who can satisfy *her* emotional needs. This would seem to be the ideal basis for a lasting relationship. But note: the young man is motivated primarily by *his* personal interest, and the young woman is motivated primarily by *her* personal interest. Although they profess love for *each other,* the reality is that they each love *themselves,* and the other is but someone whom they expect will please them. Should anything occur — the other partner is not pleasing them as they had expected, or if they meet someone who they think can better please them — the relationship is at risk of falling apart.

It may be difficult for us to understand how marriages were once made, with the parents of the couple arranging the engagement. In absence of passion and self-love, what was the basis for such marriages? It was a sense of responsibility to establish a family to whom the couple could transmit the legacy of Sinai. Certainly, the relationship was to provide satisfaction for both partners. However, if the level of satisfaction was not what each might have wished, the basis of the relationship was not weakened, and accommodation could more easily be reached. There was a common goal and purpose to the marriage rather than self-seeking interests. This enabled the development of a more mature love.

BEREISHIS / GENESIS: Chayei Sarah

The Torah tells us, "He (Isaac) married Rebecca, she became his wife and he loved her." The love developed *after* she became his wife. I can understand that. I saw it work.

> *My parents' marriage was essentially similar to that of Isaac and Rebecca. The marriage was arranged by their parents, and my father met my mother for the first time after the chuppah (marriage ceremony). Self-love did not enter into their relationship at its incipience nor at its end.*
>
> *My father was extremely well-versed in medicine, and when he found out that he had cancer of the pancreas, he felt there was no purpose in undergoing chemotherapy. "Inasmuch as it is not going to prolong my life, there is no reason to suffer the side-effects," he said. I had to agree.*
>
> *The doctor, however, told my mother that while chemotherapy in this condition was not of much value, it could extend his life for two or three months. My mother was adamant that chemotherapy be used, even if it would add only one day to his life.*
>
> *My father said to me, "I'm sorry that the doctor gave Mother misinformation. However, if I refuse chemotherapy, then when I die, mother may have regrets. She may feel guilty that she did not insist on chemotherapy: 'If only he would have had chemotherapy, he might have lived.' I don't want Mother to feel guilty, so I will submit to the distress of chemotherapy. I've done many things for Mother, and this gives me a chance to do one last thing for her."*

This marriage was not one of self-love.

Even when the couple know each other before the wedding, a sincere effort at making one's own needs subordinate to those of the other partner can make the marriage one of true love.

Thoughts on Shidduchim

The narrative of the *shidduch* of Isaac and Rebecca is the one place in Torah that refers to this subject, and it does so at uncharacteristic length. R' Avraham Pam states that this should serve as a focal point for guidance on *shidduchim*, and he gives some excellent advice (*Atarah LeMelech* pp. 26-33). Inasmuch as this book is not available in English, I would like to present some of the highlights.

The pivotal role of *middos* in choosing a husband or wife has already been mentioned. The information the young man receives about the young woman is that her *middos* are superb. She is kind, considerate and is engaged in *chesed* activities. Occasionally, after the marriage, the husband may find that his wife is a difficult person. He may conclude that he was given erroneous information about her, or perhaps she underwent a personality change.

R' Pam says that neither of these may be the case. Rather, the husband's behavior toward his wife may be such that it does not elicit consideration and kindness. He may not be sensitive to her needs, and may become angry easily. He may not treat her with the respect the Talmud requires. How can she be expected to respect and love him when she is embittered by his behavior toward her?

R' Pam's words are a breath of fresh air. So often it is thought that it is the wife's responsibility to initiate the respect and love in the marriage. R' Pam's position is supported by Rambam, who states the rules for the behavior of both partners in a marriage, requiring mutual respect and love. However, it is not accidental that Rambam *first* cites the husband's responsibilities in the relationship (*Hilchos Ishus* 15:19-20). It is the husband's responsibility to behave in a manner that will be conducive to eliciting love and consideration.

R' Pam addresses another important issue. There are many people who insist that their children's wedding be held in the beginning of the Hebrew month, when the size of the moon is on the increase, because that is a good *siman* (favorable omen). They consider it *mazaldig*. Some specify that the wedding be on a Tuesday, because in the six days of creation, the phrase "God saw that it was good" appears twice in the narative of Tuesday, hence it is a good *siman* and *mazaldig*. Families may have traditions about things that are *mazaldig* and are, therefore, a blessing to the young couple.

R' Pam cites the practice of eating certain foods on the first night of Rosh Hashanah because they are a *siman* for good things. We eat the apple and honey as a *siman* for a sweet year. We eat foods whose names indicate abundance, as a *siman* that we should have abundant merits. The Mishnah Berurah says that we must be particularly cautious not to have disputes or arguments on Rosh Hashanah, because this may undo all the favorable omens.

How foolish, then, for parents who wish to have their children's marriage begin with *mazal*, to get into arguments about arrangements of the wedding. They may bicker about who should be honored with reciting the *berachos* under the *chuppah*. They may argue over whether each set of parents should conduct their child to the *chuppah* or whether the two fathers should conduct the *choson* and the two mothers the *kallah*. As the Mishnah Berurah says, such arguments may undo all the *mazal* they wish for their children

I wish to add that the greatest source of *berachah* is *emes* (truth). A relationship that is based on less than truth is at great risk of failure. It is understandable that neither side wishes to reveal anything negative about the physical or emotional health of the *choson* or *kallah* for fear that it would discourage the *shidduch*. In my experience, those cases in which significant information was subsequently discovered (which is virtually inevitable) the lack of trust resulting from the deception casts a dark shadow on the marriage.

The Chafetz Chaim dedicated his entire life to eliminating *lashon hara*. However, he cites the verse, "You shall not be a gossipmonger among your people; you shall not stand aside while your fellow's blood is shed" (*Leviticus* 19:16), and comments that the approximation of these two phrases means that although it is forbidden to speak defamingly about another person, the exception to this is when you have factual information about a candidate for a *shidduch* which you know the other side would take seriously. In such cases, you are *obligated* to reveal this information, and failure to do so is a transgression of "you shall not stand aside while your fellow's blood is shed."

In a marriage, truth and harmony between husband and wife are the best *siman* for enduring happiness.

BEREISHIS / GENESIS: Chayei Sarah

פרשת תולדות
Parashas Toldos

וַיֶּעְתַּר יִצְחָק לַה׳ לְנֹכַח אִשְׁתּוֹ כִּי עֲקָרָה הִוא
Isaac entreated God opposite his wife because she was barren (25:21)

The Power of Prayer

Rashi explains that "opposite his wife" means that Isaac was standing opposite Rebecca when she was praying. The Midrash says that the patriarchs and matriarchs were childless for so long because God wished to hear their prayers (*Yevamos* 64a).

It is unthinkable that God, in His infinite benevolence and *chesed* (loving-kindness) would allow *tzaddikim* to suffer just because He desired to hear their prayers.

If we have any difficulty in understanding this Midrash, it is because we lack an understanding of prayer. The prayer that we are familiar with bears no resemblance to the prayer of our *tzaddikim*. Our *Shacharis* (morning service) often consists of rushing through the prescribed prayers in the *siddur* in 30 minutes or less. The *Amidah* is recited in five minutes or less.

This is not what prayer was intended to be. The Talmud bewails the deterioration of prayer even in their own time by noting that the pious people of earlier days would spend an hour in meditation before the *Amidah* and a full hour reciting the *Amidah*. It would then require another hour before they were able to descend from the intensity of their spiritual experience to be able to address the tasks of daily living (*Berachos* 30b). Our prayer has no resemblance to the prayers of earlier *tzaddikim*.

After the patriarch Abraham concluded his prayer to spare the population of Sodom, the Torah says, "God departed when He had finished speaking to Abraham" (*Genesis* 18:33). Abraham's prayer was a dialogue with God, and the *Shechinah* (Divine Presence) had been with him. We find similar expression in reference to the *Shechinah* resting on Jacob (ibid. 35:13).

The word for prayer, *tefillah*, can also mean "bond" (*Rashi, Genesis* 30:8). True prayer binds a person to God. It is an experience which elevates a person spiritually.

R' Shneur Zalman, author of *Tanya*, said that he was weighing the choice of whether to go to the Vilna Gaon, under whose tutelage the emphasis was on Torah scholarship, or to go to the Maggid of Mezeritch, where the emphasis was on *tefillah*. "I knew something about Torah," R' Shneur Zalman said, "but I knew nothing about *tefillah*." R' Shneur Zalman's "knowing nothing" about *tefillah* was a quantum leap beyond our most intense prayers, yet he felt it needed perfection.

The prayers of the patriarchs and matriarchs was such that it led to ever greater spirituality. To be the progenitors of the Jewish nation, they had to rise to the loftiest level of spirituality, and this could be accomplished only through prayer. It was for this reason that they were barren. They could not conceive and raise Isaac and Jacob until they had achieved this extraordinary spirituality, of so bonding with God that the Talmud refers to them as being the "Divine chariot."

We would do well to reflect on the nature of prayer, that it is a bonding with God. Perhaps we would not feel under pressure to finish the services so quickly.

וְיַעֲקֹב נָתַן לְעֵשָׂו לֶחֶם וּנְזִיד עֲדָשִׁים וַיֹּאכַל וַיֵּשְׁתְּ וַיָּקָם וַיֵּלַךְ וַיִּבֶז עֵשָׂו אֶת־הַבְּכֹרָה

וַיִּגַּשׁ וַיִּשַּׁק־לוֹ וַיָּרַח אֶת־רֵיחַ בְּגָדָיו וַיְבָרֲכֵהוּ

Jacob gave Esau bread and lentil stew, and he ate and drank, got up and left; thus Esau spurned the birthright (25:34)

So he (Jacob) drew close and kissed him; he (Isaac) smelled the fragrance of his garments and blessed him (27:27).

The Essence of a Jew

These two verses tell us much about the psychological makeup of a Jew, indicating the depths to which a person may sink and the dazzling spiritual heights to which one may rise from the depths.

The birthright at that time consisted of the privilege to do the Divine service. The firstborn son was essentially a priest. This privilege was transferred to the *Kohen* branch of the tribe of Levi following the sin of the Golden Calf. By selling this sacred privilege for a pot of lentil stew, Esau evidenced his disdain for the Divine service.

The account provided by the Midrash gives us an interesting insight. Esau could not reject this sacred privilege without somehow justifying it to himself. As we know, rationalizations do not have to be good. Even a weak rationalization may suffice to justify one's actions.

The Midrash states that Jacob was cooking lentils because that was the traditional food for mourners. The patriarch Abraham had just died, and Jacob was preparing the traditional mourner's food. When Esau entered, he asked Jacob who had died. When Jacob said that Abraham had died, Esau exclaimed, "What! A great *tzaddik* like Abraham died? Then there is no justice in the world. If there were a God, he would not have allowed so great a *tzaddik* to die." For Esau, this "gross injustice" was adequate reason for rejecting belief in God and the birthright privilege of priesthood.

Gross injustice? Abraham lived to be 175 years old, which the Torah terms "a good old age" (*Genesis* 25:8). There was nothing unjust at all about a *tzaddik* living to that age. Why did Esau consider Abraham's death at age 175 as indicating that there was no God and no justice? Because he wanted to free himself of the restrictions and responsibilities a believer assumes.

BEREISHIS / GENESIS: Toldos

This tactic has continued throughout the ages and is very much with us now. People who wish to be free, to do as they please and not be bound by the restrictions and responsibilities of Torah, look for any reason to discredit Torah. The reason does have to be any more valid than Esau's viewing Abraham's death as unjust. Any rationalization can suffice.

But within every Jew there is a Divine spark which is never extinguished, and given the right circumstances, even someone who is distant from Torah can rise to spiritual heights.

The Midrash cites the verse "he smelled the fragrance of his (Esau's) garments and he blessed him (Jacob)," and comments that the Hebrew word for garment, *beged*, appears in the Torah without vowel markings and can also be read as *boged*, which means "betrayer" or "defector." The patriarch sensed the quality of Jewish defectors, and found that even they were worthy of his blessing.

The Midrash relates that when the Romans sacked Jerusalem, they told Joseph Meshisa, who had defected to the Romans, to go into the Temple and take anything he wished. When Joseph emerged with the Menorah, the Romans said, "That was not intended for personal use. Go take something else." At this point Joseph refused, saying, "It is enough that I aggrieved my God once. I will not do it again." The Romans put him on the torture rack and tortured him mercilessly, and Joseph cried, "Woe is to me that I angered my God!" (*Bereishis Rabbah* 65:22).

Joseph Meshisa had not only betrayed his people, but had been degraded to the point where he was willing to enter the Temple — which even the Romans were hesitant to do — and took the Menorah for himself. When the Romans told him that this was not appropriate for personal usage, he realized how decadent he had become, and the spark of his *neshamah* was aroused to the point where he accepted torture, crying only for how sinful he had been.

At one point, God told Abraham that his descendants would be "like the stars of the sky." At another point, He said that they would be "like the sand on the seashore." The Midrash says this is characteristic of Jews. They can rise to unparalleled heights "like the stars of the sky," or they can be as low as "the sand on the seashore."

Every Jew has the Divine spark within him. Every one can turn this spark into a bright light.

וַיִּגַּשׁ יַעֲקֹב אֶל־יִצְחָק אָבִיו וַיְמֻשֵּׁהוּ וַיֹּאמֶר הַקֹּל קוֹל יַעֲקֹב וְהַיָּדַיִם יְדֵי עֵשָׂו

Jacob drew close to Isaac his father who felt him and said,
"The voice is Jacob's voice, but the hands are Esau's hands" (27:22)

Beware of Your Environmental Influence!

The Torah commentaries elucidate the incomparable insights whereby the Torah teaches us proper living.

Rashi comments on the above verse, "The voice is Jacob's, who speaks gently: 'Please, rise up.' But Esau speaks with arrogance: 'Get up, father!'"

R' Henoch Lebovitz asks, "How can it be that Esau spoke harshly and disrespectfully to his father? The Midrash says that Esau gave his father more than a hundred-fold the honor that the Talmudic sage, Rabban Shimon ben Gamliel, gave to his father. When attending his father, Esau wore his finest clothing out of respect for his father. How is it, then, that he spoke disrespectfully to him?"

R' Lebovitz's answer is something that we should all take to heart. If a person becomes accustomed to coarse language, it may become so much a part of him that he cannot speak politely even if he tries. Esau could change his clothes out of respect for his father, but having picked up the coarse language of his peers, he was unable to control the way he talked.

At the workplace or in the office, we often associate with people whose speech is less than delicate. Expletives and vulgar terms may pepper their conversational diet. Under protection of freedom of speech, the radio and television spew obscenities. If we are not extremely cautious, we may pick up this language and, what is worse, bring it home to our children.

It has been proven that people can be affected even by subliminal stimuli, and certainly by more overt and forceful actions. Just as coarse language is contagious, so are other aspects of behavior. Our business dealings may bring us into contact with people whose *middos* are not praiseworthy. We may not realize that they are influencing us and that our own behavior is deteriorating. Without being aware of the changes in us, we are helpless to prevent them.

Our only safeguard is to be on the alert, and to make a concerted effort not to pick up the speech and traits of the environment in which we live.

וְיִתֶּן־לְךָ הָאֱלֹקִים מִטַּל הַשָּׁמַיִם וּמִשְׁמַנֵּי הָאָרֶץ

הִנֵּה מִשְׁמַנֵּי הָאָרֶץ יִהְיֶה מוֹשָׁבֶךָ וּמִטַּל הַשָּׁמַיִם מֵעָל

"And may God give you of the dew of the heavens and of the fatness of the earth" (27:28, Isaac's blessing to Jacob)

"Behold, of the fatness of the earth shall be your dwelling and of the dew of the heavens from above" (27:39, Isaac's blessing to Esau)

The Source of Blessing

Although the blessings to Jacob and Esau appear similar, there are two striking differences between them. To Jacob, Isaac said, "may God give you," whereas in Esau's blessing he does not invoke the Name of God. Secondly, in Jacob's blessing, the blessing of "the dew of the heavens" precedes the blessing of "the fatness of the earth," whereas in Esau's blessing the order is reversed.

Although Isaac thought he was blessing Esau, the Divine Spirit motivated him to give Jacob the blessing appropriate for him. Jacob was to know that everything he possesses, even if it appears to be the result of his own efforts, is a gift from God. Moses warned the Israelites that when they inherit the Promised Land and become affluent, they should not think that it was their skill, prowess and work that produced their affluence, but that it was God Who gave them the ability to acquire wealth (*Deuteronomy* 8:17-18). Jacob's descendants can have this faith, but to Esau's descendants it is an alien concept. Living by the sword, Esau's descendants gained their wealth by plunder and robbery.

The Divine Spirit also bestowed upon Jacob the awareness that the goal and purpose of life is spiritual, "the dew of the heavens." This is achieved via the fulfillment of the Divine will. Inasmuch as one cannot fulfill the mitzvos without the physical means to do so, earthly belongings, "the fatness of the earth," are a necessity, but they should be seen only as a means, not as an ultimate goal.

Esau, on the other hand, lives for earthly pleasures. "The fatness of the land" is primary, and any spirituality is but an afterthought.

The two nuances are related. We can live spiritual lives only if we are aware that all mundane possessions are Divine gifts. If we lose sight of our utter dependence on God, we can degenerate into creatures that seek only physical pleasures, and we thereby lose the dignity of spirituality that elevates us above all other living things.

כִּשְׁמֹעַ עֵשָׂו אֶת־דִּבְרֵי אָבִיו וַיִּצְעַק צְעָקָה גְּדֹלָה וּמָרָה עַד־מְאֹד וַיֹּאמֶר לְאָבִיו בָּרֲכֵנִי גַם־אָנִי אָבִי

When Esau heard his father's words [that Jacob had received the blessings], he cried out an exceedingly great and bitter cry, and said to his father, "Bless me too, Father!" (27:34)

Causing Distress: a Grievous Sin

The Midrash states that because Jacob had caused Esau anguish, his descendants had to suffer the anguish of the threat of extermination by Haman, where Mordechai "cried out an exceedingly great and bitter cry" (*Esther* 4:1). Although Jacob heeded his mother to obtain Isaac's blessings and was obligated to obey her, and although he caused anguish only to Esau, who was not deserving of his father's blessings, this was nevertheless considered so grave a sin that it exacted Divine retribution on his children, to live under the fear of extermination. R' Reuven Grozovsky calls our attention to this, and points out how extremely cautious we must be not to hurt another person's feelings, regardless of how uncouth that person may be.

The Torah treats offending another person most seriously. The Torah states, "You shall not cause pain to any widow or orphan" (*Exodus* 22:21), and Rashi explains that the prohibition of causing anguish applies to *everyone,* and that the Torah mentions widows and orphans because they are defenseless and are, therefore, more likely to be victims of abuse. The Torah continues, "If you dare to cause him pain, then if he shall cry out to Me, I shall surely hear his outcry. My wrath shall blaze" (ibid. 22:22-23).

This prediction was fulfilled when we suffered the terror of Haman, because our ancestor Jacob had caused Esau to cry out in pain.

R' David Lebovitz carries this a bit further. He says that inasmuch as Jacob was ordered to take the blessings by his mother, he was compelled to do so and would not have been culpable for causing Esau anguish. However, he says, given that he had no choice but to hurt Esau, he should have felt the distress at having to do so. Parents who submit their child to a painful life-saving treatment have no choice, but they suffer the anguish at having their child feel pain. It was Jacob's lack of feeling distress for causing Esau to suffer for which he was held culpable.

There may be times when we have no choice but to act in a way that may hurt others. If we truly have no choice, then we are not culpable for what we do, but we will have to answer to God if we do not commiserate with the person's distress.

פרשת ויצא
Parashas Vayeitzei

וַיַּחֲלֹם וְהִנֵּה סֻלָּם מֻצָּב אַרְצָה וְרֹאשׁוֹ מַגִּיעַ
הַשָּׁמָיְמָה וְהִנֵּה מַלְאֲכֵי אֱלֹקִים עֹלִים וְיֹרְדִים בּוֹ

*He dreamt. And behold! A ladder was set earthward
and its top reached heavenward; and behold!
angels of God were ascending and descending on it* (28:12)

Fear of Failure

There is a principle that the actions of the patriarchs were prototypical for their descendants (based on *Sotah* 34a). There is an important teaching in the Midrashic comment on Jacob's dream.

The Midrash states that Jacob had a vision of the rise and fall of four empires under which Israel was exiled: Babylonia, Media (Persia), Greece and Edom. The angels representing these four empires were ascending and descending the ladder. God said to Jacob, "Ascend the ladder," but Jacob said, "I fear that if I ascend, I will have to descend also." God said, "Do not fear. You will ascend and you will not descend" (i.e., you will be elevated and you will not fall). However, Jacob feared and did not ascend. God said to Jacob, "Had you ascended, you would not have fallen. Inasmuch as you did not have trust in Me and did not ascend, your descendants will be in exile in these four empires" (*Vayikra Rabbah* 29).

Etz Yosef explains that the patriarch Jacob was unsure of himself and feared that he may forfeit God's blessing by committing a transgression. We find this again when he was about to encounter Esau, that he was not confident that he deserved Divine protection (*Genesis* 32:11). Etz Yosef said that this is in contrast to Abraham, who believed that God's infinite kindness assured fulfillment of His promise even if he were not deserving (*Ramban, Genesis* 15:6). According to the Midrash, God's reprimand to Jacob was that if he had had the trust of Abraham and ascended, his descendants would have been punished if they sinned, but would not have lost their sovereignty and gone into exile.

This Midrash has a practical application in our lives. In *Angels Don't Leave Footprints* and in *Life's Too Short*, I pointed out that people who have low self-esteem and unwarranted feelings of unworthiness are prone to avoid initiating endeavors because of a dread of failure. No one likes failure, but a person with good self-esteem can take failure in stride.

There are few people who have had uninterrupted strings of success. Most people encounter disappointments in some ventures, but this does not crush them. They reorganize, gather their strength and go on with life. A person with low self-esteem is likely to see a failure as a confirmation of his feelings of inadequacy, and this can be so fearsome that he avoids taking the risk. Of course, by not trying, one cannot succeed. *Success can occur only if one has the strength to withstand failure.*

The Midrash teaches us that we must have the courage to advance ourselves. We must pray for God's blessing. While there is no guarantee that we will succeed, we should realize that *not trying* results in the greatest failure of all.

וַיִּיקַץ יַעֲקֹב מִשְּׁנָתוֹ וַיֹּאמֶר אָכֵן יֵשׁ ה' בַּמָּקוֹם הַזֶּה וְאָנֹכִי לֹא יָדָעְתִּי

Jacob awoke from his sleep and said, "Surely God is present in this place and I did not know!" *(28:16)*

Know God in All Your Ways

Rashi (28:11) quotes the Midrash that this was the first night that Jacob slept. During the fourteen years he spent at the academy of Shem and Eber, he spent his nights studying Torah.

The Talmud (*Berachos* 63a) says that there is a brief passage upon which the entire body of Torah is dependent: "In all your ways know God" (*Proverbs* 3:6). Rambam and countless other commentaries refer to this statement, saying that one should serve God not only with the actual performance of mitzvos, but with all one's daily activities. A person should eat and sleep with the intent that food and rest are essential to have a healthy body, which enables one to do the mitzvos properly. Someone who is weak and exhausted cannot concentrate on Torah study or do mitzvos properly. One engages in work and business to provide the needs for one's family, and to acquire the means to do the mitzvos. Money is necessary to give *tzedakah*, to purchase *tefillin* and *tzitzis*, to build a succah, to pay for an *esrog* and for matzoh and to fulfill all the mitzvos. If one partakes of worldly goods for the purpose of being able to serve God properly, then all one's actions become part and parcel of Torah and mitzvos.

The Baal Shem Tov said that earlier generations were able to tolerate fasting without compromising their energies. As generations have become weaker, depriving oneself of food and engaging in other forms of self-flagellation may impair one's ability to engage optimally in Torah and mitzvos.

It is related that one Friday afternoon, the Maggid of Mezeritch sent a messenger to R' Zusia of Anipole, requesting that he desist from reciting *Shir HaShirim* (*Song of Songs*), because it was creating such a tumult in heaven that it disturbed the Maggid's sleep. *Chassidim* said that there is nothing remarkable in the fact that R' Zusia's recitation of *Shir HaShirim* caused a tumult in heaven or that the Maggid could detect this. What was surprising was that the Maggid's sleep was more important than R' Zusia's recitation of *Shir HaShirim*.

The *tzaddik* of Apt said that this was the discovery that the patriarch Jacob made and that he transmitted to future generations. Until now he had believed that one could serve God only while awake. In his sleep on the future site of the Temple he experienced a Divine vision, and realized that one could be in communion with God even while one slept. "Jacob awoke from his sleep and said, 'Surely God is present in this place and I did not know!'" i.e., "I did not know that I could relate to God even during sleep."

Serving God in our daily, mundane activities is not exclusive to great *tzaddikim*. The Talmudic statement, "There is a brief passage *upon which the entire body of Torah is dependent*: 'In all your ways know God,'" makes this obligatory for everyone.

וַיֹּאמֶר הֵן עוֹד הַיּוֹם גָּדוֹל לֹא־עֵת הֵאָסֵף הַמִּקְנֶה הַשְׁקוּ הַצֹּאן וּלְכוּ רְעוּ

He (Jacob) said, "Look, the day is still long; it is not yet time to bring the livestock in; water the flock and go on grazing" (29:7)

Middos (Character Traits) Can Be Infectious

Jacob was rather harsh in reprimanding the shepherds. Wasn't it obvious that the stone covering the well was so massive that it required many men to move it? The Rabbi of Gur (Imrei Emes) said that Jacob was aware of this, but that he rebuked them for not trying to move it. But is it not possible that they had in fact tried but could not move it? Yes, but just because they failed once, why were they not trying again? But how did Jacob know that they had not tried repeatedly? Was his rebuke justified?

R' Samson Raphael Hirsch sheds light on this episode by asking, why was it necessary to cover the well with so massive a stone? Could they not have covered it with something not quite as heavy? He answers that the shepherds were suspicious of one another, and feared that a lighter cover would enable one of them to uncover the well on his own and take an unfair share of the water for his flock. In order to prevent this, they made it impossible to have access to the water unless they were all present.

Jacob understood this, and reasoned that people who had no trust in one another were likely to be indolent and not exert themselves. Traits are infectious. Trust and diligence are likely to go hand in hand, as are distrust and sloth. Jacob knew that they had not even tried to uncover the well.

Even in a competitive world, we should have faith that what God decreed for us to have cannot be taken from us. Begrudging other people's success because we may think that it comes at our expense is a contemptible character trait, and unless we rid ourselves of this trait, it may affect other aspects of our character.

Character traits are not likely to exist in isolation. True faith in God and to *fargin* others (be happy for someone else's good fortune) tend to go together.

וַיַּעֲבֹד יַעֲקֹב בְּרָחֵל שֶׁבַע שָׁנִים וַיִּהְיוּ בְעֵינָיו כְּיָמִים אֲחָדִים בְּאַהֲבָתוֹ אֹתָהּ

So Jacob worked seven years for Rachel, and they seemed to him a few days because of his love for her (29:20)

One Day at a Time

Some of the commentaries note that this appears to be the reverse of what we usually experience. Being separated from someone one loves makes each day of separation feel like an eternity. How could it be that Jacob's love for Rachel made seven years seem like but a few days?

I am indebted to one of my patients for an insight into this verse. This young man

BEREISHIS / GENESIS: Vayeitzei

was recovering from an addiction to alcohol. He had become dependent on alcohol, and the thought that he could never drink again was intolerable. When he joined the fellowship of Alcoholics Anonymous, he was told not to focus on the rest of his life, but to deal with just this day. "It is not impossible for you to abstain from drinking just today, is it? Then focus only on what you must do today. There is nothing you can do today about tomorrow's sobriety, so there is no point in contemplating it."

I have found this principle in the works of *mussar*. The *yetzer hara* (evil inclination) says, "What point is there in trying to observe all the Torah prohibitions? There is no way you can do so for the rest of your life. You are certain to violate Torah in quest of your desires. Why fight a losing battle? Why struggle and deny yourself so many pleasures when you are doomed to fail at it? You might as well just give in now." The response to the *yetzer hara* should be, "I do not have to deal with the rest of my life today. I know that today I can withstand temptation, and that is all I am concerned with. When tomorrow comes, I'll deal with that challenge then."

The literal translation of the verse above is not "they seemed to him a *few* days." The Hebrew word *achadim* means "single days." The delay of seven years would have been very difficult to manage. Jacob, therefore, did not think of seven years, but took each day as it came. He could tolerate the deprivation *today*, and that was all that was necessary.

This is an important lesson for us. It is commonplace for people to make "New Year's resolutions," and these are soon broken. The reason for this is that a year is too great a task to undertake. One should resolve, "I will not lose my temper *today*," or " I will not smoke *today*" or "I will adhere to my diet *today*." Reducing challenges to smaller segments of time makes them much more manageable.

וַתַּהַר וַתֵּלֶד בֵּן וַתֹּאמֶר אָסַף אֱלֹהִים אֶת־חֶרְפָּתִי

*(Rachel) conceived and bore a son, and said
"God has taken away my disgrace"* (30:23)

Understanding Human Traits

When discussing Biblical personalities, we should bear in mind the Talmudic statement that if we consider ourselves as humans, we should think of the *tzaddikim* of earlier times as being angels (*Shabbos* 112b). In several places the Torah describes seemingly wrongful behavior by these angelic people, and we must understand that these are but microscopic flaws in otherwise perfect diamonds. An infinitesimally small speck that would not even be noticeable elsewhere may flaw a diamond. Acts which would not even deserve mention if we were to do them are considered noteworthy faults in Torah characters. The description of these acts by the Talmud is much different from what we may gather from a reading of the Torah text. Why, then, does the Torah present them as though they were indeed grievous sins? Because Torah means "teaching," and it is intended to guide us in behavior of which *we* may be capable.

Let us consider the matriarch, Rachel. The Midrash states that Rachel was aware that her father, Laban, might substitute Leah in her place at the wedding, and she provided Jacob with secret signs by which he could detect the ruse. At the last moment, realizing that exposing the subterfuge would publicly humiliate her sister, Rachel gave Leah the secret signs. Think of it! In order to spare her sister *a single moment* of embarrassment, Rachel was ready to give up for *her entire lifetime* the person she wanted to marry. This level of selflessness and spirituality is far beyond what we can conceive.

When Leah began having children, Rachel envied her sister. Her desire to have a child was so great that she said to Jacob, "Give me children—otherwise I am dead." Life without children was meaningless to Rachel, and she preferred death to childlessness.

Then the long hoped-for event occurred. Rachel conceived and bore a healthy child. What joy this must have brought her! Suddenly she embraced life again. It is difficult to imagine a greater delight than Rachel had when she gave birth to a son. However, when the son was born, Rachel said, "God has taken away my disgrace." What disgrace? Listen to what the Midrash says. "As long as a woman does not have a child, she has no one to blame for things going wrong. When she has a child, she can blame the child. 'Who broke the dish? Your son! Who ate the figs? Your son!'" (*Bereishis Rabbah* 73:5). Rashi cites this Midrash in explanation of the "disgrace" from which Rachel was relieved now that she had a child. She could now blame mishaps on the child!

Is it conceivable that after years of being barren and pained by her sister's fertility, and after declaring that she would rather die than be childless, the matriarch Rachel, whose spirituality was beyond our grasp, would have so petty a thought: "Good! Now I can blame the child when something breaks." This seems to be the height of absurdity.

The Torah is an eternal teacher, and makes use of this incident to alert us to our propensity to place blame on others, and relates what must be an absurdity in order to call our attention to this human frailty.

I once said, only half in jest, that there are four essentials to human life: (1) food and water; (2) clothing; (3) shelter and (4) *someone to blame.*

The dynamics of blame are simple. If I must acknowledge an error or wrongdoing, then I am obligated to make amends and make the necessary changes in myself to avoid repetition of the act. But we instinctively resist change. We are creatures of habit and we are set in our ways. Changing ourselves is most uncomfortable. People who are fully aware that cigarettes can cripple them or even cause their demise find it difficult to change. People will fabricate the most ingenious excuses to explain away their behavior so that there is no need for them to change.

But without change, there can be no progress. The resistance to change must be overcome. We must learn to accept blame rather than project it onto others.

Rashi's first interpretation is that the "disgrace" Rachel referred to was that if she remained childless, she might ultimately be given to Esau in marriage (*Tanchuma*). "When Jacob returns home, my father may say that he can take the mothers of his children with him, but I would have to remain, and he might give me away to Esau" (*Midrash HaGadol*). Why, then, does Rashi add the "Now I will have someone to blame" interpretation? Only to stress for us the ubiquity of this tendency so that we may guard against it.

Being cognizant of our lapses is not only a virtue, but also a vital ingredient of progress.

BEREISHIS / GENESIS: Vayeitzei

וַיֹּאמֶר לָהֶן רֹאֶה אָנֹכִי אֶת־פְּנֵי אֲבִיכֶן כִּי־אֵינֶנּוּ אֵלַי כִּתְמֹל שִׁלְשֹׁם . . .
קוּם צֵא מִן־הָאָרֶץ הַזֹּאת וְשׁוּב אֶל־אֶרֶץ מוֹלַדְתֶּךָ

[Jacob said to Rachel and Leah] "I have noticed that your father's disposition is not toward me as in earlier days . . . (God said to me) 'Arise, leave this land and return to your native land'" (31:5-13)

Indifference to Evil

The usual interpretation of this verse is that Jacob noticed a change in Laban's behavior toward him. It was no longer friendly, and was perhaps even hostile.

One of the Torah commentaries offers an additional interpretation that is an important lesson for us. The literal translation of the Hebrew is, "I see your father's face, and it is not to me as it was in earlier days." Jacob was saying, "In the past, when I saw your father, I saw the evil in him and it repelled me. Now, I seem to be more tolerant of him. He does not appear to me to be as evil as he once did. If I have adapted so that I am not repelled by evil, then I must leave. I have been associating with him for too long, and I have become callused to his corrupt ways. If so, then remaining here can corrupt me."

With this interpretation, the Torah is warning us about a common phenomenon which presents a serious threat to our moral integrity. *We tend to develop an indifference to wrongdoing.* The first time something unethical or scandalous occurs, we react with vehemence. As the same act is repeated, it loses it opprobrium. Indeed, the Talmud says that when a person commits the same sin several times, he may no longer recognize it as a sin (*Yoma* 86b).

Just several years ago, the first physician-assisted suicide became public knowledge, resulting in an outpouring of condemnation from an outraged populace. Then more cases were reported, and one could see that with each report there was less reaction. This progressed not only to indifference but also to the approval of physician-assisted suicide by several state legislatures.

The first reports about teenage gang wars and killings sent chills up and down our spines. Today, we may not even hear of them, and if we do, our reaction may be, "So what else is new?"

We still react with anger at school shootings, but we must admit that we do not react with the intense horror that we once did. In fact, because the carnage at the Columbine school was so severe, school shootings of lesser severity are almost ignored by the media.

The patriarch Jacob was sensitive to this, and when he realized that Laban's corruption did not elicit as intense a repulsion, he knew it was time to leave.

It is related that outside of a corrupt community, a man walked to and fro with a placard that read, "Sinners! Repent your evil ways." Someone asked him, "Do you really think you are going to change this community?" The man answered, "No, but my protesting will help me avoid becoming like them."

We must be on our guard. More than ever, we need to study our ethical works. Evil does not change its character when it is repeated. We dare not allow ourselves to become indifferent to it.

וַיִּחַר לְיַעֲקֹב וַיָּרֶב בְּלָבָן וַיַּעַן יַעֲקֹב וַיֹּאמֶר לְלָבָן מַה־פִּשְׁעִי מַה חַטָּאתִי כִּי דָלַקְתָּ אַחֲרָי

Jacob spoke up and said to Laban, "What is my transgression? What is my sin that you have [so] hotly pursued me?" (31:36)

Our Efforts Indicate Our Values

When Rachel left, she stole her father's idols and concealed them. Laban pursued Jacob and angrily demanded, "Why did you steal my gods?" (*Genesis* 31:30).

One of the Torah commentaries said that Jacob's statement, in addition to being a complaint against Laban, was also a self-reprimand by Jacob. In essence Jacob was saying, "Here Laban forms a search group to pursue me for seven days in order to retrieve his worthless idols. And am I, knowing the true God, exerting as much effort to come close to Him?"

How much we value something is indicated by how much effort we are willing to exert to acquire or retain it. A recovering drug addict who is told that he must attend regular meetings of a recovery group may say, "I don't have a car. I don't have any way to get to those meetings." I then say, "Be truthful with me. If you wanted to get cocaine and did not have any transportation, what would you do?" Invariably the person admits that he would walk miles even in icy weather to get his drug. I then say, "If you are not willing to make the same effort to avoid the drug use as you would to get the drug, I suspect that you are not ready to recover yet."

Let us be truthful with ourselves. If the weather is inclement, we may justify praying at home and not going to the *minyan* (quorum for prayer service). Does the same amount of snow or sleet also deter us from going to the office?

Parents may not be aware that actions of this nature send subtle yet powerful messages to their children. I have spoken with children who went "off the *derech*" (deviated from Torah observance). Their parents were most distraught, and tried to impress their children with how vital Torah observance was to them. These children point to their parents' behavior, and say that the parents regularly gave greater importance to their business than to mitzvos. Yes, they observed the mitzvos, but they would not extend themselves for mitzvos to the same degree that they would for business. "They are asking me to give up my friends. For me that is a major sacrifice. I don't have any other friends. I haven't seen them make major sacrifices for what they say is important."

There are people who spend an entire night outdoors waiting for the ticket booth to open so that they can obtain tickets to a sports event. Would we really do the same to be certain that we did not miss a mitzvah?

When Jacob saw the effort that Laban exerted to retrieve his idols, he took himself to task. Seeing the effort that some people put forth for things of questionable importance, we should do a soul-searching on how much effort we are ready to expend for proper observance of mitzvos.

פרשת וישלח
Parashas Vayishlach

וַיִּשְׁלַח יַעֲקֹב מַלְאָכִים לְפָנָיו אֶל־עֵשָׂו
Jacob sent angels ahead of him to Esau (32:4)

Peace Requires Personal Contact

For years Esau had hated Jacob. "Esau harbored hatred toward Jacob because of the blessing with which his father had blessed him" (*Genesis* 27:41). In an effort to appease Esau, Jacob sent messengers with lavish gifts for him. The messengers reported that the gifts had not altered Esau's attitude. "He is heading toward you with an army of 400 men" (ibid. 32:7).

It is related that there was a falling-out between R' Shneur Zalman, author of *Tanya*, and R' Baruch of Mezhibozh, the grandson of the Baal Shem Tov. Various attempts by intermediaries failed to bring about a reconciliation.

R' Baruch then said, "The Torah tells us that even angelic intermediaries could not defuse Esau's hatred toward Jacob. It was only when the two met personally that Esau overcame his hatred. When there is antagonism between two people, efforts to bring about peace via intermediaries are usually futile. The two opponents should meet face to face to iron out their differences."

Sometimes the dislike of a person may be due to misconceptions one has of him. Abraham Lincoln once said, "I do not like that man very much. I should get to know him better." A better knowledge of a person can eliminate such misconceptions.

The Talmud says, "Do not judge a person until you reach his place" (*Ethics of the Fathers* 2:5). Although this is usually understood to mean that you should withhold judgement until you understand the other person's circumstances, it can also be taken literally: Do not judge a person until you reach him personally. A face-to-face encounter may clarify his behavior.

Dramatic changes in feelings can occur when there is a direct relationship.

וַיִּירָא יַעֲקֹב מְאֹד וַיֵּצֶר לוֹ
Jacob became very frightened and it distressed him (32:8)

The Incalculable Merit of a Mitzvah

Although God had promised to protect him, Jacob was afraid that the merits of Esau's mitzvos might tip the balance in his favor, to the point where God's promise would no longer be binding and Esau would be allowed to triumph.

Esau's mitzvos? Why, Esau was a scoundrel of the first order! The Midrash states that Esau committed the most grievous sins. And if he did have any mitzvos, how could they possibly outweigh Jacob's abundant mitzvos? Jacob studied Torah day and night for 14 years at the academy of Shem and Eber. He did not neglect any of the mitzvos during his 20 years with Laban (*Rashi, Genesis 32:5*). What reason was there to suspect that Esau had greater merits?

The Midrash states that Jacob feared that Esau had the merit of two great mitzvos which he lacked: (1) Esau lived in Eretz Yisrael while Jacob was in Mesopotamia, and (2) Esau was in the presence of Isaac and fulfilled the mitzvah of honoring his parents (*Bereishis Rabbah 76:2*).

The Gaon of Vilna longed to go to Eretz Yisrael, and was distressed that his plans were thwarted. He pointed out that the mitzvah of living in Eretz Yisrael is so great that Jacob feared it might give Esau the upper hand over him, even though Esau was otherwise a *rasha*.

The second mitzvah of extraordinary merit is honoring one's parents. Jacob did not willfully neglect this mitzvah. He had to leave home at his mother's behest, because Esau swore to kill him. Although Esau was a *rasha*, Jacob feared that the great merit of this mitzvah might earn him Divine favor.

The Midrash states that the choicest of the patriarchs, Jacob, and the greatest of the prophets, Moses, were both afraid that the merit of even a single mitzvah by an adversary might outweigh their many merits. When Moses went to battle with Og, the king of Bashan, God reassured him that he had no reason to fear. Why did Moses fear Og? Because, as the Midrash says, Og was the fugitive who informed Abraham that his nephew, Lot, had been taken captive, and Moses feared that the merit of his service to Abraham might transcend all his merits! This, despite the fact that Og's motive was hardly altruistic. The Midrash states that Og hoped that Abraham would be killed in battle and that he could then marry Sarah. Yet, although his intentions were nefarious, the act of service to Abraham was so meritorious that it gave Moses reason to fear Og.

We may not adequately appreciate the greatness of a mitzvah.

> *A person who was a flagrant violator of Torah once said to R' Levi Yitzchok of Berditchev, "God said that he would punish those who violated the Torah. Well, I have transgressed all the Torah prohibitions, and just look at me! I am wealthy, happy and lack for nothing!"*
>
> *R' Levi Yitzchok replied, "My child, how do you know that God punishes the sinful? Because you read it in the Shema. You should know that the mitzvah of reading the Shema even once is so great, that even if you had ten times the wealth you have it would not be adequate reward for that one mitzvah."*

We are blessed with the opportunity to do many mitzvos. We should appreciate their incomparable value.

וַיִּוָּתֵר יַעֲקֹב לְבַדּוֹ וַיֵּאָבֵק אִישׁ עִמּוֹ עַד עֲלוֹת הַשָּׁחַר

Jacob was left alone and a man wrestled with him until the break of dawn (32:25)

The Danger of Isolation

The Midrash states that the person who attacked Jacob was the guardian angel of Esau. The commentaries add that this angel represents the *yetzer hara*, the prime spiritual force of evil that wished to vanquish Jacob and his descendants.

BEREISHIS / GENESIS: Vayishlach

The rabbi of Slonim interprets this verse to provide us with an important lesson. He points out that the Hebrew word *vayivoser* can also mean "to be superfluous," and the message of the verse is that Jacob felt that he was superfluous when he was alone, isolated and detached from others.

The Psalmist says, "For I have said that the world is built upon *chesed* (loving-kindness)." The chassidic writings interpret this verse as a reason for Creation. Although we cannot have any concept into the essence of the Divine attributes, we are told that God created the world because "it is in the nature of the good to do good" and without a world, there would be no recipients for God's goodness.

We are supposed to emulate the Divine attributes, and the foremost obligation of man is to do *chesed*. But *chesed* cannot be done in a vacuum. The phrase, "God said 'It is not good that man be alone,'" (*Genesis* 2:18) means not only that a person should not be without a spouse, but also that "there can be no goodness when man is alone." Goodness requires that there be a relationship, a recipient of one's *chesed*. Inasmuch as the purpose of creation was for man to emulate God in doing *chesed*, failure or the inability to do *chesed* leaves a person unfulfilled.

In my writings on self-esteem (*Angels Don't Leave Footprints*) I pointed out that we value things for one of two reasons: (1) they are functional or (2) they are ornamental. If you have a grandfather clock whose mechanism breaks down, you may keep it as a handsome piece of furniture. If your can-opener no longer works, you discard it. Since it has no esthetic component, it has no value if it is not functional.

On what basis can a person have a sense of self-worth? Few people are so handsome as to be ornamental, and even those who are exceptionally handsome lose their beauty as they grow old. Man's true worth is in his function, and inasmuch as a major function of man is to do *chesed*, the inability or failure to do *chesed* deprives a person of a source of self-esteem.

One of the tactics of the *yetzer hara* is to crush a person by depriving him of the ability to do *chesed*. The person who is isolated from others and cannot give of himself to others may lose his sense of self-worth. My years of working with people who are addicted to drugs or alcohol has convinced me that one of the factors that lead to addiction is self-centeredness. One recovered alcoholic expressed it this way: "I could look up at people or I could look down my nose at them. They were either far above me or beneath me, but I never felt that I belonged. Alcohol gave me the feeling that I belonged." This person escaped from the distress of isolation via the anesthetic effects of alcohol.

Feeling that one does not belong causes a person to feel superfluous. The rabbi of Slonim found this message in the verse which he translated as, "Jacob felt superfluous because he was alone." The low self-esteem and depression incident to isolation renders a person vulnerable to the attack of the *yetzer hara*.

Doing *chesed* is not only a great mitzvah, but it also helps a person to have a sense of worthiness and self-esteem.

וְהוּא עָבַר לִפְנֵיהֶם וַיִּשְׁתַּחוּ אַרְצָה שֶׁבַע פְּעָמִים עַד־גִּשְׁתּוֹ עַד־אָחִיו:
וַיָּרָץ עֵשָׂו לִקְרָאתוֹ וַיְחַבְּקֵהוּ וַיִּפֹּל עַל־צַוָּארָו וַיִּשָּׁקֵהוּ

*He (Jacob) himself went on ahead of them and bowed earthward
seven times until he reached his brother. Esau ran toward him,
embraced him, fell upon his neck and kissed him (33:3-4)*

Mutuality of Feelings

A superficial reading of these verses raises the question, if Jacob had already reached his brother, why did Esau have to run toward him?

There is a nuance in this verse that should be noted. The Hebrew reads "*ad gishto ad achiv*, until he reached *until* his brother," whereas it would seem to be grammatically correct to say *ad gishto el achiv*, until he reached *up to* his brother.

This nuance provides the answer to the first question. Let us go back to Rebecca's words to Jacob when she instructed him to go to Laban. "And remain with him a short while until your brother's wrath subsides." The next verse is usually translated, "Until your brother's anger against you subsides" (*Genesis* 27:44-45), which is redundant. Some commentaries, therefore, point out that the second verse lends itself to the translation, "Until the anger of your brother subsides *from you*." They explain, how was Jacob to know when Esau's anger has subsided? The answer is based on the verse, "As water reflects face to face, so the heart of man to man" (*Proverbs* 27:19). You can gauge how a person feels toward you by how you feel toward him. Rebecca was, therefore, saying, "Remain with him a short while until your brother's wrath subsides," and you will know that this has happened "when the anger of your brother subsides *from you*," i.e., when you no longer feel anger toward him.

When Jacob saw Esau approaching, he "bowed earthward seven times," *from a distance*, each time decreasing his anger toward Esau, "until he reached *until* his brother," i.e., until he achieved a feeling of brotherly affection for Esau. By following the verse in *Proverbs,* he thereby caused Esau to feel positively toward him, so that "Esau ran toward him, embraced him, fell upon his neck and kissed him."

The Torah is telling us how to convert an adversary to a friend: Do your utmost to feel positively toward him. Chances are that he will then begin to feel positively toward you.

וַיֹּאמֶר נִסְעָה וְנֵלֵכָה וְאֵלְכָה לְנֶגְדֶּךָ . . . וַיֹּאמֶר עֵשָׂו
אַצִּיגָה־נָּא עִמְּךָ מִן־הָעָם אֲשֶׁר אִתִּי וַיֹּאמֶר לָמָּה זֶּה

He [Esau] said, "Travel on and let us go — I will proceed alongside you."
Then Esau said, "Let me assign to you some of the people who are with me."
And he [Jacob] said, "To what purpose?" (33:12-15)

Dangerous Associations

Having apparently dispensed with his hatred of Jacob, Esau now offers to help him. "Come, let us travel together, or at least let me have some of my people help you." Jacob refuses Esau's offer, and proceeds alone.

The commentaries say that Esau is the personification of the *yetzer hara* that seeks to destroy Judaism. At first, Esau is overtly hostile, but he then changes his tactics to become overly friendly.

Judaism has been threatened many times by hostile enemies and has repeatedly suffered from their persecutions. However, there is a greater danger to Judaism than their hostility, and that is the association with them and the assimilation that ensues. It has been pointed out that in the half century following the Holocaust, we have lost more than six million Jews due to intermarriage.

We read in the Haggadah an excerpt from the declaration of the *bikkurim* offering, where one recounts the formative years of Judaism. In relating the history of the Exodus, one says, "The Egyptians mistreated us" (*Deuteronomy* 26:6). R' Chaim Halberstam of Sanz points out that the Hebrew word for "mistreated," *vayoreu*, can also be translated as "befriended," and that the captivity in Egypt was destructive in two ways: persecution and assimilation. In fact, the Midrash says that only one-fifth of the Israelites left Egypt, because four-fifths had assimilated with the Egyptians (cf. *Rashi, Exodus* 13:18).

One of my patients was a highly successful professional who was a secular Jew. Although he was not observant, he could not accept his son marrying a non-Jewish woman. He said, "Had I known that this would be the result, I would have practiced keeping kosher. When you don't eat with non-Jews the chances of intermarriage are lessened."

Esau twice offered to be of assistance to Jacob by accompanying him, and Jacob politely declined. Jacob's refusal to associate with Esau was intended as a guide for future generations. Courteous and considerate relationships with our neighbors, of course. Fraternization, no.

וְתִמְנַע הָיְתָה פִילֶגֶשׁ לֶאֱלִיפַז בֶּן־עֵשָׂו וַתֵּלֶד לֶאֱלִיפַז אֶת־עֲמָלֵק

Timna was a concubine of Eliphaz, son of Esau, and she bore Amalek to Eliphaz (36:12)

To Be Always Sensitive and Respectful

Of what possible use is this piece of information to us?

It tells us of the origin of Amalek, whose bitter hatred and cowardly attack of the liberated slaves after the Exodus resulted in the statement, "The Name of God is not complete and the throne of God is not perfect as long as Amalek survives" (*Rashi, Exodus* 17:16). How did this venomous hatred develop?

The Talmud says that Timna, Amalek's mother, was a member of a royal family. She desired to convert to Judaism. However, Abraham, Isaac and Jacob each refused to convert her. She then said, "I prefer to be a maid servant (i.e. concubine) to this nation rather than a princess elsewhere," and she married Isaac's grandson, Eliphaz the son of Esau. She then bore Amalek who became the archenemy of Judaism "*because Timna had been rudely rejected*" (*Sanhedrin* 99b).

We venerate the patriarchs, Abraham, Isaac and Jacob, and we dare not be critical of them in any way. The Talmudic sages' veneration of the patriarchs far exceeded ours, yet they made the point of saying that the patriarchs should not have rudely rejected Timna.

R' Chaim Shmulevitz cites this Talmudic statement. He points out that Abraham was aggressive and tireless in bringing pagans to the realization of the true God. "Abraham would convert the men, and Sarah would convert the women" (*Rashi, Genesis* 12:5). This legacy was transmitted to Isaac and Jacob. If the patriarchs refused to accept Timna when she asked to be converted, it was only after much deliberation which led them to conclude that she was not suitable for conversion. Without question, they were correct in their decision. However, the Talmud says, in refusing to accept her conversion, they should not have done it in a manner that she felt to be a rejection. Timna's bitterness at being rejected was infused into Amalek, from whose venom Jews have continued to suffer throughout history. As we know, Haman was a descendant of Agag, king of the Amalekites.

How terribly far reaching Timna's rejection was! Although the refusal was justified, it should have been done in a manner that would not have aroused such bitterness.

This is a most important lesson. There are many times when we must turn down a request, but at all times we must maintain a sensitivity to a person's feelings. If we have one job opening available and twenty applicants, we can hire only one and must turn away nineteen. If a young man and a young woman meet for a *shidduch* and either one is not interested in the relationship, one must refuse. You cannot hire twenty people because you feel sorry for them and one cannot consent to a *shidduch* because one is reluctant to reject the other. However, refusals must be handled with the utmost sensitivity and consideration. This is where Hillel's principle must be applied: "Do not do to another person what you would not wish done to you" (*Shabbos* 31a). We have all experienced refusals. Whereas we are always disappointed when our request is denied, we are not always hurt. In refusing a request, we should put ourselves in the other person's position and treat him as we would wish to be treated.

How sensitive must we be to avoid rejecting someone? Let me share with you a trivia to which I was alerted. When ending a telephone conversation, and after the last word was uttered you *immediately* hear a click, does that not make you feel that the other party was in a hurry to cut the conversation short? It takes only two seconds to wait until the other party hangs up the phone. These two seconds can prevent the other party from thinking you were not exactly enthralled to talk with him.

We may not be able to avoid disappointing others, but we can certainly avoid offending them.

פרשת וישב
Parashas Vayeishev

וְיִשְׂרָאֵל אָהַב אֶת־יוֹסֵף מִכָּל־בָּנָיו כִּי־בֶן־זְקֻנִים הוּא
Israel loved Joseph more than all his sons because he was a child of his old age (37:3)

Living in an Alien Environment

Onkeles translates the Hebrew word for "a child of his old age" as "a wise child." Rashi cites the Midrash that states that Jacob transmitted to Joseph all that he had learned in the academy of Shem and Eber. The Torah describes Jacob as being "a wholesome man, abiding in tents," i.e., a scholar, from the moment he matured (*Genesis* 25:27). Jacob certainly received much teaching from Isaac, yet the Midrash specifies that what he transmitted to Joseph was what he had learned at the academy of Shem and Eber rather than what he had learned from his father.

R' Yechiel Meir of Ostrovza cites the Midrash that when Rebecca sent Jacob away to Laban, Jacob spent fourteen years at the academy of Shem and Eber before proceeding to Haran as his mother had instructed. Jacob felt that the teaching he had received from his father was inadequate because it taught him how to conduct himself in a decent environment, in the presence of Abraham, Isaac and Rivkah. But now he was going to live in an alien environment with the corrupt Laban. He needed new information and expert knowledge on how to maintain his integrity and spirituality when exposed to noxious influences. In preparation for this challenge, Jacob spent *fourteen years* under the tutelage of the academy of Shem and Eber.

Inasmuch as it was God's design that Joseph live in Egypt and rise to a position of power, God inspired Jacob to transmit to Joseph all that he had learned during the fourteen years at the academy of Shem and Eber. It was this special knowledge that would enable Joseph to remain a *tzaddik* in the decadent environment of Egypt.

How important this message is for us today! Young people go off to colleges where the campuses are saturated with drugs and immorality. People go into the modern commercial world which is sadly lacking in ethics and morality. How adequately are they prepared to withstand the noxious influences that prevail in these environments? Coming from the saintly home of Isaac, Jacob nevertheless felt he needed *fourteen years* of special preparation before going into an alien environment. Do we spend a fraction of that in preparation? We do everything possible to immunize ourselves against physical diseases. How much do we do to immunize ourselves against influences that threaten the health of our *neshamah*?

The great Gaon of Vilna would review the second chapter of *Path of the Just* (*Mesillas Yesharim*) no less than *thirteen times* before venturing out of his home. Do we do anything to prepare ourselves to diffuse the influence of the street?

Inasmuch as my correspondence with the Steipler Gaon has been published (*Kariana D'igrissa*) I can cite what he wrote to me when I told him that I was planning to study medicine.

> "Inasmuch as the environment you will be in is totally secular, with no faith and with total absence of a sense of duty to God, there is great danger that one exposed to this environment may suffer ideational and behavioral (middos) deterioration. Rambam says that a person is deeply influenced by the people and friends with whom he associates, and one needs much Divine mercy that one's faith and fear of God do not come to ruin.
>
> "I believe it is essential to take protective measures to avoid being swept away by the secular current. It is, therefore, essential (1) to set aside a minimum of two hours daily for Torah study, and if possible, to find a God-fearing Torah scholar with sound intellect as a Torah-study partner; (2) to pray all services with a minyan, and at the end of the Amidah to pray intensely for Divine protection against improper thoughts; (3) to go to the mikveh regularly; (4) to be most cautious in proper observance of Shabbos. The entire day of Shabbos should be devoted to Torah and Divine service, to avoid weekday type of conversation, and to avoid reading anything other than Torah writings, such as newspapers. The holiness of Shabbos is protective for the whole week; (5) to set aside no less than 15 minutes study of the works of chassidus and mussar every day. You should constantly remember that everything in existence, all senses and all intellect, are but a spark of Divinity, and that without Divine loving-kindness a person would be nothing at all. This should bring about humility, which leads to fear of sin, to piety and to Divine inspiration."

Jacob and Joseph were adequately protected for venturing into a secular environment. We must be cautious to follow their example.

וְיִשְׂרָאֵל אָהַב אֶת־יוֹסֵף מִכָּל־בָּנָיו כִּי־בֶן־זְקֻנִים הוּא

Israel loved Joseph more than all his sons because he was a child of his old age (37:3)

Experience in Parenting

If we were asked the reason for Jacob's favoring Joseph, we would probably say that it was because he was Rachel's child. After all, Jacob wanted Rachel as his wife, and was deceived into marrying Leah. The Torah is explicit that "he loved Rachel more than Leah" (*Genesis* 29:30). Is it any wonder that he had special affection for Joseph? Yet the Torah gives a different reason, "because he was a child of his old age," and Rashi adds that Jacob transmitted more knowledge to Joseph than to his other sons.

The Torah may be sending us a subtle message. We cannot fathom the Divine wisdom, so I will never understand why God arranged it so that we are wisest in our old age. The most momentous decisions of our lives are not made when we are senior citizens. It is when we are young that we decide whom to marry, what career to choose, where to live, etc. This is when we could benefit most from mature wisdom. We also have and raise our children long before we attain our maximum wisdom. Do we make mistakes in raising our children? Of course! How could it be otherwise? We may do so with the best intentions, but we simply do not have access to the wisdom of later years. Many senior citizens look back at their younger years and say that if they had had the wisdom they now have, they would have raised their children differently.

It may, therefore, be that a child born when the parent was older was given a more wholesome upbringing than his older siblings. This may be one reason why Joseph was superior to his brothers, why Jacob taught him more and why he loved him most.

What, then, is the message? It is that we should be aware that as young parents, lacking the experience gathered as we advance in age, we should not rely on our intuition and inherent wisdom to raise our children. We should seek guidance on parenting from our elders and from other competent authorities on child-rearing, to compensate for our lack of experience. Perhaps then we will not have to say as we look back, "I wish I had done it differently."

וַיִּרְאוּ וְהִנֵּה אֹרְחַת יִשְׁמְעֵאלִים בָּאָה מִגִּלְעָד וּגְמַלֵּיהֶם נֹשְׂאִים נְכֹאת וּצְרִי וָלֹט

They saw behold! — a caravan of Ishmaelites was coming from Gilead, their camels bearing spices, balsam and lotus (37:25)

Divine Justice Is Perfect

Of what use is it for us to know what merchandise this caravan was carrying? Rashi explains that these merchants generally transported malodorous substances, but in order to protect Joseph from the irritation of offensive odors, God engineered it so that they were carrying fragrant merchandise.

The author of *Nesivos Noach* remarks that Joseph was suffering the horrendous trauma of being torn away from his loving father and being sold into slavery, not knowing whether he would ever be freed or ever see his father again. Compared to this overwhelming agony, what difference could it possibly make to him whether the odors to which he was subjected were pleasant or not?

That is precisely the point, the *Nesivos Noach* says. For reasons known only to Him, God had decreed that Joseph undergo the agony of being sold into slavery. However, God did not permit even the slightest distress beyond that which He had decreed. It was Divinely decreed that Joseph had to experience this suffering, but what was not decreed, what he had not deserved, he was not subjected to.

This verse is, therefore, a profound teaching of the faith which we must have in the Divine justice. We may not be able to understand why we are subjected to distress, but we can be certain of one thing: we will not be made to suffer even one iota more than what God judged is to be our lot.

Moses, being denied his lifelong wish to enter the Promised Land, said, "The mighty One—perfect is His work, for all His paths are justice; a God of faith without iniquity, righteous and fair is He" (*Deuteronomy* 32:4).

If we could understand everything, there would be no need to have faith. The caravan's carrying fragrant spices is a testimony to the absolute perfection of the Divine judgment.

וַיַּכֵּר יְהוּדָה וַיֹּאמֶר צָדְקָה מִמֶּנִּי

Judah recognized and he said, "She is right. It is from me" (38:26)

Gratitude and Confession

The Midrash lauds Judah's courage in admitting that he was the father of Tamar's child, because he could easily have denied it. The Midrash states that Judah received this trait from his mother, Leah, because when he was born, she said, "This time let me gratefully praise God" (*Genesis* 29:35; *Bereishis Rabbah* 71). The Hebrew word for "giving thanks," *hodaah*, is also the word for "confess." Leah was indeed grateful, but we do not find her confessing anything. Although the same word has two meanings, how does Judah's ability to confess derive from his mother's ability to be grateful?

R' Samson Raphael Hirsch frequently points out that words that are similar are somehow related. This must be more so when the words for two different concepts are identical.

There is a very profound relationship between the ability to confess and the ability to be grateful. Both are the result of self-esteem.

Many people have difficulty in expressing gratitude, because it makes them feel obligated and beholden to their benefactor. This psychological truth is clearly stated in the Talmud (*Avodah Zarah* 5a). The resistance to express gratitude appears to be innate. A mother may tell her five-year-old child, "Say 'thank you' to the nice man for the candy," but the child may only grunt. A person with low self-esteem sees being beholden to anyone as a dependency on others, and considers being dependent as demeaning. He may not only be resistant to *express* gratitude, but may also turn off any *awareness* of gratitude. A mature person with good self-esteem is not threatened by feeling gratitude. He can take appropriate dependency in stride.

This also holds true for the ability to confess a wrong. A person with low self-esteem is apt to deny having done wrong. He may not admit a misdeed even to himself, let alone to others. Confessing a wrong can be crushing. A person with good self-esteem, on the other hand, realizes that even the finest human being may err, and he may have little difficulty in confessing.

When I lecture on self-esteem, people invariably ask, "What can we do to help our children build their self-esteem?" My answer is that the first thing is to have good self-esteem yourself. Self-esteem is contagious. Parents who feel positive about themselves provide an atmosphere where the child can feel positive. Parents with low self-esteem act in a way that transmits negative feelings to their children.

Leah had reason to have low self-esteem. Jacob preferred her sister to her, and she had participated in deceiving him. When the Torah says that God saw that Leah was despised (*Genesis* 29:31) it does not mean that Jacob despised her. The patriarch did not despise his wife. It means that Leah despised *herself* for participating in the deception. The names Leah gave her first three children all indicate how poorly she felt about herself. By the time she bore Judah, her self-esteem had improved to the point where she could express gratitude. She transmitted her positivity to Judah, who was, therefore, able to confess.

The Midrash that equates the ability to be grateful with the ability to confess is teaching us an important psychological concept: self-esteem enables a person both to be grateful and to confess a wrong.

The Qualities of Leadership

The Davidic dynasty of kingship stemmed from Judah, whose actions laid the foundations for true leadership.

The Torah relates that Judah was involved in a relationship, which, if exposed, would humiliate him. The only person who could expose him was about to be executed, and his secret would have been safe forever.

What have we seen from modern leaders, from executives to clerics to congressmen, to senators to presidents? Denial, cover-ups and failure to accept responsibility for one's actions. We have a legal system that is purportedly to assure justice, to punish the criminals and protect the victims. Instead, the system seeks to absolve people from the consequences of their actions.

Judah had the integrity and courage to publicly confess his actions. Just a few moments of silence would have prevented his actions from ever coming to light. Judah could have had a foolproof cover-up, but he chose to be truthful and accept responsibility. This is the prime ingredient for leadership.

There are numerous times in our lives when we have the choice of accepting responsibility for our actions or denying them and covering-up. The message of the Torah is clear. Forthrightness earns one honor and dignity.

The temptation to cover up mistakes and justify oneself can be extremely strong, and only with an unwavering dedication to truth can one withstand this test of integrity.

> *In his younger years, R' Yisroel of Salant began giving lectures on Talmud in Vilna, and local scholars were enchanted by his brilliance. However, there were several people who were envious of him, and sought to embarrass him. They engaged one of the foremost scholars in Vilna to challenge R' Yisroel and refute his interpretations of the Talmud. R' Yisroel was able to successfully rebut all this scholar's objections.*
>
> *One time this scholar raised an objection which R' Yisroel could not rebut. R' Yisroel admitted that he had been mistaken and descended from the*

platform. He later confided to his students that when the scholar raised this objection, "I promptly thought of five different ways in which I could have justified my position, and any of the five would have been an adequate rebuttal. However, I felt that none of these was in fact valid, and the objection the scholar raised was correct."

R' Yisroel continued, "Don't think for a moment that I wasn't tempted to defend my position. I could further justify giving these rebuttals in order to preserve the dignity and authority of a Rosh Yeshivah. But I rebuked myself, and said to myself, 'Yisroel, where are your mussar principles? How can you justify defending something that is not true?' At that point I admitted I was wrong and left the lectern. But it was not easy."

If someone of R' Yisroel's extraordinary spirituality felt that he had to struggle to overcome the urge to justify a mistake, how much more vulnerable are we to admit a mistake!

It irritates me when people say that they find the biographies of our *tzaddikim* to be counterproductive. "They are depicted as angels, with no human frailties. Angels cannot serve as models for us."

The above incident of R' Yisroel of Salant shows that he was not an angel. No, he was superior to angels. Angels do not have to struggle to overcome urges. R' Yisroel is an example of what a human being can be if he sincerely dedicates himself to be everything that he can be.

וַיְהִי אַחַר הַדְּבָרִים הָאֵלֶּה חָטְאוּ מַשְׁקֵה
מֶלֶךְ־מִצְרַיִם וְהָאֹפֶה לַאֲדֹנֵיהֶם לְמֶלֶךְ מִצְרָיִם

And it happened after these things that the cupbearer of the king of Egypt and the baker transgressed against their master, against the king of Egypt (40:1)

To Be on Constant Alert

Rashi states that the transgression of the baker was that a small pebble was found in the king's bread. He was punished for this by being sentenced to a year in prison.

The first paragraph of the *Shulchan Aruch* states, " 'I have set God before me always' (*Psalms* 16:8) is a major principle of Torah because a person's behavior when he is alone in the privacy of his home is not like his behavior when he is in the imminent presence of a king. How much more so if one realizes that he is in the presence of the Great King, Almighty God, whose glory fills the universe: He would have the reverence, humility and fear of God."

Our *tzaddikim* never lost sight of being in God's presence. Everything that transpired was contemplated as to how it applied to their service of God.

The Alter (Elder) of Kelm once found a small chip of wood in his bread. This immediately brought to mind the story of the king of Egypt's baker who was imprisoned for allowing a pebble to be in the king's bread. The Alter cogitated, "A defect in a person's bread is hardly grounds for so severe a punishment. No one will be punished for this chip of wood in the bread,

BEREISHIS / GENESIS: Vayeishev

especially since it was totally accidental. Why, then, was the king's baker punished so harshly? It was because when one serves or relates to the king, the standard of perfection is much greater than when relating to other people. One must exercise much greater caution to prevent any defects. In serving the king, even a small defect is a major offense.

"I am in the service of the King of Kings. Is my behavior before him without defect? Have I been cautious enough to avoid even accidental infractions?"

I think that if any of us found a tiny foreign object in our food, we would discard it without giving it a second thought. That is the difference between us and *tzaddikim*. They lived according to the first paragraph of the *Shulchan Aruch*. They were always on the alert that they were in the presence of God and must behave accordingly.

וְעָשִׂיתָ-נָּא עִמָּדִי חָסֶד וְהִזְכַּרְתַּנִי אֶל־פַּרְעֹה . . .
כִּי־גֻנֹּב גֻּנַּבְתִּי מֵאֶרֶץ הָעִבְרִים

[When Joseph gave a favorable interpretation to the dream of the Chamberlain of the Cupbearers, he said,] "Do me a kindness, if you please, and mention me to Pharaoh for indeed I was kidnapped from the land of the Hebrews" (40:14-15)

We Are All Citizens of Our Homeland

When the Israelites left Egypt, they took the remains of Joseph with them, and he was buried in Shechem. Moses pleaded with God to be permitted to enter the Holy Land, and when this was denied him, he asked to be buried there. God said, "Joseph admitted that he was from the land of the Hebrews, and he, therefore, deserved to be buried there. You heard the daughters of Jethro refer to you as an Egyptian (*Exodus* 2:19) and you remained silent and did not protest that you are a Hebrew. You, therefore, shall not be buried in the land of the Hebrews" (*Devarim Rabbah* 2:8).

R' Yechiel Meir of Ostrovza asks, why was Moses punished? Joseph was indeed raised in Eretz Yisrael and was in fact kidnapped there. Moses, however, was born and raised in Egypt. Why was it so great a transgression that he did not say that he was from the land of the Hebrews? Factually, he was not.

The rabbi of Ostrovza answers that once God had promised the Holy Land to the descendants of Abraham, Isaac and Jacob, the Land was indeed theirs. All their descendants, regardless of where they were born and raised, are citizens of the Land of the Hebrews and should proudly identify themselves as such. Although Moses was born and raised in Egypt, he should have protested being referred to as an Egyptian. Like Joseph, he was displaced from the Land of the Hebrews.

The words of this great sage are most important to us today. Whether we live in America, England, Australia or anywhere else on earth, we are citizens of the Land of our forefathers.

וַיָּשֶׁב אֶת־שַׂר הַמַּשְׁקִים עַל־מַשְׁקֵהוּ . . .
וְאֵת שַׂר הָאֹפִים תָּלָה כַּאֲשֶׁר פָּתַר לָהֶם יוֹסֵף

He [Pharaoh] restored the Chamberlain of the Cupbearers to his cupbearing. But the Chamberlain of the Bakers he hanged, just as Joseph had interpreted to them (40:21-22)

Life Is Action

At first glance, the two dreams seem to be very similar, yet Joseph gave them so radically different interpretations. And if we say that Joseph's interpretations were totally by Divine inspiration and were not dependent on the content of the dream, why does the Torah bother to tell us the dreams in such detail?

R' Elchanan Wasserman said that a closer scrutiny of the text reveals a major difference between the two dreams. The Chamberlain of the Cupbearers related, "I *held* Pharaoh's cup in my hand, and I *took* the grapes, I *pressed* them into Pharaoh's cup and I *placed* the cup on Pharaoh's palm" (*Genesis* 40:11). He was active in the dream. The Chamberlain of the Bakers, on the other hand, said, "Three wicker baskets were on my head, and in the uppermost basket were all kinds of Pharaoh's food. And the birds were eating them from the basket on my head" (ibid. 16-17). In contrast to the Chamberlain of the Cupbearers, he is inactive, doing nothing whatsoever. "This," says R' Elchanan, "indicated to Joseph the two different interpretations. Action represents life, inaction represents death."

According to R' Elchanan, we are as alive as our actions. Furthermore, they were not just any actions, but productive actions. In the dream, the Chamberlain of the Cupbearers was fulfilling his assignment, and that is life. The Chamberlain of the Bakers did nothing. For all we know, all the baked goods were baked by others. He evidenced no signs of productive activity. That is being lifeless.

In addition to the activities that we do in daily living, we should realize that every person has a mission. Moses tells us, "For if you will observe the entire commandment that I instruct you, to perform it, to love God, to walk in His ways and to cleave unto Him" (*Deuteronomy* 11:22). That is our mission, and if we act to achieve our mission to cleave unto God, then "You, who cling unto God, are all alive this day" (ibid. 4:4).

❦

Reconciliation with Love — a Chanukah Message

It is no coincidence that Chanukah occurs during the week that we read about the epic of Joseph and his brothers.

Chanukah is widely celebrated with considerable fanfare. What is so special about Chanukah that it receives such acclaim?

Although the miracle of the oil is significant, the stunning military victory, whereby a handful of warriors defeated the mighty army of the Syrian Greeks and restored the independence of Israel, would seem worthy of at least as much attention as the miracle of the oil. Yet, the military victory is mentioned only as an addendum to the *Amidah*, whereas the miracle of the oil dominates the holiday. The huge variety of exquisite Chanukah menorahs indicate the extraordinary importance of the miracle of the oil in Judaism. Why?

R' Avraham Pam raises another interesting question. Granted, there was a miracle of the single vial of oil burning for eight days. However, the Talmud says that there were ten miracles that regularly occurred in the Temple (*Ethics of the Fathers* 5:7). None of these are commemorated. What is so special about the miracle of the oil?

R' Pam cites the halachah that for communal rituals, the prohibition against *tumah* (ritual impurity) may be waved. Many commentaries, therefore, ask why was there a need for a miracle at all? It was permissible to light the Menorah even with ritually impure oil.

The *P'nei Yehoshua* answers that precisely because it was permissible to use impure oil, the miracle demonstrated the intensity of God's love for Israel, that the Menorah illuminated the Temple for eight days with just the single vial of pure oil. There was no purpose for this miracle other than to show God's love for Israel.

R' Pam notes that many of the Jews at that time had defected to Hellenism, and that they returned to Torah observance with the triumph of the Macabees. He points out that when a couple reconciles after separation, the relationship often becomes one of peaceful coexistence, but the quality of love that they initially had for each other is rarely restored.

Not so when Jews do *teshuvah*. Rambam says that although a sinful person distances himself from God, once he does *teshuvah* he is near, beloved and dear to God. It is not that God "tolerates" the *baal teshuvah*, but rather that He loves him as He would the greatest *tzaddik*. As the prophet says, "I will remember for you the loving-kindness of your youth, when you followed Me into the desert, into a barren land" (*Jeremiah* 2:2). The love of yore is fully restored.

This is the significance of the miracle of the oil. It teaches us that with proper *teshuvah* our relationship with God is restored, as if we had never sinned.

This is also the message of Joseph and his brothers. Joseph did not simply forgive them and suppress his resentment for their abuse of him. Rather, he loved them and cared for them as if nothing had happened, telling them that he feels toward them as he does to Benjamin, who was not involved in his kidnapping (*Rashi, Genesis* 45:12).

The celebration of Chanukah is, therefore, more than the commemoration of a miracle. We are to emulate the Divine attributes (*Shabbos* 133b). Just as when God forgives His love for us is completely restored, so must we be able to restore the love for one another when we mend our differences.

As we watch the Chanukah candles, let us think about the light they represent: the bright light of a love that is completely restored (*Atarah LeMelech* p. 189).

פרשת מקץ
Parashas Mikeitz

וַיְהִי מִקֵּץ שְׁנָתַיִם יָמִים וּפַרְעֹה חֹלֵם

It happened at the end of two years to the day: Pharaoh was dreaming (41:1)

Endeavor and Trust

Pharaoh's dream led to Joseph's release from prison. The Midrash states that Joseph's imprisonment was extended by two years because he asked the Chamberlain of the Cupbearers to remember him to Pharaoh. Seeking help from a human being showed a lack of trust in God, for which Joseph was punished to remain in prison for two additional years. Yet, the Talmud says that although we should pray for Divine help, one should not rely on miracles (*Pesachim* 64b). It was thus appropriate for Joseph to take some action to bring about his liberation.

The words of the Midrash are cited as being contradictory. The Midrash praises Joseph for his trust in God, while also criticizing him for enlisting the help of the Chamberlain of the Cupbearers. Various solutions to reconcile these apparently conflicting statements are proposed by Torah commentaries.

> *It is related that one Friday morning, the Baal Shem Tov knocked on someone's door and promptly left. When the person answered the door, there was no one there. The only person in sight was walking down the street. He hurried after the Baal Shem Tov and asked him, "Were you the one who knocked on my door?"*
>
> *"Yes," the Baal Shem Tov answered.*
>
> *"What was it that you wanted, and why did you leave after knocking?" the man asked.*
>
> *The Baal Shem Tov said, "I have no provisions for Shabbos, and I am certain that God will provide for me. The Torah says 'God will bless you in all that you do' (Deuteronomy 15:18), which means that a person must do some action to draw down the Divine blessing. However, that does not mean that the specific action one does is the vehicle whereby God will provide for him. I had to do some action, so I knocked on your door, but you may not be the one through whom God wishes to provide for me. That is why I left."*
>
> *A somewhat similar story is told of a chassidic rebbe. He was asked for his*

berachah (blessing) by a person whose business had failed and was in deep debt. The rebbe told the man to buy a sweepstake ticket. When the man did not win, the rebbe was deeply disappointed and complained to a tzaddik, "My berachos are ineffective." The tzaddik said, "In the morning service we say, 'Who among all Your handiwork, those above and those below, can tell you what You should do?' You should have given that person a berachah that he should prosper. Your mistake was in telling him to buy a sweepstake ticket. It is not your position to dictate to God how to bring about this person's prosperity."

The Midrash states that Joseph was both right and wrong. It was proper for him to do an action, to ask the Chamberlain of the Cupbearers to remember him to Pharaoh. It was *not* proper for him to believe that this would be the way his salvation would come about. God could have engineered things any other way to achieve the same result.

This is an important concept. Yes, we do make endeavors, and it is appropriate that we should do so. However, I am certain that we can think of instances when the result we desired came about in a way other than that which we had planned. We should, therefore, do something reasonable to earn our livelihood, but we should have faith that whatever God has destined for us to have will come about in the way that God chooses, rather than the way we choose.

וְהִנֵּה שֶׁבַע פָּרוֹת אֲחֵרוֹת עֹלוֹת אַחֲרֵיהֶן מִן־הַיְאֹר רָעוֹת מַרְאֶה וְדַקּוֹת בָּשָׂר וַתַּעֲמֹדְנָה אֵצֶל הַפָּרוֹת עַל־שְׂפַת הַיְאֹר: וַתֹּאכַלְנָה הַפָּרוֹת רָעוֹת הַמַּרְאֶה וְדַקֹּת הַבָּשָׂר אֵת שֶׁבַע הַפָּרוֹת יְפֹת הַמַּרְאֶה וְהַבְּרִיאֹת

Then behold! — seven other cows emerged after them out of the River — of ugly appearance and gaunt flesh; and they stood next to the [healthy] cows on the bank of the River. The cows of the ugly appearance and gaunt flesh ate the seven cows of beautiful appearance (41:3-4)

Avoid Toxic Associations

Every element in the dream was symbolic of something. Of what significance is the phrase, "and they stood next to the [healthy] cows on the bank of the River?"

Every letter in the Torah is meaningful. The teaching in this phrase is that the sickly cows, which symbolized famine and evil, could engulf the healthy cows, which symbolized abundance and good, *only because they stood next to them*. Evil can never affect and triumph over good if it is kept at a distance.

This message is of utmost importance today. We tend to be oblivious of destructive influences in our environment. We have a false sense of security, believing that we will not be affected.

The adage that an ounce of prevention is worth a pound of cure is so true. Many years ago, serious use of drugs was essentially confined to the inner city, to a population that was deprived and despaired of participating in the American dream. No one was alarmed. There was no reason to suspect that drug addiction would invade suburbia, the college campuses and affluent families. Little was done to combat the drug problem when it was a rather self-contained fire. Only when it spread and became a conflagration, an all-alarm fire, did the country become alert. Unfortunately, efforts to extinguish this consuming flame have failed. All we are able to do now is to rescue isolated individuals.

The immorality that prevails in today's society is unprecedented. We and our children are exposed to it. How much are we doing to avoid being influenced by our environment?

Rambam says that if a person cannot find a decent community in which to reside, he should move to the wilderness. It is difficult to follow this advice. Our homes and our workplaces are in the populated areas and it is unrealistic to move to the wilderness. But at the very least, we should be aware of the danger to which we are exposed, and do everything possible to avoid the toxic effects of the environment.

Our homes should become spiritual citadels of ethics and morality. Our personal lives should be exemplary. Much more effort should be put on refinement of our *middos*. The study of *mussar* should not be relegated to classes in yeshivos, but should be a daily event in every home. Yes, there are ways of teaching principles of *mussar* even to small children. We need only realize how important this is to prevent our children from being contaminated by the decadence of modern society.

"Seven other cows emerged after them out of the River—of ugly appearance and gaunt flesh; and they stood next to the [healthy] cows on the bank of the River. The cows of the ugly appearance and gaunt flesh ate the seven cows of beautiful appearance." We must take great caution that we are not engulfed by the destructive influences that stand alongside us.

וַיֹּאמֶר יוֹסֵף אֶל־פַּרְעֹה חֲלוֹם פַּרְעֹה אֶחָד הוּא אֵת אֲשֶׁר הָאֱלֹקִים עֹשֶׂה הִגִּיד לְפַרְעֹה: שֶׁבַע פָּרֹת הַטֹּבֹת שֶׁבַע שָׁנִים הֵנָּה . . . יִהְיוּ שֶׁבַע שְׁנֵי רָעָב: הוּא הַדָּבָר אֲשֶׁר דִּבַּרְתִּי אֶל־פַּרְעֹה אֲשֶׁר הָאֱלֹקִים עֹשֶׂה הֶרְאָה אֶת־פַּרְעֹה

Joseph said to Pharaoh, "The dream of Pharaoh is a single one; what God is about to do, He has told to Pharaoh: The seven good cows — they are seven years ... There shall be seven years of famine. It is this matter that I have spoken to Pharaoh: What God is about to do He has shown to Pharaoh" (41:25-28)

Sensitivity in Speech

I never cease to marvel at the infinite wisdom contained in the Torah. In studying the Talmud and the laws that the sages derived from the Torah, we may sometimes wonder how the text indicates these derivations. R' Meir Simchah HaKohen of Dvinsk (*Meshech Chochmah*) often provides the insights which show us how the sages studied Torah. We may read the text and even study it with several commentaries, yet not be aware of the content of the Torah.

For example, there is a nuance in the above text which calls for an interpretation. At one point Joseph says, "What God is about to do, He has *told* to Pharaoh" and just a bit later he says, "What God is about to do He has *shown* to Pharaoh." Why does the verb change from "told" to "shown?"

Our great Torah scholars knew how to study Torah. The Talmud (*Pesachim* 3b) says that a person should avoid being the bearer of bad tidings, citing the verse, "He who speaks evil is a fool," (*Pesachim* 10:18). However, there are times when we have no choice, and we have to inform someone of bad news. The Talmud says we should avoid shocking the person, and preferably give him a clue from which he can gather the truth, which you may then confirm for him.

R' Shlomo Kluger says that this is the teaching conveyed by the change of verbs in the above verses. God modeled proper communication for us. Joseph said that for the prediction of the years of plenty, "He has *told* to Pharaoh: The seven good cows are seven years." This was a message of good news, and was delivered in a straightforward manner. However, in predicting the years of famine, God did not convey it the same way. Rather, "what God is about to do He has *shown* to Pharaoh." God shows a symbol from which a person can gather the unpleasant information.

The Torah teaches us *middos* as well as mitzvos. We must excercise sensitivity in our speech and choose our words so that they can be accepted.

וַיַּרְא יוֹסֵף אֶת־אֶחָיו וַיַּכִּרֵם וַיִּתְנַכֵּר אֲלֵיהֶם
Joseph saw his brothers and he recognized them, but he acted like a stranger toward them (42:7)

The Importance of Self-Esteem

Jacob grieved relentlessly over the loss of his beloved son whom he assumed to be dead, and he refused to be consoled. "I will go down to the grave mourning for my son" (*Genesis* 37:35). Joseph knew what kind of agony his father was suffering. Even if he was not able to communicate to him when he was a slave of Potiphar or when he was in prison, he was certainly able to do so once he became viceroy of Egypt. Why did he not inform his father that he was alive and alleviate his profound grief?

Furthermore, Joseph is referred to in Torah writings as "Joseph the *tzaddik*." Is it characteristic of a *tzaddik* to wreak vengeance and torment his brothers the way Joseph did? We would expect that as a *tzaddik*, he would not harbor a grudge and would forgive them.

The explanation I heard from my late brother, R' Shlomo, addresses these questions and provides an answer that is both ethically and psychologically sound.

If Joseph had forgiven his brothers for their shameful act, he would have been the magnanimous person who, from the goodness of his heart, forgave his offenders. The brothers would have forever been the groveling penitents who would have to eternally bear the guilt of their behavior. There would be no opportunity for them to make any amends. They would never again be able to face Joseph or their father. Their spirits would have been totally crushed.

Joseph wished to avoid this. He wished to give his brothers an opportunity to redeem themselves and retain their self-esteem.

The Talmud says that true and effective *teshuvah* is achieved only if the person is placed in the same circumstances of his sin and under the same temptation.

Joseph, therefore, designed it so that this would occur. After his absence, Benjamin, the youngest of Jacob's sons and the only other child of his beloved Rachel, had now become Jacob's favorite child. Joseph arranged to have Benjamin brought to him, and he singled out Benjamin for special treatment, giving him five times as much as he gave the brothers. He then engineered it so that Benjamin was suspected of thievery, and said that he was going to keep Benjamin as a slave. He had set the stage for the litmus test. Would the brothers act as they had toward him, saying, "Let Benjamin stay here. This is a good way for us to be free of his favoritism," and again be indifferent to their father's feelings as they were when they sold him into slavery? Or had they realized and repented their mistake, and were ready to sacrifice themselves to return Benjamin to their father?

When Judah said that he must return Benjamin to his father and offered to stay as a slave in his place, Joseph saw that the brothers had thereby corrected their behavior and had done proper *teshuvah*. They had redeemed themselves and would no longer have to bear the guilt and shame for their sin. Joseph was now prepared to reveal his identity to them. Far from being a vengeful torment, Joseph's actions were in their interest, enabling them to redeem themselves and walk with their heads raised high.

What about Jacob's agony? Joseph knew his father well. He knew that, painful as the ordeal was, Jacob would gladly accept years of suffering in order to provide his children with the opportunity to gain self-respect. This could not have been achieved in any other way, and Joseph was certain that he was doing what his father wished.

This interpretation shows us the overriding importance of self-esteem. One psychologist writes, "If you have given your child self-esteem, you have given him everything. If you have not given him self-esteem, then whatever else you gave him is of little value." Self-esteem is *the* major component of a healthy personality.

We should be aware of this. Sometimes we say or do things to another person that may depress his self-esteem. We should be aware that this is a kind of psychological homicide. The Torah repeatedly emphasizes the importance of upholding every person's dignity. The saga of Joseph and his brothers teaches us to what extent we must go to preserve a person's feelings of self-respect and dignity.

וַיַּכֵּר יוֹסֵף אֶת־אֶחָיו וְהֵם לֹא הִכִּרֻהוּ

Joseph recognized his brothers, but they did not recognize him (42:8)

The Power of Denial

Psychology describes the phenomenon of *denial*. Denial does not mean that a person is denying something in the usual sense of the word "deny" as a disclaimer. A person who denies something may be telling the truth if the fact is correct, or he may be lying. In either case, the person *is aware* that he is denying something. The term "in denial" as used in psychology, refers to a person being *unaware* of some aspect of reality. The person is *not* consciously lying. He will swear repeatedly to what he believes is the truth. Somewhere, deep down in the hidden recesses of his subconscious mind, there is an awareness of the fact, but since the person has no access to this awareness, it is of no use to him.

Very often, the reason for the unawareness of reality is that this particular aspect of reality is too painful to accept. To protect the person from the distress of knowing this reality, the mind turns off the awareness.

Who is capable of denial? Everyone. What about highly intelligent people? They are even *more* prone to denial than people of lesser intellect.

The Rabbi of Gur made a penetrating comment on a verse in the Torah. The Torah relates that when the matriarch, Sarah, was told that she would bear a child at the age of 90, she laughed "inwardly," thinking, "How can I bear a child at my old age?" God then said to Abraham, "Why did Sarah laugh? Is there anything that is beyond God?" Abraham reprimanded Sarah, but "Sarah denied, saying 'I did not laugh' for she was frightened." Abraham then said to her, "No, you laughed indeed" (*Genesis* 18:12-14).

The Rabbi of Gur says that it is impossible to think that Sarah lied. The Midrash tells us that Sarah was totally free of sin (*Bereishis Rabbah* 58:1). He, therefore, interprets the verse as saying not that Sarah *denied*, but that Sarah was *in denial*. Her disbelief that she could carry a child was *bekirbah*, "inward," deep in the recesses of her subconscious. Sarah was not even aware of this thought. Only God, who knows a person's innermost thoughts and feelings, was aware of it. When Abraham reprimanded her for this thought, Sarah could not even imagine that she could have harbored disbelief of God's omnipotence. Her reverence of God was so great that a thought such as this was beyond her. The verse thus reads, "Sarah was *in denial* because she was so God-fearing." Sarah was certain that she was speaking the truth when she said, "I did not laugh." Sarah did not deny or lie. She had no access to her subconscious.

As we study the saga of Joseph and his brothers, we cannot but wonder how they did not suspect the identity of Joseph. Rashi says that Joseph's features were similar, if not identical, to Jacob's (*Genesis* 37:3). And although Rashi notes that when the brothers sold him he was seventeen and now at thirty he had grown a beard (ibid. 42:8), that still does not rule out that he was very similar to Jacob, who likewise had a beard.

But let us go further. The Midrash says that when Joseph sought to imprison Simon, Simon fought off all the guards who tried to subdue him. Joseph then sent his son, Menashe, who struck Simon only once. Simon fell to the ground and said, "That blow came from someone of our family." Should this not have aroused suspicion?

When they feasted at Joseph's residence, "They were seated before him, the firstborn according to his seniority and the youngest according to his youth. The men looked at each other in astonishment" (ibid. 43:33). Rashi adds that Joseph said, "Reuben, Simon, Levi, Judah, Issachar and Zevulun, the sons of one mother, sit in this order." He then sat Dan and Naftali, children of Bilhah, together, and Gad and Asher, children of Zilpah, together. Finally he said of Benjamin, "He does not have a mother, nor do I, so he will sit next to me."

When you take all these together, it is difficult to see how the brothers did not think this was Joseph. The only explanation is that *they were in denial*. They had hated Joseph for his dreams and had dismissed them as absurd. "Would you then reign over us? Would you then dominate us?" (ibid. 37:8). To recognize that they were wrong and that Joseph's dreams had indeed come true was so unacceptable to them that they were *in denial.* Their defense mechanism of denial blinded them to the perception that this could be Joseph.

When the Torah forbids a judge's taking a bribe, it says "for the bribe *will blind the eyes of the wise*" (*Deuteronomy* 16:19). Rashi quotes the Talmud, that it is *physically impossible* for a judge who has taken a bribe not to be partial to that litigant. Just as a bribe can blind one to the obvious, so can an intense desire to not be aware of something.

Inasmuch as denial is a subconscious process, there is no way that a person can say, "I am not in denial." A person cannot be aware that he is denial. How then can we protect ourselves from being blind to reality? Only by listening to teachers and sincere friends who are objective and can see that which we cannot see.

R' Elimelech of Lizhensk advises that one should have a trusted friend in whom one can confide everything, and that one should regularly reveal to this friend all one's actions and thoughts. This is an excellent guideline. A trusted friend can help us avoid dangerous denial, falling into a pit which we are unable to see.

וַיֹּאמְרוּ אִישׁ אֶל־אָחִיו אֲבָל אֲשֵׁמִים אֲנַחְנוּ עַל־אָחִינוּ אֲשֶׁר רָאִינוּ
צָרַת נַפְשׁוֹ בְּהִתְחַנְנוֹ אֵלֵינוּ וְלֹא שָׁמָעְנוּ עַל־כֵּן בָּאָה אֵלֵינוּ הַצָּרָה הַזֹּאת:
וַיַּעַן רְאוּבֵן אֹתָם לֵאמֹר הֲלוֹא אָמַרְתִּי אֲלֵיכֶם לֵאמֹר אַל־תֶּחֶטְאוּ בַיֶּלֶד

They then said to one another, "Indeed we are guilty concerning our brother, inasmuch as we saw his heartfelt anguish when he pleaded with us and we paid no heed; that is why this anguish has come upon us." Reuben spoke up to them, saying, "Did I not speak to you saying, 'Do not sin against the boy?'" (42:21-22)

Teshuvah Must Be Complete

What was the purpose of Reuben's remark? The brothers were obviously repenting what they had done. Was it appropriate to rub salt into their wounds and say, "I told you so?"

The Midrash praises Reuben as a champion of *teshuvah* (*Bereishis Rabbah* 40:18). Reuben recognized that the brothers' *teshuvah* was incomplete.

The Midrash states that the brothers had deliberated at length about Joseph, and had come to a decision that his behavior was in fact a crime punishable by death. It was only Judah's intervention that commuted the death sentence to being sold into slavery. Reuben noted that the brothers did not repent their judgment and their action, but only the fact that they had caused Joseph anguish. They were still self-righteous about their decision.

Reuben was not telling them, "I told you so." The Torah states that when Reuben objected to their killing Joseph and said to throw him into a pit, it was with the intention of rescuing him and returning him to his father (*Genesis* 37:22). Reuben was not present when the brothers sold Joseph. He was now telling them that their repentance was lacking, because they were only repenting the anguish they caused him, but still believed that their action was justified. For their *teshuvah* to be complete, they must admit that they were wrong.

There is a tendency for people to defend their wrong actions, and at best, make

BEREISHIS / GENESIS: Mikeitz [91]

only a partial concession that there was something inappropriate about what they did. The Torah is teaching us to yield our self-righteousness and be big enough to admit we were wrong.

וַיִּשָּׂא מַשְׂאֹת מֵאֵת פָּנָיו אֲלֵהֶם וַתֵּרֶב מַשְׂאַת בִּנְיָמִן מִמַּשְׂאֹת כֻּלָּם חָמֵשׁ יָדוֹת וַיִּשְׁתּוּ וַיִּשְׁכְּרוּ עִמּוֹ

He [Joseph] had portions that had been set before him served to them, and Benjamin's portion was five times as much as the portion of any of them. They drank and became intoxicated with him (43:34)

The Joy of Spiritual Achievement

Rashi says that since the day that the brothers sold Joseph, neither he nor they drank wine until this day.

The Rabbi of Aleksander (*Yismach Yisrael*) says, we can understand why Joseph drank that day: because he was reunited with all his brothers. But why did the brothers drink? If they had deprived themselves of wine in atonement for selling their brother, why was this day different? At this point they did not know the identity of Joseph.

The *Yismach Yisrael* says that after they had sold Joseph, they realized how destructive it was to be envious, and they were determined to extirpate this trait from their character. However, they had no way of knowing whether they had succeeded in this. When Joseph gave Benjamin five times as much as he gave them and they did not feel even a twinge of envy, they rejoiced. They had overcome the root of their sin. This was adequate reason for allowing themselves to drink wine. They celebrated their spiritual achievement.

R' Chaim Vital says in *Shaarei Kedushah* that it is more difficult to correct a bad character trait than to complete the entire Talmud. Just as when one completes the Talmud it is customary to celebrate with a *seudas mitzvah* (feast), so one may celebrate the eradication of a bad character trait. And just as when completing the Talmud one should not become vain but realize that it was by the help of God that one was able to achieve this and look forward to increasing one's learning, so also with the elimination of a bad character trait. One may rejoice at the achievement, but realize how much more one must do to further refine one's character.

The accomplishment of any spiritual advance is a reason for celebration, but also a reminder of how much more one must do.

This may help answer the question raised by the Talmud (*Megillah* 16b), why did Joseph give more lavish gifts to Benjamin than to the other brothers (45:22)? Why repeat the discriminatory favoritism that caused the entire saga? It was because Joseph recognized that the brothers had succeeded in ridding themselves of envy, and that special treatment of Benjamin would not irritate them.

פרשת ויגש
Parashas Vayigash

וַיִּגַּשׁ אֵלָיו יְהוּדָה וַיֹּאמֶר בִּי אֲדֹנִי
יְדַבֶּר־נָא עַבְדְּךָ דָבָר בְּאָזְנֵי אֲדֹנִי

Then Judah approached him and said, "If you please, my lord, may your servant speak a word in my lord's ears" (44:18)

The Power of Soft Speech

Judah indicated that he wished to speak very softly, virtually whispering "a word in my lord's ears." What was the purpose of that? Furthermore, why does the Torah bother to tell something that does not appear significant?

Ah! Torah is always teaching us something.

There is great emphasis today on methods of communication. Difficulties in relationships are often attributed to problems in communicating.

It is related that a pastor left his sermon on the lectern. An observer noted that he had made marginal notes on the method of delivery. One note said, "Go slowly and emphasize." Another said, "Gesture upwards." At one point the note read, "Argument very weak here. Yell loudly!"

If what you have to say really has merit, you will make yourself heard if you speak softly. Shouting is a giveaway that your argument is weak.

Solomon says, "The gentle words of the wise are heard above the shouts of a king over fools" (*Ecclesiastes* 9:17). A soft voice can actually drown out a shout.

Judah believed that his argument for the release of Benjamin was very convincing. In order to impress Joseph that what he was about to say was valid, Judah said, "I am going to say it to you softly."

And why does the Torah tell us this? To teach us effective communication. If you have a valid argument and you bellow it, the other person will tune you out. Instead of listening to the content of your argument, he will prepare a rebuttal. Shouting and harsh words betray the weakness of your argument. Speaking softly and gently will enable you to be heard.

BEREISHIS / GENESIS: Vayigash

וְעַתָּה לֹא־אַתֶּם שְׁלַחְתֶּם אֹתִי הֵנָּה כִּי הָאֱלֹקִים
וַיְשִׂימֵנִי לְאָב לְפַרְעֹה . . . וּמֹשֵׁל בְּכָל־אֶרֶץ מִצְרָיִם

"And now: it was not you who sent me here, but God; He has made me a father to Pharaoh and ruler throughout the entire land of Egypt" (45:8)

A Lesson in Faith

Anyone reading the saga of Joseph and his brothers cannot but not reflect on one glaring omission: How did Jacob react when he found out the truth, that his sons had sold their brother into slavery? It is clear that he found out. After Jacob died, the brothers said to Joseph, "Your father gave orders before his death, saying, 'Thus shall you say to Joseph: "O please, kindly forgive the spiteful deed of your brothers"'" (*Genesis* 50:16-17). Rashi says that this was a fabrication, because Jacob knew that Joseph was not vengeful. Nevertheless, this indicates that Jacob knew what had happened. How did he react, and why does the Torah not tell us this?

Ohr HaChaim says that Joseph's statement, "It was not you who sent me here, but God" was not lip service to assuage his brothers' consciences, but a genuine conviction that they were merely instruments whereby God sought to make Joseph the ruler of Egypt and save the country from famine. After giving his brothers the opportunity to redeem themselves, Joseph did not bear any ill-will toward them. In fact, when they told Joseph that his father had instructed him to forgive them, Joseph wept because he thought that Jacob considered him capable of holding a grudge.

Although we are not told of Jacob's reaction, we see in the next portion of the Torah that Jacob blessed all his sons, referring to their sin only indirectly and with subtlety (*Rashi, Genesis* 49:6). They had been so ruthless to put him in unspeakable agony for twenty-two years, and he blesses them!

Ohr HaChaim says that like Joseph, Jacob sincerely believed that the brothers were not guilty of so heinous a sin, because they were but instruments of the Divine will. He accepted his twenty-two years of suffering without questioning the Divine justice, and inasmuch as he was convinced that all that had happened was by God's design, he did not condemn his sons for selling their brother into slavery, duping him to believe that Joseph had been killed by a wild beast, and having him endure twenty-two years of grief.

That is why the Torah does not relate Jacob's reaction. *There was no reaction*, and the very fact that Jacob did not react is the most important lesson in faith.

The Midrash says that the Torah was given as "black fire inscribed on white fire" (*Rashi, Deuteronomy* 33:2). The "black fire" is the ink of the letters that are written, and the "white fire" is the blank space, that which is unwritten. The Torah's omitting the report of Jacob's reaction is as much a lesson for us as what is written. It is a teaching of the extremely high level of faith of which a human being is capable: accepting twenty-two years of suffering and not condemning his sons, because of his faith that this was the handiwork of God.

וְהִנֵּה עֵינֵיכֶם רֹאוֹת וְעֵינֵי אָחִי בִנְיָמִין כִּי־פִי הַמְדַבֵּר אֲלֵיכֶם

"Behold! Your eyes see as do the eyes of my brother Benjamin that it is my mouth that is speaking to you" (45:12)

Proper Speech: the Uniqueness of Man

Rashi comments that the words, "my mouth is speaking to you" mean "in *lashon hakodesh* (the holy tongue)." Purportedly, this means that Joseph offered as proof of his identity that he knew Hebrew.

But in what way was this a proof? Until now, they communicated through an interpreter, whom they assumed to be an Egyptian who obviously knew Hebrew.

Rashi's words may have an additional meaning. All matter is divided into four categories: *domem* (inanimate), *tzomeach* (vegetative), *chai* (living) and *medaber* (speaking). The last is the category of man, the only being that can speak.

But is this really so? Is man the only creature that can communicate by sound? We know that many forms of life communicate by sound. Are the sounds they make not a form of speaking? Granted, human speech is much more sophisticated, but that makes it only *quantitatively* distinct from animal verbalizations, but it is not a qualitative distinction. More types of sounds and a greater vocabulary are not enough to give man the distinction of being *medaber*.

The uniqueness of man is not just that he has a more sophisticated form of speech, but that he can elevate his speech to being holy. By using his speech properly, by not speaking foolishly, by avoiding defamatory speech and carrying tales, man can sanctify his speech. This is something that animals cannot do, and it is this ability to sanctify speech that merits the designation *medaber*.

Although the brothers' action cannot be justified, Joseph was not totally innocent. The Torah says that "he would bring evil reports about them to his father" (*Genesis* 37:2). The Midrash states that all the evil reports were groundless, and Joseph was, therefore, guilty of *lashon hara*. During his enslavement and imprisonment, Joseph did *teshuvah* to purify himself of *lashon hara*.

However, the halachah states that an offense against another person is not forgiven until one makes proper amends and asks for forgiveness from that person. In revealing himself to his brothers, Joseph wished to tell them that he had repented for the *lashon hara* he had spoken about them. "I have corrected that defective trait. I have sanctified my speech. I am now truly a *medaber*," Rashi's comment means more than that I speak Hebrew. Being polylinguistic does not yet warrant the designation of *medaber*. One is a *medaber* only if one's *lashon* is *kodesh*, only if one sanctifies his speech.

We should indeed take pride in having the gift of speech, but unless we sanctify our speech, we are not yet unique. Avoiding the abuse of this precious gift is what makes us unique as humans.

וַיְדַבְּרוּ אֵלָיו אֵת כָּל־דִּבְרֵי יוֹסֵף אֲשֶׁר דִּבֶּר אֲלֵהֶם . . . וַתְּחִי רוּחַ יַעֲקֹב אֲבִיהֶם

When they related to him all the words that Joseph had spoken, the spirit of their father Jacob was revived (45:27)

A Definition of Life

Rashi comments on the phrase "the spirit of their father Jacob was revived" as meaning that the Divine spirit which had departed from him during the years of grief now returned to him.

There are numerous references to the word *chai* that deserve our attention. When Joseph revealed himself to his brothers, he asked, "Is my father still alive (*chai*)?" What could be the meaning of this question? Judah had just pleaded for the release of Benjamin because, "If I return without him, my father will die" (*Genesis* 44:31). Obviously, Jacob was alive. Later, Jacob says, "My son Joseph still lives (*chai*)." This begs for an interpretation of *chai*.

It is of interest that the next portion of the Torah, which tells of Jacob's death, is called *Vayechi*, "he lived." The portion of the Torah that tells of the matriarch Sarah's death is *Chayei Sarah*, "the life of Sarah." Is it not strange that the we use the term *chai* in referring to death?

The Talmud says, "The righteous are considered alive even after their death, whereas the wicked are considered dead even when they live" (*Berachos* 18a). The Torah considers human life to be spirituality rather than biology. Animals, too, breathe, look for food, seek shelter, reproduce and care for their young. Some show a degree of intelligence. Man is more than just an animal with greater intelligence. Man is a creature that can be master of his biology rather than a slave to it. I elaborated on Torah spirituality in *Twerski On Spirituality*.

A human being without spirituality is nothing more than an animal with intellect. He lives biologically, but is spiritually dead.

In the Joseph saga, an obvious question is raised. Why did Joseph, after coming to power, not get a message to his father that he was alive and well? Joseph knew how Jacob must be agonizing over his assumed death. The answer is that Joseph knew that Jacob had prophetic vision. He was certain that Jacob knew exactly what had happened to him and where he was. It did not occur to Joseph that Jacob was deprived of the Divine spirit. When Judah told him that Jacob said, "You know that my wife bore me two sons. One has left me and I presumed: Alas, he has surely been torn to pieces, for I have not seen him since!" it was then that Joseph realized that Jacob had lost the Divine spirit. This is why he asked, "Is my father still *chai*?" Of course he knew that Jacob was alive, but to exist without the Divine spirit was not being *chai*.

When the brothers told Jacob that Joseph was alive and was ruler of Egypt, Jacob feared that twenty-two years in the decadent environment of Egypt may have corrupted Joseph. He may not be the spiritual person he once was. When they told him how spiritual Joseph was, Jacob said, "Then my son is still *chai*, truly living, and has not deteriorated to being an intellectual animal." Having emerged from his grief, the Divine spirit returned to him, and "the spirit of their father Jacob came back to life." Jacob was once again *chai*.

The spiritual achievements of a person survive one's physical existence. We are the beneficiaries of the spiritual achievements of the *tzaddikim* of the past. As long as their spirit lives, they are alive. Indeed, "the righteous are considered alive even after their death." This is why the portions of the Torah that tell of the death of Sarah and Jacob are *Vayechi* and *Chayei Sarah*. The Torah narrates their physical death, but tells us that they are very much alive.

The quest for eternal life is universal. I addressed this in *Light at the End of the Tunnel*. The Torah's use of the word *chai* teaches us how to achieve an eternal existence.

וַיִּסַּע יִשְׂרָאֵל וְכָל־אֲשֶׁר־לוֹ וַיָּבֹא בְּאֵרָה שָּׁבַע וַיִּזְבַּח זְבָחִים לֵאלֹקֵי אָבִיו יִצְחָק:
וַיֹּאמֶר אֱלֹקִים לְיִשְׂרָאֵל בְּמַרְאֹת הַלַּיְלָה וַיֹּאמֶר יַעֲקֹב יַעֲקֹב וַיֹּאמֶר הִנֵּנִי:
וַיֹּאמֶר . . . אַל־תִּירָא מֵרְדָה מִצְרַיְמָה . . . וְיוֹסֵף יָשִׁית יָדוֹ עַל־עֵינֶיךָ

So Israel set out with all he had and he came to Beer-sheba where he offered sacrifices to the God of his father Isaac. God spoke to Israel in night visions and He said, "Jacob, Jacob!" And he said, "Here I am." And He said "Have no fear of descending to Egypt . . . and Joseph shall place his hand on your eyes" (46:1-4)

Faith in Divine Benevolence

Virtually every year when the Torah portion of *Vayigash* was read, my father repeated the same explanation of these verses. He knew that we knew it, and the repetition could only have been to further impress this teaching upon us. What is noteworthy in these verses is that the Torah says "*Israel* set out" and "God spoke to *Israel*," then suddenly changes to "Jacob, Jacob!" Why the change and why the repetition? Also, there is no indication that Jacob feared going to Egypt that warranted the reassurance, "Have no fear." And just what is meant by "Joseph shall place his hand over your eyes?" Finally, the Zohar makes a cryptic comment on this verse: "This is the secret of the *Shema*." How are we to understand this?

My father explained that the patriarch Abraham represented *chesed* (loving-kindness) and Isaac represented *gevurah* (stern judgment). Jacob is referred to as "the choicest of the patriarchs," the name "Israel" representing *chesed* and the name "Jacob" representing *gevurah,* thereby combining both traits in *tiferes* (splendor).

Previously, Jacob had invoked, "God of my father Abraham and God of my father Isaac" (*Genesis* 32:10) and "Had not the God of my father—the God of Abraham and the Dread of Isaac been with me" (ibid. 31:42). However, here, he brought offerings to "the God of his father Isaac," to whom he had earlier referred to as "the Dread of Isaac," with no mention of "God of Abraham." This indicated that he was in a state of dread, and this is why God says to *Israel*, "Jacob, Jacob!" i.e., "you are also Israel, but you are only exhibiting the trait of Jacob, which represents the Dread of Isaac." This is why God reassured him, "Have no fear."

The additional reassurance was that Jacob should know that everything God does is *chesed*. Sometimes it is manifest *chesed*, and sometimes God's loving-kindess is disguised and is cloaked as *gevurah*, which appears as harsh and inspires dread. But even *gevurah* is Divine benevolence. It is just that with our human perception we are unable to see the *chesed* that is concealed by the cloak of *gevurah*.

The episode of Joseph is an example of *chesed* that appears to us as *gevurah*. What could have been worse for Jacob than to experience the loss of his beloved son, Joseph? The Midrash says that when Jacob complained, "God has turned away from me," God said, "I am manipulating things to make his son viceroy of the greatest empire in the world, and he is complaining." Jacob complained because, having been temporarily deprived of prophetic vision, he saw things with human perception, and what he saw was terribly distressing. He was unable to see the *chesed* that was concealed by *gevurah*.

My father cited the chassidic writings that point out that the Divine appellation, *Hashem,* refers to *chesed* and *Elokim* refers to *gevurah*. We should have unquestioning faith in God and realize that *gam zu letovah*, (this, too, is for good) even that which may appear to us as being bad is in fact good, but it is "a blessing in disguise." This is what is meant by the words of the *Shema: Hashem* (manifest *chesed*) and *Elokeinu* (*gevurah*) are *Hashem echod,* all *chesed. Gevurah,* too, is in essence *chesed*, albeit in disguise.

Our limited human perception conflicts with our faith. We may see things as being terrible because we cannot see through the cloak of *gevurah.* As testimony that our faith is firm and that it overrides our human perception, we cover our eyes when we recite the *Shema.* This is a gesture which says that we are willing to disregard our human perception in favor of our faith in God's eternal benevolence.

This is what the Zohar meant, referring to the verse "Joseph shall place his hand over your eyes" as being "the secret of *Shema.*" The episode of Joseph, which had appeared to Jacob as the worst tragedy that could possibly befall him, is a testimony that "*Hashem* (manifest *chesed*) and *Elokeinu* (*gevurah*) are *Hashem echod,* all *chesed.*"

We all experience adversity in our lives. This teaching should strengthen our faith, to enable us to accept adversity with the serenity that comes from the conviction that *gam zu letovah*. Everything God does is for an ultimate good, even though we may not be able to see it.

וַיֶּאְסֹר יוֹסֵף מֶרְכַּבְתּוֹ וַיַּעַל לִקְרַאת־יִשְׂרָאֵל אָבִיו גֹּשְׁנָה וַיֵּרָא אֵלָיו וַיִּפֹּל עַל־צַוָּארָיו וַיֵּבְךְּ עַל־צַוָּארָיו עוֹד

Joseph harnessed his chariot and went up to meet Israel his father in Goshen. He appeared before him, fell on his neck, and he wept on his neck excessively (46:29)

Single-Mindedness of Purpose

Rashi states that Joseph personally harnessed his chariot, in diligence to honor his father. Then Rashi makes a rather cryptic statement. On the words "He appeared before him," Rashi comments, "Joseph appeared to his father." Just what is Rashi adding to the text with this comment? The Torah says "he appeared before him," which obviously means that Joseph appeared to his father.

R' Elyah Lopian gives a penetrating interpretation to Rashi's comment.

We have come to appreciate the power of focusing energy on one point. People trained in karate can break a thick board by striking it with their bare hand because they have learned how to harness the energy that is spread over the entire body to a single point. The power of the laser beam results because the light waves are focused.

The Torah tells how Jacob was able to remove the huge boulder from the mouth of the well, even though several shepherds together could not do it. Rashi says that it was as simple as removing the cork from a bottle (*Genesis* 29:10). How did Jacob do this? We say in our prayer for rain that Jacob "dedicated his heart and rolled the stone from the well of water." The Hebrew word for "dedicated" is *yichad*, which means "to make one." When Jacob saw Rachel with her father's flock, he was able to focus and bring all his energies to one point.

Our thoughts and emotions are rarely single-minded, focusing on a single point to the exclusion of all else. We may have a thought or emotion that is dominant, but there may be other thoughts or feelings present.

When Joseph went to meet his beloved father after an absence of twenty-two years, his emotions were very intense, as is evident by his "excessive weeping." However, there was another issue involved. Joseph knew how much his father loved him, and how joyous his father would be to see him. To meet his father would be fulfilling the mitzvah of honoring his father.

There were, therefore, two thoughts and feelings in Joseph's heart and mind. (1) The mitzvah of bringing happiness to his father and (2) his desire to see his father. The average person could have both simultaneously. Joseph knew that one would detract from the other. He wished to have nothing on his mind other than pleasing his father, and in order to do this he had to set his own feelings aside temporarily.

This, R' Lopian says, is what Rashi is telling us. The sequence of the verse tells us of Joseph's extraordinary spirituality. "He appeared before him," Rashi says means that "Joseph appeared to his father." Joseph's only thought was to appear before his father and bring him joy. This was not to be diluted by his own desire to see his father again. It as only *after* he had fulfilled this mitzvah with single-mindedness that "he fell on his neck, and he wept on his neck excessively."

We fulfill the mitzvos of the Torah, but we must admit that it is not with the channeling of all our thoughts and feelings to a single focal point. Rashi is teaching us the goal toward which we should strive.

וַיֹּאמֶר יַעֲקֹב אֶל־פַּרְעֹה יְמֵי שְׁנֵי מְגוּרַי שְׁלֹשִׁים וּמְאַת שָׁנָה מְעַט וְרָעִים הָיוּ יְמֵי שְׁנֵי חַיַּי

Jacob answered Pharaoh, "The days of the years of my sojourns have been a hundred and thirty years. Few and bad have been the days of the years of my life" (47:9)

Acceptance of the Past

The *Daas Zekenim* cites a Midrash that God rebuked Jacob: "I rescued you from Esau and Laban, I returned Dinah and Joseph to you, and you complain that the years of your life have been few and bad? I will, therefore, decrease the years of your life." Indeed, Jacob lived to one hundred forty seven, whereas Isaac lived one hundred eighty years.

The Midrash states that when Jacob mourned for Joseph, he said, "God has turned away from me." God said, "I am designing things to make his son viceroy over the greatest empire in the world, yet he is complaining that I have turned away from him." However, Jacob was not punished for this complaint, whereas he was punished for referring to his life as "few and bad years." Why the difference?

As we have noted, we must exercise great caution when referring to the patriarchs. Because of their enormous spirituality, they were held to a much higher standard than we are. Yet, the Torah and the Talmud describe their flaws as though they were in fact more serious transgressions, to teach us to apply these teachings to our own lives even though we are at an infintely lower level of spirituality.

There are two statements in the Talmud that, at first glance, appear to be conflicting. The Talmud says that a person who complains because of his suffering is not held culpable if he questions God's judgment (*Bava Basra* 16b). On the other hand, the Talmud says that a person must praise God for the bad that happens to him as well as for the good (*Berachos* 54a), reciting the blessing *Baruch Dayan Ha'emes* (Blessed is the True Judge).

The answer is that when a person is in agony, he cannot be expected to exercise the highest quality of judgment. There is a virtually reflex response of anger against whoever one holds responsible for inflicting the pain. A person cannot be held culpable for a reflex action, hence, even an expression of anger toward God is not a sin. However, once the pain has subsided, a person should be able to exercise better judgment, and a person with firm faith in God's benevolence should be able to say about the distress of the past, *gam zu letovah*, that somehow there is a concealed good in the painful episode.

When Jacob complained at the time he was suffering from the disappearance and the assumed death of Joseph, he was not held culpable. However, now that he was reunited with Joseph and was not presently in distress, he was held culpable for saying that the years of the past were bad. As one *tzaddik* said, we may say that our circumstances are very bitter, because life-saving medicines may taste bitter, but we may not say that things are bad, because nothing that is bad issues from God.

We may not be held to the standard of Jacob, but we are expected to accept the suffering *of the past* with faith that what happened was indeed just, because God is a *dayan emes*, a true Judge.

# פרשת ויחי
Parashas Vayechi

בְּבֹאִי מִפַּדָּן מֵתָה עָלַי רָחֵל בְּאֶרֶץ כְּנַעַן בַּדֶּרֶךְ בְּעוֹד כִּבְרַת־אֶרֶץ
לָבֹא אֶפְרָתָה וָאֶקְבְּרֶהָ שָּׁם בְּדֶרֶךְ אֶפְרָת הִוא בֵּית לָחֶם

"When I came from Paddan, Rachel died on me in the land of Canaan on the road, while there was still a stretch of land to go to Ephrath; and I buried her there on the road to Ephrath, which is Bethlehem" (48:7)

The Right Thing for the Right Reason

Rashi says that Jacob was explaining to Joseph why he did not bury Rachel in the Tomb of the Patriarchs, yet he was requesting that he be buried there. Jacob said, "It was not because the distance to Hebron was long, because Bethlehem is near Hebron. It was also not because of bad weather that I did not take her to Hebron, because it was the dry season. I buried her there because God instructed me to do so, so that when Jews would be driven into exile, they could pass her gravesite and beseech her to intercede with God on their behalf."

R' Chaim Shmulevitz asks, why all this lengthy explanation? Had Jacob simply said, "God told me to do so," Joseph would have believed him. R' Shmulevitz derives an important lesson from this. If we have a personal reason and a strong interest in doing something, we may convince ourselves that it is the will of God that we do so. We are very clever in rationalizing and deceiving ourselves. Only when we have no personal gain, when it is not for our comfort or convenience, can we be sure that it is indeed God's will and not our own.

How cautious we must be not to deceive ourselves about our motivation for our actions. Not only must we be careful not to justify a wrong action, but we must also make certain that the *right* things we do are for the right reason.

The Midrash says that when Jacob encountered Esau, he concealed Dinah in a box, lest Esau be attracted to her. For this he was punished: she was taken by Shechem. God said, "Because you denied her to a descendent of Abraham, she will be taken by a pagan."

What did Jacob do wrong? Is it conceivable that he should have allowed a scoundrel like Esau to marry his daughter? The commentaries answer that Jacob was justified in hiding Dinah, but that when he closed the box, he did so tightly, saying, "Now Esau will not see her." In other words, his denying her to Esau was with a touch of malice toward Esau, and this feeling was improper. Jacob did the right thing and even for a good reason, but there was also a wrong reason involved, and for this he was held culpable.

BEREISHIS / GENESIS: Vayechi

Had the distance to Hebron been long or had the weather been inclement, Jacob could not have been certain that he was burying Rachel elsewhere because it was God's wish. The fact that this was more convenient for him would have made Jacob suspect his own motivation. This is why he elaborated to Joseph, "I did so because it was God's wish. I know this to be true, because there was no personal interest involved."

It is so easy to convince ourselves that what we are doing is right. We should be alert to our vulnerability to self-deception. When making important decisions, where one of the options is the more desirable, we would be wise to solicit the advice of an objective person who is not subject to our distortions.

רְאוּבֵן בְּכֹרִי אַתָּה כֹּחִי וְרֵאשִׁית אוֹנִי יֶתֶר שְׂאֵת וְיֶתֶר עָז: פַּחַז כַּמַּיִם אַל־תּוֹתַר

שִׁמְעוֹן וְלֵוִי אַחִים . . . בְּסֹדָם אַל־תָּבֹא נַפְשִׁי . . . כִּי בְאַפָּם הָרְגוּ אִישׁ

"Reuben, you are my firstborn, my strength and my initial vigor,
foremost in rank and foremost in power. [Because of your]
water-like impetuosity—you cannot be foremost"

"Simeon and Levi . . . into their conspiracy may my soul not enter! . . .
For in their rage they murdered people" (Genesis 49:3-6)

When Judgment Is Impaired

It is noteworthy that in reprimanding Reuben, Simeon and Levi, the patriarch denounces the *manner* in which they acted even more than the acts of which he disapproved. "Because of your water-like impetuosity . . . for in their rage."

The greatest source of human error is the failure to deliberate. When emotions run amok, a person is capable of doing things one would never do if one gave it some thought. The Talmud says that when a person is in rage, "all the forces of hell dominate him" (*Nedarim* 22a). I.e., one is taken over by destructive forces that determine one's behavior. This is also true of impulsive and impetuous behavior. One's critical faculties are suspended.

Animals act on impulse. Whatever urges they experience cause them to act. They do not weigh the pros and cons, they do not consider the long-term consequences of their actions and they do not seek the counsel of those who are wiser. A distinguishing feature of man is that he can deliberate before he acts. Failure to do so reduces one to a sub-human state. The act in itself is of secondary importance. Even if a particular act is not patently destructive, and even if the act *per se* is commendable, if it was done in haste or in rage without adequate forethought, it is wrong.

The Talmud says that after Rachel's death, Jacob favored Bilhah over Leah. Reuben was zealous for his mother's honor, and he removed Jacob's bed from Bilhah's tent into Leah's tent. Perhaps he could not be faulted for the act, but he acted impetuously, and that was wrong.

As the firstborn, Reuben should have been the leader of Israel. He was to have the priesthood and the kingship, but he forfeited the leadership because he acted impetuously, in haste and without thinking. That is irresponsible for a leader.

We may not be leaders of nations or communities, but we may be the leaders in our families. One of the most important traits to impress upon our children is to think before acting. We have countless opportunities to model this for them. We are often provoked to anger. If we show our children that rather than acting reflexively we deliberate before we act, we are teaching them one of the most valuable lessons in life.

וַיִּקְרָא יַעֲקֹב אֶל־בָּנָיו וַיֹּאמֶר הֵאָסְפוּ . . .
הִקָּבְצוּ וְשִׁמְעוּ בְּנֵי יַעֲקֹב וְשִׁמְעוּ אֶל־יִשְׂרָאֵל אֲבִיכֶם

וְזֹאת אֲשֶׁר־דִּבֶּר לָהֶם אֲבִיהֶם וַיְבָרֶךְ אוֹתָם אִישׁ אֲשֶׁר כְּבִרְכָתוֹ

Jacob called for his sons and said,
"Assemble yourselves . . . Gather yourselves and listen,
O sons of Jacob, and listen to Israel your father" (49:1-2)
This is what their father spoke to them and he blessed them,
each according to his appropriate blessing (49:28)

Jacob's Blessing: Brotherhood and Self-Realization

The Talmud (end of *Uktzin*) says that the only vessel that can contain blessings is *shalom* (peace). Prior to giving them his blessings, Jacob twice indicated the importance of togetherness: *assemble* and *gather*. Fragmentation and divisiveness can undo even the greatest blessings.

It is significant that in blessing them, Jacob referred to both his names, Jacob and Israel. He was named Jacob (*Yaakov*) because when he was born he held on to the heel (*ekev*) of Esau. The name, Jacob, thus represents the person at birth, the genetic endowments and the potential. The name, Israel, was given to him after he wrestled with an angel and triumphed; Israel meaning, "You have striven with the Divine and with man and have overcome" (*Genesis* 32:29). Israel, therefore, represents Jacob's achievements, his ability to be master over both human and superhuman forces.

It is of interest that we do not find manifest blessings in Jacob's words. He seems, rather, to be describing the character traits of each of his sons. The Torah tells us that indeed, "He blessed them, each according to his appropriate blessing."

Jacob knew his children. He instructed them to each fulfill his unique potential, maximizing the particular talents, skills and character strengths with which he was created.

This is the greatest blessing of all. Jacob did not bless them with wealth or other external acquisitions. The latter may not be a blessing at all. The true blessing is for a person to become everything that he can be.

This is an important teaching for parents. Sometimes parents set their minds on what they would like their child to be, not taking into consideration the child's interests and abilities. All parents want the best for their child. However, they may think they know what is best for the child, whereas what they really desire is that the child fulfill *their* aspirations for him. The patriarch teaches us that we must get to know our children and help them develop and realize their own unique potential.

In these few words, Jacob conveyed the essence of blessings: brotherhood, working at achievement (Israel) and developing one's innate endowment to its fullest (Jacob).

וַיִּשְׂאוּ אֹתוֹ בָנָיו אַרְצָה כְּנַעַן וַיִּקְבְּרוּ אֹתוֹ בִּמְעָרַת שְׂדֵה הַמַּכְפֵּלָה

His sons carried him to the land of Canaan and they buried him in the cave of the Machpelah field (50:13)

Becoming Indifferent to Injustice

The Talmud states that when the sons brought Jacob to Machpelah, Esau objected to his being buried there, claiming that he was Isaac's heir. Although he had sold the extra portion that the firstborn son receives (*Genesis* 25:33), he nevertheless had equal rights with Jacob and protested his burial there. The sons claimed that Jacob had purchased the rights to Machpelah from him. "Where is the deed?" Esau asked. The sons said that it remained in Egypt. Esau insisted they prove Jacob's ownership with the deed, and they sent Naftali to bring it.

Jacob's grandson, Chushim the son of Dan, was hard of hearing and was unaware of what was happening. "Why isn't Grandfather being buried?" he asked. When they told him that they were awaiting Naftali's return with the deed, Chushim exclaimed, "What! And until then Grandfather's burial will be delayed?" He arose in anger and killed Esau (*Sotah* 13a).

R' Chaim Shmulevitz asks, "Why was Chushim the only one who reacted?" He answers that because the sons had entered into a discussion and negotiations with Esau, their sense of outrage faded away. Because Chushim was deaf and had not been party to the discussion, his reaction to the delay in burial was outrage.

R' Shmulevitz points out the danger of losing one's sense of outrage. We can attest to this from our own experience. Shooting by students at schools still occurs, but it does not elicit the sense of horror that the first shooting did. We have become inured to what was once a shocking act.

The media saturate us with accounts of violence and scandals. We hardly react to these anymore, accepting them as, "Well, that's the way it is." The perpetrator of a crime is not the villain he once was. Our attitude towards horrible acts is similar to that of bad weather. We are no longer shocked by outrageous acts.

We must be careful not to lose our sensitivity to wrongdoing. Indifference to injustice is essentially condoning injustice.

וַיִּרְאוּ אֲחֵי־יוֹסֵף כִּי־מֵת אֲבִיהֶם וַיֹּאמְרוּ לוּ יִשְׂטְמֵנוּ יוֹסֵף וְהָשֵׁב יָשִׁיב לָנוּ אֵת כָּל־הָרָעָה אֲשֶׁר גָּמַלְנוּ אֹתוֹ

Joseph's brothers perceived that their father was dead, and they said, "Perhaps Joseph will nurse hatred against us and then he will surely repay us all the evil that we did him" (50:15)

Passive Aggression

Rashi states that the Hebrew word *lu*, that is here translated as "perhaps," does not have this meaning elsewhere. Usually, *lu* is an expression of wishfulness. It may well be that the usual meaning of *lu* is appropriate here, and that the brothers were indeed saying, "We wish that Joseph will repay us all the evil that we did him."

Joseph was exceedingly kind to his brothers, and supported their families. He told his brothers that he sincerely believed that they had been but instruments of God whereby He wanted to make him viceroy of Egypt. He told them that he bore no resentment toward them. As we saw earlier, Joseph did not wish to be the magnanimous forgiver. Rather, he sought to give his brothers an opportunity to redeem themselves, which they indeed did. Nevertheless, they were unable to accept forgiveness and they retained their guilt.

It was because of this lingering guilt that they were unable to tolerate Joseph's kindness. It would have been easier to accept frank punishment from Joseph than his persistent kindness. They, therefore, said, "*Lu, we wish* Joseph would punish us for what we did. We would then be able to feel that we expiated our sin."

The messages conveyed here are twofold. (1) A person should be able to accept forgiveness, and (2) a punishment of kindness can be more painful than a lashing.

In our Friday night *zemiros* (*Kol Mekadesh*) we say, "Extend Your kindness to those who know You, O jealous and vengeful God." It may appear odd to address God as jealous and vengeful when one is seeking kindness. What the poet is saying is, "If I deserve to bear Divine vengeance, then punish me with kindness."

The Torah forbids taking revenge (*Leviticus* 19:18). Yet, we are to emulate God, and God is described as being vengeful. The answer to the contradiction is to be vengeful the way God is. If you wish to be vengeful, do it by extending kindness.

וַיְנַחֵם אוֹתָם וַיְדַבֵּר עַל־לִבָּם
Thus he [Joseph] comforted them and spoke to their heart (50:21)

Words of Consolation

One of the mitzvos is to console the bereaved. We generally fulfill this mitzvah by visiting the family during the *shivah* (seven days of mourning). In many cases, such as when an elderly parent dies, making a *shivah* call is not a great challenge. It is the way of the world that when one has lived a long life, one passes on. True, one can sorely miss an elderly father or mother, but the grief is not overwhelming. Visitors may share memories they had of the departed person, and this may be a comfort to the family.

But there are times when, God forbid, a young person dies, or one loses a child. This is not the way of nature, and the pain can be excruciating. People are at a loss for words. What can one say, other than the prescribed blessing, "May God console you among the other mourners of Zion and Jerusalem?" Because there seems to be nothing one can say, and to speak about the departed person may only aggravate the pain, a person may feel awkward. Platitudes may be irritating. Some people have said that in such cases they are reluctant to make a *shivah* call.

There is truth in the adage that, "Joy that is shared is doubled and sorrow that is shared is halved." The comfort is not in what one says, but in what one feels. Sharing the sorrow may not relieve it, but when others share the pain, it helps the sufferer bear it.

Rashi explains the phrase "he comforted them": Joseph told his brothers that he was grateful for their presence, because the Egyptians now knew that this former slave came from a highly respected family. But the Torah tells us that this was not enough. As we have seen (v. supra), the brothers could not wholly accept Joseph's forgiveness. The Torah then tells us that he "spoke to their heart." Here Rashi does not tell us what words he used, because it was not a matter of words but of feelings. Feelings can be conveyed without words. One heart can speak to another heart silently.

Halachah dictates that when one makes a *shivah* call, one should not initiate conversation. If the mourner wishes to converse, then he will initiate conversation. Sometimes the mourner does not have to hear, but feel. If one genuinely feels the pain that the mourner feels, it will convey itself, and while this may not relieve the pain, it does help a person bear it when he feels that others share his grief.

To truly share pain, one must have *ahavas Yisrael*, love for one's fellow Jew. It is by refining our character and eliminating the negative traits that we can empathize and identify with those who suffer and provide a modicum of consolation.

ספר
שמות

SHEMOS/EXODUS

Introduction to Shemos/Exodus

The Book of Shemos/Exodus tells of the formation of the Jewish nation. It begins with the descent to Egypt of the twelve sons of Israel and their families. They enjoyed a period of prosperity as long as Joseph was viceroy. The circumstances of the Israelites in Egypt changed gradually but radically, resulting in their enslavement and inhumane treatment. God charged Moses with the task to liberate them, and at Sinai they received the Torah and became the Jewish nation. Not too long afterwards they committed the sin of worshipping the Golden Calf, incurring the wrath of God, and it was only Moses' intercession that saved them from extinction. They regained God's favor, and God instructed them to construct a Sanctuary where His presence would always be in their midst.

The first mitzvah in the Book of Shemos is the establishment of the calendar. In contrast to others, the Jewish calendar is lunar rather than solar. Whereas the light of the sun is essentially uniform, the light of the moon waxes and wanes. From total darkness, a tiny sliver of light appears, gradually increasing to a full moon, then decreasing until the light disappears. But even when the sky is totally dark, it is only a matter of days before the light returns and increases again.

The history of the Israelites in the Book of Shemos is much like the moon that regulates their year. They began their existence with a life of comfort and luxury, which was followed by a crushing enslavement. This was followed by a glorious emancipation and the dazzling spiritual heights of Sinai. This gave way to a precipitous decline, which was followed by the spirituality of the Sanctuary.

The history of the Jewish nation since then follows much the same pattern: light alternating with darkness. We have had periods of glory alternating with periods of depression. The Book of Shemos and the lunar calendar that regulates our lives teach us that even when we may be experiencing a period of utter darkness, we should remember that light is soon to appear. There is never any reason for despair.

R' Nachman of Braslav says that hopelessness is nonexistent. There are indeed times when one *feels* hopeless, but one must remember that this feeling is a delusion. Just as a psychotic person may have a hallucination, a sensory experience of something that does not exist in reality, says R' Nachman, so may a mentally healthy person experience a feeling which to him seems very real, but it is in fact hallucinatory and delusional.

The Baal Shem Tov said that one should not refer to a distressing experience as "bad," but as "bitter." Everything that emanates from God is good, although it may be painful. A life-saving medication may be very bitter, but it is good.

Torah is reality, and the Book of Shemos is a lesson in reality.

פרשת שמות
Parashas Shemos

וּבְנֵי יִשְׂרָאֵל פָּרוּ וַיִּשְׁרְצוּ וַיִּרְבּוּ וַיַּעַצְמוּ
בִּמְאֹד מְאֹד וַתִּמָּלֵא הָאָרֶץ אֹתָם

*The Children of Israel were fruitful, teemed, increased
and became strong — very, very much so;
and the land became filled with them* (1:7)

Assimilation: a Provocation

Midrash (*Yalkut*) comments, "The Egyptian *theaters* became filled with them."

R' Yehoshua Leib Diskin and R' Yosef Dov Soloveitchik (*Beis HaLevi*) both state that the Egyptians and the Israelites lived in peace as long as the Israelites remained in Goshen. They were indebted to Joseph for having saved the land from famine and for enriching the royal coffers. As long as the patriarch Jacob and his sons were alive, the Israelites remained in Goshen. After their death, the Israelites began moving out of Goshen, mingling with the Egyptian population, adopting their customs and "filling their theaters." It was this that turned the Egyptians against the Israelites.

Beis HaLevi cites the verse, "You shall be holy for Me, for I, God, am holy, and *I have separated you from the peoples to be Mine*" (*Leviticus* 20:26). It is God's will that Jews remain distinct and separate from other peoples. When they try to assimilate, God turns their gentile neighbors against them to preserve the separation. The more that the Jews attempt to blur the separation, the more anti-Semitism increases.

It is high time that we accepted this historical truth. When we are distinct as Jews, in our appearance and lifestyle, our gentile neighbors may tolerate us. When we lose our distinction and try to assimilate with them, their animosity toward us increases.

For decades, the Anti-Defamation League waged a battle against resorts and country clubs that were "restricted;" i.e., off limits to Jews and African-Americans. What a foolish battle! Which Jews were they restricting? Jews who observed kosher would not enter these places even if they were invited and provided with free meals. What interest would an observant Jew have in a place where he could not even drink a glass of water? The Jews they wished to exclude were those who had abandoned Torah observance. Had the ADL directed their enormous efforts to encourage Jews to keep kosher, the restrictions against Jews would have been dropped.

Commenting on the miracle of Purim, R' Tuvia Tavyomi cites the Talmudic statement that Haman's decree to exterminate the Jews was brought about because they partook of the feast of Ahasuerus, at which they consumed non-kosher food and wine (*Megillah* 12a). He comments that this aggravated Haman's anti-Semitic fervor. As long as Jews were segregated and could not intermingle with the general population, they did not pose a serious threat. There was no reason to fear that they would ever come to power. However, when he saw that they had abandoned the dietary laws which kept them separate, he was afraid that they might eventually infiltrate the power structure. When he saw that Mordechai was indeed in the royal court, his worst fears came true (*Imrei Tal*).

In 1965 there was an exclusive club in Pittsburgh that did not admit Jews. I was probably the first Jew who set foot there. I came to lunch meetings with my brown-bag kosher lunch. I represented no threat to them. I would not accept a membership there if they had handed it to me on a golden platter.

It has been said that those who do not learn from history are doomed to repeat it. We would be wise to avoid this painful repetition.

וַיָּקָם מֶלֶךְ־חָדָשׁ עַל־מִצְרָיִם אֲשֶׁר לֹא־יָדַע אֶת־יוֹסֵף

*A new king arose over Egypt,
who did not know of Joseph* (1:8)

Emotional Flexibility

The Talmud quotes two opinions: It was either a new king or the existing monarch with new policies, who acted as if he "did not know of Joseph" (*Sotah* 11a). The Midrash follows the second opinion, and states that when the Egyptians turned against the Jews, Pharaoh refused to go along with them and they deposed him for three months, until he yielded to their wishes (*Shemos Rabbah* 1:9).

Is it not amazing that the king who said to Joseph, "Since God has informed you of all this, there can be no one so discerning and wise as you" (*Genesis* 41:39), now says to Moses, "Who is God that I should heed His voice to send out Israel? I do not know God" (*Exodus* 5:2)?

R' Meir Rubman cites *Mishnas R' Eliezer*: "The reason the Torah is so harsh regarding an ingrate is because denial of gratitude toward another person is tantamount to denial of gratitude toward God. Today one denies gratitude toward a fellow man, and the next day he denies gratitude toward God. All of Egypt knew that Joseph had saved their land, as did Pharaoh. However, Pharaoh chose to deny gratitude toward Joseph, and thereafter denied God, saying, "Who is God that I should heed His voice? I do not know God" (*Lekach Tov, Shemos* p. 5)

How we relate to God depends on how we relate to other people. When the Baal Shem Tov was asked, How can one develop a love for God? How can one love a Being that one cannot see or have any sense experience of Him? He responded, "Love your fellow man. This will lead you to love of God." Indeed, the Talmud says that the way a human being can cleave unto God is to emulate His traits: "Just as He is merciful, you should be merciful" (*Shabbos* 133a).

R' Yehudah Leib Chasman shares another insight with us. The Midrash says that

Pharaoh initially resisted his people's demands that he enslave Jews, because he felt indebted to Joseph and to Jacob's blessing the land. However, when expedience required that he persecute the Jews in order to retain his throne, he became a cruel tyrant, enslaving them and ordering their children to be killed. This shows us that a person is capable of altering his emotions. A person may not say, "That's me. That's just the way I am."

Pharaoh underwent an emotional change because of his desire to keep his position. Just as a person can alter one's emotions negatively, so can one change one's emotions positively. Pharaoh was motivated by expedience. A person can also be motivated by a sincere conviction to do what is right. One need only realize which emotions are proper and have a sincere desire to cultivate them.

People who do not wish to put forth the effort to modify their character traits may say, "I was born that way." R' Shneur Zalman says in *Tanya*, "It is an inborn capacity that the intellect can be master over the emotions." The ability to change is an inborn trait. In fact, it is the most significant distinguishing feature between man and other living things. A person who denies his ability to alter his character is lowering himself to a subhuman level. Our dignity should not allow us to do this.

וַתִּקְרָא שְׁמוֹ מֹשֶׁה וַתֹּאמֶר כִּי מִן־הַמַּיִם מְשִׁיתִהוּ

She (Pharaoh's daughter) called his name Moses (Moshe), as she said, "For I drew him from the water" (2:10)

Inculcating Values

The Midrash says that Moses had many names. At birth, Amram called him "Chaver," and his mother called him "Yekuthiel." Miriam called him "Yered," and Aaron called him "Avi Zanoach" (*Yalkut Shimoni, Shemos* 166). Yet, he is referred to in the Torah only as "Moshe," the name given him by Pharaoh's daughter, and even God did not call him by any other name (*Shemos Rabbah* 1:26).

Is it not strange that although he was known by other names for the first three months of his life, the names given to him by his parents and by Miriam and Aaron, who were both prophets, were superceded by the name given to him by Pharaoh's daughter?

Pharaoh's daughter knew of her father's decree. By saving a child of the Hebrews, she was putting herself at great risk. Because of her *mesiras nefesh*, her willingness to sacrifice herself to save the child, the name Moshe prevailed. The origin of the name, "For I drew him from the water," therefore, represents *mesiras nefesh*.

Moses never forgot that his very existence was the result of her *mesiras nefesh*, and this trait was indelibly etched into his character. When God threatened to annihilate the Israelites because of the sin of the Golden Calf and to rebuild the nation from him, Moses interceded, saying, "If You do not forgive them, erase me from the book that You have written" (*Exodus* 32:32). Throughout the entire forty years of his stewardship, Moses was prepared to sacrifice himself for his people. When Moses pleaded for his life, to be able to enter the Promised Land, God said that this could come to pass only if He retracted the forgiveness for the Golden

Calf worship. Moses said, "Let Moses and even a hundred like him perish, but let not the minutest harm come to even one of my people" (*Devarim Rabbah* 7:11).

The fact that God called Moses by no other name indicates the importance of early impressions on children. The name Moshe was dearest to God because it was Pharaoh's daughter's *mesiras nefesh* that was impressed upon Moses and that qualified him to be the leader of Israel.

The Talmud says that when a child is old enough to speak, the parents should teach him the verse, "The Torah that Moses commanded us is the heritage of the Congregation of Jacob" (*Deuteronomy* 33:4). We generally assume that this is to impress the child with the legacy of Torah. But perhaps it is even intended more as a reminder to the parents that it is their values that the child will adopt, just as Moses adopted the *mesiras nefesh* of Pharaoh's daughter.

וַיְהִי בַּיָּמִים הָהֵם וַיִּגְדַּל מֹשֶׁה וַיֵּצֵא אֶל־אֶחָיו וַיַּרְא בְּסִבְלֹתָם

It happened in those days that Moses grew up and went out to his brethren and observed their burdens (2:11)

The Making of a Leader

In the text of the Torah there is a significant gap. The Torah tells nothing about Moses from the time that that his mother, Jocheved, turned him over to the daughter of Pharaoh, until he went out and saw the suffering of the Israelites.

The Midrash says that Moses was a precocious child, and we may assume that he was aware of his Jewish origin. But from the time he was taken into Pharaoh's palace at age 2 (*Shemos Rabbah* 1:31) until the time he went out among the Israelites and killed the Egyptian who was beating a Jew (*Shemos* 2:11), the Torah tells us nothing about him. He obviously grew up in the royal court. According to the Midrash, there was an interval when he was ruler of Ethiopia (*Yalkut Shimoni, Shemos* 168).

The Midrash says that the patriarch Jacob spent 14 years in the academy of Shem and Eber. This learning period was over and above what he had learned from Isaac. Where was Moses educated? Hardly in Pharaoh's palace or on the throne of Ethiopia.

The emphasis of this book is on *middos*, and justly so. Torah is the Divine wisdom, and Moses achieved the wisdom of Torah because he excelled in *middos*.

"It happened in those days that Moses grew up and went out to his brethren and observed their burdens." Rashi comments, "He set his eyes and heart to feel their anguish." The Midrash states that when Moses saw the hard labor of the Israelites, he put his shoulders under their burdens to carry their load (*Shemos Rabbah* 1:27). How much could this possibly contribute to alleviating the burden of hundreds of thousands of slaves? The purpose was not to relieve their burden, but rather to feel the suffering that they were experiencing. Feeling sorry for them was not enough. Moses wanted to feel the pain so he could better understand their predicament.

R' Yeruchem Levovitz cites the Talmud that one of the essential traits to acquire Torah is to share the burden of another person (*Ethics of the Fathers* 6:6). He states that *all the mitzvos of the Torah are dependent on this trait, which is the very foundation of Torah and mitzvos, not only those mitzvos between man and fellow man, but also those between man and God* (*Daas Chochmah U'Mussar* vol. 4 pp. 29-32). Not only does one develop proper behavior toward others, but one can also achieve an understanding of the Divine will.

We can feel for other people in several ways. We can *sympathize* or feel sorry for them. We can *empathize* with them, and attempt to see reality as they see it. Or, we can *identify* with them and actually feel their pain. Moses was able to identify.

R' Yaakov Neiman states that identifying with another person's feelings can be achieved only if one sets one's self aside, effacing one's ego. This humility is also one of the requisites for acquisition of Torah. To the degree that one lacks humility, one lacks the capacity to identify. It was Moses' extreme humility that enabled him to identify.

R' Neiman says that even if someone knows all of the Talmud and all the halachic writings, he has not *acquired* Torah unless he has achieved the ability to identify and share the pain of others (*Darkei Mussar* p. 100).

The Midrash states that God spoke to Moses for seven days prior to the revelation in the burning bush, but Moses paid no heed. He did not know that it was God speaking to him, but made no attempt to find the source of the voice because he was in the employ of Jethro, hired to care for the flock, and felt that he had no right to divert his attention from the flock (*Shemos Rabbah* 2:10). We find in halachah that a laborer may not divert from his work. Moses knew this intuitively. The Midrash says that even when he saw the burning bush, he did not leave the flock, but only turned to observe it better, and that is when God said to him, "I am the God of your father."

The Midrash says that one of the sheep ran off and Moses ran after it to retrieve it. When he saw the sheep had gone for water he said, "I didn't know that you were thirsty. You must be exhausted." He then carried the sheep back to the flock (*Shemos Rabbah* 2:2).

The *Zohar* (2:21) says that just as iron is drawn to a magnet, so Moses felt a pull to Sinai, where he had the revelation. It is clear that a person who refines his *middos* develops an attraction to and a closeness to God.

"Remember the Torah of Moses, My servant" (*Malachi* 3:22). It is the Torah of Moses. It was given to him and became his acquisition because of his humility and his ability to identify and share the burden of others.

וַיִּירָא מֹשֶׁה וַיֹּאמַר אָכֵן נוֹדַע הַדָּבָר

Moses was frightened and thought, "Indeed, the matter is known" (2:14)

The Far-Reaching Consequences of Lashon Hara

Rashi says that Moses had wondered, Why should the Israelites be singled out to suffer more than other nations? But now the "matter is known." It is because they carry tales about one another.

The Chafetz Chaim asks, inasmuch as the Midrash says that in Egypt the Israelites were idol worshippers, why did Moses not attribute their suffering to this grievous sin rather than to *lashon hara*?

The Chafetz Chaim cites the Talmud, "He who commits even a single transgression gains himself a single accuser" (*Ethics of the Fathers* 4:13). Every sin results in the creation of an accuser who brings the sin before God.

"However," the Chafetz Chaim said, "the created accuser is similar in character to the sin that begot it. Sins which do not involve speech create accusers that are mute, and they cannot, therefore, bring charges to God. *If a person commits a sin involving speech, the created accuser can speak.* It then not only relates the sin that begot it, but also relates all the other 'mute' sins which cannot speak for themselves. Therefore, Moses felt that even idolatry would not have warranted a harsh judgment had it not been for the sin of carrying tales that created an accuser that could speak and bring the sin before God" (*Talelei Oros, Shemos* p. 53).

The Chafetz Chaim dedicated his life to the eradication of *lashon hara*, describing the multiple transgressions it involves. However, this insight is perhaps the most poignant: *We may not suffer the consequences of other sins if we do not transgress with improper speech.*

This concept may explain another rather puzzling statement. Following the horrible massacres of Jews by Chmielnicki in 1748-9, R' Yom Tov Heller (author of *Tosafos Yom Tov* on the Mishnah) said that this suffering was brought about because Jews conversed in shul during services. R' Heller composed a special prayer of blessings for all who showed reverence for the shul and prayer by maintaining silence during services.

Here, too, we may ask, were there not other sins, perhaps far more severe, that Jews had committed? Why place the onus on talking during services, which is, after all, not a Scriptural prohibition?

The Chafetz Chaim's comment explains this as well. Other sins, even if grave, were mute and could not voice any persecutory accusations. The sin of speaking in shul was one that created a persecutory angel that could speak, and who could thus present his condemning evidence before the heavenly tribunal.

If we have not been careful about our speech before, this insight should make us aware of the far-reaching consequences of *lashon hara* and of conversing during services.

וַיַּרְא וְהִנֵּה הַסְּנֶה בֹּעֵר בָּאֵשׁ וְהַסְּנֶה אֵינֶנּוּ אֻכָּל: וַיֹּאמֶר מֹשֶׁה אָסֻרָה־נָּא
וְאֶרְאֶה אֶת־הַמַּרְאֶה הַגָּדֹל הַזֶּה מַדּוּעַ לֹא־יִבְעַר הַסְּנֶה...
וַיֹּאמֶר אָנֹכִי אֱלֹקֵי אָבִיךָ אֱלֹקֵי אַבְרָהָם אֱלֹקֵי יִצְחָק וֵאלֹקֵי יַעֲקֹב

He [Moses] saw and behold! the bush was burning in the fire but the bush was not consumed. Moses thought, "I will turn aside now and look at this great sight—why will the bush not be burned?" And He [God] said, "I am the God of your father, the God of Abraham, the God of Isaac and the God of Jacob" (3:2-6)

The Nucleus of Divinity

How does God's statement satisfy Moses' question?

My father conveyed an interpretation by his grandfather, Zeide R' Motele. The *sneh*, a bush that is barren of both leaves and fruit, represents a person who is devoid of both mitzvos and Torah knowledge. Yet, this person is capable of having a burning passion for God. Yaavetz says that during the Inquisition, Jews who were not observant of mitzvos in the least went to the stake exclaiming *Shema Yisrael*, surrendering their lives rather than renounce their faith.

The question Moses raised was, if a person is capable of such total devotion to God, "Why does the barren bush not glow? Why do we not see this passion in him at other times?"

God's answer was that in every Jew there is a spark of a passion to unite with God. This is a heritage passed down by the patriarchs Abraham, Isaac and Jacob to all Jewish *neshamos*, whether Jewish by birth or by choice, as evidenced by the martyrdom of Graf Petotski, the Righteous Proselyte of Vilna. This nucleus of Godliness longs for union with its Source.

The nucleus of Godliness that is within every Jew may be likened to the molten rock in the center of the earth that is at an extraordinary high temperature and is under great pressure. This molten rock slowly pushes its way through fissures and crevices in the earth's crust. No one is aware of the molten rock beneath the earth's surface until one day it breaks through the surface as a volcano, spewing its lava miles into the air.

So it is with the nucleus of Godliness that lies deeply concealed within a person, and one may not be aware of its existence. Like the lava, it relentlessly pushes its way to the surface. Once it makes its breakthrough, it can appear with an explosive force.

What causes the breakthrough? R' Shneur Zalman explains that the bond that ties the nucleus of Godliness to its Source is the Torah. Violation of the Torah estranges this nucleus by setting up barriers between it and God. The *yetzer hara* is cunning, and deludes a person into thinking that he can maintain a closeness to God even when he disobeys His will. However, when a person is confronted with renouncing God, the *yetzer hara* can no longer delude him that he can relate to God while rejecting Him. At this point the person is willing to give up his life rather than to be separated from God.

This was Moses' first lesson of the essence of a Jew, a lesson which he never forgot. In spite of the obstreperous behavior of the Israelites during the forty years in the desert, and the many times they angered God, Moses always pleaded for them. He knew that in their essence they were devoted to God and wished to unite with Him.

This is something which every Jew should bear in mind. We cannot possibly achieve true happiness if we are distanced from our Source. There is a force within us that strives to unite with God. To deny that innate Godliness its wish is to be in conflict with oneself. Strengthening the bond between ourselves and God by observing His will eliminates the internal conflict that robs us of peace of mind and peace of soul.

וַיֹּאמֶר בִּי אֲדֹ-נָי שְׁלַח-נָא בְּיַד-תִּשְׁלָח

He replied, "Please, God, send through whomever You will send" (4:13).

How Considerate We Must Be

The Yalkut explains that Moses' reluctance to become the deliverer of Israel was because he was concerned that his brother Aaron, who was three years his senior and had prophesied before he did, might be offended that he was passed over in favor of his younger brother. This is why God assured Moses, "Is there not Aaron, your brother the Levite? I know that he will surely speak; moreover he is going out to meet you and when he sees you he will rejoice in his heart" (*Exodus* 4:14).

R' Nosson Zvi Finkel, the Alter (Elder) of Slobodka, said, "Pause and think for a moment. Hundreds of thousands of Jews are suffering indescribable enslavement. Their children are being killed. God tells Moses, 'You can deliver these people from their suffering,' and Moses refuses the mission because he is concerned that his brother's feelings may be hurt! This gives you an idea of how grave a sin it is to hurt a person's feelings."

How did Moses dare to refuse an assignment by God for this reason? Because he knew that it could not possibly be God's will that he cause his brother distress, and he awaited God's reassurance that Aaron would not be offended.

R' Chaim Shmulevitz expresses a similar thought. The Midrash states that when God commissioned Moses to liberate the Israelites, Moses said, "Master of the Universe! I cannot go without taking leave from my father-in-law, Jethro. He was hospitable to me when I was homeless" (*Shemos Rabbah* 4:2). Again, every moment of delay prolongs the Israelites' suffering, but Moses says that he cannot be rude and ungrateful to Jethro. Moses knew that it would be God's will that he not be an ingrate (*Sichos Mussar* 32, 5732).

How did Moses know that this was God's will? He knew that God could deliver the Israelites miraculously without Pharaoh's permission. Yet He sent Moses to obtain Pharaoh's consent, because it was only appropriate to give Pharaoh an opportunity to avoid severe punishment. Moses knew that because God valued decent behavior, He would not want him to be inconsiderate.

The will of God regarding gratitude is evident in the Torah. "You shall not reject an Egyptian, for you were a sojourner in his land." Rashi comments, "Even though they threw your newborn into the river, you must remember that they had been your hosts." The debt of gratitude that Jacob and his family incurred when they lived in Egypt is not negated by subsequent Egyptian cruelty.

When God told Moses to give Pharaoh the courtesy of sending out the Israelites rather than taking them out by force, Moses understood how important acknowledgement of gratitude is to God.

These Torah teachings should make us give serious thought to how sensitive we are to other people's feelings, and to alert us to be grateful for any favor we receive.

פרשת וארא
Parashas Va'eira

וַיְדַבֵּר אֱלֹקִים אֶל־מֹשֶׁה וַיֹּאמֶר אֵלָיו אֲנִי ה׳

God [Elokim] spoke to Moses and said to him, "I Am Hashem" (6:2)

Bitter, but Not Bad

When God is referred to by the appellation "Elokim" rather than "Hashem," that indicates an attribute of stern judgment. Rashi says that God reprimanded Moses for having said, "Why have You done evil to this people, why have You sent me? From the time I came to Pharaoh to speak in Your Name he did evil to this people, but You did not rescue Your people" (*Exodus* 5:22-23).

What was wrong with what Moses said? The leader of Israel must be an advocate for his people, and when necessary, plead their case before God. Furthermore, instances where the prophets complained to God abound. The Psalmist says, "My God, my God, why have You forsaken me?" (*Psalms* 22:2). "You have given us up like sheep to be eaten ... You sell Your people for worthless gain ... Why do You wish to appear as if asleep?" (ibid. 44:12-24). "Why, O God have You forsaken us forever?" (ibid. 74:1). These seem to be even greater statements of protest than that of Moses.

R' Yaakov Neiman says that Moses was not reprimanded for having challenged God, but for having used an improper expression: "Why have You done *evil* to this people?" God does no evil. Everything that God does is good. As noted, the Baal Shem Tov says that when a person experiences adversity, he should not say, "This is bad," but rather, "This is bitter." A life-saving medication may taste very bitter, but it is good. A surgical procedure may be very painful, but if it saves one's life, it is good (*Darkei Mussar*).

A mature adult will swallow a bitter medication because he knows it is for his own good. A child cannot understand this, so he will resist taking the medication. We should have the maturity of knowing that even the most distressing things are for an ultimately good cause. Like a child, we may resist what is good for us.

The Psalmist complains about his suffering, but does not call it evil. We may complain when we are in pain, but we should have faith in God's infinite goodness.

הֵן בְּנֵי־יִשְׂרָאֵל לֹא־שָׁמְעוּ אֵלַי
וְאֵיךְ יִשְׁמָעֵנִי פַרְעֹה וַאֲנִי עֲרַל שְׂפָתָיִם

*"Behold, the Children of Israel have not listened to me,
so how will Pharaoh listen to me?
And I have sealed lips"* (6:12)

Good, Not Better Than

Rashi says that this is one of ten *a fortiori* arguments that we find in the Torah. Many of the commentaries question the logic of this argument. The Torah says that the reason the Israelites did not listen to Moses was because "of shortness of breath and hard work" (*Exodus* 6:9). Inasmuch as Pharaoh was not a victim of such oppression, perhaps he might listen.

My grandfather, the Rebbe of Bobov, gave a novel interpretation to this verse. He cited the verses: "The prophetic burden of the word of God, through Malachi. 'I loved you,' said God, and you said, 'How have You loved us?' 'Was not Esau a brother of Jacob'—the words of God—'yet I loved Jacob but I despised Esau,' " (*Malachi* 1:1-3).

My grandfather asked, "In what way was this prophecy a burden? It is such an uplifting statement: 'I despise Esau and I love Jacob.' A prophecy that expresses God's love for Israel is hardly a burden."

He answered that there are two ways whereby a father can love a son. One way is that the son has earned the father's love. He is gentle, considerate, studious and courteous. It is also possible that the son is none of these and has really not earned love. However, he has a brother who is an absolute scoundrel, and compared to his renegade brother, he is a *tzaddik*. The father loves him because by comparison to his brother, who causes the father much grief, he is so much better.

Malachi conveyed the words of God: "I love Jacob, because he is a brother to Esau, whom I despise because he is a rogue. Compared to Esau, Jacob is a *tzaddik*." The prophet said, "If God cannot find anything more laudable to say about the Israelites other than they are not as bad as the pagans, then this is indeed a burdensome prophecy for me. We should merit God's love because we earned it."

Moses was an advocate for the Israelites. He had come to them with the joyous message of deliverance, that God would liberate them from their cruel enslavement, yet they turned a deaf ear to him. Moses pleaded for them: "They rejected me because they were oppressed, 'of shortness of breath and hard work.' However, I know that when I come to Pharaoh, he will reject me even though he lives in leisure. Therefore, the Israelites are not as bad as Pharaoh." Then Moses added, "If I have nothing more favorable to say about the Israelites other than they are better than Pharaoh, then 'I have sealed lips.' I am without words. This is hardly what I wish to say about my people."

We should seek to improve ourselves spiritually. Living in an environment which is so immoral and corrupt, we may tend to think that because we are not as decadent as our neighbors, that is adequate spirituality. This is a mistake. We must strive to be virtuous on our own, rather than being satisfied because we may be better than the wicked. We should constantly seek to advance ourselves spiritually.

SHEMOS / EXODUS: Va'eira

וַיְדַבֵּר ה' אֶל־מֹשֶׁה וְאֶל־אַהֲרֹן וַיְצַוֵּם אֶל־בְּנֵי יִשְׂרָאֵל
וְאֶל־פַּרְעֹה מֶלֶךְ מִצְרָיִם לְהוֹצִיא אֶת־בְּנֵי־יִשְׂרָאֵל מֵאֶרֶץ מִצְרָיִם

God spoke to Moses and Aaron and commanded them to the Children of Israel and regarding Pharaoh, king of Egypt, to take the Children of Israel out of the land of Egypt (6:13).

Respectfully Yours

This verse appears redundant. Just two verses earlier, the Torah says, "God spoke to Moses, saying, 'Come speak to Pharaoh, king of Egypt, that he send the Children of Israel from his land'" (*Exodus* 6:10-11). Rashi explains that the second verse means that God told them to speak respectfully to the king of Egypt.

Is this not a bit strange? Moses was going to warn Pharaoh about the ten plagues that he would suffer. In the presence of all the ministers in the palace, Moses was going to speak harshly to Pharaoh. How can this be respectful?

R' Yehudah Leib Chasman says that there was no way out of delivering the warnings to Pharaoh. However, although what had to be said had to be said, it could still be said respectfully rather than with indignation. Indeed, we see that when Moses told Pharaoh about the plague of the firstborn, at which time Moses was angry, he nevertheless said, "Then all these servants of yours will come down to me and bow to me, saying, 'Leave—you and the entire people that follows you'" (*Exodus* 11:8). Rashi says that Moses really meant that Pharaoh himself will come and bow to him and plead for him to take the Israelites out of Egypt, but out of respect for the king he said "all these servants of yours will come down to me and bow to me" (*Ohr Yahel,* 2).

The Torah is teaching us that even when we must reprimand or punish someone, we should make every effort to avoid insulting him. This is so important in disciplining children. Obviously, children must be reprimanded when they do wrong, and sometimes it is necessary to punish them. However, we should be most cautious to do so in a manner that does not humiliate the child or crush him.

Children who were insulted when they were disciplined are likely to develop feelings of shame and worthlessness which may accompany them throughout their lives. If parents would realize how destructive low self-esteem is to their children, they would be much more careful in how they discipline them. Emotional abuse of a child is as serious an offense as physical abuse. Yet, parents who would never think of breaking a child's arm or leg may not give much thought to the words they use in a reprimand.

Children must be taught right from wrong, but they should be helped to retain their dignity.

הוּא אַהֲרֹן וּמֹשֶׁה . . . הוּא מֹשֶׁה וְאַהֲרֹן

This was the Aaron and Moses this was the Moses and Aaron (6:26-27)

True Equality

Rashi says that the reason Moses is sometimes mentioned before Aaron and at other times Aaron is mentioned before Moses is to tell us that they were both equal, "as one." The latter qualification means that at a spiritual level they were perfectly identical. The Seer of Lublin asked, how can two people be perfectly alike? The Midrash says that just as no two people are absolutely identical in appearance (even identical twins have minor differences), no two people are absolutely identical in ideas (*Tanchuma Pinchas* 10).

The Seer cites the Talmudic statement (*Chullin* 89a) that "what the Torah says of Moses and Aaron is greater than what it says about Abraham because Abraham said, 'I am but dust and ash' (*Genesis* 18:27), whereas Moses said, 'For what are we?' (*Exodus* 16:8)." Although Abraham's humility was indeed profound, "dust and ash" are nevertheless tangible substances. Moses' and Aaron's expression of humility exceeded Abraham's because the expression "*what* are we?" is a total self-effacement, i.e., "we are nothing."

Two substances, the Seer said, cannot be exactly identical, but two "nothings" can be identical. One non-existence is no different than another. It was because of Moses' and Aaron's absolute self-effacement that the Torah refers to them as identical.

There are many proponents of equality. However, a closer look at these will reveal that "some are more equal than others." Few of those who carry the banner of egalitarianism are profoundly humble. Their espousal of equality lacks sincerity because true equality would require a leveling, a measure of self-effacement that they do not possess.

The Seer's comments teach us that if we are to be sincere in the pursuit of equality, we must be ready to relinquish our own ego. To the degree that we lack self-effacement, our ideal of equality is spurious.

וַאֲנִי אַקְשֶׁה אֶת־לֵב פַּרְעֹה
וְהִרְבֵּיתִי אֶת־אֹתֹתַי וְאֶת־מוֹפְתַי בְּאֶרֶץ מִצְרָיִם

*"But I shall harden Pharaoh's heart and I shall multiply
My signs and My wonders in the land of Egypt"* (7:3)

Recovery Follows Crisis

Virtually all the commentaries struggle with this question: If God hardened Pharaoh's heart so that he would not yield after each punishment, what justification was there for further punishment? Can a person be punished for doing something when he had no choice?

It may be chutzpah, but I would like to suggest an answer which was not available to the commentaries.

First, God did not harden Pharaoh's heart for the first five plagues. In these the Torah says, "Pharaoh's heart *was hardened*." It was not until the sixth plague that God hardened Pharaoh's heart.

Forty years of working with alcoholics enabled me to understand Pharaoh's obstinacy. The alcoholic can suffer blow after blow, each time swearing off drinking: "I will never touch another drop as long as I live!" Invariably, he resumes drinking soon afterward. I recall one man whose drinking resulted in severe pancreatitis, which caused such horrific pain that it was not relieved even by morphine. He cried bitterly, "If you can only get me over this pain, Doc, I swear I will never, never even look at alcohol." Three weeks after being released from the hospital, he was drunk. Alcoholics who go through the ordeal of a liver transplant may drink at their first visit outside of the hospital.

Pharaoh acted like a typical alcoholic. When he felt the distress of a plague, he pleaded with Moses, promising to send out the Israelites. No sooner was the plague removed, than he retracted. To me, this behavior is not at all unusual.

But what happened with the sixth plague? It appears that if God had not hardened Pharaoh's heart, he would have yielded. In order to explain this, you must bear with me while I describe a case.

Jim was a very bright, resourceful young man, who got a job with a major construction firm. He was so efficient that he received promotion after promotion, eventually becoming second in command to the CEO at an unprecedented young age.

Jim drank excessively, and his wife's appeals fell on deaf ears. When she told him that she could no longer tolerate it, he said that she was free to leave. She took their three young daughters and left.

Jim continued to work, but eventually the drinking impaired his performance. When his peers pointed this out to him, he said, "They're just jealous of my position." One day the CEO fired him.

Jim would sit in the tavern, expecting that any moment a head-hunter would recruit him to be the CEO of a Fortune-500 firm. He drank away all his savings, then drank away his home, then drank away his car and lived on welfare.

At age 49, Jim admitted himself to my hospital. He was down, yet the next day he signed himself out of the hospital against medical advice.

Two years later, Jim was back. "I know you're mad at me, Doc," he said, "for walking out on you last time."

I said, "Jim, you walked out on yourself, not on me."

Jim nodded. "I'll do anything you say."

I asked Jim, "What makes you more ready now than two years ago?"

Jim responded, "You know what you get for selling your blood? Sixteen beers."

"When you sell for blood for beer, that is hitting rock-bottom," I said.

Jim shook his head. "No, Doc," he said. "I've been doing that for a year."

"Then what brought you in today rather than a year ago?" I asked.

Jim said, "When I was with the firm, I practically ran the United Way drive myself. This past week I've been panhandling quarters on Liberty Avenue. I can't live with that."

Every alcoholic has his individually unique "rock-bottom" which is the point at which he recovers. Jim's loss of his family, his home and his car; sleeping in doorways; and even selling his blood for alcohol were not his rock-bottom. Begging quarters was.

Here is the crucial point to understand. *If, due to pressure, the alcoholic stops drinking before he has reached his particular rock-bottom, he generally relapses.* Sustained recovery occurs only if the person has reached what was for him rock-bottom.

Now let us return to Pharaoh. The Torah says that when the Egyptian army was drowned in the Reed Sea, "none remained *until* one" (ibid. 14:28). I.e., one did remain: Pharaoh. On the verses, "For now I could have sent My hand and stricken you and you would have been obliterated from the earth. However, for this have I let you endure, in order to show you My strength" (*ibid.* 9:15-16), the Midrash comments that God saved Pharaoh, who later became king of Ninveh, and was its king in the episode of Jonah (*Yalkut Shimoni, Shemos* 176).

Incidentally, we can now better understand the reaction of the king of Ninveh. Is it not surprising that when a man suddenly appears, crying in the streets, "In 40 days Nineveh will be destroyed!" that he is taken seriously? Today, if a man shouted something like that in the streets of Washington, D.C. he would be hospitalized as a lunatic. Yet, the king of Nineveh promptly donned sackcloth, fasted and ordered the entire populace to do *teshuvah* to save the city. This was only because the king, who was Pharaoh, knew from bitter experience that there can be a prophet whose words must be taken seriously.

It was God's will that Pharaoh become king of Nineveh. For this it was necessary *that Pharaoh's surrender to God be absolute and permanent.* Had Pharaoh yielded after the fifth or any subsequent plague, *that would not have been his bottom*, and he would have relapsed, again denying God. Inasmuch as it was God's design that Pharaoh survive and become king of Nineveh, he could not be permitted to yield due to pressure before he reached *what God knew was his rock-bottom*. It was for this reason that God hardened his heart to sustain him so that he could reach the point where his recognition of God would be permanent and enduring.

My purpose in this commentary is not to just cite explanations of the Torah, but rather to derive teachings that we can apply in our own lives.

We all have a bit of the alcoholic's tendencies within us. We resolve that we will not repeat a wrong act, and after a period of time elapses, we do it again. Have you never said, "I will never again allow myself to lose my temper like that?" And what happened?

If instead of simply making a promise not to lose control of our temper, we did some serious, persistent study of the *mussar* works on rage, until we felt so crushed by the evil of rage that this episode constituted a "rock-bottom," we could make the necessary character transformation so that we would not subsequently relapse. We should not need to wait for a tragic, destructive "rock-bottom" to bring us to our senses.

כִּי יְדַבֵּר אֲלֵכֶם פַּרְעֹה לֵאמֹר תְּנוּ לָכֶם מוֹפֵת
וְאָמַרְתָּ אֶל־אַהֲרֹן קַח אֶת־מַטְּךָ וְהַשְׁלֵךְ לִפְנֵי־פַרְעֹה יְהִי לְתַנִּין

*"When Pharaoh speaks to you, saying, 'Provide a wonder for yourselves,'
you shall say to Aaron, 'Take your staff and cast it down
before Pharaoh — it will become a snake' "* (7:9)

Sensitivity to Other's Feelings

When God told Moses to instruct Aaron to turn the water of the Nile into blood (*Exodus* 7:19), Rashi explains that Moses was not to smite the river because it had protected him when he had been put in a basket on the river. But why was Aaron, rather than Moses, told to cast the rod before Pharaoh and turn it into a snake?

When God commissioned Moses to deliver the Israelites, Moses said, "What if they will not believe me, for they will say, 'God did not appear to you?'" God then told Moses to cast down his rod, and it turned into a snake (ibid. 4:3). Rashi says that God chose this particular miracle to indicate His displeasure with Moses for having spoken derogatorily about the Israelites, suspecting that they would not believe him.

The Talmud says that at the end of days, the animals will ask the snake, "The lion and the wolf kill for food. What gain do you have for killing someone with your venom?" The snake will answer, "What gain does a person have when he harms someone with slander?" (*Arachin* 16b). The snake has, therefore, become the symbol of *lashon hara.*

Of course, once Moses received the Divine reprimand, he did *teshuvah.* The Talmud says that if a person committed a sin and did *teshuvah*, one is not allowed to remind him of having sinned (*Bava Metzia* 58a). For Moses to have turned the rod into a snake would be a reminder of his previous transgression. The execution of this miracle was, therefore, delegated to Aaron.

The Torah is teaching us how sensitive we must be to another person's feelings. If we know that something we say, even in a jest, may evoke discomfort in another person, we should refrain from saying it. Hillel interpreted the verse, "You shall love your fellow as yourself" (*Leviticus* 19: 18) as meaning, "Do not do to another what you would not want done to you." We should be considerate and sensitive to other people's feelings just as we wish others to be considerate and sensitive to us.

וְשַׂמְתִּי פְדֻת בֵּין עַמִּי וּבֵין עַמֶּךָ
"I shall make a redemption between my people and yours" (8:19)

Internal Freedom

The Baal HaTurim cites two other places where the term *pedus* (redemption) is found: "Redemption He has sent to His people" (*Psalms* 111:9), and "with Him there is redemption in infinite abundance" (ibid. 130:7).

R' Shalom Rokeach of Belz says that there are three types of redemption, corresponding to three types of *galus* (Diaspora). One *galus* is when Jews are oppressed by non-Jews. A more difficult *galus* is when Jews are oppressed by fellow Jews. The severest *galus* is when a person is oppressed by himself.

In the Haggadah *From Bondage to Freedom* I pointed out that there can be a tyranny in the absence of an external taskmaster, and that is when a person is enslaved by his desires and urges and loses his freedom of choice. A striking example of this is the person who is addicted to drugs, who is under so intense a compulsion to use drugs that he cannot exercise the ability to choose his actions. He must do whatever it takes to procure his drug. But drugs are not the only tyrants. Some people are so driven by greed, lust or the desire for acclaim that they are essentially powerless to make proper choices. When a person loses his freedom to choose wisely, he is in an internal *galus*, oppressed by himself. Redemption from this oppression is the most difficult of all. When one is oppressed by others, one is aware of it. When one is a captive of one's own irresistible drives, one may not even be aware of it. One may have the delusion that he is free.

What is true of the individual may be true of the nation as a whole. Historically,

Jews have been deprived of their freedom by oppressors. However, we have too often surrendered our freedom, failing to exercise our right to be unique. We have developed an attitude of subservience, assuming that we must subjugate ourselves to the dictates of our environment. This is an internal *galus*.

R' Shmuel of Mohilev was discussing the concept in Talmud of the two redeemers, the Mashiach who is descendant of Joseph and the Mashiach who is a descendant of David. Someone asked why there is a need for two redeemers. R' Shmuel responded, "One is to take the Jews out of *galus*, and the other is to take the *galus* out of the Jews." We need to be redeemed from our own tyranny.

In the Haggadah I noted that in the order of the Seder, the eating of the matzah precedes the eating of the *maror* (bitter herbs). This appears to be chronologically reversed. The *maror* symbolizes the bitterness of the enslavement, whereas the matzah represents the liberation, so the symbol of liberation should follow that of the enslavement.

However, the Israelites were in an internal *galus*, as is evident when they longed for return to Egypt, making peace with being enslaved (*Exodus* 16:3). They were not even aware how bitter it is to be deprived of freedom. We eat the matzah first as a lesson that only after we experience freedom can we realize that being enslaved is indeed bitter.

We need to strive for our freedom, both as a nation and as individuals.

וַיִּשְׁלַח פַּרְעֹה וְהִנֵּה לֹא־מֵת מִמִּקְנֵה יִשְׂרָאֵל
עַד־אֶחָד וַיִּכְבַּד לֵב פַּרְעֹה וְלֹא שִׁלַּח אֶת־הָעָם

*Pharaoh sent and behold, of the livestock of Israel not even
one had died yet. Pharaoh's heart became stubborn,
and he did not send out the people* (9:7)

Reinforcing Obstinacy

Moses warned Pharaoh that on the following day there would be an epidemic among the livestock of the Egyptians, and that the livestock of the Israelites would be unharmed (*Exodus* 9:3-4). On the following day, the predicted epidemic occurred. From the text it appears that when Pharaoh found out that the livestock of the Israelites were spared, he became even more stubborn than before, rather than becoming more flexible.

The Torah is describing a not uncommon phenomenon. When two people are engaged in a debate, they may exchange arguments more or less logically. If one delivers a proof that invalidates the other's position, the defeated person may lash out with an argument that is patently absurd.

There is often great resistance to admitting one is wrong. When such realization occurs, a person may feel so threatened by being defeated that he reacts like a mother bear whose cubs are threatened, with behavior that may be irrational.

On more than one occasion, I have seen chess players who, when they realized that they were going to be defeated, tipped the chessboard. This is an obvious admission of defeat, yet the vanquished player cannot get himself to say, "The game is yours. You won." There seems to be an innate resistance to verbalizing these words. Angrily upsetting the chessboard, albeit an admission of defeat, is easier than to say, "You win."

This is the meaning of the above verse. Pharaoh saw that the epidemic occurred according to Moses' prediction and that furthermore, none of the Israelite's livestock were affected. And his reaction? To become even more stubborn than he had been.

Many of the other Egyptians were also unable to concede. Moses predicted a destructive hailstorm, and advised Pharaoh to tell the people to take all their belongings into their homes to save them from the hailstorm. "Whoever among the servants of Pharaoh feared the word of God chased his servants and his livestock into the houses. And whoever did not take the word of God to heart, left his servants and livestock in the field" where they were indeed destroyed by the hailstorm (ibid. vs. 19-25).

Seven times previously Moses had predicted a plague, and each time the Egyptians saw his predictions come true. Now Moses warns them of a destructive hailstorm and even advises them to take protective action. How could anyone in his right mind risk losing his belongings? But that is the nature of obstinacy, not to yield even if being stubborn will prove disastrous.

We often find ourselves in an argument where we defend our position. We must be able to accept being wrong, and when we realize that we have lost, admit it with grace.

פרשת בא
Parashas Bo

וַיִּפֶן וַיֵּצֵא מֵעִם פַּרְעֹה

And he [Moses] turned and left Pharaoh's presence (10:6)

Decency Indicates Integrity

The theme of this book is learning proper *middos* from the Torah. The Midrash on this verse is an excellent example of this. The Midrash states that Moses turned away because he saw Pharaoh's ministers taking counsel with each other.

> In Czarist Russia it was not uncommon for Jews to be arrested on suspicion of treason. Anti-Semitism was rampant, and anyone who wanted to make trouble for a Jew would accuse him of plotting against the Czar.
>
> One such case involved R' David, rabbi of Bechov, who was arrested despite his protests of innocence. After several days in prison, he was brought before a board of inquiry. Several of the members of the panel began to discuss something that they did not wish R' David to overhear, so they spoke in French. R' David turned and walked away.
>
> The presiding officer reprimanded R' David for his disrespect in walking away from the panel. R' David said, "Your honor, I did not mean any disrespect. It was evident that you were speaking to each other in French rather than in Russian because you did not want me to listen to your discussion. However, I am fluent in French, and it would have been dishonest of me to overhear something that you wanted to keep secret. That is why I walked away."
>
> The panel was taken by surprise by this show of honesty, and decided that a person of such integrity was speaking the truth when he protested his innocence. They promptly released him.
>
> R' David later explained to his friends that it would not have occurred to him to walk away from the panel, until he remembered the Midrash that Moses turned away when he saw Pharaoh's ministers taking counsel. "Obviously, it is not proper to eavesdrop and overhear when others wish to discuss something in secret."

A lesson in decency derived from the Torah spared R' David's life.

וְהָיְתָה צְעָקָה גְדֹלָה בְּכָל־אֶרֶץ מִצְרָיִם . . . וּלְכֹל בְּנֵי יִשְׂרָאֵל
לֹא יֶחֱרַץ־כֶּלֶב לְשֹׁנוֹ לְמֵאִישׁ וְעַד־בְּהֵמָה

*There shall be a great outcry in the entire land of Egypt . . .
But against all the Children of Israel, no dog shall
whet its tongue, against neither man nor beast* (11:6-7)

Neutrality Is Not Always a Virtue

This was Moses' statement to Pharaoh when he predicted the death of the firstborn.

In Brisk a bitter feud once broke out between two groups. R' Yoseph Dov Soloveitchik appealed to one of the influential citizens, asking him to use his prestigious position to bring the two camps to a peaceful resolution. The man declined the rabbi's request, and when R' Yoseph Dov told him that it was a mitzvah to bring peace to two warring parties, the man said, "I think it is a greater mitzvah to remain neutral and not get involved." This was a rather impudent comment to the rabbi.

R' Yoseph Dov then said, "I was always puzzled by the verse in the Torah, 'But against the Children of Israel, no dog shall whet its tongue.' For what purpose does the Torah tell us this?

"The Talmud says that when the Angel of Death enters a community, the dogs weep. When the prophet Elijah enters the community, the dogs are playful" (*Bava Kamma* 60b).

R' Yoseph Dov continued, "On the night of the plague of the firstborn, there was a conflict. The prophet Elijah is the one who is the harbinger of redemption, so he was there that night. But so was the Angel of Death, to smite the firstborn. The dogs were, therefore, in a quandary. Should they weep because of the Angel of Death or be playful because of Elijah? The dogs decided to remain neutral. That is why the Torah says, 'No dog shall whet its tongue.' Remaining neutral when one can bring peace among feuding people is appropriate for dogs, not for intelligent people."

R' Yoseph Dov's comment was, of course, a witticism. The plague of the firstborn was by the hand of God, not by the Angel of Death. However, his point is valid. The Talmud says that "bringing peace between a man and his fellow" is a great mitzvah for which one is rewarded in both this world and in the eternal world (*Shabbos* 127a). One should not shun this mitzvah, hiding behind a cloak of neutrality.

הַחֹדֶשׁ הַזֶּה לָכֶם רֹאשׁ חֳדָשִׁים רִאשׁוֹן הוּא לָכֶם לְחָדְשֵׁי הַשָּׁנָה

*"This month shall be for you the beginning of the months,
it shall be for you the first of the months of the year"* (12:2)

The Sanctity of Time

The Talmud (*Rosh Hashanah* 22a) derives the mitzvah of establishing the calendar according to the lunar cycle from this verse. When witnesses reported that they had seen the new moon, the Sanhedrin would pronounce the beginning of the month with the declaration, "It is sanctified. The month has been sanctified."

The sanctification of space did not occur until after the sin of the Golden Calf (*Sforno, Exodus* 20:21). Prior thereto, the only sanctification was of time. "God blessed the seventh day and sanctified it." Although the Torah states that it is Shabbos that is sanctified, the Torah commentaries say the sanctity of Shabbos extends over the first three days of the week, and the latter three days take on the sanctity of the upcoming Shabbos (*Korban Nesanel, Gittin* 77a). Prior to the sin of the Golden Calf, the *Shechinah* (Divine Presence) was everywhere. "Wherever I permit My Name to be mentioned I shall come to you and bless you" (*Exodus* 20:21). After the sin of the Golden Calf, God instructed the Israelites to build a Sanctuary. Due to their fall from the spiritual heights of Sinai, they forfeited the ubiquitous *Shechinah*, which now would be in a circumscribed place. But although there was a contraction of the holiness of space, the sanctity of time remained intact.

Just as one must have great reverence for a sacred place, so must one have reverence for time. It is forbidden to be wasteful of time. *Bitul* Torah, wasting time that could be devoted to Torah study, is more grievous than most severe sins (*Jerusalem Talmud, Chaggigah* 1:7). If one is engaged productively in the necessities of life, that is not considered *bitul* Torah. However, wasting time is disrespect of something holy.

Modern technology has provided us with many time-saving devices. Being given additional time is like being given holy books. One would never think of treating holy items with contempt. Neither should we be contemptuous of time.

בָּרִאשֹׁן בְּאַרְבָּעָה עָשָׂר יוֹם לַחֹדֶשׁ בָּעֶרֶב
תֹּאכְלוּ מַצֹּת עַד יוֹם הָאֶחָד וְעֶשְׂרִים לַחֹדֶשׁ בָּעָרֶב

In the first [month], on the fourteenth day of the month in the evening shall you eat matzos, until the twenty-first day of the month in the evening (12:18)

Matzah: Bread of Freedom

Although in the Haggadah we say that we eat matzah on Passover because the Israelites left Egypt in such haste that their dough did not have a chance to rise, the fact is that on the first day of Nissan, God instructed that matzah be eaten on Passover. Just what is the significance of matzah that made it relevant to Passover even before the Exodus? Furthermore, whereas the halachah is that if a small piece of non-kosher food is accidentally mixed into a batch of kosher food, if the ratio of kosher to non-kosher is greater than 60:1, the food is kosher. This is not so in regard to *chametz*. A miniscule fragment of *chametz* that falls into a vat of thousands of gallons renders the entire vat prohibited. What is there about the prohibition of *chametz* that makes it more stringent than other forbidden foods?

The Bnei Yissaschar provides an answer. Matzah and *chametz* symbolize two opposite attitudes. In the baking of matzah, there is someone in control, manipulating the matzah from the moment water is added to the flour until it is baked.

Nothing happens to it spontaneously. With *chametz,* on the other hand, the dough is set aside for a period of time and allowed to rise by itself. The dough undergoes a significant change spontaneously, without anyone making it happen.

Judaism believes that nothing in the world happens of itself. At every moment, God is in control of the world. Except for decisions on moral and ethical behavior, for which a person has freedom of choice, everything else is ordained by God. Laws of nature are principles by which God manages the world. Why things happen the way they do is beyond our ability to understand, because we cannot fathom the Divine wisdom. But we must know that nothing, even the smallest occurrence that is not a matter of free will, is controlled by God.

A person can be enslaved by his own drives as well as by a taskmaster. Ironically, someone who thinks he has control of his fate is not truly free. He is driven to acts that are futile, because whatever is destined to be will be.

The Chafetz Chaim gave a parable of a person who was traveling by train, and was pushing against the wall of the wagon. He explained, "I'm trying to make the train go faster." His act is as futile as the person who tries to earn more money by working longer hours. A person can be truly free only if he is free of drives that dominate him. Matzah, therefore, is the bread of freedom because it represents total control by its maker, with nothing occurring on its own. The message of matzah is that nothing in the world occurs unless God decrees it. "A person's earnings are decreed on Rosh Hashanah" (*Bava Basra* 10a). If a person believes this, he will not be enslaved by an insatiable drive to make more money.

In celebrating our freedom from enslavement, which includes being a slave to one's drives, we eat the matzah. Even the tiniest morsel of *chametz,* which symbolizes spontaneous happenings, is forbidden. To believe that there is anything, however miniscule it may be, that is beyond control of God is antithetical to true freedom.

One might ask, if matzah represents *hashgachah pratis* (Divine providence), why are we not required to eat matzah all year round? Why is *chametz* permitted at all?

The answer is that once we have reinforced our faith in *hashgachah pratis* by eating matzah on Passover, we have been given guidelines how to protect ourselves from the concept of spontaneity, symbolized by *chametz.*

The Torah states that meal-offerings on the Altar were not permitted to be *chametz* (*Leviticus* 2:11). There are two exceptions to this rule: the offering of *shtei halechem* (two loaves of *chametz*) on Shavuos and the ten loaves of *chametz* which accompanied the *korban todah,* the thankfulness offering.

On Shavuos, which commemorates the giving of the Torah when we rededicate ourselves to its study and observance, the offering is one of *chametz.* If we study Torah diligently and observe the mitzvos, we can avoid the error of spontaneity. Similarly, if we cultivate the *middah* of gratitude and thank God for everything, we are attesting that everything comes from Him. This allows us to eat *chametz* all year round and not forget the principle of the matzah on Passover.

וּקְחוּ לָכֶם צֹאן לְמִשְׁפְּחֹתֵיכֶם וְשַׁחֲטוּ הַפָּסַח

"Acquire for yourselves one of the flock for your families and slaughter the Pesach-offering" (12:21)

The Family: Basis of Judaism

This is the first mitzvah given to the Jews at the time of their liberation from enslavement in Egypt.

The greatest miracle of the Exodus is not the dividing of the waters of the Reed Sea nor any of the plagues. These pale before the miracle of a people, cruelly dehumanized for decades, becoming a nation of unprecedented spirituality, exclaiming at Sinai *naaseh venishmah*, we will do and we will listen. How could such a miraculous transformation occur?

The Divine wisdom was that the first mitzvah after throwing off the shackles of slavehood should be a *family* mitzvah. A strong family bond is the key to spirituality. When family members join and reinforce each other's dedication to God by performing a mitzvah together, the path to spirituality is open.

Unfortunately, in western civilization there has been fragmentation of the family. Not only is there often rare contact with the extended family, but even the nuclear family has sustained damage, with far too much domestic strife and parent-child separation. In many families, the Passover *seder,* a remnant of the *Pesach-offering* is the only time that the family may come together.

In the traditional Jewish family, the sense of *mishpachah* was primary. There was greater unity within the family and more consideration of other family members. The family was a unit that stood for something. Today, the divisive attitude of "do your own thing" has pulled family members apart. Too often, the family cannot stand for anything, because every member has his/her own agenda.

The Psalmist says, "How good and how pleasant when brethren dwell together" (*Psalms* 133:1). In my clinical practice I have seen far too many instances of the family being fractured.

Sibling rivalry is as old as the world. Yet, the sense of *mishpachah* was often able to overcome differences within the family. Today, where sibling rivalry exists, there is no glue that can bond brothers and sisters.

The first mitzvah of Passover should serve as a beacon of what is necessary for us to be truly spiritual and to be a nation: *mishpachah*.

וְהָיָה כִּי־יֹאמְרוּ אֲלֵיכֶם בְּנֵיכֶם מָה הָעֲבֹדָה הַזֹּאת לָכֶם: וַאֲמַרְתֶּם זֶבַח־פֶּסַח הוּא לַה׳ אֲשֶׁר פָּסַח עַל־בָּתֵּי בְנֵי־יִשְׂרָאֵל בְּמִצְרַיִם בְּנָגְפּוֹ אֶת־מִצְרַיִם

It shall be that when your children say to you, "What is this service to you?" you shall say, "It is a Pesach feast-offering to God, Who passed over the houses of the Children of Israel when He smote the Egyptians" (12:26-27)

Questions, Yes. Contempt, No

According to the Haggadah, this is the question posed by the "wicked son." However, whereas the Torah gives the response, "It is a *Pesach feast-offering* to God, Who passed over the houses of the Children of Israel when He smote the Egyptians," the Haggadah makes no mention of this. Rather, it says to rebuff him with the statement, "Had you been in Egypt, you would not have been delivered."

A careful study of the Torah text provides the answer. In *Exodus* 13:14, the Torah says, "And it shall be when your son *will ask you* 'What is this?' you shall say *to him*, 'With a strong hand God removed us from Egypt.'" In the verse cited above, the Torah does not say "when your children *will ask* you," but "when your children *say* to you." The Torah also does not say "you shall say *to him*," but rather "you shall say," not addressing the child.

A question deserves an answer. The wicked son is not asking a question; he is making a statement. In a scoffing manner he *saying*, not asking, "Of what use is this ancient, obsolete ritual to you anyway?" He is not interested in an answer, so there is no point in giving him one. Solomon says, "A conceited fool has no desire for understanding; but only wants to express his own view" (*Proverbs* 18:2).

However, when there are scoffers around who depreciate the Torah, we must reinforce ourselves so that we should not fall under their influence. Therefore, although the Torah says that there is no point in responding to the scoffer, "You shall say, *(to one another)* 'It is a *Pesach-offering* to God.'"

The author of the Haggadah analyzed the text of the Torah carefully, and his interpretation teaches us not to get involved in a discussion with someone who is not interested in learning, but is merely provocative. Also, when there are threats to our principles, we should stand together in mutual reinforcement of our beliefs.

וְהִגַּדְתָּ לְבִנְךָ בַּיּוֹם הַהוּא לֵאמֹר בַּעֲבוּר זֶה עָשָׂה ה׳ לִי בְּצֵאתִי מִמִּצְרָיִם

And you shall tell your son on that day, saying, "It is because of this that God acted on my behalf when I left Egypt" (13:8)

Visualizing the Exodus

The Haggadah says that the mitzvah of narrating the story of the Exodus is on the night of the fifteenth day of Nissan, when the matzah and *maror* (bitter herbs) are before our eyes on the *seder* table. This is derived from the above verse. The phrase, "It is because of *this*" indicates that one is referring to some object, i.e., the matzah and *maror*.

The Alter (Elder) of Kelm says that the patriarchs had an intellectual knowledge of God, which was sufficient for them. However, for the average person, an intellectual knowledge is inadequate to bind him to the will of God. Our conviction of the reality of something we see with our own eyes is greater than something whose reality is known to us only because we can reason to its existence. God, therefore, showed the Israelites the awesome miracles of the Exodus, to impress upon them a firm conviction of His sovereignty over the world.

As the generations became more distant from the Exodus, the sense impression of the miracles faded, and we are now left with only an intellectual knowledge of the Exodus. To reinforce our conviction of the events of the Exodus, we use tangible objects, such as matzah and *maror*, to stimulate a sense impression.

R' Shlomo Wolbe, in *Alei Shur*, says that we must use the powers of our imagination to strengthen our convictions. The Torah says, "Beware for yourself, lest you forget the things that your eyes have beheld and lest you remove them from your heart all the days of your life ... the day that you stood before God at Horeb ... You stood at the foot of the mountain, and the mountain was burning with fire up to the heart of heaven ... God spoke to you from the midst of the fire" (*Deuteronomy* 4:9-12). This was said to the people who personally witnessed the revelation at Sinai, but it applies to us as well. With our imagination we must see ourselves as our ancestors were at Sinai, seeing the mountain aflame, hearing the thunder, witnessing the lightning and hearing the sound of the shofar.

The Haggadah says that in every generation, a person is obligated to *see* himself as though he was personally delivered from Egypt. We must visualize in our minds the plagues inflicted upon Pharaoh, the scene of three million people leaving Egypt and the dividing of the Reed Sea.

The accoutrements of the *seder* are indeed helpful, but we should use the powers of our imagination to experience the Exodus.

פרשת בשלח
Parashas Beshalach

וַיְהִי בְּשַׁלַּח פַּרְעֹה אֶת־הָעָם וְלֹא־נָחָם אֱלֹקִים דֶּרֶךְ אֶרֶץ פְּלִשְׁתִּים כִּי קָרוֹב הוּא כִּי אָמַר אֱלֹקִים פֶּן־יִנָּחֵם הָעָם בִּרְאֹתָם מִלְחָמָה וְשָׁבוּ מִצְרָיְמָה

It happened when Pharaoh sent out the people that God did not lead them by way of the land of the Philistines, because it was near, for God said, "Perhaps the people will reconsider when they see a war, and they will return to Egypt" (13:17)

Tolerance of the Diaspora

It is rather difficult to fathom the mentality of the Israelites who were freed from Egyptian bondage. The Torah tells us that they were subjected to back-breaking labor, and that their newborn sons were thrown into the Nile. The Midrash adds that Pharaoh had their children slain so that he could bathe in their blood. If a Jew did not supply his quota of bricks, his child would be cemented into the wall. Yet on several occasions, when conditions in the desert were arduous, they expressed a longing for Egypt and a willingness to return. But it would seem that anything, even death, would be preferable to the inhuman cruelty they suffered in Egypt!

The Divine promise was, "I shall take you out from under the burdens of Egypt" (*Exodus* 6:6). R' Yitzchok Meir of Gur says that the Hebrew word for "burdens" (*sivlos*) also means "tolerance." The Israelites had become tolerant of their enslavement in spite of its inhuman conditions. They had adjusted and accommodated to what appears to us to be intolerable.

Every narrative in the Torah is a teaching for all generations.

> *R' Nochum of Czernoble lodged at an inn, and as was his custom he arose at midnight to recite the lamentations over the fall of Jerusalem and the loss of the Temple. The innkeeper, hearing his wailing, arose to see what the trouble was, and could not understand why R' Nochum was sitting on the ground, crying. R' Nochum explained how we continually mourn the loss of our land and our exile into the Diaspora. He explained that we cry to God to hasten the ultimate Redemption, when Mashiach will take us out of exile and lead us back to Jerusalem.*
>
> *The innkeeper asked, "Will we all go to Jerusalem?"*
>
> *"Of course," R' Nochum said.*

> *"But what will be with my little farm, my cows and chickens?" the innkeeper asked.*
>
> *"What account are they compared to our being in exile?" R' Nochum said. "We are repeatedly attacked by the Tartars. They carry out pogroms, killing and pillaging our people. In Jerusalem we will be free of such persecutions."*
>
> *The innkeeper was not satisfied. "I must ask my wife about this," he said.*
>
> *When the innkeeper told his wife what R' Nochum said about the Redemption by Mashiach, she said, "How can we leave our farm and the cows and chickens that we worked so hard to get?" The innkeeper then explained how we would be free of the destructive pogroms by the bands of Tartars. The wife thought a bit, then said, "Go tell the rabbi that when Mashiach comes, he should take the Tartars to Jerusalem, and we can live here in peace."*

We may laugh at this, but let us be honest with ourselves. We have our comfortable, furnished homes, and we enjoy our lifestyle in exile. When we hear the sound of the shofar of Mashiach, summoning us all to follow him to the Holy Land, will we all be willing to leave everything behind and follow him to Jerusalem?

Perhaps like the innkeeper's wife and like our ancestors of the Exodus, we may have adjusted to life in exile. It is amazing to what we can accommodate. Like Moses, Mashiach will lead us to a life of spiritual heights. We must be truthful with ourselves. What are our aspirations? Are we ready to trade in our physical comforts to be in the presence of the Glory of God that will again reside in Jerusalem?

וַיְהִי בְּשַׁלַּח פַּרְעֹה אֶת־הָעָם וְלֹא־נָחָם אֱלֹקִים דֶּרֶךְ אֶרֶץ פְּלִשְׁתִּים כִּי קָרוֹב הוּא כִּי אָמַר אֱלֹקִים פֶּן־יִנָּחֵם הָעָם בִּרְאֹתָם מִלְחָמָה וְשָׁבוּ מִצְרָיְמָה

It happened when Pharaoh sent out the people that God did not lead them by way of the land of the Philistines, because it was near, for God said, "Perhaps the people will reconsider when they see a war, and they will return to Egypt" (13:17)

Our Capricious Memory

In the previous essay we expressed our dismay at how the Israelites, who had suffered so bitterly during their enslavement in Egypt, could possibly have wanted to return there. The author of *Shaar Bas Rabim* provides us with an important psychological insight.

Please allow me a bit of levity to share an appropriate anecdote.

> *A candidate for reelection was making the rounds of his constituency to reinforce his support. He addressed one of his constituents, saying, "Clem, I'm sure I can count on your vote."*
>
> *"Nope," Clem said, "I think I'm gonna vote for the other guy."*
>
> *"Why would you do that?" the candidate asked. "Did you forget how much I did for you? Don't you remember when your farm was up for sheriff's sale, I was able to get you a government loan to keep the farm?"*
>
> *"Yep," Clem said. "I remember."*

> "And when your son was drafted into the army and you said you needed him on the farm, I got a hardship exemption for him. Remember that?"
>
> "Yep," Clem said.
>
> "Have you forgotten how I was able to get your mother into a nursing home without cost to you? Don't you remember that?"
>
> "Yep," Clem said. "I remember."
>
> "Then why are you going to vote for my opponent?" the candidate asked.
>
> Clem answered, "Well, what have you done for me lately?"

Some people's memories do not go beyond yesterday. The years of favors Clem received had no impact on what he was going to do now.

That is how it was with the Israelites who left Egypt. Although they had suffered inhumane cruelty for decades, the last day was one on which the Egyptians lent them gold, silver and garments (*Exodus* 12:36). When Pharaoh sent them off, he said to Moses, "Please bless me" (ibid. v. 32). The last day was a pleasant one, on which they were enriched and honored. This single pleasant day obscured the decades of suffering, and because of this recent benevolent attitude of the Egyptians, the Israelites would have readily returned there.

Shaar Bas Rabim is pointing out to us that the Torah is teaching us the frailty of human thought and reaction. We must beware not to be deluded, to allow a brief recent event to cloud our minds and gives us a false perception of reality. Before being convinced of any appreciable change in any relationship, we should have firm and enduring indications that there has indeed been a change.

וַיִּקַּח מֹשֶׁה אֶת־עַצְמוֹת יוֹסֵף עִמּוֹ
Moses took the bones of Joseph with him (13:19)

Personal Contact with a Tzaddik

The Talmud says that when the Israelites left Egypt, Moses sought to take the bones of Joseph with him for burial in the Promised Land, as Joseph had adjured them to do (*Genesis* 50:25). However, he did not know where Joseph was buried. Serah, the daughter of Asher, was the sole survivor of Joseph's generation, and she told Moses where Joseph had been interred (*Sotah* 13a).

What was Moses' problem? Why didn't Moses speak to God directly, as he had at other times? "God would speak to Moses face to face, as a man would speak with his fellow" (*Exodus* 33:11). Why did he not simply ask God where Joseph was buried? On several occasions, when Moses was uncertain of something, he said, "Stand and I will hear what God will command you" (*Numbers* 9:8). And again, "Moses brought their claim before God" (ibid. 27:5).

Perhaps the Talmud wishes to teach us something. There simply is no substitute for being in the presence of a *tzaddik* and observing his behavior. That is a foolproof way of developing the awe of the majesty of God and devotion to Him. The most learned person's knowledge cannot equal what one can learn from a *tzaddik*. When R' Baruch Ber would give a lecture of *mussar* to his students, he would tearfully say, "What can I teach you? If only you had been able to see the master (R' Chaim of Brisk), you would have had a more intense *mussar* experience than anything I can teach you."

For all of Moses' unparalleled greatness, he had never seen the patriarch Jacob nor the *tzaddik* Joseph. Serah was an old woman who was far less learned than Moses, but she had been in the presence of Jacob and Joseph. Moses felt that even the teachings received directly from God could not equal what Serah had observed in Jacob and Joseph.

If we were wise, we would question the elderly among us who were fortunate to be in the presence of the great *tzaddikim* of the previous generation. There is so much we could learn from them.

וְאַתָּה הָרֵם אֶת־מַטְּךָ וּנְטֵה אֶת־יָדְךָ עַל־הַיָּם וּבְקָעֵהוּ

"Lift up your staff and stretch out your arm over the sea and split it" (14:16)

Unexpected Salvation

The Talmud says that a person's livelihood is as difficult to come by as was the splitting of the sea (*Pesachim* 118a). R' Yechiel Meir of Gostanin asked, Where is the similarity between one's livelihood and the splitting of the sea?

He answered, "When the Israelites found themselves trapped between the sea and the oncoming Egyptian army, 'they cried out to God' (*Exodus* 14:10). They prayed for Divine salvation, but they did not know in what manner it would take place. Perhaps God will smite the Egyptian army as He did with the 10 plagues in Egypt. It did not occur to anyone that God would save them by splitting the sea. Their salvation came about in an unexpected way.

"This is equally true of a person's *parnassah* (livelihood). We are indeed required to do something to earn a living. 'God will bless you in your handiwork that you may undertake' (*Deuteronomy* 14:29). However, that does not mean that one's livelihood will occur by the particular way a person chose to earn it. It may come from a totally unexpected source, just as the Israelites' salvation came about in an unexpected way."

The Talmud says that neither poverty nor wealth depends on the type of work one does. A person should choose work that is clean and uncomplicated, and pray to God for success.

> R' Levi Yitzchok of Berditchev once stopped a person who was hurrying through the marketplace. "Where are you going?" he asked.
>
> The man replied, "I'm sorry, Rabbi, but I can't stop to talk with you. I am going after my parnassah."
>
> R' Levi Yitzchok asked, "How do you know that your parnassah lies ahead of you, and that you are running toward it? Maybe it lies behind you, and you are running away from it."

If we recognize that our livelihood comes from God's blessing, we would do the minimum work necessary and pray to God for success. We would have far more time to devote to Torah study, prayer and performing mitzvos. And if we eliminated the frenzy consequent to driving ourselves to earn more, we would also minimize a host of health problems. It has been said that people squander their health in order to acquire money, then squander their money in effort to restore their health.

Trust in God and living a spiritual life is beneficial for the body as well as the soul.

אָז יָשִׁיר־מֹשֶׁה וּבְנֵי יִשְׂרָאֵל אֶת־הַשִּׁירָה הַזֹּאת לַה׳
וַיֹּאמְרוּ לֵאמֹר אָשִׁירָה לַה׳ כִּי־גָאֹה גָּאָה

Then Moses and the Children of Israel chose to sing this song to God, and they said the following: "I shall sing to God for He is exalted" (15:1)

Exalting the Name of God

While the Song of Triumph does tell about the Israelite's miraculous salvation, the opening verse is, "I shall sing to God for He is exalted." Even more than their own salvation, the Israelites rejoiced in the *kiddush Hashem*, that God's Name was glorified. *Kiddush Hashem* should be the prime motivator in the life of a Jew.

It is of interest that in the *kaddish*, the traditional prayer for the deceased, there is no reference to death or to any type of memorial service. Rather, the *kaddish* is, "May His great Name grow exalted and sanctified." True, there are rituals of mourning and there is the Yizkor service. But when a life has been ended, the survivors should make a commitment that their lives should contribute to the exaltation of God's Name.

In the *Shema*, we say, "You shall love your God with all your heart" (*Deuteronomy* 6:5). The Talmud interprets this verse to mean, "You shall make God beloved." If a Torah-observant person is courteous and scrupulously honest, people will say, "How wonderful the Torah is, that it teaches people to behave so beautifully," thereby bringing glory to God, a *kiddush Hashem*. If he behaves otherwise, people will say, "See, Torah observance does not produce fine character," and this a *chillul Hashem*, profaning the Name of God.

The first *berachah* recited to a couple after they have been joined in wedlock is, "Blessed is God, Who has created everything for His glory." The relevance of this in the marriage ceremony is that if the newlyweds exhibit the *middos* (laudable character traits) that bring glory to God, the *middos* will make their marriage blissful, free of the altercations that may occur between husband and wife.

We are often in doubt whether or not to do something. An excellent guideline to do what is right is to ask, "Will this act contribute in any way to the greater glory of God?" If it does not, then even if it does not profane the Divine Name, serious consideration should be given whether or not to do it.

Moses taught the Israelites that even before they express their gratitude toward God for their salvation, they should be most thankful that it exalted God's Name.

There is great reward for one who recites the Song of Triumph every morning with *kavannah* (concentration). Understood properly, it can set the tone for the entire day.

שָׂם שָׂם לוֹ חֹק וּמִשְׁפָּט
There He established for [the nation] a decree and an ordinance (15:25)

The Uniqueness of Shabbos

Rashi states that in Marrah God gave the Israelites the mitzvah of Shabbos. Why was the mitzvah of Shabbos given in Marrah, prior to Sinai? Why was it not given along with all the other mitzvos?

The author of *Siduro shel Shabbos* explains that this indicates the uniqueness of Shabbos. The Midrash states that God said to Moses, "I have a special gift in My treasure house. Its name is Shabbos. Tell the Children of Israel that I wish to give it to them" (*Shabbos* 10b).

Prior to the giving of the Torah, God said to Moses, "Go tell the Children of Israel, 'You have seen what I did to Egypt, and carried you on the wings of eagles and brought you to Me ... and now you shall be a nation of priests and a holy people.'" The Israelites responded, "Everything that God has spoken, we shall do" (*Exodus* 19:8). It was by virtue of this expression of unconditional acceptance of the sovereignty of God that the Israelites merited receiving the Torah. They thus "earned" the Torah.

God wanted the Israelites to know that Shabbos was different. It was an outright gift. In distinction from the rest of the Torah, they did not have to "earn" Shabbos.

Siduro shel Shabbos explains that there are two levels of affection of a father to his child. One is a love simply because it is his child. The father has love for a newborn infant even though the infant has not done anything to arouse the father's love. As the child grows and does things that bring pleasure to the father, a second type of love develops in response to the child's achievements. If the child does not behave properly, this second type of love does not develop, but the biological love of the father for the child is unaffected. We can see this in the case of King David's son, Absalom, who rebelled against his father and pursued him to kill him. Yet, when Absalom was killed, David grieved bitterly. "My son, Absalom! My son, my son, Absalom!" (*II Samuel* 19:1).

Similarly, God's love for Israel is increased when Jews fulfill His mitzvos. But even when they do not do His will, the Divine love of a father for his child is not diminished. Shabbos, which is God's gift to Israel, is given to them whether or not they are deserving of it. It is not contingent upon their merits.

God may respond to Israel just as a father responds to a child who elicits his love. However, before creation, there was no one in existence to elicit the Divine love. The act of creation was, therefore, an outpouring of Divine benevolence that was not in response to anyone's merits. This is why we refer to Shabbos in the *kiddush* as "in commemoration of the works of creation." Shabbos and creation are similar in that both were initiated by God, rather than being a response to our merits.

The giving of the mitzvah of Shabbos at Marrah is, therefore, a testimony of God's unconditional love for His children. When we observe the Shabbos, we should be appreciative of this special relationship we have with God.

וַיִּלּוֹנוּ [וַיִּלּוֹנוּ] כָּל־עֲדַת בְּנֵי־יִשְׂרָאֵל עַל־מֹשֶׁה
וְעַל־אַהֲרֹן בַּמִּדְבָּר . . . כִּי־הוֹצֵאתֶם אֹתָנוּ אֶל־הַמִּדְבָּר הַזֶּה
לְהָמִית אֶת־כָּל־הַקָּהָל הַזֶּה בָּרָעָב וַיֹּאמֶר ה׳ אֶל־מֹשֶׁה הִנְנִי
מַמְטִיר לָכֶם לֶחֶם מִן־הַשָּׁמָיִם וְיָצָא הָעָם וְלָקְטוּ דְּבַר־יוֹם בְּיוֹמוֹ

The entire assembly of the Children of Israel complained against Moses and Aaron in the Wilderness... "You have taken us out to this Wilderness to kill this entire congregation by famine." God said to Moses, "Behold! — I shall rain down for you food from heaven; let the people go out and pick each day's portion on its day" (16:2-4)

The Foundation of Social Justice

The Torah tells us about the miracle of the manna. Each person picked precisely one measure for each member of the household. If one picked more than that, the excess rotted. If one picked less, the measure filled by itself.

The provision of the manna began on the fifteenth day of Iyar (*Exodus* 16:2), one month after leaving Egypt. Rashi says that until this day they ate the food they had taken with them from Egypt. R' Mendel of Rimanov points out that it was only by a miracle that the food they took from Egypt could last for thirty days. Why, then, did this miracle not continue for a longer time?

R' Mendel says that the manna was a necessary precursor for accepting the Torah. The Torah forbids stealing and coveting others' possessions. It forbids lying, cheating, taking usury and all methods of unlawful enrichment. These laws are in opposition to the innate acquisitive drives within people. How can people abide by laws that defy innate drives?

The manna served as a lesson that a person would get only that which he actually needed. If he had less, God would increase his portion to meet his needs. If he took more than his needs, his greed would result in the excess portion rotting. Once the Israelites developed the trust that God would provide for their needs and that accumulating excess was futile, they could accept laws that opposed their acquisitive drives.

> *A man once complained to R' Mendel that a competitive store had opened not too far from his business. R' Mendel said, "Have you ever observed a horse drinking from a brook? The horse taps with its hoof while drinking. This is because when it sees its reflection in the water, it thinks that there is another horse there who will drink all the water. It taps with its hoof to drive the other horse away.*
>
> *"Do not be like the horse. God can provide enough parnassah (livelihood) for both of you."*

Without a firm belief that God will provide one's needs, the innate acquisitive drives may lead a person to acquire wealth by improper means. The lesson of the manna, that each person gets what he needs, was a necessary precondition for the laws of the Torah.

In front of the Ark in the Temple in Jerusalem, there was a container of manna. This served as a reminder that if we have faith in God and live spiritual lives, God will provide us with what we need. But note, He will provide us with what we *need*, but not necessarily with all that we *want*.

Of course, if we led truly spiritual lives, we would not want more than our needs. The extent of our desires is an indication of how spiritual we are.

וְנַחְנוּ מָה כִּי תַלּוֹנוּ [תַלִּינוּ] עָלֵינוּ
"For what are we that you should incite complaints against us?" (16:7)

True Humility

The Talmud says that Moses' expression of humility exceeded that of the patriarch Abraham. Abraham said, "I am but dust and ashes," whereas Moses said, "What are we?" (*Chullin* 9a).

Some commentaries say that the superiority of Moses' humility was that he said, "we are *what*." "What" is a non-tangible, whereas dust and ashes, albeit very low, are nevertheless substances.

> R' Meir Shapiro of Lublin gave another explanation. He related the following story.
>
> On the High Holidays, it was R' Yonasan Eibeschitz's practice to stand near someone who was praying sincerely with a broken heart, in order to be inspired to greater kavannah (concentration). At the minchah of Yom Kippur, he found an elderly man, a rather simple person, who was saturating his machzor with his tearful praying. He heard the man recite the prayer at the end of the Amidah (silent prayer), which reads, "I am dust in my life and will surely be so in my death." The man commented tearfully, "Yes, in my life I am dust, and how much more so when I die."
>
> R' Yonasan was overjoyed to have found someone so humble and sincere, and he stood near him on Yom Kippur, listening to the man's heartrending prayers. At the Torah reading, this man was called for the fourth aliyah (called to the reading of a Torah portion). He became irate and shouted at the gabbai (shul officer), "You give me the fourth aliyah, and you gave this other person the third! Why? Is he a more honorable person than I am?"
>
> R' Yonasan was shocked. He said to the man, "Didn't you just say yesterday that you were dust even in your life?"
>
> "Of course," the man said. "I was talking to God, and before Him, I am nothing but dust. But compared to this other man, why, I am more honorable than him."
>
> R' Meir Shapiro commented, "The patriarch Abraham was indeed very humble, but the expression 'I am but dust and ashes' was spoken before God. The Torah says that Moses was the most humble person on earth (Numbers 12:3), which means that he considered himself less than all other people. When he said 'what are we,' he was speaking to a group of discontents, and he considered himself even less than them. That is the paragon of humility."

The greatness of the humility of Moses is that he was so profoundly humble even though he knew that he was the only person who spoke to God directly. He knew he had liberated the Israelites from Egypt and received the Torah. Moses was not unaware of his enormous stature, yet he felt humble even in comparison to the ingrates.

We must not deny our abilities, strength and knowledge. However, this should not make us vain. Self-awareness and humility are perfectly compatible, as Moses has taught us by example.

פרשת יתרו
Parashas Yisro

וַיִּשְׁמַע יִתְרוֹ כֹהֵן מִדְיָן חֹתֵן מֹשֶׁה אֵת
כָּל־אֲשֶׁר עָשָׂה אֱלֹקִים לְמֹשֶׁה וּלְיִשְׂרָאֵל עַמּוֹ

Jethro, the minister of Midian, the father-in-law of Moses, heard everything that God did to Moses and to Israel, His people (18:1)

Durability Requires Personal Effort

Rashi comments that Jethro was moved to join the Israelite nation because he had heard of the miraculous dividing of the waters of the Reed Sea and because he heard of the battle with Amalek. In the Talmud, these two reasons are given separately by two sages, yet Rashi combines these two diverse opinions. Why did Rashi feel that it was the combination of these two that moved Jethro?

R' Samson Raphael Hirsch says that as great as the miracles of the Exodus were, there is a principle that one should not rely on miracles (*Pesachim* 64b). A person must put forth the necessary effort to extricate himself from trouble.

Jewish history contains many miracles, from the manifest supernatural miracles of the exodus to the miracles concealed under a cloak of natural events, such as Purim. Without Divine intervention, the Jewish nation could not possibly have survived.

Human effort without Divine intervention could not have preserved us throughout history. On the other hand, we are instructed not to rely on miracles. The secret of Jewish survival is that we have struggled for our existence, and God has enabled us to succeed.

The miracle of the Reed Sea alone would not have caused Jethro to become part of the Jewish nation, because miracles are unreliable. However, unaided human effort is not enough to preserve us. The miracle of the Reed Sea happened without human effort, as Moses said, "God shall do battle for you, and you shall remain silent" (*Exodus* 14:14). Therefore, when Jethro also heard that the Israelites did battle with Amalek, putting forth their own effort, he concluded that this combination of human effort with Divine intervention would give the Jewish nation endurance.

This should serve as a guide for us. We cannot sit in the passenger seat and expect God to do the driving. On the other hand, Moses warned us not to think that "my strength and the might of my hand have made me all this wealth" (*Deuteronomy* 8:17). We must do whatever we can on our behalf, but we should realize that our success is the outcome of God's blessing.

וַיִּשְׁמַע יִתְרוֹ כֹהֵן מִדְיָן חֹתֵן מֹשֶׁה אֵת כָּל־אֲשֶׁר עָשָׂה אֱלֹקִים לְמֹשֶׁה וּלְיִשְׂרָאֵל עַמּוֹ

Jethro, the minister of Midian, the father-in-law of Moses, heard everything that God did to Moses and to Israel, His people (18:1)

Hearing and Listening

The Talmud says that every day a voice issues from Sinai and proclaims, "Woe to them, to the people, because of their insult to Torah" (*Ethics of the Fathers*, 6:2). The Baal Shem Tov asked, of what purpose is this voice if no one hears it? We can better understand the Baal Shem Tov's answer today because of the discovery of "subliminal stimuli." The Baal Shem Tov says that when a person has even a momentary thought that perhaps he should become more spiritual, it is because at that time his *neshamah* heard the proclamation from Sinai. Even though his ears did not pick up audible sound waves, he nevertheless absorbed it at some level.

In the *haftarah* for this week's portion we read a verse: "Surely you hear, but you fail to understand" (*Isaiah* 6:2). Isaiah proceeds to explain, "The heart of this people is fattened, its ears are heavy, and its eyes are sealed; lest it see with its eyes and hear with its ears and its heart understand, so that it will repent and be healed." This is the crucial phrase: "*so that it will repent and be healed.*" An understanding would lead to a change of lifestyle. Humans are creatures of habit. Change is uncomfortable, so it is resisted.

Isaiah stated an important psychological principle: We see what we want to see and hear what we want to hear. We effectively block out things which we do not want to know.

But the blockage is not complete. We may not be *aware* of things we do not want to know, but the knowledge does reach into our subconscious mind, and periodically it breaks through to our awareness. If we would be wise, we would listen to the subliminal voice and make salutary changes in our behavior.

The Torah tells us the greatness of Jethro. Others heard what Jethro heard. "Peoples heard—they were agitated" (*Exodus* 15:14). They heard but they did not listen. Amalek, too, heard, but it did not deter them from attacking the Israelites. Jethro heard and listened, and the Torah praises him.

We should avoid the closure of our senses and thoughts that Isaiah describes. True, we may have to change, but the dignity of the human being is that he can improve himself. We should live up to our dignity.

עַתָּה יָדַעְתִּי כִּי־גָדוֹל ה' מִכָּל־הָאֱלֹהִים

"Now I know that Hashem is greater than all the gods" (18:11)

The Voice of Experience

Rashi comments that Jethro knew all the other religions, and there was not one type of idolatry that he had failed to worship. He came to the realization that all the gods he had worshipped were false, and the God of the Israelites was the only God. Perhaps it was this statement that earned Jethro the great honor of having an entire portion of the Torah bear his name.

There is a fad among some Jewish young people to seek out Oriental faiths. This is tragic, because the overwhelming majority have never adequately studied the Jewish faith. But they should also be deterred from this for another reason: Many who sought other faiths have, like Jethro, eventually come to Judaism.

Solomon says, "It is better to hear the reproof of a wise man than to listen to the song of fools" (*Proverbs* 7:5). A more accurate translation of this verse was provided by R' Simchah Bunim of P'shis'che: "It is better to hear the reproof of a wise man *from* a person who has listened to the song of fools." A person who is reprimanded by a scholar may say, "What does he know? He spends all his time in books. If he was aware of what goes on in the real world, he would sing a different tune." However, if the same reproof comes from a person who has been out in the real world and has experienced many of its delights, yet teaches that these have little or no true value, his words may be better received.

Many of those who were enamored by the mysticism of Oriental faiths have come back and declared that they did not find the nirvana they had expected. Having seen this futility, they now turn to Judaism.

Why make an unnecessary trip? In *Path of the Just*, R' Moshe Chaim Luzatto says that people in a maze may tread many paths in an attempt to reach the exit. A person placed in an elevated position, who can see the entire maze and which path is the one that leads to the exit, shouts, "Don't go that way. It gets you nowhere! Follow the path that I am pointing out." How foolish it would be to disregard his advice!

We do not have infinite time, and we cannot afford costly mistakes. We would be wise to listen to those who have tried other ways and found the way of Torah to be best.

וְאַתָּה תֶחֱזֶה מִכָּל־הָעָם אַנְשֵׁי־חַיִל יִרְאֵי אֱלֹקִים . . . וְשַׂמְתָּ עֲלֵהֶם שָׂרֵי

"You shall discern from among the entire people men of accomplishment, God-fearing people . . . and you shall appoint them as leaders" (18:21)

To Learn from Everyone

Following Jethro's advice, Moses set up a judicial system with various categories of judges to whom he delegated authority. The obvious question is, Was Jethro so much wiser than Moses, that he saw a need which Moses had not recognized? Furthermore, inasmuch as God approved of this, why did God not instruct Moses on this? Why did it have to wait for Jethro?

The answer to this can be found in *Genesis* (1:26), in the phrase, "God said, 'Let us make Man.'" Rashi explains that the Torah uses the expression "let *us*" because God took counsel with the angels regarding the creation of man. Although God obviously does not require advice from anyone, He did this to teach us that regardless of how wise and learned a person may be, one should always be willing to learn from and to consult with someone of lesser stature.

Moses was certainly capable of designing a judicial system, and God could have instructed Moses to do so. The reason it was arranged so that Jethro should recommend this is to impress upon us again the lesson of "let us make man," that Moses was willing to take advice from Jethro.

Inasmuch as this precedes the account of the giving of the Torah, we may assume that the principle of accepting advice from less learned people is a prerequisite for Torah. Indeed, the Psalmist says, "From all those who have taught me, I have learned understanding" (*Psalms* 119:98), and the Talmud says, "Who is a wise man? One who learns from every person" (*Ethics of the Fathers* 4:1).

Patients may ask their physician to call in a consultant on their case. Some doctors do so gladly, but others seem to take offense, as though this implies that they were not sufficiently competent. These doctors will consult only an outstanding specialist or the head of the department in the university medical school. They feel that consenting to consult anyone of lesser stature is demeaning.

People who are reluctant to ask advice from those who are not manifestly superior must have an ego problem, causing them to be so sensitive that they perceive this as an insult. People with a healthy ego have no problem asking anyone for advice.

In *Angels Don't Leave Footprints* I asserted that an inflated ego is actually the result of underlying feelings of inferiority. I was thrilled to find support for this in *Rabbeinu Yonah al HaTorah*, where he states that *gaavah* (vanity) is a desperate attempt by a person to cope with feelings of worthlessness. A person who feels competent and secure will have no need to develop *gaavah*.

Acquisition of Torah requires humility (*Ethics of the Fathers* 6:6). Therefore, prior to giving the Torah, we were taught humility. This was achieved when Moses accepted advice from Jethro, indicating a willingness to learn from everyone.

This lesson is every bit as valid now as it was at Sinai. We should be able to be always teachable, and as the Talmud says, from everyone.

וַיִּחֲנוּ בַּמִּדְבָּר וַיִּחַן־שָׁם יִשְׂרָאֵל נֶגֶד הָהָר

And they encamped in the Wilderness and Israel encamped there, opposite the mountain [Sinai] (19:2)

Torah and Unity

As we have seen, the narration that precedes the giving of the Torah is more than just historical. It indicates the prerequisites of Torah.

Rashi points out that the Hebrew word for encamped is *vayichan*, **he** camped, rather than *vayachanu*, **they** camped. Furthermore, the Ten Commandments were also spoken in the singular, **Anochi Hashem Elokecha,** your God in the singular, rather then the plural **elokeichem.** The singular form of the verb is utilized because there was such complete unity among the Israelites that they were like one person, hence the entire nation could be addressed in the singular.

The Torah was given to each individual, and every person is required to fulfill the 613 mitzvos. It is obvious that technically this is impossible. There are some mitzvos whose performance is restricted to *Kohanim* (priests), which *Yisrael* cannot perform. A person whose firstborn child is a girl cannot fulfill the mitzvah of *pidyon haben* (redemption of the firstborn son). Mitzvos that apply to judges do not apply to lay people. How can any single person fulfill all 613 mitzvos?

Torah scholars have provided the answer. When a person puts on the *tefillin* (phylacteries) on his arm and head, it is not just the arm and head that have the mitzvah, but the whole person. Similarly, when people are united, they are as one, and a mitzvah performed by one person is shared by those with whom one is united.

How tragic that we have allowed ourselves to be divisive. Fragmentation not only weakens our nation, but deprives a person of acquiring the merit of those mitzvos which he is unable to perform.

Every human trait may have positive applications, even something as repulsive as selfishness. We should realize that eliminating the divisiveness that reigns among us is not merely altruistic. It is of inestimable personal benefit.

לֹא־תַעֲשֶׂה לְךָ פֶסֶל

"You shall not make yourself a carved image [idol]" (20:4)

The Essence of Idolatry

The practice of idolatry is mind-boggling. How can an intelligent person think that an image that he fashioned with his own hands is a god? Moses repeatedly cautions against idolatry, and the frequent denouncing of idolatry by the prophets indicates that it was a widespread practice. Could our ancestors possibly have been so foolish as to believe in idols?

The Talmud clarifies this for us. "The Israelites knew that the idols were worthless. They were only looking for a public sanction to gratify their lust" (*Sanhedrin* 63b). In other words, idolatry really has little to do with graven images, but with the concept that underlies them. The word of God in the Torah is restrictive and prohibits many of our physiological urges, and defying authority would result in distressful guilt. The solution? Create a new authority, a new god who will tell you what you want to hear and allow you to do whatever you wish.

Rather than doing what God wishes, the idolater does what *he* wishes. Instead of worshipping God, the idolater worships himself. With or without a graven image, having as one's goal in life the gratification of all one's desires *is* idolatry.

Today's practice of legalizing things that were previously taboo is reminiscent of idolatry. Abortion was once equivalent to murder; now the fact that it is sup-ported by tax money has made it a virtue. Euthanasia was once an abomination; now, under the euphemism of "death with dignity," it is respectable. Just several years ago, the country was outraged by an incident of physician-assisted suicide; now it has been legitimized by several legislatures. Casino gambling is legal, and there is consistant pressure to legalize drugs. The prevailing opinion is that a person should not be denied anything he desires. This is idolatry.

The verses in the Ten Commandments are so appropriate: "I am the Lord your God ... You shall not make *yourself* a carved image." Do not become a self-worshipper. Do not become your own idol.

לֹא תִשָּׂא אֶת־שֵׁם־ה' אֱלֹקֶיךָ לַשָּׁוְא
"You shall not take the Name of HASHEM your God in vain" (20:7)

The Challenge of Honesty

This commandment forbids swearing falsely. The Talmud says that when God spoke this commandment, the entire world trembled (*Shavuos* 39a). What is so outstanding about this particular commandment that makes it so formidable?

The author of *Chezyonos Avraham* says that this commandment was a prerequisite for all the commandments that follow.

Our capacity to rationalize is remarkable. The human mind is ingenious in producing logical reasons for something one wishes to do. Rationalizations, of course, are nothing but *good* reasons to cover up the *true* reason. The danger of rationalization is that we may delude ourselves to actually believe the conjured up reasons.

People have justified stealing and cheating, saying that they use the money for worthy causes. Some people who do not observe Shabbos may say that the laws of Shabbos are obsolete. For example, making a fire was prohibited because it involved work, but pushing a button to turn on a light is not work. The real reasons for these justifications is that they wish to satisfy their desires, so they rationalize in order to eliminate any obstacles. However, if they had to swear to the reason for a particular act, the severity of the transgression, "God will not absolve anyone who takes His Name in vain," might break through their self-deception. If the rationalization was eliminated, they would be discouraged from doing the forbidden act.

This commandment is, therefore, fundamental to observance of the entire Torah. The convulsions of the earth when this commandment was pronounced served to impress upon the Israelites its awesome nature, and made them cognizant of the importance of adhering to the truth.

לֹא תַחְמֹד בֵּית רֵעֶךָ לֹא־תַחְמֹד אֵשֶׁת רֵעֶךָ וְעַבְדּוֹ וַאֲמָתוֹ וְשׁוֹרוֹ וַחֲמֹרוֹ וְכֹל אֲשֶׁר לְרֵעֶךָ
"You shall not covet your fellow's wife, his manservant, his maidservant, his ox, his donkey and all that belongs to your fellow" (20:14)

All or Nothing

R' Yitzchak Silberstein relates that he was approached by a man who said that he lacked for nothing, yet whenever he saw that his neighbor had bought a new car, he felt a sharp pang of envy. He realized that envy is a very despicable trait, but try as he might, he could not rid himself of it.

R' Silberstein realized that this man was incapable of understanding profound Torah and didn't know how to respond. Then it occurred to him to say, "Doesn't your neighbor suffer from a stomach ulcer?"

"Yes, he does," the man said.

"There you have your answer. Things come in packages. If you want *what he has, you must accept everything he has, including having a stomach ulcer."*

"No, no!" the man exclaimed. "I'll never again want what he has."

R' Silberstein says that it occurred to him that perhaps this is what the Torah means when it says, "You shall not covet all that belongs to your fellow." If you want something that another person has, you must be willing to accept everything he has (Aleinu Leshabe'ach vol. 1).

I recall Moshe and Chaim, two friends who hailed from the same village in Europe. Moshe was very industrious. When he came to America he opened a small laundry, which he gradually expanded to several laundries and linen supply companies. Moshe was extremely wealthy, but suffered from severe stomach ulcers. In those days, treatment consisted of a very restricted diet, primarily milk and crackers.

Chaim was the proprietor of a small corner grocery store and was a person of meager means. One time, Moshe asked Chaim how he was faring. "Not good," Chaim said. "I have to get up before dawn to go to the market, then I stand on my feet in the store until late at night. And what do you think I earn from all this? Barely enough to afford dark bread and a radish."

"You are a fool, Chaim," Moshe said. "If I would be allowed to eat dark bread and radish, I would gladly give you all my laundries."

It has been said that if all a person's circumstances were put into a bundle, and the bundles placed in a room where anyone was free to pick whichever bundle he wished, everyone would pick his own.

R' Silberstein's interpretation and response were correct. "You shall not covet *all that belongs to your fellow.*" When you feel envious of someone, remember that the "all or none" principle applies. If you are not ready to accept someone else's misery, you should not be desirous of having his good fortune.

פרשת משפטים
Parashas Mishpatim

וְאֵלֶּה הַמִּשְׁפָּטִים אֲשֶׁר תָּשִׂים לִפְנֵיהֶם
"These are the ordinances that you shall place before them" (21:1)

Torah Jurisprudence

In this portion of the Torah we find laws relating to property damage, personal injury, bailee responsibility and theft.

The chassidic master of Apt was once challenged by a government official: "Why do your rabbinic courts dispose of a case so hastily? We have lawyers that study both sides of the case and gather evidence. After the court rules, there may be a number of appeals. In this way we know that justice is carried out."

The rabbi responded with a parable:

A wolf once made off with a lamb from the flock, but was accosted by a lion who took the lamb from him. The wolf protested, but the lion said that as the king of all animals he has a right to all prey. However, the lion agreed to take their dispute to the fox, the wisest of all animals. The fox ruled that the wolf indeed had legitimate possession, but that as king of the forest, the lion also had rights. Therefore, the fox ruled, they should share the lamb equally, and he proceeded to divide the lamb.

However, because one piece was larger than the other, the fox nibbled off a bit to make them equal. He nibbled off a bit too much, so that now the other piece was larger. In order to make the halves equal, the fox nibbled off each until almost nothing was left.

"That," the rabbi of Apt said, "is your system of justice. With endless litigation, the lawyers end up receiving most of the money, and both litigants are losers. In a rabbinical court, both sides have their say, the ruling is swift and object of the dispute is not consumed by lawyers."

I cite this because it gives us insight into Torah jurisprudence. The rabbi of Apt lived nearly 200 years ago. His parable is even more appropriate today than it was then.

וּמַכֵּה אָבִיו וְאִמּוֹ מוֹת יוּמָת

*One who strikes his father or his mother
shall surely be put to death* (21:15)

וּמְקַלֵּל אָבִיו וְאִמּוֹ מוֹת יוּמָת

*One who curses his father or his mother
shall surely be put to death* (21:17)

The Sin of Verbal Abuse

Ramban says that cursing one's parents is even more grievous a sin than striking them. Hostile words may be worse than hostile deeds.

King Solomon says, "The words of a contentious person are like self-justification; and they penetrate into the innermost recesses" (*Proverbs* 18:8). R' Samson Raphael Hirsch comments, "A habitually irascible man is as if possessed by a passion for quarreling. His agitation carries him away to irresponsible utterances. His words seem to sound like self-justification, like defense. However, instead of fending off the insult, instead of confining himself to refuting unjustified aggression, he offends his adversary with insults which penetrate into the depths of his being. Instead of protecting himself, he destroys the other" (*Wisdom of Mishlei,* p. 106).

In my book *The Shame Borne in Silence*, I point out the gravity of verbal abuse between spouses. Sometimes a spouse will say that he/she was provoked by the partner, and that the abusive words were in self-defense. R' Hirsch rebuts this argument of self-defense: "Instead of protecting himself, he destroys the other."

The Gaon of Vilna, in his commentary on Mishlei, states that insulting words may be more harmful than physical blows. Insults "penetrate into the innermost recesses." Physical injuries may heal. The wounds inflicted by verbal abuse may never heal.

Injuring another person, whether physically or emotionally, is a Biblical prohibition. There is no exception if the other person is one's spouse. To the contrary, halachah requires that husband and wife be most respectful to each other. Lack of respectful communication, especially in the family, is a form of abuse. Because "familiarity breeds contempt," we should be especially cautious to be respectful to those with whom we are familiar.

וְכִי־יִפְתַּח אִישׁ בּוֹר אוֹ כִּי־יִכְרֶה אִישׁ בֹּר וְלֹא יְכַסֶּנּוּ
וְנָפַל־שָׁמָּה שּׁוֹר אוֹ חֲמוֹר: בַּעַל הַבּוֹר יְשַׁלֵּם כֶּסֶף

*If a man shall uncover a pit, or if a man shall dig a pit
and not cover it, and an ox or a donkey fall into it,
the owner of the pit shall make restitution* (21:33-34)

Sensitivity and Consideration

The Talmud says that any object left in the thoroughfare that can cause one to stumble and fall is the equivalent of an uncovered pit.

There is a moral derivative to this verse. One should be cautious to never do anything that might cause harm to another person. The extent to which our *tzaddikim* observed this can be seen from the following incident.

SHEMOS / EXODUS: Mishpatim [151]

The Chafetz Chaim was walking with his students and noticed a piece of paper in the street. Thinking that it might be a fragment of a sefer (Torah writing) that must be treated respectfully, the Chafetz Chaim picked it up. When he saw that it was not of a sacred nature, he left it on the street. A few moments later, he retraced his steps and picked up the paper. He explained to his students, "Just as I thought that this might be a fragment of a sefer, that may occur to another passerby, who will bend down to pick it up. Once I had the paper in my hand, if I threw it down, I would be responsible or causing another person to make an unnecessary exertion.

"The Torah says that if a person removes the cover from a pit, it is he and not the person who dug the pit that is liable for any damages. Similarly, once I picked up the paper, it would be me rather than the person who threw it down initially who would be responsible for causing someone to bend down to pick it up."

How cautious we must be to not cause even the slightest harm to anyone, even inadvertently.

וְנִקְרַב בַּעַל־הַבַּיִת אֶל־הָאֱלֹקִים אִם־לֹא שָׁלַח יָדוֹ בִּמְלֶאכֶת רֵעֵהוּ
The householder shall approach the court that he had not laid his hand upon his fellow's property (22:7)

Closeness to God

The Hebrew word for "court" in this verse is *elokim*, whose most frequent usage is to mean "God." R' Meir of Premishlan said that the verse can be read as, "A householder can approach God if he has not laid his hand upon his fellow's property." The "householder" is a lay person, who may not be an accomplished Torah scholar. However, he can come into a close relationship with God if he has been honest and has not taken anything to which he had no right.

One opinion in the Talmud is that the first question a person will be asked on his Judgment Day is, "Did you transact honestly?" (*Shabbos* 31a). This question is posed even before one is asked if he set aside time for Torah study. It is clear that honesty in respecting property rights and not taking anything which is not legitimately one's own is of the highest priority.

The Talmud says, "The property of others should be as dear to you as your own. Just as a person takes care that his money not be taken, so he must be protective of the money of others" (*Avos D'Rabi Nosson* 17:2). "'He that is clean of hands and pure of heart ... shall receive a blessing from God' (*Psalms* 24:4-5). This teaches that one who abstains from unlawful possession, his prayer is pure" (*Shemos Rabbah* 22:4).

Our Torah personalities were paragons of honesty, most scrupulous to avoid encroaching on other people's property and rights.

In 1948, when Jerusalem was under siege, there was a scarcity of water and there were long lines of people at the water-dispensing stations. One time, the wife of R' Isser Zalman Meltzer went to bring water, and in a short time returned with a container of water. She called to her husband to help her carry up the water.

R' Isser Zalman said, "Before I can take the water, I must know how you returned so soon. Did you push yourself ahead of people standing in line? Were you given preference because you are my wife? If you did not wait your turn with others in line, then we cannot use the water, because it comes on the account of having stolen other people's time by causing them to wait longer." Only after his wife convinced him that she had waited in line for her turn did R' Isser Zalman agree to use the water.

We must be protective not only of other people's property, but also of their time and effort.

כָּל־אַלְמָנָה וְיָתוֹם לֹא תְעַנּוּן
You shall not cause pain to any widow or orphan (22:21)

Compassion for the Underprivileged

How sensitive we must be to the underprivileged can be seen from the following story.

During one of his travels, the Baal Shem Tov lost his way in a forest, and even after several days, could not find his way out. When Friday came, he was distressed that he would not have a minyan (quorum of ten) for Shabbos services, and no wine or challah for Kiddush. Toward evening he saw a small hut and knocked on the door. He was greeted by a very gruff woodsman. "What do you want here?" the man asked.

The Baal Shem Tov said that he had been lost in the woods for several days and would like to be in a home for Shabbos. "Go away!" the man said. "I have no room for you." Only after repeated pleadings did the man allow him into his hut. "You can stay here," he said, "but I don't want to hear a word from you."

Friday night, when the woodsman and his wife sat at their table, the Baal Shem Tov asked if he could join in the Kiddush. The woodsman shouted at him, "Go back to your bed! I don't want to see or hear you!" The Baal Shem Tov bewailed that he could not recite the Kiddush. Shabbos morning the Baal Shem Tov began to pray out loud, and the man silenced him. "Didn't I tell you that I didn't want to hear you?" All day Shabbos the woodsman spoke disparagingly to the Baal Shem Tov.

After Shabbos was over, the woodsman's wife asked the Baal Shem Tov, "Don't you remember me? I used to be your kitchen-help. I was an orphan and had to support myself.

"One time, I did something wrong in the kitchen and your wife scolded me. You saw this and you said nothing. At that time there was a decree from heaven that because you did not come to the aid of an orphan, you would lose your share in the Eternal World.

"My husband is one of the hidden tzaddikim. He prayed that you should not be punished so severely. It was decreed that you could atone for your

SHEMOS / EXODUS: Mishpatim

misdeed by suffering the deprivation of one Shabbos. We engineered it so that you would be brought to us and we would make you suffer over Shabbos. Now you have been forgiven."

The woodsman then shed his disguise, and revealed himself as one of the thirty-six hidden tzaddikim. The two spent the entire night in discussion of the secrets of Torah.

All of the Baal Shem Tov's extraordinary merits could have been nullified by his failure to come to the aid of an orphan. We must take precautions not to cause pain or anguish to anyone. How much more so when the individual is in unfortunate circumstances. How careful we must be not to aggrieve a widow or orphan, or as Rashi says, any underprivileged person.

מִדְּבַר־שֶׁקֶר תִּרְחָק

Distance yourself from a false word (23:7)

Preventing Lying

There are many rabbinic ordinances enacted as precautionary measures to prevent one from transgressing a Scriptural prohibition. However, this is the only instance where the Torah itself adds a precautionary measure. It is not satisfied with saying, "You shall not lie to one another" (*Leviticus* 19:11), but adds, "*Distance* yourself from a false word."

Just what is meant by "Distance yourself?" It means that one should act in a way that there will be no need to lie. Think about what you are about to do. Is there a possibility that you may at some time have to deny that you did it? If so, then do not do it. That is how you can distance yourself from falsehood.

The prophet equates God with truth (*Jeremiah* 10:10). Any breach of truth draws one away from God.

There may be a short term gain from lying, but the only long term profit is in truth.

R' Refael of Bershed was delivering a sermon on the evils of falsehood, when one of the congregants left the room. The man later explained, "Rabbi, you were making me feel unbearably guilty. I am a retail merchant, and I cannot tell the whole truth about my wares. Do you expect me to close my shop and go begging?"

R' Refael said, "You will not sustain a great loss if you tell the truth about an item on which you make only a one kopek profit. Just tell the truth about such items for a week, then come back to me."

After a week the man reported that he had indeed told the truth about one-kopek-profit items. "Good," R' Refael said, "now you will have no difficulty in telling the truth about two-kopek-profit items." In this way, the man eventually told the truth about all his merchandise. His reputation as an honest merchant garnered him a large clientele, and he earned much more than if he had lied about the products.

The Talmud says that a wise person is one who can envision the outcome (*Tamid* 32a). This does not mean that one should be a prophet. Wisdom consists of seeing the long term consequences of one's actions rather than just the immediate effects.

Distancing oneself from falsehood not only prevents one from transgressing the prohibition of lying, but also results in behavior that is both ethical and profitable.

שֵׁשֶׁת יָמִים תַּעֲשֶׂה מַעֲשֶׂיךָ וּבַיּוֹם הַשְּׁבִיעִי
תִּשְׁבֹּת לְמַעַן יָנוּחַ שׁוֹרְךָ וַחֲמֹרֶךָ

*Six days shall you accomplish your activities,
and on the seventh day you shall desist,
in order that your ox and donkey may rest* (23:12)

Shabbos and Character Traits

There are some verses on which Rashi comments, "this verse demands an interpretation"; i.e., it cannot be taken literally. The above verse is one that demands an interpretation.

The Talmud says that if a person observes Shabbos properly, it is as if he observed the entire Torah, whereas if one violates Shabbos, it is as if he violated the entire Torah (*Jerusalem Talmud, Nedarim* 3). The Torah repeats the commandment of observing Shabbos several times, and it is one of the Ten Commandments. Yet, if we take the above verse literally, "*in order that* your ox and donkey may rest," it would seem that the sole purpose of Shabbos is to provide respite for work animals. That can hardly be true. We must, therefore, look for another meaning in this verse, and the Torah commentaries provide it for us.

The *mussar* authorities say that the ox is the symbol of strength and energy, while the mule is a symbol of indolence and obstinacy. This is why, when the Torah wishes to tell us that a combined effort by two people or animals of opposite nature is prohibited, it states, "You shall not plow with an ox and a mule together" (*Deuteronomy* 22:10; *Chinuch, Mitzvah* 550).

We have a variety of character traits, in some of which we take pride, others we may wish to disown. The chassidic and *mussar* writings say that all human traits can be channeled into constructive channels. A person may wish to deny his feelings of aggression or obstinacy. There is no need do deny these. Rather, they should be directed toward constructive goals.

In psychology, there is the concept of *sublimation.* It is theorized that the subconscious mind can redirect an unacceptable drive toward proper goals. Thus, psychologists say, an astronomer who peers through a telescope or a scientist who looks through a microscope has converted a voyeuristic drive into a constructive curiosity. Although sublimation is certainly a beneficial mechanism, it is not accomplished consciously. The person has no awareness of the origin of his scientific curiosity.

Our ethicists say that there is no need to deny or repress any urge or drive. These are part of our physiological makeup. Rather, we should allow ourselves to be aware of them and consciously redirect them. But this requires introspection and self-examination, something which most people have little time to do. We are too occupied with our daily activities to take time out for meditation, contemplation and soul-searching.

SHEMOS / EXODUS: Mishpatim

Shabbos provides the opportunity for introspection. "Six days shall you accomplish your activities, and on the seventh day you shall desist." Desist and refrain from all your usual activities. Freeze your aggressive, assertive, indolent and obstinate traits. Let them not be manipulated by subconscious mechanisms. Allow them to be at rest, where you can examine them and see what you can do with them.

This is indeed a worthy function of Shabbos. It gives a person the opportunity to enhance one's spirituality by becoming the finest human being one can be.

פרשת תרומה
Parashas Terumah

דַּבֵּר אֶל־בְּנֵי יִשְׂרָאֵל וְיִקְחוּ־לִי תְּרוּמָה

"Speak to the Children of Israel and let them take for Me a portion [a donation for the Sanctuary]" (25:2)

To Accept with Grace

Many of the Torah commentaries offer an explanation why the term "let them *take* for Me" is used instead of the more appropriate "let them *give* to Me." With so many explanations available, an additional one might seem superfluous. Inasmuch as each verse in the Torah may have countless messages, there is perhaps yet another message in this verse.

It is generally assumed that there may some hesitancy in giving, because people are by nature acquisitive and wish to hold on to their belongings. Taking, however, is assumed to be relatively easy because everyone likes to receive. This is not universally true. Some people feel that accepting help of any kind is demeaning. They may be so fiercely independent that they will jeopardize their health and even their lives rather than accept help. It is true that the Talmud praises a person who lives an austere life rather than accept *tzedakah*, but it is critical of a person who rejects help when it is really essential. R' Ovadiah MiBartenura says that a person who has no mercy on himself is unlikely to be merciful to others (*Pe'ah* 8:9).

> *One of my patients, a woman who was recovering from alcoholism, confided in a friend that her furnace had broken down in the midst of a frigid spell and that she had slept three nights in an unheated apartment. Her friend said, "You could have stayed at my house for those three nights." She responded, "I don't like to impose on anyone."*
>
> *I called this patient and I told her that I was disappointed because I was hopeful that she could be helpful to newcomers in recovery. She said, "Please, you can call on me at any time." I said, "I'm sorry, but I cannot. Anyone who cannot accept help has no right to give it."*

There is a time for everything. There is a time when we should be independent and self-sufficient, and a time when we should accept help and even ask for it. People who cannot accept appropriate help are invariably people with unwarranted low self-esteem. This feeling may have many undesirable consequences, as I pointed out in *Angels Don't Leave Footprints* and *Let Us Make Man*. Some people may refuse legitimate help because they do not wish to feel beholden to a benefactor.

Perhaps this is why the Torah uses the expression "let them take for me" rather than "let them give to me." We should indeed be willing to give, but we must also be able to take when it is necessary. Inability to take when it is essential is not a commendable character trait.

דַּבֵּר אֶל־בְּנֵי יִשְׂרָאֵל וְיִקְחוּ־לִי תְּרוּמָה
Speak to the Children of Israel and let them take for Me a portion [a donation for the Sanctuary] (25:2)

Retaining Enthusiasm

The Midrash says that when the Israelites at Sinai declared "*naaseh venishmah*, we will do and we will obey" (*Exodus* 24:7), God said, "Speak to the Children of Israel and let them take for Me a donation for the Sanctuary." This Midrash differs with another Midrashic opinion, that the commandment to build a Sanctuary was not given until after the episode of the Golden Calf.

The Baal Shem Tov explains this Midrash according to a frequently observed phenomenon. People may be inspired by an impressive happening or by a brilliant orator to do a good deed, anything of service. We are seized with enthusiasm and are ready to overcome all challenges. But then we go home, and how quickly our fiery enthusiasm may wane. Our feeling the next day may be, "It really is a good cause, but I just don't have the time. I'm so busy. I can't get deeply involved in this. I do believe in this worthy project, but it is not realistic for me to undertake an active role."

The Baal Shem Tov, therefore, taught that when something arouses you to a good cause, *do something immediately to implement your good intentions.* Do not put it off until the next day or until you are called upon, because by that time the finest resolve may have dissipated. Do something *promptly*. Once you have made an actual beginning, it is much easier to continue the effort.

In physics, there is a concept of *inertia*. For example, if you wish to move a very heavy box, you may have to exert much energy at first, but once it has been moved from its place of rest, it is much easier to move it still further. There is also a "law" of spiritual inertia. It may take a great deal of effort to start doing something, but once you have started, it may require much less effort to keep it going. This is why the Baal Shem Tov recommended taking some action promptly to initiate one's good intentions.

This may be the message of the Midrash. The enthusiasm of the declaration *naaseh venishmah* was indeed very wonderful, but God knows human nature, that after a bit of time this enthusiasm might be lost. He, therefore, instructed Moses to *immediately* have the Israelites do a mitzvah, to contribute to the building of the Sanctuary.

R' Yoel Teitelbaum of Satmar used this principle to explain the verse, "The Children of Israel went and did as God commanded Moses and Aaron, so did they do" (*Exodus* 12:28). The words "so did they do" appear redundant. R' Yoel says that the commandment to bring the Passover offering was given to the Israelites on the first day of Nissan, whereas the actual offering was not brought until the fourteenth day of Nisan. During these two weeks, there was ample time for their enthusiasm for the mitzvah to have waned. However, the Torah states that "they went and did *just as God commanded Moses and Aaron, so did they do,*" i.e., with the same fervor and excitement as on the day they received the commandment.

We should keep this psychological principle in mind, so that we may implement our noble intentions.

> *There is an interesting anecdote regarding Shimon Nathaniel Rothschild of Frankfurt, Germany, who was approached in the street by a man who poured out his tale of woe about how he had fallen upon hard times. Rothschild was very moved by this man's distress, and not having any money with him at the moment, he removed his gold watch chain and gave it to him. The man was bewildered and said, "How can I take your watch chain? If you wish to help me, I can come to your home tomorrow and you can give me whatever you wish."*
>
> *"No," Rothschild said. "At this moment I feel your distress and wish very much to help you. By tomorrow, this compassion may well have dissipated."*

Solomon said, "Do not say to your fellow, 'Leave and come back; I will give it tomorrow,' when it is [already] with you" (*Proverbs* 3:28).

We should exploit the enthusiasm of the moment. It may not come again.

כָּל־אִישׁ אֲשֶׁר יִדְּבֶנּוּ לִבּוֹ תִּקְחוּ אֶת־תְּרוּמָתִי
"From every person whose heart motivates him you shall take My portion" (25:2)

Heartfelt Donations

Contributing to a worthy cause is a mitzvah regardless of one's motivation. The desire to receive praise as a donor does not detract from the mitzvah. However, there is one motivation that essentially undoes the mitzvah. Allow me to share with you something I heard from my father.

The Talmud says, "Poverty follows the poor" (*Bava Kamma* 92a). It explains that when the poor brought the offering of their first-ripened fruits (*bikkurim*) to the Temple, their baskets were kept in the Temple, whereas the silver and gold vessels brought by the wealthy were returned to them.

> *R' David of Tolna said, "I once sent word to my chassidim that I was coming to their town for a visit. The news was received with general jubilation. One chassid, a man of very meager means, returned from shul very happy. 'The Rebbe is coming to town!' he said. Abruptly his mood changed. 'Why are you sad?' his wife asked. 'You were just so delighted that the Rebbe is coming.' The man said, 'I am happy, but it is customary to give the Rebbe money for tzedakah, and I have nothing to give him.'*
>
> *"'Don't let that worry you' his wife said. 'I'll do some baking and sell my cakes, and you will have a ruble to give the Rebbe.' The man's joyous mood returned.*
>
> *"The same morning, a wealthy man returned from shul in a downcast*

SHEMOS / EXODUS: Terumah

mood. 'What's wrong?' his wife asked. 'Did anything happen?' 'Not really,' the man said, 'but the Rebbe is coming to town, and he is going to put the touch on me for tzedakah. I can see 50 rubles going down the drain.'"

R' David said, "I must accept the wealthy man's donation because I have no right to deprive the recipients of tzedakah, but the single ruble that was given with joy is much dearer to me than the 50 rubles that were given with resentment."

"I surmise," R' David said, "that something similar occurred with bikkurim. A man who owned a small patch of land with a few trees was jubilant. 'Some of the fruits are ripening,' he exclaimed. 'I can take them to the Temple in Jerusalem.' But then his mood changed. 'I don't have a decent vessel to carry the fruits,' he said. 'Don't you worry,' his wife said. 'Our daughter and I will weave a beautiful basket for you.' The mother and daughter then worked with sincere devotion to weave a basket for the bikkurim. Every square inch of the basket was made with love of the mitzvah.

"A wealthy man who owned many orchards was told by one of his laborers that some of the fruits were ripening. 'So, what about it?' he said. 'Well, isn't it time for you to take the first-ripened fruits to Jerusalem?' the laborer said. 'Oh, for heaven's sake!' the wealthy man said. 'Another trip to Jerusalem! I don't have the time to be running to Jerusalem repeatedly. I have business to attend to here.' After a bit he said, 'I guess I have no choice but to go. But last year there were some show-offs who flaunted their wealth by bringing the fruit in silver vessels. I'll bring mine in a gold vessel, and let them turn green with envy!'"

R' David said, "The baskets that were woven with love were dear to God and were kept in the Temple. The gold and silver vessels that were intended to provoke envy in others were returned to their owners. God has no use for such gifts."

In instructing Moses to gather donations for building the Sanctuary, God said, "From every person whose heart motivates him you shall take My portion." Only heartfelt donations were welcome, not donations that were given in order to provoke envy in others.

The ideal *tzedakah* is that which is given whole-heartedly to obey the mitzvah. *Tzedakah* that is given for acclaim is also worthy and acceptable. But *tzedakah* given with a desire to hurt others is tainted and is not welcomed by God.

וְעָשׂוּ לִי מִקְדָּשׁ וְשָׁכַנְתִּי בְּתוֹכָם
*'They shall make a Sanctuary for Me —
so that I may dwell among them"* (25:8)

Shelah HaKadosh says that this verse can also be translated as, "They shall make a Sanctuary for Me, and I will dwell *within* them;" i.e., within each individual. Every person should make himself into a Sanctuary wherein the Divine Presence can rest.

> *On one of his travels, the townsfolk complained to the Baal Shem Tov that on Yom Kippur, the chazzan had chanted the Al Chet (confession of sins) with a merry melody instead of a more appropriate somber refrain. When the Baal Shem Tov asked the chazzan why he did this, the latter replied, "If I was hired to clean the king's palace, wouldn't I be happy that I am making the palace more suitable for the king? When I confess my sins, I am sweeping away all the objectionable material within myself to make a place where God would wish to reside. Should I not rejoice over this?" The Baal Shem Tov was very moved by the explanation.*
>
> *When R' Mendel of Kotzk first came to R' Simchah Bunim of P'shis'che, the latter asked him, "Young man, where can one find God?" R' Mendel said, "God is everywhere." R' Simchah Bunim again asked, "Young man, where can one find God?" R' Mendel answered, "His glory fills the entire universe." R' Simchah Bunim again asked, "Young man, where can one find God?" R' Mendel said, "If my answers do not satisfy you, then you tell me." R' Simchah Bunim said, "God can be found wherever one permits Him to enter." The Torah says that we must behave in a manner that does not cause God to turn away from us (Deuteronomy 23:15).*

The Talmud says that God shuns a person who is vain and arrogant. "I cannot dwell together with him" (*Arachin* 15b). "I abide in exaltedness and holiness—but am with the contrite and lowly of spirit" (*Isaiah* 57:15).

A recovered alcoholic said, "When I stopped drinking, I felt a terrible void within me. That was the space where God belonged. How foolish of me to have tried to fill that space with alcohol!" People who do not drink may try to fill that space with money, power, acclaim or any one of a variety of pleasures.

R' Simchah Bunim was right. Every person has a space where God belongs. We must make that space available so that God can enter it.

וְעָשִׂיתָ מְנֹרַת זָהָב טָהוֹר מִקְשָׁה תֵּיעָשֶׂה הַמְּנוֹרָה
יְרֵכָהּ וְקָנָהּ גְּבִיעֶיהָ כַּפְתֹּרֶיהָ וּפְרָחֶיהָ מִמֶּנָּה יִהְיוּ

You shall make a Menorah of pure gold, hammered out shall the Menorah be made, its base, its shaft, its cups, its knobs and its blossoms shall be [hammered] from it *(25:31)*

Man Begins, God Completes

Rashi calls our attention to the wording of this verse, which begins with "*You shall make* a Menorah," but closes with "shall the Menorah *be made*." The intricate designs of the Menorah were not to be made separately and then attached to it. Everything had to be hammered out from a single piece of gold. Inasmuch as this was beyond human ability, God instructed Moses to put the gold ingots into the fire, and the Menorah emerged, fashioned by God.

This is an important lesson. We are obligated to do what is right and proper and demanded of us, but we are not always able to bring things to completion. But this does not give us permission to sit back and do nothing. We must do whatever is within our ability to do and trust in God for a favorable outcome. This is a delicate balance which is often ignored. Some people insist on doing everything themselves, refusing to accept the limitations of reality. They become frustrated when they cannot control everything, even when clear thinking indicates that there are things beyond one's control. On the other hand, some people who realize that they cannot control the outcome may sit back and do nothing. "What's the use?" they say. "I cannot make things turn out the way I want anyway."

The Menorah teaches us the proper balance. We must do what we can. When we have made a sincere effort, it is then that God will help us bring it to completion. "God will bless you in all that you do" (*Deuteronomy* 15:18).

The Baal Shem Tov uses this concept to explain a rather puzzling verse in Psalms. "Yours, O God, is kindness, for you repay each man according to his deeds" (*Psalms* 62:13). If God rewards a person only according to his deeds, that is simply justice. In what way is this a kindness?

The Baal Shem Tov says that a person only initiates the deed, but God brings it to completion, God rewards the person as if he had completed the entire deed himself. That is beyond what the person deserved, and that is a Divine kindness.

"*You shall make*" and "*it shall be made.*" The Menorah was a source of light. This lesson illuminates for us a proper path in life.

וְשַׂמְתָּ אֶת־הַשֻּׁלְחָן מִחוּץ לַפָּרֹכֶת וְאֶת־הַמְּנֹרָה נֹכַח הַשֻּׁלְחָן עַל צֶלַע הַמִּשְׁכָּן תֵּימָנָה וְהַשֻּׁלְחָן תִּתֵּן עַל־צֶלַע צָפוֹן

You shall place the Table outside the Partition, and the Menorah opposite the Table on the south side of the Tabernacle, and the Table you shall place on the north side (26:35)

The Physical and the Spiritual

The Torah commentaries state that the Torah is a guide to proper living, and that everything in the Torah is directed toward refinement of character. We might wonder, in what way is the detailed description of the construction of the Sanctuary a guide? Inasmuch as the Torah is eternal, of what value is our knowledge of the arrangement of the furnishings of the Sanctuary applicable to us today?

The above verse, with two references where the Table should be placed, appears a bit cumbersome. It would have been much more concise to say, "Place the Table outside the partition on the north side." A sentence structure in the Torah that appears awkward is an indication that the verse contains a message.

The Table and the Menorah represent two aspects of life. The Table and the showbread represent the physical aspect of life, the food we need for survival, and the Menorah represents the spiritual aspect.

When life begins, the infant knows only his physical needs and their gratification. The juvenile mind cannot conceptualize or understand spirituality. We thus begin life with our physical and material drives being dominant. When one reaches the age of reason, the spiritual aspect of life sets in, and should achieve primacy. The physical needs should eventually become subordinate to the spiritual. Inasmuch as one cannot achieve spiritual goals unless one is physically healthy, one must provide the body with all its essential needs. However, this should not be as in childhood, when satisfying one's hunger or resting to overcome weariness were dominant.

Too often, however, maturation is limited to the acquisition of knowledge. We may learn how to do things we could not do in childhood, but the goal in life may remain unchanged. There are brilliant people who have earned advanced degrees, even doctorates, yet whose goal in life is primarily pleasure-seeking. Although their intellect has certainly advanced, their philosophy of life has remained essentially juvenile. They began life with the primacy of the Table, and in maturity, the Table, representing physical gratification, is still primary. The only change is from the simple menu of the infant to sophisticated gourmet cooking. No "Menorah" has been introduced to alter their direction in life.

This is why the Torah goes out of its way to describe the placement of the Table and the Menorah. The beginning of life is indeed with the Table, but at some later date, the Menorah must be given primacy. After that, the Table is still very much a part of life, but is now subordinate to the Menorah. Maturity is not limited to intellectual progress, but requires that spirituality becomes the goal of life, and physical needs only the means.

פרשת תצוה
Parashas Tetzaveh

וְאַתָּה תְּצַוֶּה אֶת־בְּנֵי יִשְׂרָאֵל וְיִקְחוּ אֵלֶיךָ שֶׁמֶן זַיִת זָךְ כָּתִית לַמָּאוֹר

You shall command the Children of Israel that they should take for you pure olive oil pressed for Illumination (27:20)

The Danger of Cultism

Many commentaries note that from the birth of Moses onward, there is not one portion of the Torah in which Moses' name is not mentioned, with the exception of this week's portion, *Tetzaveh*. Baal HaTurim says that this is because, when pleading for forgiveness for the sin of the Golden Calf, Moses said to God that if He will not forgive the Israelites, "erase me now from the book that You have written" (*Exodus* 32:32). Although God did forgive them, Moses' words were nevertheless effective, because "the curse of a righteous person is fulfilled even if uttered on a conditional basis" (*Berachos* 56a). Other commentaries have offered other explanations.

The explanation of R' Zalman Sorotzkin is impressive. The readings of the Torah are so arranged that the portion of Tezaveh almost invariable occurs in the week of Adar 7, *the birth date and day of death of Moses*. One might have thought that this day would have special significance in Judaism. In order to de-emphasize the birth date and date of death of Moses, the sages arranged the readings so that the portion of Torah in which his name is *not* mentioned is read that week.

This is a far-reaching observation, and calls for a delicate balance. Moses was the greatest of all prophets, the lawgiver who transmitted God's word to us. Moses was a teacher: *Moshe Rabbeinu*. But he was only the *agent* of God, not the principal.

There is a tendency among people to deify their leaders. The Roman emperors became gods. In my writings on self-esteem (*Let Us Make Man, Angels Don't Leave Footprints, Life's Too Short*) I pointed out a number of mechanisms whereby a person with low-self esteem may try to gain a feeling of worthiness. One of these is a form of hero worship, whereby a person sets someone up as the ultimate in greatness, and by identifying with him and becoming his devotee, one participates in the greatness which one has imparted to his totem. The ultimate in this defense mechanism is to elevate someone to godhood and identify with him. This is essentially the dynamics of cults.

The Talmud says that it was the *eirev rav*, a group of Egyptians who had joined the Israelites in the Exodus, who were responsible for the Golden Calf. This is borne out by the statement that the worshippers of the Golden Calf said, "This is *your* god, O Israel, which brought *you* up from the land of Egypt" (*Exodus* 32:1-4), which indicates that it was a group of outsiders who were addressing the Israelites. Although the *eirev rav* had witnessed the dividing of the waters of the Reed Sea and the revelation at Sinai, they were unable to grasp the concept of an abstract God. They developed a "Moses cult," and when they thought that Moses had died, they said to Aaron, "Make for us gods that will go before us."

Unfortunately, during their enslavement in Egypt and exposure to the Egyptian culture, some of the Israelites had become vulnerable to Egyptian thought, and they did not subdue the *eirev rav*. Under Moses' continued tutelage and admonitions against all forms of idolatry, they developed a firm faith in God rather than in man or a totem. When Bilam sought to cast an evil spell upon Israel, he found himself unable to do so and exclaimed, "It is God Who brought them out of Egypt" (*Numbers* 23:22). With a firm faith in God, Israel is immune to curses.

R' Sorotzkin's insight enables us to understand why the Passover Haggadah, which is a detailed account of the Exodus, omits the central character of the story: Moses. It is because we must remember that, "It is God Who brought them out of Egypt."

Humans have their frailties, and one of these weaknesses is to deify great leaders. We must be cautious not to succumb to this tendency. We must honor our great leaders, revere them and most of all, learn from them, but we do not worship them or pray to them.

וְאַתָּה תְּצַוֶּה אֶת־בְּנֵי יִשְׂרָאֵל וְיִקְחוּ אֵלֶיךָ שֶׁמֶן זַיִת זָךְ כָּתִית לַמָּאוֹר

You shall command the Children of Israel that they should take for you pure, olive oil pressed for illumination (27:20)

Mitzvos Are to Our Advantage

The Talmud interprets the phrase "they should take for you" to mean that "the light is for you. I do not need it" (*Menachos* 86b). Clearly, the Creator of all light, Whose pillar of fire illuminated the way for the Israelites during their forty-year sojourn in the desert, hardly needs the little flames of the Menorah to provide light for Him. The light of the Menorah was for the Israelites, a testimony that the Divine Presence was with them.

"For a mitzvah is a shining lamp, and Torah is a beam of light, and the course of life lies within the admonition of education" (*Proverbs* 6:23). Just as the Menorah was not to provide light for God, neither are the mitzvos of the Torah to benefit Him. "The mitzvos were given for no other reason than to refine Israel" (*Vayikra Rabbah* 13:3).

The light of the Menorah was to burn continually (*Exodus* 27:20). This indicates that we must constantly have the awareness that we are the beneficiaries of the mitzvos.

It does not take much thinking to realize that the Shabbos is a precious gift. Rather than just a day on which work is restricted, proper observance of Shabbos is a delight, akin to the delight of Gan Eden (Paradise). Some of the other mitzvos can also be seen as rather obvious lessons for us, such as the commemoration of the Exodus on Passover, or the forgiveness of sins on Yom Kippur. Other mitzvos, however, may not present an obvious lesson. How do we benefit from taking the four species on Succos or from never wearing a garment of an admixture of linen and wool?

We can hardly expect to grasp the depth of meaning of mitzvos by a superficial reading of the Torah, or even by studying the *Shulchan Aruch* on how the mitzvos should be performed. We have a rich treasury of interpretation of Torah in the works of the Torah commentaries and the writings of *chassidus* and *mussar*. Exten-sive and intensive study of these can help us understand what the mitzvos do for us.

There is one category of mitzvos, *chukim* (ordinances), which are Divine decrees that are beyond the capability of the human mind to understand. The light of the Menorah should remind us that these, like all the other mitzvos, are for our benefit.

וְאַתָּה תְּצַוֶּה אֶת־בְּנֵי יִשְׂרָאֵל וְיִקְחוּ אֵלֶיךָ שֶׁמֶן זַיִת זָךְ כָּתִית לַמָּאוֹר

You shall command the Children of Israel that they should take for you pure, olive oil pressed for illumination (27:20)

Light: a Unifying Force

In the previous Torah portion, the Torah says, "Speak to the Children of Israel and let them take for Me a portion, i.e., a donation for the Sanctuary" (*Exodus* 25:2), and the commentaries point out that *"give to Me"* would have been more appropriate than *"take for Me."* We have a similar situation here. It would have been more appropriate to say "they should *give* to you" rather than "they should *take* for you."

When referring to light, "give" and "take" are interchangeable. If you turn on a light for yourself, the room becomes bright for everyone else as well, and if you turn on a light to illuminate a room for others, you benefit from the light as well. Light is always shared, hence when you "take" light you also "give" it.

Perhaps this is the reason why the Menorah is a symbol of Judaism, and why lighting the Menorah is of such great importance. The Midrash states that when Aaron saw that neither he nor his tribe participated in the inauguration of the Sanctuary, his heart fell. God then said to him, "Your portion is greater than theirs, because you will be kindling the Menorah" (*Tanchuma, Numbers* 5). Light is not restricted by boundaries, hence it brings people together. The Talmud says that the light of the Menorah was a testimony that the Divine Spirit rested with Israel. This is because there is nothing so dear to God as unity among Jews, and when Jews are together, His imminent Presence is with them.

The Talmud places great emphasis on kindling the Shabbos candles, stating that they are a source for *shalom bayis*, peace and harmony within the family. A husband and wife should know that there can be no confined personal interest in marriage. If something is good, it is good for both, and if something is bad, it is bad for both. Nothing in a marriage should be advantageous for one partner and disadvantageous for the other.

"For a mitzvah is a lamp and the Torah is light; and reproving discipline is a way of life" (*Proverbs* 6:23). Properly observed, the ethical teachings of Torah are a light which is shared, bringing together husband and wife, man and fellow man. The mitzvos are the lamp, the vehicle whereby one illuminates one's world.

"To kindle a lamp continually" (*Exodus* 27:20): The principle of the light of the Menorah should be with us constantly.

יַעֲרֹךְ אֹתוֹ אַהֲרֹן וּבָנָיו מֵעֶרֶב עַד־בֹּקֶר

Aaron and his sons should arrange it [the light of the Menorah] from evening until morning (27:21)

Teaching All Students

The Talmud states the quantity of oil placed into the Menorah was enough to last through the longest winter nights. Although the summer nights were much shorter, the quantity of oil was not decreased. Long nights and short nights were alloted the identical amount of oil.

Why was this necessary? Obviously, the quantity of oil needed for a five hour night is only half that needed for a 10-hour night. This is what R' Moshe Feinstein said in *Kol Ram*: In Torah literature, olive oil represents Torah wisdom, and Torah wisdom should be taught equally to all, without discrimination.

This message is desperately needed today. Unfortunately, some educators are interested only in bright students, and neglect those students who may not be able to grasp Talmudic discussions quickly or profoundly. This has resulted in the weaker students developing an antipathy toward Torah study. Some of the youngsters who have come to my attention for treatment of drug abuse listed one of their reasons for leaving yeshivah and joining the youngsters in the street as, "I was bored in yeshivah. The teacher never explained things so that I could understand them. He paid attention only to those students who could stimulate him."

One of my instructors once said to me, "I prepared the Talmud lecture only for you and your *chaver* (study partner)." He thought he was paying me a compliment. Somehow he didn't realize that he was addressing only two out of twenty students in the class, and that the rest of the class was left behind in boredom.

I cannot refrain from expressing my criticism of those educators who neglect the weaker students. If one of their own children was not the brightest, would they not seek to bring out the best in him, to maximize his potential? The obligation of a Torah educator toward a student should be no less than to one's own child. "Whoever teaches another person's child Torah is expected to relate to him as if he gave birth to him" (*Sanhedrin* 19b). I suspect that these educators select the brightest students for their institution because they wish to boast of producing Torah geniuses. This is an ego drive rather than a true dedication to Torah teaching.

The *Kohen* who kindled the Menorah provided the same quantity of oil for the short nights as for the long nights. Just as he did not discriminate, neither should a Torah instructor discriminate.

וְהֵם יִקְחוּ אֶת־הַזָּהָב וְאֶת־הַתְּכֵלֶת וְאֶת־הָאַרְגָּמָן
וְאֶת־תּוֹלַעַת הַשָּׁנִי וְאֶת־הַשֵּׁשׁ

***They shall take the gold, turquoise, purple
and scarlet wool and the linen*** (28:5)

Preparation for a Mitzvah

The Alter (Elder) of Kelm asks, inasmuch as the materials for the vestments are listed in the specific instructions for fashioning each of them, e.g., "They shall make the Ephod of gold, turquoise, purple and scarlet wool and twisted linen" (*Exodus* 28:6), what is the purpose of prefacing the instructions with the general statement, "They shall take the gold, turquoise, purple and scarlet wool and the linen" (ibid. v. 5)? He answers that before the craftsmen began fashioning the vestments, they took the materials with the *kavannah* (intent) that they were going to use them for the mitzvah. The preparation for doing a mitzvah requires proper *kavannah*.

> *An example of the importance of proper preparation for a mitzvah is in an anecdote of the tzaddik of Sanz. He was on his way to shul when he abruptly stopped and turned back home, then promptly set out again for shul. To his curious followers he explained, "I realized that when I left the house for shul, I had not had the kavannah that I was going to shul. I had to go back and leave for shul with the proper kavannah."*

We do many mitzvos, but too often they are done out of rote. We say the blessing after meals, but generally with little or no preparation. In many *sidduurim* there are prefatory verses to some mitzvos, such as "Behold, I am prepared and ready to perform the commandment of counting the Omer as is written in the Torah," but even though we may recite prefatory prayers, we may still be derelict in having adequate *kavannah*.

The Talmud says that the pious people of yore would spend a full hour in meditation before praying (*Berachos* 30b). Although we may not be able to spend a great deal of time in preparing ourselves for the performance of mitzvos, we are certainly able to devote a few moments to thinking about the mitzvah, that we are doing it to fulfill the Divine wish and to thereby draw ourselves closer to God. The preparatory *kavannah* greatly enriches the performance of a mitzvah and its impact upon us.

פִּי־רֹאשׁוֹ בְּתוֹכוֹ שָׂפָה יִהְיֶה לְפִיו סָבִיב מַעֲשֵׂה אֹרֵג

***Its head opening [of the Robe] shall be folded over within it,
and its mouth [opening] shall have a border all around*** (28:32)

Silence Is Golden

The Midrash says that each of the vestments of the *Kohen Gadol* (High Priest) symbolized a particular transgression of the people for which he sought forgiveness. The Robe (*Me'il*) represented the transgression of improper speech. This is indicated by the phrase in the above verse, "its mouth shall have a seam."

The sins of *lashon hara* (defamatory speech), carrying tales or insulting a person are extremely grave. But there are other types of speech that require our attention, especially to withhold from making even justified comments out of consideration for others.

> At one time, my grandfather, the Rebbe of Bobov, moved to Tchebin, where the great Torah scholar, R' Dov Weidenfeld, was the local rabbi. The two were once at a wedding celebration, and a discussion arose about whether providing the drinks for the wedding feast is the obligation of the groom's or bride's family. My grandfather commented that the opinion of Tosafos (a Talmudic commentary) is that it is the groom's family's responsibility. The rabbi of Tchebin, whose Talmudic erudition was encyclopedic, remarked, "There is no such opinion of Tosafos," to which my grandfather did not respond. Months later, the rabbi of Tchebin was lecturing on a portion of the Talmud when he exclaimed, "The Rebbe of Bobov was right! Tosafos does indeed say that." He then said to his students, "Can you appreciate the greatness of the Rebbe of Bobov? He knew to which Tosafos he was referring, and he could have told me that I was wrong. Yet, he preferred to allow himself to be thought to be in error rather than to risk embarrassing me!"
>
> A similar episode happened when the Talmudic scholar, R' Shmuel Rosovsky, visited the two Talmudic giants, the Chazon Ish and the Steipler Gaon. He presented them with his analysis of a topic in the Talmud. The two listened attentively and complimented him on his insight. Upon returning home, R' Rosovsky was curious about what comments the Steipler Gaon might have made on the subject in his writings on the Talmud. He found that the Steipler Gaon had preceded him in the analysis which he thought to be his novel interpretation. The Steipler Gaon could have commented, "Your interpretation can be found in my writings." Yet, he not only withheld such comment, but also complimented him on his brilliant analysis.

How difficult it is to keep silent when you can say, "Your comment is anything but new. I pointed that out a long time ago." It takes great character strength to restrain oneself in consideration of another's feelings.

A Miracle Within Nature

In years that are not Jewish Leap Years, Purim generally falls during the weeks when these portions of the Torah are read. It is, therefore, appropriate to include a Purim message here.

Commenting on the verse, "And these days of Purim should never cease among the Jews" (*Esther* 9:28), the Midrash states that even when all the other festivals are discontinued, Purim will always remain. The commentaries give various interpretations on what this Midrash may mean but it is evident from this Midrash that Purim has extraordinary significance, and surpasses in importance even the Scriptural festivals of Passover, Shavuos and Succos. What is it that gives Purim such great significance?

R' Levi Yitzchok of Berditchev explains that supernatural miracles, great as they may be, are of only a temporary duration. The salvation of the Israelites by the dividing of the waters of the Reed Sea was indeed an exceptional occurrence, but it was witnessed only by that generation, and for us it is a historical incident. We do not expect miracles of that type to occur.

The salvation of Purim, however, did not consist of any supernatural miracle. Every event could be seen as a perfectly natural happening. A king becomes intoxicated and in his drunken rage has the queen executed. He chooses a Jewess as his new queen, and she conceals her origin. Her uncle, who is in the royal court, discovers a palace intrigue to assassinate the king, and the queen reports this to the king, thereby saving his life. The anti-Semitic prime minister extracts a decree from the king to exterminate the Jews in his kingdom. The king is reminded that it was a Jew who saved his life. The queen turns the king's wrath against the prime minister, who is executed. The queen reveals her Jewish origin, her uncle is appointed as prime minister and the Jews are saved.

It is only when the entire sequence of events is put together that one sees the guiding Hand of God saving His people. In all likelihood, during the Purim episode, someone in shul related, "Did you hear what happened yesterday? The king was drunk and flew into a rage and had the queen executed!" A listener probably said, "I couldn't care less about what the king does. Politics is not my thing." At no point did anyone realize that a miracle was in the making.

Miracles such as these are with us today. No laws of nature are suspended, but the guiding Hand of God causes "natural" events to occur in such a way that results in our salvation.

The realization that everything in the world is orchestrated by God is a fundamental principle of Judaism. This teaching of Purim should be with us 354 days of every year. As we say in the *Amidah*, "for Your miracles are with us every day." This belief enables us to entrust our lives to the care of God, and should stimulate us to live our lives according to His commandments.

וְיָדְעוּ כִּי אֲנִי ה׳ אֱלֹקֵיהֶם אֲשֶׁר הוֹצֵאתִי אֹתָם
מֵאֶרֶץ מִצְרַיִם לְשָׁכְנִי בְתוֹכָם אֲנִי ה׳ אֱלֹקֵיהֶם

*"They shall know that I am HASHEM, their God,
Who took them out of the land of Egypt to rest My
Presence among them, I am HASHEM, their God"* (29:46)

When Familiarity Does Not Breed Contempt

R' Henoch of Aleksander said that he was once a follower of a particular rabbi, but the closer and more intimately he came to know him, the more he realized that he was less of a great tzaddik than he had thought him to be, and consequently his respect for him diminished. "When I came to Kotzk," R' Henoch said, "the closer I came to the Rebbe and the more I got to know him, the more my respect and admiration for him grew, until I was in utter awe of his greatness.

"It was then," R' Henoch said, "that I understood the verse, 'They shall know that I am their God, Who took them out of the land of Egypt to rest My Presence among them, I am their God.' People who worship false gods become disillusioned with them as they come closer to them. Not so with *the true God. The closer one comes to Him, the more one stands in awe of His infinite greatness. That is what the verse says: 'When I make My Presence among them, then they shall know that I am their God.'"*

Judaism thrives on knowledge of God. Historically, one of the very first things established in a new Jewish community was a *cheder* where young children could learn the Bible in the original. Other religions kept the Bible as the sole possession of the religious elite. This was possible when books were copied laboriously by hand and were scarce. It is a matter of recorded history that when the printing press was invented, the Church forbade the printing of the Bible. Indeed, when the Bible became accessible to all, the opposition to the Church escalated, leading to the Reformation.

Torah education is the foundation and lifeblood of Judaism. Giving children anything less than a thorough Torah education is alienating them from God.

The popular aphorism, "Familiarity breeds contempt" is true only under circumstances where a more intimate relationship reveals defects. In Judaism, greater familiarity with God breeds love and reverence for Him.

פרשת כי תשא
Parashas Ki Sisa

> הֶעָשִׁיר לֹא־יַרְבֶּה וְהַדַּל לֹא יַמְעִיט מִמַּחֲצִית הַשָּׁקֶל
>
> *The wealthy shall not increase and the destitute shall not decrease from half a shekel* (30:15)

Emunah (Faith) — the Foundation of Judaism

Rashi explains that the half-shekel donations were used for the silver bases of the boards that formed the walls of the Sanctuary. All the other parts of the Sanctuary, its appurtenances and the vestments of the *Kohanim* (priests), were made from donations which were "from every person whose heart motivates him" (*Exodus* 25:2), with the wealthy contributing more and those of lesser means contributing less. R' Yosef Zvi of Salant asks, why were the silver bases singled out, that they were not made of free-will donations, but rather of the compulsory half-shekel?

As was noted, the teachings of the Torah apply to every age, and everything in Torah has a message. The Torah commentaries say that all the detailed instructions about the construction of the Sanctuary, if properly understood, are guidelines to proper living.

The Talmud says that Moses taught us 613 mitzvos. King David subsumed then under eleven principles, Isaiah subsumed them under six principles, Michah under three and Habbakuk under the single principle: "A righteous person lives by his *emunah*" (*Makkos* 24). If a person has a sincere and unwavering faith in God, this will lead him to acceptance of the entire Torah. In other words, *emunah* is the foundation of the entire Torah.

People vary in their Torah knowledge. One may be a great scholar while another may have scant knowledge of Torah. However, *there cannot be any quantification of emunah*. The least learned person is required to have as complete an *emunah* as the most erudite scholar. True, the *quality* of *emunah* may vary according to one's depth of understanding, but quantitatively, all are equal. If a person says that he accepts all of Torah except for one item, it is tantamount to rejecting the entire Torah (*Sanhedrin* 91a).

It is for this reason, R' Yosef Zvi says, that the silver for the bases of the Sanctuary was donated equally by all. This is to teach us that in regard to *emunah*, the foundation of Torah, there is no stratification. Both the "wealthiest" in knowledge and the most "destitute" have equal obligations in acceptance of the entire Torah.

בֵּינִי וּבֵין בְּנֵי יִשְׂרָאֵל אוֹת הִוא לְעֹלָם
"Between Me and the Children of Israel it [Shabbos] is a sign forever" (31:17)

The "Sign" of Shabbos

The unparalleled importance of Shabbos is evident from the Talmudic statement that if one observes Shabbos properly, it is equivalent to observing the entire Torah, and if one violates Shabbos, it is equivalent to transgressing the entire Torah (*Jerusalem Talmud, Nedarim* 3). What is it that gives Shabbos this unique status?

> *The Chafetz Chaim explained with a parable. A proprietor of a store had to close down because business was poor. However, because his name was displayed on the store front, people assumed that he would reopen one day. Indeed, when economic conditions improved, the store was reopened. When the economy deteriorated again, the store was again closed. This cycle was repeated several times.*
>
> *One time when he closed his store, the proprietor removed the sign bearing his name. People then knew that this time the store was closed for good. Had there been any hope that he would again reopen, he would not have removed the sign.*

This, the Chafetz Chaim said, is the reason for the exclusive importance of Shabbos. By observing Shabbos, one asserts his belief that God created the world in six days and rested on the seventh day. In contradistinction to a world that just "happened" to come into existence as a result of a freak accident, a created world has a purpose. Even if one might deviate from observance of the Torah, the knowledge that there is a Creator leads one to reflect that there is a purpose to existence and that the Creator revealed that purpose. This belief enables one to return to live according to the will and commandments of the Creator. If one rejects Shabbos, the fundamental principle that underlies acceptance of the Divine will is eliminated, and there is little reason to expect that one will observe God's commandments.

Shabbos is a sign. It is equivalent to the sign on the store. As long as the sign is intact, there is hope that one will observe the rest of the Torah. Removal of the sign is an indication that one has abandoned Torah.

We must preserve the Shabbos "sign" forever.

וְשָׁמְרוּ בְנֵי־יִשְׂרָאֵל אֶת־הַשַּׁבָּת לַעֲשׂוֹת אֶת־הַשַּׁבָּת לְדֹרֹתָם בְּרִית עוֹלָם . . . וּבַיּוֹם הַשְּׁבִיעִי שָׁבַת וַיִּנָּפַשׁ
The Children of Israel shall observe the Sabbath, to make the Sabbath an eternal covenant for their generations . . . and on the seventh day He rested and was refreshed (31:16-17)

A Taste of Paradise

"*To make* the Sabbath?" Inasmuch as Shabbos is a period of rest and inaction, the term "to make" seems out of place. This term is repeated when the Torah says, "These are the things that God commanded, *to do* them. On six days, work may be done, but the seventh day shall be holy for you, a day of complete rest" (*Exodus* 35:1-2). "Complete rest" implies "non-doing." Why then the phrase "that God commanded *to do* them?" There can be only one conclusion. "The seventh day shall be holy for you" does require *doing*. While Shabbos is indeed a day of abstinence from work, we must *do* something to *make* it holy.

The Talmud says that Shabbos is "a taste of Paradise." Simply abstaining from work is not Paradise for anyone other than a sluggard. Shabbos is much more than that.

Assume that you have just invested a huge sum of money in components of the finest sound system available. It is supposed to make you feel as though you are in the choicest seats in the concert hall. This is something you've been dreaming of for years! With great excitement and anticipation, you connect all the components, place the speakers where you think they should be, put in a brand new CD of Beethoven's Fifth Symphony conducted by Arturo Toscaninni and you relax in your recliner for the beatific experience.

But what is wrong? The music sounds no different than on your battery operated tape recorder! Is this the system for which you spent thousands of dollars? With disappointment and some anger, you call the store where you bought it. They tell you they will send someone over to check it.

The service person arrives, and after checking the equipment, he says that it was not assembled properly. He disconnects the wires, attaches them where they belong and spaces the speakers appropriately. "Now sit back and listen," he says.

You are suddenly transported to the finest seats in Carnegie Hall. The music surrounds you. The strings, the wind and the percussion instruments are right before you. You can touch the music as well as hear it. It was worth the investment. The system is everything it was promised to be. It just had to be assembled properly.

SHABBOS! A taste of Gan Eden. Indeed, one sixtieth of Gan-Eden, the Talmud says (*Berachos* 57b). Yes, it is indeed pleasant. The Friday night services are more or less o.k., depending on who serves as the *chazzan*. *Kiddush* is nice. The wine was a good choice. The challah, gefilte fish, chicken soup, roast, *tzimmis* and compote—really delicious. Shabbos morning, the Talmud *shiur* was interesting, and the services were decent, although there was a bit too much talking in shul. The kugel, chopped liver, egg salad, cholent and cold cuts—no denying it, they are delicacies. The Shabbos afternoon nap was refreshing, and the friends who came over were enjoyable. No question about it. Shabbos is a very pleasant day.

But a taste of Gan Eden? Is Gan Eden going to be only 60 times as pleasant as the Shabbos we experience? That is something of a disappointment. True, if the delicacies in Gan Eden are 60 times as good as those of the Shabbos table, they must really be something special. Yet, all our lives we are striving to earn the bliss of Gan Eden, and if that's all it is going to be, well . . .

But what is wrong? We have all the proper equipment. All the laws of Shabbos are strictly observed. We rest on Shabbos. There is no work on Shabbos, no driving, no cooking and no working the computer. We pray, and we read the Torah. We do everything right, don't we?

Yes, all the parts of the system are present, but perhaps they have not been connected properly. The Torah says that on the seventh day, *shavas vayinafash* (*Exodus* 31:17). *Shavas* means that God rested. Sforno says that *vayinafash* means "the seventh day has an extra spirit, an additional understanding to grasp what God intended with the completion of His work, as He said, 'Let us make man in our likeness.'" Apparently, on Shabbos we are to reach a level of spirituality that makes us like unto angels and even unto God. Do we come anywhere near that on Shabbos?

Yes, we have the equipment, but perhaps it has not been properly assembled.

R' Chaim of Chernovitz wrote *Sidduro shel Shabbos* (The Order of Shabbos), in which he explains the sanctity of Shabbos. People testified that on Shabbos, R' Chaim was physically taller than during the weekdays.

Are we capable of reaching such heights of spirituality? Well, have we really tried?

We cannot say that something is not realistic until we have tried. Even if we cannot reach the dazzling heights of spirituality as did some of our *tzaddikim,* we can certainly do better, so that our concept of Gan Eden will be something more than 60 times kugel.

The key to the "taste of Paradise" was given to us in the account of creation: "Thus the heaven and the earth were completed" (*Genesis* 2:1). Our ethical works say that just as God's Shabbos was a completion of creation, with everything in perfect place and nothing more to be done, so our observance of Shabbos should be a similar completion of the workweek, *with nothing more to be done.* Everything in our lives is in perfect order. We do not owe any money, and no one owes us money. Friday afternoon we were worried about the merchandise that should have arrived several days earlier. With the onset of Shabbos, the merchandise has arrived. Shortly before Shabbos we looked at the unfinished kitchen and were aggravated at the contractor's tardiness in getting it installed on time. Friday night after *kiddush,* the kitchen looks completely finished, to the minutest detail. We do not have the faintest thought of what we wish to do next week, because there is nothing more to do. All the many worries of the work week have suddenly evaporated, because we live in the perfect world of Shabbos.

But is it realistic that one can look at an unfinished kitchen (which was to have been completed a month ago) and see a beautiful kitchen with handsome cabinets and glistening counters? Yes, it is possible, if one attains a high level of spirituality.

> Our tradition has many examples of the level of spirituality that can be reached on Shabbos. One of my favorite stories is that of the disciples of the Baal Shem Tov who, one Friday night, saw a rather simple person whose face radiated with light. "What is this man's secret?" they asked. The Baal Shem Tov said, "Let's follow him home and see."
>
> The man entered a small hut and greeted his wife with a hearty, "Good Shabbos." Peering through the window, they saw a sparsely furnished room which testified to the austere conditions of the household. A wooden table was covered with a plain white cloth, and the two candles shed a warm glow. The man sang the Sholom Aleichem with a lively refrain welcoming the angels, then sang Aishes Chayil (Woman of Valor). Then he said to his wife, "Please bring the special wine."
>
> The wife brought two loaves of bread. He washed his hands and recited the proper blessing, then chanted the Kiddush. After he ate of the challah, he said, "We have never yet had such a fine wine! Can you please bring in the fish?"
>
> Moments later the wife served him a dish of beans. "Hm!" he said,

smacking his lips. "This fish is unusually delicious." He sang a Shabbos song and said, "I'm ready for the soup." The wife appeared with another dish of beans. The man complimented his wife, "This soup is simply superb." He sang another Shabbos song and said, "Can we have the roast meat and tzimmis?" Again the wife served him a dish of beans. "How wonderful the roast meat and tzimmis are," he said.

The Baal Shem Tov said to his disciples, "Our ancestors in the desert had the manna, a food from heaven, in which they could taste anything they wished. This man's love for God and Shabbos have enabled him to reach a level of spirituality that he can taste the finest delicacies in a dish of beans."

If a person can taste fish, soup, roast meat and *tzimmis* in beans, it is also possible to look at an unfinished kitchen and see it as completed.

The earthly world is where we work to earn the merits of Gan Eden, to be in the immanent presence of God and to delight in the radiance of His glory. Once our earthly stay is over, there is nothing more to be done. That should be the Gan Eden of Shabbos, to delight in the radiance of Torah, in our prayers and in Torah study. There is nothing to distract us from this delight, because there is nothing more we must do.

On Friday night, my mother would serve *farfel tzimmis*. She would refer to this as "the Baal Shem Tov's *tzimmis*," using the symbolism of the word *farfel* for its similarity to the Yiddish word "*farfallen*," which means "over and done with." As she served the *farfel tzimmis*, she would say, "Whatever happened until now is *farfallen*." In other words, we were not to bring any of the past into Shabbos. Everything in the past is over and done with. We live in a stage of completion, with nothing on our minds to distract us from bonding with God through Torah and prayer.

This is what we must *do* to *make* Shabbos holy.

We are meticulous in the *shavas*, the rest from work. Let us see what we may do to realize the *vayinafash*, to approach the Divine intention of, "Let us make man in our likeness."

וַיִּקַּח מִיָּדָם וַיָּצַר אֹתוֹ בַּחֶרֶט וַיַּעֲשֵׂהוּ עֵגֶל מַסֵּכָה
וַיֹּאמְרוּ אֵלֶּה אֱלֹהֶיךָ יִשְׂרָאֵל אֲשֶׁר הֶעֱלוּךָ מֵאֶרֶץ מִצְרָיִם

He took it [the gold] from their hands and bound it up in a cloth, and fashioned it into a molten calf. They said, "This is your God, O Israel, which brought you up from the land of Egypt" (32:4)

How to Not Serve God

It is simply unthinkable that people who witnessed the revelation at Sinai and who declared *naaseh venishmah* (we will do and we will obey, *Exodus* 24:7), eliciting the Divine praise, "Who revealed to My children the secret phrase which the heavenly angels use?" (*Shabbos* 88a), would after a brief interval worship a golden calf as a god. The Midrash says that the episode of the Golden Calf was the work not of the Israelites, but of the *eirev rav* (Egyptians who joined them in the Exodus). This is supported by the statement, "They said, 'This is *your* God, O Israel,'" which indicates that a group of non-Israelites was addressing the Israelites. However, this does not free the Israelites of their complicity. They so outnumbered the *eirev rav* that they could have easily subdued them. How are we to understand their passive participation in the Golden Calf episode?

Most Torah commentaries say that the Israelites never accepted the absurd assertion of the *eirev rav*. They remained faithful to the God whose voice they had heard at Sinai say, "You shall have no other gods before me." What they did do was to agree to adopt the practices of the Egyptian religion in their service of God. They had not yet heard Moses' warning, "Beware for yourself lest you be attracted after them and lest you seek out their gods, saying 'How did these nations worship their gods, and even I will do the same.' You shall not do so to Hashem your God, for everything that is an abomination of Hashem that He hates, have they done to their gods; for even their sons and daughters have they burned in the fire for their gods" (*Deuteronomy* 12:30-31). Why, then, was their sin so grave?

The sin of the Israelites was not that they violated the first of the Ten Commandments. Rather, they transgressed one part of the second commandment which reads, "You shall not recognize the gods of others in My presence. *You shall not make yourself a carved image.* You shall not prostrate yourself to them nor worship them" (*Exodus* 20:3-4). The phrase "You shall not make yourself a carved image" stands independently of "prostrating to them or worshiping them." The Israelites rationalized that this prohibition did not apply if they fashioned an image and used it in the service of worshiping God. Their sin was in "second guessing" the word of God.

There is only one way of worshipping God, and that is by the way the Torah dictates and which was transmitted to us by the Oral Law. Innovations in the worship of God are not permitted, regardless of how benign the intent is.

The gravest sin in Jewish history was the result of relying on one's logic to decide what God desires. His will was made abundantly clear to us by the words of the Torah and by the interpretations which were transmitted by Moses to the prophets and to the sages in an uninterrupted chain of authority.

As we look back upon the folly of the Israelites who committed the sin of the Golden Calf, we should be cautious not to repeat it. Recent social events wherein behaviors that were previously held to be unacceptable have been sanctioned and legalized have proven the wisdom of Moses' words, "for everything that is an abomination that Hashem despises, have they done to their gods; for even their sons and daughters have they burned in the fire for their gods." Unaided human logic can be insidious and deceptive.

וַיְהִי כַּאֲשֶׁר קָרַב אֶל־הַמַּחֲנֶה וַיַּרְא אֶת־הָעֵגֶל וּמְחֹלֹת
וַיִּחַר־אַף מֹשֶׁה וַיַּשְׁלֵךְ מִיָּדָו אֶת־הַלֻּחֹת וַיְשַׁבֵּר אֹתָם תַּחַת הָהָר

It happened as he [Moses] drew near the camp and saw the calf and the dances, that Moses' anger flared up. He threw down the Tablets from his hands and shattered them at the foot of the mountain (32:19)

Never Accept Tales

There is a remarkable Midrash which states that when God said to Moses, "Go, descend — for your people that you brought up from Egypt have become corrupt," Moses held on to the Tablets and did not believe that the Israelites had sinned. He said, "If I do not see it, I do not believe it," for the Torah says, "It happened as he [Moses] drew near the camp and saw the calf and the dances," hence, he did not break the Tablets until he saw it with his own eyes.

The Midrash continues, "Woe unto those people who testify to what they did not see. Is it possible that Moses did not believe it when God said to him, 'your people have become corrupt?' But Moses wished to teach the Israelites proper behavior. Even if one hears something critical from a trustworthy person, one is not permitted to accept his word and take action on it if he does not see it himself" (*Shemos Rabbah* 46:1).

The Midrash seems to say that Moses did in fact believe God, but that he acted *as if* he did not in order to set an example for the people. However, the Midrash earlier is very clear: "Moses held on to the Tablets and *did not believe* that the Israelites had sinned. He said, '*If I do not see it, I do not believe it.*'"

The resolution of this apparent contradiction is that Moses did *not* believe God *because he knew that God did not wish that he believe Him*. Moses knew that God desires only what is proper, and inasmuch as it is proper not to believe anything negative about others unless one sees it oneself, God did not want Moses to believe Him. Moses did not act "as if." His example and teaching were factual.

We find a similar incident when God told Moses to go to Egypt to deliver the Israelites from their enslavement. Moses said, "I must first ask permission from my father-in-law, Jethro" (*Rashi, Exodus* 4:18). How dare he refuse to follow God's command until he received Jethro's permission? R' Chaim Shmulevits explains that Moses understood God's will, that inasmuch as Jethro was hospitable to him when he fled from Pharaoh, God would not want him to depart without seeking his permission.

The Torah forbids speaking *lashon hara* (defamatory speech) and *rechilus* (talebearing). The Chafetz Chaim says that one who accepts *lashon hara* or *rechilus* is as sinful as the one who spreads them. In fact, even when one does see an apparent wrongdoing with one's own eyes, one should still give the person the benefit of doubt and assume that there must be compelling reasons for the person's action (*Ethics of the Fathers* 1:6).

If we observe Hillel's principle, "Do not do anything to others that you would not want done to you," we can avoid both speaking and listening to *lashon hara* and *rechilus*.

וּמְשָׁרְתוֹ יְהוֹשֻׁעַ בִּן־נוּן נַעַר לֹא יָמִישׁ מִתּוֹךְ הָאֹהֶל

His servant, Joshua son of Nun, a lad, would not depart from within the tent (33:11)

The Torah Apprenticeship

Rashi cites the Midrash, that Moses wished that his sons should succeed him as leaders of Israel, but God said that Joshua deserves to be rewarded for never leaving Moses' side (*Numbers* 27:16-22). This "reward" is not in the sense of compensation. Rather, the leadership was given to Joshua because his constant attendance to Moses made him the most qualified.

Torah knowledge is indeed invaluable. However, the Talmud states that serving a Torah scholar surpasses what one may learn from him didactically (*Berachos* 7b). Just as in parenting, when children learn behavior by observing their parents, so, too, do we learn best from the examples set for us by great Torah personalities.

> *I was privileged to be in the company of my uncle, the Rebbe of Bobov, shortly after he came to America. The house he lived in was shared by a number of immigrants who came to America after the Holocaust. There was a rather strange set-up in that house. The telephone in the Rebbe's office had an extension in the living quarters, and on the latter phone there was a "privacy button" which cut off the office phone. Any number of times the Rebbe had said to the other residents, "You are free to use the phone, but please, before you turn the privacy button, listen whether there is a conversation on the office phone. It is very annoying to abruptly be cut off in the midst of a conversation."*
>
> *One day I was in the Rebbe's office, and he was on the phone having an important discussion. He stopped in the middle of a sentence and slowly replaced the receiver on the hook. I knew what had happened. Someone upstairs had cut him off.*
>
> *The Rebbe turned toward the window and began humming a tune, drumming on the desk with his fingers. After several moments he arose and smiled, then took me by the hand and said, "Let's go up and remind them again not to turn on the privacy button when there is a conversation taking place on the phone."*
>
> *We can well imagine what the average person's reaction might be: slamming down the receiver and running upstairs in a rage to chastise the residents for their thoughtlessness. What I learned about anger management from the Rebbe in those few moments was far more impressive than even lectures or book learning of mussar.*

We may not have the opportunity to be in direct contact with the *tzaddikim* of our time, but we are fortunate that we have biographies of some of our great Torah personalities. Many accounts of their behavior have been recorded, and if we are serious in the desire to improve our character traits, we can benefit greatly by reading them.

Some people have said that these biographies are of little help to them because "they describe these people as being angels rather than human beings. We cannot be expected to become angels." I suspect that this may be nothing more than a rationalization to free one of the obligation of character improvement. The Chafetz Chaim was not an angel. He was very much a human being, but a great human being. This human being closed his store in the morning as soon as he had earned enough to provide for him for that day, and the rest of the day was spent in Torah study. There would be ample time tomorrow to take care of tomorrow's needs.

This was not the work of an angel, but of a human being who had developed a profound trust in God, who had a firm conviction that Torah study and mitzvos is the purpose of man's creation, and that consequently anything that did not contribute to that goal was unnecessary and to be avoided. This attitude is not that of an angel, but of a person who has firm convictions and is willing to do what is necessary to implement them.

We hope to teach our children by example. Perhaps they would learn better by example if we demonstrated that we, too, learn by example.

ה' ה' קֵל רַחוּם וְחַנּוּן אֶרֶךְ אַפַּיִם וְרַב־חֶסֶד וֶאֱמֶת:
נֹצֵר חֶסֶד לָאֲלָפִים נֹשֵׂא עָוֹן וָפֶשַׁע וְחַטָּאָה וְנַקֵּה לֹא יְנַקֶּה

Hashem, Hashem, God, Compassionate and Gracious, Slow to Anger, and Abundant in Kindness and Truth; Preserver of Kindness for thousands of generations, Forgiver of Iniquity, Willful Sin and Error (34:6-7)

Magnanimity

These are the Thirteen Divine Attributes of Mercy that God revealed to Moses.

The Talmud states, "Whenever Israel sins, let them perform before Me this order, and I shall forgive them" (*Rosh Hashanah* 17b). Yet, the Talmud sharply criticizes anyone who says that God will overlook people's sins (*Bava Kamma* 50a). The commentaries explain that "forgiveness" is not the same as "overlooking." Forgiveness must be earned, and a person is forgiven only when he deserves to be forgiven.

Our ethical works state that God conducts the world according to firm principles of justice. One of these principles is that it is just to act toward a person as that person acts toward others. The Baal Shem Tov said that this is the meaning of the verse, "God is your shadow" (*Psalms* 121:5). Just as one's shadow mimics one's every move, so does God act correspondingly to how a person acts. If a person is magnanimous and readily forgives personal offenses, then it is just that God forgive that person's misdeeds.

> *The tzaddik of Sanz was lavish in his giving of tzedakah. When he gave tzedakah to a person who was a known scoundrel, some of his followers protested that the scoundrel did not deserve the tzaddik's bounty. The tzaddik said, "If I give tzedakah even to people who are undeserving, then I may hope that God will give to me even though I am undeserving. But if I restrict my tzedakah only to people who are worthy of it, how can I ask God to give anything to me?"*

The Talmud states that Jerusalem was destroyed because people exercised the letter of the law (*Bava Metzia* 30b). If they exercised the letter of the law, why were they punished? It is because they refused to be magnanimous and yield, insisting on getting everything that the law entitled them to receive. In judging their sins, God, too, exercised the letter of the law and refused to yield.

We may think that when we forgive an offense, we are being charitable to the offender. The fact is that we are the beneficiaries of kindnesses we do to others.

Is being kind and forgiving to others self-serving? Perhaps, but this is a kind of selfishness that is "kosher."

פרשת ויקהל-פקודי
Parashas Vayakhel-Pekudei

אֵלֶּה הַדְּבָרִים אֲשֶׁר־צִוָּה ה' לַעֲשֹׂת אֹתָם:
שֵׁשֶׁת יָמִים תֵּעָשֶׂה מְלָאכָה וּבַיּוֹם הַשְּׁבִיעִי יִהְיֶה לָכֶם קֹדֶשׁ

These are the things that God commanded to do them. On six days, work may be done, but the seventh day shall be holy to you (35:1-2)

Mitzvos à la Torah

These two portions of the Torah, *Vayakhel* and *Pekudei*, describe the fashioning and construction of the Sanctuary. Moses prefaces this with an admonition to observe Shabbos. Rashi says that this was to instruct the Israelites that although building the Sanctuary was a great mitzvah, it does not supercede the restriction of work on Shabbos. This was because they might have thought that the prohibition of work on Shabbos might be suspended in favor of the construction of the Sanctuary.

It is understandable that a person's zeal for mitzvos might lead to the idea that some prohibitions may be waived for their performance. The Talmud has a concept of *mitzvah haba'ah b'aveirah*, a mitzvah that comes about via a transgression, and it states that if one does this, one does not have the merit of the mitzvah but does incur the sin of the transgression.

The Talmud says that if a person makes bread from stolen wheat and recites the blessing of *hamotzi*, this angers God (*Bava Kamma* 94a). One may not earn money dishonestly in order to give *tzedakah*, and one may not violate Shabbos in order to attend prayer services. R' Yisroel of Salant noted the hypocrisy of people trying to get to the front row to better hear a discourse on *mussar* from the rabbi, rudely pushing others out of their way to get there.

R' Yisroel knew human psychology. We are very adept at justifying our behavior, especially when we can use a mitzvah as a rationalization.

Moses' admonition against building the Sanctuary on Shabbos is the prototype for avoiding performance of mitzvos via transgressions. Mitzvos are such only when performed the way Torah dictates.

SHEMOS / EXODUS: Vayakhel-Pekudei

וְכָל־חֲכַם־לֵב בָּכֶם יָבֹאוּ וְיַעֲשׂוּ אֵת כָּל־אֲשֶׁר צִוָּה ה'

וְכָל־אִשָּׁה חַכְמַת־לֵב בְּיָדֶיהָ טָווּ

מִלֵּא אֹתָם חָכְמַת־לֵב לַעֲשׂוֹת ... כָּל־מְלָאכָה

וְעָשָׂה בְצַלְאֵל וְאָהֳלִיאָב וְכֹל אִישׁ חֲכַם־לֵב אֲשֶׁר נָתַן יְקֹוָק חָכְמָה וּתְבוּנָה בָּהֵמָּה לָדַעַת לַעֲשֹׂת אֶת־כָּל־מְלֶאכֶת עֲבֹדַת הַקֹּדֶשׁ

וַיַּעֲשׂוּ כָל־חֲכַם־לֵב בְּעֹשֵׂי הַמְּלָאכָה אֶת־הַמִּשְׁכָּן

Every wise-hearted person among you shall come and make everything that God has commanded (35:10)

Every wise-hearted woman spun with her hands (35:25)

[He [God] filled them with a wise heart to do ... every craft (35:35)]

Bezalel shall carry out — with Oholiab and every wise-hearted man within whom God had endowed wisdom and insight to know and to do all the work for the labor of the Sanctuary (36:1)

The wise-hearted among those doing the work made the Tabernacle (36:8)

Emotional Intelligence

The repeated references to the trait of "wise-hearted" cannot be without significance.

On the verse, "Every man whose heart inspired him came" (*Exodus* 35:21), Ramban comments that none of the Israelites had learned the skills necessary for the work of the Sanctuary and the vestments. However, because they were intensely motivated to do the Divine will, *they discovered that they were in fact able to do the skilled craftsmanship*. This might be interpreted as a miraculous endowment of skills they had not had. However, the words of Ramban indicate that it was not an endowment of something new. Rather, it was a discovery that they had these skills within them.

This is an important lesson. Clinically, I repeatedly encounter people who are not aware of their inherent skills and personality assets. In my writings on self-esteem I point out that not only are many people oblivious of their personality assets and potential, but even when these are pointed out to them, they persist in denying them. One can only wonder why intelligent people are not able to accept such factual information.

It is not uncommon in psychotherapy to repeatedly point out something to a patient, but it does not have the slightest impact upon him. After regularly pointing this out for a year and a half, there is a sudden insight. The patient may then say, "Doctor, I've been coming here for a year and a half. Why haven't you ever pointed this out to me before?"

During the year and a half of therapy, when the therapist interpreted the patient's symptoms, the patient said, "I understand everything you've said, but it doesn't make me feel any better." I can conclude only that intellect is subordinate to emotion, and that intellectual knowledge that is not accompanied by emotional knowledge is ineffective. If there are emotional factors that do not allow a person to accept something about himself, whether it is something good or something bad, no amount of intellectual information will register.

According to Ramban, this is what happened with the Israelites. Many people did not have an inkling that they had the requisite skills for the intricate work in crafting the vessels, vestments and curtains of the Sanctuary. But their devotion to God and their desire to do His will resulted in "their hearts being elevated in the ways of God" (*II Chronicles* 17:6). Their spirits soared, and the emotional fervor enabled them to discover the skills within them.

We usually think of wisdom as associated with the mind and brain rather than with the heart. We associate the heart with emotions rather than with wisdom. The Torah repeatedly refers to the "wise-*hearted*" to indicate the overriding influence of emotion over intellect, and that only when one's emotions permit can one implement the powers of the intellect.

We have untouched reserves of both physical and mental abilities. Under conditions of stress, people have been known to perform physical feats that they never thought were within their capacities. There is reason to believe that some geniuses were not of such superior intellect, but rather that their emotional investment allowed them to fully utilize their potential.

This is an important principle in education. If we can stimulate interest and desire for knowledge in children, they are likely to excel in their studies. A good teacher is, therefore, one who can reach the students in a way that they become "wise-hearted."

וַיָּבֹאוּ הָאֲנָשִׁים עַל־הַנָּשִׁים כֹּל נְדִיב לֵב הֵבִיאוּ
חָח וָנֶזֶם וְטַבַּעַת וְכוּמָז כָּל־כְּלִי זָהָב

The men came with the women; everyone whose heart motivated him brought bracelets, nose-rings, rings, body ornaments — all sorts of gold ornaments (35:22)

Passion for Mitzvos

Ramban says that when Moses called for donations for the Sanctuary, the women preceded the men with their gifts. On the other hand, at the tragic episode of the Golden Calf, the Midrash states that the women refused to yield their jewelry for the sinful act, and that the men took it by force. The Midrash says that not a single woman among all the Israelites participated in the worship of the Golden Calf.

Verses 35:26-27 state: "All the women whose hearts inspired them with wisdom spun the goat hair. The tribal princes brought the precious gems for the settings of the Ephod." The approximation of these two verses leads the Midrash to comment that the women spun the goat hair on the goats before it was shorn, which was a rare skill. On the other hand, the Hebrew word *nessiim*, the tribal princes, is written in the Torah minus the vowel *yud*. This is because the princes said, "Let everyone make their donations, and we will then bring whatever is lacking" and the absence of the *yud* indicates that they were derelict in delaying their gifts.

R' Reuven Grozovsky says that the purpose of a mitzvah is not the product of one's action, but the refinement of character and the drawing closer to God that it brings about. This is why the Talmud says that if a person attempted to do a mitzvah, but circumstances beyond his control prevented him from carrying out his intention, God considers it as if he had in fact performed the mitzvah (*Berachos* 6a). Although a tangible goal was not achieved, the function of the mitzvah was fulfilled.

God could have provided everything for the Tabernacle. The purpose of having people donate the necessary materials was to bring about a change in them. The tribal princes failed to grasp this, and as a result of their laxity, they failed to achieve the improvement in oneself which the women did with their zeal for the mitzvah.

The two verses indicate the polar extremes. The women were so overcome by the zeal to participate in the Sanctuary that they did not wait for the goat hair to be shorn, whereas the princes were lax in bringing their gifts.

Here and elsewhere, the Torah praises the virtue of the women, whose devotion to and belief in God surpassed that of the men. The Midrash says that it was by the virtue of the women that the Israelites were delivered from Egypt (*Sotah* 11a). When the Israelites reacted with a loss of trust in God upon hearing the report of the spies who scouted Canaan, it was only the men who were faithless. The women wished to proceed to the conquest of Canaan.

It is incomprehensible that some people contend that the Torah considers men more worthy than women. As we have noted, this is blatantly false. The duties assigned to different people are not an indication of their value. I am not a *Kohen*, and I do not have any of the mitzvos assigned to *Kohanim*, but this does not make me feel less worthy.

As I sit in my study and look at the many volumes written by Torah scholars, it occurs to me that when these scholars were in their formative years, their fathers were either engaged in Torah study or at work. Their love for Torah study could not have come primarily from their fathers, and their lifelong dedication to Torah could have had its roots only in their mothers' devotion to Torah. By the time they were sent to *cheder* at age five or six, the love for Torah had already been implanted by their mothers. The wise Solomon said, "Do not forsake the Torah of your mother" (*Proverbs* 1:8).

When you next pick up a work by one of the great Torah scholars, it would be well to remember that the inspiration for their Torah study came from their mothers.

וַיֹּאמֶר מֹשֶׁה אֶל־בְּנֵי יִשְׂרָאֵל רְאוּ קָרָא ה' בְּשֵׁם בְּצַלְאֵל בֶּן־אוּרִי בֶן־חוּר לְמַטֵּה יְהוּדָה . . . לַעֲשׂוֹת בְּכָל־מְלֶאכֶת מַחֲשָׁבֶת

Moses said to the Children of Israel, "See, God has proclaimed by name, Bezalel son of Uri son of Hur of the tribe of Judah . . . to perform every craft of design" (35:30-33)

Eliminating Anger

What did Moses mean by "See?" What were the Children of Israel supposed to see?

The Daas Zekeinim MiBaalei HaTosafos says that Moses assumed that he would be designated to fashion the Sanctuary, but God said to him, "It is not going to be as you assume. Rather, the grandson of Hur, who was killed by the Israelites for opposing the making of the Golden Calf, he will make the

Sanctuary, which is to serve as a forgiveness for the worship of the Golden Calf."

R' Henoch Lebovitz remarks that logically we might have reasoned that Bezalel was unfit for this assignment, because he might be harboring a resentment toward the Israelites for the killing of his grandfather, and he might not throw himself wholeheartedly into the work to achieve forgiveness for them. The selection of Bezalel tells us that God knew that Bezalel had eliminated every trace of anger and resentment toward the Israelites. It was this enormous self-mastery that made him the ideal person to build the Sanctuary to achieve forgiveness for the Israelites.

In relating Moses' last blessing of the Israelites, the Torah says, "This is the blessing that Moses, the man of God, bestowed upon the Children of Israel before his death" (*Deuteronomy* 33:1). Why does the Torah choose only here to refer to Moses as "the man of God?"

The Ohr HaChaim notes that immediately preceding this, God told Moses to ascend to the mountain of Nebo and that he was to die there, since he could not enter the Promised Land "because you did not sanctify Me among the Children of Israel" (ibid. 32:48-51). The latter event resulted when the Israelites provoked Moses demanding water, and instead of speaking to the rock as God had instructed him, he smote the rock (*Numbers* 20:7-14). Thus, the petulance of the Israelites led to Moses being deprived of his lifelong wish to enter the Promised Land. One might think that Moses harbored a resentment against the Israelites for being the cause of his dying before entering the Holy Land, and even if he did not wish them any harm, he would hardly bless them. The Torah, therefore, testifies that Moses blessed the Israelites wholeheartedly, without the slightest vestige of anger toward them. This warranted his being called "the man of God." Moses had truly adopted the Divine attributes.

The Baal Shem Tov explained the verse, "God is your shadow at your right" (*Psalms* 121:5), as meaning that just as one's shadow mimics one's every move, so does God relate to a person corresponding to one's actions. Moses was not as directly affected by the worship of the Golden Calf as was Bezalel, whose grandfather was killed by the Israelites because of it. Bezalel's ability to wholeheartedly forgive the Israelites earned him the capacity to achieve Divine forgiveness for the sin of the Golden Calf.

The Torah tells us these things as a lesson, that we, too, must endeavor to eliminate anger and resentment toward those who have provoked or harmed us.

Lest one might argue that such extraordinary self-mastery was indeed within the capacity of Biblical characters like Moses and Bezalel, but cannot be expected of us, let me cite two anecdotes of people who were virtually our contemporaries.

> *One of the people whom the Chafetz Chaim had engaged to sell his books gave the sage money from the sales. The calculation revealed that the amount of money should have been significantly larger. The man pleaded that his wife was constantly hounding him for money. "She embitters my life," he said, and he admitted that to appease her he gave her some of the money from the sale of the books. The Chafetz Chaim sympathized with the man, and said that he forgave him the money he had siphoned off for his wife.*
>
> *After the man left, he heard someone calling him. He saw that the*

Chafetz Chaim was running toward him, carrying a package. "Here," the Chafetz Chaim said, "is a beautiful scarf for your wife. Bring this to her as a gift. This will help diminish her irritability toward you."

Another anecdote is that of R' Aaron Roth of Jerusalem, author of Shomer Emunim. A local shoemaker had once publicly insulted him. One Erev Yom Kippur, the sage took a few friends with him and went to the shoemaker's home. "It has been some time since I've seen you," he said, "and I assume you have been avoiding me because you are angry with me. I've come to apologize and to ask forgiveness for whatever I might have done to offend you."

The Israelites were supposed to "see" the selection of Bezalel and derive a lesson in proper *middos*.

Overhauling one's character to eliminate all anger and resentment is possible even for us. We just must be willing to make the requisite effort.

וַיָּבֹאוּ כָּל־הַחֲכָמִים הָעֹשִׂים אֵת כָּל־מְלֶאכֶת הַקֹּדֶשׁ . . . וַיֹּאמְרוּ אֶל־מֹשֶׁה לֵּאמֹר מַרְבִּים הָעָם לְהָבִיא מִדֵּי הָעֲבֹדָה לַמְּלָאכָה . . . וַיְצַו מֹשֶׁה . . . אִישׁ וְאִשָּׁה אַל־יַעֲשׂוּ־עוֹד מְלָאכָה לִתְרוּמַת הַקֹּדֶשׁ וַיִּכָּלֵא הָעָם מֵהָבִיא

All the wise people came — those performing all the sacred work . . . and they said to Moses, "The people are bringing more than enough for the labor of the work" . . . Moses commanded . . . "Man and woman shall not do more work toward the gift for the Sanctuary!" And the people were restrained from bringing (36:4-6)

Responding to Need

R' Mendel of Rimanov remarks that Moses' proclamation appears a bit wordy. It would have been simpler had he said, "We have enough material. Do not bring any more." Why, "Man and woman shall not do more work?"

The Rebbe of Rimanov answered that as long as the work of the Sanctuary was in progress, it stimulated the people to donate. When the work was discontinued, the stimulus to give was removed, and it was only then that Moses could restrain the people from bringing.

This teaches us something about the character of the Jewish people: *They respond to need.* There is some mysterious force, a kind of wireless communication, that tugs at the heart of the Jew, and he responds.

Over the years, I have known of synagogues that have been in financial difficulty. However, I have never known a synagogue to close because of lack of money. A synagogue closes only when it can no longer muster a *minyan*. I am also not aware of a yeshivah that had to close because of lack of funds. As long as there are students and a dedicated staff, somehow the yeshivah survives.

Therefore, said the Rebbe of Rimanov, in order to stop donations, Moses had the craftsmen discontinue the work. The cessation of the work conveyed the message that there was no longer a need, and that is when the donations stopped.

וַיַּעַשׂ בְּצַלְאֵל אֶת־הָאָרֹן עֲצֵי שִׁטִּים
Bezalel made the Ark of acacia wood (37:1)

Sense of Personal Duty

Rashi says that because Bezalel dedicated himself to the work of the Ark more than others, it bears his name: the Ark that Bezlael made.

In *Exodus* 25:10, the Torah says, "They shall make an Ark of acacia wood." The Midrash notes that for all the other appurtenances of the Sanctuary, God said to Moses, "*You* shall make," but in the case of the Ark, He said, "*They* shall make." The Midrash explains this exception; God said to Moses, "Let everyone participate in the fashioning of the Ark, so that all will have the merit of Torah" (*Shemos Rabbah* 34:3). There seems to be a bit of a conflict here. God instructed that everyone should share in the construction of the Ark, yet it appears as though Bezalel did it almost single-handedly.

R' Boruch Sorotzkin says that the message herein is that when Torah is involved, one should not assume that others will do their part, but rather act as if one were the only person who could carry out the responsibility. Although all the Israelites were obligated to share in the Ark, Bezalel approached it as if he were the only one available to fashion it.

There is the well-known story of the shul that asked all its members to donate a cup of wine. Each member reasoned that everyone else would donate wine, so he could get away with putting in a cup of water. When they came to fetch wine from the barrel, it was all pure water! That is what may happen when one relies on others to do the task. Every person may rationalize that others will do it.

R' Sorotzkin's observation is relevant to all mitzvos as well as to Torah. When there is something to be done, do not rely on others, even if they share the responsibility. Act as if you were the only person available and capable of doing the task.

וַתֵּכֶל כָּל־עֲבֹדַת מִשְׁכַּן אֹהֶל מוֹעֵד וַיַּעֲשׂוּ בְּנֵי יִשְׂרָאֵל כְּכֹל אֲשֶׁר צִוָּה ה' אֶת־מֹשֶׁה כֵּן עָשׂוּ
All the work of the Tabernacle, the Tent of Meeting, was completed, and the Children of Israel had done everything that God commanded Moses, so did they do (39:32)

We Have Control Only over Our Actions, Not the Outcome

It would seem that logically, the order of this verse should reversed; i.e, "The Children of Israel did everything that God commanded Moses, so did they do, and all the work of the Tabernacle, the Tent of Meeting, was completed." Why does the Torah tell us that the Tabernacle was completed before it says that the Israelites did as they were commanded?

The answer is that if the order were reversed, it would indicate that *because* the Israelites did the work, that is why the Tabernacle was completed. The fact is that the Tabernacle was actually completed by God, after the Israelites did all they were commanded. The completion of the Tabernacle was indeed the result of their

SHEMOS / EXODUS: Vayakhel-Pekudei

effort, but their effort alone could not have done it. It was because they *tried their utmost* that they merited that God should complete it.

This is a lesson that we should apply in every walk of life. In virtually everything we do, there are many factors beyond our control that can affect outcome. We are responsible only for what we do, not for what ultimately emerges.

This does not hold true in commerce. A person may begin a business with total disregard for every principle of economy, and if he makes a windfall profit, he is considered to be an excellent businessman. On the other hand, if one prepares carefully for a business venture, attending to every detail properly, and the business fails, he is thought of as a poor businessman. People will invest their money with the one who has the best outcome, not with the one who has the best method.

We are so involved in economics, that we may apply commercial principles to our personal lives and ethical issues. Parents who tried to raise their children in the best possible way, but have a child with errant behavior, tend to feel guilty that they were not good parents. I have seen instances where parents who were self-indulgent and totally neglected their children had a child who turned out to be a fine person and a credit to society. The parents who cared and tried are good parents, even though the child turned out to be a disappointment. The parents who were negligent were bad parents, even if their child grew up to be a great person.

We pray every day that God remember for us the merits of the patriarchs, Abraham, Isaac and Jacob. Of Abraham God said, "For I have loved him, because he commands his children and his household after him that they keep the way of God, doing charity and justice" (*Genesis* 18:19). God loved Abraham for doing his best to teach his children to walk in God's ways, but Abraham's son, Ishmael, did not follow his father's teachings. Similarly, Isaac had a son, Esau, who was a scoundrel, but that does not detract from Isaac's great spirituality. Neither Abraham nor Isaac are held responsible for the unfavorable outcome of their children.

The phraseology describing the construction of the Tabernacle makes this point. We must do what we can, but we must realize that the final product is really out of our hands.

ספר ויקרא

VAYIKRA/LEVITICUS

Introduction to Vayikra/Leviticus

"Each person shall revere his father and mother." "Do not put a stumbling block before the blind." "Do not insult the deaf." "Do not hate your brother in your heart." "Love your fellow as you do yourself." "Leave the corners of your field, stalks of grain that have fallen and sheaves that have been forgotten for the poor." "Do not lie or deceive." "Do not lend your money in usury." "Stand up before the elderly and show respect to the wise." These are some of the laws in the Book of Leviticus. We can readily see the great value in these laws, both for their social function and individual character refinement. However, there are many laws in Leviticus that pertain to rituals, some of which are beyond our understanding. Ritual law is strengthened by the other (logical) laws.

The Talmud says that when God spoke the first two commandments, "I am your God and you shall have no other gods before Me," the nations of the world said, "God is interested in His own glory." However, when they heard, "Honor your father and mother," they realized that God was not interested in His own glorification. Inasmuch as the latter commandment is obviously intended for the betterment and refinement of mankind, so must the first commandments be for the betterment and refinement of mankind (*Kiddushin* 31a).

This applies also to the Book of Vayikra/Leviticus. The Lawgiver Who dictated the laws of ethical behavior and social justice also specified that a person who recovered from *tzaraas* (a skin disease mistakenly referred to as leprosy) requried purification with a complex ritual that we cannot undertand. We can only conclude that just as the logical laws are for our betterment, so are those that escape our understanding.

It is traditional that when a child begins to learn Torah at age five, he is taught the first few verses of Vayikra relating to the sacrifical offerings. The reason generally given is that children are holy. "Let the holy children learn about the holy services in the Temple."

A common practice when a child begins Torah study is to treat him with sweets, so that he may associate Torah study with sweetness. Perhaps this is another reason why children begin with Vayikra, so that they should know that even those mitzvos that we do not understand are also sweet.

The word *Vayikra* is written in the Torah with a diminutive *aleph*, and we point out to children that the diminutive *aleph* represents diminutive people; i.e. children. This is a way we encourage them to identify with the Torah. It is *their* Torah, for the little people.

As adults, we should embody the concepts that we teach children. Torah is sweet, all of it. And it is *our* Torah. It belongs to every individual.

פרשת ויקרא
Parashas Vayikra

וַיִּקְרָא אֶל־מֹשֶׁה וַיְדַבֵּר ה' אֵלָיו מֵאֹהֶל מוֹעֵד

"He [God] called to Moses, and God spoke to him from the Ohel Moed [Tent of Meeting]" (1:1)

Proper Decorum

The Midrash calls attention to the fact that although Moses had attained an intimate relationship with God—"God spoke to Moses as a person would to his friend"—Moses nevertheless did not enter the *Ohel Moed* until God called and invited him in. This is to teach us that a person should always behave courteously and respectfully.

Then the Midrash continues with a startling statement. "If a Torah scholar does not have the knowledge to act respectfully, then a dead carcass is better than him" (*Vayikra Rabbah* 1:15). Why does the Midrash use such unusually harsh words, particularly in light of the Talmud's emphasis that a person should avoid coarse language (*Pesachim* 3a)? Could it not have indicated its disapproval with a less offensive term?

The answer is that a Torah scholar, or for that matter anyone who is looked upon as being Torah observant, is essentially a representative of God and Torah, and people look upon his behavior as that which Torah prescribes. If such a person acts in a disrespectful manner, people will attribute his behavior to Torah teachings, and he thereby commits a *chillul Hashem*, besmirching Torah and profaning the Divine Name. This is an unforgivable sin.

A dead carcass emits an offensive odor, which causes people to avoid coming in contact with it and becoming contaminated. A Torah scholar who behaves improperly does not ward off people. To the contrary, because of his erudition he may attract people. If his actions result in people emulating him, he causes them to act improperly and become contaminated. He is, therefore, worse than a dead carcass.

The sin of besmirching Torah through one's behavior is so grave, that here the sages felt that only the most graphic language could express their opprobrium.

Every Torah-observant person should realize that he is an ambassador of Torah and act accordingly.

וַיִּקְרָא אֶל־מֹשֶׁה וַיְדַבֵּר ה׳ אֵלָיו מֵאֹהֶל מוֹעֵד
He [God] called to Moses, and God spoke to him from the Ohel Moed [Tent of Meeting] (1:1)

True vs. Affected Humility

In the Torah scroll, the word for "He called," *vayikra*, is written with a diminutive *aleph*. Without the *aleph*, the word would be *vayikar*, which means "He happened upon him," a rather defamatory term used when God spoke to the villainous Bilaam (*Numbers* 23:4). The Baal HaTurim explains that because of his profound humility, Moses wanted to use the word *vayikar* in regard to how God spoke to him. Inasmuch as God commanded him to write *vayikra*, Moses wrote a diminutive *aleph*.

Some commentaries note that when the Torah was given at Sinai, God called to Moses several times (*Exodus* 19:3, 20), and Moses wrote the word *vayikra* without a diminutive *aleph*. Why the difference?

R' Yitzchok of Vorki explained that sometimes a person may feign humility, when he publicly belittles himself. This is in fact vanity rather than humility, because he is trying to give the impression that he is humble.

When God called to Moses at Sinai, it was in the presence of the entire congregation of Israelites. To have asserted his diminutive status before the eyes of everyone at that time would have been flaunting his humility, which is vanity rather than humility. Moses, therefore, did not make any pretense of humility. When he was called to the *Ohel Moed*, however, no one but Moses heard the call (Rashi). Here the expression of humility was genuine and sincere.

There are people who try to impress others with their humility. This affected humility is the polar opposite of true humility.

Humility is the finest of all character traits, but it must be sincere.

Another significance of the diminutive *aleph* is that in addition to being the name of a letter, *aleph* is a word that means "learning." The message of the diminutive *aleph* is that one can learn only when one is humble. There are some very bright people who do not learn much because they think they already know everything. Vanity is an obstacle to learning.

The mountain of the Sinai range where the Torah was given is the lowest in the range. This was to teach the Israelites that one can acquire Torah only if one is humble.

Repeatedly in Torah literature, Torah is symbolized by water, and it is pointed out that just as water always flows to the lowest level, so Torah flows to those who think of themselves as least. The greatest acquisition of Torah was by Moses, of whom the Torah says was "the most humble of all men on earth" (*Numbers* 12:3).

The diminutive *aleph* represents both Moses' profound humility and the lesson that only with humility can one gain knowledge.

אָדָם כִּי־יַקְרִיב מִכֶּם קָרְבָּן לַה׳
If a person among you brings an offering to God (1:2)

The Two Aspects of Man

Rashi notes that the Torah uses the word *adam* for "person" rather than the more frequently used word *ish*, and explains its use as meaning that just as Adam did not serve God with anything acquired dishonestly because nothing in the world belonged to anyone else, so must a person who brings an offering make certain that the offering was acquired honestly.

There may be an additional significance to the choice of the word *adam* as designating man. The first human was called Adam because his origin was from earth, *adamah*. This term connotes man's humble origin, as expressed by the patriarch Abraham, "I am but dust and ashes" (*Genesis* 18:27). Following the example of the patriarch, a person must always bear in mind that he is a mortal being, of little significance in the cosmos.

But it is only man's body that is of little significance, because it was the body that was formed from earth. Man has another component, the vital spirit that inhabits his body, that was instilled in him by the Divine breath, and hence is Godly in nature. The word *adam* also relates to the word *adameh*, "I shall be akin, I shall be similar," and this refers to the way man bears a semblance to God. "In the likeness of God did He create him" (ibid. 5:1) refers to the Divine *neshamah* (soul) which is Godly.

Man, therefore, is comprised of two components: the lowly earth and the Divine soul. Both are represented by the word *adam*.

As praiseworthy a trait as humility is, it may conceivably result in a person feeling so insignificant that he gives no serious consideration to his actions. Of what consequence can this body be if it originated from dust and will return to dust? This may result in a carefree attitude of abandon. To counter this, a person must remember that he was created in the likeness of God, and that he is, therefore, immeasurably great. Every move he makes is extraordinarily significant.

The word *korban* is generally translated as "sacrifice" or "offering." Both are inexact. One is not giving up anything nor making a gift to God. *Korban* means "drawing close," and closeness to God can be achieved only when one is humble, because God shuns vanity. But this humility must be tempered with man's awareness of his Divine origin, which places upon him the obligation of the Divine attributes. Furthermore, it is the craving of the Divine *neshamah* to be reunited with its Creator that attracts man to God.

A closeness to God can be achieved only when a person appreciates and implements both aspects of *adam*.

אָדָם כִּי־יַקְרִיב מִכֶּם קָרְבָּן לַה׳ . . . יַקְרִיב אֹתוֹ לִרְצֹנוֹ

If a person among you brings an offering to God
. . . he shall offer it of his own will (1:2-3)

No False Piety

Korban, drawing closer to God, requires sincerity and a surrender to God of one's will.

As we noted above, Rashi says that the Torah uses the word *adam* for "person" rather than the more frequently used word *ish*, and explains its use as meaning that just as Adam did not serve God with anything acquired dishonestly because nothing in the world belonged to anyone else, so must a person who brings an offering make certain that the offering was acquired honestly.

There is also another similarity to Adam which is essential for a *korban*, and that is that one must be sincere in one's service of God and not try to impress others with his piety. The Talmud uses the expression *genevas daas*, which is essentially "stealing" another person's judgment. Deceiving others in any way is depriving them of an accurate judgment of reality and is seen as a form of theft.

Adam did not try to impress anyone with his piety. There was no one to impress. This quality of sincerity must accompany a *korban*, because otherwise it is dishonest.

The Torah further specifies that bringing an offering should not be a mere ritual. It is not the animal that one must sacrifice, but rather one's own animal nature. There is that part of us that craves gratification of our animalistic desires. That is the will of the body rather than that of the *neshamah*. The Talmud says, "Make His will your will," and "Set aside your will before His" (*Ethics of the Fathers* 2:4). Man's animalistic drives stand as a barrier between man and God, and it is by subjugating these drives that one allows for the supremacy of the *neshamah*. Therefore, the essence of the *korban* is the "offering of his will to God."

This verse thus contains all the elements necessary for a relationship with God: humility, an awareness of one's Divine *neshamah*, sincerity and a subjugation of one's personal drives before the will of God.

וְהוּא עֵד אוֹ רָאָה אוֹ יָדָע אִם־לוֹא יַגִּיד וְנָשָׂא עֲוֹנוֹ
If a person is witness — has either seen or known of it —
if he does not testify out he shall bear his sin (5:1)

When Silence Is Not Golden

The Talmud considers the sin of *lashon hara* to be grievous, equivalent to the three cardinal sins of adultery, idolatry and murder. The Chafetz Chaim dedicated his life's work to the eradication of *lashon hara*. However, in the above verse we see that there are times when it is a sin to keep silent. If a person has information that is beneficial to another person, providing their information may not fall under the category of *lashon hara*. Indeed, there are situations where it is obligatory to reveal such information. The Chafetz Chaim elaborates on this in Chapter 9 of *Rechilus* (tale-bearing). A typical example is if someone is about to enter into a contract with a person whom you know to be a swindler, you are required to reveal this information to prevent the person from being cheated. Failure to reveal this information is a violation of "Do not stand idly by when your fellow's blood is shed" (*Leviticus* 19:16).

Unfortunately, some people may withhold such information, under the misconception that it is *lashon hara*. They would do well to study the chapter cited and consult a halachic authority about whether or not they should reveal what they know.

A young man is recommended to the parents of a young woman who are interested in a *shidduch* (marriage match) for their daughter. You happen to know that several years earlier, the young man suffered a severe depression and underwent psychiatric treatment. Understandably, great caution was taken to avoid this becoming public knowledge. As a close friend, you were privy to this. You know that the parents of the young woman would consider this to be very serious. According to the Chafetz Chaim, you are obligated to apprise the young woman's parents of this information *even if you were not asked*. Perhaps one might consider this to be a betrayal of one's closest friend. However, if all the conditions specified by the Chafetz Chaim are met, you *may not* keep your silence. Inasmuch as this is a weighty decision, with the possible transgression of *lashon hara* on the one hand and the transgression of "Do not stand idly by when your fellow's blood is being spilled" on the other hand, a halachic authority should be consulted about what one should do.

We must be careful not to allow our emotions to determine our behavior. What we may feel is right and proper is not always so. What is right and proper is that which halachah prescribes.

וְהָיָה כִי־יֶאְשַׁם לְאַחַת מֵאֵלֶּה וְהִתְוַדָּה אֲשֶׁר חָטָא עָלֶיהָ

When one shall become guilty regarding one of these matters, he shall confess what he had sinned (5:5)

Admitting One Was Wrong

Forgiveness for a sin can come only if one is sincere in the recognition that one has done wrong. This is by no means easy. A genuine confession requires more than regret of a particular act.

In regard to the sin-offering one brings for an inadvertent sin, the Torah says, "If he becomes aware of the sin *that he sinned*" (*Leviticus* 4:28). The words "that he sinned" appear redundant. The Torah means to tell us that a sin, even an inadvertent sin, does not occur in a vacuum. The person must have had an attitude that rendered him vulnerable to committing a forbidden act. It is not enough that he is remorseful for the act. Rather, he must do a thorough soul-searching to discover what character defects allowed him to commit the sin. Sincere *teshuvah* requires a "character overhaul." As Rambam says, the personality who emerges after *teshuvah* must be a different personality than the one that sinned. One must recognize that one's entire lifestyle had been flawed. This recognition is a formidable challenge.

R' Chaim Shmulevitz says that the patriarch Abraham's trial to sacrifice his son, Isaac, was more than the loss of his son. For decades Abraham had denounced idolatry, particularly the abominable practice of human sacrifice. What would he now say to all those people to whom he had repeatedly condemned human sacrifice as something that God could never desire? He would have to admit that he had been in error his entire lifetime! That Abraham was willing to repudiate his lifelong teaching indicated his loyalty to God (*Sichos Mussar* 5731:11).

In my work treating alcoholics, their recovery requires more than simply abstaining from alcohol. Unless one's personality undergoes significant change, one will relapse into drinking. A man with over twenty years of sobriety put it succinctly: "The man I once was drank, and the man I once was will drink again. I can be sober only if I am no longer that person who drank." This change requires more than remorse for one's behavior. It requires a painstaking analysis of one's character traits, discovering one's character defects and eliminating them.

This is the essence of confession. It is not accomplished in an instant. Rather, it takes years of diligent effort.

נֶפֶשׁ כִּי־תִמְעֹל מַעַל וְחָטְאָה בִּשְׁגָגָה מִקָּדְשֵׁי ה׳

*If a person behaves unfaithfully and sins
unintentionally against any of God's holy things* (5:15)

Deceptive Appearances

R' Samson Raphael Hirsch's philological genius is evident in his commentary on this verse and provides a lesson which is hidden in the text of the Torah.

The Hebrew word for "unfaithful behavior" is *me'ilah*. R' Hirsch suggests that the close similarity with the word *me'il*, the cloak worn by the High Priest, is not incidental. He supports his thesis with the fact the word *beged*, a garment, is spelled exactly the same as the word *boged*, which, like *me'ilah*, refers to deception and violation of trust. That both these words have similar double meanings, R' Hirsch contends, cannot be coincidence. A garment, R' Hirsch says, is something whereby a person presents himself to the world. One cannot know the true essence of a person merely by his external appearance.

The Talmud, contrasting the evil Balaam with the patriarch Abraham, says, "What distinguishes the disciples of Abraham from the disciples of the wicked Balaam?" and goes on to enumerate the character traits of the disciples of each (*Ethics of the Fathers* 5:22). One of commentaries asks, Why does the Talmud refer to the differences between their *disciples*? Why not simply say what distinguished Balaam from Abraham? He answers that from outward appearances, one might not detect the true essence of Balaam. He was a prophet who spoke to God (*Numbers* 2:11-12). He may have had a refined physical appearance and dressed similar to the patriarch. His true nature was revealed by his disciples. Of Abraham, the Torah says that he instructed those who would follow him to adhere to the ways of God, to do justice and righteousness. The disciples of Balaam were corrupt and degenerate, because that is what he conveyed to them.

Some people may purportedly appear to be upright, but this appearance is misleading. Behind the cloak of piety there may lurk dishonesty and corruption. The *me'il* may be a cloak that is masking the true essence, the *me'ilah*. A *beged* may give a superficial appearance which disguises the underlying personality.

By use of these words, R' Hirsch says, the Torah cautions us not to be deceived by external appearances.

וְכִפֶּר עָלָיו הַכֹּהֵן לִפְנֵי ה׳ וְנִסְלַח לוֹ
עַל־אַחַת מִכֹּל אֲשֶׁר־יַעֲשֶׂה לְאַשְׁמָה בָהּ

*The Kohen shall provide him atonement before God, and it shall be
forgiven him for any of all the things he might do to incur guilt* (5:26)

Spiritual Growth

The Seer of Lublin commented on this verse, that after a person achieves forgiveness for a particular sin, he is then in a position to discover that there were other things he did to incur guilt. It is much like an object which is covered with a heavy layer of dust. Only after the dust is removed might one be able to see a defect in the object. So it is with sin. As long as one bears the sin, he may be oblivious to other wrongs that he committed. It is only after he has been forgiven and is relieved of the sin that he can be sensitive to other things he did.

Sin creates a barrier between man and God. As long as one bears the sin, he may be unable to appreciate the majesty of God. His psychological defenses of rationalization may result in his justifying his action, and his resistance to feeling guilt may result in frank denial of any wrongdoing. Awareness of the majesty of God Whom he defied with his acts would cause him much distress, which the psychological defense mechanisms forestall. Once he is relieved of the sin, he is free to appreciate the majesty of God.

The *neshamah* craves a relationship with God. The guilt of sin causes a person to keep his distance from God. If the sin is forgiven, one can come closer to God, and the closer one draws to God, the greater is one's awareness that his actions were improper.

The Seer said that this is the meaning of the verse: "For with You is forgiveness, so that You may be feared," (*Psalms* 130:4). One who is distant from God cannot stand in utter awe of Him. After forgiveness, one is closer to God and can stand in awe of Him.

Rambam received a letter from a student who said that he did not feel he had any sins to confess on Yom Kippur. Rambam answered that this indicated that he did not have a concept of the majesty of God. If he did, he would be aware that he had not acted according to His will.

This is why *teshuvah* is never ending. The more one does *teshuvah*, the more one sensitizes oneself to discover how one's behavior was inadequate. *Teshuvah*, therefore, provides for an ongoing spiritual growth throughout all of one's life.

פרשת צו ֍
Parashas Tzav

צַו אֶת־אַהֲרֹן וְאֶת־בָּנָיו לֵאמֹר זֹאת תּוֹרַת הָעֹלָה
Command Aaron and his sons, saying, "This is the law of the elevation offering" (6:2)

The Fallibility of Emotion

The unusual term "command" rather than the more frequent "speak" or "say" caused the Sages to comment that the *Kohanim* were instructed to pay particular attention to the elevation-offering because it represented a "financial loss" to them (*Rashi*). The financial loss is generally understood to mean the fact that in contrast to other offerings, from which the *Kohanim* received portions of meat, the elevation-offering was totally consumed by flame. Inasmuch as the *Kohanim* received nothing to eat from this offering, they might be negligent in fulfilling the specifications of the ritual.

This is nothing less than mind-boggling. The meat from the offerings was so abundant that the *Kohanim* could not possibly eat all of it in the short period of time prescribed for its consumption, and any leftover meat had to be burned. Why would the *Kohanim* feel deprived if they did not receive any meat from the elevation-offering? Furthermore, this commandment was given to Aaron and his sons, people of immense spirituality. How could they possibly be suspected of negligence because they would not receive a portion of meat?

The Torah means to teach us something about the nature of human emotions: *They are not subject to logic.* Logically, the *Kohanim* had no use for additional meat, and highly spiritual people would hardly be affected by a portion of meat. The point is that the human acquisitive drive can be so powerful that it defies rational thought.

There are multibillionaires who could not possibly use all their wealth if they lived for a thousand years, yet they are driven to make more money. The multi-billionaire, J. Paul Getty, was asked, "How much is enough?" He answered, "Just a bit more." Even though he could not possibly have any use for "a bit more," he was nevertheless driven to add to his immense wealth.

Of course the *Kohanim* had no need for additional meat. Logically, they should not have been affected in the least by the lack of meat from the elevation-offering. But this is precisely the point: *The acquisitive drive is not subject to logic.* Furthermore, even highly spiritual people are not free of an acquisitive drive. Every person is capable of acting irrationally when his acquisitive drive is thwarted.

This lesson is certainly appropriate for us. We may occasionally be driven to do things that are grossly absurd, but which we may rationalize as making sense. We must be on constant guard not to be overwhelmed by emotion, and particularly when our acquisitive drive is involved, we must exercise extra caution to assure that our logical thinking prevails.

וְהָאֵשׁ עַל־הַמִּזְבֵּחַ תּוּקַד־בּוֹ לֹא תִכְבֶּה

*The fire on the Altar shall be kept burning on it,
it shall not be extinguished* (6:5)

Think Positive

Many books have been written on the value of positive thinking. There is no doubt that an upbeat attitude can affect not only our behavior, but also the function of our bodies. Repeated studies, spurred by Norman Cousins' *Anatomy of an Illness*, have demonstrated that patients who have a positive attitude may have better and more rapid recoveries. Various suggestions have been given for how to achieve an upbeat attitude even in the face of adversity.

R' Shneur Zalman, the Baal HaTanya, suggested a unique translation of the above verse. It can read, "The fire on the Altar shall be kept burning *within him* (the *Kohen*). *You shall extinguish the negative.*"

It has been suggested that the symbolism of the offerings on the Altar is that we should recognize that the animal nature within us must be subdued and subjugated to the Divine *neshamah*. This can be accomplished when one has a passionate desire to unite with God, because the *neshamah* is, in fact, Godly in nature. "He (God) blew into his nostrils a breath of life" (*Genesis* 2:7). The Zohar comments that when one exhales, one breathes out something from within oneself, hence when God "blew into his nostrils a breath of life," He (so to speak) "exhaled" from within Himself. The *neshamah* is the breath of life of Divine origin, and it craves being reunited with its Source. The barrier to this reunion is the mundane desires of the earthly body. When these are subjugated to the *neshamah*, the barrier is removed and the *neshamah* can unite with God.

Our history is replete with *tzaddikim* who were able to maintain their composure and were not crushed by adversity. The Psalmist says, "He will not fear bad tidings; his heart is steadfast, trusting in God" (*Psalms* 112:7). And again, "As for me, nearness of God is my good" (ibid. 73:28). A person who has a burning passion for uniting with God can withstand adversity, and can think positively even under the most stressful circumstances.

This, said R' Shneur Zalman, is the meaning of the above verse. One who has the sublimating fire of the Altar within him can always extinguish the negative.

חָק־עוֹלָם לְדֹרֹתֵיכֶם מֵאִשֵּׁי ה' כֹּל אֲשֶׁר־יִגַּע בָּהֶם יִקְדָּשׁ

An eternal portion for your generations, from the fire-offerings of God; whatever touches them shall become sacred (6:11)

Contact vs. Absorption

If a food or vessel touches the meal-offering in such a way that it absorbs its flavor, it must be treated with the same stringency as the sacred meal-offering, because it takes on the latter's character. Mere contact without absorption does not make it sacred.

> *A young man would come in periodically and spend some time among the disciples and chassidim of R' Shneur Zalman. One time R' Shneur Zalman called the young man aside and said that he had heard he was associating with freethinkers, some of the haskalah movement who had become intoxicated with secular studies and had drifted away from Torah, considering the ideologies that were being taught in the universities as being superior to the ancient wisdom of Torah. R' Shneur Zalman warned the young man that such associations are dangerous to his spiritual well-being, because he is vulnerable to their seduction.*
>
> *The young man responded, "You have no need to worry, Rabbi. I am not easily influenced. You see, I have been associating with your chassidim, and they have not influenced me to become a chassid."*
>
> *R' Shneur Zalman responded, "There are two different halachos that relate to being in contact with something sacred vs. something profane. If food touches something which is tamei (contaminated), it becomes tamei by mere contact. On the other hand, if it were to touch the sacred meal-offering, it does not become sacred unless it absorbs therefrom. Sanctity cannot be acquired unless you absorb it within yourself, whereas tumah can be acquired simply by superficial contact.*
>
> *"You have not tried to absorb what my chassidim teach," R' Shneur Zalman said, "and that is why it has not affected you. However, when you associate with these freethinkers, even superficial contact is enough to affect you negatively."*

This is something we should bear in mind. Contact with any type of negative influence should be assiduously avoided. It is not necessary to have an intense relationship in order to be negatively affected. One can suffer spiritual deterioration even by superficial contact. On the other hand, if we wish to elevate ourselves spiritually, it is not sufficient to merely be in touch with spiritual people. We must make a concerted effort to incorporate their teachings.

As important as this is for ourselves, it is of even greater importance for our young children. There is much in our environment that is harmful to their moral and spiritual well-being. We should not be lulled by a false sense of security that exposure to these influences is harmless. Quite the contrary, it is easy to become "contaminated" by the immorality in our environment, and we should protect our children from sources of spiritual harm just as we would from serious contagious diseases. On the other hand, it is not enough to bring them into shul or give them a token Jewish education. If we wish them to become truly spiritual people, we must provide them with appropriate teachings and an environment which will enable them to absorb Torah values.

בְּמְקוֹם אֲשֶׁר תִּשָּׁחֵט הָעֹלָה תִּשָּׁחֵט הַחַטָּאת
In the place where the elevation-offering is slaughtered shall the sin-offering be slaughtered (6:18)

The Primacy of Human Dignity

This verse seems to be a bit wordy. The Jerusalem Talmud says that the Torah wishes to indicate that the slaughter of the sin-offering is done in the same area as is an elevation-offering. This insures that an individual bringing the offering is not identified as having committed a sin. Observers may assume that he is bringing an elevation-offering. The Torah teaches us this to impress upon us the need for preserving the dignity of every person, even one who has sinned.

This is so important that it bears some elaboration. The Talmud states that if someone humiliates another person in public, he forfeits the rewards of all the mitzvos he had done (*Ethics of the Fathers* 3:15). Think of it! A person who was observant of Torah an entire lifetime and at age 80 humiliates someone publicly and does not apologize, all his mitzvos are wiped out! This would not have resulted had he committed a sin as serious as eating *tereifah*!

We are fortunate in having biographical accounts of our *tzaddikim*, who modeled for us how we must preserve a person's dignity.

> *The great sage, R' Akiva Eiger, was recognized as a Talmudic genius at a young age. When he became a choson his future father-in-law wished to impress the scholars of his town with his good fortune, and when the young Akiva came to visit, the local Torah scholars were invited to meet him. To his astonishment, the young Akiva kept silent, to the point where the father-in-law felt he had been deceived about him. After several days, Akiva asked to meet with the scholars, and he expounded for hours on Torah in a manner that left them breathless.*
>
> *The young Akiva explained that another young man, also reputed to be a fine Torah scholar, had been in town visiting the home of his father-in-law. "Had I expounded when this young man was in town, the local scholars would have thought little of this young man. I, therefore, decided that it was better that they consider me an ignoramus than to upstage this young man."*

As a young man, R' Yisroel of Salant, the founder of the *mussar* movement, delivered lectures on Talmud in the Vilna yeshivah. Gradually, students of the older Rosh Yeshivah began to gravitate to R' Yisroel's lectures. Fearing that the older scholar would be embarrassed, R' Yisroel resigned his position.

> *R' Moshe Kliers was the Askenazic rabbi of Tiberias. One Friday it became known to him that the eruv, which allowed people to carry things on Shabbos, was not in compliance with halachah, although it had been*

approved by the Sephardic rabbi. On Sunday, R' Moshe went to the Sephardic rabbi and said that he was having difficulty understanding a particular portion of the Talmud, and sought the latter's explanation. Together they studied the section dealing with the laws of eruv, and eventually the Sephardic rabbi remarked, "I have overlooked this opinion, according to which the eiruv is pasul (disqualified)."

The Sephardic rabbi recognized that this had been the way R' Kliers wanted to apprise him of his error. "Why did you not declare the eruv to be pasul on Friday?" he asked. R' Kliers answered, "Many halachic authorities consider the eruv to be kosher. Had I declared it to be pasul, that would have been embarrassing to you. All authorities agree that to cause a person to be embarrassed is a grievous sin. It was preferable by far to rely on those authorities that consider the eruv to be kosher than to risk embarrassing you."

From the Scriptures to the Talmud to our contemporary *tzaddikim,* the primacy of preserving a person's dignity is emphasized.

The Shabbos of Greatness

In most years, the Shabbos on which we read *Parashas Tzav* is *Shabbos HaGadol,* the "great" Shabbos, which comes before Passover. Countless explanations have been given for the appellation *Shabbos HaGadol.*

The Midrash states that on this Shabbos, the Israelites in Egypt acquired sheep for the Passover offering. The sheep was an Egyptian totem, and many of the Israelites had fallen under the sway of Egyptian idolatry. Sacrificing the sheep was a repudiation of paganism and an open defiance of Egyptian rule.

The essence of idolatry is not the worship of an icon. Jews were never so foolish as to believe that an animal, a tree or a statue was a god. Rather, because the ethical and moral teachings of God are restrictive, people may establish a religion and a godhead that allows them to gratify their desires without feeling guilt that they are transgressing a Divine commandment. The Talmud states this very clearly: "The Israelites knew that the idols were without substance. They were simply looking for a sanction to permit them to indulge in forbidden relationships" (*Sanhedrin* 63a).

People who are driven by powerful cravings may rationalize, and rather than resist the compulsion, they may try to justify their behavior. Idolatry is nothing but a self-deceiving rationalization.

The idea for my Haggadah, *From Bondage to Freedom,* came from a recovered drug addict. Attending his father's *seder,* he interrupted his father when the latter began reciting *Avadim Hayinu* (we were slaves unto Pharaoh). "Father," he said, "can you truthfully say that you, personally, were ever a slave? You may not be able to appreciate what it is to be free. *I* can say that I was a slave. When I was in my addiction, I had no freedom at all. I was under the tyranny of drugs. I did many things that I never thought myself capable of doing. I did them because I had no choice. I was a slave to drugs and they were my master. Today I can make choices. Today I am free."

VAYIKRA / LEVITICUS: Tzav

Drugs are not the only form of enslavement to which people are subject. People who smoke in spite of the knowledge that they are destroying themselves are slaves to nicotine. Some people who are dangerously overweight are a slave to food. Some people are driven mercilessly to achieve acclaim, and others to accumulate more wealth than they could ever consume. All of these drives are essentially tyrannical dictators that control a person.

The sacrifice of the sacred sheep was a rejection of idolatry. It was a repudiation of the compulsivity of our mundane drives. It was our Declaration of Independence, not only of our freedom from the rule of Pharaoh, but also from the ruthless tyranny of our internal drives. We would now be free to choose what is right and proper, even if it is in defiance of a bodily urge.

A child is dominated by bodily drives. He does not have the intellectual capacity to distinguish good from bad, right from wrong. This is why a child is not held legally responsible for his actions. As he matures, he gains intellect, and as an adult, he is held responsible for his actions. The rule of the intellect rather than that of internal drives is what distinguishes an adult from a child.

The Hebrew word for a minor is *katan*, and for an adult, *gadol*. The Shabbos on which we rejected rule of the body in favor of rule of the intellect is the Shabbos on which we asserted our maturity as a *gadol*. Perhaps this is one of the many meanings of *Shabbos Hagadol*. With the sacrifice of the totem and the repudiation of idolatry the Israelites established themselves as dignified, mature adults.

The Gift of Spirituality

The festival of Passover is far more than an Independence Day celebration. The Torah writings say that the happenings of the first Passover set a precedent, and that all subsequent Passovers have the magic of that momentous event.

A high level of spirituality is not easily achieved. It requires much effort in divesting oneself of character defects that are antagonistic to spirituality. Some of these may be deeply engrained and may resist being eliminated.

The Israelites in Egypt were at the lowest possible level of spirituality. The Midrash states that of the 50 levels of *tumah* (spiritual decadence), they were at the 49th, and the Ari z"l said that had they not been delivered from Egypt at that precise moment, they would have descended into the depths of *tumah* from which they could never have emerged.

Yet in that sorry state, the Israelites were privileged to a Divine revelation, as the Haggadah says, "'With great awe' refers to the revelation of the *Shechinah* (Divine Presence)." Several days later, at the dividing of the Reed Sea, there was a Divine revelation so intense that the least of the Israelites had a prophetic vision greater than that of the prophet Ezekiel (*Rashi, Exodus* 15:2). For there to be so great a spiritual experience while not having emerged from so lowly a state was a unique phenomenon.

The Chassidic writings say that this set a precedent for the future, that on Passover it is possible for a person to make a leap into spirituality even if one has not yet divested oneself of character defects. They say that this is the meaning of the *berachah* we recite to commemorate the miracles of Chanukah and Purim:

"Blessed are You ... Who has wrought miracles in those days *at this time.*" This time, the present, the days on which the miracles occurred, is a propitious time for miracles. Similarly, the days of Passover are propitious for repetition of the unique phenomenon of achieving spirituality when one is in a state that would make this impossible at other times.

The Haggadah commentaries call our attention to the formula for the order of the *seder*: *kadesh, urchatz*, recite the *kiddush* and wash the hands. They point out that this may also mean *kadesh*, become holy and *urchatz*, wash yourself. Usually one must cleanse oneself of all defects before one can acquire holiness. On Passover the sequence may be reversed. One may acquire holiness even if one has not prepared oneself adequately.

The Psalmist says, "Desist from evil and do good" (*Psalms* 34:15). One must first abandon all improper behavior before doing good. However, it can also be read as "Desist from evil *by doing good.*" "A small amount of light can banish a great deal of darkness" (*Tzedah LaDerech* 12). Passover is the time when this can best be accomplished.

Passover is *zeman cheirusenu*, which is not simply the time when we *became* free, but the time when *we were freed*, the time when God delivered us from enslavement. Just as one may be a slave to a cruel taskmaster, one may also be enslaved by the tyranny of one's bodily drives or by addictive habits. Breaking loose from these may be very difficult, but is much easier on Passover. All that is necessary is a sincere desire to become spiritual, and the Divine blessing will enable one to achieve that desire.

פרשת שמיני
Parashas Shemini

וַיְהִי בַּיּוֹם הַשְּׁמִינִי קָרָא מֹשֶׁה לְאַהֲרֹן וּלְבָנָיו וּלְזִקְנֵי יִשְׂרָאֵל

It was on the eighth day, Moses summoned Aaron and his sons and the elders of Israel (9:1)

The Constriction of Sanctity

This was the eighth day of the consecration of the *Mishkan* (Sanctuary), the day on which the Divine service in the *Mishkan* began. It was a day of unprecedented joy, a day on which God rejoiced as with Creation. Yet, the Midrash states that wherever we find the word *vayehi* (it was), it is indicative of some tragic occurrence. The Midrash says that the tragic occurrence on that day was the death of Aaron's sons, Nadab and Abihu.

R' Yisroel of Rizhin gives an additional explanation for the word *vayehi*. The original Divine will was that the *Shechinah* (Divine Presence) should be manifest everywhere in the world, as was said after the giving of the Torah at Sinai, "Wherever I permit My Name to be mentioned, I shall come to you and bless you" (*Exodus* 20:21). It was not until the sin of the Golden Calf that the universality of the immanent Divine Presence was lost, and was now circumscribed within a structure (*Sforno, Exodus* 25:9). The *Mishkan*, for all its holiness, was nevertheless a reminder of the loss the world sustained as a result of the sin of the Golden Calf. Therefore, although it was a joyous occasion, the consecration of the *Mishkan* had an element of sadness, and this is a reason for the term *vayehi*.

There are various interpretations of the sin of the Golden Calf, some of which are relevant to our own shortcomings. We have never totally rectified the sin of the Golden Calf. This requires an unshakeable faith in God and a devotion of *naaseh venishmah* as was had at Sinai. Only this can restore the presence of the *Shechinah* everywhere.

We are to never forget the sin of the Golden Calf. "Remember, do not forget, that you provoked your God in the Wilderness" (*Deuteronomy* 9:7).

Joy and sadness can coexist. When we enter the shul to pray, we should rejoice that we have a place where there is greater immanence of the *Shechinah*, but we should also remember that if *Klal Yisrael*, the entire Jewish people, behaved in a way that would rectify the sin of the Golden Calf, we would merit the return of the universal Immanence of the *Shechinah*.

וַיֹּאמֶר מֹשֶׁה אֶל־אַהֲרֹן קְרַב אֶל־הַמִּזְבֵּחַ וַעֲשֵׂה אֶת־חַטָּאתְךָ

Moses said to Aaron, "Come near to the Altar and perform the service of your sin-offering" (9:7)

The Importance of Empathy

Rashi says that Moses had to urge Aaron to perform the service because Aaron was embarrassed by his participation in the sin of the Golden Calf (*Exodus* 32:35). Moses, therefore, said to him, "Why do you feel embarrassed? This is why you were chosen."

The *Otzar Chaim* cites an explanation of this. One of the commentaries says that Aaron was far too spiritual to have volitionally participated in the sin of the Golden Calf. The Talmud says that God protects the righteous from sin (*I Samuel* 2:9). He says, therefore, that it was destined that Aaron have a trace participation in the sin of the Golden Calf, because inasmuch as he was to be the one to perform the sin-offerings for forgiveness for the nation, he, too, had to have a taste of the sin.

It is virtually impossible to do anything wholeheartedly for a person unless you empathize with him. Empathy is not sympathy. Empathy is seeing the world as the other person sees it.

> *R' Mendel of Lubavitch (Tzemech Tzedek) was receiving chassidim when he secluded himself for several hours before continuing. He explained, "When someone consults me for help in doing teshuvah, I must first find a trace of his sin in myself before I can help him. The Baal Shem Tov said that inasmuch as a person is often oblivious of his own faults, God arranges it that he see them in other people. The world is like a mirror. What you see in others is a reflection of yourself.*
>
> *"When the last person told me of his sin, I searched within myself to find where I had a trace of it, but after a thorough soul-searching I could not find any. That meant that I had developed a blind spot to my own faults. I, therefore, said Tehillim (Psalms) for several hours until I could overcome my denial and find that fault in myself."*

This is why Moses said to Aaron, "Come near to the Altar and perform the service of your sin-offering and provide atonement for yourself and for the people" (*Leviticus* 9:7). Only by recognizing one's own errors and accepting forgiveness for them can one achieve forgiveness for others.

This is an important lesson. In order to be of help to others, we must be able to set aside our perception of the world. We must feel what they feel, and only then can we be of true help to them.

Another interpretation is that Aaron was chosen as High Priest in spite of his involvement in the Golden Calf episode to demonstrate the power of *teshuvah*. Once a person has done appropriate *teshuvah*, his sin is erased, never to be brought to mind. The prophet says, "I have erased your sin like a fog (that has dispersed)" (*Isaiah* 44:22). Just as there remains no trace of a fog that has cleared, so there is no trace of a sin for which one has done proper *teshuvah*.

But what about the Psalmist's statement, "My sin (*chait*) is before me always"? (*Psalms* 51:5). This seems to imply that one should never forget one's sin. The resolution to this is that the word *chait* means "lack" or "defect." A person who has committed a sin should realize that there was something in his personality that rendered him vulnerable to committing the sin. This character lack or defect could conceivably lead him to repeat the sin. He must, therefore, remain on guard and maintain a state of alertness so that he should not succumb to that defect. The sin for which he did adequate *teshuvah* need not be remembered, because it was totally erased. What one should remember is one's vulnerability, so that a repetition of the sin is avoided.

In that same psalm, David says, "Erase all my iniquities" (ibid. v. 11), and "Then I will teach transgressors Your ways, and sinners will return to you" (ibid. v. 15). The knowledge that *teshuvah* completely removes one's sins encourages the sinful to do *teshuvah*.

This is what Moses told Aaron: "You were chosen to become High Priest to teach people the power of *teshuvah*; that not only are one's sins erased, they also do not constitute an impediment to reaching the highest level of spirituality."

וַיִּקְחוּ בְנֵי־אַהֲרֹן נָדָב וַאֲבִיהוּא אִישׁ מַחְתָּתוֹ וַיִּתְּנוּ בָהֵן אֵשׁ וַיָּשִׂימוּ עָלֶיהָ קְטֹרֶת וַיַּקְרִיבוּ לִפְנֵי ה' אֵשׁ זָרָה אֲשֶׁר לֹא צִוָּה אֹתָם

The sons of Aaron, Nadab and Abihu, each took his fire-pan, they put fire in them and placed incense upon it; and they brought before God an alien fire that He had not commanded them (10:1)

Spirituality Needs No Alien Stimulus

Rashi cites the statement of R' Yishmael in the Talmud that the transgression of Nadab and Abihu was that they drank wine before entering the Sanctuary. This statement appears remarkable. The Torah is explicit that their sin was the introduction of an alien fire. How and why does R' Yishmael give another reason, which seems to contradict the Scripture?

The answer is that R' Yishmael is not at all contradicting the Scripture. Rather, he is offering an interpretation thereof. While *eish zarah* is literally "an alien flame," it is also figuratively "an alien passion." R' Yishmael's interpretation is of singular importance today.

Nadab and Abihu were extraordinarily great men, so much so that Moses said that he considered them greater than himself and Aaron (*Rashi, Leviticus* 1:3). If they drank wine before entering the Sanctuary, it was not because they were out partying. Rather, they knew that in the Sanctuary they would have a spiritual experience. They believed that by drinking wine they would attain a state of mind more conducive to a spiritual experience. After all, the psalmist says, "Wine makes glad the heart of man" (*Psalms* 104:15). By relieving a person's tension, wine enables one to have greater joy, and joy can enhance a spiritual experience. It was for the intensification of the spiritual experience that they drank wine.

Why, then, were they so severely punished? *Because one should not seek to enhance a spiritual experience by artificial means.* Intense spiritual experiences should come as a result of prayer, Torah study and meditation, with contemplation on the Infinite, and not by altering the metabolism of the brain with a chemical.

In recent times we have suffered a plague of drug use which has destroyed many lives, ruined the minds of countless youth, and still poses a threat to the very survival of our society. Several decades ago, there arose a false prophet who advocated "mind expansion" by use of potent mind-altering chemicals such as LSD, claiming that it would give people a perception of reality that they could not achieve otherwise. Many people believe that intoxicating the brain with alcohol, marijuana or other chemicals improves one's functioning. Many minds have been destroyed as result of this misconception.

R' Yishmael's point is that one should not seek spiritual enhancement by altering one's state of mind with a chemical. Nadab and Abihu's attempt to do so was introducing "an alien fire" into the Divine service. Now, as then, chemical alteration of one's state of mind is destructive.

I arrived at this interpretation of R' Yishmael's statement as a result of my clinical experience in treating people who have resorted to chemicals to alter their state of mind. I was thrilled to subsequently discover that several Torah commentaries had offered this interpretation.

וַיֹּאמֶר מֹשֶׁה אֶל־אַהֲרֹן הוּא אֲשֶׁר־דִּבֶּר ה' לֵאמֹר
בִּקְרֹבַי אֶקָּדֵשׁ וְעַל־פְּנֵי כָל־הָעָם אֶכָּבֵד וַיִּדֹּם אַהֲרֹן

Moses said to Aaron, "Of this did God speak, saying:
'I will be sanctified through those who are nearest Me,
thus will I be honored before the entire people;'"
and Aaron was silent (10:3)

Humility and Acceptance

Referring to Aaron's silence in accepting the harsh Divine judgement, the Sifra says that there were three individuels who serenely accepted the Divine judgment: Abraham, who said, "I am but dust and ashes" (*Genesis* 18:27); Aaron, in the above verse, and David, who said, "I am a worm, and no longer a man" (*Psalms* 22:7).

The obvious question is that the Sifra does not cite exactly where Abraham and David accepted the Divine judgment with serenity. Rather, it lists where they expressed their humility. What is the relevance of humility to acceptance?

The question of why the righteous suffer is as old as history. The Talmud says that Moses posed this question to God, and God told him that is one secret that cannot be revealed to him as long as he inhabits a mortal body (*Berachos* 7a). Yet, throughout the ages, people have struggled with this question. This is the theme of the Book of Job, which the Talmud says was written by Moses (*Bava Basra* 14b). Various explanations are offered, but all are rebutted. The final answer is that this is something beyond human understanding, and the righteousness of God's judgement must be accepted on faith.

Acceptance by faith and surrendering the effort to grasp something logically is possible only if one recognizes the limitations of the human mind. "As high as the heavens over the earth, so are My ways higher than your ways, and My thoughts than your thoughts" (*Isaiah* 55:9). People who accept only that which they can understand and reject anything that is beyond their understanding are actually worshipping the human mind. One who deifies the human mind cannot worship God.

The Talmud says that one must praise God for the bad as for the good (*Berachos* 54a). This is referred to as *tziduk hadin*, justifying a harsh Divine judgement.

The paragons of humility, Abraham, Aaron and David, were able to accept the Divine judgment because they did not try to understand God. In spite of their great intellect, they recognized the limitations of the human mind.

This is the reason for the Sifra's statement. Humility and acceptance are inseparable.

וַיִּקְצֹף עַל־אֶלְעָזָר וְעַל־אִיתָמָר בְּנֵי אַהֲרֹן הַנּוֹתָרִם לֵאמֹר . . . וַיִּשְׁמַע מֹשֶׁה וַיִּיטַב בְּעֵינָיו

He [Moses] was wrathful with Elazar and Ithamar, Aaron's remaining sons . . . Moses heard and he approved (10:16-20)

Anger and Error

Moses had instructed Elazar and Ithamar to eat of the offerings of the consecration even though they were in mourning, because God had so commanded. When he discovered that they had not eaten from the *Rosh Chodesh* offering, he became angry and reprimanded them. When Aaron pointed out to Moses that he was in error, Moses conceded.

The Midrash states that three times Moses was angry and each time he erred (*Vayikra Rabbah* 13:1). The Sifra cites a difference of opinion between Chananiah ben Yehudah, who says that the anger caused the error, and R' Yehudah, who says that the error caused the anger.

We have a principle that although the position of two Talmudic sages may be polar opposites, both are nevertheless true (*Eruvin* 13b). *Otzar Chaim* says that this teaches us that both can occur: Anger may lead to error, and error may lead to anger.

The Talmud says that when a person is in rage, "If he is wise, his wisdom is suspended" (*Pesachim* 66b). In rage, one may lose control of both one's thoughts and one's actions, because "all the forces of hell dominate him" (*Nedarim* 22a). One cannot exercise good judgment under such conditions.

Although we may accept that "to err is human," a person may nevertheless be very angry with himself for having made a mistake. Clear thinking will result in the awareness that no one is infallible. We make mistakes and we should learn from our mistakes. These can be invaluable learning experiences. There is no reason to be angry at oneself for having erred, since anger is likely to lead to further errors.

Chananiah ben Yehudah and R' Yehudah are both right. We must avoid rage, and we must be able to adapt properly to our mistakes.

וַיִּשְׁמַע מֹשֶׁה וַיִּיטַב בְּעֵינָיו
Moses heard and he approved (10:20)

Truth Is Not Negotiable

The Midrash says that when Aaron questioned Moses' instructions, saying that perhaps God had not told him what Moses claimed He did, Moses said, "You are right. I forgot what I had heard from God."

R' Chaim Shmulevitz points out that Moses was confronted with an awesome decision. Moses was the sole conduit of the word of God, and there was no way to verify his instructions. If he were to admit that he had forgotten and had erred in conveying God's words, how would that impact on the authenticity of the entire Torah? Might people not say, "If Moses could have erred in one thing, perhaps he erred in others as well." Admitting that he had erred in this one instruction would place the validity of the entire Torah in jeopardy throughout eternity. Was this not adequate reason for Moses to stand his ground and say, "Do as I said. That is God's wish?"

But Moses knew that truth should never be compromised. He was obligated to speak the truth. Whatever consequences might flow from that was not his responsibility. Speaking falsehood cannot be justified. His responsibility was to adhere to the truth. The authenticity of Torah throughout eternity was God's responsibility, not his (*Sichos Mussar* 5731:11).

How often do we deviate from the truth for reasons far less momentous than that available to Moses? Many people think that a "white lie" is exempt from the Torah prohibition against lying (*Leviticus* 19:11). The frequently quoted axiom that one may lie to restore peace is inaccurate. Rashi states that one "may alter things" for the sake of peace (*Genesis* 18:13, 50:16), which means that one may say something which is not frankly untrue, but which can be interpreted in several ways. The Talmud does not sanction outright falsehood for any reason. Even "altering things" is only permitted for the sake of restoring peace.

Adhering to absolute truth is not always easy, but we have no option. Not only is truthfulness mandated by Torah, but it is also crucial in parenting. Children cannot distinguish "white lies" from any other color. Parents who are not truthful are modeling lying for their children, and should not be surprised when their children lie to them.

We declare, "*Moshe emes v'soraso emes.*" The truth of Torah is evidenced by Moses' refusal to deviate from truth, regardless of the consequences. We should follow his example.

אַךְ אֶת־זֶה לֹא תֹאכְלוּ . . . אֶת־הַגָּמָל . . . וּפַרְסָה אֵינֶנּוּ . . .
וְאֶת־הַשָּׁפָן . . . וּפַרְסָה לֹא יַפְרִיס . . . וְאֶת־הָאַרְנֶבֶת . . . וּפַרְסָה לֹא הִפְרִיסָה
"This is what you shall not eat . . . the camel . . . but its hoof is not split . . . the hyrax . . . its hoof will not split . . . the hare . . . its hoof was not split (11:4-6)

Never Despair of a Jewish Neshamah

This portion of the Torah enumerates the kosher and non-kosher animals. In the English translation of the Chumash, all of the three above verses are translated as "its hoof is not split." However, in the Hebrew, three tenses are used: "*is* not split, *will* not split, *was* not split." This cannot be without significance.

Although the Torah is speaking about the non-kosher animals which we must reject, there is a message for us regarding our relationship with people, said R' Yisroel of Salant. We can reject something only if there is no hope whatsoever of any redemption.

As objectionable as a person's present behavior may be, if he had a respectable heritage, i.e., family roots of decent people, we should realize that he undoubtedly has a nucleus of fine character traits within him, which can be unearthed and nurtured. Even if one lacks such a heritage, there is always the possibility that one may change in the future. There are countless instances of people who have made major lifestyle changes, even late in their lives. Rejection can be justified only if there is no redeeming feature either in the past, present or future. Since such criteria can never be met, there are no grounds for ever rejecting anyone.

There are times, or course, when a person's improper behavior warrants a modicum of rejection, but even then the rejection should not be absolute. The Talmud is critical even of the prophet Elisha for totally rejecting his errant servant, Gehazi. If distancing someone is called for, "One should always push aside with the left (i.e., weaker) hand and attract with the right (i.e., stronger) hand" (*Sotah* 16a). The force of attraction should exceed the force of rejection.

R' Yisroel of Salant was the father of the *mussar* movement, which calls for highly ethical behavior. Yet he states that although we must denounce improper behavior, we should always look for redeeming features that will enable us to salvage even the most sinful person.

פרשת תזריע-מצורע
Parashas Tazria-Metzora

Higher than Angels; Lower than Animals

The previous portion of the Torah delineated those animals which are *tamei* (unclean) and which may not be eaten. The Midrash states that after discussing unclean animals, the Torah then cites conditions which render a person *tamei*. Rashi says that just as animals preceded man in creation, the laws pertaining to animals precede those pertaining to man.

There is also a Midrash that states that if a person lives a proper life as befits a human being, he is considered the first of creation, because the Divine idea of creation was that there should be a human being that would recognize and worship God. If, however, man fails to develop his unique abilities, he is told, "The lowly insect preceded you in creation."

Precisely because a human being has a physical body that has many animalistic drives, a person who subdues these drives in the interest of drawing closer to God actually surpasses angels in spirituality. Angels are holy because they were created holy, whereas man becomes holy through his own effort. However, man may descend to a level beneath that of animals. Animals have inborn limitations to their bodily drives. They eat to provide the necessary nutrients for the body, and then they stop. They mate to preserve the species, and then they stop. Even predatory animals kill only for their food, but when they are not hungry, they will not kill unless provoked. Animals drives are in the interest of survival.

Man, on the other hand, is not bound by such limitations. Man may indulge far in excess of bodily needs, and man may pervert his urges. Indeed, man may indulge himself to the point of self-destruction. Furthermore, whereas predatory animals kill only for self-survival, man's aggressiveness can be totally senseless. When a person corrupts his bodily drives, he sinks to a level lower than animals.

When a person fulfills himself spiritually, he becomes the primary goal of creation, and he not only precedes animals, but also precedes angels, who were not created until the second of the six days. However, if he fails to live a spiritual life, he deteriorates to a level beneath an insect.

Although the human ego-drive may lead a person astray, there is one aspect of the ego-drive that is constructive. We should be proud to be the goal of creation, superior even to angels.

אָדָם כִּי־יִהְיֶה בְעוֹר־בְּשָׂרוֹ . . . לְנֶגַע צָרָעַת

If a person (adam) will have on his skin . . .
a tzaraas affliction *(13:2)*

Vulnerability to Lashon Hara (Defamatory Speech)

The Talmud is very clear that the affliction of *tzaraas* (the exact nature of which is unknown to us) is a punishment for having spoken *lashon hara*.

The Hebrew word the Torah uses for "person" in the above verse is *adam*. There are several other Hebrew words for "person": *enosh, ish, gever*. The ethical writings state that each refers to a level of spirituality, and *adam* represents the highest level. We must understand, therefore, the Torah's choice of the word *adam* for a person afflicted with *tzaraas*.

The Chafetz Chaim said that the juxtaposition of this portion of the Torah to that of the previous portion dealing with nonkosher animals is to teach us that people who may be meticulously careful about what goes into their mouths should be equally as scrupulous about what comes out of their mouths. There are sins which a Torah observant person would never do, but as for *lashon hara*, it is a rare person who is saved from it (*Bava Basra* 164b). Hence, even a spiritual person, *adam*, is vulnerable to *lashon hara*.

The Midrash relates that a peddler went through the streets shouting, "Who wishes to buy an elixir of life?" R' Yannai, who was engrossed in his Torah study, asked to see his wares. The peddler said to him, "For you I have nothing." Upon R' Yannai's insistence, the peddler took out a Book of Psalms and showed him the verse, "Who is the person who desires life and loves days that he may see good? Keep your tongue from evil and your lips from deceitful speech" (*Psalms* 34:13-14). R' Yannai then said, "All my life I have been reciting this psalm, but I never understood it until this peddler pointed it out to me" (*Vayikra Rabbah* 16:2).

This Midrash has puzzled many Torah scholars. What was in these verses that he had never grasped previously? The words of the psalm could not be any clearer: Guarding one's tongue from *lashon hara* is conducive to long life.

Perhaps we may understand this by examining the Talmudic statement that the remedy for *lashon hara* is the study of Torah (*Arachin* 15b). A number of commentaries ask, In what way is Torah study a penance for *lashon hara*? The halachah is that if you have offended someone, it is essential that you make amends to that person and ask his forgiveness. They answer that it is not the study of Torah *per se* that constitutes penance. Rather, the study of Torah will enable a person to understand the gravity of *lashon hara* so that he will do what is necessary for penance.

The gravity of *lashon hara* can be seen in the episode of Joseph and his brothers, which was brought about by his speaking derogatorily about them (*Genesis* 37:2), and in what happened to the prophetess, Miriam, when she spoke improperly regarding Moses (*Numbers* 12:1-10). To this very day, we are suffering the consequences of the *lashon hara* delivered by the spies to Moses (ibid. 13:31-32). This should make one cognizant of how far-reaching the effects of *lashon hara* can be, and how diligent one must be to do proper *teshuvah*.

While the mitzvah of studying Torah is extraordinarily great (*Shabbos* 127a), the Talmud points out that Torah can be a double-edged sword. "If one merits, Torah can be an elixir of life; if one is not virtuous, Torah can be a deadly poison" (*Yoma* 72b).

How penetrating these words are! If used improperly, Torah can be destructive.

The impact of derogatory speech depends on the character of the speaker. If a person who has little credibility makes a negative comment about someone, people are likely to dismiss it as worthless babble. However, if the speaker is a person of stature, a scholar whose opinion carries some weight, the attitude towards his words is, "If he says so, it must be true. He knows what he is talking about." The more learned a person is and the higher he is held in esteem, the more his words are taken seriously.

The Baal Shem Tov taught that every human character trait can be put to good use. But what about vanity? This is so abominable a trait that it repels the Divine Presence (*Arachin* 15b). How can vanity ever have a positive application?

We can see, however, that even vanity can have a redeeming feature. Before making a negative comment about someone, do not be humble and think of yourself as an insignificant person whose words will not be heeded. This is the time when vanity can temporarily be put to good use. "I must be careful of what I say. People are not likely to dismiss my words lightly. I am an important person, and my words can have a great impact."

The greater a Torah scholar a person is, the more he must be careful of his speech. The words of an esteemed Torah scholar will be taken seriously. If he speaks negatively about someone, he has allowed his Torah scholarship to become a negative force. The Midrash says that *lashon hara* destroys three people: the speaker, the listener and the one about whom it is spoken (*Devarim Rabbah* 5:10). If Torah scholarship gives credibility to one's *lashon hara*, it indeed becomes "a deadly poison."

The man who was peddling the "elixir of life" was not an unlearned person. He was trying to teach people *mussar*. He did not believe that a great Torah scholar like R' Yannai was in need of his teaching. When he told R' Yannai that his teaching about *lashon hara* was not relevant for Torah scholars, R' Yannai remarked, "I was unaware that people had this mistaken impression. To the contrary, it is those who are Torah scholars who have great need for this elixir of life, because Torah has value only if one is virtuous. Negligence on the part of a Torah scholar, particularly in speaking *lashon hara,* can seriously distort the value of Torah."

We can be spared from *lashon hara* if we incorporate the second half of the verse, "loves days that he may see good." In his introductory morning prayer, R' Elimelech of Lizhensk says, "Help us to see the good in our fellows, and not their defects."

If we concentrate on looking for the good in people, we will have no need to make negative comments about anyone.

אָדָם כִּי־יִהְיֶה בְעוֹר־בְּשָׂרוֹ שְׂאֵת . . . לְנֶגַע צָרָעַת

If a person will have on the skin of his flesh . . .
a tzaraas affliction (13:2)

The Mystery of Suffering

The affliction of *tzaraas* is the only condition which the Torah attributes to a specific sin: *lashon hara*. "Beware of a *tzaraas* affliction. Remember what God did to Miriam" (*Deuteronomy* 24:8-9). This refers to Miriam's unjust criticism of Moses (*Numbers* 12:10).

Our people have experienced suffering in its many forms, as a nation as well as individually. Every so often, someone suggests a reason for suffering. This is presumptuous, because while there may be various reasons for suffering, they are largely unknown to us.

The question of why things happen has been instrumental in advancing human knowledge. Many scientific discoveries have resulted from man's attempt to understand and explain things. Whether an apple did or did not fall on Isaac Newton's head, something aroused his curiosity as to why things fell to the ground, and so he investigated and formulated the Law of Gravity. Life-saving penicillin was discovered because of Fleming's curiosity as to why there was no bacterial growth around the mold on the petri dish. It is only natural for people to be curious why things happen.

Curiosity is one thing. Obstinacy in insisting that every question must have an answer that we can understand is something else. Perhaps we feel that not being able to find an answer is an insult to our competence. There is nothing wrong with realizing our human limitations. There are many things that are unknown, and even if we see the unknown as a challenge and try to investigate it, we should realize that we may not be able to know everything.

There are things in Judaism about which our knowledge is limited or even non-existant. For example, we believe that God has infinite foresight and knows the future. We also believe that a person has the freedom of choice to do right or wrong. This raises a question that has been discussed by many theologians: If God knows what I am going to do tomorrow, how can I have free choice? I cannot do anything other than what God knew I was going to do.

Rambam says that the reason we see this as a conflict is because we equate God's knowledge with our own. If we have certain knowledge of what is going to happen, it cannot happen differently. However, God's knowledge is totally different than ours, and His knowledge does not conflict with free will. What is God's knowledge like? That we cannot possibly know, because God's knowledge is inseparable from Him. Just as we cannot have an understanding of God, we cannot have an understanding of His knowledge (*Hilchos Teshuvah* 5:5). Ravad criticizes Rambam for raising a question to which he cannot give a logical answer. But Rambam's position is that it is perfectly proper to have insoluble mysteries. We do not have to have a concrete answer to everything. We must learn to live with mystery, with the unknowable.

There are many things that we must accept as facts and proceed from there. For example, when oxygen and hydrogen combine in a specific ratio, they form water. That is a natural phenomenon. Why they form water rather than another compound is unknown. However, we accept this fact and see what useful applications we can derive from this fact.

Throughout history, we have observed the fact that there is suffering in the world. We have sought to explain it, particularly why the innocent suffer and why bad things happen to good people. The theme of the Book of Job is the mystery of the suffering of good people.

As previously noted, the Talmud says that Moses' request of God, "Let me know Your ways" (*Exodus* 33:13) was to understand why the righteous suffer, but God denied him this knowledge (*Berachos* 7a). The Talmud says that it was Moses who wrote the Book of Job, wherein several explanations are offered, but all are rebutted. It would be most presumptuous for us to try to understand something that escaped Moses' understanding.

Yet many of our ethicists have investigated the question of suffering. I believe that they were not in search of an explanation. They obviously did not try to grasp something that was beyond the grasp of Moses. The *reason* for suffering is known only to God. All we can do is try to derive some useful lesson from suffering. While we may not be able to know *why* there is suffering, we may be able to see how we can benefit from this perplexing phenomenon.

R' Baruch Ber Lebowitz was engaged in a Torah discussion with R' Chaim of Brisk, and he remarked, "Why does the Torah say this?" R' Chaim corrected him. "We may not ask *why* the Torah says something. That is God's wisdom and is beyond our ability to understand. We can only ask, 'What can we derive from what the Torah says?' "

The chassidic master, R' Avraham Yaakov of Sadigur, said of his brother, R' Dovid Moshe of Tchortkov, "When my brother says Tehillim, he says it with such devotion that God says, 'Dovid'l, you may have the entire world and do with it whatever you wish.' But my brother is very trustworthy, and he returns the world to God exactly as he got it. Now, if God would make me that offer, I would make some changes."

R' Avraham Yaakov was saying that the rebbe of Tchortkov had such perfect faith in the Divine justice, and so believed that everything that happened in the world was right, that he would not change things if he could. Of himself, R' Avraham Yaakov said that he had not achieved so absolute a faith, and that if it were within his power, he would make some changes in the world.

I am far, far beneath the level of the rebbe of Sadigur. Although I profess to have *emunah*, and when I suffered losses I recited the *berachah* of *Baruch Dayan Ha'emes*, Blessed be the Judge of Truth, I could not avoid feeling that it was an intellectual expression. I was in pain, and I felt otherwise in my heart.

Oh, if God would only let me operate the world! All children would be born healthy, without physical or mental defects. There would be no leukemia or cancer. People would be healthy until they reached the end of their allotted time on earth.

The Talmud says that the righteous suffer in this world in order to increase their reward in the Eternal World. We find different attitudes toward suffering in the Talmud. R' Eliezer welcomed his suffering, calling his pains "my friends" (*Bava Metziah* 84b). On the other hand, R' Elazar said, "I do not want the suffering and I do not want its reward" (*Berachos* 5b). This was not a rejection of suffering but was in response to the question whether he wished to suffer.

There is a difference between *pain* and *suffering*. People who have been given morphine for severe pain, if questioned carefully, may say, "The sensation is still there, but it doesn't bother me." Suffering may be an *interpretation* of pain rather than a sensation on its own.

Inasmuch as there is no decisive halachah on this issue, I favor the latter position. I have a very low pain threshold, and I find even a toothache intolerable. I am not even interested in knowing *why* my tooth hurts. That is for the dentist to know. I just want relief.

As a psychiatrist, people come to me with their problems, some of which are heart-rending. I am happy when I can do something to relieve their distress, but I am most frustrated when I am powerless to do so. I suffer along with them, and as you may surmise, I do not handle suffering well.

Sometimes I identify with my great-grandfather, Zeide Reb Motele of Hornosteipel. He was a chassidic rebbe to whom many people came to unburden themselves of their misery. One day, after absorbing many tales of woe from the people who sought his blessing to extricate them from their plights, he abruptly tore open his shirt, bared his chest and exclaimed, "Master of the universe! Look into my heart. I cannot take any more."

Ah! But I am not Zeide Reb Motele. He genuinely cared for others. I care for myself.

> *In my last year of medical school, I received a call late one night from a hospital, because a patient requested a rabbi. I found a distraught women standing over an incubator. Her infant had been born with what was at that time an irreparable heart defect. Her baby was going to die. Tearfully, she turned toward me and said, "Why, rabbi, why?" I stood there in utter silence, crying along with her. I said a brief prayer with her and left. The words of Moses came to my mind, when he complained to God that his efforts to have Pharaoh free the Israelites resulted in aggravating their suffering. "Why did You do evil to this people? Why did You send me?" (Exodus 5:22). If Moses could complain, so may we.*
>
> *The following morning I told my father about this experience. He said, "Was your frustration due to the woman's pain, or because you were unable to help her?" He was right. One of the reasons I had left the rabbinate for medicine was because I felt I could do more for people as a doctor than as a rabbi. Now I was both, and in spite of having the tools of the two greatest healing professions, I was totally impotent. I could not handle the assault to my ego. I am sure that Moses and Zeide Reb Motele genuinely cared for others and shared their pain, whereas I was caring primarily for myself and was nursing my wounded ego.*

Sometimes we can see, if only in retrospect, the good that resulted from suffering. Many times we cannot, even in retrospect. I am sure that the intensely painful experience of the distraught mother had a profound impact on her emotional makeup, but I cannot fathom why it had to come this way. I can only resort to God's words to Job: "And where were you when I created the world?" In other words, there is a master plan knowable to only a Being who has infinite knowledge of time and space. We may think of a jigsaw puzzle of a thousand pieces. One who has only one piece of the puzzle may say, "This piece doesn't make any sense." Of course, it cannot make any sense unless it fits in with the other 999 pieces which one does not have.

Some things do lend themselves to our understanding. For example, the Talmud says, "God gave Israel three good gifts, and all were given only through suffering. They are: Torah, Eretz Yisrael and the World to Come" (*Berachos* 5a). It is common experience that we have greater feeling and appreciation for things we acquire through suffering than for things that come to us easily, especially gifts. The more effort we put into achieving or acquiring something, the more meaning and value it has for us, because we have put part of ourselves into it. The Talmud says that *tzaddikim* value their possessions even more than their own bodies, because they scrupulously avoid anything that they did not earn honestly (*Sotah* 12a). Their bodies were given to them, whereas they worked hard for their possessions. In order that we properly treasure Torah, Eretz Yisrael and the World to Come, we have to experience suffering to acquire them.

> *The chassidic master, R' Baruch of Medzhibozh was reciting the prayer prior to the Friday night Kiddush. When he came to the verse, "I thank You, God, for all the kindnesses that You have done for me, and for all the kindnesses that You will do for me in the future," he paused. "Why do I have to thank God in advance for future kindnesses? I can wait and thank Him when they occur." After meditating a few moments, he said, "I understand why. The kindnesses may come packaged in suffering, so that I will not be able to recognize them as kindnesses when they occur." Thereupon he began weeping. "How tragic it is," he said, "that God will be doing kindnesses for me and I will be unable to appreciate them."*

The Midrash says that when Jacob mourned the loss of his beloved son, Joseph, he said, "God has turned away from me." God said, "Here I am manipulating things to make his son viceroy over the greatest empire on earth, yet he complains" (*Bereishis Rabbah* 91:13). If the great patriarch had difficulty in accepting suffering as a kindness in disguise, what can we expect of ourselves?

While we wish that it would come via a more pleasant route, suffering is often a wake-up call. We are often so frenetically engaged in the activities of life that we may give little thought to the purpose of life. It is when we suffer that our focus may change. Suffering may change our perspective and we may assign different values to things. As Solomon said, "It is better to go to the house of mourning than to the house of feasting, for that is the end of all man, and the living should take it to heart" (*Ecclesiastes* 7:2). There is not much that one learns at a feast.

As a physician, I have observed people reject values that they had never questioned before, and consider new paths in life. I addressed this phenomenon in *Light at the End of the Tunnel*.

Suffering may alter a person's sensitivity. In experiencing our own suffering, we may develop a connection with the suffering of others of which we may not have been aware. A wise psychotherapist said to me, "Out of suffering come the strongest souls. God's wounded often make His best soldiers."

We may not have satisfactory answers to some questions. The phenomenon of suffering will forever remain a mystery. Its uses need not be so.

וְרָאָהוּ הַכֹּהֵן וְטִמֵּא אֹתוֹ

***The Kohen shall look at it and declare him tamei [contaminated]** (13:3)*

The Power of a Word

Until the *Kohen* declares the person to be *tamei*, he is not in state of contamination. The presence of the lesion in and of itself does not deem the person *tamei*.

This is totally different than the diagnosis of a lesion by a physician. If a person has a malignant lesion, it does not become malignant by the doctor's diagnosis. It is what it is, and the doctor only describes its condition. Not so with *tzaraas*. The words of the *Kohen* give the lesion its status.

As was noted earlier, the affliction of *tzaraas* is a punishment for *lashon hara*. Some people may think that aggressive actions may be harmful, but that mere words are not significant. By this halachah the Torah indicates the power of the word. It is not the reality that confers a state of *tumah* on the person, but the *word* of the *Kohen*.

This is a lesson for the person who was careless with his speech. It shows him just how powerful "mere" words can be.

בָּדָד יֵשֵׁב מִחוּץ לַמַּחֲנֶה מוֹשָׁבוֹ

He shall dwell in isolation;
his dwelling shall be outside the camp (13:46)

The Curse of Isolation

One Friday, when R' Aryeh Levin davened Minchah at the Kosel, he saw a woman crying bitterly. To his inquiry about her distress, she said that her son was hospitalized in isolation in a Jerusalem hospital for lepers. R' Levin decided to visit the hospital, where he found that there were twelve Jews along with three hundred Arabs. Upon seeing him, the Jews burst into tears. "We have not had a visitor for years," one man said. R' Levin made it his business to visit them every Friday. Once time they said to him, "Each time you come, we think this is the last time we will see you. All we do here is await death. No one has ever been discharged from this place."

When the Jews asked for kosher food. R' Levin's wife would cook for them, and he personally brought the food to them. On Rosh Hashanah his son accompanied him to blow the shofar for them.

One time, R' Levin asked the Rebbe of Sochachov to assist him in bringing food to the patients in the leper hospital in Bethlehem. He noted that R' Levin went into each patient's room to exchange a few words with them.

"Why do you take so much time to visit this Arab hospital?" the Rebbe asked. "Don't they have their own clergy?" R' Levin answered, "There is one Jewish patient there who needs my visit. Once I am there, I will not discriminate, and I visit all the patients."

R' Levin's biography is entitled *A Tzaddik in Our Time*. How apt.

כִּי תָבֹאוּ אֶל־אֶרֶץ כְּנַעַן . . . וְנָתַתִּי נֶגַע צָרַעַת בְּבֵית אֶרֶץ אֲחֻזַּתְכֶם
וּבָא אֲשֶׁר־לוֹ הַבַּיִת וְהִגִּיד לַכֹּהֵן לֵאמֹר כְּנֶגַע נִרְאָה לִי בַּבָּיִת

"When you arrive in the land of Canaan . . . and I will place a
tzaraas affliction upon a house in the land of your possession, The
one to whom the house belongs shall come and declare to the Kohen,
'Something like an affliction has appeared to me in the house'" (14:34-35)

Blessings in Disguise

Why should the owner say, "Something *like* an affliction has appeared to me in the house?" Why not say, "An affliction has appeared to me in the house?" The Divine statement, "I will place an affliction upon a house in the land of your possession" appears to be a promise rather than a punishment. Rashi explains that the Cannanites used to hide their treasures in the thick walls of their houses. The affliction in the house resulted in the walls being demolished, which would expose the hidden treasure. Thus, the affliction in the house was a blessing rather than a punishment.

This is why the owner should not say, "An affliction has appeared to me in the house." An affliction is a punishment, whereas the lesion in the wall of the house was a blessing leading to discovery of hidden treasure. Therefore, all he may say is "It seems to me like an affliction."

This has far-reaching application. We all experience unpleasant things which at the moment are distressing and appear to be bad. In many instances, we realize much later that what we had assumed to be bad was really a good in disguise.

The Baal Shem Tov said that when an adversity occurs, one should not say, "It is bad." God does not do bad things. Rather, we may say, "This is a bitter happening." Some life-saving medications may have a bitter taste.

Remembering this should help us keep our bearings in times of adversity.

כִּי תָבֹאוּ אֶל־אֶרֶץ כְּנַעַן אֲשֶׁר אֲנִי נֹתֵן לָכֶם לַאֲחֻזָּה
וְנָתַתִּי נֶגַע צָרַעַת בְּבֵית אֶרֶץ אֲחֻזַּתְכֶם
וּבָא אֲשֶׁר־לוֹ הַבַּיִת וְהִגִּיד לַכֹּהֵן לֵאמֹר כְּנֶגַע נִרְאָה לִי בַּבָּיִת

"When you arrive in the land of Canaan that I give you as a possession, and I will place a tzaraas affliction upon a house in the land of your possession. The one to whom the house belongs shall come and declare to the Kohen, 'Something like an affliction has appeared to me in the house'" (14:34-35)

The Importance of Attitude

The Talmud states that the affliction in the house may be a punishment for begrudging things to others (*Arachin* 16b). The Hebrew word for *tzaraas* can be broken down to read *tsar ayin*, an oppressive eye, referring to refusal to share one's things with others. "A person may have asked a neighbor to lend him an item, but the neighbor claimed he had no such item. The affliction in the house requires the owner to remove everything from the house (*Leviticus* 14:34), at which time his claim that he did not possess the requested item will be publicly proven to have been untrue" (*Vayikra Rabbah* 17:3).

It is also possible to be a *tsar ayin* even if one does lend his belongings or gives *tzedakah*. One can do so with a demeaning attitude that causes the recipient to feel humiliated. It is not uncommon for people to look upon recipients of *tzedakah* as *schnorrers*, and even if one does give *tzedakah*, one may do so with a condescending attitude.

People who are in need of help are often broken in spirit because of their dependence on others. It is a great mitzvah to be encouraging and uplifting to them. We should remember that when we give *tzedakah*, we receive much more than we give (*Vayikra Rabbah* 34:10). If our attitude toward *tzedakah* is begrudging, the pain we inflict upon the recipient may outweigh the good we do for them.

The Torah says, "When you lend money to My people, to the poor with you" (*Exodus* 22:24). The commentaries remark that everything in the world belongs to God. In His infinite wisdom, He has given more to some, less to others. The wealthy should know that their wealth has been given to them merely for safekeeping, and that they must give of it to the poor. "To the poor with you" means that the share of the poor is with the wealthy, who should know that their wealth has been given to them merely for safekeeping, and that they must give of it to the poor, because it is their rightful possession. This is why the Torah emphasizes "the land of Canaan *that I give you* as a possession." Remember that it is My land, and that it is given to you with the understanding that you will share your portion with the needy. R' Yishmael cites the verse, "the one to whom the house belongs" will suffer the affliction in the house; i.e., one who thinks that the house is exclusively his, rather than a gift from God which he should share with the less fortunate (*Arachin* 16b).

If one is aware that the *tzedakah* he gives is merely that which rightfully belongs to the poor, one will not give grudgingly.

The Folly of Vanity

The *haftarah* for *Tazria* is a portion found in *II Kings* 5:1-19, and relates a fascinating story.

Naaman, a general of the army of Aram, suffered from *tzaraas*. A young Jewish girl who had been taken captive by Aram and who was a servant in the house of Naaman told of the many miraculous healings performed by the prophet Elisha. When Naaman came to Elisha's house with his entire retinue, the prophet sent him a message that bathing seven times in the Jordan River would heal him, Naaman became enraged. "I thought that he would heal me with some special ritual. As for bathing in the Jordan, the rivers of Aram are far superior to the Jordan!" and he left in fury.

Naaman's servants prevailed upon him to do as the prophet said, and when he did bathe seven times in the Jordan, his *tzaraas* cleared.

R' Yehudah Leib Chasman points out that Naaman had certainly exhausted all the available treatments for this terrible affliction. When he was promised a cure, what difference did it make what the cure was? Should he not, in desperation, have grabbed at even a straw? Especially since he had heard of the miraculous healings wrought by the prophet, he should have promptly seized the opportunity. Instead, his ego got in the way. "The rivers of Aram are far superior to the Jordan!"

This shows us how vanity can affect our thinking. Because he felt that the prophet had slighted the rivers of Aram and infered that the Jordan was somehow superior to them, he turned a deaf ear to what ultimately proved to be his cure.

Had his servants not prevailed upon him, he would have continued to linger in the misery of *tzaraas* for the rest of his life.

R' Chasman cites this as an important lesson for us. Vanity may blind us to what is in fact in our best interests. If we keep our ears open to the words of the wise and set aside our petty pride, we will be spared the serious pitfalls of vanity.

פרשת אחרי מות ·§
Parashas Acharei Mos

וַיְדַבֵּר ה' אֶל־מֹשֶׁה אַחֲרֵי מוֹת שְׁנֵי בְּנֵי אַהֲרֹן בְּקָרְבָתָם לִפְנֵי־ה' וַיָּמֻתוּ

God spoke to Moses after the death of Aaron's two sons, when they approached before God and they died (16:1)

Breaking Through Denial

God instructed Moses to tell Aaron that he may not enter the Holy of Holies except on Yom Kippur, lest he die as did his two sons. Rashi explains the reason for citing the death of his two sons with a parable. A doctor may warn a patient against certain practices, but the patient may not heed him. However, if he says that these practices may kill him as they did another patient, he is more likely to listen.

R' Isaac Sher points out how ineffective a mere verbal prohibition may be. Moses was talking to the High Priest Aaron, who was his equal in spirituality. Is there the slightest doubt that Aaron would have obeyed Moses' instruction, even without the graphic reminder of his sons' death? But the Torah means to teach us, R' Sher said, that as long as person inhabits a physical body, a drive to do something may not be thwarted by a didactic warning alone. Even for someone as spiritual as Aaron, the prohibition had to be reinforced by a graphic description of the consequences. How much more so should we, who are at a far lower spiritual level, realize the danger of ignoring the consequences of prohibited acts.

It is important for us, and especially parents, to realize that we are today faced with a challenge so severe that even personal experience with grave consequences is not a deterrent. I am referring to the problem of drug use, especially among youngsters. Repeated studies have shown that educating young people about the dangers of drugs and that they may be fatal does not deter them. Taking them to prisons and showing them what happens when one is arrested for a drug related crime is ineffective. Even when they have personally witnessed a close friend die of drug use, this does not deter them. The drive to use drugs is inordinately strong.

All youth are at risk, even those from the finest families who did not experience any deprivation. We should not be lulled by a false sense of security. Parents should educate themselves about the facts of drug use, and do their utmost to thwart the desire for drugs in their children.

Civilization today, due to the unprecedented progress of science and technology, is the most hedonistic in history. So many sources of distress have been eliminated and so many sources of pleasure have been added, that there is a prevailing attitude that the goal in life is to derive as much pleasure as one can. Even Torah observant people may share in this attitude. It is this pursuit of pleasure, now accepted as a norm, that plays a significant role in young people's use of drugs to experience a high.

While it is certainly appropriate to enjoy good things of the world, the purpose and goal of life must be something beyond that. Lecturing children has proved inadequate. Parents who model a truly spiritual goal and the pursuit of spirituality rather than the pursuit of pleasure, can imbue their children with an attitude toward life that may discourage their recourse to drugs for their pleasurable effects.

The effectiveness of intellectual knowledge is limited. The Alter (Elder) of Kelm said that even a thorough knowledge of the entire Torah is no assurance that one will behave properly. It is easy to know what *others* should do, but one may not be able to apply intellectual knowledge to oneself.

It is related that the Gaon of Vilna was able to review two entire complex tractates of Talmud, *Zevachim* and *Menachos,* in a single night. He also spent an entire night repeatedly reviewing the first Mishnah in *Peah,* which cites the mitzvos of *tzedakah* and *gemilas chasadim.* The two difficult tractates are primarily concerned with rituals in the Temple which are not applicable at this time, hence an intellectual knowledge sufficed. The single Mishnah of *Peah,* however, deals with practical mitzvos, and the Gaon felt that an intellectual knowledge of them was inadequate. He reviewed this Mishnah numerous times to make certain that its content had impressed on him emotionally as well as intellec-tually.

It is indeed important that we teach our children by conveying to them the content of Torah, but we should realize that in order for them to implement these teachings in their behavior, we must model it for them.

לְאֹהֶל מוֹעֵד הַשֹּׁכֵן אִתָּם בְּתוֹךְ טֻמְאֹתָם
The Tent of Meeting that dwells with them in the midst of their impurities (16:16)

God Is Present Where He Is Welcomed

"Even when they are in a state of contamination, the Divine Presence is with them" (*Yoma* 57a).

Although disobeying the Divine will sets up a barrier between man and God, it is somewhat like a one-way mirror. We cause ourselves to be distant from God, but He is never distant from us. This is rather easy to understand. We sometimes see children who reject their parents, but regardless of how defiant the child may be, the parents' love for him is as intense as ever, and they long for his return to them.

When R' Mendel of Kotzk first joined the court of R' Simchah Bunim of P'shis'che, the latter asked him, "Young man, where is God?" R' Mendel answered, "The entire world is full of His glory." R' Simchah Bunim repeated, "Young man, I asked you, where is God?" R' Mendel answered, "There is no place that is devoid of Him." R' Simchah Bunim persisted, "Young man, I am asking you, where is God?" R' Mendel said, "If my answers do not satisfy you, then you tell me." R' Simchah Bunim said, "God can be found wherever He is welcomed."

"He who is haughty of eye and large of desire, him I can not tolerate" (*Psalms* 101:5). Of a vain and arrogant person the Talmud quotes God as saying, "He and I cannot share the same dwelling" (*Arachin* 15b). God is indeed everywhere, but He withdraws His presence from a vain and arrogant person.

Committing a sin is not necessarily a denial or rejection of God. A person may simply have been overwhelmed by an urge that he did not suppress, or may not have realized that a sin causes him to be distant from God. However, a vain, egotistical person is one who is his own god. Inasmuch as there cannot be two gods, if a person thinks himself to be god, he cannot believe in the true God. There is no form of idolatry as absolute as the person who worships himself.

In my writings on self-esteem, I suggested that vanity and conceit are desperate defenses whereby a person tries to cope with a sense of unworthiness. I was thrilled to find that no less an authority than Rabbeinu Yonah validates this concept. "The vain person seeks to compensate for his feeling of defectiveness by means of grandiosity" (*Rabbeinu Yonah al HaTorah,* p. 156). A person with healthy self-esteem does not seek the praise and recognition of others to remind him that he has value.

If a person truly believes that he possesses a Divine *neshamah*, he will realize that he has great worth, and even if he may have gone astray in his behavior, he is nevertheless worthy by virtue of his Divine *neshamah*. Anyone with a profound feeling of unworthiness must be in denial that he has within himself the breath of God.

Man's closeness to God is by virtue of his *neshamah*, which craves to be united with its Source. Denial of having a Divine *neshamah* precludes a close relationship with God.

God is with us even if we have sinned. As long as we feel a desire to be close to God, we know ourselves to be of His essence, and that we are capable of becoming more spiritual. This opens the door to *teshuvah*, and this is why the above verse is contained in the narrative of the Yom Kippur service.

וְכָל־אָדָם לֹא־יִהְיֶה בְּאֹהֶל מוֹעֵד

Any person shall not be in the Tent of Meeting (16:17)

The Meaning of Solitude

This portion of the Torah conveys the instructions of the service of the High Priest on Yom Kippur, the one day of the year on which he may enter the inner chamber of the Sanctuary or Temple, the Holy of Holies. The Torah states that no one may be in the Sanctuary when the High Priest enters the Holy of Holies.

We find something analogous to this at Sinai, when God told Moses that only he could approach Him, and that all others had to remain at varying distances (*Exodus* 19:24, *Rashi*). These two auspicious occasions required solitude, in which one man was alone with God. Indeed, the Jerusalem Talmud states that even the heavenly angels were not permitted to be in the Sanctuary when the High Priest entered the Holy of Holies (*Yoma* 5:5). There was to be total solitude, only man with God.

As a rule, isolating oneself from others is not advantageous. We should learn to live together, to share with one another and to yield our own comfort and convenience to be of help to others. But every so often, a person should have some solitude, away from everything and everyone. Many of our great leaders set aside specific periods of time for *hisbodedus*, solitude and meditation.

At such times, a person should consider what it would be like if there were no other beings in the world, only himself and God. What would his behavior be like then? No one around to impress, no one to appease, no one to imitate, no one else's values to adopt, just oneself and God. One would certainly seek an intense closeness with God and do everything possible to achieve it.

After such solitude and reflection, one must return to reality. There *are* other people around: our families, our friends, our community. It is inevitable that we will be distracted from a constant and total communion with God, but we can then ask ourselves, How much distraction is absolutely necessary? Do we allow our relationships with others to unnecessarily distract us from our relationship with God? Do we perhaps do things because we wish to impress others with our importance, things that we would not do in the absence of people? Do we perhaps do things to ingratiate ourselves to people so that we can derive some benefit from them, things that we would not do if no others were around?

If we begin with the proposition that total absorption with God is the ideal, and consider how much we allow ourselves to be distracted from the ideal, we may be motivated to change our priorities. Our daily life habits may cause us to sometimes act like automatons. We should set aside some time for solitude and reflection, so that we can be truly intelligent and spiritual people.

This is what we may learn from the solitude of the High Priest on Yom Kippur. Granted, it is but a brief period of time in the entire year, but it should serve as a reminder of what the ideal goal in life should be, and enable us to maximize our attainment of that goal.

וְכִפֶּר בַּעֲדוֹ וּבְעַד בֵּיתוֹ וּבְעַד כָּל־קְהַל יִשְׂרָאֵל

He shall provide atonement for himself, for his household and for the entire congregation of Israel (16:17)

A Psychotherapeutic Error

In discussing the proper formula for *vidui* (confession), the Talmud (*Yoma* 36b) cites the verse, "We have sinned with our fathers, we have caused iniquity and wickedness" (*Psalms* 106:6). The Hebrew term used for "sin" is *chait*, which denotes an unintentional transgression. The words used for "caused iniquity and wickedness" are *avon* and *pesha*, which refer to willful and defiant transgressions.

MaHarsha points out that we implicate our ancestors only in regard to *chait*, inadvertent sins, but not to willful sins.

People who consult psychotherapists for emotional problems are asked about their childhood experiences, and particularly how they were treated by their parents. Not infrequently, the therapist will attribute the patient's emotional problems to faulty parenting. While it cannot be denied that early experiences may have great impact, it is important that parents should not be vilified. Unfortunately, there are some parents who are negligent or abusive, but the vast majority of parents wish to do the best for their children. They may indeed make mistakes in parenting, but these are generally done with good intentions. It is even possible that parents who have consulted purported experts in child rearing may have been given wrong advice. Although children may suffer from parental mistakes, we should bear in mind that these were most often inadvertent rather than willful errors.

In some cases, the awareness that one's problems are the result of faulty parenting has turned children against their parents. This accomplishes nothing therapeutically, and the rift that is created between children and parents deprives both of one of the most meaningful relationships in life. Both parents and children are made to suffer needlessly.

Except in those cases where there has been frank abuse, we should realize that our parents' errors are not a reason for resentment. Rather than dwell on parents' mistakes, we would achieve much more if we addressed our own behavior. It has been correctly said, "Even if you are what your parents made you, if you stay that way, it's your own fault."

The words in the psalm are well chosen. We should not impart any malice to our parents. Even if they erred, they invariably meant well.

דַּבֵּר אֶל־בְּנֵי יִשְׂרָאֵל וְאָמַרְתָּ אֲלֵהֶם אֲנִי ה׳ אֱלֹקֵיכֶם

"Speak to the Children of Israel and say to them: 'I am your God'" (18:2)

The Responsibility of Being Jewish

I have tried to avoid repeating what I wrote in *Living Each Week*. However, I wish to elaborate on something I wrote there, because it is of crucial importance. It complements something I refer to in the piece that follows titled *The Absolute of Morality*.

The above verse is somewhat enigmatic. The Ten Commandments begin with the statement, "I am the Lord, your God," because the belief in God is the basis for Judaism and a prerequisite for everything in the Torah. What is the purpose of its being restated here?

I believe that this fundamental principle is stated here as an introduction, to impress upon us that the verse that follows immediately is equally vital to Judaism and is essential for there to be a relationship between God and Israel. The verse that follows is: "Do not perform the practices of the land of Egypt in which you dwelled; and do not perform the practices of the land of Canaan to which I bring you." What is there in this rather non-specific verse that makes is so pivotal as to warrant it being introduced by the opening words of the Ten Commandments?

Furthermore, just what is meant by the prohibition against emulating the practices of the Egyptians and the Canaanites? Everything that we may not do is stated explicitly in the Torah. We may not eat non-kosher foods, we may not have forbidden relationships, we may not work on Shabbos, we may not worship alien gods, we may not lie, steal, kill, etc. What is this general statement adding to what has been explicitly forbidden?

The answer lies in the Talmudic statement (*Berachos* 63a), "What verse in the Torah is fundamental to everything else in the Torah? 'Know Him in all your ways'" (*Proverbs* 3:6). The Talmud is telling us that just as "I am the Lord, your God" is the foundation of Torah, so is "Know Him in all your ways."

In some other faiths there is a dichotomy: "Give to God what is to God and to Caesar what is to Caesar." I.e., there is a separation between activities of life that pertain to religion and those that are distinct from religion. Worship and certain rituals are the arena of religion. Working, eating, relaxing, socializing and other activities of daily life are not affected by religion. One works to earn a livelihood, and that has nothing to do with God. One may enjoy a hearty meal, and that has nothing to do with God.

In Judaism there is no such dichotomy. The verse, "Know Him in *all* your ways" means that *everything* a person does must be related to the service of God. Working, eating, relaxing, socializing and other activities of daily life are no less religious functions than are observing Shabbos, hearing the shofar or eating matzah on Passover.

Halachah states that if someone hires a worker to chop wood, he must pay him for the time he takes to sharpen his axe. Making the necessary preparations for performing the task for which he was hired is an integral part of the task.

The purpose of a Jewish person's life is to develop a close relationship to and unite with God. This is accomplished by fulfilling the will of God as it is expressed in the mitzvos of the Torah. There are prerequisites to the performance of these mitzvos. A person must have the means and must be physically and emotionally capable of doing so.

Everything a person does that enables him to perform the mitzvos is, like the worker's sharpening his axe, an integral part of the mitzvos. Inasmuch as sleeping, eating, working and other activities of living are necessary for optimum functioning, these can be an integral part of the mitzvos, *provided that one intends them to be such.*

The practices of the Egyptians and Canaanites to which the Torah refers are not the prohibited acts. Rather, they are permissible behaviors. However, whereas people in the Jew's environment may eat solely for the gustatory delight, sleep for the pleasure of sleeping and recreate for the fun of it, the Jew must sublimate these activities. He should eat to have the energy wherewith he can observe the mitzvos, sleep in order to have the requisite rest for optimum function, and do the things that contribute to physical and emotional well-being so that he can best strive to achieve his ultimate goal: a close relationship with God. He thus "knows God" in all his ways.

In *Kedoshim*, the portion of the Torah that follows, Ramban states that it is possible for a person to be in technical compliance with all the Torah requirements, yet be vulgar rather than spiritual. One can be grossly self-indulgent without transgressing any specific prohibition. Such behavior distances one from God. A person may indeed partake of the goods of the world and enjoy them, but the pursuit of pleasure should not be one's ultimate goal. Animals act only to satisfy their bodily drives. The dignity of man demands that his behavior be motivated by something more than gratifying one's animalistic drives.

This is why the Torah states, "I am your God" as a preface to the commandment not to engage in the practices of the Egyptians and the Canaanites. In order to reach God a Jew must live a thoroughly spiritual life. He must work, eat, sleep, socialize and recreate in a way that will bring him closer to God. He must elevate himself far above lower forms of life. The responsibility of the Jew is to achieve the true dignity of being human.

כְּמַעֲשֵׂה אֶרֶץ־מִצְרַיִם אֲשֶׁר יְשַׁבְתֶּם־בָּהּ לֹא תַעֲשׂוּ
וּכְמַעֲשֵׂה אֶרֶץ־כְּנַעַן אֲשֶׁר אֲנִי מֵבִיא אֶתְכֶם שָׁמָּה לֹא תַעֲשׂוּ
וּבְחֻקֹּתֵיהֶם לֹא תֵלֵכוּ אֶת־מִשְׁפָּטַי תַּעֲשׂוּ וְאֶת־חֻקֹּתַי תִּשְׁמְרוּ
לָלֶכֶת בָּהֶם אֲנִי ה' אֱלֹקֵיכֶם: וּשְׁמַרְתֶּם אֶת־חֻקֹּתַי וְאֶת־מִשְׁפָּטַי
אֲשֶׁר יַעֲשֶׂה אֹתָם הָאָדָם וָחַי בָּהֶם אֲנִי ה'

"Do not perform the practice of the land of Egypt in which you dwelled; and do not perform the practice of the land of Canaan to which I bring you, and do not follow their traditions. Carry out My laws and safeguard My decrees to follow them; I am your God. You shall observe My decrees and My laws, which man shall carry out and by which he shall live—I am God" (18:3-5)

The Absolute of Morality

These verses are somewhat strange, because they really say nothing new. We have already been specifically instructed about the various mitzvos. What is being added here?

There are various categories of mitzvos, including those that are completely beyond logical understanding, such as *shaatness* (the prohibition of combining linen with wool) or the mixing of meat and milk. There are other mitzvos which are perfectly understandable, such as the prohibition of stealing, murdering and lying. Obviously one who observes *shaatness* and *kashrus* is doing so because these are Divine commandments. However, when one abstains from stealing, killing or other objectionable acts, this may not be because of the Torah prohibition but because of the awareness that these are morally wrong.

The problem with the latter is that standards of morality that are based on human logic are precarious. The human mind is capable of rationalizing and modifying morality to meet a person's needs or desires. For example, just several decades ago, abortion was forbidden in this country and was looked upon as tantamount to murder. Today, it is not only permissible, but it is funded by taxpayers' money. In a relatively brief period of time, the pendulum has swung from something being considered criminal to its being a basic human right which the country should make available to every woman. It might be thought that this radical change is due to the country becoming more enlightened, but I believe that there is a hidden reason, which is being sanitized by an affectation of idealism.

There have been unprecedented medical and technologic advances in the past several decades. Prior to widespread immunization, antibiotics, corticosteroids and other "wonder drugs," prenatal care and the revolutionary surgical procedures, the average life span in the United States was in the forties. Infant mortality was high. *People were a necessary commodity for social survival.* There could be no consideration of "zero population growth" as desirable, because the commodity of human beings was of great value to the country. Prior to the proliferation of countless labor-saving devices, human energy was needed to produce all of our needs. Aborting a potential resource was a crime against society.

Immunization essentially eradicated the epidemic childhood diseases. Antibiotics brought the great killer, pneumonia, under control and closed every tuberculosis hospital in the country. More people survived into adulthood and lived much longer. Suddenly, a major concern was *overpopulation*. A bill was introduced into Congress to eliminate tax exemptions for more than two children. The human being was no longer a vital commodity. It was this change that permitted the change in attitude toward abortion. Destroying a vital commodity is bad, but destroying a non-vital commodity may not be bad.

To someone who believes in the inherent sanctity of human life and that it is not merely a commodity to be valued according to the marketplace laws of supply and demand, abortion is the same evil today that it was 100 years ago. The moral degeneration evident in people's personal behavior is another example of how human intelligence can modify anything to comply with human desires.

That a nation's morality can be corrupted is related in the stories of the sinful cities of Sodom and Gemorrah. But we do not have to reach back to ancient history for this phenomenon. In our own time, Nazi Germany acted upon its decision that destroying Jews was morally correct.

It is against this that the Torah warns us. There are indeed some mitzvos, laws, "which man shall carry out and by which he shall live," that are advantageous to society. One might wish to place the social commandments of Torah in this category, and tamper with them according to human understanding and intelligence. Therefore, God says, "You shall observe My decrees and My laws, because I am God Who dictates them, and not merely because you think they are right and proper. The latter concept might allow you to amend them as you see fit, whereas My laws are eternal and immutable."

Man's tampering with morality threatens to destroy humanity, as is evidenced by the AIDS epidemic. Hence, "Do not perform the practice of the land of Egypt in which you dwelled; and do not perform the practice of the land of Canaan to which I bring you," because in these countries, morality was dictated by human intelligence. Then, as is tragically true today, legislatures and courts were the authorities that set moral values. Rather, "You shall observe My decrees and My laws, which man shall carry out and *by which he shall live*—I am God." This is the only assurance of life.

אֶת־מִשְׁפָּטַי תַּעֲשׂוּ וְאֶת־חֻקֹּתַי תִּשְׁמְרוּ לָלֶכֶת בָּהֶם אֲנִי ה' אֱלֹקֵיכֶם וּשְׁמַרְתֶּם
אֶת־חֻקֹּתַי וְאֶת־מִשְׁפָּטַי אֲשֶׁר יַעֲשֶׂה אֹתָם הָאָדָם וָחַי בָּהֶם אֲנִי ה' אֱלֹקֵיכֶם

*"Carry out My laws and safeguard My decrees to follow them;
I am your God. You shall observe My decrees and My laws, which man
shall carry out and by which he shall live. I am your God"* (18:4-5)

Spiritual Progress

The Hebrew words translated here as "to follow them," *laleches bahem*, literally mean "to go in them." *Ksav Sofer* says that this is indeed the intention of the Torah, that one must constantly "go" and "proceed" in the mitzvos, and not remain static and stagnant.

The Talmud says that one mitzvah leads to another mitzvah, and one sin brings another sin in its wake (*Ethics of the Fathers* 4:2). Yet, we have seen that some people may do a mitzvah but do not follow it with other mitzvos. Putting on *tefillin* and davening are certainly mitzvos, but people do not necessarily proceed to do other mitzvos afterward.

Let us look at the context in which the Talmud makes the above statement. "*Run to perform even a minor mitzvah, and flee from sin*, because one mitzvah leads to another mitzvah, and one sin brings another sin in its wake." Perhaps the phenomenon that one mitzvah begets another is only when one "runs to perform it," i.e., when one diligently pursues the performance of a mitzvah. Any manner in which a mitzvah is done is indeed meritorious, but the unique characteristic of it leading to other mitzvos is only when it is actively pursued. While we certainly have a mitzvah when we put on *tefillin,* we cannot truthfully claim that we "pursue" this mitzvah. If someone asks for *tzedakah*, we give it, but how often do we run after someone to give *tzedakah?* This is true of other mitzvos as well. We may do them, but we do not often "pursue" them.

On the other hand, we do pursue ways in which to increase our earnings. If we were to hear of an opportunity to turn a handsome profit, we would very likely make every effort to realize this. If a promising business venture required travelling to a distant city, we would probably do so. We do not necessarily wait for business opportunities to knock at our door. Rather, we may actively pursue them.

Spiritual progress requires pursuit of mitzvos, because only then will one mitzvah lead to another. If we properly appreciated the value of mitzvos and realized that they are as essential to life as the money we earn, we would exert the same effort to acquire mitzvos as we do to acquire more money.

The two verses cited above state this principle. Carrying out the Divine commandments, *laleches bahem,* in a way that one will progress spiritually, that one mitzvah will lead to another, can come about only if "by which *he shall live*," i.e., if a person values them as one does his livelihood.

During the eight days of Passover, we do not don *tefillin*. After the close of the eighth day of Passover, R' Levi Yitzchok of Berditchev sat all night by the window, anxiously looking for the first sign of dawn, when he would be permitted to fulfill the mitzvah of *tefillin*. That is an example of "pursuing" a mitzvah. We can achieve spiritual growth, but not by waiting for spiritual opportunities to come to our door. If we exert ourselves in the pursuit of mitzvos, we will grow spiritually.

פרשת קדושים
Parashas Kedoshim

דַּבֵּר אֶל־כָּל־עֲדַת בְּנֵי־יִשְׂרָאֵל וְאָמַרְתָּ אֲלֵהֶם קְדֹשִׁים תִּהְיוּ

"Speak to the entire assembly of the Children of Israel and say to them, 'You shall be holy'" (19:2)

The Body of Torah

Rashi cites the Midrash that makes a bold statement: The reason this portion of Torah was delivered to the entire assembly of Israel is because it contains the greater part of the body of the Torah. In spite of the Talmudic admonition to be as diligent in performing a "minor" mitzvah as a "major" mitzvah because one cannot know the value of mitzvos (*Ethics of the Fathers* 2:1), the Midrash considers the mitzvos in this portion of the Torah to be most important.

The mitzvos in this portion of the Torah relate primarily to interpersonal relationships: respect of parents; providing for the poor; avoiding theft, deceit, lying, false oaths, withholding a worker's wage, giving improper advice, showing favoritism in judicial decisions; carrying tales, harboring resentments, seeking revenge; being as considerate of others as one is of oneself. These mitzvos constitute the "greater part of the body of the Torah."

In *Deuteronomy* (7:12) Rashi cites the Midrash that the Divine rewards will come primarily for observance of the commandments that people may regard as relatively unimportant, which they figuratively "tread on with their heels." Our ethicists repeatedly bewail the phenomenon that some people are most scrupulous about the ritual mitzvos, but may take liberties with improper business practices, *lashon hara* (defamatory speech), taking revenge or harboring resentments.

When I lecture regarding the problem of spouse abuse, someone points out that there are some Torah observant people who are abusive to their spouses. I respond that this is impossible, because a person who is abusive to one's spouse is in frank violation of Torah, and cannot be considered to be Torah observant any more than a person who eats *tereifah* or violates Shabbos.

We must rid ourselves of the erroneous idea that Torah observance is primarily of ritual nature. The Midrash cited by Rashi leaves no room for any argument. This portion of the Torah, which contains the mitzvos regulating interpersonal behavior, constitutes the "greater part of the body of Torah."

אִישׁ אִמּוֹ וְאָבִיו תִּירָאוּ וְאֶת־שַׁבְּתֹתַי תִּשְׁמֹרוּ

***Your mother and father you shall revere,
and My Sabbaths you shall observe*** (19:3)

Reverence for Parents

The Talmud interprets the juxtaposition of these two commandments to mean that although one must honor one's parents, one may not comply with their instruction to commit a transgression, such as to violate Shabbos.

There is also another message herein. Although one may not commit a sin at a parent's behest, one must nevertheless be respectful in one's refusal. Halachah says that in such instances one should say, "But father, does not the Torah say otherwise?"

This halachah is of special importance today. There are families who are not observant of mitzvos whose child has become a *baal teshuvah*. The son or daughter can no longer share in non-kosher meals or in activities on Shabbos. Some parents react with anger and object to the child's becoming observant. Sometimes it is because they think that Torah observance is obsolete and irrational, and sometimes it is because they see it as a rejection of their values. The child's choice of a lifestyle different from theirs is taken as a personal affront. In many instances they forget that *their* parents were observant, and that they had rejected their parents' lifestyle.

Regardless of the reason for the parents' objection, one must know that in adopting a Torah lifestyle, one must abide by halachah, including the halachah that one must retain reverence for one's parents even when there is a sharp disagreement. There is no halachah that requires that the parents speak respectfully to their children, although this is highly desirable. If parents berate a child and criticize his Torah observance, the child must remember that this does not exempt him from respecting his parents, and his disagreement with them must be with an attitude of respect.

Unfortunately, there is not much one can do when the parents' objections are an ego issue. However, if parents see that Torah observance requires that their child must respect them, their attitude toward this lifestyle may become more favorable.

לֹא־תָלִין פְּעֻלַּת שָׂכִיר

***You shall not withhold a
worker's wage*** (19:13)

Tzedakah Does Not Negate Obligations

R' Zusia of Anipole lived in dire poverty, but was always in a cheerful mood. When asked, "How can you recite the blessing thanking God for providing you with all your needs, when you are so sorely lacking?" R' Zusia responded, "God knows what my needs are better than I do. He knows that one of my needs is poverty."

One time, R' Zusia's wife told him that she was ashamed to be seen by her neighbors wearing the same dress all the time, and asked him for money for a new dress. R' Zusia saved kopek after kopek until he *eventually accumulated enough money for a new dress. Happily, his wife ran off to the tailor to have a dress sewn.*

When she went to get the dress, R' Zusia's wife noticed that the tailor was dejected. He told her that his daughter was soon to be married, and that he could not afford to make her a dress. "My daughter was here yesterday," the tailor said, "and when she saw this dress, she assumed I had made it for her. When I told her that it was for someone else, she began crying. I am heartbroken for her." R' Zusia's wife was overcome with pity for the young woman and said, "Please, give the dress to your daughter. My husband will care for me even if I do not have a new dress."

When the wife told R' Zusia about this, he praised her for the great act of tzedakah that she had done, gladdening the heart of a bride-to-be. Then he said, "Did you pay the tailor for his work?"

"Pay him?" she asked. "Why, I let him have the dress! Why should I pay him?"

R' Zusia said, "When you engaged the tailor to sew the dress for you, you became obligated to pay him for his work. He did his job faithfully, and he deserves his wage. You then made a decision to give the dress away. It makes no difference whether you had taken the dress, given it to someone else or given it to the tailor himself. He relied on that income to feed his family, and your act of tzedakah does not free you of your obligation to pay him for his work."

Our great *tzaddikim* had a Torah perspective. The logic of halachah supersedes our own logic.

לֹא־תַעֲשׂוּ עָוֶל בַּמִּשְׁפָּט
You shall not commit a perversion of justice (19:15)

The Perversion of Justice

R' Simchah Bunim of P'shis'che said that this means, "Do not pass unjust laws, because these pervert justice."

R' Simchah Bunim's interpretation was meant for our time. Our society is in great danger of approaching the degeneracy of Sodom and Gomorrah. Had these cities merely been sinful, they would not have been destroyed. God is ever patient and would have given them the opportunity to correct their ways. What sealed the doom of Sodom and Gomorrah was that they had a corrupt standard of justice. They had legalized every crime and every perversion. Inasmuch as corrupt behavior was legally sanctioned, there was no possibility of *teshuvah*.

It is not difficult to rationalize. "You will never stop people from gambling, so let us legalize gambling. You will never stop people from using drugs, so let us legalize drugs." One may even make a convincing argument that legalizing drugs would significantly lower crime. We must be wary of this tendency. If something is ethically and morally wrong, it cannot become right by an act of the legislature.

In prohibiting a judge from taking a bribe, the Torah says, "A bribe will blind the eyes of the wise and make just words crooked" (*Deuteronomy* 16:19). Rashi states that if a judge accepts a bribe, it is impossible for him to remain objective. This is as true of society as a whole as it is of a judge. We may be "bribed" by desires we have. It is only natural for people to seek comfort and convenience. We must realize that our desire for comfort and convenience may influence our thoughts and judgments. If we feel, for example, that legalization of drugs will relieve society of crime, we may be "bribed" to think that this is right, and give little thought to moral and ethical considerations. When Nazi Germany decided that the elimination of Jews was to its advantage, killing Jews became morally acceptable and was legalized.

Morality and ethics are absolute. They do not change with time, place or condition. We must be careful that we do not rationalize to pervert justice.

הוֹכֵחַ תּוֹכִיחַ אֶת־עֲמִיתֶךָ

You shall reprove your fellow (19:17)

Everyone Needs Discipline

The Talmud says that Jerusalem was destroyed because they "did not give reproof to one another" (*Shabbos* 119).

The author of *Binah Leltim* points out that the ones who give reproof are, of course, the spiritual leaders. Then "one another" means that the spiritual leaders did not give reproof to each other. They chastised the lay public, but failed to give admonishment to each other.

No human being is free of character defects, and it is axiomatic that we are blind to our own faults. The most spiritual of all people may be in need of having his shortcomings called to his attention. Some *tzaddikim* were known to have specifically hired someone to give them reproof.

> *It is difficult to think of anyone more spiritual than the great Gaon of Vilna. Knowing that no one would dare rebuke him, he appealed to R' Yaakov Krantz, the Maggid of Dubnow, to give him reproof. But what defect could one possibly find in the great Gaon? The Maggid said to him, "You are a tzaddik because you have secluded yourself and study Torah all day. You are never exposed to any situation where one is tempted to sin. That is no trick. Anyone can be a tzaddik if he does that. Let me see you go out to the marketplace and mingle with people. If you will be a tzaddik then, that is some trick."*
>
> *The gaon humbly accepted this chastisement, but then commented, "So who says I have to be a trickster?"*

If people of the caliber of the Gaon felt that they needed reproof, what can anyone less than that say? Yet some people are offended if they are criticized. This labels them as unwise, because Solomon says, "Admonish a wise man and he will love you" (*Proverbs* 9:8).

> *When R' Yehudah Aryeh of Gur (Sfas Emes) was a youngster, he once stayed up all night studying Torah. He went to bed only shortly before*

dawn, and when he did not awaken at daybreak, his grandfather (Chiddushei HaRim) reprimanded him. The young Yehudah Aryeh accept the reprimand silently. Later, a friend asked him, "Why did you not tell your grandfather that you had been up all night studying Torah?" R' Yehudah Aryeh said, "What! And lose the opportunity to receive reprimand from my grandfather?"

R' Yehudah Aryeh cited the reprimand that Moses gave to the tribes of Gad and Reuven, because he had understood that they wished to shirk their duties in the conquest of Canaan. They explained to Moses that this was not at all their intention. "Why did they accept the rebuke?" R' Yehudah Arye asked. "They could have made their intentions clear to Moses." He answered, "They remained silent because they knew that it was a golden opportunity to receive reproof from Moses, and they did not wish to lose it. So it is with me and my grandfather."

Solomon rightly said, "Admonish a wise man and he will love you."

לֹא־תִשְׂנָא אֶת־אָחִיךָ בִּלְבָבֶךָ . . . לֹא־תִקֹּם וְלֹא־תִטֹּר

You shall not hate your brother in your heart
. . . You shall not take revenge
and you shall not bear a grudge (19:17-18)

The Folly of Resentments

The translation of *lo sitor* as "you shall not bear a grudge" is rather incomplete. Rashi explains that *lo sikom* means that one should not take active revenge, whereas an example of *lo sitor* is when the person who refused to lend you his axe asks to borrow your saw. Refusing to lend it to him is a violation of *lo sikom*. Lending it to him and saying, "You may have my saw, even though you do not deserve it. You refused to lend me your axe when I needed it, but I am not like you." *Lo sitor* is more than bearing a grudge. It is *acting* on the feeling.

One may ask, "How can the Torah command me not to hate someone? This person offended or harmed me. How does the Torah expect me to control my feelings toward him? It is enough that I control my actions, but I have no control over my feelings."

Let me share with you something that I learned from treating alcoholics. At one meeting of recovered alcoholics, one man described how he was dealt with unfairly. "But I must divest myself of my resentments, because if I do not, it will lead me to drink again." Someone suggested, "These people could not care less how you feel toward them. They will not lose sleep or get headaches or indigestion. *You* will be the one who will have these symptoms. What sense does it make to punish yourself for *their* bad behavior?" Another person said, "Harboring a resentment is allowing someone whom you don't like to live inside your head without paying rent." The logic of these statements is irrefutable.

If a person were permitted to act on a grudge, one might argue that there might be a purpose in harboring a resentment. "Just wait! The time will come when he will need a favor from me. I'll show him that I am a *mentsch*, not a scoundrel like him." Inasmuch as the Torah forbids this by the admonition *lo sitor*, there is simply

VAYIKRA / LEVITICUS: Kedoshim

no way that one can ever implement taking action on a grudge. It is, therefore, not only a useless feeling, but also one that takes its toll on a person. The recovered alcoholic was right. It is utter folly to punish yourself for someone else's misdeed.

This is what Solomon meant. "Anger lingers in the bosom of a fool" (*Ecclesiastes* 7:9). You may not have had any choice about *feeling* anger when you were provoked or offended, but if you allow that anger to linger on and become a grudge, that is indeed foolish. We now have the answer to the question, How can the Torah demand of me not to hate someone who has offended me? The answer is that inasmuch as you may not take any action on that hate, harboring it will hurt no one except yourself, and you would hardly want to do that.

The sequence of the verses in the Torah is clear. "You shall not hate your brother in your heart … You shall not take revenge and you shall not bear a grudge." If you observe the latter, your good judgment will allow you to rid yourself of self-defeating hate.

לֹא־תִשְׂנָא אֶת־אָחִיךָ בִּלְבָבֶךָ . . . וְאָהַבְתָּ לְרֵעֲךָ כָּמוֹךָ

You shall not hate your brother in your heart … You shall love your fellow as yourself (19:17-18)

Preserve a Fraternal Relationship

My father's study was often the setting for his adjudication of disputes. One time I heard much shouting emitting from his study. When I asked him what the furor was all about, he said that there were four brothers who were wrangling over the division of their father's estate. The dispute had become so heated that they had developed a venomous hatred toward each other.

"I now understand something that has always perplexed me," my father said. "Why, in regard to a brother, does the Torah say, 'Do not hate him,' whereas in regard to a stranger, the Torah says 'Love your fellow as yourself.' Now I see why. There may be times when brothers argue over a father's estate. The Torah says, 'Perhaps I cannot expect you to love your brother under these circumstances, but at least do not hate him.'"

It is unfortunate that such incidents occur. Family relationships are sometimes shattered because of wrangling over an inheritance. The Torah therefore pleads, "Do not let such quibbling turn into hatred of a brother."

וְאָהַבְתָּ לְרֵעֲךָ כָּמוֹךָ

You shall love your fellow as yourself (19:18)

The All-Encompassing Principle

Earlier we noted Rashi's comment explaining that this portion of the Torah was addressed to the entire assembly of Israel because it contains the greater part of the body of Torah. It is possible that "contains the greater part of the body of Torah" refers to the above verse. Indeed, R' Akiva said that this verse is "the all-encompassing principle of Torah" (*Jerusalem Talmud, Nedarim* 9:4).

R' Akiva's statement is sometimes translated as, "This verse is the *cardinal* or *primary* rule of Torah." This is an inaccurate translation. R' Akiva's words are that this is a *klal gadol*, which means "a great, all-encompassing principle" of Torah, and this has a broad implication.

A *klal* is a general principle under which there are many *pratim* (specifics). Each specific item must have the characteristic of the *klal*. If any specific item does not have the characteristic of the *klal*, then it does not belong there. For example, "animate objects" is a *klal*. A rock lacks the characteristic of animation, hence it cannot be classified under that *klal*.

One of the ethicists said that inasmuch as "You shall love your fellow as yourself" is the "great *klal*" of Torah, this means that it encompasses all 613 mitzvos, and that each mitzvah must partake of the characteristic of the *klal*. Every mitzvah must relate to *ahavas Yisrael* (love for a fellow Jew), and must contribute to *ahavas Yisrael*. Therefore, he concludes, if a person does not have an increase in *ahavas Yisrael* after the performance of a mitzvah, that mitzvah was not done properly. A properly performed mitzvah *must* contribute to *ahavas Yisrael*.

This statement was nothing less than shocking. I had considered some mitzvos I had done as being properly performed. My *tefillin* are top quality, and there were at least some times when I had proper *kavannah* (concentration). The matzah I ate at the *seder* was of the highest quality *shmurah* (supervision). The sounding of the shofar that I heard on Rosh Hashanah was without fault, and the *esrog* (citron) that I used for the mitzvah of the four species on Succos was free of the slightest blemish. I felt I had fulfilled these mitzvos properly. But I must confess that I did not feel an increase in *ahavas Yisrael* after these mitzvos. The argument that R' Akiva's *klal* necessitates *ahavas Yisrael* as an ingredient in every mitzvah is unassailable. Where was I lacking?

It then occurred to me that I was overlooking something I say in davening every day. Is it not tragic that we may verbalize without thinking about what we are saying?

Prior to the opening prayer, *Baruch She'amar*, there is a short Kabbalistic declaration of intent that includes the phrase, "I pray in the name of all Israel." This is not the same as praying *for* Israel, which we do abundantly in the *Amidah* and other prayers. Rather, this is a declaration of intent that I am not praying alone, but that I wish to share my prayer with all Israel. Whatever merits accrue from my prayer are not exclusively mine, but belong to all Israel.

I found this same declaration of intent preceding the mitzvos of putting on the *tallis* and *tefillin* and the Counting of the Omer. Further research revealed that it is recommended that this declaration is recited prior to every mitzvah one performs.

If there were true unity among Jews, this declaration would not be necessary. Just as the mitzvah of shofar accrues to the entire person rather than just to the ear, so would the mitzvah of every Jew accrue to the credit of all Jews *if they were united as one body*. Alas, that highly desirable state does not exist, so we must make a declaration that we wish to share the mitzvah with all of Israel. Of course, *all* of Israel means without exception, and indeed, *ahavas Yisrael* should be without exception.

R' Eliyahu Dessler says that there is a common misconception that you give to whomever you love. The reverse is true: you love to whomever you give. When you give to someone, you invest part of yourself in him, and since every person loves himself, you now love that part of you that resides in the other person (*Michtav MeEliyahu* vol. 1 p. 36).

If we listen to the words we say and are sincere, then we can fulfill R' Akiva's principle. By sharing our mitzvos with others, we can generate *ahavas Yisrael*.

וְאָהַבְתָּ לְרֵעֲךָ כָּמוֹךָ אֲנִי ה'

You shall love your fellow as yourself, I am God (19:18)

As Yourself

When the proselyte asked Hillel to condense the entire Torah and teach it to him in the brief time that he could stand on one foot, Hillel said, " 'You shall love your fellow as yourself,' that is the essence of Torah. All the rest is commentary." Given the centrality of this verse, it is not unusual that it has been given numerous interpretations. Let us look at some of them.

The Baal Shem Tov said that just as you love yourself in spite of your shortcomings, so you should love another person in spite of his shortcomings.

On the verse, "God is your shade at your right hand" (*Psalms* 121:5), the Baal Shem Tov commented that just as a person's shadow mimics his every move, so God acts toward a person the way that person acts toward others. Therefore, he said that the verse can also be read as, "You shall love your fellow, because I, God, will be like you." If you will be forgiving to others, I will be forgiving to you. If you will insist on exacting unrelenting justice, I will do likewise to you.

Arvei Nachal writes if another person is in the same business as you, you may feel that he is a competitor, and that may cause you to dislike him. Therefore, the Torah emphasizes, "You shall love your fellow *who is* as yourself."

> R' Yisroel of Rizhin said that there were two people who were devoted friends. One was falsely accused of treason and was sentenced to death. The friend intervened, saying, "He is innocent! Free him! It was I, not he, who committed the treason, and it is I who should be executed, not he." The other friend said, "Don't believe him! He is just trying to protect me. I was the traitor." When the king heard of this, he said that someone who is willing to give up his life for another person could not be guilty of treason, and he freed the man. He then called both friends and said, "I have never seen such a devoted friendship. Take me into your circle. I wish to be part of such a selfless relationship."
>
> "This is the meaning of the verse," R' Yisroel said. "If you love your fellow as yourself, then I, God, wish to be in a relationship with you."

מִפְּנֵי שֵׂיבָה תָּקוּם וְהָדַרְתָּ פְּנֵי זָקֵן

In the presence of an old person shall you rise, and you shall honor the presence of a sage (19:32)

The Wisdom of Age

The manifest mitzvah is to show respect for the elderly and the learned. R' Pinchas Horowitz (*Haflaah*) said that this verse has additional meaning.

The secular and the Torah views on the origin of man are widely divergent. Secular science sees man as having evolved from lower forms of life. This concept leads to the conclusion that mankind has been progressing, and that we are an improvement over our ancestors. It came as no surprise, then, when the generation of the '60s openly advocated rejecting the advice of anyone over the age of 35. Wisdom rests in youth, who are more advanced than their parents.

The Torah perspective is the polar opposite. Each ensuing generation is a bit more removed from the generation that stood at Sinai and heard the voice of God. Each ensuing generation is less authoritative on Torah matters. After the closing of the Mishnah, the next era of Torah scholars could interpret the Mishnah, but could not argue against it. After the Talmud was sealed, halachic authorities might favor the position of one of the rabbinic disputants, but could not argue against a Talmudic ruling. This pattern has continued to the present. Earlier Torah scholars are more authoritative than those who follow them.

"Every person is required to say, 'When can my deeds equal those of my ancestors?'" (*Tanna D'bei Eliyahu Rabbah* 28). We may have much more advanced technology than our ancestors, and we may be more advanced in *how* to live, but our ancestors were wiser in knowing more about the *why* of life. We may be more advanced in the means of life, but they were more advanced in the goals of life. Computers, microwaves and jet travel notwithstanding, our ancestors had a better grasp on the value of time than we do.

Respecting and honoring the elderly goes farther than offering them your seat on the bus. It also means that we should respect their Torah values.

כְּאֶזְרָח מִכֶּם יִהְיֶה לָכֶם הַגֵּר הַגָּר אִתְּכֶם וְאָהַבְתָּ לוֹ כָּמוֹךָ
The proselyte who dwells with you shall be like a native among you, and you shall love him like yourself (19:34)

A Tragic Violation

Rashi cites the Talmud which says that it is forbidden to say to a proselyte, "Just a while ago you were worshipping idols and eating *tereifah,* and now you want to participate in the Torah that was given to us by God" (*Bava Metzia* 59b). R' Yeruchem Levovitz that says the acceptance of a proselyte is not a matter of courtesy. It is required by Torah, and rejecting a proselyte is a violation of a Torah commandment.

The Chafetz Chaim says that *lashon hara* is not limited to speech. A derogatory gesture is also *lashon hara.* Similarly, one transgresses the Torah commandment not only when one *verbally* reminds a proselyte of his past, but also when one does so by one's behavior.

If the Torah forbids provoking anguish of a proselyte, how much more so is it forbidden to remind a *baal teshuvah* of his non-observant past. Indeed, we are explicitly prohibited from telling a *baal teshuvah,* "Remember your sinful behavior" (see *Chafetz Chaim* 4:1).

Alas! Some people who are observant of everything else in the Torah may be derelict in observing this commandment. Any number of *baalei teshuvah* have said, "You exerted much effort to be *mekarev* me (make me Torah observant), but when it comes to a *shidduch*, I am often rejected because of having once been non-observant. Where is 'Love your fellow as yourself? Where is 'Love the proselyte like yourself?'" This is a serious indictment.

Some people may contend that they are uncertain of the sincerity of a *baal teshuvah's* commitment. This is hardly valid when the young man or woman has shown themselves to be dedicated to Torah observance for years.

The acceptance of a *baal teshuvah* is not a matter of courtesy. R' Yeruchem reminds us that it is a Scriptural mitzvah, no different than *tefillin*.

וִהְיִיתֶם לִי קְדֹשִׁים כִּי קָדוֹשׁ אֲנִי ה' וָאַבְדִּל אֶתְכֶם מִן־הָעַמִּים לִהְיוֹת לִי

"You shall be holy for Me, for I, God, am holy; and I have separated you from the [other] peoples to be Mine" (20:26)

Assimilation Is the Problem, Not the Solution

R' Chaim of Volozhin's comment on this verse was prophetic. "If you will be holy unto Me, then I will separate you from other peoples. If you transgress the Torah and are not holy unto Me, then *the other peoples will separate you from them*" (*MeShulchan Govoha, Vayikra* p.175).

Some people, distressed by anti-Semitism, think that if Jews would shed their religious practices and adopt the customs and practices of their non-Jewish neighbors, this would eliminate anti-Semitism. How wrong they are! People who carry hatred for Jews do not want them in their midst. They do not want them to marry their sons and daughters. They do not feel threatened by those Jews who would never consider fraternization or intermarriage.

A Jewish organization fought to have the "Restricted" clauses eliminated from country clubs and hotels. "Restricted" meant that Jews were not welcome. Just a bit of thought would indicate that they were not trying to bar those Jews who observe kosher. The latter would not join a *tereifah* country club or vacation in a *tereifah* hotel if they were invited and hosted free of charge! What would a *kashrus*-observant Jew do in a place where he cannot partake of any food or drink? The "Restricted" clause was intended to exclude those Jews who had abandoned the observance of kosher.

History has proven that assimilation does not diminish persecution. The most assimilated country, Germany, was the origin of the Holocaust.

If we will be true to Torah, God will see to it that we remain distinct without harm befalling us.

פרשת אמור
Parashas Emor

וְקִדַּשְׁתּוֹ כִּי־אֶת־לֶחֶם אֱלֹקֶיךָ הוּא מַקְרִיב
קָדֹשׁ יִהְיֶה־לָּךְ כִּי קָדוֹשׁ אֲנִי ה' מְקַדִּשְׁכֶם

"You shall sanctify him (the Kohen), for he offers the food of your God; he shall remain holy to you, for holy am I, God, Who sanctifies you" (21:8)

Reverence, Yes; Worship, No

It is of interest that wherever the Torah refers to the sanctity of the *Kohen*, it says, "For I am God Who makes *him* holy" (21:16, 22:9, 22:16). The exception is in the above verse which dictates that we revere the *Kohen* for his holiness, and closes with, "For holy am I, God, Who sanctifies *you*." Inasmuch as it speaks about the sanctity of the *Kohen,* it would appear to be more appropriate to say, "Who sanctifies *him*" as it does elsewhere, rather than, "Who sanctifies *you.*"

What we have here is a Torah guideline to help us avoid a serious error. We must be very careful how we relate to our spiritual leaders. There is a healthy, constructive attitude, but there can also be an unhealthy attitude.

We must, of course, have spiritual leaders. The Talmud says, "Accept a teacher upon yourself" (*Ethics of the Fathers* 1:6). This is binding on everyone. No person, not even a learned person, should be without an authoritative Torah guide. We are very vulnerable to be biased by personal interests that may distort our judgment. But although we must revere our spiritual leaders, we must be cautious that we do not deify or worship them.

There is a healthy attachment to a teacher or spiritual leader, but it is not beyond the possibility that, as a result of one's psychological needs, a person may turn such a relationship into "hero worship," akin to the cult phenomenon which has unfortunately lured some young Jews.

I believe that hero worship is the consequence of a lack of self-esteem. Many people have unwarranted feelings of low self-esteem. The feeling of unworthiness is an intensely painful emotion. I elaborated on this in *Angels Don't Leave Footprints* and *Let Us Make Man*, describing a number of ways in which people may seek relief from this agony.

The dynamics of hero worship are quite simple. If I view myself as being unworthy and having little redeeming value, I may seek relief from this feeling by attaching myself to someone whom I think of as having great value. By identifying with that person and feeling myself to be one with him, I, too, can have value. This attachment may be reinforced if the hero is a person who seeks aggrandizement and encourages such attachment. The attachment to the hero may be so strong that the person allows himself to be totally controlled by him. This is not the same as accepting guidance from a spiritual leader, but rather a total surrender of oneself.

I suspect that something like this may have occurred in the episode of the worship of the Golden Calf. Our sages tell us that it was the *eirev rav*, the Egyptians who accompanied the Israelites in the Exodus, who were responsible for the Golden Calf. These people had been idolaters and had no concept of an abstract God. They had formed a "Moses cult," and when they thought Moses had died, they replaced him with an idol.

The best prevention against developing hero worship is a healthy self-esteem. There should be no need of so desperate a defensive maneuver as to fuse oneself with a hero and lose one's identity. Having a feeling of worthiness can forestall such a pathological identification.

This may be the message in the verses cited in regard to the *Kohen*. He should be respected and revered because God has sanctified him. However, we should remember that our self-worth does not emanate from the *Kohen*. Rather, it comes from God; "for holy am I, God, Who sanctifies *you*." We have great value independent of the *Kohen*, because God has sanctified us and has instilled a *neshamah*, a part of His essence, within us. We, therefore, identify with God, rather than with a flesh and blood person, and we should have no need for hero worship.

וּבָא הַשֶּׁמֶשׁ וְטָהֵר וְאַחַר יֹאכַל מִן־הַקֳּדָשִׁים כִּי לַחְמוֹ הוּא

After the sun has set, he shall become purified; thereafter he may eat from the holies, for it is his food (22:7)

The Essence of Teshuvah

The Torah is referring here to a *Kohen* who has become *tamei* (ritually impure), who is not permitted to eat *terumah* (the tithe) until he has purified himself. The Hebrew reads, *ve'achar*, afterward, he may eat the tithe. R' Yehoshua Trunk of Kutna said that *ve'achar* may also mean "another," in which case the verse reads, "*another* may eat the holy food." After going through purification, the *Kohen* should be *another* person, not the same person he was before.

This is an important lesson in *teshuvah*, as Rambam states (*Hilchos Teshuvah* 2:4), that the penitent must be able to say, "I am a different person. I am no longer the person who committed the sin."

This enables us to understand another statement of Rambam that poses some difficulty for commentaries. In *Hilchos Teshuvah* 2:2 Rambam states that the degree of *teshuvah* must reach the point where God will testify that the person will no longer repeat the sin. This raises a question. Inasmuch as a person at all times has free will insofar as good and evil is concerned, and God does not control a person's moral behavior, how is it possible that God will testify that the person will never again repeat the sin? This is incompatible with the principle that a person always has a free choice to do right or wrong. The classic example is the High Priest Yochanan, who, after eighty years of faithful service, defected to the Saducees. It cannot be said with certainty of anyone that he will never sin again.

In order to understand Rambam's statement, we must realize that given a person's level of spirituality, there are some things that he is simply incapable of doing. For example, imagine a devoted Torah scholar who arises at dawn to study Torah, immerses in the mikvah, prays for two hours with great *kavannah* (concentration) and follows this with Torah study; this person is not going to stop at a fast food chain for a cheeseburger. The possibility of his eating *tereifah* is not within reality. However, it is conceivable that someone may tell him something about another person that is *lashon hara*, and that he may listen to it. Listening to *lashon hara* is as grievous a sin as speaking it. How is it that although it is impossible for him to eat *tereifah*, it is possible that he may listen to *lashon hara*? The answer is that although he is at a level of spirituality that makes eating *tereifah* an impossibility, he does not have the degree of spirituality that would make listening to *lashon hara* as impossible as eating *tereifah*.

If this person realizes that he committed a sin by listening to *lashon hara*, sincerely regrets it and resolves to never listen to *lashon hara* again, his *teshuvah*, says Rambam, is inadequate. Resolving not to do something is not enough. The person must do whatever it takes to elevate his level of spirituality to the point where listening to *lashon hara* is as impossible as eating *tereifah*. He will then have undergone a change in character, so that *he is no longer the same person as the one who listened to lashon hara.* He will be able to say, as Rambam requires, "I am a different person. I am no longer the person who committed the sin."

A person's *teshuvah* is complete when he has achieved this level of spirituality. God may indeed testify that *at this level of spirituality*, the person is no longer capable of committing the sin. It is, however, possible that the person may fall from this spiritual level, and if that occurs, he may indeed commit the sin again. God is not testifying that the person will not commit the sin again. That is a matter of free choice. What God is attesting to is that his *teshuvah* has elevated him to a spiritual level, which, *as long as he maintains it*, will preclude his committing the sin again.

This, according to R' Yehoshua Trunk of Kutna, is what the Torah is telling us. The process of purification should not be perfunctory. Rather, it should lead to the *Kohen* undergoing a change in character, attaining a higher level of spirituality, so that he is no longer the same person. This is what the Torah means by, "*another may eat the holy food.*"

Of course, this lesson is not restricted to a *Kohen*. Every person who regrets having committed a misdeed should seek to enhance his spirituality to the point where the inappropriate act is no longer a possibility.

וְכִי־תִזְבְּחוּ זֶבַח־תּוֹדָה לַה' לִרְצֹנְכֶם תִּזְבָּחוּ
When you slaughter a thanksgiving offering to God, you shall slaughter it to gain favor for yourselves (22:29)

The Mystery of Suffering

The Hebrew text lends itself to an additional translation: "When you slaughter a thanksgiving offering to God, you shall slaughter it with your full will" (*Ksav Sofer*).

Thanksgiving (*todah*) offerings were brought by a person who survived danger. In psalm 107, King David mentions four conditions which obligate a person to express his gratitude to God: deliverance from the dangers that beset those who travel through the wilderness; deliverance from imprisonment, from illness and from the perils of the sea.

While a person who survived danger may indeed be grateful, his gratitude may be somewhat muted because he may feel that God could have prevented the danger. A person who recovers from illness is indeed grateful, but may think, "I'd rather that God had prevented me from suffering in the first place." This gratitude is not felt with one's entire heart.

Although we may not understand why there is suffering, and we certainly do not need to justify God, we may be able to see what can be gained from suffering.

Suffering is something that enhances communication among people, brings them together and allows some of their finest character traits to emerge. Most people do not share much of their lives with others, except perhaps with close family members. But when misfortune occurs, people who did not know or care about the existence of others suddenly come forth, extending themselves in every possible way to be of help. We have seen the scenes after tornadoes or floods ruined people's homes. People seem to suddenly materialize to offer help. Where were they before the disaster occurred? Why, they were minding their own business, and when we mind our own business we are isolated from each other. Suffering makes us realize that there is something more to life than minding one's own business. We become caring, sensitive people.

Suffering may be a wakeup call for a person who is so busy going through the motions of living that he never stops to think what is the meaning of his life. I addressed this issue in *Light at the End of the Tunnel*. Many people who experienced suffering have said that their values had changed radically. Things that were once important have diminished in importance, whereas things that had been neglected become significant.

Suffering may enhance a person's prayer and bring one closer to God. It may shake a person loose from his conviction that he is the master of his own life. It may bring him face to face with his mortality. Suffering may bring out strengths that a person never knew he had.

Because suffering is so painful, it is understandable that we may try to render ourselves numb to it. However, if we succeed in doing so, we have not only blocked ourselves from feeling pain, but from other feelings as well. We may anesthetize our whole feeling system, and not be able to feel love, joy or compassion for others.

Although we would rather do without suffering, we should not overlook what we may gain from it. This is why the Talmud says that a person must praise God for the bad as well as for the good. The benefits we derive from suffering are a gift, and although we would rather have received the gift in more pleasant wrappings, a gift is a gift and we should acknowledge it.

This is what *Ksav Sofer* meant with his interpretation of the verse, "When you slaughter a thanksgiving offering to God, you shall slaughter it with your *full* will." When we are delivered from danger, the suffering we experienced should not detract from our gratitude. We should be grateful for our deliverance, and also for what we gained from suffering.

וְלֹא תְחַלְּלוּ אֶת־שֵׁם קָדְשִׁי וְנִקְדַּשְׁתִּי בְּתוֹךְ בְּנֵי יִשְׂרָאֵל

"You shall not desecrate My holy Name, rather I should be sanctified among the Children of Israel" (22:32)

Dearer than Life

This verse is the source of the mitzvah of *kiddush Hashem*, which is that a person should accept martyrdom rather than deny God. Unfortunately, this mitzvah has too often been fulfilled in Jewish history. Jews have given up their lives when put to the ultimate test of their faith.

Although *kiddush Hashem* is generally thought of as martyrdom, one does not have to give up one's life to fulfill this mitzvah. Anytime that a Jew behaves in a manner that brings honor to God, and people can point to him saying, "That is the beauty of obeying the Torah," that is a *kiddush Hashem*.

We are required to think of *kiddush Hashem* every time we recite the *Shema*. This *mesiras nefesh*, willingness to give up one's life rather than deny God, is required of every Jew, not just a *tzaddik*.

A philosopher said, "If there is nothing for which a person would give up his life, then life has no value." I developed this theme in *Dearer than Life*. It helps understand why *mesiras nefesh* is so important in Judaism.

The chassidic master of Karlin said, "No act can be true, if it is without *mesiras nefesh*." This is a rather odd statement. According to halachah, we are required to meditate on *mesiras nefesh* only when reciting the *Shema*. What does it mean that everything we do should involve *mesiras nefesh*?

For any act to have meaning and value, it must have a purpose. For life to have meaning and value, it must be purposeful. Everything a person does consciously has a purpose. Even if nothing tangible results from an act, as when one moves one's arms and legs in exercise, there is nevertheless a purpose to the act, whether to strengthen one's muscles, lose weight or improve a skill. Rational people do not do things that have no purpose.

A person cannot feel his life has much value if it has no purpose. Life is a means to whatever end one has adopted. If there is nothing that is worth more than life, then the *means*, which is *living*, takes on a greater value than the end. This is essentially an internal contradiction. For life to have meaning and value, there must be something important enough for which a person would surrender his life.

This is the concept of *mesiras nefesh*, and this is what the Rebbe of Karlin meant. If an act is not part of an ultimate purpose for which a person would have *mesiras nefesh,* the act has little meaning.

For the Jew, the ultimate purpose should be to do the will of God. If one has *mesiras nefesh* for this, it gives great meaning and substance to all the mitzvos.

בַּחֲמִשָּׁה עָשָׂר יוֹם לַחֹדֶשׁ הַשְּׁבִיעִי . . . תָּחֹגּוּ אֶת־חַג־ה' . . . וּשְׂמַחְתֶּם לִפְנֵי ה' אֱלֹקֵיכֶם שִׁבְעַת יָמִים

On the fifteenth day of the seventh month you shall celebrate a festival before God and you shall rejoice before God for a seven-day period (23:39-40)

True Simchah

In this portion of the Torah we are instructed to celebrate the Festivals. The above verse is about the festival of Succos, and we are told to rejoice. It is significant that the Torah emphasizes the joy of Succos twice more, in *Deuteronomy* 16:14 and 16. What is so special about Succos that it is singled out for joy?

True, Succos comes at the end of the harvest, when the abundant crops brought in from the field can certainly provide a feeling of happiness. However, it is unlikely that the Torah would emphasize the joy over material riches.

The *succah* is a temporary dwelling, usually dismantled after the festival is over. As such, it serves as a reminder that our stay on the earth is a temporary one. Our permanent home is in the Eternal World.

> *A wealthy businessman who visited the Chafetz Chaim was surprised to see that the sage lived in such sparse quarters, and he offered to pay for more spacious and comfortable quarters.*
>
> *The Chafetz Chaim asked him, "What is your home like?"*
>
> *The visitor said, "I have a large salon, a spacious dining room, a study, several bedrooms, all lavishly furnished."*
>
> *"And when you are away from home on business, do you also have such accommodations?" the Chafetz Chaim asked.*
>
> *"No," the man answered. "When I am on the road I have a room in a hotel."*
>
> *"It is the same with me," the Chafetz Chaim said. "In the Eternal World I have a spacious home. But I am here on earth for a rather brief journey to earn my provision for my permanent home. My stay on earth is like a business trip, and like you, when I am on the road, one room suffices."*

One might think that inasmuch as the *succah* symbolizes our mortality and the limited time we have on earth, Succos would be a very solemn festival, hardly one of exhilaration. But lo! It is just this festival of which we say in our prayers is, "the time of our gladness," as the Torah describes it.

A person who accumulates great wealth may indeed enjoy it, but the time in which he can enjoy it is so limited. It is only the denial of one's mortality that allows one to be happy. It was well said, "Many people live as if they would never die, and they die as though they had never lived." The Torah attitude is just the reverse of the secular attitude. It is precisely because we know that our existence will extend far beyond the limited period of our physical lives that we can feel happiness.

If a person who brings in an abundant harvest lived only for his earthly existence, his joy would be marred by the awareness of his mortality, and would depend on his ability of denial. Recognizing one's mortality and realizing that our sojourn on earth enables us to bring in an abundant harvest of mitzvos to our Eternal Home, allows us to have unlimited joy.

That is the charm of the *succah*.

וּלְקַחְתֶּם לָכֶם בַּיּוֹם הָרִאשׁוֹן
פְּרִי עֵץ הָדָר כַּפֹּת תְּמָרִים וַעֲנַף עֵץ־עָבֹת וְעַרְבֵי־נָחַל

You shall take for yourselves on the first day the fruit of the citron tree [esrog], the branches of date palms [lulav], twigs of a plaited tree [myrtle, hadasim] and brook willows [aravos] (23:40)

Everyone Is Essential

The Midrash says that the four species represent four types of people. The citron, which has both taste and fragrance, represents the person who has both Torah knowledge and good deeds. The dates of the date palm have taste but no fragrance, and they represent the person who has Torah knowledge but lacks good deeds. The myrtle has fragrance but no taste, and it represents people who have good deeds but lack Torah knowledge. The willow has neither taste nor fragrance, and represents people who are devoid of both Torah knowledge and good deeds (*Vayikra Rabbah* 30:12).

In order to fulfill the mitzvah, the four species must be bound together; i.e., the *lulav,* the *hadasim* and the *aravos,* and held together with the *esrog.* If any one of the four species is missing, the mitzvah is not fulfilled.

Similarly, every Jewish person is an essential part of the Jewish nation. Some people may be more learned and may have performed more mitzvos, but in terms of comprising the Jewish nation, everyone is equal.

It is said that every Jew is represented by a letter of the Torah. If any letter is missing in a Torah scroll, that disqualifies it for use. It makes no difference whether the missing letter was in the Ten Commandments or in the conversation of the shepherds of Laban. Just as a Torah scroll that is missing a letter, any letter, is incomplete, so is the Jewish nation incomplete if any Jew is lacking.

Another aspect of this mitzvah is that taking each of the four species separately does not fulfill the mitzvah. The three species must be bound together, and the *esrog* held adjoining them. That is how the Jewish people should be, bound and close to one another.

"And you shall rejoice before God for a seven day period." If we can achieve unity, that is indeed cause for joy.

VAYIKRA / LEVITICUS: Emor

בַּסֻּכֹּת תֵּשְׁבוּ שִׁבְעַת יָמִים

You shall dwell in the succah for seven days (23:42)

The Importance of Hospitality

The chassidic master, R' Pinchas of Koritz, was beloved by his community. His home was constantly buzzing with people. Some sought advice, some sought his blessing and some simply wished to unburden themselves of their troubles. But all this distracted him from his Torah study and prayer, and he was much distressed by this. He, therefore, prayed to God, "Let the people not love me. Let them leave me alone."

The next day, no one came to R' Pinchas' home. He had a difficult time finding ten people for a minyan. However, he was happy because he could pray as long as he wished, and his Torah study was not interrupted.

One day, R' Pinchas' wife said to him, "I don't understand what has happened. The people in the marketplace seem to be avoiding me. They always used to talk to me, but now when I try to talk to them, they turn away."

R' Pinchas explained to his wife that he had prayed for solitude, and apparently his wife was given the status along with him. R' Pinchas' wife said that she was not pleased with being shunned, but if this was necessary to allow him to devote all his time to Torah study and prayer, she was willing to accept it.

Every Succos, many people helped R' Pinchas put up his succah, but this Succos no one came to help. R' Pinchas had to put up his succah single-handedly, but he was willing to forego the help as long as he was free to devote himself totally to the Divine service.

Every Succos, R' Pinchas' succah was full of friends who joined him in the meal, but this Succos he was alone. R' Pinchas regularly welcomed the ushpizin (the succah guests, Abraham, Isaac, Jacob, Moses, Aaron, Joseph and David) to his succah. This Succos, R' Pinchas saw the patriarch Abraham standing outside the succah. He invited the patriarch to come in, but Abraham said, "I do not enter a succah where there are no guests."

R' Pinchas realized that he had erred. As important as Torah study and prayer are, they should not be at the expense of closeness with people. He then prayed to have his charm returned to him. Soon his home was buzzing again with many visitors.

The Talmud says that receiving guests surpasses in importance even welcoming the Divine Presence (*Shabbos* 127a). Our homes should always be open to others, and we should offer our hospitality to everyone.

כַּאֲשֶׁר יִתֵּן מוּם בָּאָדָם כֵּן יִנָּתֶן בּוֹ

Just as he will have inflicted a wound on a person, so shall be inflicted upon him (24:20)

Projection

This portion of the Torah deals with personal injury. The Talmud says that the Oral Law, transmitted through the generations, was that the above verse, as well as "an eye for an eye," are not meant to be taken literally. Rather, one must compensate the victim for the injury.

The *Kometz HaMinchah* translates this verse a bit differently. "As one caused a defect in another, so it shall be given to him."

The Baal Shem Tov taught an important psychological insight. Inasmuch as people are generally *in denial*, they may be unaware of their character defects. Therefore, God shows them their character defect in another person. "The world is a mirror," the Baal Shem Tov said. "The faults you see in others are your own."

One might say, "Why is this a general rule? I just happened to see someone in a rage. How does that prove that I do not have control over my anger?"

Let us reflect on, "I just happened to see." If you put several people on a busy street corner for several minutes, then asked them to report what they saw, you would likely get a different response from each one. They were all witnesses to the same scene, in which many things were happening. Yet, each person saw something different than the others. This is because the mind has a selective filter. If we were at all times aware of all the stimuli bombarding our senses, our minds would be overwhelmed and we could not possibly function. The filtering system, therefore, blocks out most stimuli and allows us to focus on just a few.

There is no escaping the fact that there must be some reason why, out of the myriad of stimuli, the filtering system selects those of which the person becomes aware. The Baal Shem Tov's point is that the selectivity is determined by *what one wants or needs to become aware of.* One factor governing this selectivity is one's own character makeup.

Our psychological defensive system operates to minimize our discomfort. It is easier to accept a character defect within oneself if it occurs in others as well. Therefore, the mind's filtering system is motivated to allow these particular stimuli to come to one's awareness, and blocks out those which serve no psychological purpose for the individual.

If we bear this in mind, we will be able to avoid *lashon hara*. Saying something derogatory about someone else is an indication that we, too, have that character defect. Why would anyone wish to disclose his own character defects to the world?

This, *Kometz HaMinchah* says, is the message of the above verse: "As one caused a defect in another, so it shall be given to him." The faults you attribute to others are probably your own.

פרשת בהר
Parashas Behar

וְסָפַרְתָּ לְךָ שֶׁבַע שַׁבְּתֹת שָׁנִים שֶׁבַע שָׁנִים שֶׁבַע פְּעָמִים . . . וְהַעֲבַרְתָּ
שׁוֹפַר תְּרוּעָה . . . וְקִדַּשְׁתֶּם אֵת שְׁנַת הַחֲמִשִּׁים שָׁנָה וּקְרָאתֶם דְּרוֹר בָּאָרֶץ

*You shall count for yourself seven cycles of sabbatical years . . .
You shall sound a broken blast on the shofar . . . You shall sanctify
the fiftieth year and proclaim freedom throughout the land* (25:8-10)

The Control Issue

In *Successful Relationships*, I discussed the issue of "control," and suggested that the most frequent disruptive factor in human relationships, whether husband-wife, parent-child, employer-employee, friend-friend or any other relationship, is the attempt by one person to control another person. Even though the futile and destructive efforts to control others should be clearly evident, this behavior nevertheless persists, to everyone's detriment. The resistance to releasing control is discussed in an essay by R' Chaim Zaichek (*Chochmas HaMatzpun*, *Vayikra* p. 662).

In Leviticus 25:39-40 the Torah states that a master may not abuse an indentured servant, and that after six years of service or in the Jubilee Year, he must let him go free. Toward the end of the period of the first Temple, the Israelites were in violation of this law and refused to emancipate their servants. The prophet, Jeremiah, admonished them sharply, and initially they freed their servants but soon thereafter reneged and took them back. Jeremiah then told them that their defiance of the Torah commandment to release their servants evoked the Divine wrath, and that they would be punished by being conquered by enemies and driven from the land (*Jeremiah* 34).

The Jerusalem Talmud (*Rosh Hashanah* 3:5) states that prior to their deliverance from the Egyptian enslavement, when the agony of slavery was still fresh in the minds of the Israelites, God commanded them to observe the law of freeing their indentured servants after six years. Of all 613 mitzvos, God instructed them on this mitzvah because their personal suffering as slaves would enhance their obedience. Yet, despite their history of suffering as slaves, and despite the prophet's exhortation that they would be severely punished, the Israelites could not overcome their desire to be masters over their servants.

The *Chinuch* (mitzvah 331) states that the proclamation of freedom by sounding the shofar on Yom Kippur of the Jubilee Year was to arouse people's emotions and awaken their spirituality. The fact that the emancipation was to become effective throughout the entire land, shared by all, would lower the resistance of masters to free their servants. This was to take place on no other day than Yom Kippur, on which people's spirituality would be on a high level.

R' Zaichek points out that all this indicates two things: that there is an intense drive to be master over others, and the great difficulty in yielding control.

I have observed this unfortunate phenomenon in ruined relationships. People have sacrificed their personal happiness and that of their household because of their reluctance to yield control. Abuse of spouse and children, whether physical or emotional, is nothing other than the drive to control gone to an extreme.

I suspect that the need to control others may stem from feelings of inadequacy and poor self-esteem. The sensation that one has power over another person may boost a faltering self-esteem. If the person felt better about himself, he might not need to exert his power over other people.

The need to control others is most unhealthy. It does not mean that one is a powerful person. To the contrary, it is an indication that a person is trying to overcome his sense of weakness by dominating others. A truly powerful person is a person who is master over himself, who can exert self-control rather than control others (*Ethics of the Fathers* 4:1).

The bond within a family should be love. But love is impossible when there is control. People seek to control others primarily by intimidation. They should be aware that love and fear are mutually exclusive. Intimidation results in resentment, not in love.

Although the mitzvah of the Jubilee Year is currently not in effect, the lesson of this mitzvah should guide us in our lives. Let us not forget that the prophet said that the refusal to relinquish control would have dire consequences. This is as true now as it was then.

וְקִדַּשְׁתֶּם אֵת שְׁנַת הַחֲמִשִּׁים שָׁנָה וּקְרָאתֶם דְּרוֹר בָּאָרֶץ לְכָל־יֹשְׁבֶיהָ יוֹבֵל הִוא תִּהְיֶה לָכֶם וְשַׁבְתֶּם אִישׁ אֶל־אֲחֻזָּתוֹ וְאִישׁ אֶל־מִשְׁפַּחְתּוֹ תָּשֻׁבוּ

You shall sanctify the fiftieth year and proclaim freedom throughout the land for all its inhabitants; it shall be the Jubilee Year for you, you shall return each man to his ancestral heritage and you shall return each man to his family (25:10)

Responsible Freedom

The Jubilee Year was a dramatic event and, in a way, a social upheaval. Properties that had been sold during the previous forty-nine years were returned to their original owners. Fields were left barren, all the produce of the land was common property and all indentured servants were released. "Proclaim liberty throughout the land," but note, "each of you shall return to his family."

In our own times, we, too, have experienced a dramatic event and a social upheaval: the decade of the '60s. This was the decade in which there was a proclamation of so-called "freedom:" Authority was rejected, convention was repudiated and accepted social norms were cast aside. No longer would young people be fettered by obsolete ideas. The rallying cry was, "Do your own thing!" Children leaving the family to live on their own became the norm, listening to parental advice became anathema and marriage was replaced or frequently terminated by divorce. Loyalty to one's family and family stability were discarded in this new era of "freedom." The prophets of "liberty" were intoxicated with breaking the yoke of discipline and restraint.

Several decades later, we are reaping the bitter fruits of this great emancipation. Our youth are plagued with drugs; their young, developing minds poisoned by marijuana, ecstasy, cocaine and heroin. There has been an outbreak of undiscriminating violence, with utter disregard for human life. This is the heritage of the '60s.

This is very different from the liberty proclaimed in the Jubilee Year. There were indeed some radical social and economic changes, but the underlying theme was "each of you shall return to his family." Every person would return to one's family. The family unit was predominant. Parents were respected, and their words were heeded.

Grandparents were revered, and spouses were faithful to one another. There was a family bond, strengthened by the elders of the family and by a sense of moral responsibility. The freedom of the Jubilee Year was not the recklessness and carelessness that characterized the "freedom" of the '60s, which has had so many negative results. Rather, it was one that strengthened both the individual and society.

The Torah says that the Ten Commandments were insribed on two tablets. The Talmud says that the Hebrew word for "inscribed," *chorus*, can also be read as *cherus*, freedom. True freedom depends on living according to the Ten Commandments: accepting the authority of God; revering one's parents; avoiding illicit relationships, theft and murder. Only then can we have a viable society, with respect for property and respect for life.

"You shall return each man to his family." If you wish to have true freedom, strengthen and preserve the family.

וְכִי־תִמְכְּרוּ מִמְכָּר לַעֲמִיתֶךָ אוֹ קָנֹה מִיַּד עֲמִיתֶךָ אַל־תּוֹנוּ אִישׁ אֶת־אָחִיו . . . וְיָרֵאתָ מֵאֱלֹקֶיךָ כִּי אֲנִי ה' אֱלֹקֵיכֶם

When you make a sale to your fellow or make a purchase from the hand of your fellow, do not deceive one another... and you shall fear your God; for I am your God (25:14-17)

Avoid Deceptiveness

I wish to call your attention to a halachah of which some people may be unaware. The Talmud says that it is deceptive and forbidden to intentionally mislead a person into thinking you are going to buy something from him when you have no intention of doing so. It is certainly permissible to shop around and inquire about prices from different vendors if your intention is to buy from whoever makes you the most reasonable offer. However, if you have decided to buy an item from a catalog, and you go to a store to see the item and inquire from the salesman about the details of the item that you have no intention of buying from that store, you are misleading that merchant and the Torah forbids this.

I mention this because some people think this is permissible. "Why, everyone does it." Even if this is true, it does not make it right.

There are several places where the Torah says, "you shall fear your God." This statement invariably accompanies a mitzvah which is dependent on one's thoughts and feelings, and are not discernable to any outsider. Whereas theft is an act which can be exposed, misleading someone may never be revealed. This is why the Torah says, "you shall fear your God," because before God, everyone's thoughts are revealed.

Fear is not necessarily a harmful sensation. To the contrary, fear may help us avoid harm, as when we fear exposing ourselves to danger. The fear of God is constructive, and that is why one of the first verses of the Torah we teach our children is, "The beginning of wisdom is the fear of God" (*Psalms* 111:10).

Our *yetzer hara* may try to delude us that deceptions such as misleading a merchant are not prohibited, and furthermore, no one would ever know. While a person may be able to save a few dollars by deception, one should remember that the fear of God is in order to prevent harm to ourselves. It is foolish to expose oneself to harm for a short term gain.

וְכִי־יָמוּךְ אָחִיךְ וּמָטָה יָדוֹ עִמָּךְ וְהֶחֱזַקְתָּ בּוֹ . . . אַל־תִּקַּח מֵאִתּוֹ נֶשֶׁךְ וְתַרְבִּית

If your brother becomes impoverished and his means falter . . . you shall strengthen him . . . Do not take from him interest and increase (25:35-36)

Endearing a Mitzvah

One of the most prominent citizens of Pressburg came to R' Moshe Schreiber (Chasam Sofer) and asked for a private audience. He burst into tears and told the rabbi that although he had always been a successful businessman, he had recently suffered unexpected losses and was on the verge of bankruptcy. "As soon as I default on my first loan, the word will get out and I will be ruined. Furthermore, I have never missed a trip to the marketplace in Leipzig, which is coming up shortly. If I don't go to Leipzig, people will suspect that something is wrong. I don't even have enough money for the trip," he said.

"What are the expenses of a trip to Leipzig?" R' Schreiber asked.

"I used to travel in luxury," he said. "I cannot even think of that. Just to get there and have accommodations would cost one hundred gulden."

"One hundred gulden, is that all?" R' Schreiber asked. He opened his drawer and took out the money that comprised his entire savings. "I will lend you one hundred gulden. Go to Leipzig and may God bless you with success."

The man refused to take the money. "I didn't come to you for money," he said, "but just to unburden myself of my distress." R' Schreiber insisted, however, that he take the money.

At Leipzig, the man met a merchant who suggested that he buy a huge amount of coffee, and knowing him to be a prosperous businessman, he sold it to him on credit. The next day there was a sizeable increase in the price of coffee and he sold it at a large profit. He made several other transactions which were very profitable, and was convinced that the Chasam Sofer's blessing had brought him this good fortune. "I must bring the rabbi a gift," he said. Knowing that R' Schreiber was a mayvin (expert) on diamonds, he bought a diamond ring.

On returning to Pressburg he returned the hundred gulden and gave the rabbi the ring. The rabbi admired the ring. "It is indeed a beautiful diamond," he said. He continued to examine the ring, repeatedly praising its beauty, its color, its purity. He then gave the ring to the merchant, saying, "It is a very beautiful ring. Use it in good health."

"But I brought the ring for you, rabbi," the merchant said. "It was only by virtue of your blessing that I had this extraordinary success."

The Chasam Sofer said, "Had I not lent you the money, I might have accepted the gift. However, inasmuch as I lent you the money, taking anything more than what I lent you might constitute taking interest."

After the merchant left, one of the Chasam Sofer's students asked him, "Why were you so lavish in praising the ring?"

The Chasam Sofer answered, "Businessmen lend money, and they have the opportunity to fulfill the mitzvah of not lending on interest. As a rabbi, when do I have the opportunity to fulfill this mitzvah? No one comes to me for a loan. Here I was presented with the unusual opportunity to fulfill this mitzvah by refusing the ring. The ring was a vehicle whereby I could fulfill this mitzvah by returning it. How could I not praise something that enabled me to fulfill a mitzvah?

We are blessed with the opportunity to do mitzvos. We should cherish these precious opportunities.

וְחִשַּׁב עִם־קֹנֵהוּ מִשְּׁנַת הִמָּכְרוֹ לוֹ עַד שְׁנַת הַיֹּבֵל

He shall make a reckoning with his purchaser from the year he was sold to him until the Jubilee Year (25:50)

Faith in the Ultimate Redemption

This verse is stated in regard to a Jew who sold himself into servitude to a non-Jew who is under Jewish jurisdiction. It is a mitzvah upon his relatives to buy his freedom, but the Torah prescribes that the owner must be properly compensated. Inasmuch as all slaves went free in the Jubilee Year, the value of each year of service depended on which year of the Jubilee cycle he sold himself. For example, if he sold himself for $1,000 in the twenty-fourth year of the cycle, he would have to work for the next twenty-five years. Each year was, therefore, worth $40. If his relatives redeemed him after he worked for five years, they would have to pay the owner for the remaining twenty years, i.e., $800. If they did not redeem him until he had worked for fifteen years, they would have to pay for only the remaining ten years, i.e., $400. The longer he remained in service, the less the price of redemption.

> Members of the Chafetz Chaim's family related that late at night when he assumed everyone was asleep, he would seclude himself in a dark room. Eavesdropping, they heard him express gratitude to God for all the kindness He had done for him, enumerating many incidents in his lifetime for which he was grateful.
>
> His tone of voice would then change, and he began pleading the cause of Israel before God. He would say, "You gave us a holy Torah, but it was a sealed book. Israel produced prophets, the sages of the Talmud and Torah scholars, who deciphered your Torah and made it accessible to all, revealing Your will to Israel. And what did Israel get in return? Persecution and massacres!
>
> "Nevertheless, we were steadfast in preserving Your Torah, taking it with us when we were expelled and driven from one country to another.
>
> "You established a time for the ultimate Redemption. If Israel had enough merits, we would be redeemed before that time. In Your Torah You state that the longer one remains in servitude, the less is the price of redemption. Israel has been exiled and subjugated to foreign nations so long, that it should no longer require many merits to warrant our Redemption.
>
> "How long must we yet wait? We are as broken as shattered earthenware. Not one Jew in the world is whole. We cannot hold out much longer. You are our closest relative, and You must redeem us from our servitude and exile."

The Chafetz Chaim was in the presence of R' Yosef Dov Soloveitchik (Beis HaLevi) when the leaders of the community of Brisk asked R' Yosef Dov to become their rabbi. At first he declined, because after leaving the position in Slutzk, he decided that he would not take another position. Tending to community affairs detracted him from Torah study. The representatives of Brisk said, "How can you refuse us? Twenty-five thousand Jews in Brisk are waiting for you."

R' Yosef Dov was shaken by these words and said to his wife, "Please give me my kaftan and hat. I must go to Brisk promptly. Twenty-five thousand Jews must not be made to wait!"

The Chafetz Chaim said, "If R' Yosef Dov would not keep twenty-five thousand Jews waiting, how can Mashiach keep hundreds of thousands of Jews waiting? It must be only because we are not clamoring sufficiently for his coming." Tearfully, he would say, "Yes, we pray 'We are anxiously waiting for You,' but I am afraid these are only words, but they do not come from the heart. If we were sincere in pleading for the Redemption, Mashiach would certainly come."

Let us put our hearts into our prayers. Sincere prayer can hasten the Redemption.

אֶת־שַׁבְּתֹתַי תִּשְׁמֹרוּ וּמִקְדָּשִׁי תִּירָאוּ אֲנִי ה'

"My Sabbaths shall you observe and My Sanctuary shall you revere—I am God" (26:2)

Reverence for the House of God

Perhaps the reason for the juxtaposition of these two mitzvos is because, unfortunately, the greatest irreverence of the House of God is on Shabbos, when people thoughtlessly profane the sanctity of the synagogue by conversing during services. I have mentioned this elsewhere in this book, but it is of such importance that it bears repetition.

I am certain that if those people who carry on conversation during prayers were in the presence of a high government official or even at a meeting presided on by the CEO of their firm, they would not be disrespectful. To place respect of God beneath that of humans is a desecration of holiness of the highest order. How can parents expect their children to respect them when they model for them disrespect of God? It is not only the children of the talkers who are negatively affected, but the children of other congregants who see the disrespect for God condoned.

I know of at least one synagogue where a group of worshippers left to form their own *minyan* because the conversation during services was intolerable. I deplore breakaway *minyans* because they foster fragmentation and disunity. However, in this case, I believe that the breakaway was justified.

R' Yom Tov Heller (*Tosafos Yom Tov*) attributed the horrible Chmielnicki pogrom to the brazen disrespect for God shown by those who talk during services. Here is an excerpt of the blessing he composed for those who refrain from this.

May He Who blessed our forefathers, Abraham, Isaac and Jacob, Moses, Aaron, David and Solomon, bless those who guard their tongue and refrain from conversing during prayers and the reading of the Torah. May all the blessings in the Torah and the Books of the Prophets come upon him. May he see his children upright and healthy, and may he prosper in this world and have a share in the Eternal World, Amen.

Is it not the height of folly to forfeit such wonderful blessings?

I urge worshippers in all synagogues to do everything within their means to curb conversation during services, and may they merit great reward for bringing honor to the Divine Name.

פרשת בחקתי
Parashas Bechukosai

אִם־בְּחֻקֹּתַי תֵּלֵכוּ וְאֶת־מִצְוֹתַי תִּשְׁמְרוּ וַעֲשִׂיתֶם אֹתָם

"If you will follow My decrees and observe My commandments and perform them" (26:3)

To Labor in Torah

"Following My decrees" and "observing My commandments" appear to be a redundancy. Rashi, therefore, comments that "If you will follow My decrees" refers to "toiling in Torah."

A young man complained to the Chafetz Chaim that he had not been successful in acquiring Torah knowledge despite years of Torah study. The Chafetz Chaim replied that there is no mitzvah to become a *lamdan* (a scholar of Torah) or a *gaon* (genius in Torah). There is only a mitzvah of "toiling in Torah," pursuing Torah study diligently.

It is certainly gratifying to be an accomplished Torah scholar, and it is certainly pleasant to have students who are fine Torah scholars. Unfortunately, there are young men who are unable to grasp Talmud easily, and too often they are neglected in yeshivos. They sense that their instructors are disappointed in their learning, and they share in this disappointment. They receive little, if any, recognition. Feeling that they have no hope of becoming Torah scholars, they give up on Torah study. Some of these young men who leave the yeshivah because of their disappointment take to the streets, drift away from Yiddishkeit and often become drug users.

If the lesson of the Chafetz Chaim was heeded, these young men could be saved. If they could genuinely feel that their *trying* to understand the Talmud is appreciated regardless of whether or not they succeed, and if they received recognition for their effort, they would be better motivated to continue Torah study.

Torah instructors should not give up on slow learners. Where would we be today if R' Akiva would have been subject to the attitude that so often prevails in the yeshivos today? Without R' Akiva, much of the Talmud would be missing.

> *What was R' Akiva's beginning? At age 40 he was uneducated and knew nothing. He tried to learn Torah, but to no avail. One time he saw a*

depression that had been formed in a rock by dripping water, and he reasoned, 'If water can make an impression on hard rock, then Torah can make an impression on me.' He then returned to Torah study.

R' Akiva took his son with him and went to a beginner's class. 'Teach me Torah' he said. The teacher wrote aleph beis on his tablet, and he studied it. Eventually he learned the entire Five Books of Moses.

He then went to R' Eliezer and R' Yehoshua. 'Teach me to understand the Mishnah,' he said. When they taught him one halachah, he sat by himself and reviewed it. He would ask them, 'Why is there an aleph here? Why is there a beis here?' Eventually he progressed to become the greatest of the Talmudic sages.

R' Shimon ben Elazar said, 'Let me give you a parable that explains R' Akiva. A stone cutter was hewing tiny pieces of stone from a mountain and throwing them into the Jordan River. Onlookers asked him, 'What are you doing?' He answered, 'I am dismantling this mountain and throwing it into the river.' They said to him, "That is ridiculous. You will never be able to dismantle this mountain.' He paid them no mind, but kept on hewing small pieces of stone.

That's how R' Akiva was. The entire Torah appeared to be a huge mountain that he could never digest, but he did not care. He just continued learning bit by bit (Avos D'Rabi Nosson 7).

If students who have difficulty excelling in Talmud were impressed with the fact that the effort they put into Torah study is as dear to God, *to their teachers, principals and parent* as the scholarship of the most brilliant student, the tragedy of losing them from Yiddishkeit might be avoided.

אִם־בְּחֻקֹּתַי תֵּלֵכוּ וְאֶת־מִצְוֹתַי תִּשְׁמְרוּ וַעֲשִׂיתֶם אֹתָם

"If you will follow My decrees and observe My commandments and perform them" (26:3)

Spiritual Progress

The literal translation of the above verse is, "If you will *walk* in my decrees." R' Simchah Bunim of P'shis'che pointed out that whereas the heavenly angels do not progress in holiness and remain forever in the state in which they were created, man should not remain static, but advance in spirituality every day of his life. This is what the prophet means: "If you walk in My ways and safeguard My charge I shall permit you movement among these immobile [angels]" (*Zechariah* 3:7). God has enabled us to have "movement," i.e., to grow in spirituality in contrast to angels that remain stationary.

R' Saadiah Gaon once lodged at an inn, and because the innkeeper did not know his identity, he was not accorded the honor due him but was treated decently like any other customer. Someone who did recognize him informed the innkeeper who his guest was. The innkeeper then apologized profusely to the Gaon.

"Why are you apologizing?" the Gaon asked. "You treated me very well."

The innkeeper said, "But if I had only known who you were, I would have served you with greater respect."

The Gaon became tearful. "Today I have a better understanding of God than I had yesterday. If only I had known yesterday what I know today, I would have served God with much greater fervor."

Let us be truthful with ourselves. Were our prayers today recited with greater *kavannah* than our prayers yesterday? Have we progressed spiritually in the last day? Is every day of our lives one of spiritual advancement? If not, then we are derelict in our roles as human beings. We do have the capacity to grow spiritually, and it is wrong to not do so.

The fact is that there is no standing in one place. If we are derelict in advancing ourselves spiritually, this failure sets us back and we regress spiritually. We are constantly in movement. If we do not move forward, we are slipping backward.

The wording of the Torah is precise. It is not enough to simply observe the mitzvos. We must do so in a way that we progress in spirituality.

אִם־בְּחֻקֹּתַי תֵּלֵכוּ וְאֶת־מִצְוֹתַי תִּשְׁמְרוּ וַעֲשִׂיתֶם אֹתָם

"If you will follow My decrees and observe My commandments and perform them" (26:3)

Exposure to Torah

Commenting on the literal translation, "If you will *walk* according to My decrees," the Midrash cites the verse: "I considered my ways and returned my feet toward Your testimonies" (*Psalms* 119:59). King David said, "Whenever I think that I will go to a certain place or house, my feet take me to the House of Worship or the House of Study" (*Vayikra Rabbah*).

I was helped to understand the message of this Midrash in my treatment of alcoholics. The alcoholic is urged to attend meetings of Alcoholics Anonymous. Some say, "I was at some meetings, but they don't interest me." Veterans in recovery say to him, "Go anyway. Get your body to the meetings. The mind will come eventually."

The alcoholic may be reluctant to be told that he cannot drink again, and this results in his resistance to the meetings and in his lack of interest in what goes on there. He would rather avoid the meetings so that he can satisfy his desire to drink. He is told to go anyway in spite of his lack of interest. Repeated contact with people who have recovered from alcoholism will eventually bring his mind around.

This is the message of the Midrash. If you intend to go to places to satisfy your desire for pleasure and entertainment, let your feet take you to the House of Worship or the House of Study. Even if you do not have much interest in studying Torah, go anyway. Repeated exposure to Torah scholars will stimulate your interest in Torah.

It may be difficult to resist an urge to engage in pleasurable activities. What finally motivates the alcoholic to go to meetings is the awareness that his drinking is destructive. What will motivate a person to go to the House of Study is the awareness that the indulgence in pleasurable activities is ephemeral and leaves him with nothing. A life of transient pleasures is bankrupt, devoid of meaning and content. This requires thoughtful contemplation. "I considered my ways."

Profound consideration of one's ways will result in the realization that there must be more to life than fleeting pleasures. Only when one feels a sense of emptiness will one seek substance and meaning.

וְאִם אֶת־מִשְׁפָּטַי תִּגְעַל נַפְשְׁכֶם
"If you consider My decrees loathsome" (26:15)

Respecting Others' Observance

This is a very harsh expression. It is hardly likely that anyone, even a non-observant person, would consider any law of the Torah loathsome. Rashi explains that this means, "If you will spurn anyone who observes the decrees of the Torah." This is not an infrequent occurrence.

Some people think that the way they observe the Torah is the proper way, and that anyone who exceeds their standard of observance is a "fanatic." Some people who may be a bit lax in observance of Shabbos may consider those who are more strict as being fanatic. The latter may think of those who require a *mechitzah* (separation) at a wedding as being fanatic. If the latter are not particular about using only *cholov Yisrael* (supervised milk), they may think that those who are stringent about *cholov Yisrael* are fanatic. If the latter do not observe *chodosh* (prohibition of grain grown after Passover), they may consider *chodosh* observers as fanatics. I must admit that I am not without fault. I assumed that my parents' home was the highest standard of *kashrus*, and when someone asked my mother for fish because he did not wish to eat meat, I thought he was fanatic.

It seems that the definition of fanatic is someone who believes what you do, but just a bit more so. We may be convinced that our level of observance is adequate, but we should nevertheless respect those who wish to be more stringent. It is unfortunate that we are not always tolerant of those whom we label as fanatic. On more than one occasion I have seen parents disapprove of their son's choice of a wife because she comes from a family where the women cover their hair.

Being critical of someone who is "more *frum*" may simply be an ego thing. Someone who is more stringent than we are may cause us to feel that we may be somewhat delinquent.

Perhaps this is what Rashi is referring to. The Torah is critical of someone who disesteems others for being too *frum*.

וְזָכַרְתִּי לָהֶם בְּרִית רִאשֹׁנִים אֲשֶׁר הוֹצֵאתִי־אֹתָם מֵאֶרֶץ מִצְרַיִם
"I will remember for them the covenant of the ancients, those whom I have taken out of the land of Egypt" (26:45)

Remembering Our Merits

This verse comes after the *tochachah*, the admonition of what will befall Israel if it abandons the Torah. In spite of God's displeasure with Israel, He nevertheless assures us of the ultimate Redemption.

A woman came to R' Yisroel of Kozhnitz, complaining that her husband wants to divorce her because he no longer finds her attractive. R' Yisroel said, "I wish I could help you, but what can I do if he is so foolish?" The woman cried, "But it is not fair! Why doesn't he remember how much he loved me when I was young and beautiful? Can I help it if I lost my beauty as I aged?"

R' Yisroel arose and tearfully said, "Master of the Universe! Listen to this woman. She is right. It is only fair that her husband should remember what she was like when he married her. You, too, Master of the Universe, should remember what we were like when You first took us. We followed You into a barren desert, a place of no food or water, with full faith in You. You loved us then and said that of all peoples we would be Your beloved treasure. Even if we no longer have the beauty of our youth, is it fair that You turn away from us?"

In our prayers, we repeatedly mention the Exodus from Egypt. We should pray for our Redemption by virtue of the merits of our youth, of the love God had for us when He took us out of Egypt.

ספר
במדבר

BAMIDBAR/NUMBERS

Introduction to Bamidbar/Numbers

The Book of Bamidbar/Numbers relates the sojourn of our ancestors in the desert after their liberation from Egypt. Several of the episodes are of less than desirable conduct. When someone referred to the sins of the Israelites in the desert, one of the chassidic masters remarked, "And as a result of their sins, we have a significant portion of the Torah."

True, we do not seek misfortunes as stimuli to growth, and we do our utmost to avoid them. However, if they do occur, we should learn how to overcome them and emerge with greater strength.

The Torah is not a history text. The word "torah" means teaching and guiding. There are specific instructions in the Torah which constitute the 613 mitzvos, the positive commandments and prohibitions, but *all* of Torah is teaching. The various incidents narrated in the Torah are a source of the all-important body of *middos* (character traits) which are a *sine qua non* for Torah observance. Indeed, the Midrash says that the sole purpose of the mitzvos is to enable us to refine our character traits (*Vayikra Rabbah* 13:3). It is the narration in the Torah which provides the teaching of *middos*.

With this in mind, let us study the Book of Bamidbar.

פרשת במדבר
Parashas Bamidbar

Preparation for Sinai

The first portion of Bamidbar is generally read before the Shavuos festival, which commemorates the giving of the Torah at Sinai. Inasmuch as there are no coincidences, we may assume that this portion is a prerequisite for receiving the Torah.

In relating the episode at Sinai, the Torah states, "Israelites camped near the mountain" (*Exodus* 19:2). However, the Torah uses the singular *vayichan*, "he camped" rather than *vayachanu*, "*they* camped." Rashi explains that the singular indicated that all the Israelites were united as one person. It is this unity that made them worthy of receiving the Torah.

There is nothing so dear to God as unity among His children. So much so, that the Talmud states that when Jews are united, God forgives even their gravest sins (*Kallah* 8).

The Sages teach, "You have no person without his hour and no thing without its place" (*Ethics of the Fathers* 4:3). One of the chassidic masters asked, "If every person has a specific time and place, why is there so much dissension among us?" He answered, "Because many people are envious of others, and wish to occupy *their* time and place." If we were free of envy, we might achieve the coveted unity.

This portion of the Torah describes the organization of the Israelites. "The Children of Israel shall encamp, each person by his banner according to the insignia of his father's household" (*Numbers* 2:2). Each person knew his place. The *Kohanim* had their place, the Levites had their place and every single person knew his rightful place. It was this knowledge and acceptance of one's place that enabled the Israelites to be a unit rather than fragmented.

We may conceptualize unity of a nation as a symphony orchestra, where each musician has a designated assignment. If the percussionist or the flute player would balk at his assignment because the violinist plays a better part, the performance would suffer. No one musician is of greater importance than another. This is equally true of the Jewish nation. We all have specific assignments: *Kohanim*, Levites, Israelites, men, women, Torah scholars, lay people. We are one harmonious unit.

The message of Bamidbar is the message of unity: "The Children of Israel shall encamp, each person by his banner." This is why the Torah reading of Bamidbar precedes Shavuos. Unity is the prerequisite for acceptance of the Torah.

ספר במדבר: פרשת במדבר

Friend and Beloved

The Shabbos after Passover, we begin weekly readings of *Pirkei Avos, Ethics of the Fathers*. On the Shabbos preceding Shavuos, we read the sixth chapter, which is actually a compilation of Tannaic statements appended to the tractate. This chapter is referred to as *Kinyan HaTorah*, and discusses the essentials of acquisition of Torah.

The sixth chapter begins with a statement by R' Meir: "Whoever engages in Torah study for its own sake merits many things. He is called, 'Friend, Beloved.' He loves the Omnipresent, he loves (His) creatures."

One might have assumed that a person who is totally dedicated to Torah study would be called *gaon* (Talmudic genius) or *tzaddik*. Yet R' Meir circumvents the obvious, saying instead that he will be called *friend* and *beloved*.

R' Meir's statement supports the thesis of this book. The essence of Torah study goes beyond knowledge. Unless Torah knowledge is translated into *middos* (fine character traits), it is sterile. The hallmark of the sincere Torah scholar is that his character is refined so that people see him as a friend, and his actions make him beloved by all.

The Baal Shem Tov was asked, How can a person develop love for God, Who is not accessible to human senses? The Baal Shem Tov answered, "Love other people, and this will lead you to love of God." This is contained in R' Meir's statement, "He loves the Omnipresent, he loves (His) creatures."

The Shabbos preceding Shavuos, as we prepare ourselves for renewing the receiving of the Torah, we are reminded of what the ultimate purpose is: character refinement, to be recognized as *friend* and *beloved*.

וַיְדַבֵּר ה' אֶל־מֹשֶׁה בְּמִדְבַּר סִינַי בְּאֹהֶל מוֹעֵד
בְּאֶחָד לַחֹדֶשׁ הַשֵּׁנִי בַּשָּׁנָה הַשֵּׁנִית לְצֵאתָם מֵאֶרֶץ מִצְרַיִם

God spoke to Moses in the Sinai desert, in the Sanctuary, in the second month of the second year after their exodus from Egypt (1:1)

Beyond Physical Limitations

The Ohr HaChaim points out a subtle inconsistency. In regard to the place *where* God spoke, the Torah lists first the greater locality, the Sinai desert, and then the narrower, more specific site, the Sanctuary. In regard to *when* God spoke to Moses, the Torah lists first the narrower time, i.e., the month, and then the broader period, the second year. Why the inconsistency?

The Ohr HaChaim explains that it is not at all inconsistent. To the contrary, it is a most precise parallel. The intention of this syntax is to teach us that just as the "year" is more inclusive than "month," so is "Sanctuary" a broader, more inclusive term than "Sinai desert." Vast as it may be, the Sinai desert is a finite space. The Sanctuary, although it measured only one hundred by fifty cubits, was infinite.

The Midrash states that when God instructed Moses to build the Sanctuary, Moses was bewildered. "The whole universe cannot contain you," he said, "let alone a small structure." God responded, "My thinking is not like yours. Ten cubits in the width etc."

The physical dimensions may indeed be meager, but the spiritual dimensions are enormous.

When R' Levi Yitzchok of Berditchev saw a copy of the *Tanya*, he commented, "What an amazing feat R' Shneur Zalman accomplished! He contained an Infinite God in such a tiny book."

Alas! Our human senses make us think small. Several thousand miles is a great distance, and billions of miles are an enormous distance. Our ears can detect sounds only thousands of feet away, and our powerful telescopes can detect light at great, but finite distances. We are so accustomed to think in small terms that infinite greatness is an alien abstraction. Even Moses, the greatest of all prophets, was stymied by God's instruction to build Him a Sanctuary. God's lesson to Moses and to us is that a small structure can contain infinity.

The Talmud relates that King Munbaz distributed lavish *tzedakah*. His family criticized him, "Why are you dissipating the royal treasury?" Munbaz responded, "My ancestors gathered wealth in this lower world. I am investing my wealth in a supernal world." Billions of dollars constitute a great sum when measured in human terms. The money given to *tzedakah* brings infinite returns.

The careful wording in the opening verse of Bamidbar alerts us to our propensity to err in thinking of everything in the physical terms with which we are most familiar. In our physical bodies we are limited. Our *neshamah's* reach is infinite. We should overcome the limitations of the familiar and learn to think expansively: *spiritually*.

וְאֵלֶּה שְׁמוֹת הָאֲנָשִׁים אֲשֶׁר יַעַמְדוּ אִתְּכֶם לִרְאוּבֵן
אֱלִיצוּר בֶּן־שְׁדֵיאוּר ... לְנַפְתָּלִי אֲחִירַע בֶּן־עֵינָן

These are the names of the men who shall stand with you:
For Reuben, Elizur son of Shedeur ... For
Naftali, Ahira son of Enan (1:5-15)

The Guardian of Israel Neither Slumbers nor Sleeps

What possible teaching can be contained in the listing of the names of the tribal chiefs?

In his last words to the Israelites, Moses said, "He (God) encircled him (Israel), He granted him discernment, He preserved him like the pupil of His eye" (*Deuteronomy* 32:10). Moses then proceeds to describe the loving care which God provided for the Israelites during their sojourn in the desert. It is important that we remember that despite the hardships that have befallen us, we are forever under the watchful eye of God. True, we cannot understand why He has permitted us to suffer, anymore than an infant can understand why his loving and caring mother collaborates with the doctor who inflicts a painful injection to immunize him against dread disease. We must maintain our faith in God at all times.

The first name to appear is that of the tribal chief, *Elizur* אֱלִיצוּר, "My God is my preservation." The name of the last tribal chief ends with *Enan* עֵינָן, "eye." The names of the tribal chiefs that encircled Israel symbolizes Moses' description of Divine protection: "He (God) encircled him (Israel), He granted him discernment, He preserved him like the pupil of His eye." The enormous suffering which our people has sustained throughout history may present a challenge to faith. However, as the Talmud says (*Yoma* 69b), our survival in a hostile world which has repeatedly sought to destroy us is a testimony to the truth of Moses' words. It is only God who preserves us.

וַיִּתְיַלְדוּ עַל מִשְׁפְּחֹתָם לְבֵית אֲבֹתָם
They established their genealogy according to their families according to their father's household (1:18)

Better than Yichus

True, *yichus* (genealogy) has always occupied an important place in Judaism. However, its importance has sometimes been exaggerated. Personal qualifications are far more important than *yichus*.

It has been said that *yichus* is like a row of zeros, which has no value. If you put a "1" in front of them, the number is very great. Without the "1," all the zeros are nothing.

If a person has achieved deserving status, this gives his *yichus* great value. If he himself is a zero, the *yichus* is worthless.

> At a gathering of Torah scholars, each of the attendees related words of Torah that their ancestors had said. Among the scholars was R' Yechiel Meir, rabbi of Ostrovza, who was an outstanding Torah scholar, but who had no distinguished lineage. In fact, his father, a rather simple but devout person, was the proprietor of a bakery.
>
> R' Yechiel Meir felt that the other attendees were a bit too boastful about their illustrious ancestry. When it was his turn to deliver words of Torah, he said, "My father taught me that fresh bread that is newly baked is much better than bread that is several days old." With that, he delivered a scintillating Torah discourse that was totally his own.

> R' Yisroel of Rizhin's grandson married the daughter of R' Mendel of Rimanov. Before the wedding, R' Yisroel said, "It is our custom to recount the yichus before the chuppah. My great-grandfather was the great Maggid of Mezeritch, my grandfather was R' Avraham the Malach (angel). We have an unbroken chain of ancestors who had ruach hakodesh (Divine inspiration), all the way back to King David."
>
> R' Mendel of Rimanov responded in a soft voice. "My father was a simple, God-fearing man. Both of my parents died when I was a child. The dear people of the community, wanting to provide me with a means of livelihood, arranged for me to be an apprentice to a tailor so that I would learn the trade.
>
> "The tailor was an honest and pious person. He taught me, 'If something has a defect, you must repair it, and if you receive some new material, you must be very careful not to damage it in any way.' That is all the yichus I have."
>
> R' Yisroel said, "You have excelled me."

If we correct our mistakes of the past and are careful not to do anything wrong in the future, we will live an ideal Torah life. The tailor's simple but profound lesson outweighs even the glory of an illustrious ancestry.

וְחָנוּ בְּנֵי יִשְׂרָאֵל אִישׁ עַל־מַחֲנֵהוּ וְאִישׁ עַל־דִּגְלוֹ לְצִבְאֹתָם:

וַיַּעֲשׂוּ בְּנֵי יִשְׂרָאֵל כְּכֹל אֲשֶׁר צִוָּה ה' אֶת־מֹשֶׁה כֵּן עָשׂוּ:

The Children of Israel shall rest, each with his camp and each with his banner according to their hosts (1:52)

And the Children of Israel did everything that God commanded Moses, so did they do (1:54)

Accepting Assignments

Why does the Torah repeat and emphasize "so they did?"

The *Kohanim* and the Levites camped adjacent to the Sanctuary, and the other tribes were more distant from it. Among the tribes there were the elders and the judges, many of whom were far more learned than some of the *Kohanim* and Levites. They certainly could have presented a convincing argument that they were more deserving to be closer to the Sanctuary than those who had special status by accident of birth. However, the Israelites did not question God's instructions. They camped at their assigned positions.

"This you shall do for them so that they shall live and not die; ... Aaron and his sons shall come and assign them, every man to his work and his burden" (*Numbers* 4:19).

Within the tribe of Levi there were subdivisions. Some carried the tapestries of the Sanctuary, others carried the coverings and yet others carried the holy appurtenances, the Menorah, the Ark of the Covenant and the Table of the Showbread. There could certainly have been a skirmish over the various privileges. Why are the Kohathites more deserving to carry the Ark? Would it not be more equitable to have a rotation? But the Children of Israel did not question the word of God. His Infinite Wisdom designated the various assignments, and anyone who attempted an assignment which was not his would forfeit his life.

The Ark and the Menorah were certainly most dear to everyone. Why would someone be punished for wishing to be closer to the most holy objects? Did this not indicate an intense love for God? One would think this merited reward rather than punishment. Again, a very convincing argument. Setting aside logical arguments, the Levites as well as the Israelites did not question the Divine designations (*Sfas Emes, Imrei Noam*).

The various assignments did not make the Levites more worthy than the Israelites, nor the Kohathites more worthy than the Gershonites. The Children of Israel understood this.

We may take an example of something very familiar to us. Imagine if a ballplayer assigned to the outfield told the manager that he wants to be the pitcher or the catcher. These two players are more prominent, and are seen on the TV screen much more often than an outfielder, so the latter wishes to have a position where he, too, will be prominent. This does not happen and would not be tolerated. The players assume the positions designated by the manager. Each player knows that his position is as important to the team as any other. The team cannot function with only pitchers and catchers.

This lesson is relevant in every era. Whereas equality is a very alluring concept, it is simply not universally applicable. As the Israelites did, so must we assume our designated roles. *Kohanim* have their mitzvos, Levites have theirs, men have theirs and women have theirs. We are all members of God's "team" and although our assignments may vary, we are all equally dear to him.

כַּאֲשֶׁר יַחֲנוּ כֵּן יִסָּעוּ
As they encamp, so shall they journey (2:17)

When Away from Home

The Torah is relating that the formation of the Israelites when they settled for encampment was maintained when they journeyed.

R' Yehoshua Trunk of Kutna saw a message in this verse. Some people hold to a high standard of observance at home, but when en route, may take some liberties. They may eat "cold salads" in restaurants they would never frequent at home. Granted, maintaining the most demanding kashruth specifications on the road may not be easy, but one should not have two standards.

This may be the message in the above verse: "As they encamp, so shall they journey." We should be as meticulous when on the road as we are at home.

The laxity while on vacations in not a new phenomenon. One of the rabbis who vacationed at a spa observed people taking liberties with behavior that they would never do at home. He remarked, "The Talmud says that the hot springs of Tiberias are a residual from the days of the great flood (*Sanhedrin* 108a). What was the purpose of this? It was because some people may ask, 'What could the people of Noah's time possibly have done that warranted their being destroyed by the flood?' God, therefore, allowed some hot springs to remain, so that when people come to the spas and see how others behave, they will understand the reason for the great flood."

The Chafetz Chaim always traveled with a small bag which he never opened. It was later discovered that this bag contained a shroud. This great *tzaddik* wanted to be sure that he never lost sight of the Talmudic saying that to discourage one from sin, one should think of the day of death (*Berachos* 5a). If someone as saintly as the Chafetz Chaim felt that he needed this reminder when away from home, what can we say for ourselves?

וְאֵלֶּה תּוֹלְדֹת אַהֲרֹן וּמֹשֶׁה... נָדָב וַאֲבִיהוּא אֶלְעָזָר וְאִיתָמָר
These are the descendants of Aaron and Moses... Nadab, Abihu, Elazar and Ithamar (3:1-2)

The Responsibility of a Teacher

Rashi remarks that although the Torah lists only Aaron's sons, they are considered to be Moses' children as well, because Moses taught them Torah. This teaches us that if one teaches another's child Torah, it is considered as though he bore him.

This is an important principle that every teacher of Torah should bear in mind. *You must treat every child you teach as though he were your own child.* Anything less is a dereliction of a Torah teacher's obligation.

BAMIDBAR / NUMBERS: Bamidbar

Teaching children Torah is not the same as teaching the "three R's." A teacher of secular subjects fulfills his responsibility when he successfully transmits knowledge to his students. A dedicated teacher who has made a sincere and maximum effort at teaching his pupils algebra may go home with a clear conscience and sleep peacefully. The fact that one or more students were unable to grasp the subject does not disturb him. He has not been derelict in his duties.

This is not the case with someone who teaches Torah. The Torah places an awesome responsibility on a teacher of Torah. He must consider each child as if it were his own biological offspring. How would a father feel if his child did not learn well or misbehaved? That, the Torah tells us, is how a Torah teacher must feel. He should have the child evaluated for a possible learning disability. He might even try to investigate whether there may be something in the home environment that inhibits the child's learning.

If a teacher were to find out that his own child had been humiliated in class, he would be irate. If he found out that his child's teacher embarrassed his child in class, he would be incensed at that teacher. If he found out that his child's teacher directed most of his attention to the brightest students and neglected maximizing his child's potential, he would certainly react. If his child was expelled for misbehaving, he would investigate what had happened and appeal for the child's reinstatement.

Parents expect their children to love them, just as they love their children. Teachers, too, should love their students and relate to them in way that will earn their love.

In my practice, I often encounter situations of gross deviant behavior of adolescents, whether with drug addiction or defiant behavior. In extreme cases, as when the youngster is causing severe disruption that affects the siblings, the parents, who have told the child that this behavior is unacceptable, may have to evict the child from the home. This recommendation is met with great resistance, implemented with great reluctance and causes the parents much heartache and many sleepless nights. They are tortured by having evicted their child from the home.

It is not unusual that a child misbehaves in school to the point where it affects other students, and the child is expelled. However, this decision may be made with much less reluctance than exhibited by the parents. Even if the decision is correct (which is not always the case), I wonder whether the teacher or administrator agonizes over this action to the degree of having sleepless nights.

R' Yosef Zvi Dushinsky was consulted about a youngster whom the yeshivah wished to expel. The youngster's behavior was such that R' Dushinsky had no choice but to agree to expel him. *For the rest of R' Dushinsky's life, he fasted on the day he had approved of expelling the boy.* To him, this act was the equivalent of the destruction of the Temple, and it was his personal Tishah B'Av.

The prevalence of defiant behavior among youngsters today is unprecedented, but this does not absolve the Torah teacher of the responsibility to act toward a wayward student as if it were his own child. Perhaps this attitude among Torah teachers would foster a teacher-student relationship that would significantly reduce the incidence of such behavior.

הִנֵּה לָקַחְתִּי אֶת־הַלְוִיִּם מִתּוֹךְ בְּנֵי יִשְׂרָאֵל
תַּחַת כָּל־בְּכוֹר . . . מִבְּנֵי יִשְׂרָאֵל

*"Behold! I have taken the Levites from among the
Children of Israel, in place of every firstborn . . .
among the Children of Israel"* (3:12)

Avoid Tacit Approval of Wrong

Rashi explains that initially the firstborn were to perform the Divine service, but when they sinned through worship of the Golden Calf, they lost this privilege.

Those who participated in the worship of the Golden Calf were but a small minority of Israelites. In fact, they were the *eirev rav*, the Egyptians who joined the Israelites in the Exodus. Certainly, most of the firstborn were not guilty of the sin of idolatry. Why did all the firstborn lose their distinction?

When Moses descended from Sinai and saw the worship of the Golden Calf, he declared, "Whoever is for God, join me," and the entire tribe of Levi came to him (*Exodus* 32:26). Although the overwhelming majority of each of the other tribes had not worshiped the Golden Calf, they did not respond to Moses' call.

Although the majority of Israelites did not participate in the Golden Calf debacle, they did not oppose it vigorously. They remained silent, and did not rally around Moses as did the tribe of Levi. That is why they forfeited the privilege for their firstborn to be the *Kohanim*.

When there is injustice, it is incumbent upon everyone to protest and take action against it. To remain passive and silent is giving tacit approval to the injustice.

This lesson is of great importance today. During the Holocaust, there were countries who knew what was happening. They share the guilt with the Nazis. Today, there are countries that fund and actively support terrorism. They share the guilt with the actual terrorists.

This is true of the community as well as of the world as a whole. Domestic violence and child abuse are just two of the grave injustices which could be significantly reduced if not entirely eliminated if the community reacted responsibly.

In addiction treatment, there is a concept of "co-dependence." This means that when there is an active addict in the family, there are some members of the family who are actively or passively supportive of the addiction. Tolerating errant behavior is tantamount to supporting it.

Fire is not caused by oxygen, but in the absence of oxygen a fire will be extinguished. Errant behavior cannot exist in the absence of "oxygen," of an environment that gives it tacit support.

Whenever we see a *Kohen* giving the priestly blessing or being called first to the reading of the Torah, we should be reminded why the tribe of Levi earned this privilege and why the firstborn of the other tribes forfeited it.

We may not remain silent when there is injustice. The responsibility of protesting against injustice is incumbent on every individual as well as on the community as a whole. To the extent that we remain passive, to that extent we lose some of our spirituality.

פְּקֹד אֶת־בְּנֵי לֵוִי . . . מִבֶּן־חֹדֶשׁ וָמַעְלָה תִּפְקְדֵם
Count the sons of Levi ... from one month of age and up shall you count them (3:15)

Preparation for Sanctity

Earlier in this portion, Moses was told to count the Israelites "from the age of 20 years of age and up, everyone fit for military duty" (*Numbers* 1:3). Why were the Levites counted from the age of one month, whereas the Israelites were counted from the age of 20?

R' Moshe Feinstein explains that bearing arms is something that can be taught to an adult even if he had no previous preparation for military service. Holiness, however, cannot be instilled in a person later in life. Holiness must be taught from birth. Failure to do so will allow a child to formulate concepts and develop habits which are incongruous with holiness. Once these are imprinted in a child, they are not easily eradicated.

The Levites were to serve in the Temple and as teachers of Torah. Their preparation for these roles had to begin soon after birth.

This is a vital lesson for our time. The immorality and corruption that plagues modern society is without precedent. If a child is permitted exposure to these influences, they may affect his character development in a way that cannot be corrected later.

It is traditional to place a copy of psalm 121 over the crib of a newborn. From the very first moment that the infant focuses its eyes, it should see the words of the Scripture. It is also important that when the parents approach the crib, they should see the words of the psalm: "My help comes from God, Creator of heaven and earth. God is your shadow."

The Baal Shem Tov explained that "God is your shadow" means that just as a person's shadow mimics every move he makes, so does God relate to a person in a way that mimics his actions. If a person is tolerant, kind and forgiving, God will be tolerant, kind and forgiving with him. If a person is intolerant, harsh and resentful, God will act accordingly to him. If parents train the child according to these principles by modeling them in their lives, there is great hope that the child will absorb them and formulate his character accordingly.

Although the Levites had specific sacerdotal assignments, every Jewish child should be trained to be holy. We must take great caution not to expose our young children to the profane influences that saturate the media, or to an educational system that is devoid of ethical teachings. Training for an ethical life cannot begin in adulthood or even adolescence. It must begin in the very earliest phase of life.

אַל־תַּכְרִיתוּ אֶת־שֵׁבֶט מִשְׁפְּחֹת הַקְּהָתִי מִתּוֹךְ הַלְוִיִּם
Do not let the tribe of the Kohathite families be cut off from among the Levites (4:18)

Misplaced Zeal

The Torah proceeds to instruct the *Kohanim* to assign specific tasks to the Kohathites. The Midrash states that because each of them wished to have the mitzvah of carrying the holy Ark, they would compete and argue with each other, resulting in disrespect for the holy objects, for which they were punished by death (*Bamidbar Rabbah* 5).

R' Avraham Pam elaborates on this theme, pointing out that in one's zeal to do a mitzvah, one may overstep boundaries and actually commit a wrongful act. R' Pam particularly emphasizes the need to avoid arguments and strife that may result from the desire to do a mitzvah.

At one time there was dissension among the staff of the yeshivah in Radin. They tried to keep this fact from the Chafetz Chaim, but he became aware of it and called a meeting at which he said, "I will close ninety yeshivahs rather than allow a yeshivah to become a cause for argument."

R' Pam says that we must carefully weigh the consequences of our behavior. He cites as an example the mitzvah to bring cheer to a *choson* and *kallah*, which is indeed very worthy. However, he says, friends of the newlyweds may stay at the wedding for a long time, having left their parents to be baby-sitters. By tarrying at the wedding, they prevent their parents from retiring until very late, which is unfair to them. Even a hired baby-sitter should not be kept up late. The merit of the mitzvah is countered by the lack of consideration for the parents or baby-sitter.

R' Pam cites the case of a young wife who prepared dinner for her husband who usually came home at six. The husband did not come till much later, causing the wife to worry whether something bad had happened to him. When he came home, he explained that a friend of his had no other way to get to the airport, so he drove him there.

A wonderful mitzvah of *gemilas chasadim*? Not so, says R' Pam. The anxiety and worry he caused his wife countered the mitzvah of helping his friend. If he wished to do this mitzvah of *gemilas chasadim*, says R' Pam, he should have called his wife and asked for her approval to do so.

We must be extremely cautious to do what the Torah tells us is right and proper, rather than what we think is such (*Atarah LeMelech* p.123).

R' Yeruchem Levovitz echoes this concept. The Midrash states that when Pharaoh decreed that all male newborns should be killed, Amram separated from his wife, Yocheved. Miriam said to Amram, "Your decree is worse than Pharaoh's. His decree was to eliminate male children, whereas by separating, you are also eliminating the birth of female children." Amram then remarried Yocheved and Moses was born.

"How remarkable," says R' Yeruchem, "Amram, who was a great *tzaddik* who never sinned (*Shabbos* 55b) was going to commit something worse than Pharaoh's evil decree!"

R' Yeruchem said, "I have a brief handwritten note from R' Simchah Zissel of Kelm that says: 'To all great Torah scholars and influential people: If a person deviates from truth, he can cause greater damage with his efforts for what he considers righteous than the wicked Antiochus did with his decrees to uproot Torah from Israel' " (*Talelei Oros, Shemos* p.36).

וְהָיָה בִּמְקוֹם אֲשֶׁר־יֵאָמֵר לָהֶם לֹא־עַמִּי אַתֶּם יֵאָמֵר לָהֶם בְּנֵי קֵל־חָי

*"And it shall be in a place when it is said to them,
'You are not my nation,' it will be said to them [you are] the
children of the living God"* (Hosea 2:1; *Haftarah* to *Parashas Bamidbar*).

Growing Pains

The author of *Bikkurei Aviv* calls our attention to an historical pattern that was foretold by the prophet. The periods when Jews suffered oppression and persecution were often the periods of the greatest productivity in Torah study and writings. Many of our greatest *tzaddikim* emerged precisely when living conditions were unfavorable. On the other hand, when Jews lived in greater comfort and social acceptance, deviation from Torah increased.

When one Torah scholar was told, "There are good tidings. The government has granted Jews civil rights and equality with all its citizens," he responded, "You call that good tidings? I consider that a *gezeirah ra'ah* (evil decree)!"

How sad, but how true! When Jews were subject to severe discrimination, forbidden to live in large cities and refused admission to the professions, intermarriage was extremely rare. In the United States, where we enjoy unprecedented liberties and are well represented in the sciences and professions, assimilation dominates and intermarriage is at an alarming all time high.

The Talmud says that we were given three things that can be acquired only through suffering: Torah, the Holy Land and the World to Come (*Berachos* 5a). While we may complain about this and wish it were not so, the historical facts are undeniable.

I was at a meeting of recovering alcoholics where the speaker said, "I cannot think of a single thing that I ever learned from a pleasant experience, but I can list many things I learned from painful experiences."

The mother of a young man who recovered from severe drug addiction and became a successful businessman said to me, "I am so proud of Alvin. He is so wonderful. What a shame that he had to go through those horrible years of drug addiction." When I repeated her remarks to Alvin, he said, "Mom, you don't understand. I could never have become what I am now if I had not gone through that."

Of course, we wish to avoid suffering, both as individuals and as a nation. But the Torah refers to the period of enslavement in Egypt as a "purifying furnace" which separates the dross from the metal (*Deuteronomy* 4:20). In retrospect, we must recognize that the most painful periods in history were also the periods of greatest growth.

And so the prophet says that precisely when the environment we live in will reject us and say to us "you are not my nation," it is then that it will be said of us, "you are the children of the living God."

פרשת נשא
Parashas Nasso

וְהִתְוַדּוּ אֶת־חַטָּאתָם אֲשֶׁר עָשׂוּ

And they shall confess their sins that they did (5:7)

Sins Do Not Occur in a Vacuum

There is not a single superfluous letter in the Torah. Yet the words "that they did" seem to add nothing to the sentence.

The Torah is telling us that sins do not occur in a vacuum. A person must have had a mind-set that was conducive to sin in order for sin to occur. He must have done something improper which caused him to be in an altered state of spirituality that enabled him to sin.

R' Mendel of Kotzk said that the reason a person should not sin is not because it is forbidden, but because he should not have free time to sin. If a person is engaged in studying Torah, doing mitzvos and conducting himself in his daily activities according to Torah teachings, he will simply not have any available time to commit a sin. Therefore, if a person has sinned, it is not enough that he regrets his sin and resolves not to repeat it. True *teshuvah* requires that he review his behavior and see where he had been lax in leading a total life of Torah that allowed the sin to occur. He must then correct his lifestyle so that the opportunity for sin does not recur.

This is what the Torah is telling us. "They shall confess their sin," but that is not enough. They must also do some serious soul-searching and discover "what they did" that made the sinful act possible. This, too, they must confess and correct.

A recovering alcoholic who was sober for twenty years said, "The man I once was, drank. And the man I once was, will drink again." This is an important insight. The character traits that he once had resulted in his drinking. In recovery, he underwent significant personality changes which enabled him to abstain from alcohol. If he were to revert to his pre-drinking personality, he would certainly drink again.

In my book, *Addictive Thinking,* I described the nature of thinking that allows addictive behavior to occur. Sustained recovery requires changing the way one thinks. This is equally true of any improper act. The only way one can prevent a sin from recurring is by making salutary changes in one's character, thereby creating a personality that cannot do this act. Rambam states that this why *teshuvah* works. Reuven cannot be held culpable for something that Shimon did. Neither can this new person, whose previous personality was discarded, be held culpable for what a previous personality did.

The realization that "that they did," i.e., the character makeup that had existed was responsible for the wrongful deed, enables a person to divest oneself of those character traits and develop this new personality.

אִישׁ אוֹ־אִשָּׁה כִּי יַעֲשׂוּ מִכָּל־חַטֹּאת הָאָדָם לִמְעֹל מַעַל בַּה'
וְאָשְׁמָה הַנֶּפֶשׁ הַהִוא וְהִתְוַדּוּ אֶת־חַטָּאתָם ...

A man or woman who commits any of man's sins
by committing treachery towards God; that person
will be guilty — they shall confess their sin (5:6-7)

Passive Complicity

The verses open with the singular, "a man *or* woman," but close with the plural, "*they* shall confess."

The ethicist, R' Chaim Zaichek, says that this teaches us the concept that I referred to earlier, that the firstborn of the tribes forfeited the priesthood because they did not actively protest when the minority worshipped the Golden Calf. Silence in the presence of wrong is a tacit approval.

Here, too, the Torah underscores this. If an individual sins, it is not enough that he acknowledge his guilt. The community as a whole must acknowledge its dereliction. Had the community established proper rules of conduct and observed them, individuals would have been discouraged from transgressing. The community may not point a finger at the transgressor as being the only one at fault. It, too, must share in the blame for the sin of any individual.

Let me give an example. Everyone condemns drunk driving and the horror of the killing and crippling that it causes. We are told that there are "tough laws" that punish drunk drivers. Yet, it is not unusual for a vehicular homicide to be committed by a person who has had several arrests for drunk driving.

In some places, the *first* drunk-driving offense results in a lifelong revocation of a driver's license with no appeal. It is true that irresponsible people will drive without a license, but this law has had a significant effect in reducing drunk driving.

Why do we not have a similar law in the U.S.? The argument advanced is that one cannot deprive a person of a livelihood that depends on mobility. Or, why should the wife and children be made to suffer if the drunk driver cannot work without a car? But what about the people who were killed or maimed for life? What about the bereaved family members of a victim? Why is only the family of the perpetrator considered?

The incidence of drunk-driving deaths in the U.S. is high because the community gives lip service to being tough, but its failure to really take decisive action condones this heinous crime.

Whenever any crime is committed, the community should do some soul-searching for its role in allowing it to occur.

We find an additional halachah regarding "enabling" in the Talmud, which states that if a person lends someone money in the absence of witnesses and without documentation, he is in violation of the prohibition, "Do not put a stumbling block before the blind," which the Talmud interprets to mean, do not set up a condition which may cause someone to sin (*Bava Metzia* 75b). Human nature is such that a person may conveniently forget that he owes money, and without evidence of the loan, he may refuse to repay it. The person who lent him the money under conditions which permitted his denying it shares in the guilt. Therefore, although a single individual commits the crime of refusing to repay his loan, the lender, too, must recognize his guilt in permitting it to happen, hence the plural "*they* shall confess the sins that *they* did."

In treating alcoholism, drug addiction or compulsive gambling, we must make the family aware that they may often have been unwitting participants in the problem, by "enabling" the addict to continue his drug use. Sometimes the family gives the addict money or bails him out of jail. Families are notorious for paying off a gambler's debts to keep him out of jail. This may be well intended, but eliminating the consequences of the gambling enables the person to continue it.

Long before the phenomenon of "enabling" was formulated in psychology, the Torah recognized it. The person who lent someone money without evidence of the loan certainly had good intentions, but he set up a condition which was conducive to sin, and he, too, must seek forgiveness.

The above verse (*Numbers* 5:7) refers to the sin of theft. "They shall confess the sin that they committed and make restitution." Inasmuch as *teshuvah* for any sin requires confession, why does the Torah choose the sin of theft to cite the need for confession?

R' Yitzchok Meir of Gur states that according to halachah, if one uses a borrowed item for purposes other than those specified by the lender, that is tantamount to theft. For example, if one borrows an automobile with the understanding that he will drive it only within the city limits, and then takes it out to a rugged, mountainous terrain, he has essentially taken another person's property without permission.

God gave us many abilities: to see, hear, speak and act. Our lives are essentially on loan to us, and we return our spirit to Him when our allotted time us up. God gave us these abilities with specific instructions on their use. For example, we are not to look at indecency, we are not to speak or hear *lashon hara*, and there are many acts that are forbidden. If one violates these instructions, one has used a borrowed item for other than its intended use, and this constitutes theft.

Every act of transgression, says R' Yitzchok Meir, is a commission of theft. This is why the requirement for confession in *teshuvah* is specified at the sin of theft.

אִישׁ אֲשֶׁר־יִתֵּן לַכֹּהֵן לוֹ יִהְיֶה
That which a person gives to the Kohen shall be his (5:10)

To Give Is to Own

How different Torah concepts are from secular concepts! A person who has a vast amount of money in the bank is considered wealthy because he owns that money. But if all the money remains in the bank and is not shared with others, the person is merely a *shomer* (bailee), who has the money for safekeeping. He does not demonstrate ownership until he shares the money.

This is what the Torah tells us: "That which a person gives to the *Kohen* shall be his." As long as one hoards money, or exchanges it for personal possessions, it is not really his. It is only when he gives of it to others that he demonstrates that he indeed owned it (R' Yehoshua Trunk of Kutna).

The human being is a composite creature, comprised of an animal-like body and "something else." The "something else" is the aggregate of those traits which are unique to man, which we may refer to as the "human spirit." Acquisitive drives are not unique to man. The accumulation of wealth is, therefore, not a uniquely human feature. However, animals in the wild, as a rule, do not sacrifice of themselves for strangers. When we share our possessions with others, we are exercising our humanity.

Giving *tzedakah* is uniquely human. It defines us as spiritual beings.

> It is related that a Jew held a high ministerial position in a government, and some anti-Semites who begrudged him this honor sought to discredit him before the king. They told the king that this Jewish minister had embezzled huge sums of money from the royal coffers. Although the king did not wish to believe this, he nevertheless asked the Jew for an accounting of his possessions.
>
> When the minister presented the figure, the king said, "This cannot be. You own far more than what is here."
>
> The Jew responded, "Your Majesty, I know why you requested an accounting of my belongings. My adversaries have slandered me to you to make me suspect in your eyes. If Your Majesty were to believe them, you will confiscate everything I have.
>
> "When Your Majesty requested an account of my possessions, I calculated how much I gave to charity. That can never be taken from me, hence that is my only real possession."

Perhaps that is the message in the above verse: "That which a person gives to the *Kohen* shall be his." Only what we give to *tzedakah* is really our own.

אִישׁ אִישׁ כִּי־תִשְׂטֶה אִשְׁתּוֹ וּמָעֲלָה בוֹ מָעַל
Any man whose wife shall go astray and commit treachery against him (5:12)

The Insanity of Sin

The Hebrew word for going astray is *sisteh*. Inasmuch as there are no markings in the Torah, the word can also be read as *sishteh*, which means "go insane." This led to the Talmudic statement, "A person does not commit a sin unless one was overtaken by a spirit of insanity" (*Sotah* 3a). Sin is invariably the result of a person surrendering to temptation. Given that this is wrong, in what way is it insane?

To contend that 2 + 2 = 5 is insane. To believe that one is emperor of China is insane. Insanity is a break with reality.

A Jew is required to believe that one is always in the presence of God and that nothing can be hidden from God. The opening paragraph of the *Shulchan Aruch* (Code of Jewish Law) states that the awareness that one is in the presence of God discourages a person from improper behavior. One would not act indecently in the presence of even a mortal king. Committing a sin is an assertion that one is *not* in the presence of God. Unless one denies the existence of God, such an assertion is a denial of reality, hence it constitutes insanity.

The gap between mortal man and Infinite God is so vast that it cannot be bridged by anything other than the method provided by God: fulfilling His commandments. Violating His will severs the relationship between man and God. R' Shneur Zalman states in *Tanya* that no rational person would wish this relationship to be severed, and one who commits a sin is under the impression that his relationship with God can remain intact even if he sins. This is a delusion, hence it constitutes insanity.

Certainly, a person would be offended if someone called him insane. When we deviate from God's commandments, we are essentially labeling *ourselves* as insane. No rational person should wish to degrade himself in this way.

אִישׁ אוֹ־אִשָּׁה כִּי יַפְלִא לִנְדֹּר נֶדֶר נָזִיר לְהַזִּיר לַה' ...

The Torah gives the rules for a Nazirite, one who has taken
a vow not to drink intoxicating beverages for thirty days.
***A man or woman who shall dissociate himself by taking
a Nazirite vow of abstinence for the sake of God*** (6:2)

Being Humanly Holy

The Hebrew word for "dissociates," *yafli,* can also mean "to do wonders." Ibn Ezra uses this translation to interpret the verse thusly: "If a person takes a vow of abstinence, it is indeed a wondrous act, because most people indulge themselves."

R' Yechezkel Levenstein states that abstaining from pleasure is going against one's innate drives, because all living things are driven to seek pleasure. Man was indeed created with many bodily drives, but it is his mission to become master over them rather than a slave to them.

The Gaon of Vilna wrote in a letter, "It is not essential that a person engage in self-flagellation, but just that he be master over his speech and temptations."

R' Yisroel of Salant said: "It is not sufficient that a person serve God only to the extent that it causes him no discomfort. This is serving oneself rather than serving God. A person must do what is required of him, even if it goes against his natural inclinations."

The Torah says of a Nazirite, "For the crown of his God is upon his head" (*Numbers* 6:7). Animals cannot go against their nature, and angels have no temptations to subdue. Neither animals nor angels can make free choices. Only God and man can choose their actions freely, and this is what is meant by man being created "in the image of God" (*Genesis* 1:27). When a person accepts a vow to deny fulfilling his natural inclinations, he merits the description "for the crown of his God is upon his head."

It is not necessary for a person to take vows of abstinence, but it is required of us that we truly be in conscious control of our behavior (*Lekach Tov, Bamidbar* p. 64).

R' Mendel of Kotzk cited the verse, "People of holiness shall you be to Me," and commented that the Hebrew can also be translated as "You shall be *humanly* holy unto me." Angels were *created* holy. Man must *develop* holiness. Man was not intended to be an angel, but to be "humanly holy."

חֹמֶץ יַיִן וְחֹמֶץ שֵׁכָר לֹא יִשְׁתֶּה

If a person accepts upon himself to be a Nazirite, he must abstain from wine. ***Anything in which grapes have been steeped shall he not drink*** (6:3)

Parental Influence

When the heavenly angel told Samson's mother that she would conceive and bear a son, he instructed her to abstain from wine and ale, because her child will be a Nazirite (*Judges* 10:3). The restrictions of the Nazirite apply only to him. If Samson was destined to be a Nazirite, why did his mother have to abstain from wine and ale?

Thousands of years ago, the Torah taught what has just recently been discovered by science. What the mother does during pregnancy can have a profound effect on the child. Children born to a mother who drank or used drugs during her pregnancy may suffer developmental damage.

But in a broader sense, this applies to parental behavior in general. It is unrealistic to expect children to have higher standards of behavior than those of the parents. Effective parenting is achieved by modeling. If the parents justify "white lies" or less than fully honest dealings, they can hardly expect their children to be paragons of truth and honesty.

While there may indeed be genetic factors that affect behavior, most behavior is learned, and a child's most influential teachers are the parents. How can parents who shout and scream expect their children to control their anger? How can parents who smoke cigarettes expect their children to resist the peer pressure for drug use? Smoking is an unequivocal justification for getting a temporary pleasant feeling at the cost of long-term damage. This is exactly what the drug user does.

> *A chassidic master and his disciples passed a house from which loud shouting emanated. Looking through the window, they saw that a son was dragging his elderly father to the door to evict him, shouting insults at him. The disciples were surprised that the master watched this atrocity in silence. When the son had dragged the father to the threshold, the master ran into the house, seized the son by the lapels, and gave him a sound thrashing for his despicable disrespect of his father.*
>
> *The disciples asked the master why he had remained silent until that*

point. The master said, "You see, when the father was a young man, he tried to evict his father, and had dragged him up to the threshold. Therefore, he had it coming to be dragged up to the threshold, but no further."

We set a pattern for our children through our own behavior.

עַל־נֶפֶשׁ מֵת לֹא יָבֹא: לְאָבִיו וּלְאִמּוֹ לְאָחִיו וּלְאַחֹתוֹ
לֹא־יִטַּמָּא לָהֶם בְּמֹתָם כִּי נֵזֶר אֱלֹקָיו עַל־רֹאשׁוֹ

If a person took upon himself the vow of a Nazirite, the Torah says, *He shall not come near a dead person. To his father or to his mother, to his brother or to his sister—he shall not contaminate himself to them upon their death, for the crown of his God is upon his head* (6:6-7)

In Quest of Spirituality

Ralbag explains why the Torah forbids a Nazirite to come near the dead. "The reason why a dead body contaminates is because it represents the defectiveness of the physical, and the Nazirite should avoid the physical things to which he may be attracted."

R' Henoch Lebovitz comments that to the contrary, being confronted with human mortality motivates a person to spirituality, as King Solomon says, "It is better to go to the house of mourning than to go to a house of feasting, for that is the end of all man, and the living should take it to heart" (*Ecclesiastes* 7:2). We find repeated references in the Talmud that the contemplation of one's mortality discourages a person from physical indulgences. Why, then, does Ralbag say that the Nazirite, who takes a vow of abstinence in his quest for spirituality, should avoid contact with the dead?

R' Lebovitz explains that there are two paths whereby one can strive for spirituality. One way is to focus on man's sharing of physical drives with lower forms of life, and that when he indulges in gratification of his bodily desires he is acting out his animalistic traits. The Midrash states that when God admonished Adam for his sin, Adam wept, "Now my mule and I will be eating from the same trough." This is a humbling awareness that should motivate a person toward spirituality by distancing him from physical gratification. The second way is to realize the holiness of the Divine *neshamah* (soul) that he possesses, which is inseparable from its source in God. The realization of his potential for Godliness should motivate a person toward the pursuit of spirituality.

Both approaches are valid, and each has its place. The ethicists cite the phrase, "His heart was high in the way of God" (*II Chronicles* 17:6) as meaning that although pride is vanity, one may be motivated by pride to become more spiritual. Awareness of one's Godly component should make a person reach for the stars, because there is nothing spiritual that is beyond his grasp. As Rambam says, "Every person can be like Moses" (*Hilchos Teshuvah* 5:2). The dignity of man should make him pursue perfection.

The Talmud tells of a young man who had beautiful long hair. Seeing his handsome reflection in the water, he feared that he might be drawn to physical indulgences. He promptly took a Nazirite vow, which would require shaving his head. "I swear that I will cut this hair in the service of God" (*Nazir* 4:2). One who accepts *Nezirus* for such a purpose is the ideal.

A Nazirite who is so dedicated to the achievement of spirituality should focus on the Godliness of his *neshamah*. He should be thoroughly absorbed in the spiritual greatness that is within his reach. There is no need for him to concentrate on his lowly physical component and be distracted from his potential greatness (*Chidushei HaLev, Bamidbar* p. 31).

וְאַחַר יִשְׁתֶּה הַנָּזִיר יָיִן

Afterward the Nazirite may drink wine (6:20)

Make Rituals Effective

Inasmuch as this verse refers to the ritual after the Nazirite has completed the period of his vow, then he is no longer a Nazirite when he is permitted to resume drinking wine. Why does the Torah say that afterwards "the Nazirite" may drink wine?

A chassid once complained to his Rebbe that he had read in a kabbalistic book that if a person fasts forty consecutive days, he will receive prophetic powers. "I fasted forty consecutive days," he said, "but I have not received any prophetic powers."

The Rebbe said, "It is known that the Baal Shem Tov's horses traveled with extraordinary speed, covering great distances in minutes. The Baal Shem Tov would tell his driver, Alexi, to turn his back to the horses, and they would then take off, virtually flying along the road.

"The horses were accustomed to be watered and fed at every inn along the way. When they passed the first two inns and did not stop for water and hay, they began thinking, 'Perhaps we are not horses after all. Perhaps we are really human beings, who only stop for food at mealtime.' When they continued to pass more inns at which people would normally stop to eat, they thought, 'Even human beings would have stopped for food by now. Perhaps we are angels, who have no need to eat at all.' When they arrived at their destination and were given water and hay, they concluded, 'We are in fact only horses after all.'

"You see," the Rebbe said, "you can attain prophetic powers by abstaining from food for forty consecutive days only if the fasting has elevated you spiritually, so that when you resume eating, it is much different than the way you ate before the fast. Your attitude toward food should no longer be for its pleasant taste or even to satiate your hunger. You should eat solely because your body requires the nutrition to function properly, so that you would have the energy wherewith to serve God by studying Torah and performing mitzvos. But if after you complete forty days of fasting you resume eating the way you did before the fast, then your fasting has accomplished nothing. You are much like the Baal Shem Tov's horses who, when fed hay, discovered that they were not the angels they thought themselves to be."

This is what the Torah is telling us. A true Nazirite is one who accepts upon himself the abstention of a Nazirite because he wishes to become more spiritual. This person, after completing the period of his vow, should be holier than before. Although he is no longer bound by the vows, his Nazirite experience should remain with him and alter his character. If he goes back to being the person he was before his vow, his period of abstention was rather meaningless, and it is as though he had never been a Nazirite at all. It is of the true Nazirite that the Torah says, "afterwards the Nazirite may drink wine."

During the month of Elul preceding the High Holidays and during the Ten Days of Repentance, it is customary to accept more rigid practices. This is indeed commendable, but is of value only if these practices make one more spiritual. If one reverts to the behavior one had before Elul, the extra observances are of little substance.

דַּבֵּר אֶל־אַהֲרֹן וְאֶל־בָּנָיו לֵאמֹר כֹּה תְבָרְכוּ
אֶת־בְּנֵי יִשְׂרָאֵל אָמוֹר לָהֶם יְבָרֶכְךָ ה׳ וְיִשְׁמְרֶךָ

*"Speak to Aaron and his sons, saying,
'So shall you bless the Children of Israel: saying to them,
"May God bless you and safeguard you"'"* (6:23-24)

The Blessing of Self-Esteem

The words "saying to them" appear to be superfluous. The verse could have just as well said, "Thus shall you bless the Children of Israel: 'May God bless you and safeguard you.'"

R' Levi Yitzchok of Berditchev suggests a novel interpretation. The Hebrew for "say unto them," *amor lahem,* can have an additional meaning. In *Deuteronomy* 26:17 the word *he'emarta* means to distinguish or exalt. If we apply that interpretation here, the verse reads: "Thus shall you bless the Children of Israel: *distinguish them and exalt them.*" The *Kohanim,* the spiritual leaders of Israel, are instructed to give Jews a feeling of distinction and pride.

Included in the priestly blessing is, "He shall be gracious unto you." The Hebrew word for this is, "He shall give you *chein.*" *Chein* is difficult to translate with precision. It is traditionally translated as "favor." What it means in this context is "unconditional love." It can best be conceptualized as the love of a mother for her infant child. God loves Israel unconditionally, and does not reject them even when they are sinful, as the Torah says, "He rests amidst them even when they are defiled" (*Leviticus* 16:16).

Aaron, the first High Priest, is characterized as, "He loved people and brought them closer to Torah" (*Ethics of the Fathers* 1:12). Aaron loved even those who were distant from Torah. Because he made them feel lovable, they could understand that God loved them, and this brought them closer to Torah.

When bestowing the priestly blessing, Aaron's descendants recite the *berachah,* "He has sanctified us with the sanctity of Aaron." They are to follow in the footsteps of their great ancestor, and like him, make every Jew feel worthy of being loved. This, according to R' Levi Yitzchok, is the meaning of *amor lahem,* "exalt them and make them feel worthy of being loved." This is the *chein* of the *Kohanim's* blessing.

BAMIDBAR / NUMBERS: Nasso

דַּבֵּר אֶל־אַהֲרֹן וְאֶל־בָּנָיו לֵאמֹר כֹּה תְבָרְכוּ אֶת־בְּנֵי יִשְׂרָאֵל
אָמוֹר לָהֶם יְבָרֶכְךָ ה' וְיִשְׁמְרֶךָ יָאֵר ה' פָּנָיו אֵלֶיךָ וִיחֻנֶּךָּ
יִשָּׂא ה' פָּנָיו אֵלֶיךָ וְיָשֵׂם לְךָ שָׁלוֹם

*Speak to Aaron and his sons, saying, "So shall you bless the
Children of Israel: saying to them, 'May God bless you and safeguard you.
May God make His countenance shine upon you and be gracious to you.
May God lift His countenance to you and establish peace for you'"* (6:23-26)

The Blessing of Love

Immediately prior to the *Kohanim* delivering the blessing, they say, "He commanded us to bless His nation, Israel, *with love.*" Where in the above commandment do we find any reference to blessing Israel *with love*?

Perhaps the interpretation is not only that they should *deliver* the blessing with love, i.e., that the *Kohanim* should *feel* love for Israel when blessing them, but also that "with love" is the *content* of the blessing. The blessing is that *Israel* should feel love, that they should have love for one another. According to this interpretation, it lies well within the commandment.

The blessing culminates that God should bless Israel with peace. The blessing of peace can be merited only when there is love among Jews. When there is dissension and strife among Jews, they cannot expect to enjoy the blessing of peace.

We long for and pray for peace. The key to peace is in our own hands. If we can overlook the differences between us, many of which are the result of self-centeredness, and achieve love for one another, we will merit the Divine blessing of *shalom*.

In addition to meaning "peace," *shalom* can also be read as *shaleim*, "whole." If we are fragmented rather than whole, we cannot have the *shalom* of peace.

כֹּה תְבָרְכוּ אֶת־בְּנֵי יִשְׂרָאֵל . . . וְשָׂמוּ אֶת־שְׁמִי עַל־בְּנֵי יִשְׂרָאֵל וַאֲנִי אֲבָרֲכֵם

*"Thus shall you bless the Children of Israel . . .
let them place My Name upon the Children of Israel,
and I shall bless them"* (6:23-27)

Receiving God's Blessing

Rashi explains "I will bless them" means that God will concur with the blessings of the *Kohanim*. But if so, why is there any need for the *Kohanim* to pronounce the blessing? Let the blessing come directly from God.

R' Asher of Karlin said that there may be a person who may not merit the Divine blessing. Yet, if he frequents the house of worship and receives the blessing of the *Kohanim*, God assures us that their blessing will be fulfilled even if the person is not deserving of it on his own merits. Nevertheless, a person should realize that it is God's concurrence that gives the blessing its effectiveness.

A woman once came to R' Mordechai of Czernoble asking for his blessing to have a child, but in spite of her entreaties, the tzaddik did not respond, and she left broken-hearted. The tzaddik's gabbai (aide) could not understand why the tzaddik had refused to bless the distraught woman. "Go fetch the woman," the tzaddik said.

When the woman returned, the tzaddik asked her, "What did you do

when you left here?" The woman said, "I looked up to heaven and said, 'Master of the Universe! Even the tzaddik refuses to help me. I have no one to rely on other than You.'"

The tzaddik said to his gabbai, "This woman was under the impression that I have some sort of magical powers to grant her wish. She did not realize that blessings can come only from God. Now that she has turned to the true Source of all blessings, her wish will be fulfilled."

וְשָׂמוּ אֶת־שְׁמִי עַל־בְּנֵי יִשְׂרָאֵל וַאֲנִי אֲבָרֲכֵם

"Let them place My Name over the Children of Israel, and I shall bless them" (6:27)

Preparing to Receive God's Blessing

Inasmuch as God will bless us, what need is there for the *Kohanim* to do so?

There is a constant outflow of Divine benevolence, says the author of *Akeidas Yitzchok*. How much good a person receives depends on how much one has made oneself a receptacle for the Divine blessing. The source of a river provides an effluence of water, but in the course of the river there are places where the river is wide and deep, and other places where it is narrow and shallow. The difference depends on the area into which the water flows. The magnitude of the Divine blessing one receives is dependent on how ready one is to receive it.

I heard it phrased that God's blessings hover over us like airplanes hovering over an airport with no place to land. The blessings are there, but we must give them a place to land.

How does a person prepare oneself for receiving the Divine blessing? By knowing that everything emanates from God and that one's success is not the result of one's own might and cunning. The greater one's conviction that God is the source of all good, the more one is in a state to receive His blessings.

The priestly blessing is preparatory. If you know that it is God Who blesses you and protects you and that He is the source of grace and peace, then you are capable of receiving His blessing. If you have properly understood the priestly blessing and adopted it, then "let them place My Name over the Children of Israel, and I shall bless them."

וַיְהִי הַמַּקְרִיב בַּיּוֹם הָרִאשׁוֹן אֶת־קָרְבָּנוֹ נַחְשׁוֹן בֶּן־עַמִּינָדָב

The one who brought his offering on the first day was Nachshon, son of Amminadab (7:12)

No Title Necessary

It is noteworthy that all the offerings brought on subsequent days cite the leader of the tribe as the *nasi* (chief). Only Nachshon is not given this title. Did Nachshon not deserve it?

We are accustomed to according lavish honorary titles to prominent people. Is it not ironic that the greatest Jew of all, Moses, is referred to simply as Moshe Rabbeinu, our teacher? The great sage, Hillel, is not *Rabbi* Hillel, just Hillel.

The Talmud lists the various levels of honorary titles and concludes that the greatest title of all is simply the person's name (*Tosefta, Eduyos* 3:4). No trimmings. No need to gild the lily.

When the Israelites were trapped between the Reed Sea and the oncoming Egyptian army, they panicked and cried out to God for salvation. God said to Moses, "Let them move forward." It was Nachshon, with perfect faith and trust in the Divine word, who marched into the water, and it was by the merit of this demonstration of faith that the waters divided.

Everyone knew who Nachshon was. He did not need any titles.

Those who seek public acclaim and recognition should be aware that when one does the utmost to fulfill one's mission and responsibilities, that is the greatest distinction. Lavish, honorary titles are not much more than window dressing.

Indeed, the Talmud says that if one pursues acclaim, it will elude him. Those that go about doing what they should be doing and shunning acclaim will be recognized and appreciated for what they are.

The Midrash says that a person has three names: one given by his parents, one given by his peers and one that he gives to himself (*Tanchuma, Vayakhel*). The name that parents give is his legal name, the name given by his friends is his title in society and the name he gives to himself is based on his actions.

It is not Chief Nachshon, just Nachshon (R' Pinchas of Koretz).

A second interpretation is given by *Maor V'Shemesh*. He says that although Nachshon was the leader of his tribe, he was so humble and self-effacing that anyone observing him would not identify him as a leader, but simply as "Nachshon."

The Psalmist says, "The proper offering to God is a humble spirit" (*Psalms* 51:19), upon which the Talmud comments, "When the Temple existed, one who brought an *olah* offering had the merit of an *olah*, and one who brought a *minchah* offering had the merit of a *minchah*. However, a person of humble spirit has the merit of *all* the offerings, as the verse in *Psalms* indicates."

Nachshon's greatest offering was his humility. *Maor V'Shemesh* says that a careful reading of the verse (*Numbers* 7:12) is "The one who brought his offering on the first day was Nachshon," i.e., the offering *was* Nachshon himself, i.e., his humility rather than the items he donated.

In absence of the Temple, we can achieve the merits of offerings by developing our humility.

וַיְהִי הַמַּקְרִיב בַּיּוֹם הָרִאשׁוֹן אֶת־קָרְבָּנוֹ נַחְשׁוֹן בֶּן־עַמִּינָדָב
לְמַטֵּה יְהוּדָה וְקָרְבָּנוֹ קַעֲרַת־כֶּסֶף אַחַת . . . בַּיּוֹם הַשֵּׁנִי הִקְרִיב
נְתַנְאֵל בֶּן־צוּעָר נְשִׂיא יִשָּׂשכָר הִקְרִב אֶת־קָרְבָּנוֹ קַעֲרַת־כֶּסֶף אַחַת . . .

The leaders of the twelve tribes each brought an offering to the dedication of the Sanctuary. **The one who brought his offering on the first day was Nachshon, son of Amminadab, of the tribe of Judah. His offering was: one silver bowl...** *On the second day, Nethanel son of Zuar offered, the leader of Issachar. He brought his offering: one silver bowl...* (7:12-83)

Every Person Is Worthy of Honor

The Torah proceeds to list the offerings of all the tribal leaders. Although all the offerings were identical, the Torah elaborates the composition of each offering *twelve times*. This is most unusual, because not a single letter of the Torah is superfluous. Major halachos are derived from subtle nuances. The Torah could have said, "On the second day, Nethanel brought the identical offering. On the third day, Eliab brought the identical offering," and so on. What could possibly be of such great importance that the Torah lists each identical offering in detail?

R' Yechezkel Levenstein cites Ramban, who says that although the offerings were identical, each leader designed his own offering according to his own understanding. Had the Torah said, "On the second day, Nethanel brought an identical offering," and so on, it would have appeared that each one emulated Nachshon, and that would have *lessened the honor* which each leader was due. R' Yechezkel says, "The fact that the Torah went to such great length to teach this indicates the overwhelming importance for respecting a person's honor."

> The sage R' Isser Zalman Meltzer was sitting with a group of students, when one student looked out the window and said, "The Brisker Rav is coming!" R' Isser Zalman quickly arose and changed into his Shabbos kaftan and hurried down the stairs to greet the illustrious guest. He found, however, that it was not at all the Brisker Rav, but a man who bore a faint resemblance to him, and the student had mistaken the identity.
>
> To the students' great surprise, R' Issar Zalman related toward this man as though he were the Brisker Rav! He sat him at the head of the table and asked whether he could serve him anything. The man was overwhelmed, and said that inasmuch as he was about to leave to raise funds, he would like to have a letter of recommendation from the sage. R' Issar Zalman promptly wrote the letter and escorted the man down the stairs.
>
> Seeing the students' bewilderment, R' Issar Zalman said, "It is, in fact, required that we relate to every person with great respect, just as if the person was a great scholar. Look at the way the patriarch Abraham treated the angels who had appeared to him in the guise of wayfaring Arabs.
>
> "Unfortunately, we do not observe this properly, and we discriminate in how we act to people of different status. Inasmuch as Divine Providence had me prepare to receive the Brisker Rav with the honor due him, this gave me the opportunity to greet this man with the respect that is, in truth, appropriate for every person."

We are indeed creatures of habit, and we generally do not go out of our way to accord great honor to people of lesser status. The message in the Torah's detailing each leader's offering is to impress us with the need to accord respect to everyone, and most certainly to avoid the slightest trace of disrespect.

The extraordinary length the Torah goes to emphasize this point indicates its extreme importance (*Lekach Tov, Bamidbar* p. 73). (See *Living Each Week* for another interpretation.)

זֹאת חֲנֻכַּת הַמִּזְבֵּחַ בְּיוֹם הִמָּשַׁח אֹתוֹ...
זֹאת חֲנֻכַּת הַמִּזְבֵּחַ אַחֲרֵי הִמָּשַׁח אֹתוֹ

This was the dedication of the Altar on the day it was anointed ... this was the dedication of the Altar after it was anointed (7:84-88)

Maintaining Enthusiasm

Whenever a new project is initiated or a building is completed, there is a dedication ceremony at which everyone's spirits soar, and the enthusiasm of the attendees promises to make the venture a smashing success.

Alas! As time marches on, interest often wanes, and projects that were undertaken with much fanfare may find themselves struggling for survival. The enthusiasm of its initiation seems to dissipate.

A new synagogue is dedicated. Standing room only. It promises to be a citadel of spirituality and worship. Just several months later, the attendance on Shabbos is rather meager, and it is not unusual to have to look for a tenth person to complete the *minyan* (quorum of ten) for weekday services.

This is not how it was with the Sanctuary. "This was the dedication of the Altar *on the day it was anointed* ... this was the dedication of the Altar *after it was anointed*." The enthusiasm that prevailed at the dedication ceremonies continued unabated.

We may hear an inspiring sermon from a charismatic speaker, and we may resolve to make significant changes in our lives. Several days later, the sermon is forgotten and it is business as usual. The inspiration was probably due to the brilliant oratory rather than the content. This is a superficial emotion which does not penetrate into our hearts. When we are motivated to do something that will elevate us spiritually, we should keep that motivation fresh.

This theme is continued in the next portion of the Torah. "When you kindle the lamps, the seven lamps shall cast light toward the face of the Menorah" (*Numbers* 8:2). The Hebrew word for "kindle," *beha'aloscha*, means "to lift up." Rashi explains that the *Kohen* must light the wick of the lamp until the flame rises. It is not unusual for the wick of an oil lamp to flicker and extinguish. The lighting must be such that the flame is steady.

King Solomon says, "The *neshamah* (soul) of man is the lamp of God" (*Proverbs* 20:27). The human *neshamah* also needs to be "kindled" to illuminate a person's life. It is not unusual for a person to have a moment of inspiration, in which he feels a spiritual arousal. Too often, this inspiration "flickers" and is extinguished, and life goes on as if the spiritual arousal had not occurred.

The instruction is given to the spiritual leader that he is to "kindle" the light of the *neshamah* in a way that the spiritual inspiration is maintained. It is not enough to give an inspiring sermon whose effect may wane. The dedication of the spiritual leader to his flock should be such that he continues to elevate them spiritually until the flame of the *neshamah* endures.

The enthusiasm at the beginning of a Torah project or a new mitzvah is what can give it the *simchah* that should characterize our service of God. Let us not allow it to dissipate (*Iturei Torah, Bamidbar* p. 47).

פרשת בהעלותך
Parashas Beha'aloscha

בְּהַעֲלֹתְךָ אֶת־הַנֵּרֹת אֶל־מוּל פְּנֵי הַמְּנוֹרָה יָאִירוּ שִׁבְעַת הַנֵּרוֹת

When you kindle the lamps, toward the face of the Menorah shall the seven lamps cast light (8:2)

Effective Teaching

The Midrash states that the wicks were directed away from the interior of the room, to indicate that the purpose of the Menorah was symbolic of the Divine Presence rather than to provide illumination for the Sanctuary. "God provided the pillar of light to illuminate the Israelites' travel in the desert for forty years. God hardly needed the light of the Menorah to illuminate His Sanctuary."

The fact that God created the sun, which provides light for the entire world, is an even greater feat than His providing light in the desert. Why was His creation of the sun not mentioned?

A similar question may be raised about the opening verse of the Ten Commandments: "I am your God Who has taken you out from Egypt" (*Exodus* 20:2). Why not, "I am your God Who created the universe?"

The Torah is teaching us a very practical lesson. If you want to impress someone with any concept, present it to him in a way that conforms to a sense experience with which one is familiar. Abstract concepts are often difficult to grasp. Contrary to the popular aphorism, seeing is *not* believing. Seeing is a sense experience, and one is immediately convinced of the reality of something one sees. One must believe in something which one *cannot* see, hear or touch.

We *believe* that God created the sun and the entire universe, but this is a matter of faith. It is difficult to base an argument for faith on faith alone. The Israelites did not witness the creation of the sun and the universe. They *did* witness the extraordinary miracles which God wrought in Egypt, and they beheld the pillar of fire with their very own eyes. These factual experiences were the basis of their faith.

Faith requires a degree of sophistication. After decades of enslavement, the Israelites could not easily grasp abstractions, and they required miracles to develop their faith. "Israel saw the great hand that God inflicted on Egypt; and the people revered God, and they had faith in God and in Moses, His servant" (ibid. 14:31).

We should remember that children also lack sophistication, and may not easily grasp abstractions. We refer to God as "Our Father, our King." Small children, who think of God as a father, conceptualize Him as the father they know, and in their juvenile minds they attribute to God the traits that they see in their father.

We want our children to believe that God is just, true and compassionate. It is, therefore, a father's responsibility to demonstrate these traits to his children in a way that they can readily see them. If a father is not just, true and compassionate, children will develop a faulty concept of God, which may be difficult to eradicate as they mature.

לָמָה נִגָּרַע לְבִלְתִּי הַקְרִיב אֶת־קָרְבַּן ה' בְּמֹעֲדוֹ בְּתוֹךְ בְּנֵי יִשְׂרָאֵל
וַיֹּאמֶר אֲלֵהֶם מֹשֶׁה עִמְדוּ וְאֶשְׁמְעָה מַה־יְצַוֶּה ה' לָכֶם

The Torah states that there were people who were in a state of ritual impurity because they had come in contact with the dead, and they were unable to participate in the Pesach offering. They complained to Moses, *"Why should we be diminished by not offering God's offering?"* Moses responded, *"Stand and I will hear what God will command you"* (9:7-8)

Truly Virtuous Prayer

Rashi comments, "How fortunate is a mortal who can feel secure that he can turn directly to God and receive an answer." R' Yechezkel of Shinuv asks, Inasmuch as the Torah states that Moses was the most humble person on earth (*Numbers* 12:3), is this not out of character for Moses to feel that he has free access to speak with God at any time? How could someone so humble be so presumptuous?

R' Yechezkel answers that although God always hears our prayers, he does not always grant our requests. We are like a child who wants candy before supper; God knows what we cannot know or understand. Our most fervent wish may not fit into the Divine scheme of things and may not be to our own ultimate good. However, when one prays sincerely for Divine assistance to better serve God, that request is never turned away.

In a letter (*Iggeres HaRamban*), the Ramban instructs his son on proper conduct. He closes with the instruction to read the letter regularly once a week. Then Ramban makes a bold promise, that on the day one reads the letter, God will grant one's requests.

Experience appears to disprove Ramban's assurance. Many people have prayed for something on the day they read the letter, and their requests were not fulfilled.

The reason for this is that Ramban was not referring to prayer for everything a person may wish. Having instructed his son on the need to achieve proper *middos* (character traits), Ramban says, "If, after reading this letter, you will realize the importance of good *middos,* and you will ask God for help in achieving them, your prayers will be answered."

When Moses saw how heartbroken these people were because they were unable to participate in the Divine service of the *Pesach-offering,* he was certain that their sincere desire to serve God would merit a Divine response. Moses was not presumptuous. His statement, "Stand and I will hear what God will command for you," was based on his conviction of *their* merits, not his.

Yes, we pray, but our prayers are so often for fulfillment of our personal needs and desires. If we realized that attaining greater spirituality is the greatest good, and we prayed with greater sincerity for Divine assistance in becoming more spiritual, these prayers would surely be answered.

עֲשֵׂה לְךָ שְׁתֵּי חֲצוֹצְרֹת כֶּסֶף מִקְשָׁה תַּעֲשֶׂה אֹתָם

*Make for yourself two silver trumpets —
make them hammered out* (10:2)

The Fusion of Two Halves

This commandment appears to have applied to the period of the Israelites' sojourn in the desert, where the trumpets were used as a signal for assemblage or at wartime. Inasmuch as the Torah is eternal, this commandment must be relevant today as well.

R' Dov of Mezeritch points out that the Hebrew word for trumpets, *chatzotzros*, can be divided into two words, *chatzi tzuros*, "half forms." The specification that they be hammered out means that they were to be of one unit of silver, and not fashioned of assembled parts. The verse can then be read as "Make for yourself two half-forms, and make them into a single unit." This can have several interpretations.

The human being begins his life with only one driving force: the desire to satisfy one's cravings. Many human cravings are the work of the *yetzer hara*. When one reaches the age of bas-mitzvah or bar-mitzvah, one acquires a moral and ethical drive (*yetzer tov*). These two opposing drives are engaged in a constant struggle for mastery over the person.

In the *Shema* we read, "You shall love your God with all your heart" (*Deuteronomy* 6:5). The Talmud comments, "with *all* your heart means with both the *yetzer tov* and the *yetzer hara*" (*Berachos* 54a). The chassidic masters state that the *yetzer hara*, which is essentially the biologic component of the individual, is the source of human energy. The *yetzer tov* is the force that should provide direction, guiding the individual to harness the energy and channel it toward proper goals. The ultimate outcome should be that the *yetzer tov* succeeds in directing the energy of the *yetzer hara* to the point where doing the will of God becomes as natural as fulfilling any physiological drive.

We may think of the *yetzer hara* as the individual's first nature, which, by continued effort and direction to follow the dictates of the *yetzer tov*, can be transformed into a positive force, a second nature. When this is achieved, the *yetzer hara* is taken over by the *yetzer tov*, and both can function as a single unit.

This may be the message of the Divine commandment: Take the two "half-forms," the *yetzer tov* and the *yetzer hara*, each of which constitute one half of an individual's character, and fuse them into a single unit.

There is only one way such fusion can occur. The *yetzer hara* may ignore the guidance of the *yetzer tov*, but it cannot transform it into anything other than what it is: a guide for proper behavior. However, by constantly channeling the energy of the *yetzer hara* toward commendable goals, the *yetzer tov* can transform it into a positive force. A successful fusion of the two "half-forms" into a single unit is the ultimate human achievement.

A second interpretation relates to marriage. The Talmud states that a person who is unmarried lacks completion. When a man and a woman marry, the Torah states, "They shall become one flesh" (*Genesis* 2:24). This relates not only to their being united in their children, but that the two must form a single unit.

When husband and wife each have their own agenda, each seeking to achieve his or her own goals, the marriage is not a unit. Such relationships are vulnerable to fracture when stressed.

In chemistry, there is a difference between a "mixture" and a "compound." Salt which had been dissolved in water is a mixture. The water can be separated off by evaporation, and the salt then emerges in its original form. Neither element undergoes an essential change in a mixture.

In a compound, the two elements combine to form a new substance. For example, when oxygen and hydrogen combine in a specific proportion, they form water, a new substance which, although comprised of the two, is an entity in its own right. As separate elements, oxygen and hydrogen have their own natures, which are very different. When they unite, they are divested of their individual natures. The new compound, water, has only one nature.

This may be the message in the verse cited. Take two "half-forms" and make them into a single unit. Man and woman are each a half-form. When they join in a way that they are a single unit, the marriage becomes a compound instead of a mixture. It is then much more stable and durable.

עֲשֵׂה לְךָ שְׁתֵּי חֲצוֹצְרֹת כֶּסֶף . . . וְתָקְעוּ בָּהֵן וְנוֹעֲדוּ אֵלֶיךָ כָּל־הָעֵדָה . . .
וְאִם־בְּאַחַת יִתְקָעוּ וְנוֹעֲדוּ אֵלֶיךָ הַנְּשִׂיאִים

Make for yourself two silver trumpets . . . When they sound a long blast with them, the entire assembly shall gather . . . If they sound a long blast with one, the leaders shall gather to you (10:2-4)

Not Much Has Changed

One of the commentaries remarks that for gathering all the Israelites, it was obviously necessary to do so by sounding the trumpets. But why were trumpets necessary for assembling the tribal leaders? There were just a few of them, and they could have easily been called by sending a messenger.

The answer is that if they had been invited by messenger, each tribal leader might want to know if he was the first one called, or just where he was in the list of the twelve tribes. If he found out that others were called before him, he might feel offended. Why was the other tribe given priority?

Envy has plagued us since creation. Cain killed Abel because God favored his offering over Cain's. Korach fomented a rebellion against Moses that had disastrous consequences because he was envious that his cousin was made tribal chief rather than he.

One might think that these incidents would have taught us the folly of envy and of desiring greater recognition than others. Yet, we persist in harboring these petty feelings.

I have seen people recognize this folly in others, but not in themselves. They may be involved in planning a program and may say with some disdain, "We'd better include him on the program or we'll never hear the end of it." Or, "Be sure he sits on the dais. You know what happened the last time we overlooked that." Yet, if *they* are not accorded the honor they feel is due them, they may react exactly like the person of whom they are critical.

The Baal Shem Tov said that the world is a mirror. Inasmuch as we tend to be oblivious of our own character failings, God shows us them in other people. He expects us to have the insight that the faults we see in others are really our own.

Alas! Not too many people take advantage of this guide to self-awareness. We may see others as being over-sensitive and feeling slighted, yet we may be the same way.

True, human nature may not have changed since time immemorial, but that does not preclude our changing ourselves. If we can set aside pettiness, we will be happier and more respected than the people who demand respect.

וְנָסַע דֶּגֶל מַחֲנֵה בְנֵי־דָן מְאַסֵּף לְכָל־הַמַּחֲנֹת
Then journeyed the banner of the camp of the children of Dan, the rear guard of all the camps (10:25)

Mitzvos Beget Mitzvos

Inasmuch as the tribe of Dan was the last in the procession, they would pick up any stragglers and any lost objects, returning them to their rightful owners (Rashi).

> *A European Jew consulted his rabbi. His son, who had deviated from Torah observance, had emigrated to America. He became successful in business, and was sending his father money. However, since the son was not shomer Shabbos (observant of Shabbos), the father was reluctant to take money which may have been earned on Shabbos.*
>
> *The rabbi said, "It is unfortunate that your son has dropped observance of the mitzvos. The one mitzvah he is still observing is honoring his father. We may hope that observance of this great mitzvah may have an influence on him to observe other mitzvos. If you refuse the money, you will be depriving him of an important mitzvah."*

The tribe of Dan was the weakest of the tribes in dedication to and reverence for God. It was a member of the tribe of Dan who carried the idol of Michah out of Egypt into the Land of Israel. It was this tribe that produced King Yeravam, who caused the secession of the ten tribes. Because of this weakness, the tribe of Dan was given the opportunity to pick up the stragglers and to return lost objects to the tribes that preceded it, in the hope that the merit of these mitzvos would strengthen their loyalty to God and Torah (*Oznayim L'Torah*).

Attracting Jews to performance of the ritual mitzvos may be facilitated by encouraging them to do the mitzvos that relate to interpersonal conduct. Because they can more easily appreciate the justice of these mitzvos, they are more likely to practice them than those which are primarily between man and God.

The Talmud says, "One mitzvah brings another mitzvah in its wake" (*Ethics of the Fathers* 4:2). Giving *tzedakah*, doing acts of kindness and avoiding *lashon hara* (defamatory speech) can introduce a person to a comprehensive Torah life.

וְהָאסַפְסֻף אֲשֶׁר בְּקִרְבּוֹ הִתְאַוּוּ תַּאֲוָה וַיָּשֻׁבוּ וַיִּבְכּוּ גַּם בְּנֵי יִשְׂרָאֵל וַיֹּאמְרוּ מִי יַאֲכִלֵנוּ בָּשָׂר . . . וַיֹּאמֶר מֹשֶׁה אֶל־ה׳ לָמָה הֲרֵעֹתָ לְעַבְדֶּךָ . . . לָשׂוּם אֶת־מַשָּׂא כָּל־הָעָם הַזֶּה עָלָי . . . וְאִם־כָּכָה אַתְּ־עֹשֶׂה לִּי הָרְגֵנִי נָא הָרֹג

The rabble that was among them cultivated a craving, and the Children of Israel also wept once more, and said, "Who will feed us meat?" . . . Moses said to God, "Why have You done evil to Your servant . . . that You place the burden of this entire people upon me? And if this is how You deal with me, kill me now" (11:4-15)

There Is No Solution to Deception

Although I commented on this portion of the Torah in *Living Each Week*, I believe that the message herein is so important that it warrants further elaboration.

Moses' reaction to the request for meat is out of character for him. The worship of the Golden Calf was a grievous sin for which God threatened to destroy the Israelites, but Moses interceded and pleaded for them. The episode of the spies (*Numbers* 13:1-14:25) was an expression of their lack of trust in God. Again God threatened to destroy them and again Moses pleaded for them. Here, when they were dissatisfied with the manna and wanted meat, Moses throws up his hands in defeat. "Where shall I get meat to give to this entire people?" Furthermore, Moses knew full well that God could provide them with meat, as He indeed did (ibid. 11:31). The entire episode is enigmatic.

The answer lies in a comment by Rashi. On the verse, "Moses heard the people weeping in their family groups" (ibid. 11:10), Rashi comments, "They were complaining about family issues; namely, that the Torah forbade intra-family marriages." However, this is not what they said. Rather, they expressed their discontent over the lack of meat. At this point Moses said, "I can deal with any complaint they have, provided they are forthright about it. However, if they are deceitful and do not say what it is that they want, I cannot deal with that. Giving them meat is not going to satisfy them, because that is not what they are seeking. They want legalization of incest, but instead of expressing what they want, they put forth a spurious complaint."

There are many reasons why a person may be discontent. Sometimes a person knows what he wants but is reluctant to reveal his desire, and he presents a deceptive complaint. At other times, the person is dishonest with himself. He does not wish to admit his true desire even to himself, and he deceives himself.

I have described a condition which I call the "Spirituality Deficiency Syndrome." Just as there are physical deficiency diseases, such as iron deficiency or a deficiency of any of the essential vitamins, so there is also a deficiency syndrome that is due to lack of spirituality. The physical deficiencies can be rather easily diagnosed, because the physician knows the symptoms and can confirm the diagnosis by means of a laboratory test. However, the spirituality deficiency syndrome is rarely recognized. The principle symptom of spirituality deficiency is a *pervasive discontent*. This is not the same as a clinical depression. Rather, there is just a subtle feeling of unhappiness.

People may react to the spirituality deficiency syndrome in a variety of ways. The feeling of discontent is very distressing, and they may seek to relieve the distress by escaping into alcohol or drug use, overeating, gambling, losing oneself in work or by anything that affords them relief. The relief provided by any of the escapist techniques is short-lived, and when the discontent recurs, the person is likely to repeat the escapist maneuver. This may result in addiction to alcohol, food, drugs, gambling or work.

Another response may be to try to identify the cause for the discontent. A person may blame his job, his community or his spouse. He may change jobs, move to another city or divorce. None of these are the cause of his discontent, but feeling distressed and not knowing why, he may project his dissatisfaction onto anyone or anything.

Inasmuch as he has not dealt with the true cause, his deficiency of spirituality, his discontent will recur in the new job, new community or after the divorce and remarriage. In putting the blame for his discontent onto anything else other than the deficiency of spirituality, the person is *deceiving himself*. He cannot rid himself of the discontent unless he identifies the true cause and provides his spirit with its essential nutrients.

The self-deceptive placing of blame is also a major factor in young people who reject Yiddishkeit. They may express their dissatisfaction with Yiddishkeit, pointing out some gross inconsistencies and even hypocrisy in some purported Torah observant people. However, this is often spurious. The real reason may something else, such as poor self-esteem and low self-confidence, as a result of which a youngster may despair of success. It may be his way of acting out his anger toward his parents. The focus on the defects they have found in Yiddishkeit is simply a convenient scapegoat.

Whether it is one's personal sense of discontent or that of a child, it is important to avoid being misled by whatever the person chooses to blame.

Moses could deal with any problem if it were correctly identified. However he felt himself to be totally unable to deal with deceit, whether it was willful lying or self-deception. We, too, can cope effectively only with problems that are correctly identified. We must be ever on the alert that we do not deceive ourselves.

וְעַתָּה נַפְשֵׁנוּ יְבֵשָׁה אֵין כֹּל בִּלְתִּי אֶל־הַמָּן עֵינֵינוּ

"But now, our life is parched, there is nothing; we have nothing to anticipate but the manna!" (11:6)

Failure to Appreciate

Rashi comments that God remarked, "Just look at what my children complain about, the wonderful manna!"

R' Avraham Pam says that this Divine comment continues to ring in his ears to this very day: "Look at what my children complain about!"

A husband returns from work and finds toys strewn all over the floor. He may indeed have had a very stressful day at the office, perhaps being unable to find some important papers among the chaos on his desk, and angrily shouts to his wife, "What kind of junkyard is this? Why aren't the kids' toys put away?" Many young couples have gone through much agony and have spent many thousands of dollars in the hope of having a child. What would they not give to have toys strewn over the floor? God says, "Look at what my children complain about!"

A young lad comes home for supper, and sees an attractive plate of tuna fish salad and vegetables on the table. He exclaims, "Again? Tuna fish and vegetables!" His mother, who had come home from work, had managed to put together a meal for which many others would be grateful. God says, "Look at what my children complain about!"

A young man and a young woman are engaged. A wonderful *shidduch* of two lovely young people who can raise a family that will bring much *nachas* to their parents. Everyone is elated. Satan cannot tolerate such bliss. As the wedding day approaches, the young man's father says, "It has been the custom in our family for countless generations that the two fathers conduct the *choson* to the *chuppah* and the two mothers escort the *kallah*. We cannot break the family tradition."

The young woman's parents say, "It has always been our dream that just as we raised our daughter together, we would take her to the *chuppah* together. We cannot relinquish our fondest dream." The disagreement progresses to a harsh argument. What should have been the young couple's happiest day is turned into misery as their parents are obstinate. Satan rejoices that he has ruined the happiness of the young couple and the two families, but God bewails this foolish squabble and says, "Look at what my children complain about!"

Three times a day we recite the *Amidah* prayer and say, "*Modim anachnu lach,*" (we thank You.) However, our actions may betray our true feelings.

Moses' sharpest reprimand of the Israelites was that they were ingrates (*Avodah Zarah* 5a). Should we not hang our heads in shame that we so often fail to appreciate God's kindness?

וַיִּשְׁמַע מֹשֶׁה אֶת־הָעָם בֹּכֶה לְמִשְׁפְּחֹתָיו ...
וַיִּחַר־אַף ה׳ מְאֹד וּבְעֵינֵי מֹשֶׁה רָע

*Moses heard the people weeping in their family groups
... the wrath of God flared greatly
and in the eyes of Moses it was bad* (11:10)

Do We Really Desire Equality?

The interpretation given to this verse by R' Yitzchok Blazer (R' Itzele of Petersburg) shows us that human nature has not changed. We persist in some of the follies of our ancestors.

R' Itzele says that "weeping in their family groups" means that the Israelites were displeased that some families could not exercise superiority over other families.

There was no economy or commerce in the desert. There was no property ownership to distinguish the "haves" from the "have nots." Their clothes grew along with them and did not wear out. No one had "designer" clothes. Each person received an equal share of manna. There was no way in which any family could consider itself better than another family, and this grieved them sorely. "In the eyes of Moses it was bad." Moses was the humblest of all men on earth (*Numbers* 12:3). To him, their desire to be superior to others was an abomination.

Equality is a noble concept but has never sat well with humanity. Many people strive for distinction, sometimes in rather foolish ways.

> *R' Naftali of Ropschitz related that he was once in a bathhouse, and the attendant who was removing his boots pulled so hard on his legs that he winced with pain. "Please," he said to the attendant, "Be a little gentler."*
>
> *The attendant became furious. "Don't you tell me how to remove boots! There is no one in this entire country who can remove boots as well as I can."*
>
> *R' Naftali commented on this phenomenon. "Removing boots is hardly a dignified profession. Yet, this attendant took pride in his assertion that he is the most expert boot-remover in the country!"*

Some people may profess that they desire equality, but as has been so wisely said, they may nevertheless contend that "some may be more equal than others."

In the Korach rebellion (ibid. 16:1-35), Korach accused Moses and Aaron of usurping the leadership and the high-priesthood, claiming, "The entire congregation is holy." The wife of Ohn ben Peleth, one of the rebels, wisely said to her husband that this was not a revolt in the interest of equality. "If Moses is the leader, then you are the subject. If Korach triumphs, he will be the leader and you will still be a subject."

When Joshua told Moses that Eldad and Meidad were prophesying and that this was an incursion on Moses' authority, Moses said, "Are you being zealous for my sake? Would that the entire people of God could be prophets" (ibid. 11:26-29).

Let us not be deceived by lofty-sounding ideals. A true desire for equality can be achieved only by someone who is sincerely humble and is not obsessed by ego drivers.

הֶאָנֹכִי הָרִיתִי אֵת כָּל־הָעָם הַזֶּה אִם־אָנֹכִי יְלִדְתִּיהוּ כִּי־תֹאמַר אֵלַי שָׂאֵהוּ בְחֵיקֶךָ כַּאֲשֶׁר יִשָּׂא הָאֹמֵן אֶת־הַיֹּנֵק עַל הָאֲדָמָה אֲשֶׁר נִשְׁבַּעְתָּ לַאֲבֹתָיו

When the Israelites persisted in complaining to Moses about conditions in the desert, Moses turned to God, saying that he was unable to tolerate their unreasonable demands. **"Did I conceive this entire people or did I give birth to it, that You say to me 'Carry them in your bosom, as a nurse carries a suckling, to the Land that You swore to its forefathers?'"** (11:12)

The Standard of Care

The Talmud states that a rabbi must be able to tolerate his community. To what degree? "As a nurse carries a suckling" (*Sanhedrin* 8a).

The *Netziv* says, "If the infant soils himself and his clothes, would the nurse cast him away in disgust? Of course not! She would cleanse him and hold him as lovingly as she always did. This attitude is what the Talmud requires of a community leader. There are certain to be difficult people in the community who may annoy him, but he must be tolerant, considerate and caring even for the worst of them."

The *Netziv* practiced his teaching. There were people who harassed him with endless complaints, and he listened to them all attentively. If a person realized he had overstepped boundaries and had annoyed him and was about to apologize, the *Netziv* would anticipate this. He would say to the person that there was no need to apologize, because he probably had not addressed his problem adequately or made himself clear. Everyone left the *Netziv* with the feeling that the *Netziv* cared for him sincerely.

The Talmud takes for granted that a nurse would not allow anything the infant did to cause her to reject him. If this is so for a nurse, it should be even more so for a biological parent. Even when discipline is called for, parents should never act in a way to cause the child to feel rejected. This is also expected of every spiritual leader.

לֹא־אוּכַל אָנֹכִי לְבַדִּי לָשֵׂאת אֶת־כָּל־הָעָם הַזֶּה כִּי כָבֵד מִמֶּנִּי
וְאִם־כָּכָה אַתְּ־עֹשֶׂה לִּי הָרְגֵנִי נָא הָרֹג אִם־מָצָאתִי חֵן בְּעֵינֶיךָ

*"I alone cannot carry this entire nation, for it is too heavy for me.
And if this is how you deal with me, then kill me now,
if I have found favor in Your eyes"* (11:14-15)

The Value of Freedom

We have never heard Moses speak this way. It seems so uncharacteristic of the person who pleaded with God to forgive the sin of the Golden Calf, to the point of saying, "If You do not forgive them, erase me now from this book that You have written" (*Exodus* 32:32). What had the Israelites done to cause Moses to lose his patience with them?

The answer lies in an earlier verse. "And the Children of Israel wept once more, and said, 'Who will feed us meat? We remember the fish that we ate in Egypt free of charge; and the cucumbers, melons, leeks, onions and garlic. But now, our life is parched ... we have nothing to anticipate but the manna'" (*Numbers* 11:4-6).

They had been enslaved for generations by cruel Egyptian taskmasters. They were whipped if they did not make the required number of bricks. Their infants were drowned in the Nile. Their lives were one huge torture. Moses had broken their shackles and led them to freedom. He had brought them to the Revelation at Sinai where they received the Torah. And now all they could think about was the "good old days" in Egypt! How can you deal with a people who have no greater goal in life than filling their stomachs? For people who are willing to exchange freedom for fish and onions, Moses had no patience with them. We should be willing to sacrifice everything for freedom.

What was God's response to Moses' complaint? "Gather to Me seventy men from the elders of Israel. I will increase some of the spirit that is upon you and place it upon them" (ibid.11:16-17). The people demanded meat. How will empowering seventy elders with prophetic powers satisfy their demand for meat?

R' Samson Raphael Hirsch says that God's response was that if the Israelites feel a need for meat, it is because they have fallen from their spiritual status. If there will be highly spiritual people who can teach and uplift them, they will not desire earthly pleasures.

This should serve as a teaching for us. If we develop a strong desire for earthy pleasures, we should realize that we must be lacking in spirituality. If we pursue spiritual development more diligently, our desires for earthly things will diminish.

Another clue to Moses' frustration may be found in the verse, "The rabble that was among them *cultivated a craving,* and the Children of Israel also wept" (*Numbers* 11:4). It was not that the Israelites craved, but rather that they *cultivated* a craving. To have a natural desire is one thing, to *create* a desire where none existed is something else.

The Roman orgies were characterized by sumptuous meals, following which the people forced themselves to regurgitate so that they could have an appetite to indulge again. This was a behavior lower than that of animals. To eat when one is hungry is natural. To force oneself to become hungry when one is satiated is decadent.

Moses was able to tolerate the Israelites' shortcomings even when they sought physical rather than spiritual gratification. But when they began to cultivate and create cravings, they had gone too far. Not only did they wish to have physical pleasures, but *they were dissatisfied with being satisfied,* and wished to stimulate desires which they did not have naturally.

This phenomenon is with us today. The commercials on television stimulate cravings that had been non-existent. A person may not feel a need for something until the commercial makes him feel deprived for not having it.

The cultivation of desire is also responsible for the deadly epidemic of drugs that is devastating our population, especially our youth. *There is no innate desire for heroin or cocaine.* This desire is created when one uses the drug, and the newly cultivated desire takes control over the person with ruinous consequences.

The desire to cultivate and create desire is a cultural phenomenon. The drug culture did not develop and spread in a vacuum. It is a product of a culture which is dissatisfied with being satisfied and seeks artificial "highs."

The goal of much of Western civilization is not the "pursuit of happiness" as proposed in the Declaration of Independence. Rather, it has become "the pursuit of *pleasure."* As long as the goal in life is to find new sources of pleasure, there is no way that the drug epidemic can be stemmed.

It is incumbent upon parents to develop a philosophy of life within the family that differs from the prevailing pursuit of pleasure. There is nothing wrong with enjoying life, but there is very much wrong when pursuit of pleasure is the goal in life. A sincere spiritual orientation within the family is the most effective deterrent to drugs.

וַיַּעַן יְהוֹשֻׁעַ בִּן־נוּן מְשָׁרֵת מֹשֶׁה מִבְּחֻרָיו וַיֹּאמַר אֲדֹנִי מֹשֶׁה כְּלָאֵם

The Torah relates that when God endowed seventy elders with Divine spirit to assist Moses, there were two men, Eldad and Medad, who prophesied among the Israelites. Joshua saw this as an affront to Moses.

Joshua, the son of Nun, the servant of Moses since his youth, spoke up and said, "My lord Moses, incarcerate them" (11:28)

The Hazards of Zeal

The Talmud says that Joshua erred in telling Moses what to do, and this was tantamount to the disrespect of pronouncing a ruling in the proximity of one's teacher. The Talmud says that this is a grave offense. "One who pronounces a ruling in the presence of one's teacher deserves death" (*Berachos* 31b). Joshua was punished by being childless (*Eruvin* 63a).

R' Henoch Lebovitz cites the Talmudic statement that Joshua felt that Eldad and Medad deserved to be punished, because their prophesying in Moses' presence was equivalent to pronouncing a ruling in the presence of one's teacher (ibid., *Rashi*). R' Lebovitz asks, "How can it be that at the moment Joshua was indicting Eldad and Medad for ruling in the presence of one's teacher, he was committing the very same offense he was condemning?" He answers that although, as Moses' devoted servant, Joshua never ruled in Moses' presence, his zeal in defending Moses' honor so flustered his thinking that he could not see that he was committing the very offense he was condemning.

The Midrash states that at the Korach rebellion, Moses wished to discourage the tribe of Levi from joining Korach and suffering grave consequences. He spoke harshly to them, saying, "It is enough for you, children of Levi!" (*Numbers* 16:7). God said, "Because you spoke harshly to the Levites, My response to you when you wish to enter the Promised Land will also be, 'It is enough for you!'" Moses' intention was to spare the tribe of Levi from Korach's fate. In his zeal to do this, he used harsh language to them, and although this rebuke was in their best interest, God considered this something for which Moses was to be punished (*Bamidbar Rabbah* 18:18).

We must be cautious about zeal. It can cloud our judgment.

וְהָאִישׁ מֹשֶׁה עָנָו [עָנָיו] מְאֹד מִכֹּל הָאָדָם אֲשֶׁר עַל־פְּנֵי הָאֲדָמָה

The man, Moses, was exceedingly humble, more than any person on the face of the earth (12:3)

Humility: the Finest of All Traits

Of all the character traits of Moses, the Torah cites only one: his humility. Of all the undesirable character traits a person may have, there is only one that repels the presence of God: vanity (*Arachin* 15b). Here are several comments on the importance of humility.

R' Yehoshua of Ostrova said that a vain person is even worse than a liar. "A liar does not believe his own lies, whereas a vain person is convinced of his superiority."

R' Refael of Bershed said, "Some people pursue acclaim and thrive on being honored. Little do they realize that in order to receive honor, you must actually lower yourself. One can only pour into a container when it is held lower."

R' Pinchas of Koritz said, "Every sin requires some action or object. Vanity requires nothing. A person may be lying under blankets and think, 'How great I am.'"

R' Mendel of Kotzk said, "A person who seeks recognition is much like a goat that wears a bell around its neck to announce its whereabouts."

Chovos HaLevovos says, "A person who is free of all sin is at risk of the greatest character defect: to consider himself a *tzaddik*."

A vain person came to see R' Avraham the Malach (angel). He found him standing by the window, looking out. "See that hill?" he said. "It is only a pile of earth, yet it stands high as if it were superior to others."

In *Angels Don't Leave Footprints*, I cited a number of ethicists who say that humility does not mean denying one's talents and abilities. Although Moses was the humblest of all people on earth, he knew that he had achieved a level of prophesy never attained by anyone else.

When Miriam and Aaron spoke critically of Moses, God reprimanded them: "In my entire house, he (Moses) is the trusted one. Mouth to mouth do I speak to him, in a clear vision and not in riddles, at the image of God does he gaze. Why did you not fear to speak against My servant Moses?" (*Numbers* 12:7-8) These verses, just like the entire Torah, were written by Moses. He knew his uniqueness, but it not detract from his humility.

> *Truly humble people shun acclaim. R' Menachem Mendel of Lubavitch (Tzemach Tzedek) took his young son, Shmuel, with him on a journey. Shmuel wrote home about the throngs of people that had greeted his father and the great honor he had received. When the Tzemach Tzedek found the letter, he said to Shmuel, "My blood was spilling like water, and this gave you pleasure?"*

The Talmud says that the last eight verses in the Torah, which relate Moses' death, were written by Moses at God's dictation, and Moses cried as he wrote them (*Bava Basra* 15a). A chassidic master suggested that Moses was not crying because he was writing about his own death, but because God dictated, "Never again has there arisen in Israel a prophet like Moses, whom God had known face to face" (*Deuteronomy* 34:10). It gave Moses great pain to write this adulation about himself.

It is quite simple to efface oneself before a great scholar. The greatness of Moses' humility was that he effaced himself before the lowliest person: "Moses was exceedingly humble, more than any person on the face of the earth."

As pointed out, humility is not a denial of one's capacity. Moses knew that he had the responsibility of leadership, and when implementation of authority was called for, he did not hesitate to assert himself. That is true humility.

Our ethical works emphasize the importance of humility, and provide instruction on how one can know one's personality strengths, yet avoid the objectionable trait of vanity. Studying the works of *mussar* is of the utmost importance to enable one to avoid vanity while maintainng a healthy self-esteem.

פרשת שלח
Parashas Shelach

שְׁלַח־לְךָ אֲנָשִׁים וְיָתֻרוּ אֶת־אֶרֶץ כְּנַעַן
"Send forth men, if you please, and let them spy out the Land of Canaan" (13:2)

The Primacy of Respect

Rashi says that the words "if you please," means that God said to Moses, "You may send spies if it pleases you. I am not instructing you to do so."

The episode of the spies is one of the most enigmatic occurrences in the Torah. The twelve men chosen were tribal leaders, and Rashi states that they were righteous people. What happened to them that caused them to lose faith in God and discourage the Israelites from entering the Promised Land? Furthermore, Abarbanel says that Moses' complicity in sending the spies was the real reason he was not permitted to enter Canaan. In what way was Moses at fault?

Thirty-eight years later, in recounting this tragic event before his death, Moses said, "All of you approached me and said, 'Let us send some men ahead of us and let them spy out the Land'" (*Deuteronomy* 1:22). Rashi comments that the phrase "all of you" indicates that they came as a mob, the young pushing the elders out of the way to get to Moses. This was crass disrespect. Moses said, "The idea appealed to me" (ibid. 1:23). His error was that he mistook their pushing and shoving as enthusiasm for entering the Land, and this caused him to overlook their lack of respect for the elders. This misinterpretation was Moses' complicity.

Respect is primary in Judaism. "Respect is a prerequisite for Torah" (*Vayikra Rabbah* 9:3), and its vital role is repeatedly stressed in the Talmud and in ethical works. Lack of respect is a mortal sin.

"A person's agent is as oneself" (*Berachos* 34b). In halachah, an agent is a representative of the principal. In *mussar* an agent can be affected by the character of the principal. The spies were indeed decent people in their own right, but having become agents of people who were disrespectful, their characters were corrupted and their perspective distorted.

The fatal report of the spies resulted not only in the death of the generation of the Exodus, but also had a deleterious effect on our entire history. The Talmud says that the night following the spies' discouraging report that resulted in the Israelites weeping was Tishah B'Av, the 9th day of the month of Av, on which both Temples were destroyed. The weeping of that night was perpetuated throughout our history, and to this very day, we suffer the consequences of disrespect.

We can rectify the mistake of our ancestors by being fastidious in respect, not only of our elders, but of every person, young or old.

שְׁלַח־לְךָ אֲנָשִׁים וְיָתֻרוּ אֶת־אֶרֶץ כְּנַעַן

"Send forth men, if you please, and let them spy out the Land of Canaan" (13:2)

Avoiding Self Delusion

The Israelites requested that Moses send spies to scout the Promised Land. Moses yielded, and when the spies returned with a very negative report — that the Land was inhabited by powerful nations — the people despaired of conquering it.

The previous portion of the Torah closes with the incident of Miriam's punishment for speaking critically about Moses. The juxtaposition of the episode of the spies is explained by Rashi (*Numbers* 13:2): *These wicked people* (the spies) *saw what had happened to Miriam when she spoke negatively about her brother, and they did not learn from this* (that negative talk is wrong).

R' Yisrael Morgenstern of Pilov said that Rashi is not trying to tell us how wicked the spies were. Rather, he is stating an important psychological insight: *It is possible to see something with your own eyes and be totally blind to it.*

In psychology, this is known as *denial*, which is a common phenomenon. I encounter this regularly when working with people who have severe drinking problems. Their life is in a shambles due to their drinking. Everybody has pointed this out to them in the strongest terms, yet they totally deny that their drinking has anything to do with the wreckage they have wrought in the family and at work.

This phenomenon is clearly described in Scriptures: "The heart of this nation is fattened, its ears are heavy and its eyes pasted shut; lest it see with its eyes, hear with its ears and its heart will understand and it will be healed" (*Isaiah* 6:10). When a person is obstinate in his ways and does not wish to change, he can be oblivious to stark facts in front of his eyes. He does not see, hear nor understand.

We must be aware of our susceptibility to self-delusion. This is especially dangerous because the reasons for our denial are often in our subconscious. Denial is not the same as lying. A liar knows that he is lying. The person who is in denial has no idea that he is denying.

How can we defend ourselves against something of which we are not aware?

The answer is that we must seek opinions from mentors or devoted friends, people who are not rendered oblivious to our biases and who can see what we cannot see.

An honest research scientist is especially attentive to those findings that seem to *disprove* his theory. He knows that these may be easily overlooked. Many scientific studies have been found to be faulty because the researcher ignored the facts that contradicted his thesis.

Young men and young women who have become infatuated may overlook serious character defects in the other. It has been truly said that, "Love is blind." Sometimes parents' objections to one's choice of a husband or wife may not be valid, but it is wise to give them serious consideration and obtain competent counseling. This is equally true of any venture for which one has a strong desire. The stronger the desire, the more important it is to seek an objective opinion.

וַיִּקְרָא מֹשֶׁה לְהוֹשֵׁעַ בִּן־נוּן יְהוֹשֻׁעַ

Moses sent a representative from each tribe to scout Canaan. The representative of the tribe of Ephraim was Hoshea bin Nun. ***Moses called Hoshea bin Nun "Joshua"*** (13:16)

Misplaced Humility

Rashi explains that the Hebrew for "Joshua" means "God shall save." Moses was praying that God save Joshua from the complicity of the spies. The *Targum* (translation) of Yonasan ben Uziel adds to the verse, "When Moses observed his humility, he called Hoshea bin Nun 'Joshua.'"

Why did Joshua's humility necessitate that Moses pray for him?

Although humility is the finest of all character traits, there are times when a person must set his humility aside and assert himself. As we saw earlier (Beha'aloscha), although Moses was the most humble man on earth, he was able to exercise the authority of his position when appropriate.

There is a danger when humility is misplaced. King Saul was exceedingly humble (*I Samuel* 10:21-23). When Samuel told him to eliminate Amalek, Saul yielded to the will of the people and spared the livestock and Agag the king. Samuel reprimanded him for not asserting his authority and said, "*Though you may be small in your own eyes,* you are the head of the tribes of Israel, and God has anointed you to be king over Israel" (ibid. 15:17). As king, he should have carried out God's instructions and not yielded to the popular will.

Seeing how self-effacing Joshua was, Moses feared that if a difference of opinion occurred, Joshua might not stand up against the majority.

The *yetzer hara* is very cunning. Citing the virtue of humility, it may counsel us to be humble at the wrong time, and yield to popular opinion. We should take a firm stand on what is right and proper, even when there is widespread approval of something that is wrong.

While Moses prayed for Joshua, Caleb prayed for himself. Rashi says that Caleb went to the Tombs of the Patriarchs in Hebron and prayed that he not be swayed to join the other spies in discouraging the Israelites from entering the Promised Land.

Why were these prayers necessary? Whereas the ten spies had lost faith in God,

Joshua and Caleb were firm in their faith. Why did they need protective prayers?

R' Simchah Zissel of Kelm says that this teaches us that even the greatest *tzaddik* should not be overconfident when he is in a sinful environment. Peer pressure is extremely powerful and can influence a person to sin. How careful we must be to avoid an environment that rejects Torah values! If we do find ourselves in an unfavorable environment, we must take great precaution to protect ourselves from being swept along with the tide.

לֹא נוּכַל לַעֲלוֹת אֶל־הָעָם כִּי־חָזָק הוּא מִמֶּנּוּ

After scouting Canaan and seeing the giants and the fortified cities, the spies were disheartened and said, *"We cannot ascend to that people for it is too strong for us"* (13:31)

The Frailty of Effortless Convictions

Many commentaries pose the question: Inasmuch as the Israelites saw the plagues God inflicted on the Egyptians, the dividing of the Reed Sea and the many other miracles God had wrought on their behalf, how is it possible that they doubted that God would enable them to conquer Canaan?

R' Moshe Feinstein answers this question with a profound psychological insight. The belief that the Israelites had in God at that point was not based on their effort to develop a strong faith. In Egypt they had been idol worshippers (*Yalkut Reuveni, Beshalach*). Their belief in God came to them without any exertion on their part, and was based on the dramatic supernatural phenomena they witnessed. But, says R' Feinstein, although the faith based on witnessing miracles may be strong, it is nevertheless evanescent, and it may dissipate as quickly as it came.

The Midrash says that the Divine revelation at the dividing of the Reed Sea was so great that the least important person had prophetic vision that exceeded that of the prophet Ezekiel. What happened to the prophecies of all these people? It passed as quickly as it had come. Ezekiel, on the other hand, labored incessantly to achieve a level of spirituality that merited his receiving the Divine spirit. He acquired prophetic power very gradually by his own effort, and that is why it endured.

As striking as the miracles the Israelites witnessed were, they had no lasting effect. Faced with every new challenge, their faith faltered.

The Talmud says, "If someone tells you that he acquired Torah knowledge without laborious effort, do not believe him" (*Megillah* 6b). True Torah knowledge can be attained only by intense effort.

This is an important insight. We live in an era where we can get many things instantaneously that required hours in the past. We can push a button and get what we want with little effort. We may find ourselves frustrated when Torah knowledge does not come that way. Meaningful Torah knowledge requires as much effort today as it did a thousand years ago. There is no microwave for Torah knowledge.

We have been blessed with Torah tapes and other technological means of acquiring Torah knowledge. This does not do away with the need to "labor in Torah" (*Rashi, Leviticus* 26:3). Torah knowledge may be delivered to us more easily, but in order to integrate it and be positively affected by it, we must exert effort in reviewing it and in achieving a deeper understanding of it.

וַנְּהִי בְעֵינֵינוּ כַּחֲגָבִים וְכֵן הָיִינוּ בְּעֵינֵיהֶם

"We were like grasshoppers in our eyes, and so we were in their eyes" (13:33)

Emotion vs. Intellect

This verse was the origin of all my writings and emphasis on self-esteem. In this unique syntax, the Torah teaches us a psychological principle of the greatest importance: *The way you feel about yourself is how you think others perceive you.*

Rashi's comment expands upon this concept. The spies said, "We heard the Canaanites say, 'Look! There are ants crawling in our vineyards.'" The Torah says that the spies felt as small as grasshoppers, which are still much larger than ants. Furthermore, how could the spies know what the Canaanites were saying? How could they understand their language?

Rashi is teaching us that low self-esteem is progressive and self-reinforcing. If you have a distorted, negative self-concept, it is apt to further deteriorate. You may begin by feeling as small as grasshoppers, but your self-image will shrink and you will eventually think even less of yourself. In addition, you will assume that others are making negative comments about you, even if you are not privy to what they are saying. A distorted, negative self-concept can lead to paranoia.

The Midrash on this verse expounds another important psychological principle.

"God said, 'I forgive you for saying, "We were like grasshoppers in our eyes." But why did you say, "and so we were in their eyes?" How do you know that I did not make you appear to them as mighty angels? For that I do not forgive you'" (*Tanchuma*).

Why was the second statement a more grievous sin than the first?

R' Henoch Lebovitz explains that a distorted negative self-image is an emotion. I have noted in my books that there is a strange phenomenon. People who are most gifted may have the most profound low self-esteem. Their undeniable, factual achievements seem to make no impact on their self-concept. Whatever the source of low self-esteem, it is an emotion that is not altered by factual reality.

The concept that God is omnipotent is an intellectual belief. The Midrash says that when God told Moses that the Israelites should go into the sea, Nachshon went into the water up to his neck and then the waters divided. It was Nachshon's faith that enabled him to overcome the emotional fear of drowning, and it was this faith that warranted the miracle.

R' Shneur Zalman (Baal HaTanya) says that it is innate within the human being that *intellect can triumph over emotion.* When we allow our emotions to outweigh our intellect, it is a laxity and dereliction on our part.

The Midrash says that God forgave the spies for having a poor self-concept. That is an emotion which is not easily overcome. Their sin was in failing to exercise their ability to act according to their intellect. Having witnessed the many miracles of the Exodus, they knew intellectually that God could make them appear to the Canaanites as mighty angels. It was not even a lack of faith that was their sin. It was their failure of surrendering to their emotions when they should have followed their intellect (*Chidushei HaLev, Bamidbar* p. 86).

This is a teaching which we should apply regularly in our lives. As far as our distorted self-concept which depresses our self-esteem is concerned, this is something which we should seek to change by finding ways to elevate our self-esteem. But until we achieve that goal, we should not allow this emotion to determine our behavior. We should be able to act on factual reality.

But how can we know factual reality when our emotions distort our perception? *By getting an opinion of ourselves from a reliable objective observer.* If we are told that we are good, worthy and competent, we should act accordingly even if we do not feel that way.

Nachshon brought about a miracle by following his intellect rather than his emotion. You can accomplish virtually miraculous things by acting according to intellect rather than emotion.

ה׳ אֶרֶךְ אַפַּיִם וְרַב־חֶסֶד נֹשֵׂא עָוֹן וָפָשַׁע ...
"O God, Who is Slow to Anger, Abundant in Kindness, Forgiver of Iniquity (14:18)

Middos: the Essence of Godliness

Some Torah-observant people may think that because they observe Shabbos, keep kosher, pray every day, learn *daf yomi*, give *tzedakah* and fulfill all the other mitzvos, they have done all that is required in the service of God. Little do we realize that these are just the basics, the foundation of Yiddishkeit upon which we must build. Many great *tzaddikim* who were meticulously observant of Torah spent their entire lifetime trying to progress in refinement of their *middos* and come into a closer relationship with God.

> *The tzaddik R' Avraham Yehoshua Heschel of Apt related that the great chassidic master R' Elimelech of Lizhensk visited him. "One time I stepped into his room, and because he was deep in meditation, he did not hear me come in. I heard him saying to himself, 'O my soul, you are not deserving of a place in Gan Eden (Paradise).' He then went on to describe all the 'sins' he had done. [We must remember that R' Elimelech did teshuvah for possibly having hurt his mother while she was nursing him. It is difficult to imagine what his 'sins' were.]*
>
> *"He then continued his soliloquy, 'But even so, there is hope for you, my soul. Even if you are not deserving, God with His infinite kindness will allow you into Gan Eden. The Talmud says that in His abundant kindness, God clothes the naked, visits the sick and consoles the bereaved (Sotah 14a). But that is all in this earthly world. What manner of kindness can God do in the Eternal World? There is no need for food or clothes. There is no sickness and no death. The only kindness God can do in the Eternal World is to take an undeserving soul such as mine, and allow it into Gan Eden."*

Whenever we feel that we have fulfilled our obligation in the service of God, we ought to think of this and realize how far we have to go. Beyond the performance of the mitzvos is the development of *middos* (fine character traits).

Inasmuch as Torah is infinite, the potential for growth in Torah and in service to

God is infinite. Standing before infinity, one may be subject to a frustrating feeling of futility. How can I ever consider myself to have made progress on a path which is endless?

We had many great Torah personalities throughout history whose profound humility did not at all discourage them from achievement, but to the contrary, invigorated them to ever increasing efforts. But we need not have recourse to ancient history. In our own generation there was the Chafetz Chaim, a paragon of humility, whose efforts at growth in Torah and *middos* were untiring. We were privileged and blessed to be eyewitnesses to profound humility and an unrelenting striving for growth in Torah and *middos* in R' Moshe Feinstein.

The formula for the highest ethical life and achievement in Torah living, for the refinement of *middos,* was demonstrated by our *tzaddikim.* We should follow their example.

וְטַפְּכֶם אֲשֶׁר אֲמַרְתֶּם לָבַז יִהְיֶה וְהֵבֵיאתִי אֹתָם
וְיָדְעוּ אֶת־הָאָרֶץ אֲשֶׁר מְאַסְתֶּם בָּהּ

"And your young children of whom you said they will be taken captive, I shall bring them; they shall know the Land that you have despised" (14:31)

Love for the Holy Land

The Psalmist says of the spies, "They despised the desirable land; they had no faith in His word" (*Psalms* 106:24).

R' Avraham Pam asks, "Granted that the spies lacked faith in God's word that He would enable the Israelites to conquer the Land. But where is there any indication that they despised the Land? Perhaps they did love it, but were simply afraid they could not conquer it."

R' Pam answers this question by citing a halachah in the Talmud, which states that one cannot give a gift to an unborn child. Although it would certainly be beneficial to the child to acquire this gift, the transaction is not valid. However, there is one exception to this rule: one *can give* a gift to one's *own* unborn child (*Bava Basra* 142b). The reason for this, Rashbam says, is that a person's desire to give to his own child is wholehearted.

R' Pam explains that the reason that a gift to a fetus is not binding is because the donor's intention is not absolute. Not every fetus is viable. There is a possibility that the fetus may not survive. If it does survive, there is the risk that it may sustain birth damage and not be able to use the gift. These possibilities raise doubt in the donor's mind, so that his gift is with dubious intent. A transaction on a dubious basis is not binding.

A father, however, has so intense a love for his child that the possibility of things going wrong *does not even enter his mind.* His gift to his unborn child is, therefore, wholehearted, and that makes it a binding transaction.

The point of this halachah, R' Pam says, is that where there is an intense love, one does not think of what might go wrong. If the spies would have had love for the Land, the various drawbacks that discouraged them would never have occurred to them. The fact that they were aware of these drawbacks indicates that they despised the Land.

Solomon said it: "Love covers up all defects" (*Proverbs* 10:12).

This is an important psychological truth. Whenever we notice ourselves finding fault with something, we should be alert to the possibility that we see these faults because we do not like it. Too often, instead of admitting our dislike, we rationalize why we do not want something, finding defects that exist only in our imagination. We should be careful not to delude ourselves.

This is particularly important in our relationships with people. *Sinas chinam*, groundless dislike, brought disaster upon us. Because groundless dislike is so illogical, we may conjure up defects in others to explain and justify our dislike of them. We should dedicate ourselves to develop *ahavas Yisrael*, love for others. This will eliminate self-delusion.

וּפִגְרֵיכֶם אַתֶּם יִפְּלוּ בַּמִּדְבָּר הַזֶּה
"Your [dead] bodies shall drop in this Wilderness" (14:32)

Measurement of Values

Although the Israelites regretted their sin and made an attempt to conquer Canaan, the harsh decree remained. Inasmuch as they said, "We shall ascend to the place of which God has spoken" (*Numbers* 14:40), they regretted their sin. Why was their *teshuvah* not accepted?

> The Maggid of Dubnow answers with one of his inimitable parables.
>
> A man who had just recently come into wealth had a daughter for whom he sought a shidduch. One marriage broker recommended the son of a wealthy person. The young man himself was no prize, but his father's wealth was attractive. Another marriage broker suggested a fine young Torah scholar whose father was a prominent rabbi, but who had no money.
>
> The girl's father chose the Torah scholar, but told the young man's father that he expected gifts of fine jewelry for his daughter, e.g., diamond earrings, necklace, etc. When the rabbi told him that he could not possibly afford such gifts, the girl's father broke off the engagement, and did the shidduch with the wealthy man's son, who was ignorant of Torah.
>
> When friends and relatives heard of this, they reprimanded him for his folly. How could he have forfeited the opportunity to have a fine Torah scholar for his daughter? How could he prefer an ignoramus just because he came from a wealthy family? Realizing his mistake, he sent word to the rabbi that he is willing to do the shidduch with him, and will forego any demand for gifts.
>
> However, the rabbi turned him down. "If, for diamond earrings, you could prefer an ignoramus to a Torah scholar, that indicates that you do not value Torah, and I would not want my son to have you for a father-in-law."

"This," said the Maggid, "is what happened with the Israelites. Their first reaction was, 'Let us appoint a new leader and return to Egypt' (ibid. 14:5). They had expressed their longing for the fish and vegetables they had in Egypt (ibid. 11:5). Like the rabbi in the parable, God did not accept their change of heart. 'If you were ready to reject the Holy Land for fish and vegetables, then the Holy Land is not for you.'"

We show how much we value something by how cheaply we are willing to give it away.

מֵרֵאשִׁית עֲרִסֹתֵיכֶם תִּתְּנוּ לַה׳ תְּרוּמָה

One of the tithes that are given to the Kohen is *challah*.
A portion of the dough is donated to the *Kohen*.
From the first of your kneading shall you give a portion to God (15:21)

Early Impressions

This verse lends itself to a novel interpretation. The word for "kneading dough," *arisa*, has a second meaning, "cradle." The verse then reads, "From the beginning of the *cradle* a portion should be given to God."

Indeed, the custom is that when an infant is born, Chapter 121 of Psalms is displayed near the crib. It is generally assumed that this is a sort of amulet to protect the infant. Perhaps it is also that very early in life, the child should see words of Torah as his first perception of the world.

The Talmud relates that the mother of R' Yehoshua ben Chananya set his crib near the house of Torah study, so that the infant should absorb sounds of Torah at the very onset of his life.

In times past, people might have raised their eyebrows about this. What possible impact can Torah sounds or words have on a tiny infant? Recent research has indicated that it is possible for even the intrauterine fetus to be affected by things in the mother's environment.

There is a more important application of the principle of early imprinting. Some modern parents, imbued with the philosophy that children should be allowed to make their own choices of lifestyle, prefer to send the child to public school rather than to a Hebrew day school. "We do not wish to impose anything on the child. Let him be free to choose whether or not he wishes to be religiously observant."

This is a serious fallacy. There really is no neutral ground. If one is not bound by moral and ethical principles, then one is influenced by an attitude that one may do as one pleases. This imprints profoundly on a child's thoughts and feelings, and he is not "free to choose." His parents have in fact made the choice for him. It is much easier to go from a more strict to a more permissive lifestyle than the reverse.

This is the meaning of the verse, "From the beginning of the *cradle* a portion should be given to God." Training for a disciplined life according to the Torah should begin in infancy.

דַּבֵּר אֶל־בְּנֵי יִשְׂרָאֵל וְאָמַרְתָּ אֲלֵהֶם וְעָשׂוּ לָהֶם צִיצִת
עַל־כַּנְפֵי בִגְדֵיהֶם לְדֹרֹתָם וְנָתְנוּ עַל־צִיצִת הַכָּנָף פְּתִיל תְּכֵלֶת

The Torah relates an episode that occurred during the Israelites' sojourn in the desert, in which a man violated the Shabbos by gathering wood. This narration is followed by the mitzvah of *tzitzis* (fringes). *"Speak to the Children of Israel and say to them that they shall make themselves tzitzis on the corners of their garments"* (15:38)

Awareness of Our Vulnerability

The Midrash states that Moses said to God, "During the week, the wearing of *tefillin* is a reminder of one's servitude to God. Inasmuch as on Shabbos one does not wear *tefillin*, one may forget that one is bound to Torah observance. The violation of Shabbos was undoubtedly due to the lack of a reminder." God, therefore, gave the mitzvah of *tzitzis*, which are worn on Shabbos as well as on weekdays.

There are some halachic restrictions which were instituted by the sages as protective laws to prevent someone from transgressing a Scriptural prohibition. There are some people who may neglect these precautionary laws, claiming that they are in full control of their behavior and do not require these restrictions.

The purpose of *tzitzis*, the Torah says, is "That you may see it and remember all the commandments of God and perform them; and not deviate after your heart and after your eyes after which you stray" (*Numbers* 15:39).

In every generation, we had great Torah personalities who had so perfected themselves spiritually that it was virtually impossible for them to be misled by temptation. If anyone was justified in dismissing the rabbinic precautionary laws, it would have been these great *tzaddikim*. But lo and behold! They were meticulous in taking the most stringent precautionary measures to avoid transgressing. Is it not the height of arrogance for someone to say, "These *tzaddikim* may need *tzitzis* to remind them not to go astray. I, however, have no need for any reminders. I am not vulnerable to sin as they are."

If *tzaddikim* do not consider themselves immune to transgression, we should certainly not do so. It is good for a person to have self-confidence in his ability to carry out whatever his duties are, but one should not be over-confident that he is immune to sin.

On the other hand, just as one should not think of oneself as being above sin, one should not despair of reaching the heights of spirituality. The above cited verse is followed by, "So that you may remember and perform My commandments and be holy to your God" (ibid. v. 40). Even a person who is capable of being led far astray by the temptations of his heart and eyes has the capacity to be holy unto God.

These verses accurately describe the polarity, not only between people, but within each person. We are at any one time at risk of descending to the depths of depravity, yet capable of rising to the heights of holiness. The choice is ours.

פרשת קרח
Parashas Korach

וַיִּקַּח קֹרַח בֶּן־יִצְהָר בֶּן־קְהָת בֶּן־לֵוִי וְדָתָן וַאֲבִירָם בְּנֵי אֱלִיאָב וְאוֹן בֶּן־פֶּלֶת בְּנֵי רְאוּבֵן וַיָּקֻמוּ לִפְנֵי מֹשֶׁה

Korach, son of Izhar son of Kohath son of Levi separated himself with Dathan and Abiram sons of Eliab, and Ohn son of Peleth, the offspring of Reuben. And they stood before Moses (16:1-2)

To Accept with Grace

The literal translation of the Hebrew verse is, "Korach, son of ... took and Dathan and Abiram and Ohn" The Hebrew word for "took" is *vayikach*, the singular, meaning "he took." Inasmuch as there were three others, it would seem that the plural *vayikchu*, "they took" should have been used. Indeed, the next sentence begins with *vayakumu*, the plural "they stood." Why is there a change from the singular to the plural?

By this nuance the Torah teaches us that when there is opposition to a leader, a number of factions may join together, but they are united only in opposition. Each faction seeks only its own goal, and not that of its cohorts. Korach, Dathan, Abiram and Ohn were each operating in the singular, each seeking the leadership for himself. Had they succeeded in their opposition to Moses, an internecine struggle would have erupted for the leadership. However, they were blinded to this, and deluded themselves to think that they were in fact united. Therefore, the Torah uses the plural *"they* stood before Moses," because it was only in confronting Moses that they were a group rather than self-serving individuals.

The wife of Ohn son of Peleth was not deluded, and said to her husband, "What do you stand to gain by opposing Moses? If the rebellion succeeds, Korach will be the leader, and you will remain a commoner." She prevailed on Ohn to withdraw from the conspiracy.

This phenomenon has repeated itself numerous times in history. It has correctly been said that those who do not learn from history are doomed to repeat it. Even today, opposition groups form, and if they succeed, they are rapidly splintered.

We may be drawn into a group that opposes something. We should be aware that the motivation for the opposition is rarely for the benefit of the group. It is usually in the ego interests of one or more individuals, who will promptly turn against one another if their opposition is successful.

Quantum Leap to Evil I: Envy

When one reads the account of Korach's rebellion (*Numbers* 16:1-35), one is astounded by the incident. Not only was Moses the one who led the Jews from Egypt, but all the Israelites were eyewitnesses to the many miracles that were wrought through him. They saw him wave his staff over the Reed Sea, causing the waters to divide. There could be no doubt that he was commissioned by God to be the leader. How could anyone question the authenticity of Moses' leadership? It simply defies all logic.

Rashi quotes the Midrash which raises this question: How could Korach, a wise and learned person, act so foolishly? The Midrash answers that Moses had appointed another Levite to be leader of the tribe of Levi, and Korach was envious of this.

Yet, this does not fully answer the question. Can envy so deprive a person of logical thinking that one would deny the evidence of one's own eyes?

R' Chaim Shmulevitz (*Sichos Mussar* 5731:21) helps us understand this. He cites the Talmudic statement, "Envy, lust and pursuit of acclaim remove a person from the world" (*Ethics of the Fathers* 4:28). The expression "remove a person from the world" is rather strange. R' Shmulevitz explains that the usual deviation from proper behavior is a very gradual one. The Talmud says that the tactic of the *yetzer hara* is to seduce a person to commit a very minor infraction, then lead him on to progressively more serious transgressions (*Shabbos* 108b). That is the nature and order of the world. The *yetzer hara* will not entice a person into doing something patently absurd.

However, if a person is overtaken by envy, one escapes the natural order of the world. One is no longer bound by logic. The passion of envy can be so great that it can overwhelm all rational thought, and leave one vulnerable to the *yetzer hara's* seduction to behave in the most irrational manner. Envy indeed *removes a person from the natural order of the world.*

That is what happened with Korach. Moses understood this, and delayed the trial until the next day (see *Rashi* to *Numbers* 16:5).

The Korach episode conveys a most important teaching. We are all vulnerable to envy, and envy is not a difficult emotion to identify. *If you feel yourself being envious, do nothing for a while.* Envy can suspend all logical thinking and make one do things that one will regret.

If you feel envious, ventilate your feelings to a friend or write them down. Read one of the ethical works about envy. This will help you realize that envy is a futile and destructive feeling. Before doing anything foolish that may be a reaction to your envy, seek the counsel of a friend or mentor. You may avoid making serious mistakes.

Quantum Leap to Evil II: Pursuit of Acclaim

In the previous essay we noted the Talmudic statement, "Envy, lust and pursuit of acclaim remove a person from the world" (*Ethics of the Fathers* 4:28). We noted how envy can deprive a person of logical thinking. This is equally true of "pursuit of acclaim."

In my writings on low self-esteem (*Angels Don't Leave Footprints, Let Us Make Man*) I pointed out a variety of maladaptive behaviors that may result from unwarranted feelings of inferiority. One reaction is to think of oneself as superior to others and seek honor and recognition. I was thrilled to find a confirmation of this in the writings of Rabbeinu Yonah, who says, "A vain person seeks to compensate for his feelings of lack by thinking himself superior to people whom he can consider to be beneath him" (*Rabbeinu Yonah al HaTorah*, p. 156).

Korach was misled by both feelings of envy and pursuit of acclaim, hoping to depose Moses and replace him as leader. His championing of equality was merely a ploy, which was recognized by the wife of Ohn ben Peleth (v. supra).

R' Yechezkel Levenstein (*Kovetz Inyanim*) states that logical thinking will enable a person to identify those traits that are destructive. Physiological drives are essential for survival and preservation of the species, but traits such as pursuit of acclaim contribute nothing to one's survival. These are actually counterproductive, resulting in frustration and wasteful expenditure of energy. One should, therefore, recognize them as challenges to be overcome in quest of spirituality.

Ramchal (R' Moshe Chaim Luzatto) says that if it were not for pursuit of acclaim, a person could get along with the bare necessities of life. One is often motivated to acquire luxuries in order not to appear inferior to others (*Path of the Just,* Ch. 11). Exhausting oneself in attempt to acquire more than the necessities of life may indeed "remove a person from the world."

Korach was physically removed from the world. While we may remain in the world physically, we must be very cautious about traits that do not contribute to survival, some of which can figuratively "remove a person from the world."

Impediments to Faith

It is not unusual to hear the refrain that one can be a good Jew without adhering to all the mitzvos. "I believe in God," a person may say. "I am considerate, compassionate and honest, and that is really the essence of Judaism."

Some have raised the question, "How was it possible for Korach to rebel against Moses and defy his Divine commission? God said to Moses at Sinai, 'Behold! I come to you in the thickness of the cloud, so that the people will hear as I speak to you, *and they will also believe in you forever*' (*Exodus* 19:9). How could God's promise to Moses be negated?"

The Steipler Gaon answered that we must understand the nature of the Divine promise. It is an axiom of Judaism that a person has moral free will and that God does not control or interfere with a person's freedom of choice. This means that a person is free to believe or not to believe in Moses, and God did not impose this belief on anyone.

God's promise to Moses was that Israel's belief in Moses will never be undermined *by philosophical speculation*. Applying intellectual reasoning will never diminish a Jew's belief in Moses, as long as one has a mind and intellect that have not been distorted and corrupted by violation of Torah and mitzvos. However, if a person deviates from the mitzvos, this may affect his thinking so that he may become skeptical about God and Moses.

Observance of Torah applies to *middos* (character traits) as well as to practices. Envy, rage and vanity are as much a violation of Torah as eating forbidden foods. On a purely intellectual and philosophical level, Korach would not have doubted Moses. But because he was vain and envious, his distorted thinking led him to erroneous conclusions.

Similarly, one who associates with non-believers may fall under their influence. Here, too, it is not clear thinking that leads him to skepticism, but the desire to conform to his environment.

We take great pride in our reasoning abilities. We should realize how sensitive these are and how easily they can be influenced by noxious factors, leading us to false conclusions. We should protect our cherished rational thinking from being adversely affected.

וּמַדּוּעַ תִּתְנַשְּׂאוּ עַל־קְהַל ה׳ וַיִּשְׁמַע מֹשֶׁה וַיִּפֹּל עַל־פָּנָיו

When Korach accused Moses of having seized the leadership, he said, **"Why do you exalt yourself over the congregation of God?"** The Torah continues, **"Moses heard and fell on his face,"** and he then reprimanded Korach (16:3)

Accepting Critique

R' Shneur Zalman (Baal HaTanya) explains that Moses' first reaction was, "Perhaps Korach is right about me." Although Moses knew that God had designated him as the leader of Israel, he thought, "Perhaps I have let the position of leadership go to my head, and I am indeed guilty of vanity. Perhaps Korach is an agent of God to deliver well-deserved rebuke." Therefore, before responding to Korach, Moses fell upon his face to do serious soul-searching. Only after he was convinced that he had not allowed his position of leadership to affect him, did he respond to Korach."

Let us do a bit of soul-searching. What is our reaction when we are criticized? Do we not feel the blood rushing to our head as we become angry? Do we not immediately adopt a defensive posture, seeking to justify our behavior? Do we not search to respond with criticism of the other person? We may insist, "What I did was right." Or, "You are not so perfect yourself."

We should, of course, respond positively to constructive criticism. That is the only way we can grow and improve ourselves. However, we should not be hasty to totally reject even *destructive* criticism.

R' Shneur Zalman tells us that this was the greatness of Moses. He did not reject Korach's accusation out of hand, but first searched within himself to find whether it might not have some validity.

The Psalmist says, "When those who wish to harm me rise up against me, my ears hearken" (*Psalms* 92:12). Your friends are likely to praise you and not tell you your defects. Your enemies, however, will not refrain from pointing out your shortcomings. Even though their intentions may be malicious, it is worth listening to their criticism. It may contain a grain of truth.

קְחוּ־לָכֶם מַחְתּוֹת . . . וּתְנוּ־בָהֵן אֵשׁ וְשִׂימוּ עֲלֵיהֶן
קְטֹרֶת . . . הָאִישׁ אֲשֶׁר־יִבְחַר ה' הוּא הַקָּדוֹשׁ

*Moses said to Korach, "Take for yourselves fire-pans . . .
and put fire in them and place incense upon them . . . then the
man whom God will choose — he is the holy one"* (16:6-7)

Consideration for Adversaries

The Torah says that Moses was greatly distressed by Korach and he said, "I have not taken even a single donkey of theirs, nor have I wronged even one of them" (*Numbers* 16:15).

Why did Moses respond this way? Korach had not accused him of misappropriation, but of unjustly asserting his leadership.

Several verses later, Moses said, "Let each man take his fire-pan and you shall place incense on them" (16:17). Initially Moses had instructed them to put fire in their fire-pans, but later he did not mention putting in fire, only incense.

R' Aryeh Levin offers a meaningful interpretation. Initially Moses thought that by assuming the privilege of the incense offering, which is the prerogative of the priests, the fire in the fire-pans would consume the violators. But then he thought, "How can I do that to them? They are my people of whom I have always been so protective. I have never wronged any of them. How can I place them in so hazardous a position?" He, therefore, issued new instructions. "Apply the incense *without* fire. The violation will then be less severe. If God will approve of their offering, He will send down a fire. If not, they will not be harmed."

But Korach was so certain of his right to the priesthood that he did not obey Moses' amended instructions, and "they took—each man his fire-pan—and they placed fire upon them." Moses had tried to spare them, but their arrogance led to their demise.

Moses' love for his people extended even to his adversaries. He was obligated to discipline them, but attempted to do so without injuring them.

This is an important lesson. There are times when we must discipline someone, whether it be a child, a student or a stranger. We must be most cautious to do so without harming the person. Moses was careful to avoid harming even an adversary if possible. It was the persistent arrogance and defiance of Korach and his following that brought the harsh punishment upon them.

> *Our tzaddikim emulated Moses. Before R' Levi Yitzchok was rabbi of Berditchev, he was rabbi in Pinsk, where he had some adversaries. One time, when R' Levi Yitzchok was away, these adversaries put his wife and children on the wagon used to haul trash and drove them from the city. R' Levi Yitzchok's friends, outraged by this atrocity, came to R' Wolf of Zhitomir and asked that he bring the wrath of God upon these perpetrators. R' Wolf said, "I cannot do anything. R' Levi Yitzchok is standing at the Aron HaKodesh (ark of the Torah) reciting Tehillim and praying fervently that no harm come to them."*

We, too, should follow in Moses' footsteps. In the bedtime *Shema* we say, "I hereby forgive anyone who angered or antagonized me or who sinned against me. May no person be punished because of me." We should act during the day in consonance with our prayer at night.

אֱמֹר אֶל־אֶלְעָזָר בֶּן־אַהֲרֹן הַכֹּהֵן וְיָרֵם
אֶת־הַמַּחְתֹּת מִבֵּין הַשְּׂרֵפָה . . . כִּי קָדֵשׁוּ

"Say to Elazar, son of Aaron the Kohen, and let him pick up the fire-pans from amid the fire . . . for they have become holy" (17:2)

The Merit of Self-Sacrifice

R' Yoseph Shaul Nathanson says that although the fire-pans had been used for an unauthorized service and were actually used in rebellion against the priesthood of Aaron, nevertheless, inasmuch as the motive of the rebels was that they, too, should deserve to be *Kohen* like Aaron, and they were willing to risk their lives to attain the privilege of doing the Divine service, their fire-pans became holy.

This reminds me of a story that I heard from my father many times.

> When the Baal Shem Tov introduced chassidus, this aroused a strong protest from many of the Torah authorities, who suspected that this new movement was a deviation from halachah. Furthermore, coming only decades after the debacle of the false messiah, Shabbsai Zevi, there was concern that chassidus was a dangerous populist movement.
>
> When the Baal Shem Tov visited Brod, the Talmudic scholars of the famous school of Brod decided to drive him out of town. R' Chaim Sanzer, one of the leading Talmudists, was by nature a pacifist, and although he, too, opposed the Baal Shem Tov, he did not participate in the expulsion.
>
> That day, a woman consulted R' Chaim with a halachic question, and R' Chaim rendered a decision. Before retiring that night, R' Chaim reviewed all the deeds of that day, as was his custom. In rethinking the halachic question, he concluded that he had ruled wrongly. He agonized over his misjudgment, since his ruling had caused someone to transgress.
>
> R' Chaim then began a soul-searching on what could have caused him to err in a halachic decision. He concluded that his failure to join his comrades in pursuit of the Baal Shem Tov was the sin that had led to his misjudgment. To rectify this, he had to now pursue the Baal Shem Tov personally.
>
> It was late at night when R' Chaim gathered a pocket full of stones with which he was going to pelt the Baal Shem Tov. He hired a carriage and stopped at every inn. It was already dawn when he located the Baal Shem Tov, and when he saw the Baal Shem Tov reciting the morning blessings of the Torah, he could not bring himself to throw the stones at him.
>
> After finishing the blessings, the Baal Shem Tov greeted him. "Rabbi of Brod," he said, "why are you agonizing? Your halachic ruling was correct after all." The Baal Shem Tov then proceeded to show R' Chaim why his decision had been correct.
>
> R' Chaim was greatly relieved. He bid the Baal Shem Tov goodbye, and as he left, he emptied his pockets of the stones. The Baal Shem Tov followed him, picked up each stone, kissed it and put it in his pocket. "These stones," the Baal Shem Tov said, "were gathered with holy intent. They are sacred and dare not be thrown on the ground."

After relating this story, my father would point out that even the sharp differences of opinion between the early chassidim and their opponents were based on the purest motivation. He would bewail the foolish residuals of the arguments which no longer have this purity of intent.

Maintaining a feud simply because it had once occurred is senseless and is an insult to one's intelligence.

זִכָּרוֹן לִבְנֵי יִשְׂרָאֵל . . . וְלֹא־יִהְיֶה כְקֹרַח וְכַעֲדָתוֹ

As a reminder to the Children of Israel that one not be like Korach and his assembly" (17:5)

The Gravity of Dissension

Dissension among Jews is the greatest danger confronting our nation. The Midrash states that "unity among Jews is so dear to God that even if they were idol worshippers, they would be immune to punishment if only they were united" (*Tanchuma, Tzav* 7).

After the uprisings in Russia in 1904, a group of people in Radin wished to organize a separate chevrah kadisha (burial society). On Shabbos, the Chafetz Chaim stepped to the bimah (pulpit) and said:

"My dear brothers! If I were given thousands of rubles to deliver a sermon, I would refuse it. I am very old, and every moment is precious to me. I would not sell my time for any amount of money. However, I find that I must address you.

"It is more than fifty years that I have been in this community. I remember all the people who once prayed here. Where are they now? All that remains are their monuments on the cemetery. Many of you were not even born then, and some of you who were youngsters then are now amongst the aged. May we all live a long life, but let us remember that at some point we will have to give an accounting of what we did here.

"We must know that dissension is very, very grave. All the mitzvos one has done may be lost if one foments or participates in dissension.

"I am certain that if you will be called before the Heavenly Tribunal and reprimanded for causing dissension (forming a separate chevrah kadisha), you will plead innocence and in your defense you will say, 'We did not know that was wrong. We had a rabbi, Yisroel Meir, whom we considered to be a halachic authority, and he did not say anything about it!'

"I beg of you, when you come before the Heavenly Tribunal, please do not mention my name. My burden of sins is heavy enough. I cannot assume responsibility for your actions."

With this, the Chafetz Chaim burst into tears. The congregation was deeply moved, and the plan for a separate chevrah kadisha was dropped.

Factionalism has forever been our undoing. Let us remember the Chafetz Chaim's penetrating words. All the mitzvos we accumulate may be for naught if we participate in dissension. We will merit redemption if we set aside our differences and unite.

פרשת חקת
Parashas Chukas

זֹאת חֻקַּת הַתּוֹרָה

The mitzvah of the offering of the red-heifer and using its ashes in the purification of one who has come in contact with the dead is introduced with, ***This is the decree of the Torah*** (19:2)

Unquestioned Acceptance of Torah

Many of the commentaries ask why this particular mitzvah is referred to as "the decree of the Torah," as though it encompassed the entire Torah.

Rashi states that the reason for the mitzvah of the red-heifer is beyond our understanding. Even King Solomon, who understood the reasons for all the other 612 mitzvos, was stymied by the mitzvah of the red-heifer (*Midrash Rabbah*). Yet Rashi cites a reason for the red-heifer as being a sin-offering to attain forgiveness for the worship of the Golden Calf. Is this not contradictory?

Deviance from Torah observance is often the result of the attempt to apply human reasoning to the mitzvos. This is fraught with great hazard. One may make assumptions which are plausible, but may not be true. For example, one might think that the reason we are forbidden to eat pork is to prevent trichinosis. On this assumption, one might argue that if pork can be treated to eliminate the trichina parasite, the prohibition is removed. This is, of course, not the case. Pork is absolutely forbidden, independent of hygienic factors.

The mitzvos of Torah are to be observed as Divine decrees. Although we can easily understand the prohibition of theft and other social ordinances, we must observe them because they are the will of God, rather than because we understand their practicality.

Recent occurrences have demonstrated the importance of accepting the mitzvos as the Divine will. Society is moving ever closer to legitimization of euthanasia, as evidenced by the adoption of laws by several legislatures permitting physician-assisted suicide, and by the restriction of coverage for certain medical treatments in persons above age 80 in some states. The Torah prohibition of taking a human life is immutable, regardless of considerations of social expedience.

The worship of the Golden Calf was the outcome of the misapplication of human logic. Moses had said he would return at the end of forty days. When he did not return at the precise moment he was expected, some people argued that Moses must surely have died. Logic dictates that no mortal can survive forty days without nourishment. It was this fallacious conclusion that led to the Golden Calf debacle.

The mitzvah of the red-heifer, precisely because it is beyond human understanding, is the rectification of the error that led to the worship of the Golden Calf. Rashi is, therefore, not contradictory. Yes, the reason for the red-heifer is unknown, and yes, the very fact that we observe mitzvos that are beyond our understanding constitutes a rectification of the sin of the Golden Calf.

The mitzvah of the red-heifer is thus appropriately referred to as "the decree of the Torah." Its principle applies to the entire Torah. Whether or not we have a logical grasp of any of the mitzvos, they are to be observed as Divine decrees.

זֹאת הַתּוֹרָה אָדָם כִּי־יָמוּת בְּאֹהֶל
This is the teaching regarding a man who would die in a tent (19:14)

The Priority of Torah Study

The Hebrew word for "teaching" is "torah." The verse reads, "This is the Torah regarding a man who would die." The sages interpret this verse to also mean that to acquire Torah one must be ready to sacrifice one's life for it (*Berachos* 63b).

The great Torah scholar, R' Ephraim Zalman Margolis, was a wealthy businessman. He never permitted his business dealings to encroach upon the time he designated for Torah study.

One time, while he was studying Torah, his wife told him that some businessmen were calling upon him regarding a major transaction which promised to yield a huge profit. R' Margolis told her that they would have to come back at another time. When she reported that they could not come back and that if he did not receive them now the deal would not materialize, R' Margolis quoted the verse, "This is the Torah regarding a man who would die." "Suppose I were deathly ill," he said, "would the lure of profit change my status and allow me to leave my sick-bed? Any distraction from Torah study should be considered in the same way as if I were dying."

R' Margolis later discovered that he had in fact forfeited a huge profit by not participating in that particular deal. He joyfully exclaimed, "Now I have been able to understand how valuable that page of Talmud is. I paid thousands of kronen for it."

The measure of how valuable Torah study is to us may be determined by how much we are willing to sacrifice for it.

Some people may become discouraged when they do not grasp Talmudic studies as quickly as others. The Steipler Gaon urges people to persist in Torah study, because sincere and devoted study elicits Divine help. One who thinks of himself as having limited potential may excel far beyond his expectations.

The Steipler Gaon cites the case of a young man who came to the yeshivah of the Chasam Sofer, professing a desire to join the yeshivah. Inasmuch as he barely knew the alef-beis, the students thought his aspirations were unrealistic. However, the Chasam Sofer accepted him and had students donate an hour of their time to teach this young man.

In addition to not having basic Hebrew knowledge, the young man appeared to have difficulty in comprehension. Even after numerous repetitions finally seemed to give him an understanding of a subject, he would not remember it the next day. The students despaired of his ever learning anything.

But the young man persisted, and spent many hours reviewing whatever he had learned. After several years, he blossomed into a respected Torah scholar, ultimately becoming the rabbi and chief magistrate in a community. The Chasam Sofer mentions him several times in his writings (Chayei Olam).

People pray for God to bless them with prosperity. We should also pray with as much *kavannah* for God to bless us with enlightenment in Torah.

עַל־כֵּן יֹאמְרוּ הַמֹּשְׁלִים בֹּאוּ חֶשְׁבּוֹן תִּבָּנֶה וְתִכּוֹנֵן עִיר סִיחוֹן:

The Torah relates the wars between Moab and the Amorites, and says, ***Regarding this the poets would say: "Come to Heshbon — let it be built and established as the city of Sihon"*** (21:27)

A Spiritual Budget

The word that the Torah uses for "poet," *moshel*, also means "ruler." The word Heshbon is the Hebrew word for "accounting." The Talmud, therefore, offers this interpretation of the above verse: "Those who rule over themselves can make an accounting, calculating the gains and losses in life: the gain of a mitzvah as opposed to its cost, and the cost of a sin as opposed to its gain" (*Bava Basra* 78b).

Much of western civilization lives under the influence of "seizing the pleasure of the moment." The American economy is built upon credit, with people being urged to "buy now, pay later." If people would calculate the ultimate cost of credit purchases which may be outrageous, they might delay buying things until they can afford to pay for them. But persistent and impressive advertising seduces people to get what they want, and to get it *now*. Blinded by their desires, people do not calculate.

How many people who know the long term danger of smoking render themselves oblivious to it because the desire for the immediate effects of smoking overwhelms their rational thought? The Talmud's statement is correct. Only "those who rule over themselves," who are not enslaved by their physical desires, can be objective and make an accurate accounting of the positives and negatives in life choices.

Animals do not "choose." They follow their instincts and do whatever is most pleasing. They are not rulers over their lives, but merely slaves to their physical drives which they cannot resist. Human beings should take pride in being rulers. Allowing oneself to be governed by physical drives is essentially an abdication of one's humanity.

Once a person can be a "ruler" one can calculate "the gain of a mitzvah as opposed to its cost, and the cost of a sin as opposed to its gain." I would like to share an example of this with you.

Due to my extensive work in treating alcoholism and drug addiction I have been immersed among people whose entire life is focused on getting a momentary thrill for which they must pay dearly in the long run. Their addiction to chemicals has taken every vestige of self-rule from them.

> *Avi is one such person. He is an Israeli whose pursuit of the "high" of drugs led him to a career of crime. His convictions for burglary resulted in eight imprisonments for a total of sixteen of his thirty-four years. This was certainly a long term loss for a momentary "high," but Avi had no self-rule. He lived under the tyranny of drug addiction.*
>
> *After Avi underwent a successful rehabilitation, he once found an envelope with 5,000 shekels. This was ostensibly hefker (ownerless) money, which the finder has a right to keep. It just so happened that Avi knew to whom it belonged, and he returned it. What a turnaround, from burglarizing homes to returning lost money to its owner! Avi had attained self-rule.*
>
> *I learned about this incident and congratulated Avi on his great progress. Avi said, "In the days when I used drugs, I would get a high that lasted for perhaps 20 minutes. When it wore off, I felt worse than ever. The incident when I returned the money happened six months ago. Whenever I think of it, I still get a good feeling."*

When he was enslaved by his addiction, Avi could not calculate the long term cost he would have to pay for a fleeting pleasure. As a "ruler," Avi was able to make an accounting, to calculate the loss of 5,000 shekels which he could have kept as opposed to the good feeling of doing a mitzvah, which persisted for six months and would be with him forever.

We should become rulers over ourselves. Only then can we make an honest calculation, gaining the most out of life and avoiding severe losses.

אַל־תִּירָא אֹתוֹ כִּי בְיָדְךָ נָתַתִּי אֹתוֹ

When Og, king of Bashan, went to do battle with the Israelites, God said to Moses, *"Do not fear him, for into your hand have I given him"* (21:34)

The Incalculable Reward for a Good Deed

Rashi says that Moses feared that Og might be victorious because of the merit he had from informing the patriarch Abraham that his nephew, Lot, was taken captive (*Genesis* 14:13; the "fugitive" was Og, v. Rashi). However, Rashi says that Og's intent was hardly laudable. To the contrary, he hoped that Abraham would be killed in battle, and he could then marry Sarah.

Yet, Moses was concerned that his meritorious deed of enabling Abraham to save Lot would stand to his credit.

R' Yaakov Moshe Charlap comments that this shows us the great reward for doing an act of *chesed*. Even if it is done for ulterior motives, and even if the motive is reprehensible, one is nevertheless rewarded for the good that results from the act.

We find a similar concept in the mitzvah of the forgotten sheaf. "When you reap your harvest in your field, and you forget a bundle in the field, you shall not turn back to take it; it shall be for the proselyte, the orphan and the widow, so that God will bless you in all your handiwork" (*Deuteronomy* 24:19). Rashi points out that one is rewarded even though one did not intentionally leave the grain for the poor. One might argue that the reward is for not turning back to retrieve it. Rashi cites Sifri, that if a person lost money and it was found by a poor person, one has a mitzvah of *tzedakah*, even though there was not even a passive act.

The mitzvah of *tzedakah* is exceedingly great. In contrast to other mitzvos, where the intent in doing the mitzvah is important, and if one does the mitzvah out of self-interest it detracts from the mitzvah, the merit of *tzedakah* is because of the help it provides for the needy. This purpose is achieved regardless of the benefactor's intent.

Sometimes we may feel imposed upon by requests for *tzedakah*. We should remember that the reward one receives for giving *tzedakah* makes the donor a greater beneficiary of this mitzvah than the recipient.

פרשת בלק
Parashas Balak

This is a most fascinating *parashah*. Balak, king of Moab, engages the sorcerer, Balaam, to cast a curse on Israel. Try as he might, Balaam is unable to pronounce any malediction. To the contrary, his words emerge as praises and blessings. Yet, the Talmud says that except for *Mah tovu*, "How goodly are your tents, O Jacob," (*Numbers* 24:5), all the blessings reverted to curses (*Sanhedrin* 108b). This *parashah* is especially rich in commentaries.

וַיַּרְא בָּלָק בֶּן־צִפּוֹר אֵת כָּל־אֲשֶׁר־עָשָׂה יִשְׂרָאֵל לָאֱמֹרִי

Balak son of Zippor saw all that Israel had done to the Amorite (22:2)

The Bias of Nations

Moses had sent emissaries to Sihon, king of the Amorite, asking for permission to pass through their land on their way to Canaan. He assured Sihon that they would not wander from the main road, and they would not make use of their water unless they paid for it. Instead of allowing the Israelites peaceful passage, Sihon gathered his army and attacked Israel, resulting in his defeat (*Numbers* 21:21-24).

But what did Balak see? Only what the Israelites did to the Amorite, which was in self-defense. It was Sihon who was the aggressor, but Balak paid no attention to that.

The Torah is timeless. What the Torah recorded several thousand years ago is as true today as it was then. In three wars the Arab nations tried to destroy Israel, but that is not how the world sees it.

The nations of the world and even much of the media in the United States are no different today than Balak was several thousand years ago.

The message? "It is better to look to God than to trust in man. All the nations surrounded me; it was with the Name of God that I faced them" (*Psalms* 118:8-10).

Israel has only one true friend: *God*. But He is all it needs.

כִּי יָדַעְתִּי אֵת אֲשֶׁר־תְּבָרֵךְ מְבֹרָךְ וַאֲשֶׁר תָּאֹר יוּאָר

Balak summoned Balaam to cast a curse on Israel,
because Balaam had supernatural powers.
*"For I know whomever you bless is blessed
and whomever you curse is accursed"* (22:6)

Why Look Elsewhere?

Rashi asks, "Why would God give prophetic and supernatural powers to an evil person? In order that other nations should not say, 'Had You given us prophets, we too would have been spiritual.' Therefore, God gave them a prophet, yet they behaved immorally."

> R' Simchah Bunim of P'shis'che asks, "How does this rebut the complaints of the nations? They may still say, 'You gave the Jews a prophet like Moses, who taught them proper behavior. You gave us a prophet like Balaam, who was degenerate. Had You given us a good prophet, we, too, would have been spiritual.'"
>
> R' Simchah Bunim answered, "When I lost my vision, I went to Berlin to consult the leading professors of ophthalmology. While in Berlin, someone suggested I see a faith healer, who had a reputation for miracle cures.
>
> "I responded that in truth I should rely on God to heal me, and I should go to a tzaddik to have him pray for me. However, inasmuch as the Torah says (that if someone injured a person) 'he shall provide for his healing' (Exodus 21:19), and the Talmud deduces from this that one should seek medical attention (Berachos 60a), I am obliged to consult physicians. But if I were to have recourse to a supernatural healer, why should I go to someone in Berlin when I can go to the tzaddik in Kozhnitz?
>
> "This is the response that God gives to the nations. I gave prophetic powers to both Moses and to Balaam. Moses was a holy person who taught people how to live spiritually, whereas Balaam was a vulgar person who preached depravity. You had a choice of following Moses or Balaam. It was your own decision to choose Balaam, because you preferred his teachings. You have no grounds to complain."

There is a message here for us. Some young people who are disillusioned with secularism gravitate toward oriental religions. If it is spirituality one is seeking, why not research the spirituality in Judaism? Do you really think that any of the oriental religions have produced people of greater spirituality than the Chafetz Chaim?

I have met a number of young people who have become enamored of oriental religions. None of them have had a true Torah education. None of them had read *Mesillas Yesharim (Path of the Just)*. None of them had any idea as to who was the Baal Shem Tov, the Gaon of Vilna or R' Yisroel of Salant.

How tragic to journey to distant lands to seek treasure when there is a gold mine on your front lawn.

וַתֹּאמֶר הָאָתוֹן אֶל־בִּלְעָם הֲלוֹא אָנֹכִי אֲתֹנְךָ אֲשֶׁר־רָכַבְתָּ עָלַי מֵעוֹדְךָ

*The she-donkey said to Balaam,
"Am I not your she-donkey, that you have ridden upon me
all your life until this day?"* (22:30)

Do not Abuse the Gift of Speech

R' Itzele of Ponevezh once attended a community meeting where several important community issues were to be resolved. However, instead of discussing the pros and cons of the issues, a heated verbal battle erupted among the attendees. Some claimed that they were greater contributors to the community coffers and had the right to be heard first. Others claimed seniority, while yet others said that as officials of the community, they should speak first. Soon there was a clamor, with each one asserting his rights, and no one addressing the issues for which the meeting had been called.

R' Itzele pounded on the lectern and demanded silence. Out of respect for him, everyone was quiet.

R' Itzele said, "I must tell you a story which explains a portion of the Torah.

"The donkeys came before God with a bitter complaint. 'Why have we been singled out from all animals to suffer? Wild animals roam the jungles freely, and have no master over them. Cows and sheep give their milk and wool, but are left at leisure all day to graze in the pasture. We alone are beasts of burden. We know no peace. Our masters place heavy loads on our backs and whip us if we don't move fast enough for them. It would only be fair for us to be able to speak to our masters and tell them when we are tired and not to overburden us.'

"God said, 'You have a just complaint. I will give you the ability to speak.'

"So God gave Balaam's donkey the ability to speak. But instead of explaining to Balaam that there was an angel standing in her way, what did the donkey say? 'Am I not your she-donkey that you have ridden all your life until this day?' It started telling how important it was. God then took the power of speech away. 'Donkeys who know nothing other than to assert their importance do not deserve to speak.'"

We would do well to remember R' Itzele's parable.

וַיֹּאמֶר בִּלְעָם אֶל־מַלְאַךְ ה' חָטָאתִי כִּי לֹא יָדַעְתִּי כִּי אַתָּה נִצָּב לִקְרָאתִי בַּדָּרֶךְ

*Balaam said to the angel of God, "I have sinned, for I did not
know that you were standing opposite me on the road"* (22:34)

Ignorance Is Not a Defense

If Balaam was not aware of the angel's presence, why was it a sin? Because there are things which a person should know, and not knowing is a dereliction.

The chassidic master, R' Naftali of Ropschitz, had a brother, R' Yoikel of Bolchov, who was an opponent of chassidus. R' Naftali was unaware that *his brother had fallen ill, and when he learned of it, he went to visit him.*

R' Yoikel chastised R' Naftali for not having come earlier. R' Naftali said that he had had no idea that he was sick.

R' Yoikel said, "That is no excuse. Balaam said, 'I have sinned, for I did not know that you were standing opposite me on the road.' Why was it a sin? Because he should have known.

"You are a tzaddik, and everyone says that you have prophetic vision," R' Yoikel said. "You should have known that I was sick."

Even without prophetic powers, we should have sufficient interest in our relatives and friends that we should know of their circumstances, to share in their joys and to be supportive in their moments of distress. If we do not make the effort to find out, we are derelict in our duty.

The Hallmark of a Person

The Talmud gives the characteristics of the disciples of Abraham: a benevolent eye, a humble spirit and a meek soul. The traits of disciples of Balaam are: an evil eye, an arrogant spirit and a greedy soul. The Talmud then says, "How are the disciples of Abraham different than the disciples of Balaam?" (*Ethics of the Fathers* 5:22).

Why does the Talmud focus on "the disciples" of Abraham and Balaam? Why not cite the differences between Abraham and Balaam themselves?

The answer is that anyone looking at Abraham and Balaam might not be able to distinguish between the two. After all, did not Balaam subjugate himself totally to God? "If Balak will give me his houseful of silver and gold, I cannot transgress the word of God" (*Numbers* 22:18). "Balaam spoke up and said, 'Whatever God puts in my mouth, that I must take heed to speak'" (ibid. 23:12). "I cannot transgress the word of God to do good or bad on my own. Whatever God speaks, that I will speak" (ibid. 24:13). Are these not the words of a *tzaddik*? Anyone hearing Balaam might conclude that he is a very God-fearing person.

Appearances can be deceptive. There were people who were Torah scholars and who were even observant of mitzvos, yet all their disciples deviated from Torah and mitzvos. On the other hand, if one looks at the disciples of the Baal Shem Tov or R' Yisroel of Salant, one can understand the greatness of their masters.

If you wish to know the true mettle of a person, look at his disciples. The true nature of a person is revealed in those whom he taught. Their character, their behavior and their belief reflect that of the teacher.

Of course, the finest parents have had an errant child, and the finest teachers have had an errant student. However, if one looks at the body of students, one can get a fair idea of what the teacher was like.

This is an important concept in moral and ethical education. The character of the mathematician does not necessarily impact the subject he teaches. It is different when the subject is human behavior.

In the secular world, one may find books on guidelines in life written by people whose ethical and moral principles may leave much to be desired. In the Torah world this is untenable. The sixth chapter of *Ethics of the Fathers* begins with "Blessed is He Who chose *them* (the sages) and their teaching." *Them* is a prerequisite for teaching. Only those whose character is such that they deserve to be chosen are acceptable as teachers.

Before accepting anyone as authoritative on how one should live, check into how he has lived his life.

לֹא־הִבִּיט אָוֶן בְּיַעֲקֹב וְלֹא־רָאָה עָמָל בְּיִשְׂרָאֵל

"He perceived no iniquity in Jacob, and saw no perversity in Israel" (23:21)

Tireless Torah and Mitzvos

The Hebrew word *amal*, translated here as "perversity," has a second meaning, "toil." It is an expression for work, especially laborious and exhausting work. The Ohr HaChaim uses this translation to give a unique interpretation to Balaam's words: "He saw no exhaustion in Israel." Balaam perceived that even when Israel devotes itself wholeheartedly to the observance of Torah and mitzvos, it does not exhaust them.

It is a well-known fact that when someone has an overwhelming desire for something, he may be tireless in its pursuit. We have numerous accounts of the indefatigable study of Torah of our great scholars. It was not unusual for them to study Torah for eighteen hours each day.

The prophet says, "You did not call upon Me, Jacob, because you became weary of Me, Israel" (*Isaiah* 43:22). The Maggid of Dubnow explained this verse with a parable, which R' Mendel of Kotzk said was Divinely inspired.

> *A merchant alighted from a ship and hired a porter to deliver his merchandise to his home. When the porter knocked at his door, sweating profusely and breathing heavily, the merchant promptly said, "Those were not my packages that you brought!"*
>
> *The porter asked, "You haven't even seen what I brought. How can you say they're not yours?"*
>
> *"Because," the merchant said, "I deal in jewelry. My packages are light. They never would have caused you to sweat profusely."*
>
> *The Maggid said, "This is the thought that the prophet is conveying. God says, 'How do I know that you are not calling upon Me? Because you become weary and exhausted with your praying. You may be just going through the motions of prayer. Praying to Me would not cause you to be fatigued.'"*

Our devotion in prayer, our passion for Torah and our love for mitzvos should be such that we never tire in their performance.

מַה־טֹּבוּ אֹהָלֶיךָ יַעֲקֹב מִשְׁכְּנֹתֶיךָ יִשְׂרָאֵל כִּנְחָלִים
נִטָּיוּ כְּגַנֹּת עֲלֵי נָהָר כַּאֲהָלִים נָטַע ה׳ כַּאֲרָזִים עֲלֵי־מָיִם

"How goodly are your tents, O Jacob, your dwelling places, O Israel. Stretching out like brooks, like gardens by a river, like aloes planted by God, like cedars by water" (24: 5-6)

A Thinly Veiled Curse

The first of these verses, *Mah tovu*, is the opening verse of the morning service. In many communities, this verse is not recited. Although it appears to be a blessing, the feeling is that nothing benevolent could have come from the tongue of the evil Balaam. The Talmud says that all of Balaam's "blessings" reverted to being curses, except for *Mah tovu* (*Sanhedrin* 108b). Nevertheless, some authorities did not wish to cite even this blessing. They followed the principle, "Only wickedness emanates from the wicked" (*I Samuel* 24:14).

> R' Levi Yitzchok of Berditchev said that his neshamah (soul) once ascended to Heaven, and he found that there was great rejoicing there. Upon inquiring as to the reason for the joy, he was told that it had been decreed that no Jew should ever suffer poverty, and that all Jews should be blessed with abundance. R' Levi Yitzchok asked who had suggested this blessing, and he was told that surprisingly, it had come from Satan.
> "Then it must be annulled!" R' Levi Yitzchok demanded. "Nothing good can come from Satan, regardless of how seemingly benign it may appear."

What harm could possibly be contained in *Mah tovu*?

R' Yaakov Yosef of Polonya explained that the words of the true prophets are for the greater part sharp reprimands. They were critical of the Israelites' behavior and pointed out their dereliction, demanding that they correct their errant ways. They warned Israel of the grave consequences awaiting those who deviated from the Torah. Not so the false prophets. They preached that all was well and that there was no reason for concern that any harm would befall Israel.

Solomon says that the wounds inflicted out of true love and concern are trustworthy, whereas the abundant kisses of an enemy are worthless (*Proverbs* 27:6).

In my work treating people who have alcohol or drug problems, I have found these words to be of great wisdom. In my book *Substance Abusing High Achievers*, I described a case of a physician who had a severe alcohol problem, but his colleagues repeatedly covered up for him. The result of this was disastrous, and this doctor said that his colleagues almost destroyed him with their "kindness." "My colleagues were unknowing, unwitting and unwilling," he said.

R' Yaakov Yosef said that Balaam's intention was to curse Israel by telling them how wonderful they were. They were so perfect that they did not need to do anything to improve.

> R' Yitzchok Meir of Gur was a follower of the Maggid of Kozhnitz. The Maggid was very fond of his great disciple, and one time embraced and kissed him. R' Yitzchok Meir then left the Maggid and became a disciple of R' Simchah Bunim of P'shis'che. "I don't need a master who kisses me," he said. "I need a master who will make my bones tremble."

The Talmud says, "If you find a spiritual leader who is beloved in his community, it may be because he does not chastise them for their delinquencies in the observance of mitzvos" (*Kesubos* 108b). We must be cautious when we hear only praise and no rebuke. As pleasant to the ear as praise may be, it does not often stimulate a person to self-improvement.

> When R' Shimon Sofer became the rabbi of Cracow, he found more than a hundred synagogues and shtiblach (small places of worship). He realized

that this proliferation of places of worship was not the result of overcrowding, but rather of splintering, which was generally due to petty differences.

R' Sofer said, "Now I understand why the Talmud said that all of Balaam's blessings reverted to curses except for Mah tovu. Balaam's intention was to curse Israel, but in His infinite mercy, God twisted his tongue so that he pronounced blessings. When the Israelites sinned and lost favor with God, Balaam's intention to curse was realized.

"Mah tovu, however, did not have to revert to a curse. It was never a genuine blessing to begin with. With his prophetic insight, Balaam saw that Jews would be nitpicking and seeking to break away and make many places of worship. His 'blessing' that there be many 'tents of Jacob' was actually a veiled curse, and did not have to revert."

There is a principle, "In the multitude of people is the king's glory" (*Proverbs* 14:28). The finest way of honoring the Divine Name would be for large congregations to have "standing room only."

R' Sofer's comments are as timely now as they were more than a century ago. We still suffer from lack of unity. Let the establishment of new places of worship be the result only of the existing shuls becoming overcrowded.

לְכָה אִיעָצְךָ אֲשֶׁר יַעֲשֶׂה הָעָם הַזֶּה לְעַמְּךָ בְּאַחֲרִית הַיָּמִים

"Come, I shall counsel you what this people will do to your people in the End of Days" (24:14)

Balaam's Ultimate Curse

Balaam's subsequent words were prophesies, but in what way were they "counsel?"

R' Simchah Bunim of P'shis'che gave this verse another interpretation. Inasmuch as there are no vowel sounds in the Torah, the word *yaaseh* can also be read as *ye'oseh*. The verse then reads, "I shall counsel you that this people will *become* your people in the End of Days."

Balaam realized that hostile curses against Israel are futile. We have survived the curses of many enemies. We have been driven from our homeland, expelled from one country after another, suffered the massacres of the crusades, pogroms and the Holocaust. But all these calamities have not destroyed Israel.

With rates of intermarriage increasing to alarming levels, the danger to our survival is real. More Jews have been lost to our nation by intermarriage than by the Holocaust. Our most formidable enemy is assimilation.

Balaam's advice to Balak was, "You cannot destroy the Jews by hostile aggression. Their God will always leave a remnant that will rise from the ashes. You can triumph only if you convince them to abandon their God. This cannot be done by force. [This was proven in the Inquisition, where countless Jews preferred death to renouncing Judaism.] But if Jews are attracted to assimilate with non-Jews, they will leave their faith."

The Torah relates that Balak promptly tried to implement Balaam's advice. With leaders such as Moses and zealots such as Phinehas (*Numbers* 24:7), this did not succeed at the time. But alas! Today we are bereft of such leaders, and the plague of assimilation has taken a horrific toll.

It is crucial that we retain an identity and practice that resists the lure of assimilation. Foremost among the ways to achieve this is for children to know from earliest infancy that they are Jews and what it means to be Jewish. Torah education is the single most potent weapon we have against the enemy of assimilation.

A patient of mine who was not observant told me that his son was planning to marry a non-Jewish woman. He was bitterly disappointed. "If I had known that this could happen, I would have kept my home kosher even if it was not my conviction. If young people of different faiths are separated and do not socialize together, there is less chance that they will develop intimate relationships."

Some people have the mistaken idea that providing the children with the finest secular education is to their benefit. Neglecting Torah education and practices puts the child at risk of being torn from the Jewish nation. Parents should realize that to lose one's identity as a Jew is not in their best interest.

פרשת פינחס
Parashas Pinchas

וּבְנֵי־קֹרַח לֹא־מֵתוּ

Korach, the leader of the rebellion against Moses, and his co-conspirators were swallowed up by an earthquake, but *the children of Korach did not die* (26:11)

Misguiding One's Children

Korach was a very learned person. He sincerely believed that he was right in challenging Moses, and he convinced many of the elders to join him. The Midrash states that Korach's children were in a quandary. On the one hand, they did not wish to challenge Moses, but on the other hand, how could they defy their father? Initially they supported their father, but at the last moment, they deserted him and supported Moses and were spared from death.

The Midrash asks, inasmuch as Korach was so highly learned and was one of the select few to carry the Holy Ark, how could he be so foolish as to challenge Moses? The Midrash answers that Korach's prophetic vision showed him the greatness of his descendants. He reasoned that he must be right, because if he were wrong in opposing Moses, he could not possibly merit having such great offspring. His mistake was that he did not consider that his children might do *teshuvah* and achieve greatness in their own right.

Korach's failure to consider that his children might do *teshuvah* caused him to expose his children to death. This was not because he did not love his children, but because he was incalcitrant and would not consider that he may be wrong.

This strikes a familiar note. Some parents today who are not observant do not respect the halachic laws of divorce. When a marriage is terminated without a *get* (halachic divorce) children born from a subsequent marriage are considered illegitimate and may not marry into a Jewish family. Some of these children who adopt a Torah way of life find themselves severely disadvantaged by their parents' failure to consider the possibility that they will be causing their children irreparable harm.

Some modern parents do not give their children a basic Jewish education. "We don't want them to be influenced. Let them make up their own minds when they grow up." How distorted an argument! A secular education is not a neutral education which will allow them to freely choose their way of life. A secular education today essentially rejects any absolute moral standards. Children educated secularly have nothing to deter them from indulging in every possible pleasure-seeking activity. Raising children with a hedonistic attitude is hardly neutral. Furthermore, should these children choose to lead a Torah life as adults, they are at a distinct disadvantage in lacking the basics of Judaism.

Korach's self-righteousness nearly proved fatal for his children. Modern parents should avoid this tragic error.

וַיַּקְרֵב מֹשֶׁה אֶת־מִשְׁפָּטָן לִפְנֵי ה׳

The daughters of Zelophehad pleaded their case before Moses.
Since their father had no male children,
why should his descendants be deprived
of a share in the inheritance of the Promised Land?
Moses did not have an answer for them,
and he brought their claim before God (27:5)

Torah and Middos

Rashi cites the Talmud explaining that Moses had known the halachah that daughters inherit when there are no sons, but that he had forgotten it. This happened because when he set up the hierarchy of judges, he said, "If anything is too difficult for you to decide, bring it to me."

Moses was the most humble person on earth (*Numbers* 12:3), and he certainly did not have the slightest taint of grandiosity when he made the above statement. Yet, because he worded it in a way that might be seen as self-aggrandizement, he overlooked a halachah which God had taught him.

The *mussar* writings state that Moses' forgetting the halachah was not a punishment. Rather, Torah in its full truth can abide only in someone whose *middos* are of the highest order. This infinitesimally small deviation from absolute humility was enough of an infraction of *middos* to cause Moses to forget a halachah!

Which mathematician forgets a mathematical principle because he is less than perfect in character? Which geologist or chemist errs in his research because of a lack of *middos*? Do students seeking the most competent teaching in a scientific field flock to the professor who is finest in character? When prizes are presented for outstanding scientific contributions, are the personal lives of the scientists taken into account?

The incident of Moses forgetting a halachah because his words carried the slightest flavor of vanity should makes us mindful of the enormous gap between Torah and secular knowledge. Torah is Divine, and the acquisition of Torah can be achieved only by those who emulate the Divine attributes.

The qualifications for a true grasp of Torah are spelled out in the sixth chapter of *Ethics of the Fathers.* No less than forty-eight character traits are listed. Is there a university anywhere in the world that established such criteria as mandatory for a professorship?

> אֲשֶׁר־יֵצֵא לִפְנֵיהֶם וַאֲשֶׁר יָבֹא לִפְנֵיהֶם וַאֲשֶׁר יוֹצִיאֵם וַאֲשֶׁר
> יְבִיאֵם וְלֹא תִהְיֶה עֲדַת ה' כַּצֹּאן אֲשֶׁר אֵין־לָהֶם רֹעֶה
>
> Moses asked God to appoint a successor to him
> ***who will go out before them and come before them,
> and let the assembly of God not be like sheep
> who do not have a shepherd for them*** (27:17)

The Qualities of a Leader

R' Yaakov, the Maggid of Vilna, noted that for the sake of brevity, the verse could have read, "let not the assembly of God be like sheep without a shepherd." Why the expression, "who do not have a shepherd for them?"

R' Yaakov explained that there are shepherds who give the greatest care to the flock, leading them to the best grazing fields and fresh streams of water. If they are his own sheep, his intention is that the sheep produce the greatest income for him, and if he is hired to look after other people's flocks, he provides good service in order to be paid well. These shepherds are hardly interested in the welfare of the sheep *per se*. They provide good care for their own benefit.

This is not the kind of leader Moses wanted to succeed him. On a number of occasions, Moses sacrificed himself for his flock. They were dearer to him than his own life. Moses asked to be succeeded by such a leader that "the congregation of God be not like sheep who do not have a shepherd *for them*," i.e., that the shepherd's interest be for the flock rather than for himself.

Our great leaders always put others before themselves. Characteristic of this is the Chafetz Chaim.

> *One of the Chafetz Chaim's students fell gravely ill, and doctors gave no hope for recovery. The student asked the Chafetz Chaim for a berachah. The Chafetz Chaim sent him to a Torah scholar in a nearby town for a berachah and swore him to never reveal this to anyone. The student did as he was told and had a remarkable recovery. Before he married, he revealed to his kallah that he had suffered a serious illness from which he had fully recovered.*
>
> *Many years later, the wife's sister fell ill with the same disease, and again there was no hope for recovery. The wife pleaded with her husband to tell her how he had been cured so that she could save her sister's life. Eventually he was unable to ignore her pleas and, although he had been sworn to secrecy, he told her about his contact with the Chafetz Chaim.*
>
> *Shortly thereafter, the man fell ill, and again went to the Chafetz Chaim. The Chafetz Chaim was now at an advanced age and frail. "I wish I could help you now," the Chafetz Chaim said. "Many years ago when you were ill, I fasted for forty consecutive days and prayed for your recovery. I am now very old, and I no longer have the strength to do so."*

Not only was the Chafetz Chaim a leader who cared for his flock more than for himself and fasted forty days to purify himself so that his prayers for the young man would be accepted, but in his great humility, he sent the young man to someone else for a *berachah* so that the miraculous recovery should not be attributed to him (*Lekach Tov, Bamidbar* p. 282).

Those are the qualities that Moses set for a leader of Israel: humility and self-sacrifice.

Mastery over Oneself

יִפְקֹד ה׳ אֱלֹקֵי הָרוּחֹת לְכָל־בָּשָׂר אִישׁ עַל־הָעֵדָה

קַח־לְךָ אֶת־יְהוֹשֻׁעַ בִּן־נוּן אִישׁ אֲשֶׁר־רוּחַ בּוֹ

The dialogue between Moses and God is noteworthy. Moses asked for his successor to be selfless and totally devoted to the people (v. above). **"Let God, Lord of all spirits, appoint a person over the congregation"** (27:16) which Rashi explains to mean "a person who can understand and relate to each individual." God responded, **"Take to yourself Joshua, the son of Nun, a man in whom there is spirit"** (27:18)

In what way does Joshua's being "a man in whom there is spirit" satisfy the qualifications that Moses requested?

The Alter (Elder) of Novaradok explains this well. The human being is comprised of a body and a spirit. The body produces all the cravings which stimulate pursuit of self-gratification. The spirit is the force that directs the person away from self-gratification, to be devoted to a higher goal in life. These two components are engaged in a struggle for mastery over the person. To the degree that bodily drives prevail, to that degree the person is self-centered. To the degree that the spirit prevails, to that degree a person can look away from his own needs and be dedicated to his mission.

A person who is preoccupied with his own needs cannot empathize fully with others. In *Not Just Stories* I related an incident of my great-grandfather, R' Mordechai Dov of Hornosteipel (v. *Zeide Reb Motele*) who underwent an excruciatingly painful medical treatment without uttering a sound. At the doctor's astonishment of such stoicism, R' Mordechai Dov responded, "If I can withstand the pain I experience when someone comes to me for help with a problem and I am unable to help him, I can certainly withstand this pain."

The ability to relate to and understand every individual requires extraordinary empathy. Such empathy is possible only in a person who has no self-gratifying drives, who has subjugated them to the spirit. The ability to be a shepherd who cares for his flock rather than for his personal interests must be devoid of bodily drives. Only such a person can be self-sacrificing and absolutely fair to everyone.

God's response to Moses' request for a leader with such qualifications was, therefore, appropriate. "Take to yourself Joshua, son of Nun, man in whom there is spirit." Joshua had succeeded in achieving self-mastery, of vanquishing the bodily drives for gratification and making the spirit dominant (*Madregas HaAdam* vol. 1 p. 58).

Every person is engaged in the life-long struggle between the two opposing forces. Perhaps the extreme elimination of all self-gratification required of the leader is not achievable by everyone. However, let us remember that the physical component of the human being is essentially no different than that of lower forms of life. "The superiority of man over animal is naught, except for the pure soul" (Morning service, *Nusach Sefard*). Our dignity as human beings is directly proportional to the degree that we achieve self-mastery and dominance of the spirit.

פרשת מטות
Parashas Mattos

וַיְדַבֵּר מֹשֶׁה אֶל־רָאשֵׁי הַמַּטּוֹת לִבְנֵי יִשְׂרָאֵל לֵאמֹר זֶה הַדָּבָר אֲשֶׁר צִוָּה ה'

Moses spoke to the heads of the tribes of the Children of Israel saying, "This is the thing that God has commanded" (30:2)

A Clear Perspective

The word *leimor*, to say, generally means that the person hearing the message should say it; i.e., convey it to others. Ohr HaChaim notes that in this verse, the term is unclear. To whom should the Israelites say it?

Rashi comments that whereas other prophets said, "Thus spoke God," which means that they received their prophecy in a vision that they interpreted, Moses was unique in being able to say, "This is the word of God." As God said to Miriam, "I speak to other prophets in visions and dreams, but not so with Moses. I speak to him mouth to mouth" (*Numbers* 12:6-7). Moses had the ability to convey the word of God with utmost clarity.

Although the Torah says that there never again arose a prophet like Moses (*Deuteronomy* 34:10), the Zohar says that the *neshamah* of Moses is widely dispersed throughout all generations. Moses bequeathed himself to Israel, and every Jew has a trace of Moses in him.

It follows that within every Jew there is the potential of seeing the word of God with utmost clarity. Although the level of Moses is unattainable, something of Moses' perception is within us.

It was Moses' fervent wish that all of Israel rise to the level of prophesy (*Numbers* 11:29). Moses certainly wished that everyone could attain the clarity in the Divine word that he attained. He hoped that every Jew should be able to say, as he did, "This is the word of God."

This may be the meaning of *leimor* in the above verse. Moses spoke to the Israelites and said, "*May you all be able to say*, 'This is the word of God.'"

Moses' wish was often fulfilled. There are commentaries on Torah that are of the category "Thus spoke God," which convey to us a variety of meanings of the Scriptures. There are other commentaries whose insights into Torah are so clear, that there is no doubt that their interpretation is the manifest Divine wish.

But this ability is not restricted to the outstanding scholars who authored the commentaries. Everyone has a particle of Moses. If we apply ourselves sincerely and diligently to the study of Torah, we can all see with great clarity the express wish of God.

אִישׁ כִּי־יִדֹּר נֶדֶר לַה׳ . . . כְּכָל־הַיֹּצֵא מִפִּיו יַעֲשֶׂה
If a person takes a vow to God . . . he shall not desecrate his word (30:3)

Achieving Self Mastery

In an earlier selection we noted that achieving dominance of the spirit over bodily drives is the distinguishing factor of humanity. How does one come by this?

The Talmud says that a person may reinforce his motivation to doing a mitzvah or resistance against committing a sin by taking a sacred vow to do or not to do (*Nedarim* 8:1).

How does taking a vow strengthen one's resolve? First, the gravity of violating a vow is extremely great. The Talmud says that when God spoke the commandment, "You shall not swear falsely," the entire world trembled. There are known cases of people who lost huge sums of money in litigation because they refused to support their claim by taking an oath.

My grandmother told me that when she was a little girl, her father, Zeide R' Motele, told her not to use the expression, "Believe me," because that is tantamount to an oath. For the rest of her 90-plus years she never used the expression, "Believe me."

Secondly, there is a psychological reason. Ever since we were children, we have resisted taking orders. The Talmud says that a person who volunteers to do a mitzvah to which he is not obligated is not as meritorious as one who is required to do it. The latter has a more intense battle with the *yetzer hara*, because he must overcome the innate resistance to obeying an order (*Kiddushin* 31a). It is much easier to do something when it is of one's own free will.

Taking an oath to do a mitzvah or to refrain from a sin allows the person to feel that he is fulfilling a self-imposed promise rather than obeying an order. This makes compliance easier.

One might ask, is this not then following one's own will rather than obeying God's commandment? Perhaps. But this falls into the category of doing mitzvos and refraining from sin *shelo lishmah* (for less than pure motivation), which then enables a person to achieve a level of *lishmah*.

In keeping with the previous article, self-imposed reinforcement of the Divine will is very much a unique human trait. Animals cannot make such vows. This is a function of the human spirit, and elevates a person spiritually.

וַיִּמָּסְרוּ מֵאַלְפֵי יִשְׂרָאֵל אֶלֶף לַמַּטֶּה
So there were delivered from the thousands of the Children of Israel, a thousand from each tribe (31:5)

Beloved Spiritual Leaders

The term "delivered" implies that they were coerced to go. This was because they knew that after the battle with Midian, Moses would die (ibid. 31:2). They, therefore, procrastinated going to battle. Rashi comments, "This teaches how beloved leaders of Israel are. During the sojourn in the desert, they so griped and grumbled that Moses said, 'They are nearly prepared to stone me.' But when they knew he was soon to leave them, they tried to delay his death."

R' Yoel Sirkis (author of Bayis Chadash) had considerable opposition from some discontents in the community who caused him much anguish. When he was near death, members of the community gathered about him, and among them were some of his adversaries. Seeing them, R' Yoel sighed, "So, now you have come to me."

Those who had distressed him hung their heads in shame. One of them said tearfully, "Rabbi, we love you just as the Israelites did Moses. The Talmud says that if a spiritual leader is beloved to his community, it is not because he is so excellent, but because he does not chastise them on their spiritual deficiencies (Kesubos 108b). If we caused you anguish, it was because you showed no favoritism, and you rebuked us for our lack of Torah study and mitzvos. Even when we caused you grief, we knew that you were right. Our discontent was precisely because, like Moses, you were a true spiritual leader."

וַיֹּאמֶר אֶלְעָזָר הַכֹּהֵן . . . זֹאת חֻקַּת הַתּוֹרָה

Upon their return from the battle against Midian, Moses angrily reprimanded the officers for not eliminating the sinful who had demoralized the Israelites. Subsequently, when it was necessary to make the utensils taken in the booty kosher,
Elazar the Kohen said, . . . "This is the decree [for making utensils kosher]" (31:21)

The Toxicity of Rage

The Talmud says that the law was taught by Elazar because Moses had forgotten it due to his anger. "If a person becomes enraged, if he is wise, he loses his wisdom, and if he is a prophet, he loses his prophecy" (*Pesachim* 66b).

"Imagine the scene," R' Yehudah Leib Chasman says. "Elazar is delivering a Torah lecture to the Israelites, conveying to them what God had said to Moses, and Moses stands by silently, unable to speak because he had forgotten what God had told him. The Talmud says that during the mourning period following Moses' death, three hundred laws were forgotten, and Othniel ben Kenaz was able to restore them by logical reasoning. And here, Moses himself, who had received the laws directly from God, stands by silently. He forgot what God had said and did not have the ability to reason logically as did Othneil. What had happened to the great Moses? His moment of rage deprived him momentarily of both his wisdom and prophetic powers.

"The suspension of his prophetic powers and intellect was not a punishment. Far from it. Moses' wrath was directed at those who failed to protect the Israelites from improper actions, and it was thus in the interest of Israel and for the greater glory of God. Nevertheless," says R' Chasman, "Moses suffered suspension of his enormous powers because *the toxic effects of rage are a natural phenomenon*. A person who puts his hand into a fire is not 'punished' by being burned. It is a natural consequence. Similarly, the loss of one's powers due to rage is a natural consequence rather than a punishment.

"Given the frequency with which we lose control of our anger," says R' Chasman, "it is only by God's compassion that we remember anything of Torah."

R' Yisroel of Salant said that most of the transgressions of interpersonal relationships are due to uncontrolled anger. Rarely did he ever manifest anger. On those few occasions when he felt it was necessary to manifest his displeasure, he was heard to whisper to himself, "Appear angry but do not feel angry."

> Only on one occasion was R' Yisroel known to have displayed wrath. In 1848 an epidemic of cholera broke out in Vilna. R' Yisroel sought tirelessly to bring medical help and assistance to the victims. He instructed all his students to personally attend the sick on Shabbos and do everything necessary for them. He told them not to look for non-Jews to make fires and cook for the sick, because halachah dictates that when there is danger to life, the work that is otherwise forbidden on Shabbos should be done by Jews (Orach Chaim 328).
>
> One Shabbos, the grandson of a Vilna citzen, R' Yoseph, fell ill. R' Yisroel's student chopped wood, built a fire and heated water, among the other things they did for him. After the grandson recovered, R' Yoseph thanked R' Yisroel for his students' help, but added, "Perhaps it is not my place to criticize, but I think the students took unnecessary liberties with violating the Shabbos."
>
> Fearing that the students who overheard this might become lax in their efforts due to concern of violating Shabbos unnecessarily, which might jeopardize the care of others who had taken sick, R' Yisroel became visibly enraged, and in an uncharacteristically loud voice, shouted, "You simpleton! Are you going to teach me what is permissible or forbidden on Shabbos? My students were entrusted to me by their parents, and it is my responsibility to return them in good health. Do you carry that responsibility?" R' Yoseph promptly asked forgiveness for his remark.
>
> This manifestation of anger was thoroughly justified, yet it tormented R' Yisroel for the rest of his life.

How many people regret an *unjustifiable* rage? How many carry this regret for the rest of their lives?

הָאָרֶץ אֲשֶׁר הִכָּה ה' לִפְנֵי עֲדַת יִשְׂרָאֵל אֶרֶץ מִקְנֶה הִוא וְלַעֲבָדֶיךָ מִקְנֶה . . .
יֻתַּן אֶת־הָאָרֶץ הַזֹּאת לַעֲבָדֶיךָ לַאֲחֻזָּה אַל־תַּעֲבִרֵנוּ אֶת־הַיַּרְדֵּן

Having conquered Transjordan en route to Canaan,
the tribes of Gad and Reuben approached Moses.
***"The land that God smote before the assembly of Israel
it is a land for livestock, and your servants have livestock . . .
let this land be given to your servants as a heritage;
do not bring us across the Jordan"*** (32:4-5)

Prioritizing: Physical or Spiritual Needs?

Although the tribes of Gad and Reuben were foremost in the battle for Canaan, they were nevertheless guilty of rejecting their portion in Canaan in favor of the rich grazing lands in Transjordan. When the Jews were driven from the Holy Land, the tribes of Gad and Reuben were the first to be exiled. The Midrash states that this was because they had chosen Transjordan over Canaan (*Bamidbar Rabbah* 22).

R' Aharon Kotler states that the intentions of the two tribes may have seemed commendable. With abundant grazing land for their livestock, they would not have to work as hard as farmers, and they would have more time to devote to Torah study. However, the fact was that this was not their true motivation. Their decision was induced by the wealth that Transjordan would bring them, and for this they abdicated the additional mitzvos that prevailed in Canaan: *bikkurim* (the offering of the first fruits), the Omer, the offering of the loaves on Shavuos. And the result? Not only did they forfeit the mitzvos, but they were also the first to lose their land.

As we have noted, the accounts in the Torah are intended for teaching and guidance rather than history. We have so many waking hours which we allot to prayer, Torah study and work. Which of these gets the lion's share? Is it proper that we often make short order of our morning prayers in order to get to the office as early as possible?

There are some traits that are innate, and others that are developed by habit. The acquisitive drive is inborn, and since it may detract us from our spiritual goals, we should seek to attenuate it. Reinforcing the acquisitive drive by habit allows it to dominate our lives. But we should realize that any monetary gain achieved at the cost of neglecting mitzvos is not likely to endure.

We would do well to rethink our priorities (*Mishnas R' Ahron* p. 226).

גִּדְרֹת צֹאן נִבְנֶה לְמִקְנֵנוּ פֹּה וְעָרִים לְטַפֵּנוּ

The tribes of Gad and Reuven said,
"Pens for the flock shall we build here for our livestock and cities for our small children" (32:16)

A Lesson in Parenting

Rashi states that the words of Gad and Reuben, placing the provisions for their livestock before that of their children, indicates that they accorded greater value to their possessions than to their children.

We may ask, how could anyone possibly give greater importance to their possessions than to their children? We may indeed be critical of Gad and Reuben, and be totally unaware that many of us are guilty of the same thing.

At a recent meeting of representatives from various communities to cope with the increasing phenomenon of yeshivah dropouts, one person said, "When I was in yeshivah, there were dropouts who were in the street trying to entice me to join them. The reason I did not join them is because I did not want to jeopardize my relationship with my parents."

Today, many children lack such a relationship. The father returns home from work late, and equipped with a cell phone and beeper, his mealtime with the children is interrupted. Whatever time he could spend with them is commandeered by business calls.

It is related that a child asked his psychiatrist father, "How much do you charge for an hour?" The father said, "$150." The child said, "I have saved up that much. Can I have an hour of your time?"

In the previous essay we noted that the tribes of Gad and Reuben gave preference to wealth over mitzvos. Here we see that they also gave greater importance to their wealth than to their children.

There is nothing that should take preference over our children. They did not ask to be brought into a world that is fraught with so many difficulties. We brought them into the world, and it is our duty as parents to provide the best opportunity to achieve happiness. *We cannot give them happiness, but we should provide them with the means whereby they can achieve happiness.*

We must teach our children and we must discipline them, because without discipline they cannot possibly make an optimum adjustment to life. But at all times, our primary concern must be what is best for *them*, rather than what is best for *us*. If these two should conflict, the child's welfare must be given preference.

For example, there are children who are simply not academically inclined. We should have a child evaluated by a competent specialist to see whether he may have some type of learning disability which can be corrected. Many such conditions go undetected, with parents being disappointed in the child's school performance, and showing their disappointment to the child.

Occasionally, no remediable condition can be found, and although the child is of normal mentality, he is just not the scholarly type. The child may have manual or artistic talents which can be developed.

Forcing the child to be a scholar because that is what the parents want of him is like asking a child who is tone deaf to be a musician.

As parents, our perception may be distorted by our desires. We may sincerely believe that something is in the child's best interest when in fact it is something *we* desire. It is important that we get proper guidance from someone who can be objective.

We are taught the mistakes of the past so that we may avoid them, rather than to repeat them.

וִהְיִיתֶם נְקִיִּם מֵה׳ וּמִיִּשְׂרָאֵל

Moses told the tribes of Gad and Reuben that if they would keep their promise and be the vanguard in the conquest of Canaan, *"then you shall be vindicated from God and from Israel"* (32:22)

Honest Vindication

The Talmud states that a person should behave in a manner that he is beyond suspicion from people, *in the same way* that he is beyond suspicion from God, as the Torah says, "You will be vindicated from God and from Israel" (*Shekalim* 3).

R' Yisroel of Salant called attention to the words, "in the same way."

"Some people may place themselves above suspicion from others by deceit. They may use their cunning to give an appearance of absolute integrity. That is why the Talmud says that one should put oneself beyond suspicion from people *in the same way* that one is beyond suspicion from God. Just as you cannot deceive God, neither should you vindicate yourself to other people by deceit."

Recent experiences in politics and in business have proven the wisdom of R'

Yisroel's remarks. Again and again we are disappointed and disillusioned by the exposure of the dishonesty of people who had gained our trust.

In our own lives, we must be different. Our integrity should be impeccable.

R' Moshe Schreiber (Chasam Sofer) said, "All my life I agonized to put myself above suspicion. It is easier to be pure before God than before people. One who is not pure before people is more culpable than one who is not pure before God" (*Likkutei Shaalos U'Teshuvos* 59).

A person may win his case involving a monetary dispute, but if it will cast the slightest doubt on his integrity, he would do better to forego the money than to be suspected of dishonesty.

> *A man was sued in a beis-din (rabbinic tribunal), and the tribunal ruled that he must take an oath that he does not owe the money that the plaintiff claimed. He took the oath, then paid the money that was claimed. He explained, "Had I paid the money and not taken the oath, people might have said that I was lying when I denied the claim, but that the fear of violating a sacred oath brought out the truth. If I had just taken the oath, people might have said, 'For a few dollars he is willing to swear falsely.' Therefore, I swore that I did not owe the money, then I paid it. Now I am above suspicion"* (Atarah LeMelech).

How different our lives would be if we were always above suspicion!

פרשת מסעי ~§
Parashas Masei

אֵלֶּה מַסְעֵי בְנֵי־יִשְׂרָאֵל . . .
וַיִּכְתֹּב מֹשֶׁה אֶת־מוֹצָאֵיהֶם לְמַסְעֵיהֶם

These are the journeys of the Children of Israel . . .
Moses wrote their goings forth
according to their journeys (33:1-2)

Taking Inventory

The Torah commentaries say that the enumeration of the journeys and encampments was to review all that had transpired during the forty years in the desert.

A person who has a purpose and goal in life will pause every now and then to assess how much he has accomplished toward reaching his objective.

> My father would tell of a chassidic rebbe, who, on the first Shabbos after Succos, lifted his goblet of wine to recite the Kiddush, and closed his eyes in meditation. He continued to meditate for hours. The goblet of wine fell from his hand, and the chassidim at his table dozed off. Toward dawn, he awoke, refilled the goblet and recited the Kiddush.
>
> The rebbe explained to his chassidim that when a merchant goes to the market, as long as he is engaged in buying, selling, appraising and trading, he does not have the time to calculate how much profit or loss he had on each transaction. After he leaves the market and lodges at the first inn, he reviews his documents to see what he accomplished at the market.
>
> "Beginning with the month of Elul, I started to do teshuvah. It was a very busy month for me. Then came Rosh Hashanah, the Ten Days of Repentance, Yom Kippur, Sukkos and Simchas Torah, all laden with special mitzvos. There was so much happening during this period that I had no time to make an accounting of what I had achieved. This Shabbos was like the 'first inn' after the marketplace, my first opportunity to review what I had accomplished. I began meditating about this before Kiddush, and it took me a while to complete my accounting."

Many *tzaddikim* did an accounting every night to see what they had accomplished during that day, and to correct whatever deficiencies they discovered.

So it was with Moses at the end of the forty years in the desert. The Israelites were about to enter the Holy Land, and he was about to turn over the leadership to Joshua. The period of his stewardship had come to a close. It was time to see what he and the Israelites had achieved during the past forty years, hence the meticulous review of the journeys and encampments and what had transpired in each.

If we are serious about achieving a goal in our lives, we must periodically take inventory. Each night, each week, at the beginning of a new year, and perhaps on our birthdays as well. A segment of time has passed. What do we have to show for it? How can we make the next segment of time more productive?

אֵלֶּה מַסְעֵי בְנֵי־יִשְׂרָאֵל אֲשֶׁר יָצְאוּ מֵאֶרֶץ מִצְרָיִם . . . וַיִּכְתֹּב מֹשֶׁה אֶת־מוֹצָאֵיהֶם לְמַסְעֵיהֶם עַל־פִּי ה' וְאֵלֶּה מַסְעֵיהֶם לְמוֹצָאֵיהֶם

These are the journeys of the Children of Israel, who went forth from the land of Egypt . . . Moses wrote their goings forth according to their journeys at the bidding of God, and these were their journeys according to their goings forth (33:1-2)

Escaping "Toward" a Goal

Many commentaries try to explain the changing in the wording and obvious reversal of the sequence of terms: "Moses wrote their *goings forth according to their journeys* . . . and these were their *journeys according to their goings forth*."

R' Samson Raphael Hirsch says that when God made the Israelites break camp, the purpose was always to reach a fresh goal. Each journey was a progress toward a goal. But to the people it was the reverse. They were generally dissatisfied wherever they stayed. They just wanted to leave. It did not matter where they were going to next. Hence, to God it was "their *goings forth according to their journeys*," whereas to the Israelites it was their "*journeys according to their goings forth*."

> *The Maggid of Dubnow enlightens us with a parable. A young man suffered much abuse from his stepmother, and looked forward to the day that he would be able to leave home. When he was of age, his father arranged a shidduch (match) for him with a fine young woman from a good family in another city. As was the custom then, the young man did not meet his wife-to-be before the wedding.*
>
> *When they traveled to the wedding, the young man kept on remarking how far they had gone from home. The father, on the other hand, kept on remarking how much closer they were to their destination.*
>
> *The young man, the Maggid says, had no idea what awaited him, so he was much more pleased with the distance he was putting between himself and his abusive stepmother. The father, on the other hand, having met the young woman and her family, knew that his son would be received with warmth and love.*

So it was with the Israelites, said the Maggid. They had no concept of the

BAMIDBAR / NUMBERS: Masei [349]

kedushah (holiness) of the Promised Land. All they appreciated was that they were away from the cruel enslavement in Egypt, hence for them the emphasis was their *"journeys according to their goings forth."* From God's perspective, however, the goal of entering the Promised Land was primary, hence "their *goings forth according to their journeys,*"

When we are dissatisfied with something, we may try a "geographic cure," without giving serious thought to why things should really be different in the new location. If our problems are within us, we take them along wherever we go. It is far better to consider the possible merits of a new location, and to see if there is indeed valid reason why the change should alleviate our problems.

וְהוֹרַשְׁתֶּם אֶת־הָאָרֶץ וִישַׁבְתֶּם־בָּהּ כִּי לָכֶם נָתַתִּי אֶת־הָאָרֶץ לָרֶשֶׁת אֹתָהּ

"You shall possess the Land and you shall settle in it, for to you have I given the Land to possess it" (33:53)

Only Israel Is the Promised Land

Ramban says, "This is one of the positive mitzvos. God commanded them to settle in the Land and to inherit it, because He gave it to them and they dare not reject God's portion. Should they think they can conquer any other land and settle in it, they would be violating the Divine commandment."

Our only guide in life is the Torah. Sometimes we may think of ways that may seem to be beneficial, but if they are not in accordance with the Torah, they are destructive.

It is well known that Theodore Herzl, father of modern Zionism, sought a solution for "the Jewish problem." In order to avoid repeated persecutions, he felt the Jews must have a homeland. But since he felt that the Land of Israel would not be available, Herzl suggested an alternate: Uganda.

This is what can happen when one deviates from Torah. There is only one Land that God designated as the Jewish homeland: Israel. Even if all the Jews in the world settled in Uganda, it would not be a holy land. Indeed, establishing any other country as a homeland is a violation of God's will.

It is unfortunate that much of modern Israeli youth was not given a Torah education and does not feel strongly bonded to Israel. To them, it is a political entity. If life elsewhere can be more comfortable and is available, many would prefer that. They have no concept of the Land being hallowed by the patriarchs Abraham, Isaac and Jacob.

"Anyone who walks four cubits in the Holy Land merits a portion in the eternal world" (*Kesubos* 111a). Only in the Holy Land, not in Uganda or any other place on earth.

The love that *tzaddikim* had for the Holy Land was boundless. An example of this is R' Nossen Zvi Finkel, the Alter of Slabodka, who settled in Hebron. When he found stones on the road he would remove them, citing the Talmud, "R' Chanina removed obstacles (from the paths of Eretz Yisrael)," upon which Rashi comments,

"Because of his love for the Land, he removed possible obstacles so that one should not have any grounds for making critical remarks about the Land" (*Kesubos* 112a).

R' Nossen Zvi said that Eretz Yisrael was one large *Aron Hakodesh* (ark of the Torah), and all who lived in it were in an atmosphere of holiness. Of those who did not observe the Torah, he would say that they nevertheless have the merit of being in a holy environment. "We find a redeeming feature in a Jew who comes to shul only on Yom Kippur. How much more so should we value Jews who live not only in a shul, but even in the *aron kodesh* all year round."

During his last illness, when his frail health made it impossible to study Torah, he consoled himself that with every breath he was absorbing the air of the Holy Land, bringing *kedushah* into his body.

וְשָׁפְטוּ הָעֵדָה . . . וְהִצִּילוּ הָעֵדָה אֶת־הָרֹצֵחַ מִיַּד גֹּאֵל הַדָּם

In narrating the laws of the unintentional killer, the Torah says, *the assembly shall judge and the assembly shall rescue the (unintentional) killer from the hands of the avenger of blood* (35:24-25)

Beware of Unanimity

From the phrase "the assembly shall rescue," the Talmud derives the halachah that the court should make every attempt to avoid imposing a death sentence. One halachah is remarkable. If the court (of twenty-three judges) renders a unanimous verdict of guilty, the case is dismissed (*Sanhedrin* 17a).

R' Shlomo Kluger explains that there is an ongoing battle between truth and falsehood. Wherever there is truth, there will arise an opposition of falsehood. Therefore, if the majority of the judges find the defendant guilty and a minority dissent, we can assume that the truth is with the majority and that the minority represent falsehood. If, however, there is a unanimous verdict of guilt, it cannot possibly be correct, for if it were a true judgement, falsehood would find some way of making an opposing statement. Therefore, there is reason to assume that a unanimous verdict of guilt is incorrect.

When there are differences of opinion, a person can consider both sides and reach a logical conclusion. Unanimity may deprive a person of critical analysis.

We should exert caution when there is a unanimity of opinion. Few things in the world are so clear cut that there is not the slightest dissent.

ספר דברים
DEVARIM/DEUTERONOMY

Introduction to Devarim/Deuteronomy

The book of Devarim/Deuteronomy is referred to as *Mishneh Torah*, a review of the Torah. Seven days before he left this world, Moses reviewed for the Israelites the forty years of their sojourn in the desert following the Exodus from Egypt. He related the numerous incidents wherein they were rebellious, and chastised them for their disobedience.

Moses spoke these words on the shores of the Jordan, which the Israelites were soon to cross to enter the Promised Land, a journey which he would not be privileged to partake. A new era was about to begin for Israel, and knowing the obstinacy of the Israelites during the forty years of his stewardship, Moses was very apprehensive that they would deviate from the Divine commandments and lose the Holy Land. His reprimand was a desperate plea that they not forfeit the precious gift God was granting them.

Having enumerated all the warnings he could, Moses gave them his heartfelt blessing before his death. Although the Israelites had caused him much anguish during his forty years of leadership, Moses' intense love for his people obliterated any resentments that any other individual might have harbored as a result of his painful experiences at their hands.

When the Israelites sinned and God wished to destroy them, Moses repeatedly interceded, ready to sacrifice his own life for them. For Moses, life without his people would not be a life. The Zohar says that God, the Torah and Israel are one. Just as there could be no existence without God and no world without Torah, so could there be no life without the Children of Israel.

Many Torah authorities considered Devarim to be the first work of *mussar*, and repeatedly reviewed it. What follows is but a miniscule fragment of the myriad lessons in this book.

פרשת דברים
Parashas Devarim

אֵלֶּה הַדְּבָרִים אֲשֶׁר דִּבֶּר מֹשֶׁה אֶל־כָּל־יִשְׂרָאֵל . . . בַּמִּדְבָּר . . .

These are the words that Moses spoke to all Israel . . . concerning the Wilderness (1:1)

Euphemisms Can Be Misleading

Rashi states that these places that the Torah mentions are not a listing of where Moses spoke. Moses spoke at the encampment near the Jordan River. The various places cited are references to the places where the Israelites had sinned. In order to protect their honor, the Torah does not mention these sins explicitly, but rather refers to them metaphorically by mentioning the places where they occurred.

However, as we read on, Moses rebukes the Israelites with a very detailed description of their sins: their desire to return to Egypt before the crossing of the Reed Sea, the Golden Calf, the spies, the Korach rebellion and their dissatisfaction with the manna. "You have been defiant of God since the day I first knew you" (*Deuteronomy* 9:24). How do we reconcile this with Rashi's comment that Moses avoided embarrassing the Israelites by referring to their sins by implication only?

The answer is that when Moses reprimanded the Israelites, he was very specific. The verse cited above is not Moses' reprimand. Rather, it is the Torah telling us *about* Moses' reprimand. There is a difference between the two.

The Talmud states that a person should avoid using coarse expressions in his speech. When God told Noah to take into the ark seven pairs of kosher animals and two pairs of the non-kosher animals, He referred to the animals as "those that are not *tahor* (pure)" rather than use the word *tamei*, which means unclean or impure. Although there is not a single unnecessary letter in the Torah, the Torah uses a more lengthy term rather than the coarse term, *tamei*.

Some of the commentaries point out that when the Torah instructs us which animals are kosher and which are not, it uses the term *tamei* liberally, "You shall not eat the pig it is *tamei* for you" (*Leviticus* 11:7). How is this to be reconciled with the avoidance of the term *tamei* when instructing Noah?

The Maggid of Dubnow shed light on this question with one of his inimitable parables.

> *In one village there was a man whom the townsfolk had dubbed Baruch grubber yung (Baruch the unsophisticate). One day, the rabbi asked his shammes to fetch Baruch. "Which Baruch do you mean?" the shammes asked. "Baruch grubber yung?"*
>
> *The rabbi responded with a sharp rebuke. "How dare you call someone with so insulting a term?"*
>
> *"But all the townspeople call him that," the shammes protested.*
>
> *"There is room enough in Gehinnom for all of them," the rabbi said.*
>
> *Baruch had sent his son to a yeshivah, and the son turned out to be an outstanding Talmudic scholar. When the rabbi's daughter reached marriageable age, a shadchan (matchmaker) suggested the bright, young scholar, Baruch's son, as a match for her.*
>
> *The rabbi turned away the suggestion. "It is not fitting for me to have a grubber yung for a mechuten (father of my son-in-law).*
>
> *The shammes overheard the rabbi's comment and said, "Why are you using that term when you reprimanded me for doing so?"*
>
> *The rabbi replied, "It is wrong to give someone an uncomplimentary eponym, regardless of its nature. If Zalman, say, were hard of hearing, it would be wrong to refer to him as 'Zalman, the deaf one.' However, if the shul were to have a committee to choose a cantor and someone suggested Zalman for the committee, it would be permissible to say, 'But Zalman is deaf, and it is inappropriate for him to be involved in choosing a cantor.*
>
> *"You referred to Baruch as grubber yung for no purpose whatsoever. Even if it is true that he is ignorant, it is wrong to refer to a person by his defect. But to suggest him as a mechuten for me, I may say that a grubber yung is inappropriate for me."*
>
> *The Maggid continued, "The Torah teaches us this. To refer to any animal, even a pig, as tamei for no reason, is wrong. It can be identified just as well as 'not tahor,' not pure. But when it comes to telling us that pig is forbidden, we must hear, know and remember that pig is tamei for us. It is tamei, tereifah! Do not eat it!"*

The Torah teaches us that there are times when euphemisms are in order and times when they can be misleading. We must be aware that "mercy killing" is nothing less than murder. That state legislatures may legalize euthanasia does not change its character. Except for extreme health considerations, abortion is forbidden by halachah. To refer to it as a "woman's right" is a deceptive euphemism. We must be careful not to be deceived when improper actions are disguised by innocent-sounding terms.

The Torah conveys this in Deuteronomy. When Moses reprimands the Israelites, he has no difficulty in pointing out their sins explicitly. They must recognize their sins for what they were. But when he is not talking to them, and the Torah wishes to tell us what Moses' agenda will be, there is no justification for using uncomplimentary terms.

אֵלֶּה הַדְּבָרִים אֲשֶׁר דִּבֶּר מֹשֶׁה אֶל־כָּל־יִשְׂרָאֵל . . . בַּמִּדְבָּר

These are the words that Moses spoke to all Israel . . . in the Wilderness (1:1)

Accepting Rebuke

The Midrash states that all the Israelites were able to accept Moses' chastisement.

The Talmud states that if a person will not listen to your rebuke, it is better not to rebuke him (*Yevamos* 65b). Inasmuch as the Torah states that Moses spoke to *all* Israel, this indicates that all of Israel was ready to accept his rebuke.

> *A rabbi in a European community would frequently reprimand his congregation. Of course, this did not particularly endear him to them. The salary he received placed him below the poverty level. This was not unusual in the shtetl, where the rabbi's wife often had to help support the family. When the family was in dire need, the rabbi asked for an increase in his salary and was turned down.*
>
> *Addressing the community, the rabbi said, "You have no idea how much I was actually comforted by your refusal to raise my stipend.*
>
> *"All the years that I have been reprimanding you to no avail made me think that perhaps the fault is not yours. It is known that 'words that emanate from the heart will enter the heart (of another).' Perhaps the reason that my reprimand has fallen on deaf ears was that I was not sincere enough, and it was my shortcoming that made my words ineffective.*
>
> *"However, I can assure you that my request for a raise was absolutely sincere and came from very depths of my heart. I have been unable to provide for the basic needs of my family. When this request made no impact on you, I realized that it was not my lack of sincerity that was responsible for your failure to accept my rebuke. Your refusal has vindicated me."*

Yes, words that emanate from the heart will enter the heart, provided that one can hear. It is possible to render oneself deaf to even the most sincere words. We must be careful that we remain receptive.

דִּבֶּר מֹשֶׁה אֶל־בְּנֵי יִשְׂרָאֵל כְּכֹל אֲשֶׁר צִוָּה ה' אֹתוֹ אֲלֵהֶם

Moses spoke to the Children of Israel according to everything that God commanded him [to speak] to them (1:3)

The Holy Al Tadin

Inasmuch as Moses' reprimands were according to God's instructions, then when Moses said, "You have been rebellious with God from the day I knew you," this was also said according to God's instructions.

R' Zalman Sorotzkin cites Rambam, who says that Moses' sin at the Waters of Strife was that when the Israelites clamored for water, he reprimanded them by saying, "Listen here, you rebels" (*Numbers* 20:10). It was because he referred to the Israelites as rebels that he was punished by being denied entrance to Canaan. Yet, R' Sorotzkin asks, here Moses was apparently instructed by God to chide the

Israelites as being rebellious. Why was this appropriate here if it was considered a sin at the Waters of Strife?

The Talmud says, "Do not judge your fellow until you have reached his place" (*Ethics of the Fathers* 2:5); i.e., until you have experienced his circumstances. My mother used to refer to this as "the *heilige* (holy) *al tadin* (do not judge)." She would say that the single greatest cause for resentment and dissension is that people are quick to condemn others without taking into consideration their particular stresses. If one were to be in those circumstances, one might have acted similarly.

The Talmud says that the second Temple was destroyed because of *sinas chinam* (baseless hatred). Why would anyone hate another person for no reason at all? The answer is that the person *thinks* his hatred is justified because he does not take into consideration the other person's circumstances. If he only understood why that person had acted in a certain way, he would not have hated him for it. He thinks he has grounds for hating him, whereas in reality his hatred is groundless.

R' Sorotzkin says that at the Waters of Strife, the Israelites were thirsty for water. Being in the arid desert and not seeing any source for water, they panicked. True, this was indicative of their lack of faith in God, Who had provided for them miraculously since the Exodus. Nevertheless, Moses should have taken into account their sense of desperation. To refer to desperate people as rebels was wrong. The Midrash states that God chastised the patriarch Jacob for being insensitive and responding in anger toward Rachel when she complained of being childless (*Genesis* 30:2; *Bereishis Rabbah* 71:10).

In this portion of the Torah, however, the Israelites had conquered Transjordan and were on the threshold of Canaan. They were not in any way in peril. Yet, Moses sensed that they were still lacking in trust in God, as he subsequently said to them. There was no way they could justify their attitude at this point, and it was, therefore, appropriate to refer to them as rebellious.

The Midrash describes Moses' fervent pleas to be allowed to enter the Promised Land. One cannot but wonder, was this punishment not excessively harsh? According to R' Sorotzkin, Moses' transgression was indeed a grievous one. He had not observed the "holy *al tadin*."

We may not be held to the same standard as Moses, but we should always be sensitive to and considerate of others.

ה׳ אֱלֹקֵיכֶם הִרְבָּה אֶתְכֶם וְהִנְּכֶם הַיּוֹם כְּכוֹכְבֵי הַשָּׁמַיִם לָרֹב

"God has multiplied you, and behold!
you are today like the stars of heaven in abundance" (1:10)

The Rabbi's Dilemma

Rashi remarks that the Israelites were only six hundred thousand strong, which is a far cry from the number of stars. Rashi explains that what Moses meant was not that they were quantitatively as numerous as the stars, but rather qualitatively as bright as the heavenly bodies.

R' Zalman Sorotzkin asks, Why, with such praise of the Israelites, does Moses say, "I cannot carry your burden alone?" (*Deuteronomy* 1:9).

R' Sorotzkin states that this is the dilemma of the rabbi. A simple congregation accepts the leadership and authority of the rabbi. Once they become more learned in Torah and halachah, they may consider themselves capable of questioning and even challenging the rabbi. Korach received his teaching from Moses, and considered himself qualified to challenge Moses' leadership.

This was Moses' statement: "I cannot carry you alone, precisely because you have become as bright as the heavenly bodies."

This is a timely message. We are fortunate in having many worshippers who are Torah students. They may think themselves capable of rendering halachic decisions. We must be cautious that this should not result in a lessening of the rabbi's authority.

וָאֲצַוֶּה אֶת־שֹׁפְטֵיכֶם בָּעֵת הַהִוא לֵאמֹר שָׁמֹעַ בֵּין־אֲחֵיכֶם וּשְׁפַטְתֶּם צֶדֶק

"I instructed your judges at that time saying, 'Listen among your brethren and judge righteously'" (1:16)

Listening to Wise Counsel

The Talmud derives from the phrase, "Listen among your brethren," that a judge may not hear the position of one litigant in absence of the other.

When the great Talmudist, R' Yonasan Eibeschitz, was a child and conducted himself with great devotion to Torah and mitzvos, someone asked him how he was able to do so. The Talmud says that the yetzer hara (evil inclination) is present in a person from birth, whereas the yetzer tov (good inclination) does not come until age 13. Inasmuch as the only operative influence was the yetzer hara, how could he resist it?

R' Yonasan responded, "I told the yetzer hara that it is not fair to listen to one side of an argument in the absence of the opposing side, so that I could not pay it any heed until the yetzer tov was present."

If a child was able to resist the temptations of the *yetzer hara* in absence of the *yetzer tov*, how can we justify yielding to the *yetzer hara* when it is counteracted by the *yetzer tov*?

וָאֲצַוֶּה אֶת־שֹׁפְטֵיכֶם בָּעֵת הַהִוא לֵאמֹר שָׁמֹעַ בֵּין־אֲחֵיכֶם וּשְׁפַטְתֶּם צֶדֶק

"I instructed your judges at that time saying, 'Listen among your brethren and judge righteously'" (1:16)

Judging Justly and Wisely

The stories about the wise judgments of Torah scholars from the time of King Solomon onward are legion.

R' Yechezkel Landau (author of Noda BiYehudah) was consulted by two litigants, one handsomely dressed in fine attire and the other in a coachman's livery. The latter tearfully complained that he was a wealthy merchant and had hired a coachman to drive him to Prague. When they were in the thick of a forest, the coachman pulled a knife, forced him to give over his money and change clothes with him. The coachman then made him drive the horses while he sat in the carriage. "When we entered Prague I began shouting for help, and a group of people gathered. This scoundrel denied everything, saying that I was really the coachman and that he was the merchant and that I had fabricated the story. The people brought us here to you, Rabbi. Only you can help me get my money back from this scoundrel."

The man in the fine attire said, "Rabbi, this man is crazy. I have been a merchant all my life. People in my hometown can testify for me. He is humiliating me in public. Please help me shake off this insane man with his crazy story."

After questioning them both vigorously, with each one sticking to his story, R' Yechezkel said, "I cannot give a ruling now. I want both of you to be here at dawn tomorrow." He then instructed the shammes, "Tomorrow morning, put them in the room adjacent to my study, and do not let them leave or enter my study, regardless of how much they insist."

At dawn the following day, the two appeared and were seated in the room adjacent to the rabbi's study. After several hours, the rabbi returned from shul but refused to see them. Time passed and they could hear the rabbi learning. After several hours had gone by, the well-dressed man approached the shammes, "I must return home. Here is some money; let me in to the rabbi." The shammes refused, and the man had no choice but to wait.

As time passed on, the well-dressed man grew tired and began to nod off. R' Yechezkel opened his door, and seeing the man half-asleep, shouted, "You! Coachman! Come here this minute!" The well-dressed man promptly jumped up and ran to the rabbi, while the man dressed in livery remained seated.

"There you have your ruling," R' Yechezkel said. He had caught the coachman off guard, thereby revealing his identity.

A man consulted R' Elya Chaim of Lodz. A number of years earlier, he had been a member of a revolutionary group, and was the group's treasurer. When the rebel group was discovered, the government disbanded them, but he miraculously escaped. He had a huge sum of money which he was afraid to spend, lest it cast suspicion on him, because there was no way he could explain his sudden wealth. "I thought that I would lie low, and after several years went by, I could start spending it slowly, claiming that I had earned it in business. I buried the money in my cellar. From time to time I would dig it up and count it.

"A few months ago I went to dig it up, but the money was gone! Someone had somehow found out that I had hid money there. Everybody says that you are wise. Can you help me?"

"Is there anyone you suspect?" R' Elya Chaim asked.

"I don't really know. I can only tell you this," the man said. "My neighbor was always a poor laborer. In the last few months he has been spending much money, and he claims he inherited it from a rich uncle. It is possible that he may have seen me dig up the money, but I have no evidence to accuse him."

R' Elya Chaim told the man to give him a few days to think it over. He then sent for the newly-rich neighbor.

"I understand that you have had a stroke of good luck and have become wealthy," R' Elya Chaim said. "How is it that you have not come with a handsome donation for tzedakah?

"You are right, rabbi," the man said. "I was negligent. I promise I will give a donation."

R' Elya Chaim then inquired about how he came to his wealth. From the man's account, he detected that he was lying.

"I'll tell you why I sent for you," R' Elya Chaim said. "I had a police investigator here today, who asked me about you. It seems that you are being suspected of passing counterfeit money. If this is true, you could be sentenced to a long prison term."

The man turned pale and began stammering. He finally blurted out the truth. He had no idea that this was counterfeit money. It was not an inheritance, but, he is ashamed to say, he saw that his neighbor had a stash of money which he had obviously come by dishonestly, and he felt justified in taking it from him.

"Go quickly and bring the money to me. If they search your house and find the counterfeit money, you are doomed to spend years in prison."

The man promptly brought the money, which R' Elya Chaim returned to the rightful owner.

לֹא תָגוּרוּ מִפְּנֵי־אִישׁ כִּי הַמִּשְׁפָּט לֵאלֹקִים הוּא

Judges are instructed, *"You shall not tremble before anyone, for the judgment is God's"* (1:17)

Fear of God Surpasses All

R' Moshe of Kobrin said that the reverence of the Maggid of Mezeritch for his master, the Baal Shem Tov, is almost beyond description. One time the Baal Shem Tov's *tallis* slipped off his shoulder, and the Maggid attempted to lift it. When he touched the *tallis*, he began trembling uncontrollably.

After the Baal Shem Tov's death, the Maggid once found the Baal Shem Tov's handkerchief and was overcome with such great awe at the memory of the Baal Shem Tov that he fainted.

This notwithstanding, the Maggid was seated in a beis din (rabbinical tribunal) in which one of the litigants was a distant relative of the Baal Shem Tov. The Baal Shem Tov happened to enter the beis din room, and without hesitation the Maggid arose and exclaimed, "By the authority of this beis din, I decree that anyone who is not a litigant in this case vacate the room promptly."

R' Moshe said, "The enormous reverence and great awe of the Maggid for the Baal Shem Tov was overwhelmed by the concern that his presence might influence the tribunal in favor of his relative. The Maggid observed the Torah statement that 'judgment is God's,' and his fear of God superseded his fear of his master."

Whether as magistrates, spiritual leaders or as lay people, we must often render judgments. We may sometimes hesitate to take a stand on an issue because we may be afraid of provoking an influential person. If we believe a certain position to be just and true, it is a Scriptural violation to cower before an influential person, or indeed before anyone.

לֹא תָגוּרוּ מִפְּנֵי־אִישׁ כִּי הַמִּשְׁפָּט לֵאלֹקִים הוּא

Judges are instructed, *"You shall not tremble before anyone, for the judgment is God's"* (1:17)

The Acid Test

When R' Chaim Halberstam (the tzaddik of Sanz) accepted his first rabbinical position, he was consulted by a man who claimed that he had sold merchandise to the town's wealthiest citizen, and now the buyer denied that he owed him the money for it. R' Chaim sent his shammes to the wealthy man with a summons to appear for a din Torah (rabbinic adjudication).

The shammes returned with a message that the man said he had no intention of going to a din Torah. R' Chaim sent the shammes back with a second summons. The shammes returned with the message, "He said that no one dares to send him a summons. He said that he is the most influential citizen in town, and that no rabbi holds this position who antagonizes him." R' Chaim sent the shammes back with the message that if he does not respond to the summons, he will be excommunicated.

Shortly afterward the wealthy man appeared, greeting R' Chaim warmly. "Rabbi," he said, "there never was a case. This man never sold me anything. I put him up to it to bring a claim against me to see if I could you frighten you off. Now I see your integrity and that you would not yield to pressure. We are proud to have you as our rabbi."

וְלֹא אֲבִיתֶם לַעֲלֹת וַתַּמְרוּ אֶת־פִּי ה׳ אֱלֹקֵיכֶם

"But you did not wish to ascend [to Canaan] and you rebelled against the word of your God" (1:26)

We Are Free to Will

When the spies returned with the report that the inhabitants of Canaan were mighty and well fortified, the Israelites turned against Moses and said, "Let us appoint a new leader and return to Egypt."

In his chastisement, Moses said, "You did not wish to ascend." Moses' rebuke was not only that they did not trust that God would enable them to conquer the land, but that they had no desire for the Promised Land.

There are two aphorisms that sound similar but are fundamentally distinct. One is the popular saying, "Where there is a will, there is a way," and the other is the Talmudic statement, "Nothing stands in the way of will."

A bit of reflection will show that the former statement is unrealistic. There are

DEVARIM / DEUTERONOMY: Devarim

some things for which a person may have a strong will, but there is no way in which it can be realized. For example, if a person who is tone deaf wishes to be an opera singer, the strongest expression of will cannot achieve this for him. However, there is nothing that can stop him from *wishing* that he could be an opera singer.

The Talmud does not say that "where there is a will, there is a way." Rather, that there is nothing than can stop one from *willing* something, even if its actualization appears unfeasible.

There is a difference between the two. We should always desire what is right and proper. The Talmud says that if a person has a sincere desire to do a mitzvah but circumstances prevent him from doing it, God considers it as meritorious as if he had in fact done it (*Berachos* 6a). We may not be able to control circumstances, but we are able to control our will. Moses' rebuke of the Israelites was not only for not having trust in God, but for not even *wishing* to ascend to Canaan.

It is a well known fact that we have selective receptivity. We hear what we wish to hear. Joshua and Caleb assured the Israelites that they could conquer the Land. The Israelites accepted the negative report of the other spies because they had little will for the Promised Land. A sincere will could have increased their trust and brought the effort to conquer Canaan to success.

Let us remember. We may not be responsible for not implementing a mitzvah but we are held responsible for not wanting to do so.

וַיִּשְׁמַע ה' אֶת־קוֹל דִּבְרֵיכֶם וַיִּקְצֹף

Chastising the Israelites for the incident of the spies, Moses said,
"God heard the sound of your words, and He was incensed" (1:34)

Watch Your Inflection

What is meant by "the *sound* of your words"? Would it not have been sufficient to say, "God heard your words?"

Moses said, "They took in their hands from the fruit of the Land and brought it down to us; they brought back word to us and said, 'Good is the Land that God gives us. But you did not wish to ascend'" (*Deuteronomy* 1:25-26). If the report was so favorable, why did they not wish to ascend?

The spoken word is different than the written word. The tone of voice can be sarcastic and give words the diametrically opposite meaning. When the spies said, "The Land is good," the sarcastic tone of their voices indicated just the reverse.

The spies showed the Israelites the beautiful fruit they had brought. But the inflection of, "This is its fruit," conveyed the message, "Just look at the size of the fruit! Gigantic fruit, gigantic people. They are invincible" (*Midrash*).

This is what Moses meant. The words in themselves were good, but the *sound* of the words conveyed their real meaning.

We must be as careful of *how* we speak as well as of *what* we say. The Chafetz Chaim says that one can be in violation of *lashon hara* (defamatory speech) without uttering a single word. If at the mention of a person's name you grimace in a way that indicates your disapproval of him, you are guilty of *lashon hara*.

Modern psychologists speak of the importance of body language. Non-verbal communication may be even more effective than what one verbalizes. We must be as careful not to "speak" *lashon hara* with the body as well as with the tongue.

ה׳ אֱלֹקֶיךָ עִמָּךְ לֹא חָסַרְתָּ דָּבָר
"For God, your God, was with you; you did not lack a thing" (2:7)

Feeling No Lack

Solomon says, "A lover of money will never be satisfied with money" (*Ecclesiastes* 5:9). The multibillionaire J. Paul Getty was asked, "How much money is enough?" He responded, "Just a bit more."

This is true not only of money but of virtually all earthly pursuits. Our desires are like bottomless pits, leaving us devoid of lasting satisfaction.

The Talmud says, "This is the way of Torah: eat bread with salt, drink water in small measure and sleep on the ground" (*Ethics of the Fathers* 6:4). This does not mean that we must live a life of deprivation. Rather, if we can be satisfied with the bare essentials of life, then we are free to pursue the study of Torah even if we live in comfort. But if we *must* have comfort and conveniences, the pursuit of these will dominate our lives and detract from Torah.

A person whose primary desire is a closeness with God lacks for nothing. Whatever he has is satisfactory.

I was privileged to visit the Steipler Gaon. He lived in utter simplicity. He turned down gifts of money because he had no need for anything more than he had. He was much happier than many people who live in great opulence.

This was true of many of our *tzaddikim*. The Chafetz Chaim kept his store open only until he had earned enough for that particular day. He lived into his 90s and is far better remembered than some people whose constant pursuit of wealth brought their lives to a premature end, and who may be remembered only by inanimate monuments.

We are subject to two major influences; our emotions and our intellect. Our emotions may produce infinite appetites, whereas our intellect teaches us that happiness is not achieved by gratification of our earthly desires.

Our uniqueness as human beings is in our intellect. Animals, too, are driven by emotions. We ought to have sufficient pride in the dignity of being human to live our lives according to our intellect. That will confirm for us the words of Moses, that when God is with us, we lack nothing.

פרשת ואתחנן
Parashas Va'eschanan

וָאֶתְחַנַּן אֶל־ה׳ בָּעֵת הַהִוא לֵאמֹר אֲדֹנָ-י ה׳ אַתָּה הַחִלּוֹתָ לְהַרְאוֹת אֶת־עַבְדְּךָ אֶת־גָּדְלְךָ . . . אֶעְבְּרָה־נָּא וְאֶרְאֶה אֶת־הָאָרֶץ הַטּוֹבָה

"I prayed to God at that time, saying, 'My Lord, God, You have begun to show Your servant Your greatness . . . Let me now cross the Jordan and see the good Land' " (3:23-25)

Praying to Pray

The Hebrew word *leimor* actually means "to say." When it follows a phrase, it generally means that this statement should be conveyed to others. The above verse would thus read, "I prayed to God at that time *to say* 'My God, etc.'" What could be meant by "to say" in this context? To say to whom?

The Divrei Chaim explains this verse as follows: "I prayed to God. What did I pray? That at the time when I will have to plead for myself, I should be able *to say* 'My God, etc.,' " In other words, Moses prayed to God to give him the ability to pray properly.

In some prayer books there is a "prayer before praying," a beautiful preparatory prayer composed by R' Elimelech of Lizhensk, which should put a person into the proper frame of mind for praying. The Talmud says that the pious men of yore would spend an entire hour before praying, preparing themselves to pray properly.

We pray for all our needs. Inasmuch as proper prayer is certainly one of our needs, should we not ask for Divine help with this need?

> *A chassid complained to R' Mendel of Kotzk because he was beset with many serious problems. "Have you prayed to God for help?" the rebbe asked. The chassid responded, "I don't know how to pray well." R' Mendel said, "Then that is an even more serious problem than all those you mentioned, and you did not even mention that."*

We pray every day. But let us be honest with ourselves. If we had to present an important petition to a high government official, how careful would we be that it should be worded correctly and delivered properly? Do we give this much attention to our prayer?

According to the Divrei Chaim, Moses prayed for the ability to pray well. If Moses felt that he needed Divine assistance to pray, what can we say for ourselves?

אֶעְבְּרָה־נָּא וְאֶרְאֶה אֶת־הָאָרֶץ הַטּוֹבָה אֲשֶׁר בְּעֵבֶר הַיַּרְדֵּן

"Let me now cross the Jordan and see the good Land" (3:25)

The Superiority of the Holy Land

R' Yisroel of Shklov (author of Pe'as HaShulchan) left Eretz Yisrael to raise money for his community. When he visited R' Chaim of Volozhin, he complained of the stresses and difficulties of life in the Holy Land. R' Chaim, with his intense love of Eretz Yisrael, said to him, "When Moses prayed to be allowed to enter Eretz Yisrael, he said 'Allow me to see the good Land.' He wanted to see only the good of Eretz Yisrael but not any of its deficiencies."

R' Chaim then continued, "The Torah relates that when his brothers wished to kill Joseph, Reuben said, 'Throw him into this pit' (Genesis 37:21-24), which, the Talmud says, contained vipers and scorpions. Although the halachah is that if a man falls into a pit known to harbor vipers and scorpions, he may be assumed to be dead and his wife may remarry (Rambam, Hilchos Gerushin 13:17), the Torah credits Reuben with saving Joseph. On the other hand, although Judah did save Joseph's life by pulling him from the pit and selling him into slavery, the Talmud is very critical of Judah. How do we explain this?

"The answer is," R' Chaim said, "that as dangerous as the poison ridden pit may have been, it was within Eretz Yisrael. As long as someone is in the Holy Land, even perilous circumstances are survivable. But Judah sold Joseph into slavery in Egypt, and even the most secure condition in the Diaspora is of greater danger than perilous circumstances in Eretz Yisrael."

R' Chaim's message of 200 years ago is timely today.

וְאַתֶּם הַדְּבֵקִים בַּה׳ אֱלֹקֵיכֶם חַיִּים כֻּלְּכֶם הַיּוֹם

"You who cleave unto your God, you are all alive today" (4:4)

One Day at a Time

In my work treating alcoholics, I have found that the greatest success for sustained abstinence from alcohol is through participation in the program of Alcoholics Anonymous. One of the fundamentals of this program is taking "one day at a time." The addicted alcoholic cannot conceive never again being able to drink. Inasmuch as he has relied on alcohol to feel good, he sees a lifetime of sobriety as being completely unrealistic. There is no point in even trying to do the impossible. Therefore, he is taught a new philosophy, "Take one day at a time. There is nothing that you can do today about tomorrow's drinking, so there is no point in thinking about it. It is not impossible for you to stay sober just for today. That is certainly within your ability. So stay sober today, and when tomorrow comes, you can deal with its challenges then."

One of my friends would write down each day how many days he had been sober. When he died at age 83, it was found that the night before he had written the number 16,472. He had been sober for forty-six years because he took one day at a time.

The concept of taking one day at a time was promoted by Alcoholics Anonymous, which originated in the mid 1930's. More than 150 years ago, R' Moshe

Sofer (Chasam Sofer) cited the above verse as teaching this concept.

The Talmud quotes ben Sira, "Do not agonize about tomorrow's problems, because you have no way of predicting tomorrow" (*Sanhedrin* 100b). The Chasam Sofer says that this is the way one can vanquish the *yetzer hara*. If a person thinks that he must resist the *yetzer hara's* temptations throughout his entire lifetime, he might consider it impossible and may give up without trying. Therefore, Chasam Sofer says, think about resisting the *yetzer hara* only today. That is certainly within everyone's abilities.

This is what Moses told the Israelites. "You can cleave unto God and observe all His mitzvos if you think only about *living this day*. Don't take on tomorrow's challenges today."

I am indebted to one of my alcoholic patients who called me, citing the verse in the Torah which says that Jacob love Rachel so intensely, that the seven years he had to wait for her seemed to him like just a few days (*Genesis* 29:20). He noted that some commentaries say that this is contrary to nature. Separation from someone you love makes each day seem endless, rather than the reverse.

"But if you look closely at the words in the Torah," my patient said, "the answer is obvious. The Torah says that the seven years were *yamim achadim*, which means *single* days. Jacob was able to tolerate the long separation because each day he thought, 'I only have to deal with today,' and that was do-able."

It is standard operating procedure for people to make "New Year resolutions," and it is common knowledge that they invariably fail. The reason is that "I will not smoke this entire year," or "I will not eat excessively this entire year" is too great an undertaking, and one fails because one cannot conceive of succeeding. The correct thing to do is, as Chasam Sofer says, to tackle only today's problem today. Breaking a resolution down to bite-size pieces makes it feasible to keep.

כִּי מִי־גוֹי גָּדוֹל אֲשֶׁר־לוֹ אֱלֹקִים קְרֹבִים אֵלָיו כַּה' אֱלֹקֵינוּ בְּכָל־קָרְאֵנוּ אֵלָיו

"For which is a great nation that has a God Who is close to it, as is our God in all our calling to Him" (4:7).

Know God in All Your Ways

"In all our calling to Him." Some people think that they should turn to God for help only with major issues, but not with the minor problems of everyday life. This is a mistake. We must turn to God for help in everything we do.

The Chazon Ish cited the Talmud which relates that R' Huna had 400 barrels of wine that spoiled. His colleagues told him to do some soul-searching regarding the cause of this loss. R' Huna said, "Do you suspect me of having done anything improper?"

The sages responded, "Do you suspect God of doing something without just cause?" They then told him that he was not giving his sharecropper the agreed upon portion of the crop.

"But he is a thief!" R' Huna protested. "He steals from me. I have a right to withhold from him."

"Not so," the sages said. "Stealing from a thief is still theft" (*Berachos* 5b).

"Suppose," the Chazon Ish said, "that something like this would occur today.

The search for the cause would be whether the temperature in the room was improper or the humidity too high or low. Few people would search for the cause within themselves, in their ethical behavior. We should know that God regulates everything except for our free will in moral and ethical matters. As with R' Huna, nothing happens without just cause.

"How can one achieve a belief that everything happens for a valid reason?" The Chazon Ish answers, "By getting into the habit of asking for God's help in everything we do." We are indeed accustomed to saying *b'ezras Hashem* (with the help of God), but too often these words are said without much thought given to their meaning. We should give a moment's thought to *b'ezras Hashem*, so that it should constitute a true prayer.

And what if one's prayer is not answered? The *mussar* authorities say that one should not attribute this to the inadequacy or insincerity of one's prayer. Rather, one should say, "I did what I was supposed to do. I asked for God's help. I am certain that God heard my prayer. I sincerely believe that God knows what is truly best for me, and that if what I asked for was indeed in my best interest, He would have given it to me."

God is close to us "in all our calling to Him." The Talmud says that the *entire* Torah is dependent on the single verse, "Know God in all your ways" (*Berachos* 63a). If we indeed relate everything we do to the will of God, we will observe Torah properly (*Lekach Tov, Devarim* p. 42).

רַק הִשָּׁמֶר לְךָ וּשְׁמֹר נַפְשְׁךָ מְאֹד פֶּן־תִּשְׁכַּח אֶת־הַדְּבָרִים
אֲשֶׁר־רָאוּ עֵינֶיךָ . . . יוֹם אֲשֶׁר עָמַדְתָּ לִפְנֵי ה' אֱלֹקֶיךָ בְּחֹרֵב

"Greatly beware for your soul lest you forget the thing that your eyes have beheld . . . the day that you stood before your God at Horeb" (4:9-10)

Exercise Your Imagination

This was said not only to the generation that stood at Sinai, but for all generations to come. The scene of the giving of the Torah must be with us just as it was with our ancestors.

R' Shlomo Wolbe says that we must exercise our imaginative faculties and create the scene on the screen within our mind: the mountain of Sinai aflame, covered with a thick cloud, the earth trembling, the thunder and lightening, the sound of the shofar, millions of men, women and children looking up to the peak of Sinai where Moses was standing, and hearing the voice of God enunciate the Ten Commandments (*Alei Shur* vol. 1, p.104).

(Incidentally, on the verse, "You approached and stood at the foot of the mountain, and the mountain was burning with fire up to *the heart of heaven*" [*Deuteronomy* 4:11], R' Mendel of Kotzk said, "the revelation at Sinai was such that it made your heart heavenly.")

Alas! Modern technology has caused our imaginative faculties to atrophy.

When I was a child, I would listen to adventure programs on the radio, and I could vividly picture the Lone Ranger or whatever character was being enacted before the microphone. Someone was reading from a script, but in my mind the words translated into a three dimensional picture.

Just as muscles shrink and wither when they are not used, so do our imaginative faculties atrophy with disuse. The television screen depicts the scenes, and we no longer use our imagination.

We must regain our ability to imagine. We can do this by taking time to meditate.

The reason we see our dreams so vividly is because in sleep our minds are not occupied with anything else. If we learn how to meditate and focus on only one item and not be distracted by any of the myriad thoughts that may enter our mind, we will be able to create vivid scenes. We will then be able to fulfil the mitzvah of remembering Sinai.

וּפֶן־תִּשָּׂא עֵינֶיךָ הַשָּׁמַיְמָה וְרָאִיתָ אֶת־הַשֶּׁמֶשׁ וְאֶת־הַיָּרֵחַ
וְאֶת־הַכּוֹכָבִים כֹּל צְבָא הַשָּׁמַיִם וְנִדַּחְתָּ וְהִשְׁתַּחֲוִיתָ לָהֶם

*"[Beware], lest you lift your eyes to the heaven and you see the sun,
the moon, the stars and all the heavenly host,
and you will be drawn astray and bow to them"* (4:19)

The Godliness Within Us

R' Moshe Alshich asks, Why does the Torah so thoroughly condemn bowing to the heavenly host? They are all servants of God. Would a king not be pleased if people showed obeisance to his officers?

Alschich answers, "Indeed so. But if anyone were to force the king himself to bow to any one of his underlings, that would be a grave offense. Inasmuch as every Jew has a *neshamah* which is part of God Himself, bowing to any one of God's creations is coercing the Godly component within a person to bow to one of His servants. That is unconscionable."

Worshipping anything or anyone other than God is *avodah zarah* (idolatry). This is the most serious prohibition in the Torah. Should one be forced to bow down to anything other than God at the threat of being killed, one is required to surrender one's life. What makes *avodah zarah* the worst sin of all? It is that one is subjugating God Himself, represented by His presence in every person, to one of His creations.

Extending Alshich's principle, whenever a person does something improper, one forces the Godly *neshamah* within the person to participate in something it despises. Every sin thus constitutes a *chillul Hashem*, a profaning of the Name of God.

By the same token, the prohibition against *avodah zarah* should make a person aware of his uniqueness and dignity, as one is the bearer of God within oneself.

Later in this *parashah* we read, "You will seek God and you will find Him, if you seek Him with all your heart and with all your soul" (ibid. 4:29). R' Simchah Bunim of P'shis'che says that the verse can also be read, "if you seek Him *in* all your heart and *in* all your soul." People may go to far away places to try to find God, and they do not bother to look for Him where He is, so close by, within each person.

In many of my writings, I stressed the importance of self-esteem. How can a person fail to have self-esteem if one knows that God is within him?

וְיָדַעְתָּ הַיּוֹם וַהֲשֵׁבֹתָ אֶל־לְבָבֶךָ כִּי ה׳ הוּא הָאֱלֹקִים
בַּשָּׁמַיִם מִמַּעַל וְעַל־הָאָרֶץ מִתָּחַת אֵין עוֹד

*"You shall know this day take to your heart, that God is the Lord —
in heaven above and on the earth below there is no other"* (4:39)

Each Person a Whole World

The usual interpretation of "there is no other" is that there is no other God. The rebbe of Munkacz gave this verse a different twist.

The Talmud states that a person is obligated to say, "The world was created for me" (*Sanhedrin* 37a). This does not mean that one should see the world as existing in order to satisfy one's needs. Quite the contrary, each person should see himself as responsible for *tikkun haolam,* rectification of the world. This was in actuality one time in history, when Adam was the sole human being and was placed in the Garden of Eden "to keep it and work it." The rectification of the world depended on him alone.

Although today there are billions of people, a person should not be indolent and think that other people can bring about *tikkun haolam*. Rather, each person should see this as his responsibility. By fulfilling the Divine will as set forth in the Torah, one can bring about *tikkun haolam.*

This, said the rebbe of Munkacz is included in the above verse. "You shall know that God is the Lord, there is no other *person other than you upon whom this responsibility falls."*

You may ask, what can one individual accomplish? Our forefather Abraham was one individual who succeeded in ultimately turning civilization away from paganism and polytheism to the belief in one God. Abraham did not do this by preaching, but by showing kindness and consideration to others.

The Midrash states that Abraham's home was open to all wayfarers, with one door open on each of its four sides. He served travelers food and drink. When they had finished, he told them to give thanks for what they had eaten. When they thanked him, he said, "The food was not mine. It was given to us by God, and you must thank Him for it." In this way he was able to motivate people to believe in the true God.

Every person has the obligation to follow in the footsteps of Abraham. By kindness and consideration, one can exert great positive influence on others.

וְנָס אֶל־אַחַת מִן־הֶעָרִים הָאֵל וָחָי

The Torah provides a place of refuge for someone who unintentionally killed a person. Six cities of refuge were designated for the unintentional killer, **who shall flee to one of these cities and live** (4:42)

Living, Not Merely Existing

The Talmud states a fascinating halachah: If a student goes into exile to one of the cities of refuge, his teacher must accompany him. Why? Because the Torah says that he will flee to a city of refuge *and live.* Rambam explains, "People who seek wisdom in absence of Torah are considered as if dead" (*Hilchos Rotze'ach* 7:1).

Let us ponder a bit on this halachah. The unintentional killer may not leave the city of refuge until the High Priest dies, which may not occur for decades. His teacher, who was settled comfortably in his home, must uproot and relocate to a city of refuge for an indeterminate period of time, no doubt taking his family with him. Why? Because just as it would be unthinkable to fail to supply the fugitive with food and water, it is equally unthinkable to fail to supply him with Torah teaching. If this means that his teacher must relocate, so be it! The Torah says that he shall "live" in the city of refuge, and Rambam states that life without Torah is not considered life.

The human being is a composite creature, composed of an essentially animal body and a spirit. It is the spirit which gives him his uniqueness and distinguishes him from other forms of life. If a person abandons the spirit and operates only according to the dictates of the body, he is indeed alive *as an animal,* but his uniquely human component is dead.

When the Torah says that the unintentional killer shall "live" in a city of refuge, it means that he shall live as a human being. This requires that he be given the spiritual wherewithal to do so.

We recite the *berachah* for the Torah, "He has given us the Torah and He has planted eternal life within us." We should take this literally rather than figuratively. Sending one's teacher into exile because the student needs to "live" stresses this point.

We appreciate the miraculous medical advances that have added years to life. But we must be cautious that we add life to years.

לֹא תִרְצָח וְלֹא תִנְאָף וְלֹא תִגְנֹב וְלֹא־תַעֲנֶה בְרֵעֲךָ עֵד שָׁוְא

"You shall not kill, and you shall not commit adultery, and you shall not steal" (5:17).

The Progression of Sin

There is a subtle but significant difference between the Ten Commandments in Exodus and the version in Deuteronomy. In Exodus, the above verse is "you shall not kill; you shall not commit adultery; you shall not steal." There is no conjunction "and." In the Deuteronomy version, the above three commandments are linked by "and."

R' Yechiel Meir of Ostrovza sheds light on this difference. The Midrash says that the devotion of the Israelites to God at Sinai was so complete that they were freed of the *yetzer hara.* That cannot mean that they were totally devoid of temptation, because otherwise they would be similar to angels. When the angels protested the giving of the Torah to mortals, Moses argued that the Torah is not applicable to angels, because it prohibits various behaviors to which only mortals are subject. If the Israelites were totally free of the *yetzer hara,* the Torah would not be applicable to them either.

What the Midrash means, says R' Yechiel Meir, is that at Sinai the Israelites were free of the progressive nature of sin. The Talmud says that the *yetzer hara* operates by enticing a person to commit a minor transgression. Inasmuch as it is the nature of sin to be progressive, the *yetzer hara* then leads him to commit sins of increasing severity. It was this aspect of the *yetzer hara* from which the Israelites at Sinai were freed. A sin remained an isolated event, and did not bring another sin in its wake.

The Midrash says that when the Israelites committed the worship of the Golden Calf, the *yetzer hara* returned in full force. Now any sin would lead to another sin.

Therefore, R' Yechiel Meir says, in the Exodus version at Sinai, the three commandments are not joined by "and," to indicate that each sin was an isolated event, not attached to any other. In the Deuteronomy version, which Moses related after the incident of the Golden Calf had restored the potency of the *yetzer hara* to make sin progressive so that each sin led to additional sin, the three commandments are connected by "and." This indicates that a sin does not remain an isolated phenomenon, but brings further sin in its wake.

This is a crucial concept. We must at all times be on guard to avoid even the slightest transgression. In medicine we know that even if an antibiotic destroys billions of bacteria, a single surviving germ can multiply and cause serious illness. That is how we must think of sin. Even a single sin can start a progression that can lead a person to a status of depravity that he never thought possible.

הֵיטִיבוּ כָּל־אֲשֶׁר דִּבֵּרוּ. מִי־יִתֵּן וְהָיָה לְבָבָם זֶה לָהֶם לְיִרְאָה אֹתִי

When the Israelites heard the voice of God at Sinai, they feared that their souls would leave them. They asked Moses to convey the words of God to them. God said, *"They did well in all that they spoke. Who can assure that this heart should remain theirs, to fear Me"* (5:25-26)

The Importance of Gratitude

The Talmud states that Moses reprimanded the Israelites as being ingrates. "When God said, 'Who can assure that this heart should remain theirs, to fear Me,' you should have responded to God, 'You assure us! Give us a heart that will always fear You'" (*Avodah Zarah* 5a).

In what way did their failure to ask this of God make them ingrates? Tosafos explains that they did not want God to give them anything so that they should not feel beholden to Him. They were unwilling to be grateful.

Hakaras hatov (acknowledging a favor) is one of the most important *middos* (character traits) a person should develop. It may take some effort, because, like the Israelites in the desert, there is often some resistance to recognizing gratitude. Indeed, some people may be so reluctant to acknowledge a favor that they not only deny it, but may develop a resentment toward their benefactor. My grandfather, the rebbe of Bobov, once said, "I don't know why that person resents me. I never did him a favor."

> *In Kovno there was a young man who feared he would be drafted into the Czar's army, which, for an observant Jew, was a fate worse than death. When he was freed from the draft, someone hastened to bring the good tidings R' Yitzchok Elchonon, who thanked him profusely, saying, "May God bless you for bringing me good tidings! I am so grateful to you. May God grant you long life and good health. Thank you so very, very much."*
>
> *R' Yitzchok Elchonon returned to his discussion of a litigation in which he was a magistrate, when another young man burst in with the same news, apologizing for the interruption. R' Yitzchok Elchonon greeted him warmly with an expression of joy as though this was new to him, and again thanked him and bestowed a lavish blessing on him. When a third student brought the tidings, R' Yitzchok Elchonon did not say, "Thank you, but I already know of this," but again appeared to be joyfully enlightened and blessed the student profusely.*
>
> *This news was brought to R' Yitzchok Elchonon six times by different individuals, and each one received the same enthusiastic response. Each one left with the feeling that he had brought joy to R' Yitzchok Elchanan.*

R' Yitzchok Elchonon was indeed an outstanding Torah scholar whose Torah responsa are important halachic teachings. His *middos*, as the above story indicates, are of at least equal importance as guidelines for Torah living.

שְׁמַע יִשְׂרָאֵל ה׳ אֱלֹקֵינוּ ה׳ אֶחָד
"Hear, O Israel, Hashem is our God, Hashem is the One and Only" (6:4)

The Real Meaning of Shema

R' Yehudah Leib Chasman (*Ohr Yahel* vol. 3, p. 359) poses a challenging question. We generally assume that the *Shema* is our assertion of our belief in God. If so, then the sages should have formulated a declaration, "I believe that Hashem is the One and Only God." How are the words "Hear, O Israel" relevant to one's personal testimony?

R' Chasman states that over and above being a statement of one's personal faith, the *Shema* is the acceptance of a responsibility that one will behave and live his life in such a manner that *it will convince others that Hashem is the One and Only God.*

How can one's behavior affect other people's faith in God? This is explained in the next paragraph of the *Shema*, which now proves to be an elaboration of the first verse. *V'ahavta es Hashem,* which is usually translated as, "you shall love God," is interpreted by the Talmud to mean, "you shall make God beloved"; i.e., to behave in an exemplary manner so that others will appreciate the beauty of Torah and come to believe in God (*Yoma* 86a). If a person transacts fairly and honestly and communicates courteously and pleasantly, people will come to respect God's Torah.

According to R' Chasman, if a person recites the *Shema* and accepts the sovereignty of God upon himself, he has not yet completely fulfilled the obligation of the *Shema*. This is fulfilled only if his behavior is such that "Hear, O Israel" is achieved; namely, that he accepts upon himself to live in a Torah-true way so that others will wish to emulate him.

וְאָהַבְתָּ אֵת ה׳ אֱלֹקֶיךָ בְּכָל־לְבָבְךָ
"You shall love your God with all your heart" (6:5)

Obeying out of Love Rather than Fear

"Do His will out of love. One who serves out of love cannot be compared to one who serves out of fear. The one who serves his master out of fear, once [the master] overburdens him, will leave him and go his own way" (*Rashi*).

I wish these words could be displayed in flashing lights in every home. These words are the single greatest method whereby parents can prevent their children from deviating. Children who obey their parents out of fear, whether it be fear of punishment or of incurring their disapproval, may well react as Rashi says. When they feel that the parental demands of them are excessive, they may rebel or go their own way. Not so if they obey their parents out of love.

Parents' love of their children is innate. Animals, too, care for and nurture their children. *Children's love for parents must be earned.* If parents act in a way that merits their children's admiration, they will receive their love. Such children are likely to avoid doing anything that will distress their parents. Any parent who relies on authority to make his children do his wishes may find himself disillusioned and disappointed when the children do as Rashi says, "leave him and go his own way."

Parents must indeed discipline their children, but should do so in a manner that will not humiliate them and cause them shame. Discipline by intimidation evokes resentment, not love. I elaborated on this theme in *Positive Parenting*.

Our people have suffered greatly throughout our history, but we have not abandoned our faith in God. Although we have been severely challenged, we know that God's love for us is boundless, and we reciprocate our love for Him. It is this love that has enabled us to withstand suffering. Similarly, children who feel that their parents' love is unconditional are more likely to reciprocate that love and abide by their parents' wishes.

וְאָהַבְתָּ אֵת ה׳ אֱלֹקֶיךָ בְּכָל־לְבָבְךָ וּבְכָל־נַפְשְׁךָ וּבְכָל־מְאֹדֶךָ

"You shall love your God with all your heart, with all your soul and with all your resources" (6:5)

Love of God

A number of commentaries pose the question, "How can an emotion be legislated? Love develops in a relationship. Can someone be commanded to love? Furthermore, how can one develop love for God Who can neither be seen nor touched and is beyond a sense experience?"

Several answers are given. The Baal Shem Tov said that we should behave in a manner that will result in *ahavas Yisrael* (love for others). This will automatically result in *ahavas Hashem* (love for God).

One of the commentaries pointed out that true love is reciprocal, as Solomon says, "Just as water reflects one's image, so does the heart of a person reflect the heart of another person" (*Proverbs* 27:19). The blessing preceding the *Shema* describes God's intense love for Israel. Our love for God, therefore, is reciprocated.

The obvious question is, Why do we not feel this intense love for God? The answer is that Solomon speaks of the reflection in water rather than in a mirror. The difference is that a mirror can reflect an image even at a distance, whereas water will reflect an image only at close range. If one will come close to God through the observance of His mitzvos, one will feel the reciprocated love for Him.

Another answer is given in the Talmud (*Yoma* 86a), that *v'ahavta* means "you shall make God's Name beloved by others." When a Jew relates to people in a pleasant manner and transacts honestly, this causes people to admire God and His Torah. *V'ahavta* is thus a commandment of behavior rather than emotion.

One of the most interesting explanations is that of Rambam (*Yesodei HaTorah* 2:2). He raises the question, "What is the way to achieve love of God?" and answers, "If a person will meditate on His great and marvelous works and see from them His wisdom which is beyond measure and infinite, one will promptly love, praise and exalt God and have an intense desire to know Him." At first glance, this does not appear to answer the question. Awareness of God's infinite wisdom may result in adoration, but how does it produce love?

The *peirush* (commentary) on Rambam says that Rambam is redefining the word *ahavah* (love). The *ahavah* with which we are most familiar is between two people, such as parent and child, husband and wife. This *ahavah* is generally contingent on the benefits one derives from the relationship. There is a second type of *ahavah*, which is a desire to be in the close presence of someone, in an intimate relationship, as a result of the adoration of someone.

We may get an inkling of this desire if we observe the "hero worship" that some children may have for prominent sports figures. Such a child will collect pictures of his hero and is thrilled to get his autograph. He may mimic his hero's actions, and if he is asked, "If you had just one wish, what would it be?" he would probably answer, "I'd just like to be with . . ." To be close to his hero may be the child's most fervent desire.

It is the intense desire to be near God, in an intimate relationship with Him, that Rambam defines as *ahavah*. Rambam has good reason for this concept. Moses says, "(I instruct you) to love God, to hearken to His voice and *to cleave to Him*": The concept of cleaving unto God is stated several times in the Torah (*Deuteronomy* 4:4, 10:20).

In order to achieve the adoration of God that will produce this type of *ahavah*, Rambam says that one must reflect on His marvelous works. We can see this in Tehillim (*Psalms*), where King David extols the wondrous and beautiful world, exclaiming, "How abundant are Your works, God. With wisdom You made them all. The world is full of Your acquisitions" (*Psalms* 104:24), and again, "When I see Your heavens, the work of Your fingers, the moon and the stars that You have set in place" (ibid. 8:4).

The prophet bewails those who indulge in revelry. "The works of God they do not note, and the accomplishments of His hands they do not see" (*Isaiah* 5:12). Radak comments, "From the wisdom of the heavenly bodies one can reach to the honoring of God, as it is said, 'How majestic Your name is throughout the land . . . when I see Your heavens and the work of Your fingers' (*Psalms* 8:2,4), and it is said, 'The heavens relate the glory of God' (ibid. 19:2). This means that if one understands the code of creation, one will know the glory of God. The prophet says, 'Lift our eyes to high and see Who created these' (*Isaiah* 40:26), whereby he means that if one contemplates this wisdom, one can know therefrom the glory of God."

Chapter 92 of *Psalms* begins with, "A song for the Sabbath day." Yet, there is not a single reference to Shabbos in the entire psalm! Rather, the Psalmist says, "You gladden me, God, by Your accomplishments; I sing of the works of Your hands. How great are Your works, O God, how profound are Your thoughts. A simpleton does not know, and a fool does not understand this." What is the relevance of these verses to Shabbos?

The Midrash says that this psalm was composed by Adam. Shabbos marks the completion of creation. When Adam saw the wondrous works that God had created in the six days of creation, he was overcome with the infinite wisdom of God that he saw in creation. Indeed, this is beyond the grasp of fools and simpletons.

If only one understood the incomparable marvel of the human body! If all the computers in the world were combined, they would be dwarfed by the human brain, whose 14 ½ *billion* parts are in complex interaction. My professor of neurophysiology said that from the time a pitcher throws the baseball until the batter swings at it, *hundreds of thousands* of messages are transmitted throughout the central nervous system.

At the base of the brain there is the pituitary gland, the size of one's thumbnail, that continually analyzes many substances in the blood and regulates the body's production of them, keeping them within an incredibly small and precise range. Beneath the brain there is an organ, the cerebellum, which at all times registers the status of every muscle in the body. Simply changing one's glance results in the cerebellum's registering the change of position of every muscle involved, and there are twelve muscles involved in every eye movement.

As the batter's eyes follow the ball, the many movements of all the eye muscles are registered, and through complex connections, the many muscles involved in the batter's stance and swing are coordinated. A thorough understanding of the many processes involved is mind-boggling.

The chemical processes performed by the liver could not be duplicated by a fully computerized factory. The finest dialysis apparatus cannot come close to the efficiency of the millions of tiny filters in the kidney.

A physician specializing in infertility said, "I looked through the microscope at a fertilized ovum, and realized that from now on, all that would be added to it would be nutrient chemicals, and from this tiny, single cell would fashion a human being. I knew then that there is a God."

Whether one examines a leaf under the microscope or peers through a powerful telescope at the vast universe, one just begins to appreciate the infinite wisdom and majesty of God, which will indeed result, as Rambam says, in the type of *ahavah* that one would have an intense desire to be in an intimate relationship with Him.

It was his understanding of the awesome greatness of Hashem's works that led King David to say, "My soul thirsts for You; my flesh pines for You" (*Psalms* 63:2) and "Only one thing do I ask of Hashem, it is that which I seek: to dwell in the house of Hashem all the days of my life" (ibid. 27:4).

If we are lacking in this type of *ahavas* Hashem, it is because we fail to appreciate the marvels of Creation in the way King David and Rambam did.

וְאָהַבְתָּ אֵת ה' אֱלֹקֶיךָ בְּכָל־לְבָבְךָ וּבְכָל־נַפְשְׁךָ וּבְכָל־מְאֹדֶךָ

"And you shall love your God with all your heart, with all your soul and with all your recources" (6:5)

Love of God Is Natural

As previously noted, some commentaries ask, How can you legislate love? Love is an emotion. It is either there or not there. Can you order someone to love?

One answer is that within each person, there is an innate, inherent love for God that is a bequest from the patriarch Abraham. It is concealed within us, because it is overshadowed by our love for mundane things that are anathema to the *neshamah*. If we rid ourselves of the love for things restricted by Torah, the innate love for God will emerge. This theme is especially developed in *Tanya*.

The Maggid of Dubnow explains that if someone invited distinguished guests into his home, he would clean the house and make certain that there was nothing in the house that would be offensive to his guests. Similarly, the love of God cannot reside wherever there are feelings and behavior that are inimical to God.

In one of his inimitable parables, the Maggid tells of a peasant who came to a store that sold fine clothing and asked for a suit. The salesperson estimated his size and gave him a suit that was appropriate for him. The peasant put the suit on top of the coarse clothing he was wearing and complained that the suit did not fit. "You fool!" the salesperson said, "you must first take off the coarse garments you are wearing, and then the suit will fit you perfectly."

That is how it is with the love of God. It cannot fit unless we divest ourselves of the coarse love we harbor for many earthly pleasures.

We often meditate on the first verse in the *Shema*, affirming our belief in the unity of God. We then recite the remainder of the *Shema* without much meditation. However, the verse "you shall love your God" is virtually meaningless if we do not meditate on how to develop this love. We should meditate and sincerely resolve to eliminate the kinds of things that suppress the innate love for God.

וְעָשִׂיתָ הַיָּשָׁר וְהַטּוֹב בְּעֵינֵי ה'
"You shall do what is fair and good in the eyes of God" (6:18)

Individualization of a Mitzvah

Ramban says that it is impossible for the Torah to list every single proper action expected of a person. Therefore, after enumerating many mitzvos, the Torah gives a general rule: to do what is fair and proper.

The Talmud does derive a particular halachah from this verse. A person who has a property adjacent to yours has the first right of purchase, unless there are special reasons why someone else should be given preference. If this first right of purchase is ignored, the neighbor can have the sale to the third party nullified. Where is the source for this in the Torah? "You shall do what is fair and good in the eyes of God." It is fair and proper that a person should have the first right of purchase of a property adjacent to his.

There is a unique feature about the mitzvah of doing what is fair and proper. The mitzvah of eating matzah on Passover applies equally to the greatest scholar and to an illiterate person. The restrictions on forbidden foods or work on Shabbos are equal for everyone. Doing what is right and proper, however, is relative. A person of greater Torah scholarship and high ethical standards has a greater responsibility to be sensitive to what is fair and proper.

One Talmudic sage said, "What constitutes *chillul Hashem* (profaning the Divine Name)? For me, it is buying meat from the butcher and not paying for it immediately" (*Yoma* 86a). For the average Torah observant person, owing the butcher a small sum of money hardly casts any aspersions on the ethics of Torah. For a prominent Torah scholar, the possibility that someone might accuse him of reneging on his debt may be a *chillul Hashem*.

A person should recognize his place in society and realize what people may justly expect of him. To operate beneath these standards, even if one is in compliance with the letter of the law, may be a dereliction in doing what is "fair and proper."

פרשת עקב
Parashas Eikev

וְהָיָה עֵקֶב תִּשְׁמְעוּן אֵת הַמִּשְׁפָּטִים הָאֵלֶּה וּשְׁמַרְתֶּם וַעֲשִׂיתֶם אֹתָם וְשָׁמַר ה' אֱלֹקֶיךָ לְךָ אֶת־הַבְּרִית וְאֶת־הַחֶסֶד אֲשֶׁר נִשְׁבַּע לַאֲבֹתֶיךָ

This shall be the reward when you hearken to these ordinances and keep and do them, that God will safeguard for you the covenant and the kindness that He swore to your forefathers (7:12).

Look to the Future with Joy

The Midrash states that wherever the Torah says *vehaya*, "It shall be," it refers to *simchah*, a joyful occurance. On the other hand, when the Torah says *vayehi beyimay*, "It was in the days," it refers to an unhappy theme.

It is a fact. Happy people are future-oriented. Sad people are past-oriented.

A tradition in many families is to serve "farfel" at the Friday night meal. My mother referred to this as "Baal Shem Tov's *tzimmes*." The significance of this dish is a play on words. In Yiddish, *farfallen* means "bygone" and "it is over and done with, irretrievable." When my mother served the farfel, she would say, "Whatever occurred until now is *farfallen*."

Friday night marks the close of the previous workweek, with all its anguish and disappointments. Shabbos is a day of meditation and renewal. It is not merely a day of rest to "recharge one's batteries" for the next workweek. Rather, it is a day where Torah study, prayer, family unity and introspection should elevate one spiritually, so that the week that follows can be one of spiritual advancement.

Just as it is difficult to walk and take great strides with a heavy burden on one's back, so it is difficult to advance spiritually carrying a heavy burden of the past. True, we may have made mistakes. We should learn from these to not repeat them and to avoid the things that are conducive to errant behavior. Wherever possible, we should make amends for any harm we may have caused. These are the components of *teshuvah*, and Torah literature states that Shabbos is particularly propitious for *teshuvah*. But once we have done proper *teshuvah*, we should let go of the past and not allow it to hinder us in the future. That is why we eat the symbolic farfel on Friday night. "Let go of the past. It is *farfallen*."

I once saw a cartoon where one character tells the other that one should not worry about the future but think only of today. The response was, "No, that would be giving up. I still want to make yesterday better." Inasmuch as one cannot make yesterday better, why try? Correct the mistakes, resolve not to repeat them, and let that be the end of it.

"It shall be" is looking to what we can accomplish in the future. That indeed is *simchah*.

וְלֹא־תָבִיא תוֹעֵבָה אֶל־בֵּיתֶךָ
"You shall not bring an abomination into your home" (7:26)

Do Not Contaminate Your Home

The Torah instructs the Israelites to destroy the gold and silver appurtenances of idol worship that they find when they enter Canaan. Idols and their appurtenances are *cherem* (banned), and anyone possessing them will similarly be banned.

Sforno comments that possession of objects used in pagan rites will bring ruination to all one's possessions.

The Talmud says that if one goes into a rage, it is equivalent of idol worship (*Shabbos* 105b). The above restriction, therefore, applies to rage as well. Rage is an abomination. Do not bring it into your home.

When R' Zeira's students asked him to what he ascribed his longevity, he said, "I never expressed anger in my home" (*Megillah* 28). It may at times be necessary to reprimand and even sharply rebuke someone for doing wrong, and this may give the appearance of anger. But this should be an outward manifestation rather than a true rage response.

Sforno's comment applies to rage as well as to idolatry. Rage is never constructive and is always ruinous. The Talmud says that rage deprives a wise person of wisdom and a prophet of prophesy. "All the forces of hell dominate someone in rage" (*Nedarim* 22a). What could be more ruinous? Rage is so pernicious that on three occasions it distorted Moses' judgment, and according to Rambam, was the transgression which resulted in Moses' not being permitted to enter the Promised Land.

"The words of the wise are heard because they are said with calm" (*Ecclesiastes* 9:17). One may think that the gold and silver items of idol worship are valuable and can enrich one. Sforno says they will bring only ruin. One might think that shouting achieves obedience. Quite the contrary. Even if it produces momentary compliance, it may turn the listener against the enraged person.

There is nothing more precious than life. R' Zeira teaches us that we may preserve and extend our lives by avoiding rage.

וַיְעַנְּךָ וַיַּרְעִבֶךָ וַיַּאֲכִלְךָ אֶת־הַמָּן...
לְמַעַן הוֹדִיעֲךָ כִּי לֹא עַל־הַלֶּחֶם לְבַדּוֹ יִחְיֶה הָאָדָם
כִּי עַל־כָּל־מוֹצָא פִי־ה' יִחְיֶה הָאָדָם

He afflicted you and let you hunger, then He fed you the manna in order to make you know that not by bread alone does man live, rather by everything that emanates from the mouth of God does man live (8:3)

Responding to Children's Needs

This verse contains an important concept of parenting.

For there to be a healthy parent-child relationship, the development of *trust* is crucial. Children must know that their parents are there for them and that they can be relied upon to provide for their needs.

Several decades ago, a permissive attitude of parenting was promoted, advocating that children should not be allowed to experience frustration, lest it result in neurosis. This permissiveness was nothing less than disastrous. It totally failed to prepare children for the real world, in which frustration abounds. Furthermore, by not allowing children to experience needs, there was no way that they could develop the feeling that their parents would provide for their needs.

In the above verse, the Torah gives us an important guideline for developing trust in children. *If parents anticipate all their child's needs and provide for them before the child has had an opportunity to identify the need, the child never learns that his needs will be met.* A child must be allowed to feel his needs, and when the parents respond in a way that meets those needs, that is how the child learns to trust.

This is stated so beautifully and clearly in the Torah. Moses says, "He afflicted you and let you hunger, *then* He fed you the manna." Had God provided the manna before they were hungry, they never would have been able to learn trust in Him.

Of course, if parents do not understand the child's needs or allow too long a period of frustration, the child does not learn trust either. And when the child lacks the security of being able to trust, he feels he must take things into his own hands, i.e., he must control things. In *Successful Relationships* I elaborate on the problems resulting from improper use of control.

Children must be disciplined, and before they reach the age of reason, they cannot understand why they should or should not do something. At this point they must accept parental authority. However, as they mature, they should become aware that their parents were genuinely interested in their welfare and not simply exercising their authority. This can be accomplished by acting only in the children's interest. Children are sensitive, and they can feel when parents are simply domineering. The latter is "toxic control."

Good parenting requires that we walk a fine line between allowing a child to feel his needs and responding to them within a reasonable time so that the child knows that his parents understand, care and provide for him. This will decrease one factor that breeds toxic control.

לֹא עַל־הַלֶּחֶם לְבַדּוֹ יִחְיֶה הָאָדָם כִּי עַל־כָּל־מוֹצָא פִי־ה' יִחְיֶה הָאָדָם

Not by bread alone does man live, rather than by everything that emanates from the mouth of God does man live (8:3)

The Most Nourishing Food

Sometimes even gourmet food is not satisfying. While it may satisfy the palate, it may not satisfy the spirit.

R' Aryeh Levin used to care for many orphans, some of whom he raised in his own home. One of these was a young boy, Shmuel Aharon, whom R' Aryeh took under his wing in his yeshivah.

One a day a wealthy man who was childless asked R' Aryeh to transfer Shmuel Aharon to his care. R' Aryeh said, "I am reluctant to lose the mitzvah of caring for Shmuel Aharon, but I have meager means and can only give him simple food. If you will promise to provide him with the best foods available, I will agree." The wealthy man readily acquiesced to this.

After a few days, Shmuel Aharon returned to R' Aryeh. "The simple food that I ate in your home was much more satisfying than the sumptuous food I was served there." Obviously, what pleased Shmuel Aharon the most was being in the presence of a tzaddik and absorbing his spirituality. He truly fulfilled the verse, "Not by bread alone does man live, rather than by everything that emanates from the mouth of God does man live."

Periodically, the Rebbe of Gur would visit the Yeshivah Etz Chaim to test the students. He was impressed by Shmuel Aharon and told R' Aryeh that this lad was destined for greatness.

R' Aryeh valued the Rebbe's opinion and asked Shmuel Aharon, "Would you agree to become my son-in-law?" Shmuel Aharon answered, "Where could I find a better father-in-law?"

The Rebbe's prophesy proved true. R' Shmuel Aharon Yudlevitz became an outstanding Torah scholar, and eventually became the dean of Yeshivah Beis Yosef.

וְאָכַלְתָּ וְשָׂבָעְתָּ וּבֵרַכְתָּ אֶת־ה' אֱלֹקֶיךָ עַל־הָאָרֶץ הַטֹּבָה אֲשֶׁר נָתַן־לָךְ

You will eat and you will be satisfied, and bless your God for the good Land that He gave you (8:10)

True Appreciation

In the blessing after meals, we thank God not only for the food we ate, but also for delivering us from Egypt, for the Promised Land, for His covenant with us, for the Torah, for life and for His kindness.

If someone invited you for a meal, you would undoubtedly thank him. However, would you say, "Thank you for taking me into your house, for giving me a chair and seating me at the table?" Why, when we thank God for the food He has given us, do we enumerate all these other things?

It is because the comparison to being invited to a meal is not accurate. A better comparison is to someone who was stranded in an arid desert and had not had any food for several days. If a truck comes by and picks him up and the driver gives him some food and water, he will thank him profusely not only for the food and water but also for stopping to pick him up and saving his life.

This, says R' Benzion Bruk, is how we should feel toward God. He provides us not only with food, not only with the necessities of life, but also with life itself. We should indeed express our gratitude for all of these.

One of the chassidic masters asks, Inasmuch as we should recite a *berachah* for everything we enjoy in this world, how to we listen to music or enjoy fine art without a *berachah*?

He suggests that whereas the Talmud did not prescribe a *berachah* for everything, it is proper that the first time in a day that we recite the *berachah shehakol nihiyeh bidvoro* (Who created everything for His glory), we should have the *kavannah* (intention) that we wish this *berachah* to apply to everything for which no specific *berachah* was designated.

This is an excellent suggestion. We should not lose sight of the fact that everything we enjoy is a Divine gift.

וְאָמַרְתָּ בִּלְבָבֶךָ כֹּחִי וְעֹצֶם יָדִי עָשָׂה לִי אֶת־הַחַיִל הַזֶּה
וְזָכַרְתָּ אֶת ה' אֱלֹקֶיךָ כִּי הוּא הַנֹּתֵן לְךָ כֹּחַ לַעֲשׂוֹת חָיִל

You may say in your heart, "My strength and the might of my hand made me all this wealth!" Then you shall remember your God: that it was He Who gives you strength to make wealth (8:17-18)

The Delusion of Self-Sufficiency

Virtually all Torah commentaries cite this verse as crucial to one's faith and Torah observance. To think that one can achieve anything other than what God willed is heresy. Yet, most people's behavior betrays their conviction that how much wealth they accumulate is due to their effort or their business acumen.

> In Yellowstone National Park, the Old Faithful geyser erupts at regular intervals. Visitors from all over the world come to see this natural wonder.
>
> Two pranksters found a steering wheel and shaft in a junk yard. They brought it to a little hill near Old Faithful and planted the shaft into the ground. Soon a guide brought a group of tourists and told them about the marvel of Old Faithful. "This geyser has been erupting regularly since time immemorial," he said. "We are now exactly 3 minutes away from the next eruption. You can look at your watches and see for yourself." Then he continued to talk about Old Faithful.
>
> About 4 seconds before Old Faithful was to erupt, one of the pranksters shouted to the other, "O.K., Frank! Let 'er go!" The tourists looked up to see the other prankster giving the wheel a vigorous turn, and just then the geyser erupted.

An observer might not be blamed for concluding that the eruption occurs when a valve is opened. The fact is, however, that the steering wheel was just a sham. It had nothing to do with causing the eruption.

Someone who sees a temporal correlation between his efforts and his earnings may think of them as cause and effect. We are indeed supposed to do something to earn a livelihood, but how much we will accumulate is not dependent on the extent of our effort, but on the blessing of God.

וַיֹּאמֶר ה׳ אֵלַי לֵאמֹר רָאִיתִי אֶת־הָעָם הַזֶּה
וְהִנֵּה עַם־קְשֵׁה־עֹרֶף הוּא

*"God said to me, saying, 'I have seen this people,
and behold! It is a stiff-necked people' "* (9:13)

Closed-Mindedness

Sforno says that obstinacy and justice are often incompatible. A stubborn person has his mind made up and will not listen to cogent arguments that would disprove his opinion. This is why, when the Israelites sinned with the Golden Calf, God said, "I have seen this people, and behold! It is a stiff-necked people. And now, desist from Me. Let My anger flare up against them and I shall annihilate them" (*Exodus* 32:10). It was only Moses' fervent prayer that delayed God's wrath and gave them the opportunity for *teshuvah*.

How was Moses able to break through the Israelites' obstinacy? Targum Yonasan says that it was the shock of seeing the Tablets of the Ten Commandments shattered and the letters flying off into the air that broke through their stiff-neckedness.

But sometimes the stiffneckedness can be so great that even a shock does not penetrate it. R' Chaim Shmulevitz cites the incident of Chiel the Beth-elite, who built up Jericho in defiance of Joshua's curse that whoever would rebuild Jericho would lose his children. "When he laid the foundations of the city, his oldest son died, and his children continued dying until his last child died when the gates of Jericho were erected" (*Rashi, I Kings* 16:34). What greater shock can there be than for a father to see his children dying! Chiel knew of Joshua's curse, yet denied that it was affecting him.

The only protection we have against being blinded by our opinions is to keep an open mind and listen to the opinions of others. In particular, we should give extra attention to those opinions that disagree with ours, because those are the ones we are likely to reject.

But even this may not be enough. We may think we are open-minded and listening when in fact we turn a deaf ear to others. We should, therefore, pray that God grants us the ability to listen to opinions that are contrary to ours.

וְעַתָּה יִשְׂרָאֵל מָה ה׳ אֱלֹקֶיךָ שֹׁאֵל מֵעִמָּךְ כִּי אִם־לְיִרְאָה אֶת ה׳

*"Now, O Israel, what does your God ask of you?
Only to fear God"* (10:12)

What Is Our Task?

Rashi quotes the Talmudic derivation from this verse that "everything is in God's hands, except for the fear of God." God determines and controls everything, but whether a person will fear God and behave according to His will, that is entirely a free choice which is left to man.

R' Hirsch Leib of Volozhin had a student who became a very successful merchant. One time the former student visited the master, who asked him, "How are you doing?"

The merchant replied, "Thank God, I have nothing to complain about. I am in good health and I have good parnassah (livelihood)."

A bit later in their conversation, R' Hirsch Leib again asked, "And how are you doing?" Again the merchant replied that he was faring well. After some further conversation, R' Hirsch Leib again asked, "And how are you doing?"

The merchant said, "With all due respect, Rabbi, you have asked me this twice before, and I have told you that all is well with me. Why are you repeating the question?"

R' Hirsch Leib said, "Because you have not answered it. I asked you how you are doing, and you answered me about your parnassah. Your parnassah is what God is doing for you. What you should be doing is what God does not do for you. You should be setting aside time every day for Torah study, you should be davening (praying) with kavannah (concentration), you should be giving tzedakah. These are your responsibilities."

Is it not ironic that we may spend so little time each day *davening* and studying Torah, while we devote the greater part of our day to work and business? Our earnings are God's responsibility, whereas Torah and *tefillah* are ours. If we really had the *emunah* (faith) that we profess to have, our apportionment of time would be totally different.

וְעַתָּה יִשְׂרָאֵל מָה ה' אֱלֹקֶיךָ שֹׁאֵל מֵעִמָּךְ כִּי אִם־לְיִרְאָה אֶת ה'

**"Now, O Israel, what does your God ask of you?
Only to fear God"** (10:12).

Just What Is Fear of God

The great *tzaddik*, R' Yehoshua Leib Diskin, explained the differences in levels of *yiras Shamayim* (fear of God) with the following story.

"When I was a child," R' Yehoshua Leib said, "I noticed that if there was ever a shailah (question about whether a food preparation was permissible) and the rabbi ruled that it was kosher, my father would nevertheless not eat it, and would tell my mother to give it to the children. This bothered me. If it was kosher enough for us, why was it not kosher enough for him? However, out of respect for my father I never asked him.

"One time there was a fire in a nearby town that destroyed part of the shul. The flames had reached the Aron Kodesh (ark where the Torah is kept) and had scorched several of the scrolls. A representative of the town brought two of the scorched scrolls to ask my father if they were still kosher to use.

"When the man brought the scorched scrolls, I was curious about what had happened, and I asked him about the details of the fire and the shul. He then went into my father's study, and when my father saw the scorched Torahs, he promptly fainted. It was with difficulty that he was finally revived.

"I then understood that there was an enormous gap between my father's yiras shamayim and mine, and why different standards applied to us."

The term "fear of God" is often thought of as fear of being punished for disobeying Him. That is a rather immature concept. *Yiras Shamayim* means fear of losing close contact with God. When a person commits a sin, he sets up a barrier between himself and God. The relationship to God should be as vital to a person as if he were being saved by drowning only because he is holding onto a rope. The rope is his only link to safety, and he fears losing hold of it.

If a person understood that his spiritual life depends on his contact with God and that the mitzvos are the only means for that contact, his fear of violating the mitzvos would be like the fear of losing hold of the rope.

That is *yiras Shamayim*.

R' Yehoshua Leib's *yiras Shamayim* is legendary. Yet, the sight of a damaged Torah did not evoke the reaction in him that it did in his father.

Lest we become complacent about our *yiras Shamayim*, let us remember that R' Yehoshua Leib felt that he was lacking in it.

אֶת ה' אֱלֹקֶיךָ תִּירָא אֹתוֹ תַעֲבֹד וּבוֹ תִדְבָּק וּבִשְׁמוֹ תִּשָּׁבֵעַ

Your God shall you revere (10:20)

Reverence for a Tzaddik

In Hebrew there is a word that has no equivalent in English. It is the word *es* that appears before a noun with a definite article. The Talmud states that *es* is an inclusive word. One of the Talmudic sages, Shimon HaAmsoni, explained in what way each *es* was inclusive. When he came to the verse, "Your God shall you revere," and the name of God was preceded by *es*, he realized that this *es* could not be inclusive. For that would mean that there is something which we must revere just as we revere God, and that is impossible. Shimon, therefore, decided that his thesis that *es* is always inclusive is incorrect. The Talmud states that when Rabbi Akiva came, he said that this *es* can also be inclusive. It means that one should revere a Torah scholar just as one reveres God (*Pesachim* 22b).

Some commentaries ask, why did Shimon not come to the same conclusion that Rabbi Akiva did? One commentary provides a unique interpretation.

Shimon had great difficulty in equating anyone or anything as deserving the reverence we must have for God. However, when he saw Rabbi Akiva, one of the greatest Talmudic sages whose devotion to God was so absolute that he rejoiced in giving up his life for God, Shimon realized that a human being could elevate himself to a spiritual height where he merited the same reverence given to God. The pronoun "he" in the Talmud's statement "that when Rabbi Akiva came, *he* said that this *es* can also be inclusive" does not refer to Rabbi Akiva as the antecedent, but rather refers back to Shimon, i.e., when Shimon saw Rabbi Akiva, *he, Shimon*, said that this *es* was also inclusive, and means that one should revere a Torah scholar just as one reveres God.

פרשת ראה
Parashas Re'eh

רְאֵה אָנֹכִי נֹתֵן לִפְנֵיכֶם הַיּוֹם בְּרָכָה וּקְלָלָה
אֶת־הַבְּרָכָה אֲשֶׁר תִּשְׁמְעוּ אֶל־מִצְוֹת ה׳ אֱלֹקֵיכֶם אֲשֶׁר אָנֹכִי מְצַוֶּה אֶתְכֶם הַיּוֹם
וְהַקְּלָלָה אִם־לֹא תִשְׁמְעוּ . . . וְסַרְתֶּם מִן־הַדֶּרֶךְ אֲשֶׁר אָנֹכִי מְצַוֶּה
אֶתְכֶם הַיּוֹם לָלֶכֶת אַחֲרֵי אֱלֹהִים אֲחֵרִים אֲשֶׁר לֹא־יְדַעְתֶּם

"See, I present before you today a blessing and a curse.
The blessing:
that you hearken to the commandments of God that I command you today.
And the curse:
if you do not hearken . . . and you stray from the path that I command
you today, to follow gods of others that you did not know" (11:26-28)

An Immature Mentality

R' Dovid of Lelov says that the book of Deuteronomy is essentially Moses' chastisement of the Israelites prior to his death. The above verses, too, are a chastisement.

A small child who runs into the street to retrieve his ball may have to be spanked to discourage him from doing so again. Explaining to him the danger of being hit by a car is futile, because he cannot understand this. When one reaches the age of reason, an explanation that one should avoid danger is adequate.

Similarly, a small child may have to be bribed with candy to get him to do something which he does not want to do. Explaining the value of it is to no avail, because he cannot grasp this. Once a person understands that something is to his advantage, he does not need to be rewarded for doing it.

Here Moses reprimands the Israelites. "After forty years of teaching you Torah, you should understand on your own that obeying the word of God is a blessing and that transgressing His commandments is a curse. Yet, I must set before you a blessing and a curse (*Deuteronomy* 27:15-28:69), as though you were children who have not yet reached the age of reason. "How tragic that you have not matured sufficiently to wish to do good because it is good and to avoid evil because it is wrong."

We can gauge our level of maturity by how much we understand that observing the Torah is to our own advantage, and that we need not be motivated by external rewards or punishments.

רְאֵה אָנֹכִי נֹתֵן לִפְנֵיכֶם הַיּוֹם בְּרָכָה וּקְלָלָה

"See, I present before you today a blessing and a curse" (11:26)

Overcoming Blindness

R' Yitzchok Meir of Gur says that God has given a person the wisdom and understanding to be able to distinguish between right and wrong, between a blessing and curse.

We have not only the intelligence to make wise decisions but also the *ability* to do so. Yet, we often see people making unwise decisions that are to their own detriment, and they fail to use these God-given strengths in their own favor. This thought occurs to me when I see intelligent and even scholarly people smoking cigarettes, knowingly poisoning themselves. True, it would require effort and some tolerance of discomfort to break the habit, but certainly one's life is dear enough that one should willingly accept the discomfort in the interest of survival. People who readily accept the discomfort of a surgical procedure to save their lives nonetheless appear unable to do so with regard to discontinuing smoking.

The reason for this discrepancy is that one's judgment is distorted by what one would like to believe. The Torah states this very clearly: "A bribe will blind the eyes of the wise" (*Deuteronomy* 16:19). One's wisdom is ineffective when a bribe has affected one's judgment capacity. A blind person would indeed wish to avoid falling into a pit, but he cannot help himself if he cannot see it.

This is true of every unwise decision. Smoking is just one stark example. We are constantly under the influence of biases that impair our judgement.

The blind person cannot make himself sighted, but we do have the ability to overcome the blindness of our biases. We just need to be on the alert and on the defensive, realizing our vulnerability.

Moses chose his words very deliberately: "*See*, I present before you today a blessing and a curse." See, indeed. You have the ability to overcome the blindness of your biases.

רְאֵה אָנֹכִי נֹתֵן לִפְנֵיכֶם הַיּוֹם בְּרָכָה וּקְלָלָה

"See, I present before you today a blessing and a curse" (11:26)

No "Neutrality"

Sforno states, "Be cautious that you not be like other peoples who have a middle-ground. 'I present before you today a blessing and a curse.' These are the two extremes in Torah living. There is no middle-ground."

This principle is often encountered in the writings of *mussar* and *chassidus*. We tend to think that there are mitzvos, things that are obligatory, and sins, things which are forbidden. However, there is a vast area which seems to be neutral. Eating matzah on Passover is a mitzvah. Eating *tereifah* is a sin. But eating kosher food falls into neither category. It is simply permissible.

Our ethical writings eliminate this neutral category. The underlying principle of Torah living is, "Know God in all your ways" (*Proverbs* 3:6). The awareness that one was created to fulfill a mission on earth should direct all one's attention toward fulfillment of that mission: to serve God with all one's heart and with all one's might. This requires energy, which we derive from food. This requires a healthy body, which needs rest in order to function properly. One can partake of many goods in this world, and if this is done in a manner which enhances one's health and functioning, which, in turn, enables one to better fulfill one's mission, then these "permissible" actions become mitzvos. Indulgence in worldly pleasures for their own sake is a dereliction of duty. What is not good must be considered evil.

This concept, Sforno states, its unique to Judaism. In the secular world, there is a concept, "Give to God what is God's and to Caesar what is Caesar's." In Judaism, there is no such dichotomy. It is our duty to dedicate everything to the sovereignty of God.

אֶת־הַבְּרָכָה אֲשֶׁר תִּשְׁמְעוּ אֶל־מִצְוֹת ה' אֱלֹקֵיכֶם אֲשֶׁר אָנֹכִי מְצַוֶּה אֶתְכֶם הַיּוֹם
וְהַקְּלָלָה אִם־לֹא תִשְׁמְעוּ . . . וְסַרְתֶּם מִן־הַדֶּרֶךְ אֲשֶׁר אָנֹכִי מְצַוֶּה
אֶתְכֶם הַיּוֹם לָלֶכֶת אַחֲרֵי אֱלֹהִים אֲחֵרִים אֲשֶׁר לֹא־יְדַעְתֶּם

"The blessing:
that you hearken to the commandments of God that I command you today.
And the curse:
if you do not hearken . . . and you stray from the path that I command
you today, to follow gods of others that you did not know" (11:27-28).

Searching for "They Know Not What"

R' Moshe Schreiber (Chasam Sofer) notes that in regard to mitzvos, the Talmud interprets the word "today" as meaning that the mitzvos should be as fresh and exciting as if they were commanded today (*Rashi, Deuteronomy* 26:15). But, he asks, how does this apply to, "And the curse: if you do not hearken . . . and you stray from the path that I command you *today*?" It cannot possibly mean that not feeling the freshness of mitzvos each day warrants the punishment of a curse. Furthermore, the phrase "to follow gods of others" is a complete rejection of Torah rather than not feeling the freshness of mitzvos each day.

The Chasam Sofer provides us with an important psychological insight. It is natural for a person to seek novel experiences which are exciting. If a person does not feel the novelty and excitement in Torah, *he will look for this feeling elsewhere.* He will seek "gods of others that you did not know."

The Chasam Sofer's words were prophetic. It is not unusual today to see Jewish youths straying to Far Eastern religions that *"they do not know"* in the hope of finding excitement in them. This is because they have not experienced Torah and mitzvos in a way that is exciting and stimulating.

This is a phenomenon for which those who do practice Torah living must accept responsibility. True, we may be meticulous in our observance of Torah, yet it is often a matter of rote, unspirited and unexciting. If mitzvos were observed with the zest and enthusiasm as if they were just given today, there would not be a need for young people to look for excitement and inspiration elsewhere.

כִּי־תְאַוֶּה נַפְשְׁךָ לֶאֱכֹל בָּשָׂר בְּכָל־אַוַּת נַפְשְׁךָ תֹּאכַל בָּשָׂר . . .
רַק חֲזַק לְבִלְתִּי אֲכֹל הַדָּם כִּי הַדָּם הוּא הַנָּפֶשׁ וְלֹא־תֹאכַל הַנֶּפֶשׁ עִם־הַבָּשָׂר

For you will have a desire to eat meat;
to your heart's entire desire may you eat meat.
Only be strong not to eat the blood—for the blood is the nefesh [life]
—and you shall not eat the nefesh with the meat (12:20-23)

Hazard of Indulgence

The Gaon of Vilna interpreted the above verse "you shall not eat the *nefesh* with the meat" homiletically. The *nefesh* to which the Torah is referring is not only the blood of the animal, but also means the *nefesh* of the person. True, the Torah permits eating meat to satisfy one's gustatory desire. However, one must be cautious that in the process of satisfying physical desires, one should not lose one's spirituality. Hence, *do not consume your own nefesh* when eating meat.

The Talmud states, "This is the way of Torah. Eat bread with salt, drink water in small measure, sleep on the ground, live a life of deprivation, but toil in the Torah!" (*Ethics of the Fathers* 6:4). Living sparingly is conducive to spiritual excellence, whereas pursuit of physical desires detracts from spirituality.

In earlier generations, many Torah scholars fasted on a frequent basis. Their dedication to Torah study was so intense that they were simply not aware of being hungry. More recent ethical writings discourage fasting out of concern that we lack the stamina of earlier generations and our energy may be depleted by fasting. However, it is the nature of all physical desires that they are never fully satisfied. To the contrary, gratifying physical drives only intensifies them, leading to a vicious cycle that can result in indulging to excess.

The human being is a composite creature, comprised of body and soul. The two are diametrically opposed in their needs. Yielding to physical desires comes at the cost of frustrating the needs of the soul.

The Torah did indeed permit many physical gratifications, but as the Gaon of Vilna warns, we must exercise great caution that we do not consume our *nefesh* in their pursuit.

וְנָתַן־לְךָ רַחֲמִים

Following the mitzvah to totally destroy a town that was idolatrous,
the Torah says, *"He [God] will give you mercy"* (13:18).

True Compassion

The Ohr HaChaim says that carrying out the severe punishment of eradicating an entire community might affect a person's emotions and result in his becoming callous and brutal. The Torah, therefore, assures us that if this punishment is carried out as a Torah commandment, God will give one a feeling of compassion and prevent this from having a detrimental influence.

We consider compassion and mercy to be laudable traits. However, we must bear in mind when compassion and mercy may be counterproductive.

In my work treating addicts, I frequently encounter counterproductive compassion. For example, a person is apprehended burglarizing in order to support his drug habit. Family members, especially parents, may intervene to prevent their relative from being prosecuted. Or, a compulsive gambler forges checks or uses stolen credit cards. Family members may cover the debts so that he is not charged with a crime. Such compassion is ill-advised, because it eliminates the negative consequences that could bring the person to the realization that he needs help to overcome his addiction. Families have become impoverished extricating addicts from criminal charges, with the result that the addiction gets progressively worse.

In such situations, people with compassion must be convinced that true compassion consists of letting the person suffer the painful consequences of his behavior. Doing so does not render one insensitive or cruel. To the contrary, one's genuine compassion can increase if one acts in the interest of another person.

The mother who takes her infant to the doctor to be given a painful injection to immunize him from serious diseases is certainly not cruel. Her love for the child increases as she acts to protect him.

It is important to receive competent guidance when one wishes to extricate a loved one from trouble. What we think is compassion may be anything but that.

בָּנִים אַתֶּם לַה' אֱלֹקֵיכֶם לֹא תִתְגֹּדְדוּ . . . לָמֵת . . .
כִּי עַם קָדוֹשׁ אַתָּה לַה' אֱלֹקֶיךָ

You are children to your God —you shall not mutilate yourselves . . . for a dead person . . . for you are a holy people to your God (14:1-2).

Limitation of Grief

Grieving for the loss of a loved one is a normal human reaction, but halachah prescribes regulations for grief. In particular, the Talmud forbids excessive mourning (*Moed Katan* 26b).

It is only natural to mourn and weep when one has suffered the pain of a loss. However, the intensity of the pain should be somewhat mitigated by the realization that a loving father would not be cruel to a child. The knowledge that God is a loving Father should make one's acceptance of a personal loss more tolerable. "You should know in your heart that just as a father will chastise his son, so your God chastises you" (*Deuteronomy* 8:5). The pain of chastisement may indeed be intense, but faith in the absolute benevolence of God, even when it is beyond our ability to comprehend, should provide some measure of consolation.

Ramban explains that the phrase "for you are a holy people to your God" in this context refers to the eternity of the soul. As a holy people, when one leaves the earth, one enters into a more imminent presence of God. This is an additional reason why one should not mutilate oneself over a death. Whereas the pain of the loss may be intense, the knowledge that a loved one has arrived at a closer relationship with God should mitigate one's initial reaction.

Self-mutilation is not healthy grief. Inflicting wounds on oneself when someone has died may be an expression of guilt. Most often this guilt is unwarranted. However, if one feels that he had in some way aggrieved the deceased person, he should look for ways to refine his behavior so that he does not offend anyone else. This is a constructive response to legitimate guilt. Self-mutilation is destructive and accomplishes nothing.

Grief is unavoidable. We should cope with grief constructively, as befits children of God.

לֹא תֹאכַל כָּל־תּוֹעֵבָה
You shall not eat any abomination (14:3)

Preserving a Person's Honor

R' Isser Zalman Meltzer related the following story.

In a certain community, some of the townsfolk had taken a dislike to their rabbi, and tormented him in the hope that he would leave.

One day, a halachic question arose regarding whether a lesion found in a slaughtered cow was kosher or tereifah, and the rabbi erred in his decision that it was kosher. His adversaries now had powerful ammunition to declare him as being incompetent. They sent a letter to the sage R' Yitzchok Elchonon Spector, in which they presented the halachic question and the rabbi's obvious error, and asked the sage what steps should be taken with a rabbi whose incompetence resulted in the townsfolk eating tereifah. They were certain that the sage would tell them to send the incompetent rabbi on his way.

R' Yitzchok Elchonon surmised that the townsfolk were exploiting this mishap to serve their desire to fire the rabbi, and that they were hardly sincere in their championing of halachah. He wrote a lengthy responsa, in which he ingeniously justified the rabbi's decision that the lesion was kosher. Immediately after mailing the letter, he sent a telegram to the townsfolk, saying, "After mailing my responsa to you, I realized that I had erred in my thinking. Please ignore the responsa. The meat was indeed tereifah." The townsfolk could no longer accuse their rabbi of being incompetent. Even the great sage R' Yitzchok Elchonon was capable of making a similar misjudgment!

When R' Isser Zalman related this story, he would cry, saying, "Look how far one must go to protect the honor of a person. R' Yitzchok Elchonon was willing to efface himself as having made a mistake in halachah in order to preserve a person's honor. How great is our lack of such devotion for another person!"

וַאֲשֶׁר יִהְיֶה לְךָ אֶת־אָחִיךָ תַּשְׁמֵט יָדֶךָ אֶפֶס כִּי לֹא יִהְיֶה־בְּךָ אֶבְיוֹן

In commanding the law that *shemittah* absolves all debts,
and in enjoining the lender against pressing for collection of a debt
after the Shemittah year, the Torah says,
***"But over what you have with your brother,
you shall remit your authority.
May there be no destitute among you"*** (15:3-4)

Chesed Never Impoverishes

When the Chafetz Chaim was in Vienna to attend the Knessiah Gedolah (Agudah Convention), a man came to his inn to consult him about a problem. The Chafetz Chaim was having a meal at the time, and the innkeeper told the man that he could sit at the table until the Chafetz Chaim had finished.

It was the practice of the Chafetz Chaim to recite Psalm 23 at every meal. After he finished the psalm, he remarked to this man, who was a total stranger to him, that a thought had just occurred to him about this psalm, which he had recited countless times.

"King David states," the Chafetz Chaim said, "'Surely goodness and kindness shall pursue me all the days of my life.' That is a rather unusual expression. Being 'pursued' means that one is fleeing from those who wish to harm him. Goodness and kindness never harm anyone. Why would anyone be 'pursued' by goodness and kindness?

"It occurred to me," the Chafetz Chaim continued, "'that it is possible for a person who gives much tzedakah and does much chesed to feel that he is sacrificing too much by giving away money and devoting his time to chesed. He may think that doing these mitzvos may decrease his wealth or diminish his earning ability. He may see doing goodness and kindness as being detrimental to him, 'pursuing' him, as it were. David, therefore, assures a person not to fear. One will never become impoverished by acts of goodness and kindness. To the contrary, they will bring God's blessing upon him."

The man rose from his seat and bade the Chafetz Chaim goodbye. The innkeeper, seeing that the man had not consulted the Chafetz Chaim, asked him why he was leaving. "I have the answer to my problem," the man said.

"Several years ago I established a fund and a free loan service for needy scholars. Operating them was consuming much of my time, and my wife complained that I was neglecting the business. She suggested that I turn over their operation to a local agency. I did not think this was wise. When we heard that the Chafetz Chaim was here, we decided to consult him for his opinion.

"The Chafetz Chaim resolved the problem without my asking him. I can assure my wife that giving of my time to acts of kindness and goodness will never result in a financial loss."

כִּי־פָתֹחַ תִּפְתַּח אֶת־יָדְךָ לוֹ וְהַעֲבֵט תַּעֲבִיטֶנּוּ דֵּי מַחְסֹרוֹ אֲשֶׁר יֶחְסַר לוֹ

You shall open your hand [to the poor]; lend him his requirement, whatever is lacking to him (15:8)

The Ultimate in Tzedakah

Our ethical writings state that although mitzvos that are performed without proper *kavannah* (intention) are lacking in perfection, this is not true of *tzedakah*. As long as the poor are provided with their needs, the mitzvah is complete.

Nevertheless, the Talmud says that there are levels of merit even in *tzedakah*. Giving *tzedakah* secretly is of special merit.

In Cracow, the burial place of R' Yom Tov Heller, author of the illustrious commentary on the Mishnah, Tosafos Yom Tov, is near the fence, which is the least honorable plot in the cemetery in Cracow. The reason for this is as follows.

There was a wealthy man in Cracow, who, because of his tightfistedness, was known as "Shimon the miser." He never gave any tzedakah to the poor.

The butcher and the baker however were known for their lavish tzedakah. Every Friday the poor would come and receive bread and meat in abundance for Shabbos.

When Shimon the miser died, the townsfolk took out their wrath by burying him in dishonor near the fence.

The following Friday, when the poor came for bread and meat, the butcher and baker had nothing to give them. All these years, what they had given each week had been paid for by Shimon the miser, who had sworn them not to reveal that he was the benefactor, because he did not wish to receive any recognition for giving tzedakah.

R' Yom Tov Heller was overwhelmed by the spirituality of Shimon, and in his will requested that he be buried near Shimon, whom he considered to be a great tzaddik.

פרשת שופטים
Parashas Shoftim

שֹׁפְטִים וְשֹׁטְרִים תִּתֶּן־לְךָ בְּכָל־שְׁעָרֶיךָ
Judges and officers shall you appoint in all your gates (16:18).

Intake Is as Important as Output

Although the intent of the Torah is to appoint judges and officers in all *cities*, there is an additional message in the Torah's choice of the word "gates."

The Chidah cites an interpretation by R' Chaim Vital. A person's "gates" are his sense organs whereby he receives information about the outside world. Many people feel that they are responsible for their actions, but may not have any scruples about the kinds of things they hear or see. They may feel that they are in full control of their behavior, and there is no reason to fear being influenced by the kinds of things they hear or see.

Recent studies have conclusively demonstrated that children who are exposed to violence on television are more prone to behave violently. Seeing or listening to immoral stimuli does influence a person's moral values. These noxious influences are not limited to children. The Torah warns us not to "stray after your heart and your eyes" (*Numbers* 15:39). This is especially important in our days, when objectionable material can be viewed in the privacy of one's home and office. I can attest that some marriages have been ruined because of exposure to these stimuli.

We must have "judges and officers" who sit at the portals of our minds and protect us from improper intake. We must give serious consideration to what we allow to enter through our "gates."

The Sfas Emes expands on this theme. "Judges" render an opinion based on their consideration of the evidence. Their deliberation and conclusion follow logical guidelines.

Once the sentence is delivered, "officers" enforce it. At this point there is no deliberation, no logical arguments. The officers carry out the sentence, and it is not for them to consider its merit.

Similarly, we must exercise proper judgment on what we allow to enter our system. Once we are aware that something is improper, there is no further argument. The verdict of the judges must be implemented, and the ban must be observed. We must be trusted officers and not compromise on our judgment.

צֶדֶק צֶדֶק תִּרְדֹּף
Righteousness, righteousness shall you pursue (16:20)

We Are Responsible for the Process, Not the Result

R' Simchah Bunim of P'shis'che says that the repetition of the word "righteousness" means that one should pursue righteousness *with* righteousness. We may not use unjust methods even in the interest of a just cause. The end does not justify the means.

In commerce, good and bad are determined by outcome. Profit is good, loss is bad. If someone undertakes a project in a helter-skelter manner and ends up with a windfall profit, he is a good businessman. If someone does a careful market analysis, uses every bit of caution in setting up his business and goes bankrupt, he is a bad businessman.

It is unfortunate that our preoccupation with commerce has resulted in our personal lives being influenced by commercial standards. We often evaluate ethical good and bad by results rather than by process.

R' Chaim Shmulevitz cites the incident where Moses chastised the High Priest, Aaron, for burning a sacrificial offering against his instructions. Aaron argued that Moses may have erred in understanding the Divine commandment. Moses conceded that Aaron was right. "You are right. God had indeed commanded as you said, but I had forgotten" (*Leviticus* 10:20, *Zevachim* 101b).

R' Shmulevitz points out that Moses was faced with a dilemma. Inasmuch as he was the sole conduit of God's word, to admit that he had forgotten something and erred would have placed the authenticity of the entire Torah in jeopardy unto eternity. "If Moses could err in this, where else might he have erred?" It would perhaps be better if he said to Aaron, "What I instructed you was right." Moses decided that he had only one responsibility: *to tell the truth*, whatever the consequences may be. Preserving the authenticity of the Torah was God's problem, not his. His duty was to tell the truth.

There is an interesting question that arises from a unique halachah. The Talmud states that in a case of capital punishment, if all seventy-one judges of the Sanhedrin (Supreme Court) vote "guilty," the case is dismissed. The rationale is that the cross-examination of the eyewitness was so meticulous that a minor discrepancy in the testimony was usually found, and this was enough to invalidate the testimony. Therefore, if the testimony coincided so perfectly that there was not even the slightest difference between the two so that not even one of the seventy-one judges could vote "not guilty," this was ample reason to believe that the witnesses had been carefully rehearsed and that the accusation and testimony was set-up.

The votes of the Sanhedrin were oral rather than by secret ballot. The question arises, suppose that seventy judges vote "guilty," and the seventy-first judge happens to feel that the defendant was not guilty. If he casts a "guilty" vote, then the rule that a unanimous guilty verdict results in acquittal will apply, and his opinion that the defendant is not guilty will be implemented. However, if he votes "not guilty," then there is no unanimous vote of "guilty," and the verdict will be that of the majority: guilty. Should this last judge, therefore, vote "guilty" in order to achieve the acquittal that he believes to be just?

The Ohr HaChaim says that the last judge must vote his opinion of "not guilty," even though that will result in the opposite of what he believes to be just. Why?

Because a person is obligated to speak the truth as he sees it, rather than consider the result.

According to Torah ethics, the process must be righteous, because it is the process that lies in human hands. Results are up to God.

שֹׁפְטִים וְשֹׁטְרִים תִּתֶּן־לְךָ . . . לֹא־תִטַּע לְךָ אֲשֵׁרָה כָּל־עֵץ אֵצֶל מִזְבַּח ה' אֱלֹקֶיךָ
Judges and officers shall you appoint . . . You shall not plant an idolatrous tree near the Altar of God (16:18-21)

Appointment of Judges

The Talmud says that the approximation of the prohibition of planting a tree near the altar to the mitzvah of appointing judges is to teach us that appointing an unsuitable person to be a judge is as grave a sin as planting an idolatrous tree near the Altar (*Sanhedrin* 7b).

The author of *Melo HaOmer* says that there is a significance in equating an unsuitable judge with an idolatrous tree.

Other forms of idolatry are easily recognizable statues or icons. A tree that is worshipped has no identifiable signs of being idolatrous. Its appearance is innocent, a tree like any other tree. However, this innocent appearance is deceptive. If it is an object of worship, it is in fact an idol.

The same principle holds true in the choice of judges. A person may give the appearance of being righteous and competent, but this may not be his true essence. A judge must be a person of impeccable integrity. Appointing an unsuitable judge on the basis of his external appearance is, therefore, similar to planting an idolatrous tree near the Altar.

The process of appointing judges in our society is often based on political considerations and rewards for loyalty to a successful candidate rather than on the judge's merits and integrity. The Torah warns us that this does not serve the cause of justice.

כִּי־יִמָּצֵא בְקִרְבְּךָ . . . אִישׁ אוֹ־אִשָּׁה אֲשֶׁר יַעֲשֶׂה אֶת־הָרַע בְּעֵינֵי ה' אֱלֹקֶיךָ . . . וַיֵּלֶךְ וַיַּעֲבֹד אֱלֹהִים אֲחֵרִים . . . אֲשֶׁר לֹא־צִוִּיתִי
"If there be found among you . . . a man or woman who commits what is evil in the eyes of God . . . and he will go and serve gods of others . . . which I have not commanded" (17:2-3)

Participation in Non-Jewish Services

"Which I have not commanded"? The verse should more properly have said, "which I had forbidden."

R' Pinchas Halevi Horowitz (*Haflaah*) states that a person may err and think that there may be times when serving other gods is actually a mitzvah, something of which God approves. The Torah therefore says, "I did not instruct you to do such 'mitzvos.'"

The Haflaah's interpretation is nothing less than prophetic. In Eastern Europe in the 18th century it was unthinkable that anyone could possibly consider serving other gods to be a mitzvah. This phenomenon did not occur until the 20th century, when interfaith services gained popularity. Some people thought that by sharing in non-Jewish services, we would develop a more benign relationship with non-Jews and that this would reduce anti-Semitism. They saw interfaith services as a mitzvah.

DEVARIM / DEUTERONOMY: Shoftim

Recent history has proven these misguided people wrong. Whatever the causes of anti-Semitism are, they are not affected in the least by interfaith services. In fact, any attempt at eliminating the differences between Jew and non-Jew in the hope of reducing anti-Semitism cannot succeed.

There was a campaign to eliminate "restricted" ads, wherein hotel and country clubs discriminated against Jews. Just a bit of thought will indicate that these were not intended to keep out Torah-observant Jews. What would a person who observes kosher possibly do in a *tereifah* hotel? The discrimination was precisely against those who sought to mix and increase socialization with non-Jews by dispensing with the laws of the Torah.

Good intentions are not reliable. It is possible to conjure up "mitzvos" which are the antithesis of Torah.

כִּי יִפָּלֵא מִמְּךָ דָבָר לַמִּשְׁפָּט בֵּין־דָּם לְדָם
בֵּין־דִּין לְדִין וּבֵין נֶגַע לָנֶגַע דִּבְרֵי רִיבֹת בִּשְׁעָרֶיךָ

If a matter of judgment is hidden from you, between blood and blood, between verdict and verdict, between plague and plague, matters of dispute in your cities (17:8)

Divisiveness: Our Undoing Then and Now

The Midrash states that the heavenly angels asked God why so much Jewish blood has been shed, why Jews suffer from harsh judgments and why they are exiled. God said, "Because there is no peace among them."

The Ari z"l said that this is indicated in the above verse. If you wonder why Jewish blood is so readily shed, why Jews are the victims of harsh verdicts and why they are driven from country to country, it is because of "matters of dispute in your communities," because of the dissension among Jews.

Alas! We fail to learn from history. For more than 2,000 years we have suffered indescribable calamities: exile, expulsions, pogroms, the Holocaust and now terrorism. This tragic course of events resulted from only one shortcoming: divisiveness and dissension among us. The Talmud tells that if there were true unity among Jews, we would be invincible. Yet, we continue the same behavior that has been responsible for all these miseries.

We have already related that Chiel the Beth-elite, with full knowledge of Joshua's curse that anyone who built up Jericho would lose his children, defiantly rebuilt it. When he laid the foundations, his oldest child died, and his children continued dying until his youngest child died when the rebuilding was complete (*I Kings* 16:34). We might wonder: how could Chiel not see the tragic consequences of his defying the curse? But are we any different? Do we not continue to reject a certain salvation by continuing the toxic divisiveness among us?

In my work treating alcoholics I regularly see people who refuse to recognize that their drinking is the cause of their ruination. At some point, when they reach a "rock-bottom," their suffering breaks through their denial and they recognize alcohol as being the culprit.

Were the horrors of the Holocaust not a sufficiently severe "rock-bottom"? Do we have to invite additional suffering before we come to the realization that in spite of our differences, we must find ways to bridge the gaps and have true unity?

The Ari z"l's interpretation of the above verse leaves nothing to the imagination. If we ask why we have experienced so many calamities, there is only one answer: "matters of dispute in your communities."

כִּי־תָבֹא אֶל־הָאָרֶץ אֲשֶׁר ה׳ אֱלֹקֶיךָ נֹתֵן לָךְ . . .
וְאָמַרְתָּ אָשִׂימָה עָלַי מֶלֶךְ . . . שׂוֹם תָּשִׂים עָלֶיךָ מֶלֶךְ

When you come to the Land that God gives you . . .
and you will say, "I will set a king over myself" . . .
You shall surely set a king over yourself (17:14-15)

Deference to Authority

Many of the Torah commentaries ask, Inasmuch as appointing a king is a mitzvah, why did Samuel rebuke the Israelites sharply when they requested a king (*I Samuel* 8:5)?

A number of answers have been given to this question. Perhaps the most satisfying is that of the *Klei Yakar*, who directs our attention to a subtle nuance in the verses of *Deuteronomy* and *Samuel*.

It is a mitzvah to appoint a king when the intention is, "I will set a king *over myself*," i.e., when one is willing to subordinate oneself to the king's rule and accept his authority. Close attention to the request of the Israelites of the Prophet Samuel show that they requested, "Give *unto us* a king," not a king *over us* whom we will obey, but rather a king *unto us* who will cater to our wishes. It was this request that angered the prophet.

A term frequently used to refer to a rabbi is "spiritual leader." Alas! Not infrequently, the rabbi is a spiritual *follower* rather than leader.

> *Rabbi Yisroel of Salant commented on the Talmud that describes the sorry state of affairs that will prevail before the Ultimate Redemption, among them, "the face, i.e., the leaders, of the generation will be similar to dogs" (Sanhedrin 97a). He said that a dog often runs ahead of its master, but then looks back to see whether the master has turned the corner. If he sees that the master has veered off in another direction, he runs back to follow him.*
>
> *"That is how the leaders will be before the Ultimate Redemption," R' Yisroel said. "They may give the appearance of leading the community, but like a dog watching its master, they turn around to see which way the community is heading, and they follow them."*

We must accept authentic leadership and defer to authority, rather than expect the leaders to follow us.

תָּמִים תִּהְיֶה עִם ה׳ אֱלֹקֶיךָ

You shall be wholehearted with your God (18:13)

To Be with God

Alshich interprets this verse to mean that one should be sincere in his observance of Torah even when one is alone with God, when no one else sees what one is doing.

R' Mendel of Kotzk comments, "Your devotion toward God should be whole, and not fragmented. If you do some things for God and others for yourself, then you are not being wholehearted with God."

These two interpretations are complementary. The person who is observant of Torah only when others see him, but when in complete privacy may transgress Torah, is really not devoted to God at all. Rather, his public observance of mitzvos is self-serving.

The comment of R' Mendel goes a bit further. There are many permissible things that we may do primarily for our own satisfaction. One may enjoy a sumptuous kosher meal, and feel that by observing the kosher laws one is serving God. R' Mendel says that this is fragmented, because his partaking of tasty food is self-serving.

Wholeheartedness with God requires that even those permissible things we do should be directed toward the Divine service. Ideally, food should be eaten not for the gustatory delight, but because the energy derived from eating the food can be utilized in doing mitzvos.

Yet another translation of the above verse is, "Be *perfect* with your God." Man can never achieve perfection on his own. However, if one lives in a way that unites him with God, then man can indeed be perfect as he becomes one with God.

Our ethical works state that when a person sheds his ego and effaces himself totally before God, he does indeed unite with God. In this way, a human being can achieve perfection.

מִי־הָאִישׁ אֲשֶׁר בָּנָה בַיִת־חָדָשׁ וְלֹא חֲנָכוֹ
יֵלֵךְ וְיָשֹׁב לְבֵיתוֹ פֶּן־יָמוּת בַּמִּלְחָמָה וְאִישׁ אַחֵר יַחְנְכֶנּוּ

When the Israelites went to war, the High Priest announced the exemptions.
"Who is the man who has built a new house and has not inaugurated it?
Let him return to his house, lest he die in the war
and another man will inaugurate it" (20:5)

Distorted Values

On the words, "another man will inaugurate it," Rashi comments, "And this is a matter of aggravation."

The Rebbe of Gur asked, is not the person's death in war a far greater source of grief than the fact that the new house will be inaugurated by someone other than its builder?

The Rebbe answered, indeed so. And this is precisely what Rashi means. If a person is exempt from battle because he is concerned that in the event he is killed, his house will be inaugurated by a stranger, *that* is a matter of aggravation. One would assume that a person who knows that he will be exposed to danger will do proper *teshuvah*, realizing that it may be his last opportunity to do so. These are the moments in which he has an opportunity to redeem his life with *teshuvah*. If, at such a moment, the only thing that concerns a person is that the house he built may be inaugurated by someone else, that is indeed a tragic state of affairs.

Our lives have both physical and spiritual components. Our physical lives on earth are of transient nature. Our spiritual lives are eternal. If one's earthly possessions are more dear to a person than his spiritual life, it is indeed tragic.

This is hardly restricted to soldiers about to go into battle. Every day of our lives we have the choice of giving primary importance to either our spiritual or physical lives. Many people devote the lion's share of their time and energy to their physical rather than their spiritual welfare. If our physical welfare takes priority, it is indeed a tragic state of affairs.

לֹא נוֹדַע מִי הִכָּהוּ ... וְאַתָּה תְּבַעֵר הַדָּם הַנָּקִי מִקִּרְבֶּךָ כִּי־תַעֲשֶׂה הַיָּשָׁר בְּעֵינֵי ה׳

The Torah states that if a corpse is found murdered and, *"it was not known who smote him,"* then the leaders of the nearest community must bring a sacrificial offering. The Torah closes this *parashah* with, *"You shall remove the innocent blood from your midst when you do what is upright in the eyes of God"* (21:1-9)

Acknowledging a Misdeed

R' Yehudah Leib Chasman asks, What if the assailant is identified, but for any one of many reasons cannot be brought to justice? Is there then no need for forgiveness?

R' Chasman says that whenever a crime occurs, there is reason for the community to ask forgiveness. A community must share in the responsibility for a crime committed in its midst. If there was a true "zero tolerance," crime would be discouraged. We may speak of "zero tolerance," but the fact is that there are abundant loopholes that are provided for criminals.

However, if it is not known how the victim met his death, the community may rationalize: Perhaps it was an accidental death rather than murder. Perhaps the victim was the attacker and was slain by someone in self-defense. Perhaps the assailant was a robber from outside the community. There are many ways in which the community may divest itself of any culpability.

This, says R' Chasman, is the most serious sin. The prophet says, "I will judge you for saying 'I did not do wrong' " (*Jeremiah* 2:35). A person may plead something in an attempt to defend himself, and even though these excuses are not acceptable, there is nevertheless an awareness that one has done wrong. The realization that one has sinned opens the door for *teshuvah*. Failure to acknowledge that one has sinned makes *teshuvah* impossible.

Not knowing how a person met his death may allow people to deny their dereliction. This is why these specific circumstances require a ritual wherein the community considers its responsibility.

The closing verse follows the theme of mutual responsibility. "You shall remove the innocent blood from your midst when you do what is upright in the eyes of God." The greatest deterrent to crime is for everyone to do what is upright. No laws, no police system, no severity of punishment can deter crime as much as a total dedication to justice on the part of every single person in the community.

פרשת כי תצא
Parashas Ki Seitzei

כִּי־תֵצֵא לַמִּלְחָמָה עַל־אֹיְבֶיךָ וּנְתָנוֹ ה' אֱלֹקֶיךָ בְּיָדֶךָ וְשָׁבִיתָ שִׁבְיוֹ

When you will go out to war against your enemies, and God will deliver them into your hand, and you will capture its captivity (21:10)

The Cunning of the Yetzer Hara

Torah commentaries are unanimous in interpreting this verse as referring also to the internal war a person must wage against the *yetzer hara*. We are assured that if we are sincere in trying to defeat the *yetzer hara*, if only "we go out to do battle with the enemy," then God will assist us and we will triumph.

The phrase "you will capture its captivity" is interpreted to mean that we should take the stratagems of the *yetzer hara* and turn them against it. The works of *mussar* describe the cunning ways in which the *yetzer hara* tries to entice one to deviate from the proper ways of life.

In the treatment of addiction, alcohol and drugs are referred to as being "cunning, baffling and powerful." People recovering from addiction are warned to be ever on the alert for the sly ways in which they may be tricked into the use of mind-altering chemicals.

The prophet compares people who deviate from Torah to inebriates. "They are drunk, albeit not with wine; they blunder, albeit not with ale" (*Isaiah* 29:9). Perhaps an example of how cunning, baffling and powerful alcohol and drugs are can help us understand how vulnerable we may be to the cunning of the *yetzer hara*, and why we must always be on the alert for its sly tactics.

> *A doctor who specialized in internal medicine recovered from alcoholism. He then became very active in the treatment field, using his own experience to help others. Eventually he became the director of a facility to treat people addicted to alcohol and drugs. He did research in the field, published articles on the subject and lectured frequently. No one could be more intensely concerned and devoted toward the treatment of these addictions, and he regularly cautioned patients on the need to be ever alert not to relapse.*
>
> *After fourteen years of sobriety, he was found to have high blood pressure and was prescribed medication. After several months, he began experiencing unpleasant side-effects from the medication. His doctor*

discontinued this particular medication, and told him that before starting a different medication, he would have to wait a week to allow the traces of the first medication to leave his body, to avoid a possibly dangerous interaction.

"When you stop the first medication," the doctor said, "you may experience a rebound phenomenon, and your blood pressure may rise very high. So, until the week is over and you start the new medication, I want you to take 5 milligrams of Valium four times a day."

The internist said, "I can't take Valium. When I drank, I was also addicted to Valium."

"That should not be a problem," the doctor said. "I will give the medication to your wife, and she will give you one tablet four times a day for the week."

The wife filled the prescription, and gave her husband a 5 mg. tablet of Valium in the morning. Instead of swallowing it, he put it in his pocket, and did the same with the next few doses. He then took all four tablets at once to get the "high." The next day he repeated this, and on the third day, he wrote himself a prescription for fifty Valium tablets. He was right back in the throes of addiction.

Here we have a highly intelligent person, extremely knowledgeable about the dangers of addiction, yet he fell into the trap of addiction again.

Just as alcohol and drugs are "cunning, baffling and powerful," so is the *yetzer hara*. It is a mistake to think that you can outsmart it.

The only defense against the wile of the *yetzer hara* is to learn *mussar* every day, and to pray intensely to God for His assistance in resisting the *yetzer hara*.

וְרָאִיתָ בַּשִּׁבְיָה אֵשֶׁת יְפַת־תֹּאַר . . . וְלָקַחְתָּ לְךָ לְאִשָּׁה

The Torah states that if, in battle, *"You will see among its captivity a woman who is beautiful . . . you may take her to yourself for a wife"* (21:11)

The Hazard of Self-Righteousness

This unusual halachah is further complicated by Rashi's comment. "The Torah spoke only in response to the Evil Inclination. If this is not permitted, the man will transgress a prohibition and marry her anyway."

Nowhere in the Torah do we find a concession to the Evil Inclination. A person is expected to be able to restrain his own impulses and urges. Many Torah prohibitions demand self-mastery. Why is this an exception?

The Rebbe of Lublin suggested a possible reason. According to the Talmud, anyone who feared that because of his sins he would not have Divine protection in battle was exempt from going to war (*Sotah* 44a). The Shulchan Aruch states that even a relatively minor infraction, such as interrupting a prayer with conversation was an adequate reason to fear losing Divine protection (*Orach Chaim* 54).

If so, said the Rebbe of Lublin, then who *did* go to war? Only a person who felt he was totally free of even the slightest transgression. A person who is so self-righteous that he thinks himself to be so saintly is precisely the person who is suspect of yielding to the Evil Inclination.

This is an important insight. "There is no person on earth who does only good and never sins" (*Ecclesiastes* 7:20). The Talmud states that there were only four people throughout history who had not sinned. These are Benjamin, the son of Jacob; Amram, the father of Moses; Jesse, the father of David; and Kilav, the son of David (*Shabbos* 55b). How, then, can a mortal consider himself to be absolutely free of the slightest blemish? It can be only because one is oblivious of one's sins. Any person who thinks himself to be holy because he is in denial of his transgressions may indeed be suspect that he would not exercise self-restraint.

Awareness of our fallibility, recognizing our misdeeds and rectifying them by doing *teshuvah* strengthens a person's self-mastery.

כִּי־יִהְיֶה לְאִישׁ בֵּן סוֹרֵר וּמוֹרֶה אֵינֶנּוּ
שֹׁמֵעַ בְּקוֹל אָבִיו וּבְקוֹל אִמּוֹ . . . זוֹלֵל וְסֹבֵא

If a man will have a wayward and rebellious son, who does not hearken to the voice of his father and the voice of his mother . . . a glutton and a drunkard (21:18-20).

The Torah Understood Addiction

The Talmud says that the capital punishment of the wayward son was never carried out and is a technical impossibility. Why then does the Torah mention it? So that we will be rewarded for studying it (*Sanhedrin* 71a).

Is it logical to have a halachah that is a technical impossibility and is there only to be studied in theory? And what is the specific reward for this?

R' Elyah Lopian addresses this issue. He prefaces with a question. The Talmud says that the wayward son is a youth who steals to satisfy his gluttony and his craving for alcohol. The harsh punishment decreed by the Torah is not for the crime of theft, but because his behavior is certain to progress to the point where he will kill to satisfy his cravings.

R' Lopian says that the Torah relates that when God provided water for Ishmael to prevent him from dying of thirst in the arid desert, the angels protested, "Why save him? His descendants will kill Jews!" (as we so tragically know). God responded, "I do not judge people by what may transpire in the future." Why, then, is the wayward son punished for what he will do in the future?

R' Lopian answers that every person has freedom of choice in his moral and ethical behavior. Even a profligate sinner may do *teshuvah*. However, a youth who steals for food and drink has lost his freedom of choice. His cravings have overwhelmed his freedom of choice, and he is capable of eliminating anything that stands in the way of his gratifying his desires.

Anyone familiar with addiction recognizes the phenomenon R' Lopian describes. An addict essentially loses his freedom of choice and becomes enslaved by his addiction. I have repeatedly heard recovered addicts say, "When I needed drugs, I did things that I never thought myself capable of doing."

Any addiction can enslave a person, whether it be to alcohol, drugs, cigarettes or food. It is, therefore, extremely important that we take great precaution not to develop habits that can be destructive.

This is especially important for parents to know. It is not uncommon for parents to think that their son's frequent recourse to alcohol is a phase which he will outgrow. It is far more likely that the condition will progress to most serious proportions.

When parents become aware of use of drugs or excessive use of alcohol in a child, it is a mistake to think that asking or ordering him to stop will be effective. He may have lost his freedom of choice. Parents should consult someone with established competence in addiction, and follow the advice they are given.

Understanding the unrelenting course of addiction is a reward we receive from studying this portion of the Torah.

וְאָמְרוּ אֶל־זִקְנֵי עִירוֹ בְּנֵנוּ זֶה סוֹרֵר וּמֹרֶה אֵינֶנּוּ שֹׁמֵעַ בְּקֹלֵנוּ

The parents of the wayward son take him to the elders of the city and declare, *"This son of ours is wayward and rebellious. He does not hearken to our voice"* (21:20)

The Basic Rule of Parenting

The Talmud cites the verse, "He does not hearken to our voice, " and comments, "their voices must be equal" (*Sanhedrin* 71a). If the parents' voices are not equal, the wayward son is exempt from punishment.

The author of *Ollelos Ephraim* says that if the parents did not speak with one voice, the son cannot be held culpable for his misbehavior.

It is a cardinal rule of parenting that the parents should have a uniform and consistent code of parenting. If one parent is strict and the other permissive, the child is confused and may not know what is right and what is wrong.

Unfortunately, this rule too often goes unheeded. Each of the parents may have a different theory of parenting. Each parent may have received a different type of parenting, and carries this over to the next generation. Sometimes, parents even use the child against one another.

When parents run into difficulty with a child, they may seek expert counseling. As wise as this is, it is unfortunately a bit late. If the child's problem is due to faulty parenting, it may be difficult to undo the effects.

Parenting is the single greatest responsibility a person has. Children do not ask to be brought into the world. Bringing them into the world places a responsibility upon the parents to give them the best chance to achieve a constructive and happy life.

Before one is granted a driver's license, one must pass a test to assure that one understands the basic laws of driving. One is then given a road test to make certain one has the necessary technical abilities to drive an automobile.

Raising a child is at least as important as driving an automobile. What education do prospective parents receive to assure that they have the necessary knowledge to raise a child?

It is most important that a newlywed couple promptly begin learning how to be effective parents. There are a number of authoritative books on parenting. There are indeed various theories on parenting, and it is difficult to determine which is the best. However, whatever method is chosen, there should be unanimity between the parents.

The Ollelos Ephraim is correct. Parents should speak with one voice.

The Talmud also derives from the Torah that if the parents were deaf or mute, the wayward son is exempt from punishment. Their auditory system and speech abilities may be functioning perfectly well, but if parents are "deaf" to a child's needs and are "mute" in that they do not know how to speak to a child, we cannot hold the wayward youth culpable. Working with young people who have used drugs, I have often heard them say, "My parents never heard me," or "I never heard a good word from my father."

As I said in the previous essay, the Talmud says that the capital punishment of the wayward son was never carried out and is a technical impossibility. Why then does the Torah mention it? So that we will be rewarded by studying it (*Sanhedrin* 71a). If we study this chapter properly, we will learn what it is telling us about proper parenting. That is our reward.

לֹא־תִרְאֶה אֶת־שׁוֹר אָחִיךָ אוֹ אֶת־שֵׂיוֹ
נִדָּחִים וְהִתְעַלַּמְתָּ מֵהֶם הָשֵׁב תְּשִׁיבֵם לְאָחִיךָ

You shall not see the ox of your brother or his sheep or
his goat cast off and hide yourself from them;
you shall surely return them to your brother (22:1).

R' Meir Simchah of Dvinsk notes that in *Exodus* 23:5 we find a similar mitzvah to be considerate of another person's animal. That verse reads, "If you see the donkey of someone you hate crouching under his burden you shall help repeatedly with him."

On this latter verse, the Talmud asks, "How does the Torah condone hating someone?" The Talmud answers, "This means that he hates someone because that person has behaved immorally" (*Pesachim* 113a). One is permitted to despise depraved behavior.

Why, then does the Torah not use the same expression in Deuteronomy? Why does it use the term "your brother?"

R' Meir Simchah's answer is something that everyone should take to heart. It is a vital concept, whose observance could be our salvation.

The mitzvah in Exodus, R' Meir Simchah says, was given before the sin of the Golden Calf. At that time, all the Israelites were in an exceptionally elevated state of spirituality, similar to that of angels. If anyone rejected this spiritual state to engage in loathsome behavior, it was permissible to despise him. After the sin of the Golden Calf, when we no longer have this level of spirituality, we must realize how vulnerable we all are to improper behavior, and it is, therefore, forbidden to hate any person, regardless of how objectionable his behavior may be. Today we are all brothers, and the commandment, "You shall not hate your brother in your heart" (*Leviticus* 19:17) applies to everyone without exception.

The Talmud says that Jerusalem was destroyed and we were driven into exile because of the hatred and dissension that prevailed among us. We hope for the Ultimate Redemption. We can hasten the Redemption by incorporating R' Meir Simchah's teaching in our lives, and have love for one another without exception.

וְכֵן תַּעֲשֶׂה לְכָל־אֲבֵדַת אָחִיךָ אֲשֶׁר־תֹּאבַד מִמֶּנּוּ וּמְצָאתָהּ לֹא תוּכַל לְהִתְעַלֵּם

The Torah says that if one finds a lost object, he must make every effort to return it to its owner. Keeping such an item is tantamount to theft. The verse reads, *"So shall you do for any lost article of your brother that may become lost from him and you find it; you are unable to hide from it"* (22:3)

We Cannot Deceive Our Conscience

It is noteworthy that the Torah does not use the expression for other prohibitions, i.e, "You *shall not* hide from it." Rather, it says "You *are unable* to hide from it." The Torah is not only giving a commandment but is also stating a fact: you are unable to hide from a wrongful act. Inasmuch as no one knows that you found the item, there is no way you can be brought to justice. However, your conscience will not give you any peace of mind.

There are, of course, some people whom we refer to as "sociopaths," who appear to lack any conscience. However, most people do have a conscience, which will not exonerate any wrongdoing.

When guilt is the result of a wrongful act, it is a healthy feeling, not to be confused with unwarranted guilt feelings that are a psychological problem. The discomfort of healthy guilt should lead a person to rectify his misdeed and prevent its repetition. Of course, one may try to do away with the discomfort of guilt by rationalization, but this self-deception is ultimately futile. The person may then use any one of many psychological defense mechanisms, which invariably result in dysfunction.

The Midrash says that the mitzvos were given for no other reason than to refine a person's character. The mitzvah of returning a lost item is an example of this. God does not accrue any benefit when a person observes this mitzvah, but the person who observes it benefits greatly.

לֹא־תִרְאֶה אֶת־חֲמוֹר אָחִיךָ אוֹ שׁוֹרוֹ נֹפְלִים
בַּדֶּרֶךְ וְהִתְעַלַּמְתָּ מֵהֶם הָקֵם תָּקִים עִמּוֹ

You shall not see the donkey of your brother or his ox falling on the road and hide yourself from them; you shall surely stand them up, with him (22:4)

We Are Brothers unto Each Other, and Children unto God

Rashi states that the last two words, "with him" are a qualifier. One is required to help only if the animal's owner participates. However, if the owner sits back and says, "It's your mitzvah, you do it," one is not obligated to help.

Based on this, the Chafetz Chaim says that when we ask God for spiritual growth, as we say in our prayer, "and unify our hearts to love and to fear Your Name," we cannot expect God to do this for us unless we make an effort. If we sit back and ask God to do it for us, we cannot expect to be elevated spiritually.

Some commentaries seem to say that just a sincere desire to be helped spiritually is enough to warrant Divine assistance. They cite the Midrash, "Open for me a portal of *teshuvah* as tiny as the eye of a needle, and I will open for you portals so wide that wagons could go through" (*Shir Hashirim Rabbah* 5:3). *Teshuvah* can begin with just the thought that one wishes to improve, even before any specific effort is made. How do they interpret the term "with him," which indicates a need for active participation?

The answer may be that the verse in Deuteronomy refers to a brother, who is not obligated to provide assistance without the subject's participation. However, we relate to God not as brothers, but as children to a father. A loving father may grant a child's wish and fulfill his request even without the child actually doing anything.

God is a loving father. If we sincerely pray for His help in becoming more spiritual, He will certainly grant our wish.

לֹא־תַחֲרֹשׁ בְּשׁוֹר־וּבַחֲמֹר יַחְדָּו

You shall not plow with an ox and a donkey together (22:10)

To Be Considerate of Others

R' Gershon Henoch, the rebbe of Rodzin, once entered a shul in a small town. He saw a group of poor people huddling together, and the tone of their conversation clearly indicated that they were very angry. Upon inquiring the reason for their anger, he was told that a wealthy citizen of the community was marrying off a son, and had made a lavish party but would not allow the poor to partake in it.

"Come with me," R' Gershon Henoch said. He knocked on the door of the wealthy man's home, and was greeted with, "No strangers are invited today."

"I am not interested in being at the party," he said. "I am looking for the rabbi, because I have an urgent halachah question which requires the rabbi's attention."

They escorted R' Gershon Henoch to the rabbi who sat at the head of the table. "I have an urgent question to ask you," he said. "Why does the Torah forbid plowing with an ox and donkey together?"

The rabbi responded, "That is not an urgent question which justifies interrupting this wedding celebration. Furthermore, we do not look for reasons for the mitzvos of the Torah. We accept them as Divine commandments."

R' Gershon Henoch said, "But we are in fact permitted to understand some mitzvos. I beg your indulgence to hear the reason for this mitzvah.

"An ox chews its cud, whereas a donkey does not. If the donkey sees the ox chewing, it will think that the ox has been fed while it, the donkey, has not been fed. This will cause the donkey great distress, and the Torah wishes to prevent even an animal from suffering.

"So I must ask the rabbi," R' Gershon Henoch said, "if the Torah is *considerate even of a donkey, how can you be sitting at a sumptuous meal while the poor are hungry for food?"*

The rabbi promptly instructed the host to invite the poor to the wedding feast.

לֹא־יָבֹא עַמּוֹנִי וּמוֹאָבִי בִּקְהַל ה׳ . . . עַל־דְּבַר אֲשֶׁר לֹא־קִדְּמוּ אֶתְכֶם בַּלֶּחֶם וּבַמַּיִם בַּדֶּרֶךְ בְּצֵאתְכֶם מִמִּצְרָיִם

An Ammonite or Moabite shall not enter the congregation of God . . . because of the fact they did not greet you with bread and water on the road when you were leaving Egypt (23:4-5)

Behavioral Problems May Have a Subtle Beginning

The commentaries ask, inasmuch as the Ammonites and Moabites sought to destroy the Israelites, that is far worse than failing to greet them with bread and water. Why does the Torah reject them for this lesser misdeed?

R' Yaakov Neiman (*Darkei Mussar*) says that when you see someone who wishes to annihilate an entire nation, you can be certain that this cruelty developed gradually. Initially the person refrained from doing acts of kindness, and the hardening of his heart progressed to his being capable of merciless killing.

We must be on guard for things than can unwittingly result in character deterioration. I know of instances where people of good character allowed themselves to use alcohol to excess, thinking that it would not affect them negatively, and suffered severe personality deterioration.

> *One time, someone told the Alter (Elder) of Kelm about a strange phenomenon. A drunkard was lying in the gutter, and while children gathered around and jeered him, he poured forth with words of Torah. The Alter investigated and found out that this person had been a fine Torah scholar who had taken to drink, leading to such deterioration. The Alter said, "If this is what alcohol is capable of doing, I will never again allow spirits to be on my table. If alcohol can do this to a Torah scholar, it is a killer that I will not allow on my table" (Lekach Tov vol. 2 Devarim, p. 61).*

While drinking a L'Chaim has been a long standing tradition, this does not justify drinking to excess. Unfortunately, as the case above indicates, alcohol can cause the ruination of even a fine Torah scholar.

Especially in modern times, when young people are easy prey to mind-altering drugs, we should model for them that excessive drinking is repugnant.

What about Purim? Is it not a mitzvah to get drunk on Purim? The final authority on the Shulchan Aruch is the *Mishnah Berurah*, which states that the proper way to fulfill "not discerning between cursed be Haman and blessed be Mordechai" is to follow the opinion of *Rema*, who says to drink *just a bit more* than one is accustomed and to go to sleep. When one is asleep, one does not discern between cursed be Haman and blessed be Mordechai (*Shulchan Aruch, Orach Chaim* 695:2, *Mishnah Berurah* §5). There is no need to become intoxicated.

The Mishnah Berurah was written by the Chafetz Chaim. Anyone who wishes to observe this mitzvah in a manner that surpasses the Chafetz Chaim's standard must be consistent and observe *all* mitzvos in a way that surpasses the Chafetz Chaim's standards.

כִּי־תִדֹּר נֶדֶר לַה' אֱלֹקֶיךָ לֹא תְאַחֵר לְשַׁלְּמוֹ
כִּי־דָרֹשׁ יִדְרְשֶׁנּוּ ה' אֱלֹקֶיךָ מֵעִמָּךְ וְהָיָה בְךָ חֵטְא

When you make a vow to God, you shall not be late in paying it, for God will demand it of you and there will be a sin in you (23:22)

Do Not Bring About Temptation

It stands to reason that if a person reneges on a vow, he will have [commited] a sin. Why does the Torah add the phrase "there will be a sin in you" in this particular commandment, whereas it does not do so with other transgressions?

The Maggid of Dubnow answers with one of his incomparable parables.

> A man once visited a prison, and he saw the inmates all working at hard labor. He saw their food rations, which were very sparse. However, there was one cell that was comfortably furnished, and its occupant was served a good meal. "Why is this inmate receiving special treatment?" he asked.
>
> The warden explained, "He is not a criminal like the others. He was in business for years, but toward the end his business began to fail. He borrowed huge sums of money to try to rescue his business, but to no avail. He was sentenced to prison for defaulting on his debts."
>
> The visitor then went to the most luxurious hotel in the city and rented their finest suite. After dining richly for two weeks, he was given a bill, but he stated that he did not have a cent to pay. He was brought before the judge and was sentenced to hard labor.
>
> "But why am I being sentenced to hard labor?" he protested. "That man who defaulted on his debts is very comfortable in prison and does not have to do work!"
>
> The judge said, "How can you compare yourself to him? He was a decent businessman for many years. When he feared his business was failing, he tried to shore it up with borrowed money. He never intended to defraud anyone. He had every intention of paying the loans. But you knowingly ran up a huge debt that you knew you could not pay. That is a serious crime."
>
> The Maggid said, "So it is with the sin if you violate a vow. A person does not knowingly incite himself to temptation. He happened to be in a situation where his yetzer hara overwhelmed him. His sin is not as grave as yours. No one asked you to make a vow. You, of your own accord, made a pledge which you probably never intended to pay. Now you have a real sin."

While there is no excuse for sin, a person may plead for mercy because he was not strong enough to withstand temptation. But when a person brings temptation on himself, that sin is much more serious.

If one watches prurient television programs or otherwise exposes himself to things that may lead to improper thoughts and deeds, one is inviting sin. It is bad enough when one commits a sin under circumstances that whet his desires, but to create such circumstances is truly a grievous sin.

> כִּי־יִקַּח אִישׁ אִשָּׁה . . . וְהָיָה אִם־לֹא
> תִמְצָא־חֵן בְּעֵינָיו . . . וְכָתַב לָהּ סֵפֶר כְּרִיתֻת
>
> ***If a man marries a woman . . . and it will be that she will not
> find favor in his eyes . . . he wrote her a bill of divorce*** (24:1)

Shalom Bayis

Although the Torah permits divorce, every attempt is made to restore harmony in the couple. A spouse may impulsively seek a divorce, and more sober thinking may cause one to reconsider.

A man once consulted R' Aryeh Levin, stating that he wished to divorce his wife and relating a list of complaints he had about her. R' Levin said, "Marriage and divorce are the most momentous steps in life, and I cannot respond to you without giving it very serious consideration.

"I plan to spend tomorrow morning visiting the graves of tzaddikim. Perhaps you can meet me at the cemetery, and I will have an answer for you."

The next morning, the man met R' Levin at the cemetery. R' Levin said, "I could hardly sleep last night, rethinking the problems between you and your wife. As I walked around the graves here, I was deeply impressed by the realization of how brief our stay in this world is, and it is not right to spend these few years in strife."

R' Levin paused a bit, then said, "I am usually hesitant to approve of divorce. I am concerned about the happiness of both the husband and wife. But in this case, I see no reason to discourage it. You will be better off without her, and she is a young and attractive woman, and you admitted that she is a very capable and conscientious housewife. It's just that some things about her do not appeal to you. She will have no difficulty in remarrying. She has many fine qualities which are not of value to you, but they will be appreciated by her next husband.

"Just look around here at the tombstones," R' Levin said. "We don't live eternally, and in this short lifetime, why should one be miserable these few years? I think that a divorce is proper."

The man thought a bit, then said, "But maybe I should try again. As you said, she has some fine qualities and is a capable housewife."

"I said?" R' Levin remarked. "I did not say it. You did. Perhaps you were not aware of her personality before you married her, in which case the marriage was an error. But those very qualities which you do not appreciate may be very desirable to another man, and I am certain she will find someone who will appreciate her.'

The man said, "Well, perhaps I was a bit too hasty. Perhaps we can work things out between us after all."

Was R' Levin's tactic merely "reverse psychology?" Hardly. His choice of the cemetery as a meeting place was not to impress the husband that one should get the most out of a brief life, but to the contrary, that the brevity of life should make one give more serious consideration to a relationship, rather than terminate it because one has been less than satisfied.

What R' Levin achieved was not necessarily a reconciliation, but rather a reconsideration which could reveal that the marriage was indeed compatible.

זָכוֹר אֵת אֲשֶׁר־עָשָׂה ה' אֱלֹקֶיךָ לְמִרְיָם בַּדֶּרֶךְ בְּצֵאתְכֶם מִמִּצְרָיִם

Remember what God did to Miriam on the way when you were leaving Egypt (24:9).

The Remembrance of Miriam

This refers to the incident where Miriam was critical of Moses for becoming celibate. Inasmuch as there is no requirement for a prophet to be celibate, why did Moses choose to do so? For speaking this way about Moses, Miriam was punished with *tzaraas*, a severe disease affecting the skin (*Numbers* 12:1-16).

Miriam was Moses' older sister, and she was devoted to her younger brother since his birth (*Exodus* 2:1-9). She was a prophetess in her own right, and it was through her great merit that the Israelites were provided with water in the desert (*Taanis* 9a). Her comments about Moses were not derogatory; yet, because she failed to appreciate Moses' uniqueness, she was smitten with *tzaraas*.

The Chafetz Chaim bewails the prevalence of *lashon hara*, and how grave a sin it is. If the prophetess Miriam was punished so severely for a comment that was on the far periphery of *lashon hara*, then how grievous is the sin of one who makes frankly defamatory comments about another person.

How is the remembrance of the Miriam incident to discourage one from *lashon hara*? It is not enough to say the words. R' Shlomo Wolbe in *Alei Shur* says that with all the remembrances required by the Torah we must use visual imagery. In remembering the giving of the Torah at Sinai, we should visualize the three million Israelites gathered around the mountain which was aflame and trembling, the thunder and lightning, the sound of the shofar, and Moses ascending to the top of the flaming mountain. Similarly, we should visualize this holy prophetess making what might seem to be an innocent comment, yet being stricken with a disfiguring and embarassing condition. A mental picture of this tragic event is likely to make one rethink one's words.

כִּי תִקְצֹר קְצִירְךָ בְשָׂדֶךָ וְשָׁכַחְתָּ עֹמֶר בַּשָּׂדֶה
לֹא תָשׁוּב לְקַחְתּוֹ לַגֵּר לַיָּתוֹם וְלָאַלְמָנָה יִהְיֶה
לְמַעַן יְבָרֶכְךָ ה' אֱלֹקֶיךָ בְּכֹל מַעֲשֵׂה יָדֶיךָ

When you reap your harvest in your field and you forget a bundle in the field, you shall not turn back to take it; it shall be for the proselyte, the orphan and the widow, so that God will bless you in all your handiwork (24:19).

The Subconscious Mitzvah

The psychological elucidation of the workings of the subconscious mind have given us a better understanding of the Torah.

There is a discussion in the Talmud about a Jewish person who was raised in a non-Jewish environment and was never aware of Shabbos. If he later becomes aware of Shabbos and that he had done things on Shabbos which are forbidden, does he have to bring a sin-offering or not? The reasoning of

Munbuz, who says that he does not have to bring a sin-offering is that the Torah uses the word "sinner" for both intentional and inadvertent violations. Just as an intentional violator had an awareness of Shabbos, the unintentional violator is culpable only if he had an awareness of Shabbos. You cannot apply the term "sinner" to a person who had never heard of Shabbos (*Shabbos* 68b).

Why is an unintentional act considered a sin? Because there is adequate psychological grounds for holding a person responsible for even an unintentional act. Psychoanalytic theory says that there are no truly "accidental" acts. There is motivation behind every act, and if it is not conscious motivation, it is subconscious motivation. But if a person never knew of Shabbos, there could not be any subconscious motivation.

One psychologist was asked, "Do you hold a person responsible for his subconscious mind?" He responded, "And whom would you hold responsible for this person's subconscious?"

Just as there may be subconscious motivation for a sin, there may also be subconscious motivation for a mitzvah. The person who forgets a bundle of grain in the field is rewarded that "God will bless you in all your handiwork." His forgetting the bundle is a virtue, just as forgetting Shabbos is a fault.

We will be duly rewarded for all the mitzvos that we do "unintentionally," because we are motivated to do them, albeit subconsciously.

פרשת כי תבוא
Parashas Ki Savo

וְהָיָה כִּי־תָבוֹא אֶל־הָאָרֶץ אֲשֶׁר ה׳ אֱלֹקֶיךָ נֹתֵן לָךְ . . .
וְלָקַחְתָּ מֵרֵאשִׁית כָּל־פְּרִי הָאֲדָמָה . . . וְשַׂמְתָּ בַטֶּנֶא
וְהָלַכְתָּ אֶל־הַמָּקוֹם אֲשֶׁר יִבְחַר ה׳ אֱלֹקֶיךָ לְשַׁכֵּן שְׁמוֹ שָׁם

It will be when you enter the Land that God gives you...
that you shall take of the very first of every fruit of the ground...
and you shall put it in a basket and go to the place that
God will choose to make His Name rest there (26:1-2)

The Centrality of Gratitude

This is the mitzvah of *bikkurim*, of bringing the first-ripened fruit to the Sanctuary and giving thanks to God for His bounty.

There is a cryptic statement in Sifri: "Do this mitzvah, for by its merit you will enter the Land." Inasmuch as the mitzvah of *bikkurim* could not be done until *after* the Land was settled, how could the entrance to the Land be contingent on the performance of this mitzvah?

The essence of the mitzvah of *bikkurim* is *gratitude*. What the Sifri means is that by virtue of acknowledging God's bounty and giving thanks for it, they would merit inheriting the Land. One of Moses' sharpest rebukes was the Israelites' reluctance to be grateful (v. supra The Importance of Gratitude).

The importance of gratitude is evident in that the Torah does nor refer to the festival of Shavuos as the day the Torah was given, but rather as the "Day of *Bikkurim*" (*Numbers* 28:26). The mitzvah of gratitude outweighed even the momentous occasion of the giving of the Torah at Sinai.

R' Chaim Shmulevitz cites the Midrash that when God told Moses to go to Egypt to deliver the Israelites from their cruel enslavement, Moses said, "I cannot go until I take leave from Jethro, who took me into his home when I was a wanderer" (*Shemos Rabbah* 4:2). Think of it! Moses has a direct command from God, and it is to deliver the Israelites from the inhuman slavery in Egypt, but Moses says that he cannot go without taking leave of Jethro! R' Shmulevitz says that Moses knew that it was indeed God's will that he do so, because gratitude is fundamental to Godliness (*Sichos Mussar* 5732:32).

R' Shmulevitz goes on to say that gratitude is so vital a trait, that one is required to be grateful to even an inanimate object. When the Egyptians were to be smitten with the first plague of the Nile turning into blood, God told Moses to have Aaron initiate this plague. Moses was not to smite the river which had sheltered him when he was an infant. Similarly, the plague of frogs was done through Aaron, because this, too, required involvement of the river.

The river is not a sentient being that can be offended or appreciate an expression of gratitude. However, gratitude is so important a trait in character refinement that we must practice it toward even an inanimate object.

Expressing our gratitude toward God is the central theme of prayer. Our very first words upon awakening in the morning are *modeh ani,* an expression of thanks to God for giving us another day of life.

We must model gratitude for our children. Children are often reluctant to express gratitude. A mother's instruction to her five-year-old child, "Say 'thank you' to the nice man for the candy," is often met with a grunt, indicating his refusal to do so. We can only conclude that reluctance to express gratitude is innate in children, and it is important that this resistance be overcome. This can best be accomplished by the parents modeling gratitude. Husbands and wives may take for granted the things that they do for each other. Saying "thank you" when the wife serves a meal or when the husband does the dishes is an important lesson for the children.

The Midrash describes the adornments of the *bikkurim* and the special honor that was shown to those who performed this mitzvah. No other mitzvah receives such celebration. It is the Torah's way of impressing upon us that gratitude is the foundation of *middos* (desirable character traits).

וְלָקַחְתָּ מֵרֵאשִׁית כָּל־פְּרִי הָאֲדָמָה . . . וְשַׂמְתָּ בַטֶּנֶא וְהָלַכְתָּ אֶל־הַמָּקוֹם אֲשֶׁר יִבְחַר ה׳ אֱלֹקֶיךָ לְשַׁכֵּן שְׁמוֹ שָׁם

You shall take of the first of every fruit of the ground . . .
and you shall put it in a basket and go to the place
that God will choose, to make His Name rest there" (26:2).

Do Not Debase a Mitzvah

The Talmud quotes an aphorism, "Poverty stalks the poor," and gives an example the mitzvah of *bikkurim.* The Mishnah says that the gold and silver bowls in which the wealthy brought the fruits were returned to them, whereas the baskets of reeds of the poor were kept in the Sanctuary (*Bava Kamma* 92a).

> Why was this so? R' David of Talna explained.
>
> "When I sent a message to a town that I was coming for a visit, the news was received ecstatically in the shul. One of my poor chassidim came home in high spirits. "The rebbe is coming to town," he said to his wife. But then his demeanor suddenly turned morose.
>
> "What is the matter?" his wife asked. "You were just so euphoric about the rebbe's visit."
>
> The husband responded, "It is customary to give the rebbe some money for tzedakah, but I have nothing to give."
>
> "Don't let that worry you. I will do some baking and sell the pastries, and

I'll be able to put together a ruble for tzedakah." Upon hearing this, the husband's joy returned.

The same morning, a wealthy man returned from shul downcast. "What is he matter?" the wife asked. "Did anything bad happen?"

"Not really," the husband said. "The rebbe is coming for a visit."

"Why should that depress you?" the wife asked.

"Don't you understand? The rebbe is going to request a large donation for tzedakah from me. I can see another 50 rubles going down the drain."

R' David said, "It is indeed important that there is more money for the poor, but to me, the single ruble that was given out of love is dearer than the 50 rubles given grudgingly."

"That is what happened with bikkurim," R' David said. "A man who had just a few trees came home one day in a joyful mood. 'There are some ripe fruits on the trees!' he exclaimed. 'I can bring them to the Sanctuary in Jerusalem!'

"Suddenly his happy mood evaporated. 'What is wrong?' his wife asked.

" 'I just realized, I don't have a decent vessel for the fruit,' the husband said.

" 'Don't let that worry you,' the wife said. 'I will weave a basket for you that you will be proud of.' That evening the wife and daughter together wove a basket with a fervor of holiness, to fulfill the mitzvah of bikkurim.

"A wealthy man, who owned large orchards, was informed by one of his workers that some of the fruits had begun to ripen. 'Well, what of it?' he said.

" 'You will have to take them to Jerusalem, no?' the worker said.

" 'Another trip to Jerusalem!' the wealthy man exclaimed. 'I can't keep running to Jerusalem all the time. I have important business to attend to. But I guess there's no way out. Go ahead and mark the fruits to be taken.'

"After a bit, the man said, 'Last year some of the rich people showed off by bringing the fruit in silver bowls. I'll show them! I'll bring mine in a golden bowl and they'll burst with envy.' "

R' David said, "Baskets that were woven with devotion were very dear to God and were kept in the Sanctuary. But God has no use for golden bowls that were brought to arouse envy in other people. That is why the baskets of the poor were kept, and the bowls of the rich were returned to them."

It is indeed commendable that we beautify the performance of mitzvos. An attractive silver container for an *esrog* or a *megillah* should be motivated by our love for the mitzvah, but not to show others that our container is more costly than theirs.

וַיָּרֵעוּ אֹתָנוּ הַמִּצְרִים וַיְעַנּוּנוּ

The Egyptians mistreated us and afflicted us (26:6).

Influence of the Environment

While the concept of the term *vayorey'u* is indeed "mistreated," the literal translation of the word is "made bad." Furthermore, if the meaning of the verse is that the Egyptians did bad to us, the correct Hebrew expression is *vayorey'u lonu* rather than *vayorey'u osonu*. The more precise translation of this verse, therefore, is "the Egyptians *made us* bad," i.e., they corrupted us. Another possible translation of *vayorey'u* is that it is derived from the word *rey'a,* "friend," in which case the verse would read, "they befriended us."

The two meanings of the word *vayorey'u* may thus coincide. The Egyptians corrupted us both with their cruelty, which caused us to lose our sensitivity for one another, and on the other hand by befriending us. We became degenerate by associating with them.

It has been said that those who do not learn from history are doomed to repeat it. Psychology has elucidated a defense mechanism of "identification with the aggressor," wherein the victim adopts characteristics of his abuser. One would think that a child who was abused by a parent would determine that he would never harm his children the way he was harmed. Research has shown this not to be true. Parents who suffered abuse in their childhood may repeat the pattern with their children. Alshich states that the abuse suffered by the Israelites in Egypt caused them to be insensitive to each other.

The second source of corruption is perhaps more dangerous. We are profoundly influenced by our friends and our environment. So much so, that Rambam says that a person who lives in a corrupt community must relocate, and if one cannot find a community that is not corrupt, one should live in the wilderness rather than be subject to a corrupt environment.

Judaism suffered an irreparable loss with the death of six million Jews in the Holocaust. However, statistics have shown that due to intermarriage, Judaism has lost more than six million since the Holocaust. Assimilation among friends is a greater threat to Jewish survival than the brutality of enemies.

The sanctity of Jewish morals has been eroded by the permissiveness and immorality that prevails in western civilization. The Psalmist bewails, "They mingled with nations and learned their ways" (*Psalms* 106:35). That historical tragedy is unfortunately with us today.

We must be on guard in both areas, not to allow our ethics and morals to be destroyed by either version of *vayorey'u,* by abuse or by association.

וְאָמַרְתָּ לִפְנֵי ה' אֱלֹקֶיךָ . . . נְתַתִּיו לַלֵּוִי וְלַגֵּר לַיָּתוֹם
וְלָאַלְמָנָה . . . לֹא־עָבַרְתִּי מִמִּצְוֹתֶיךָ וְלֹא שָׁכָחְתִּי

*Then you shall say before God'... "I have given [the tithes]
to the Levite, to the proselyte, to the orphan and to the widow...
I have not transgressed any of your commandments
and I have not forgotten"* (26:13)

On Our Honor

Abarbanel asks, why do we not find a confession with regard to other mitzvos? There is no requirement that a person confess, "I have not stolen, I have not cheated, I have not lied, etc." Why should there be a need to confess that one has dispensed the tithes?

Abarbanel answers, "In any other interpersonal relationship where there is a question of money being owed, there is a claimant to whom a person must answer, and if there is a dispute, the matter can be taken before a magistrate. In the case of tithes, there is no claimant. A person may give the tithe to any Levite he wishes or to any needy person. If a person were to withhold the tithe, no one can press a claim. This is, therefore, a matter between man and God."

The Talmud states that when the sage R' Yochanan ben Zakkai was near death, his disciples asked him to bless them. R' Yochanan said, "May you have as great a fear of God as you do of other people." The disciples asked, "Is that all you expect of us?" R' Yochanan responded, "I wish you could even achieve that. When a person sins, he is careful that no one sees him. He does not care that God sees him" (*Berachos* 28b).

R' Yochanan ben Zakkai's disciples were extraordinarily great people, of the highest level of spirituality. The Talmud says that the great sage, Hillel, was the least of them. Yet, R' Yochanan felt that even these saintly people were vulnerable to being more concerned about what others will think of them than what God thinks of them. If this could be true of them, how much more so is it true of us.

In our morning prayers we say, "Always let a person be God-fearing privately and publicly." We should not have two standards of behavior.

הַסְכֵּת וּשְׁמַע יִשְׂרָאֵל הַיּוֹם הַזֶּה נִהְיֵיתָ לְעָם לַה' אֱלֹקֶיךָ

"Be attentive and hear, O Israel: This day you have become a nation unto God" (27:9)

The Nation of Israel – Alive and Well?

Why was this the day of nationhood? Did we not become a nation unto God at Sinai with the acceptance of the Torah?

The Chizkuni says that the covenant between Israel and God at Sinai was breached by the episode of the Golden Calf. On this day, after Moses had reviewed all the mitzvos of the Torah with them, and they heard both the blessings for observing the Torah and the dire consequences if they deviated from Torah and they again pledged themselves to God, that is when they became a nation.

World history is replete with great empires that had their rise and then fell into oblivion. There were nations far more mighty than the tiny nation of Israel, but their nationhood was based on their geographic possession of their land. One after another suffered conquest by alien powers, and when they lost their sovereignty, their nation perished. Only one nation has survived throughout history, not only after being driven from its Land, but also suffering indescribable persecutions and calamities. Yet while the mighty Hittite empire exists only in archaeological findings, the nation of Israel lives and thrives.

The secret of Israel's survival is simple. The nationhood of Israel is not contingent on a Land. Through current State of Israel is most dear to us, but we were a nation even during the two thousand years after we were driven from our Land. The nationhood of Israel is based on Jews' loyalty to God and acceptance of the Torah. Without a geographic land, we were a nation. Without Torah, we would have followed the mighty empires of history into oblivion.

It is significant that Moses spoke these words before the Israelites crossed the

Jordan into the Promised Land. This was to emphasize that our nationhood is contingent on our covenant to God rather than on possession of a Land.

History is a great teacher. While the Greek and Roman empires are essentially historical relics, *Am Yisroel Chai*, the nation of Israel is very much alive.

וּבָאוּ עָלֶיךָ כָּל־הַבְּרָכוֹת הָאֵלֶּה וְהִשִּׂיגֻךָ כִּי תִשְׁמַע בְּקוֹל ה׳ אֱלֹקֶיךָ

All these blessings will come upon you and overtake you,
if you hearken to the voice of God (28:2)

Blessings in Disguise

The term "overtake" connotes that someone is fleeing. But why would anyone flee from blessings?

In *Degel Machaneh Ephraim* the Baal Shem Tov's grandson says that God's blessings sometimes come in a form that we see as distressful, and inasmuch as we do not know their true character, we may flee from them. The Torah assures us that the good that God intends for us will come upon us even if we try to avoid it.

This is also the meaning of the verse: "May goodness and loving-kindness *pursue* me all the days of my life" (*Psalms* 23:6). We pray that if, in our limited understanding, we try to avoid a concealed kindness, that it pursue and overtake us.

> R' Levi Yitzchok of Berditchev saw a person running in the marketplace. "Where are you running to?" he asked. The man answered, "I'm running for my parnassah (livelihood)."
>
> R' Levi Yitzchok said, "How do you know your parnassah is in front of you? Perhaps it is behind you and you are running away from it."

Infants cry frantically when the pediatrician administers a painful injection to immunize them against dreaded disease, and they cannot possibly understand why the mother who loves and cares for them collaborates with the doctor to hurt them. The gap between our wisdom and the infinite wisdom of God is much greater than even that between an infant and its mother. Whereas the infant cannot be expected to accept its mother's actions as being for its welfare, we should be wise enough to know that everything that God does for us has an ultimate good, even if we see it as bad.

In *It's Not as Tough as You Think* and *It's Not as Tough at Home as You Think* I cited many examples of incidents that we thought to be terrible at the time, only to discover later that they were not the calamities we had believed them to be. In fact, some turned out to be blessings in disguise. We have all had such experiences. We should be able to extrapolate from these events to all unpleasant things that may happen to us.

תַּחַת אֲשֶׁר לֹא־עָבַדְתָּ אֶת ה׳ אֱלֹקֶיךָ בְּשִׂמְחָה

The Torah lists the dire consequences that will befall the person who deviates from the word of God, and that these will occur
"Because you did not serve God with joy" (28:47)

Misguided Joy

A superficial reading appears to indicate that if a person did everything required in the service of God but did not do so with joy, he would be visited with the dire consequences described in this portion of the Torah. It seems unreasonable that failure to feel joy in the service of God warrants such severe punishment.

R' Simchah Bunim of P'shis'che, therefore, said that the verse means, "Because you did *not* serve God, *that* was with joy. In other words, one was happy that one was not serving God; that is indeed a grave transgression."

The Talmud (*Avodah Zarah* 2a-3b) says that when Jews will be rewarded with the Ultimate Redemption, the nations of the world will complain to God, "Why are You showing favoritism to the Jews? Had you given us the Torah, we, too, would have observed it." God will then say, "Very well, I will give you the simple mitzvah of Succah. Let us see whether you will observe it."

Everyone will then build their own succah. God will then cause the sun to radiate intense heat, whereupon everyone will "kick away" at the succah and leave it, indicating that they are rejecting the mitzvah.

The Talmud asks, "But the halachah is that if one is very uncomfortable in the succah, one may leave it." The Talmud says, "The nations that leave the succah because of discomfort do so with disdain. They kick away and reject the mitzvah: But when a Jew leaves the succah because of rain or other severe discomfort, he does so with a heavy heart. He loves the mitzvah, and is greatly distressed that he cannot fulfill it."

There may be circumstances where one is unable to fulfill a specific mitzvah. A person whose circumstances do not allow him to perform a specific mitzvah should feel as distressed as if he had lost a huge profit. Being happy that one does not have to do a mitzvah indicates a very negative attitude toward Torah.

The Talmud bewails the spiritual degeneration that had occurred over time. Later generations sought ways to exempt themselves from tithing, whereas earlier generations were happy to do these mitzvos.

If we truly desire a close relationship with God, we will rejoice in doing mitzvos, because they bind us to God. At the very least, we should not be happy when we lose an opportunity to do a mitzvah.

אֵלֶּה דִבְרֵי הַבְּרִית אֲשֶׁר־צִוָּה ה' אֶת־מֹשֶׁה לִכְרֹת אֶת־בְּנֵי יִשְׂרָאֵל

These are the words of the covenant that God commanded Moses to seal with the Children of Israel (28:69)

Ignoring Helpful Warnings

The covenant refers to Deuteronomy Chapter 28, known as the *tochachah* (reprimand). It foretells the terrible consequences that will befall Israel if it deviates from the Divine commandments.

Because this chapter contains a graphic description of the dire consequences that Israel would suffer for disobeying the Torah, the reader in the shul lowers his voice while reciting them. Some people, thinking that listening to these punishments may somehow precipitate them, leave the shul when this portion is read.

The Chafetz Chaim sharply denounced this practice. Not only is failing to listen to a portion of the Torah a violation of halachah, but it is also extremely foolish.

"Imagine that someone wishes to warn a traveler to avoid a certain road because it has many dangerous pitfalls, and one can come to great harm on that road. How foolish it would be to refuse to listen to that warning.

"The *tochachah* is a warning that is intended to protect people from harm. The Torah tells us to avoid deviating from the Divine word, because it will bring about severe suffering. Refusing to listen to the warning puts one at great risk of harm."

The refusal to listen to reprimand has plagued our people throughout history. The prophets pleaded with the Israelites to abandon their errant behavior because it will result in losing their Land and being sent into exile. It is clear from the Books of the Prophets that the populace turned a deaf ear. They wished to do as they pleased and did not want to hear the truth of the tragedy that they would bring upon themselves.

Although the *tochachah* is generally considered to be a curse, a wise person recognizes it as a blessing, in that it is intended to protect people from the harm that results from failure to properly obey the Torah.

וְלֹא־נָתַן ה' לָכֶם לֵב לָדַעַת וְעֵינַיִם לִרְאוֹת וְאָזְנַיִם לִשְׁמֹעַ עַד הַיּוֹם הַזֶּה

With the Israelites standing at the shores of the Jordan, poised to cross into the Promised Land which Moses was permitted to see but not to enter, Moses said, *"But God did not give you a heart to know, or eyes to see or ears to hear until this day"* (29:3).

God Is in Nature

R' Meir Simchah HaCohen (*Meshech Chochmah of Dvinsk*) interprets the last three words of this verse to mean "*even* until this day." I.e., even today you do not understand.

Why is this? Because, R' Meir Simchah explains, Moses goes on to convey the Divine message, "I led you for forty years in the Wilderness, your garment did not wear out from on you, and your shoe did not wear out from on your foot. Bread you did not eat and wine or intoxicant you did not drink, so that you would know that I am your God" (*Deuteronomy* 29:4-5).

Moses said to them, "You know nothing other than an existence based on miracles—the manna, the well of water that accompanied them, the clouds of glory—so that you have no understanding that God is in Nature. When you plow and seed a field, it is God Who makes the grain grow. When the rain waters the field, it is God Who provides the rain. When your animals graze, it is God Who makes the grass grow."

The dangers the Israelites faced upon entering the Land and the cessation of manifest miracles were twofold. (1) They might come to believe that the productivity of the Land and their prosperity is entirely due to their own work and cunning, as Moses had warned them, "You may say in your heart, 'My strength and the might of my hand made me all this wealth' " (ibid. 8:17). (2) They might turn to worshipping the forces of nature, as did the idolatrous nations in their environs.

Moses' fears were well-founded. "For I know that after my death you will surely act corruptly, and you will stray from the path that I have commanded you" (ibid. 31:29). People conditioned to expect miracles may have a difficult time adapting to nature. This may be why the era of manifest miracles essentially came to a close. We are expected to work in nature and see God in nature.

> *The Chafetz Chaim once lodged at an inn, and the innkeeper asked him why we no longer have miracles like in the Biblical era. The Chafetz Chaim told him he would answer his question a bit later.*
>
> *Later that day, the innkeeper's daughter returned from school, and showed her parents a certificate she had received for memorizing and reciting several poems. The Chafetz Chaim asked the child to recite some of the poems for him, but the child refused. He then asked the innkeeper to prevail upon his daughter to recite some poems. The child said, "I don't want to. This certificate says that I know the poems by heart. If he does not want to believe that, he doesn't have to. I don't have to prove that to everyone. That's what the certificate is for."*
>
> *The Chafetz Chaim said to the innkeeper, "There you have the answer to your question. When people did not know that God runs the world, He demonstrated that with His miracles. He then gave us the Torah, a certificate that testifies to His sovereignty. Like your daughter said, He does not have to prove it to everyone. That is what the certificate is for."*
>
> *(Incidentally, there is a great lesson in this incident. The Chafetz Chaim told the innkeeper that he would give him an answer later. Did he have prophetic foresight that the child would come home with a certificate? I believe not. What the Chafetz Chaim did have was absolute faith that God would provide him with a way to give the innkeeper an answer that he would accept. That is emunah and bitachon, faith and trust in God at its finest.)*

The lion's share of the world's population may have a belief in God, but nevertheless sees success as depending on the amount of work they do or how wisely they invest. We should realize that although the Torah requires us to earn a livelihood, success comes only from God: "God will bless you in all that you do" (ibid. 15:18).

פרשת נצבים
Parashas Nitzavim

אַתֶּם נִצָּבִים הַיּוֹם כֻּלְּכֶם לִפְנֵי ה׳ אֱלֹקֵיכֶם
You are standing today, all of you, before God (29:1)

The Eternity of Israel

Rashi cites the Midrash explaining that Moses spoke these words immediately following the predictions of the dire consequences that would befall Israel if it deviated from the Torah (*Deuteronomy* 28:15-69) because the Israelites were terrified that they might not survive if the wrath of God was so severe. Moses, therefore, said, "You are standing today, all of you, before God. In spite of your repeated rebelliousness and disobedience, you have survived. You shall continue to survive. And insofar as the Divine chastisements may be frightening, you should know that it is the hardships that you will experience that will strengthen and preserve you."

History has proven the truth of Moses' statements. Against all possible odds, the Jewish nation has survived, and indeed, the unparalleled suffering that we have experienced throughout history has been a "crucible of iron" (*Deuteronomy* 4:20) from which we have emerged with the strength of steel.

Unfortunately, it was suffering, both individually and as a nation, that has afforded us our greatness. Painful persecution does not threaten the future of Judaism, whereas assimilation does. The Talmudic statement, "This is the way of Torah: Eat bread with salt, drink water in small measure, sleep on the ground, live in deprivation and toil in the Torah" (*Ethics of the Fathers* 6:4) has proven itself to be true. The majority of great Torah scholars lived a life of deprivation. Luxury and comfort do not appear to be as conducive to Torah scholarship as does deprivation.

A wise person said, "Think of how many things you learned as a result of pleasant experiences." Most of us would be hard pressed to list many such things, but we would have little difficulty in listing things we learned from painful experiences.

Moses' words should be reassuring to us in times of distress. We have survived, and we will survive. Like God and Torah, Israel is eternal.

DEVARIM / DEUTERONOMY: Nitzavim

אַתֶּם נִצָּבִים הַיּוֹם כֻּלְּכֶם לִפְנֵי ה׳ אֱלֹקֵיכֶם רָאשֵׁיכֶם
שִׁבְטֵיכֶם זִקְנֵיכֶם וְשֹׁטְרֵיכֶם כֹּל אִישׁ יִשְׂרָאֵל טַפְּכֶם נְשֵׁיכֶם
וְגֵרְךָ אֲשֶׁר בְּקֶרֶב מַחֲנֶיךָ מֵחֹטֵב עֵצֶיךָ עַד שֹׁאֵב מֵימֶיךָ

You are standing today, all of you, before God: the heads of your tribes, your elders, and your officers—every person of Israel; your small children, your women and your proselyte who is in the midst of your camp, from the hewer of your wood to the drawer of your water (29:9-10).

Equality Before God

There was indeed a hierarchy within the Israelite nation — the elders, the *Kohanim* (Priests), the Levites, the tribal heads, the judges. But, says Alshich, here Moses said, "You are standing before God," and before God there is no classification. And if there are any people who are special before God, their status may not correspond with that which they enjoy in the world.

The fundamental equality of all Jews can be seen in the halachah. If a person is threatened that he will be killed unless he kills another person, he is required to accept martyrdom rather than to kill. The reason the Talmud gives is, "What makes you think your blood is redder? Perhaps the blood of the other person (whom you were ordered to kill) is redder than yours" (*Pesachim* 25b). In other words, what right do you have to suppose that your life is of greater value than his?

What is the halachah if a leading scholar or philanthropist, who is the pillar of the community, is ordered, under the threat of death, to kill a person who is a vagrant, a degenerate who is a burden to the community? The halachah remains unchanged. He must accept martyrdom rather than kill. But is it not clear that the philanthropic scholar is far superior to the degenerate vagrant, and that his life is of greater value? That is true in the eyes of man, but we have no knowledge of the scale by which God evaluates people.

In human terms, there can be superior or inferior. We are finite beings, and we can see the wide gap between a person of great achievement and one of little, or even no achievement. But God is infinite, and before infinity, a fraction of a millimeter and a million miles are both equally significant or non-significant.

A community cannot function without various stratifications. There are leaders and there are followers. There are teachers and there are students. There are donors and there are recipients. There are providers of services and there are beneficiaries of services. However, no status of any kind affects the value of a person before God. We are required to emulate God's attributes. To us also, the value of life is not measurable.

This is of more than academic interest. In the early days when penicillin was a new discovery, only small amounts of the drug were available. R' Moshe Feinstein was asked, what should a doctor do if he has only a single dose of penicillin and a number of patients who require it? How should he decide to which patient it should be administered? R' Feinstein answered that he must give it to the first patient he encounters who requires it. He may not judge who is more deserving to be treated.

Today, penicillin is in abundance, but livers and kidneys for transplant are not.

Shall the available organs be given to people who are considered to be of the greatest value to the community? R' Feinstein's ruling applies. There may be medical factors which may enter into a decision, but not considerations of value. Every human life is of equal value to God, and must be so to us.

פֶּן־יֵשׁ בָּכֶם אִישׁ אוֹ־אִשָּׁה אוֹ מִשְׁפָּחָה אוֹ־שֵׁבֶט אֲשֶׁר לְבָבוֹ
פֹנֶה הַיּוֹם מֵעִם ה'... וְהָיָה בְּשָׁמְעוֹ אֶת־דִּבְרֵי הָאָלָה הַזֹּאת
וְהִתְבָּרֵךְ בִּלְבָבוֹ לֵאמֹר שָׁלוֹם יִהְיֶה־לִּי כִּי בִּשְׁרִרוּת לִבִּי אֵלֵךְ

Perhaps there is among you a man or a woman, or a family or tribe whose heart turns away from being with God... And it will be when he hears the words of this imprecation, he will bless himself in his heart, saying, "Peace will be with me, though I walk as my heart sees fit" (29:17-18)

Hazards of Emotion

The following story caused me much consternation when I first heard it from my father in my childhood. As I came to understand more about human psychology, the message of the story was validated.

> R' Mordechai of Czernoble, referred to as the Maggid of Czernoble, was known for his lavish tzedakah. All at once, R' Mordechai stopped giving tzedakah. This went so far that when he saw a woman picking up branches for kindling in his courtyard, he knocked on the window and motioned for her to leave. Then, just as abruptly, he again began giving tzedakah lavishly.
>
> Knowing that everyone was puzzled by his strange behavior, R' Mordechai explained, "I realized that my giving tzedakah was not because it was a mitzvah, but because my heart ached for the poor. While there is certainly nothing wrong with this, I was acting on emotion rather than on intellect. Allowing one's actions to be determined by emotion has great risks, because emotions can totally distort a person's judgments.
>
> "Although the emotion of feeling for the poor is desirable, the fact is that one is soothing his own conscience rather than doing what God commanded. Any emotional gratification is self-centered, and self-centeredness can lead a person to do many wrong things, rationalizing that they are right.
>
> "I, therefore, stopped giving tzedakah and trained myself to be indifferent to the poor. Once I achieved this and was no longer under the sway of emotion, I could give tzedakah because it is a mitzvah, the proper thing to do."

As a child, I was bothered by someone trying to make himself indifferent to the needs of the poor. However, as I began to understand the interaction of emotion and intellect, I could understand why R' Mordechai felt this was necessary.

If you saw that a person's judgments were fair, you would likely come to trust him. If he then made an unfair judgment, you might assume that this, too, was fair, based on his reputation for fairness.

Most of our emotions are self-centered, and we should indeed be suspicious of them. We can easily rationalize to justify our behavior, as Solomon says, "Each way of a man is right in his own eyes" (*Proverbs* 21:2). Inasmuch as emotions initiate most of our actions, we are always at risk of deceiving ourselves that what we desire is indeed right.

R' Mordechai felt that emotions are not trustworthy, and that only the unbiased intellect can distinguish right from wrong. In order to be certain that all his actions were dictated by the intellect, he sought to eliminate all actions that emanated from emotion, regardless of how worthy that emotion appeared to be.

Moses warns us against the lure of emotions. "It will be when he hears the words of this imprecation, he will bless himself in his heart, saying, 'Peace will be with me, though I walk as my heart sees fit.'" Even when one has heard the awesome punishments that will befall the person who deviates from Torah, one may still feel at peace doing what his heart desires.

We are a far cry from the spirituality of R' Mordechai, but we would do well to scrutinize the actions toward which we feel drawn.

וְהָיָה בְּשָׁמְעוֹ אֶת־דִּבְרֵי הָאָלָה הַזֹּאת וְהִתְבָּרֵךְ בִּלְבָבוֹ לֵאמֹר
שָׁלוֹם יִהְיֶה־לִּי כִּי בִּשְׁרִרוּת לִבִּי אֵלֵךְ לְמַעַן סְפוֹת הָרָוָה אֶת־הַצְּמֵאָה
לֹא־יֹאבֶה ה׳ סְלֹחַ לוֹ כִּי אָז יֶעְשַׁן אַף־ה׳ וְקִנְאָתוֹ בָּאִישׁ הַהוּא

*And it will be when he hears the words of this imprecation,
he will bless himself in his heart, saying,
"Peace will be with me, though I walk as my heart sees fit."
God will not be willing to forgive him, for then God's anger
and jealousy will smoke against that person* (29:18-19)

The Evil of Recalcitrance

The commentaries remark, If this person has not done *teshuvah*, then it goes without saying that God will not forgive him. On other hand, if he has done *teshuvah*, why would God not forgive him? Furthermore, why the expression *lo yoveh Hashem selo'ach lo*? The usual term would be *lo yislach lo Hashem*.

One of the commentaries suggests a novel interpretation. This person who wishes to follow the dictates of his heart and is not discouraged by the warnings of severe punishment, *lo yoveh*, he does not even desire that *Hashem yislach lo*, that God should forgive him. This is so brazen a defiance of God that "then God's anger and jealousy will smoke against that person."

We noted earlier that when a person rationalizes and justifies his misdeeds, he is unlikely to do *teshuvah*, since he believes he has not done any wrong. Yet, even this person may do *teshuvah* when it is pointed out to him that his rationalizations were incorrect. However, the person who sins and says that he does not care whether God forgives him is not likely to be persuaded to do *teshuvah*. He recognizes that what he did was against God's wishes, but his arrogance in rejecting God's forgiveness indeed puts him beyond forgiveness.

Forgiveness is a special, precious gift of God to man. How foolish not to avail oneself of it.

הַנִּסְתָּרֹת לַה' אֱלֹקֵינוּ וְהַנִּגְלֹת לָנוּ וּלְבָנֵינוּ עַד־עוֹלָם
לַעֲשׂוֹת אֶת־כָּל־דִּבְרֵי הַתּוֹרָה הַזֹּאת

The hidden [sins] are for God [to know], but the revealed [sins] are for us and our children forever, to carry out all the words of this Torah (29:28)

Mutual Responsibility

The covenant that Moses sealed with the Israelites was in addition to that at Sinai, where each person accepted observance of the Torah on himself. This covenant is one of mutual responsibility. We are responsible for another person's misdeeds if we are derelict in helping him. to the degree that we are capable of helping him observe the Torah

The Chafetz Chaim gives an example of Reuven having guaranteed a loan for Shimon. If Reuven sees that Shimon is about to make a foolish investment with the borrowed money, he will do everything possible to stop him, because if Shimon loses the money and is unable to repay the loan, Reuven will have to repay it. Shimon cannot say to Reuven, "It's my money and I can do with it whatever I wish." He indeed may spend his own money as he wishes, but this is money for which Reuven is liable, and Reuven has a right to protect himself.

The above verse states that we are not responsible for others' sins that we know nothing about, but those that are revealed and known to us are in fact our responsibility.

The principle of mutual responsibility requires that we try to discourage fellow Jews from transgressing the mitzvos of the Torah. Granted that we may not be able to preach to others in a convincing way, but there are things that we can do. If we have friends who do not observe Shabbos, we may invite them to spend a Shabbos with us. If we can show them the beauty and spirituality of Shabbos, they may become interested in knowing more about Shabbos.

But for this to be effective, our observance of Shabbos must be such that it is in fact a spiritual experience. The true spirit of Shabbos requires a harmony within the home, and divesting oneself of all the worries of the weekdays. The Talmud says that when Shabbos begins, a person should feel that all his needs have been met and that he lacks for nothing.

If people saw the euphoria and peace that Shabbos brings to those who observe it, they would certainly wish to know how they could achieve these for themselves.

This is equally true for all the mitzvos of the Torah. We do indeed perform them, but we may do so in a manner that would not encourage others to wish to emulate us. Mutual responsibility, therefore, requires that we perfect our observance of mitzvos in more than a mechanical manner. When our faces radiate the joy of a mitzvah, we will have fulfilled our responsibility to others.

וְהָיָה כִי־יָבֹאוּ עָלֶיךָ כָּל־הַדְּבָרִים הָאֵלֶּה הַבְּרָכָה
וְהַקְּלָלָה אֲשֶׁר נָתַתִּי לְפָנֶיךָ וַהֲשֵׁבֹתָ אֶל־לְבָבֶךָ

*"It will be that when all these things come upon you—
the blessing and the curse that I have presented
before you—then you will take it to your heart" (30:1)*

Intellect and Emotion

Earlier we noted that R' Mordechai of Czernoble felt that acting according to one's emotions can be misleading, and that a person should, therefore, be guided by intellect. This is true when the motivation originates in emotion. There can also be the reverse, when something originates in the intellect and needs to be extended to emotions.

Emunah (faith and trust in God) begins in the intellect. Knowledge of God is cognitive. The Torah says "You shall know this day (cognitive) and take to your heart (emotive) that Hashem, He is the God" (*Deuteronomy* 4:39). One may have *emunah* based on the *mesorah*, the transmission of belief from parent to child, or by reasoning, as the patriarch Abraham did, and coming to the conclusion that the world must have had a Creator. Both methods are cognitive.

"Now, O Israel, what does God ask of you? Only to fear Him, to go in all His ways and to love Him" (ibid. 10:12). After a person has an intellectual belief in God, one is required to develop the emotions of reverence and love for Him.

Rambam says that one can develop reverence and love for God by appreciating the grandeur of Creation (*Yesodei HaTorah* 2:2). R' Shneur Zalman in *Tanya* adds that inasmuch as the *neshamah* is Godly, it craves to unite with its source in God. Furthermore, there is concealed within us a nucleus of reverence and love for God that was bequeathed to us by the patriarch Abraham, and needs only to be exposed. This can be done by eliminating the barriers that stand between man and God, which are the earthly physical indulgences. The latter are antagonistic to the spiritual desires of the *neshamah*, and when they are removed, the nucleus of reverence and love is exposed, and the craving of the *neshamah* for God is experienced.

We thus have a dual task: to bring the emotions under the control of the intellect, and to endow the intellect with the fervor of emotion. "Then you will take it to your heart."

כִּי הַמִּצְוָה הַזֹּאת אֲשֶׁר אָנֹכִי מְצַוְּךָ הַיּוֹם לֹא־נִפְלֵאת הִוא מִמְּךָ וְלֹא־רְחֹקָה הִוא
לֹא בַשָּׁמַיִם הִוא . . . כִּי־קָרוֹב אֵלֶיךָ הַדָּבָר מְאֹד בְּפִיךָ וּבִלְבָבְךָ לַעֲשֹׂתוֹ

"For this commandment that I command you today—it is not hidden and it is not distant. It is not in heaven . . . Rather it is very near to you — in your mouth and your heart to perform it" (30:11-14).

A Divine Torah for Mere Mortals

In psychology we find discussion of "the disowned self;" i.e., there are facets of an individual's personality which one may deny having. There may be a feeling that is so repulsive to us, that we cannot admit, even to ourselves, that we are capable of having anything so abhorrent. Ideas and feelings such as these may be repressed; i.e., they are buried in the subconscious part of the mind, hopefully never to come to one's awareness.

An idea buried in the subconscious does not just remain dormant. Rather, it seeks to break into consciousness. A person must exert energy in order to keep the idea repressed, and sometimes one may develop one or more defenses to reinforce the repression. These defenses are often the cause of psychological symptoms.

There is a much more efficient way of managing unacceptable ideas and feelings. A person should realize that a human being is a composite creature, consisting of an essentially animal body and a Divine human spirit. The body has all the desires and impulses of an animal, and the function of the spirit is to master these, and ideally, to channel these energies constructively. Lust can be transformed into desires for spiritual goals, anger can be converted to intolerance of injustice, envy can be directed to wishing to achieve the spiritual heights of *tzaddikim,* etc. Every impulse can be sublimated, but instead of sublimation operating on a subconscious level, it can be a conscious process. As long as an impulse is in the subconscious and a person is not aware of its existence, there is an internal struggle against an unknown enemy. If the idea or feeling can be admitted to consciousness, one is then in a better position to deal with it.

The Midrash says that when Moses ascended to heaven to receive the Torah, the heavenly angels objected, saying to God, "The Torah is too holy to be given to mortals who will not appreciate it and revere it. Let the Torah remain here, among us." God told Moses to rebut the angels' argument. Moses said, "The Torah says 'You shall not covet your neighbor's wife.' Does that apply to you? The Torah says, 'You shall not steal.' Are you capable of stealing anything? The Torah says, 'You shall not murder.' Can you kill one another?" With this argument, Moses triumphed over the angels and brought the Torah to us.

The point of this Midrash is that angels are totally spiritual and do not need a Torah. It is precisely because of the animal component in man that we need a Torah. If a person wishes to know what impulses are part of human nature, he need only read the 365 prohibitions of the Torah. Every one of them is a commandment to avoid doing something which our animal body desires! Why, then, should a person disown any feeling as though having it means that one is decadent? There is no reason to disown any thought or feeling. We need only realize that this originated from our animal-like body, and that it is our duty to master it.

Tiferes Yisrael on the Mishnah cites a Midrash that a king who had heard of Moses' greatness sent his artists to the Israelite encampment in the desert to draw a picture of Moses. When they returned, he gave the picture to his physiognomists, the wise men who were capable of describing a person's character by a study of his face. The physiognomists reported that this picture was of a person who was narcissistic, arrogant, lustful and capable of the worst kind of behavior. This was so incongruous with what he had heard about Moses that he decided to see for himself.

Upon meeting Moses, he saw that the picture his artists had drawn was precise to the minutest detail. He asked Moses how his physiognomists could have been so wrong. Moses explained that the physiognomists can describe only the character traits with which a person was born. "All those things they said of me are innate. I was born with all those traits. However, I transformed them all and channeled them toward positive and desirable goals" (*Tiferes Yisrael,* end of *Kiddushin*).

This is what Moses was telling the Israelites. "The Torah is not in heaven. It was not intended for angels who have no improper impulses. It is a Torah for mortals, for human beings whose animal bodies can generate desires that a person may wish to disown as being alien. It is not necessary to do so. We have the strength and capacities to be master over our behavior.

"It is very near to you, in your mouth and in your heart to perform it."

Rambam says that every person can be like Moses. What he means by this is that every person is capable of consciously sublimating all the drives that originate from our physical bodies. There is no need to disown any part of one's self.

הַעִדֹתִי בָכֶם הַיּוֹם אֶת־הַשָּׁמַיִם וְאֶת־הָאָרֶץ הַחַיִּים וְהַמָּוֶת נָתַתִּי לְפָנֶיךָ הַבְּרָכָה וְהַקְּלָלָה וּבָחַרְתָּ בַּחַיִּים לְמַעַן תִּחְיֶה אַתָּה וְזַרְעֶךָ

"I have placed life and death before you, blessing and curse; and you shall choose life, so that you will live, you and your offspring" (30:19)

Why Would Anyone Not Choose Life?

This is a rather strange admonition. Why did Moses instruct the Israelites to choose life? Why would anyone not choose life? Furthermore, the statement "so that you will live, you and your offspring" implies that a person might not choose life for his children. How can that possibly be?

Treating alcoholics and other chemically dependent people over the past four decades has given me the answer to these questions. I regularly see people who do *not* choose life for themselves, and also jeopardize the lives of their families. It is not that they *willfully* choose death. Their addiction to alcohol and drugs so blinds them to reality and so distorts their judgment that they are unable to see that they are choosing death or ruination for themselves and their loved ones. They simply cannot see reality.

This is equally true of compulsive gamblers, who may mortgage their homes, forge their wives' signatures to their savings, sell their wives' jewelry, empty the children's savings accounts and accrue hundreds of thousands of dollars of debt. They may impoverish their parents. The destruction that they wreak on those they love the most is indescribable. Yet, though they may be highly intelligent people, they do not see the destructive nature of their actions.

A far more common self-destruction is cigarette smoking, which has been demonstrated to be injurious to life and health. People who smoke are choosing death over life.

The medical community is alarmed over the increase in obesity, with the frequent complications of high blood pressure, heart disease and diabetes. Yet, obesity is now the nation's largest health problem.

There are other lifestyles which may not be as obviously destructive as these addictions, but are nevertheless harmful. People who are workaholics and drive themselves incessantly to succeed in their business or profession are placing themselves at greater risk for heart disease.

The question is no longer, Why was it necessary for Moses to instruct people to choose life over death? Rather, the perplexing question is, Why do people ignore this lifesaving admonition?

פרשת וילך
Parashas Vayeilech

בֶּן־מֵאָה וְעֶשְׂרִים שָׁנָה אָנֹכִי הַיּוֹם לֹא־אוּכַל עוֹד לָצֵאת
וְלָבוֹא וַה׳ אָמַר אֵלַי לֹא תַעֲבֹר אֶת־הַיַּרְדֵּן הַזֶּה

*"I am 120 years old today; I can no longer go out
and come in, for God has said to me,
'You shall not cross this Jordan' "* (31:2)

Joy in Growth

In *Living Each Week* I cited the comment of the Rebbe of Gur who explained that Moses lived for only one purpose: to do the Divine mitzvos and to elevate himself spiritually. At this point in his life, he had maximized the spirituality he could attain. There was only one way that he could still grow spiritually, and that was by the performance of the mitzvos that are applicable only in the Holy Land and that he could not perform elsewhere. Moses pleaded to be allowed to enter the Holy Land so that he could do these mitzvos. When his pleas were turned down and he saw that there was no way he could further grow spiritually anymore, he accepted death. For Moses, a life that was without spiritual growth was not worth living.

Moses made it very clear that *simchah* (joy) was an essential component of the Divine service. He warned the Israelites of the dire consequences that would befall the person, "Because you did not serve God with joy" (*Deuteronomy* 28:47).

R' Samson Raphael Hirsch points out that the word *same'ach* (happy) is related to and perhaps derived from the same source as *tzome'ach* (growth). True happiness can come only from growth, especially spiritual growth. A life devoid of spiritual growth is devoid of *simchah*.

There is an important message in the relationship of *someach* to *tzomeach*. Elsewhere I have cited the Talmud that we should learn some things from observation of nature (*Eruvin* 100b). We might learn from nature by observing how lobsters grow.

Lobsters are confined within a rigid shell. As the lobster grows, the shell becomes too confining and oppressive. It then sheds its shell and grows a more spacious one. As the lobster continues to grow, each new shell eventually becomes oppressive, leading to the formation of a larger one. *The stimulus that enables the lobster to grow is the discomfort it feels when its shell becomes oppressive.* If the lobster would not feel discomfort, it would remain forever tiny.

Growth is often accompanied by discomfort. "For with much wisdom comes much suffering" (*Ecclesiastes* 1:18). Yet, *tzome'ach* is related to *same'ach*. Hence, there can be *simchah* even when one experiences discomfort. This is why we find that our great *tzaddikim* welcomed *yissurim* (suffering). The spiritual growth that was stimulated by the discomfort more than compensated for the suffering.

We live in an era where scientific advances have given us unprecedented comfort in living. Western civilization has become essentially hedonistic. Whereas it is perfectly normal to seek relief from pain, we are at risk of rejecting all types of discomfort, including those that are the stimuli for spiritual growth. If we eschew spiritual growth because of the discomfort that may accompany it, we may also be lessening the amount of true *simchah* that we can achieve.

On the day of his death, *Vayeilech Moshe*, Moses progressed. Moses had one last opportunity for growth, to fulfill the mitzvah of giving reproof and blessing.

Moshe Rabbeinu, Moses our teacher. He taught us and continues to teach us that growing and fulfilling oneself is the source of true *simchah*.

מִקֵּץ שֶׁבַע שָׁנִים . . . בְּחַג הַסֻּכּוֹת . . . הַקְהֵל אֶת־הָעָם הָאֲנָשִׁים . . .
לְמַעַן יִשְׁמְעוּ וּלְמַעַן יִלְמְדוּ . . . וְשָׁמְרוּ לַעֲשׂוֹת אֶת־כָּל־דִּבְרֵי הַתּוֹרָה הַזֹּאת

At the end of seven years... during the Succos festival...
Gather together the people... so that they will hear and so that they
will learn ... and be careful to perform all the words of this Torah (31:10-12)

The Spiritual Harvest

At this gathering, *Hakhel*, the king read passages from the Book of Deuteronomy which pertained to devotion to and reverence of God and the covenant between God and Israel.

What is the significance of convening this gathering on Succos? It would seem that Shavuos, on which the Torah was given and the covenant between God and Israel was sealed, would be an appropriate time for this gathering. Or perhaps on Passover, which commemorated the deliverance from Egypt and the extraordinary miracles which God wrought for the Israelites. But why Succos, which was essentially the celebration of the harvest: "When you gather in from your threshing floor and from your wine cellar" (*Deuteronomy* 16:13)?

Among all the festivals, Succos stands out as the festival of joy: "And you shall be completely joyous" (ibid. v. 15). While there was indeed the joy of bringing in an abundant crop, this was overshadowed by the spiritual joy. The Talmud describes the celebration of *Simchas Beis HaSho'evah*, the Celebration of the Water-Libation, when the courtyard of the Temple was flooded with light, and the elders danced and sang, some saying, "Fortunate are those whose youth did not disgrace their later years," while others said, "Fortunate are those whose later years compensated for their youth" (*Succos* 53a). This was a spiritual celebration, and as the Psalmist said, "You have put joy in my heart, more than when their grain and their wine increase" (*Psalms* 4:8).

The gathering to hear the reading of the Torah on Succos emphasized the pivotal role of *simchah* in the observance of Torah.

There are two opinions in the Talmud about what Succos commemorates. One opinion is that it commemorates the protective Clouds of Glory that encircled the Israelites during their sojourn in the Wilderness, and the other is that it represents the thatched huts in which the Israelites lived in the desert (*Succos* 11b). Commemorating and reinforcing the concept of Divine protection is a reason for celebration, but what is so special about thatched huts?

Our ethical works point out that the succah must be constructed as a temporary dwelling, symbolizing our temporary existence on earth, during which we have the opportunity to accumulate the merits of performing the mitzvos. It is the harvest of mitzvos that we gather and take to our home in the Eternal World. Both the Clouds of Glory and the thatched huts have spiritual symbolism.

The assignment of spiritual joy to the harvest season can be understood with a parable the Baal Shem Tov gave to someone who asked why we have foods of gustatory delight on Shabbos, which is a spiritual day. The Baal Shem Tov said that a king once exiled his wayward son to a remote part of his realm. When the period of exile was over, the king sent a message to the prince that he may return to the palace. The prince was so overjoyed with this news that he wished to sing and dance. However, the villagers would not be able to understand this strange behavior. He, therefore, threw a party for the villagers, and when they were in high spirits, they sang and danced. The prince joined them, but while they were dancing because of their being satiated with good food and wine, the prince danced because he was going to return to the palace.

The Baal Shem Tov said that the *neshamah* wishes to celebrate Shabbos spiritually, but the *neshamah* is housed in a physical body which does not appreciate spirituality. We, therefore, give the body tasty foods which it can enjoy. In this way, both the *neshamah* and the body can rejoice; the *neshamah* with the holiness of Shabbos, and the body with delicacies.

So, too, with the spiritual celebration of Succos. Our physical selves rejoice with the grain harvest, while our *neshamos* rejoice with the spirituality of Succos.

The *simchah* of Succos makes this festival a propitious time for Torah teaching. The message for us is clear: to rejoice in the study and observance of Torah.

וְהָיָה כִּי־תִמְצֶאןָ אֹתוֹ רָעוֹת רַבּוֹת וְצָרוֹת וְעָנְתָה הַשִּׁירָה
הַזֹּאת לְפָנָיו לְעֵד כִּי לֹא תִשָּׁכַח מִפִּי זַרְעוֹ כִּי יָדַעְתִּי אֶת־יִצְרוֹ

...''It shall be that when many evils and distresses come upon it, then this song shall speak up before it as a witness for it shall not be forgotten from the mouth of its offspring, for I know its inclination'' (31:21)

God Provides a Plea in Our Defense

Malbim interprets this verse as a Divine promise to be forgiving when the Children of Israel will do teshuvah.

Malbim cites the Talmud which states that the prophet Elijah pleaded for the Israelites who had become idolatrous, saying to God, "It was You Who made it possible for them to go astray," and that God admitted, "Yes, I created the *yetzer hara*" (*Berachos* 32b). God accepts part of the responsibility for our sins, having created so powerful a *yetzer hara*.

Forgiveness requires *teshuvah*: regret for having sinned and a sincere resolution not to repeat the sinful act. But why is *teshuvah* effective? If a person commits a crime and pleads before the judge, "I'm sorry I did it and I promise I will never do it again," this will hardly stop the judge from imposing a penalty.

Teshuvah is effective because God understands how vulnerable we are to the cunning and temptations of the *yetzer hara*. Therefore, if we realize that we have been duped by the *yetzer hara*, God takes this into consideration.

The chassidic master, the Shpoler Zeide, used to plead for his people, "Master of the universe! You have placed temptations before people's eyes, but the punishments of Gehinnom (hell) are described in the books. If You had placed Gehinnom right before people's eyes and the temptations in the books, I assure You, no one would sin."

There is no justification for sin, but if a person who has sinned does *teshuvah*, God assumes part of the responsibility and forgives the sin.

This, Malbim says, is the promise in the above verse. "It shall be that when many evils and distresses come upon it, then this song shall speak before it as a witness . . . for I know its inclination." When the troubles that befall Israel will cause us to do *teshuvah*, God promises to forgive, because He knows the power of the evil inclination. This song, the Torah, "shall not be forgotten from the mouths of its offspring," and it will be a witness to plead in our behalf.

A person may be discouraged from doing *teshuvah*, thinking, "What's the use? I cannot expect God to forgive me for having disobeyed Him for so long." God promises that if a person does *teshuvah*, He will enter a plea in his behalf, assuming part of the responsibility for the person's behavior.

It is never too late for *teshuvah*.

הֵן בְּעוֹדֶנִּי חַי עִמָּכֶם הַיּוֹם מַמְרִים הֱיִתֶם עִם־ה' וְאַף כִּי־אַחֲרֵי מוֹתִי

"Behold! While I am still alive with you today, you have been rebels against God—and surely after my death" (31:27).

Rebelliousness Cannot Be Sublimated

The translation of this verse is inaccurate. A more precise translation of the Hebrew is, "you have been rebels *with* God."

What Moses was bemoaning was a particularly dangerous form of rebellion against God: using the very teachings of Torah to be disobedient. The rebellion of Korach is an example. Korach did not challenge the authenticity of Torah. Rather, because God referred to the Israelites as "a holy people" (*Exodus* 19:6), Korach claimed "the entire assembly—all of them—are holy." This was a rebellion *with* God, using His words to disobey Him.

Moses predicted the future. There are those who disobey the Torah in the Name of God, as for example, permitting driving to services on Shabbos, or increasing the number of Jews by sanctioning conversions to Judaism that are not valid in halachah. They may argue that insisting on compliance with Torah is so demanding that it will drive people away from Judaism, hence it is better to abrogate portions of the Torah to make is easier for people to observe Torah.

The *yetzer hara* is very cunning. It knows that if it tells a person to willfully disobey the word of God, one will not heed it. It, therefore, deludes a person to think that God really prefers that he do the particular act, that indeed, it is a mitzvah.

One of the most serious violations of the Israelites involves the episode of the spies who caused the Israelites to feel that they could not conquer Canaan. The Zohar says that the spies knew very well that God would make them triumphant. However, they reasoned that their life in the desert was idyllic. Their food came down from heaven as the manna, the well of Miriam followed them on all their journeys, their clothes and shoes never wore out, and the Clouds of Glory not only protected them but also cleaned their clothes. Being free of all normal activities to sustain life, they could study Torah all day. If they entered the Promised Land, the miracles would cease. They would have to work the land for food, dig for water, spin the wool and harvest the flax to make clothing. If they would have to spend so much time on mundane activities, there would be little time for Torah study, and Torah study is a great mitzvah. They, therefore, discouraged the Israelites from entering the Promised Land. Better to live the idyllic life in the desert and be able to devote their entire day to Torah study.

The refusal to conquer Canaan was a flagrant defiance of God's command, but they justified it and considered it a mitzvah because they reasoned that this would indeed be in the service of God. How foolish, to think that they could better serve God by disobeying Him!

Moses realized how distorted a person's thinking can become, and he warned the Israelites, "You have been rebellious *with* God." If they were only rebellious *against* God, they could be more easily set straight. This was so much more difficult when their rebelliousness was disguised as a mitzvah, as being *with* God rather than against Him.

We should be on the alert to defend ourselves against the cunning of the *yetzer hara*. A sin remains a sin even when one thinks it may have a salutary effect.

פרשת האזינו
Parashas Haazinu

הַאֲזִינוּ הַשָּׁמַיִם וַאֲדַבֵּרָה וְתִשְׁמַע הָאָרֶץ אִמְרֵי־פִי

*"Give ear, O heavens, and I will speak;
and may the earth hear the words of my mouth"* (32:1)

The Consequences of Sin

Rashi says that Moses called upon the heavens and the earth to be witnesses that he warned Israel not to deviate from the Torah, and that if they did so, the heavens would punish them by withholding rain and the earth would punish them by refusing to yield its produce.

How are we to understand that the heavens and earth should listen and hear, and that they should inflict punishment upon the sinful? Most commentaries interpret Moses' words as poetic. However, there may be more than an allegorical interpretation.

Solomon says, "Evil will pursue the sinful" (*Proverbs* 13:21). In other words, the punishment for a sin need not be imposed upon a person externally but is contained within the sin itself. The Midrash states, "God looked into the Torah and created the world" (*Yalkut, Proverbs* 8:30). The Torah was the blueprint for Creation, and the operation of the world is contingent upon the laws of the Torah. Violation of the Torah will result in malfunction of the world.

How a particular individual is affected by a sin is a matter of Divine Providence. The harmful consequences of a sin may affect others. The dereliction of a mechanic in the maintenance of an airplane may cause great harm to others rather than directly to the perpetrator, who may indeed be punished for his negligence. However, the evil of his delinquency may immediately affect others.

So it is with violation of the Torah. How God deals with a sinful person is dependent upon His judgment. The justice of God is not to be doubted, as Moses says, "The Mighty One!—perfect is His work, for all His paths are justice" (*Deuteronomy* 32:4). We may ask, as the prophet does, "Why do the wicked succeed?" (*Jeremiah* 12:1), but the answer is beyond the human capacity to understand. The Talmud says that even Moses was denied the explanation for this (*Berachos* 7a). But the fact is that sin brings destruction in its wake.

Rashi's interpretation of the words of Moses, that the heavens and the earth will inflict punishment for deviation from the Torah, can therefore be understood as the natural consequences of sin. As the Yalkut says, the Torah was the design for the world. Violation of Torah results in upsetting the laws of nature.

This should make us aware of the awesome responsibility each person carries. Deviant behavior brings harm to the world, and even if one is not immediately affected by it, as in the case of the negligent mechanic, the harm is inevitable.

Just as we wish not to be harmed by the truancy of others, we must be cautious not to act in a way that will harm others.

הַצוּר תָּמִים פָּעֳלוֹ . . . קֵל אֱמוּנָה וְאֵין עָוֶל צַדִּיק וְיָשָׁר הוּא

"The Rock!—perfect is His work . . . a God of faith without iniquity, righteous and fair is He" (32:4)

The Unfathomable Mystery

The question of why the Jewish nation has gone through repeated episodes of unparalleled suffering has been repeatedly raised. There is no satisfactory logical answer.

We believe that God is righteous and fair, and that what has happened to us is beyond our understanding.

Moses was the one to express trust in the Divine judgment in defiance of all logic. The Midrash states that Moses entered 515 pleas requesting that the decree against his entering the Promised Land be revoked. These pleas were well-founded in logic, and God did not refute the logic of Moses' arguments. Rather, God said, "Enough! Do not speak to Me further about this matter" (*Deuteronomy* 3:26). Although Moses knew that his arguments were valid, he submitted to the infinitely greater Divine wisdom, declaring, "a God of trust without iniquity, righteous and fair is He."

> *During World War I, when people were terrified of the dangers that engulfed them and they despaired of surviving, the Chafetz Chaim said, "There is no reason for despair.*
>
> *"The Talmud says that on the first day of Adam's life, when the sun set and darkness came upon him, Adam said, 'Woe unto me! My sin has caused the world to fall into darkness. Certainly God is going to destroy the world.' He and Eve wept all night.*
>
> *"When the sky brightened with dawn and sunrise, Adam said, 'Darkness is not the end of the world. It is a natural phase, to be followed by light.'*
>
> *"Never having experienced darkness before," the Chafetz Chaim said, "Adam felt that it was the end of the world. The darkness we are in now is not the first time that we have experienced terror and suffering? Have we not had many periods of darkness in our history? As painful as they may be, there is no reason to despair. Every period of darkness in Jewish history has been followed by light."*

Our faith must supersede logic. The mystery is unfathomable. The Chafetz Chaim said, "For the one who has faith, there are no questions. For the one who lacks faith, there are no answers."

שִׁחֵת לוֹ לֹא בָּנָיו מוּמָם דּוֹר עִקֵּשׁ וּפְתַלְתֹּל

***"Corruption is not His—the blemish is His children's,
a perverse and twisted generation"*** *(32:5)*

Distortion of Logic

What is meant by "perverse and twisted?"

In *Addictive Thinking*, I described a number of ways an alcoholic can distort logic, convincing himself and others that what he says is perfectly reasonable. A closer analysis reveals the logic to be grossly defective.

For example, there are people who are reluctant to attend a meeting of Alcoholics Anonymous for fear that they might be exposed as alcoholic, but they are not concerned that their being arrested several times for drunk driving or their appearing intoxicated in public and acting foolishly will expose their problem in a much worse fashion. Or a person who has repeatedly gotten into trouble for drinking after promising that he would never touch a drop again refuses treatment because, "I can stop by myself." He believes his own lies.

This kind of thinking is not unique to the alcoholic. It is just more prominent. "Perverse and twisted" thinking is not at all uncommon in many people.

King Solomon accurately describes the thinking of a lazy person, and this is elaborated in *Yalkut* (*Proverbs* 22). "A lazy person is told, 'Your teacher is in town. Go learn Torah from him,' and he responds, 'I am afraid of meeting a lion on the way.' He is told, 'Your teacher is in the country,' and he responds, 'I am afraid there is a lion in the streets.' He is told 'But your teacher is in your house,' and he responds, 'The door is probably locked and I can't get in.' He is told, 'No, the door is open,' and he responds, 'I can't go now. I am too tired. I must rest a bit.'"

People may defend their behavior, believing their own excuses. "All of a person's ways are right in his own eyes" (*Proverbs* 16:2). The defects may be our own, but we may not recognize them, either rationalizing them or projecting them onto others.

If one does not recognize that what he does is wrong, there is no way he will correct it. That is why Moses warns us against "perverse and twisted thinking." The only way to protect ourselves against self-deception is "Ask ... your elders, and they will tell you" (*Deuteronomy* 32:7). Seeking competent advice and guidance can deter us from serious error.

שְׁאַל אָבִיךָ וְיַגֵּדְךָ זְקֵנֶיךָ וְיֹאמְרוּ לָךְ

***"Ask your father and he will relate it to you;
your elders and they will tell you"*** *(32:7)*

Modeling Deference to Authority

One of the most prevalent problems within families in our time is the refusal of children to accept the authority of their parents. There appears to have been a general erosion of authority that is usually attributed to the upheaval of the "sixties." Whatever the cause, respect for authority has dwindled. When I was in grade school, the fear of the principal was second only to fear of God. Today, principals have far greater fear of the students than the students have of them. In the secular world, court orders are frequently defied. In the non-Jewish religions, the authority of the church is often challenged. These environmental factors have had an impact on the Jewish family, and parental authority is very often ignored.

If we wish our children to respect our authority, we must model for them how this is done. Children do not learn much from lecturing, but may learn a great deal from modeling. If they do not see their parents deferring to authority, they are unlikely to defer to their parents.

This may be the message of the above verse: "Ask your father and he will relate it to you; your elders and they will tell you." The child will accept guidance from his parents if he sees his parents accepting guidance from *their* elders.

Unfortunately, we may be hard pressed to find instances where we defer to the authority of elders. Deference does not mean asking the rabbi for a decision on a question of halachah. Deference is when you have an opinion that you believe is right, but the halachic authority disagrees with you. If you accept an opinion that is contrary to yours, then you have modeled deference to authority.

Alas! If we search through our daily lives for instances where we have set aside our own opinion in deference to a rabbi, we are not likely to find many. Too often, if the rabbi disagrees with our opinion, we may seek out another rabbi who agrees with us. This is modeling rejection of authority, and if we act in this way, we cannot expect our children to be different. Youngsters are certain they are right. We must show them that even when we firmly believe we are right, we yield to authority. Children are more likely to listen to their parents when parents listen to their elders.

> *An example of deference to authority is that of R' Isser Zalman Meltzer. After he became rabbi of Slutzk, he found that his involvement in community matters encroached severely on his Torah study. Worst of all were Thursdays and Fridays. In those days there were no ready-for-the-pot chickens. The housewife bought a chicken and in the process of eviscerating it, found a lesion which required a rabbinic decision whether the chicken was kosher. In preparation for Shabbos, many chickens were brought to him for a decision on their kosher status, and on these two days he had virtually no time to learn. He agonized over this and concluded that he must vacate the position as rabbi of the community and seek an academic position as head of a yeshivah. Before acting on this decision, he sought the counsel of his mentor, R' Chaim Soloveitchik of Brisk.*
>
> *R' Isser Zalman explained the reason for his decision, citing several points in favor of having an academic position, which would allow him to advance in Torah scholarship, rather than being a community rabbi, which would stifle his growth in Torah.*
>
> *R' Chaim listened attentively, then said, "Each of the reasons is grounds enough for vacating the position as community rabbi, and when you add them up, the logic is overwhelming in favor of your decision. But there is one point that outweighs them all: this is simply not done! Never has a rabbi relinquished community duties in favor of an academic position. It is simply not done! And as far as having adequate time for Torah study, you will just have to make time."*

R' Isser Zalman's reasons for his decision were indeed validated by R' Chaim, but the ruling was that he must remain as rabbi. Against his own judgment, R' Isser Zalman did not leave his position, because R' Chaim had ruled otherwise.

That is deference to authority.

לוּ חָכְמוּ יַשְׂכִּילוּ זֹאת יָבִינוּ לְאַחֲרִיתָם

"Were they wise they would comprehend this, they would discern it from their end" (32:29)

Eventually Why Not Now?

No one wants to contemplate their end. Most people act as if they were going to live forever. It has been quipped that we live as if we will never die, and we die as if we never lived. This is a denial of reality, and one cannot possibly have an optimum adjustment to life if one denies reality.

We may verbalize an awareness of our mortality, but our actions betray our feelings. How different our behavior would be if we had an emotional grasp of our mortality.

Both as a rabbi and as a physician, I have attended people in the last days of life when their denial had broken down and they felt that their lives were coming to an end. Many have said, "If I had to do it over again, I would have spent more time with my children. I wish I had gotten to know them better." No one has ever said, "My one regret is that I did not spend more time at the office."

Why is it that this wisdom often comes when one can no longer put it to use?

But that is the irony of life: Our wisdom comes too late.

In my rehabilitation center, adolescents are admitted for treatment of alcoholism and drug addiction. When an adult patient sees a youngster being admitted, he may say, "I wish I had been that lucky, to have been treated for my addiction when I was 15. Here I am at 49, having gone through two unsuccessful marriages and having no contact with my children from either marriage. Everything I could have had in life was lost as a result of my drinking. I have no family, no home, no job."

I suggest to this man, "Why don't you speak with this youngster and tell him how fortunate he is to have an opportunity to overcome his addiction?"

A bit later this patient says, "I tried to talk to the kid, but he won't listen. He's here because the judge ordered him here. He's going to go back out and get high. But I wasn't any different than that kid. I didn't listen to people who told me that alcohol was going to destroy me."

If only we were wise! Moses says that if we were wise, we would contemplate our end when we were young. We would then live so that we would not have anything to regret when we near our end.

לִשְׁמֹר לַעֲשׂוֹת אֶת־כָּל־דִּבְרֵי הַתּוֹרָה הַזֹּאת
כִּי לֹא־דָבָר רֵק הוּא מִכֶּם כִּי־הוּא חַיֵּיכֶם

"To be careful to perform all the words of this Torah. For it is not an empty thing for you, for it is your life" (32:46-47)

The Supremacy of Torah

Why was it necessary for Moses to even say that Torah is not "an empty thing?" Furthermore, he continues, "for it is your life." It is conceivable that one would say about an item, "It is not worthless. It does have some value." But it is too drastic a contrast to say, "It is not worthless, it is your very life."

Moses was speaking prophetically to our generation, as he stated so clearly, "Harm will befall you *at the end of days*, if you do what is wrong in the eyes of God" (*Deuteronomy* 31:29).

The Jerusalem Talmud makes a sharp comment: "If you think the Torah is empty, it is the fault of your perception" (*Pe'ah* 1:1).

We are the beneficiaries of unprecedented scientific advances. Who would have dreamt that a human being would walk on the moon, that computers would be invented that can make thousands if not millions of complicated calculations in seconds, or that doctors would replace diseased kidneys, livers and even hearts. Even these epochal achievements pale before the possibilities that lie in the future: eliminating all disease by genetic engineering.

The undeniable accomplishments of science may cause parents to give their children an education that will provide them access to the world of science. However, parents may be so enthralled by the marvels of science that they may lose sight of the fact that science can provide only for the "how" of life, but not for the "why" of life. Even breaking the DNA code does not give a person an ultimate purpose for life.

The Midrash says, "You may believe that there is knowledge in the secular world, but do not believe that there is Torah in the secular world" (*Eichah Rabbah* 2:17).

Is it not paradoxical that in this age of scientific miracles, when we have the possibility of living in comfort as never before, that the drug epidemic is ravaging our youth, and that rampant violence and immorality threatens the very survival of mankind?

Some parents would never tolerate that their children be given a scanty secular education, but are perfectly willing to allow their children to be ignorant of Torah. How foolish to allow the "how" of life to totally obscure the importance of the "why" of life, of giving life meaning and value.

Yes, Moses was speaking to our generation, to which he had to say, "Be careful to perform all the words of this Torah. For it is not an empty thing for you, for it is your life."

וַיְדַבֵּר ה' אֶל־מֹשֶׁה . . . עֲלֵה אֶל־הַר הָעֲבָרִים הַזֶּה . . . וּמֻת בָּהָר
אֲשֶׁר אַתָּה עֹלֶה שָׁמָּה . . . כִּי מִנֶּגֶד תִּרְאֶה אֶת־הָאָרֶץ וְשָׁמָּה לֹא תָבוֹא

"God spoke to Moses . . . 'Ascend to this mount . . . and die on the mountain where you will ascend . . . For from a distance shall you see the Land, but you shall not enter there' " (32:48-52)

Dearer than Life

In an earlier article (Joy in Growth), I pointed out that for Moses, the meaning of life was to grow in spirituality, which is accomplished by performance of mitzvos. Having risen to the zenith of spirituality, the only possibility for further spiritual growth was the performance of those mitzvos that can be performed only in the Holy Land. Inasmuch as God decreed that he was not to enter the Holy Land, Moses saw no purpose in a life where there could be no spiritual growth, and willingly resigned himself to dying.

From his fervent pleas, as described in the Midrash, we can understand how Moses must have felt in not having the opportunity to do new mitzvos. His acceptance of death could not have been with the joy that characterized his spiritual growth.

The Gaon of Vilna says that God, therefore, gave Moses an opportunity to fulfill a new mitzvah, and formulated Moses' death in a way that it constituted two mitzvos, a positive command and a negative prohibition: "Ascend to this mountain... and die on the mountain where you will ascend... For from a distance shall you see the Land, but you shall not enter there." By ascending the mountain, by not entering the Land and by dying on the mountain, Moses performed a new mitzvah, and at the last moment of his life was able to elevate himself above his dazzling spiritual heights.

Before performing a mitzvah, it is customary to declare, "I am hereby performing this mitzvah as God commanded." It is related that before his death, the Baal Shem Tov said, "I am hereby performing the mitzvah according to the Divine command, 'For you are dust, and to dust shall you return' " (*Genesis* 3:19).

Although there are many people who are observant of Torah, their performance of mitzvos is often perfunctory. It is not unusual to see people reciting the morning prayers in a rather hurried fashion, then running off with enthusiasm to the office or place of business where they hope to earn money. They may not reflect on the fact that the reward of doing a mitzvah properly far exceeds any monetary gain.

The Talmud relates that R' Akiva rejoiced at the opportunity to give up his life for God. Great *tzaddikim* were able to rejoice with *mesiras nefesh* (self-sacrifice). We should, at the very least, be able to have great joy when performing mitzvos that do not require any sacrifice.

פרשת וזאת הברכה
Parashas VeZos HaBerachah

וְזֹאת הַבְּרָכָה אֲשֶׁר בֵּרַךְ מֹשֶׁה אִישׁ הָאֱלֹקִים אֶת־בְּנֵי יִשְׂרָאֵל לִפְנֵי מוֹתוֹ
And this is the blessing that Moses, the man of God, bestowed upon the Children of Israel before his death (33:1)

Reprimand Can Be a Blessing

It would seem that this chapter should have begun with, "This is the blessing" rather than with, "*And* this is the blessing." The conjunction "and" implies that this, too, is a blessing, i.e., in addition to the foregoing portion. But the previous portion, *Haazinu*, hardly appears to be a blessing. Rather, it is a very sharp reprimand.

The Torah is telling us that not only are the manifest blessings in this portion of the Torah blessings, but that the reproof in *Haazinu* is also a blessing. As Solomon says, "The wounds inflicted by someone who loves you are trustworthy, whereas the kisses of an enemy are superfluous" (*Proverbs* 27:6). Bilaam heaped lavish blessings on Israel (*Numbers* 23:7-24:9), yet the Talmud says that all his blessings reverted to curses (*Sanhedrin* 105b). It was Moses' love for and devotion to Israel that caused him to reprimand them for their failings and to warn them of the grave consequences that will result from straying from the teachings of Torah.

Solomon says "Do not admonish a scoffer, lest he hate you; admonish a wise man, and he will love you" (*Proverbs* 9:8). A wise person will appreciate that admonishment is a blessing, in that it helps a person lead a decent and proper life.

King David said, "When those who would harm me rise up against me, my ears hear (their doom)" (*Psalms* 92:12). *Akeidas Yitzchok* (*Kedoshim*) points out that the verse ends with "my ears hear," and that "their doom" is an interpretation of the verse. However, the verse can also mean, "When my enemies agitate me, I listen." David is saying that listening to his friends does little for his spiritual growth, because they are likely to praise him. One does not learn much from praises. However, one's adversaries are prone to criticize, and may point out one's defects that friends may overlook. Criticism may stimulate growth, and growth is a blessing.

The portion of *VeZos HaBerachah* is a manifest blessing. By using the conjunction "*And* this is the blessing," the Torah is telling us that *Haazinu*, too, is a blessing. A sincere reprimand from someone who cares for you should be considered a blessing.

וְזֹאת הַבְּרָכָה אֲשֶׁר בֵּרַךְ מֹשֶׁה אִישׁ הָאֱלֹקִים אֶת־בְּנֵי יִשְׂרָאֵל

And this is the blessing that Moses, the man of God, blessed the Children of Israel (33:1)

Goodness That Is Sweet

Shevet Yehudah says that this verse can be read as, "This is the blessing that Moses blessed," i.e., Moses blessed the blessing. Even blessings should be blessed.

We believe that everything God does is for the good. However, in the *Amidah* we say, "Who bestows beneficial kindnesses." Is it not redundant to say "benefical kindnesses?" Are not all kindnesses beneficial? Similarly, on Rosh Hashanah Eve we pray for a "good and sweet year." All of God's actions are good and kind, but inasmuch as they may come disguised and packaged in distress, we pray for goodness and kindness that are sweet as well as beneficial.

Someone complained to the Chafetz Chaim about bad things that happened to him. The Chafetz Chaim corrected him. "You may say that these things were bitter, because a life-saving medicine, while undeniably good, may taste bitter. But do not say they are bad. Everything emanating from God is good, even if we experience it as bitter."

Moses referred to the enslavement in Egypt as "the iron crucible" (*Deuteronomy* 4:20), which Rashi describes as something which purifies gold and purges it of foreign elements. "The reason God subjected the Israelites to the harsh and cruel years of the Egyptian exile was to purge them of their basic qualities and make them eager to accept a Torah that would place many limitations on their natural and habitual desires" (*HaKsav V'HaKabbalah*).

The purification of Israel was an unquestionable good, but Moses knew first-hand how terribly painful it was. He therefore "blessed his blessings," so that they should all be effective in a sweet way.

תּוֹרָה צִוָּה־לָנוּ מֹשֶׁה מוֹרָשָׁה קְהִלַּת יַעֲקֹב

The Torah that Moses commanded us is the heritage of the Congregation of Jacob (33:4)

The Acquisition of Torah

The Talmud says that as a soon as a child can speak, the father should teach him Torah. Which part of Torah? The verse, "The Torah that Moses commanded us is the heritage of the Congregation of Jacob" (*Succah* 42a).

Why this was particular verse chosen as the very first Torah words that a child should be taught? *Tosefes Berachah* answers that a minor is not competent to enter into a transaction. Hence, he cannot take possession of anything. However, if he is an heir to a bequest, it automatically becomes his. An inheritance does not require an act of acquisition. While a minor cannot acquire by transaction, he can *inherit*.

Every Jewish child is an heir to Torah. If a child inherits a property, it is the responsibility of parents or parental surrogates to look after the property, since the child is unable to do so. If the others fail to look after the child's interests, they are derelict in their responsibilities.

Inasmuch as Torah is a child's inheritance, it is the duty of parents to see that it does not fall into disrepair as a result of neglect. Failure to preserve a child's Torah inheritance for him is a serious dereliction.

Is it not shameful that many Jewish children know who Henry Wadsworth Longfellow and Walt Whitman were, but have no knowledge of R' Yehudah Halevi? They may know about Patrick Henry but not about R' Akiva. They may be familiar with the name "Hillel" only because it is the name of a college campus organization, but they do not have an inkling who this great sage was. In absence of a knowledge of Torah which would give meaning to their lives, they may drift off to destructive cults.

Parents who fail to provide children with a proper Jewish education are betraying a lack of respect for their heritage. How can we expect to be respected by others if we lack self-respect?

A Jewish child who enters the world owns the Torah. It is the parents' sacred duty to cultivate this possession for him.

וּלְלֵוִי אָמַר . . . כִּי שָׁמְרוּ אִמְרָתֶךָ וּבְרִיתְךָ יִנְצֹרוּ

Of Levi he said . . . "They have observed Your word and Your covenant they preserved . . . (33:8).

Nurturing Torah

In the Hebrew text, the word for "observed" is *shomru*, and the word for "preserved" is *yintzoru*. R' Yechezkel Abramski said that these two words are not completely synonymous. A *shomer* is a guard who sees that no harm should come to his charge, but he does nothing to improve it. A *notzer* is one who cares for something in a way that improves it. A *shomer* of an orchard guards against thieves or animals that might take the fruit. A *notzer* is one who waters the plants, weeds the soil and fertilizes it, so that the trees produce more and better fruit.

The Levites, who were assigned the task of teaching Torah to Israel, had to fulfill both functions. They had to be the guardians of the Torah to see that its laws were not tampered with, and they had to teach Torah in such a manner that expanded the wisdom of Torah.

Before his death, the King of Prussia told his son to make sure that he expanded the borders of the kingdom. When the son said that he felt the kingdom was large enough, his father said, "If you do not expand it, it will eventually shrivel."

The Torah, being the Divine wisdom, is infinite. There is no end to what we can learn from Torah. There are seventy different facets to Torah (*Osiyos D'R' Akiva*), and each facet can again be presented in many ways.

Historically, there were the Saducees, who claimed to accept only the written Torah without the Oral Law that accompanied it. Even though they zealously guarded the Written Torah, the Saducees disappeared from the map. The Oral Torah, which teaches us how to live according to the written Torah, has allowed generations of Torah scholars to continually draw refreshing waters from its infinite well. To the degree that we are *notzrim*, caretakers of the Torah who nurture it, to that degree we survive. A *shomer* may patrol the orchard to make sure that no one breaks in, but unless there is a *notzer*, someone who cares for the trees, they may wither.

The function of the Levites is now incumbent on every Jew, to both guard and nurture the Torah.

וּלְזְבוּלֻן אָמַר שְׂמַח זְבוּלֻן בְּצֵאתֶךָ וְיִשָּׂשכָר בְּאֹהָלֶיךָ

Of Zebulun he said, "Rejoice, O Zebulun in your excursions, and Issachar in your tents" (33:18)

Can Money Bring Happiness?

Rashi cites the Midrash, which describes the partnership between Zebulun and Issachar. Zebulun engages in commerce, and supports Issachar's devotion to Torah study.

The idea that Zebulun should rejoice in his commercial undertakings raises some questions. Moses is certainly referring to joy that is sustained rather than ephemeral joy.

My forty years of psychiatric practice has brought me in contact with wealthy clients, whose commercial success afforded them little happiness. Rather than this being an isolated phenomenon, I believe that the words of Solomon indicate that it may be universal. After describing the utmost in luxury, comfort and wealth that was his, Solomon states, "I did not deprive myself of any kind of joy. Indeed, my heart drew joy from all my activities. Then I looked at all the things that I had done, it was clear that it was all futile and a vexation of the spirit" (*Ecclesiastes* 2:10-11). Fleeting joy, only to result in frustration.

"One who loves money will never be satisfied with money" (ibid. 5:9). "Sweet is the sleep of the laborer, whether he eats little or much; but the satiety of the rich does not let him sleep" (ibid. 5:11).

The satiety of the rich does not let him sleep because it is so ephemeral. The appetite for more wealth feeds upon itself.

> *One of the first stories I heard from my mother in my childhood was that of a poor man who was granted a wish. He wished that he would have a purse that would never be empty. He was given a magic purse which contained a dollar, and when he removed the dollar another dollar appeared in its place. After several weeks he was found dead atop a huge pile of dollars.*

Solomon tells how wealth can bring happiness. "Honor God with your wealth; then your provisions will be filled with satisfaction" (*Proverbs* 3:9-10). And of those who support Torah he says, "She (wisdom of Torah) is a tree of life for those who hold on to her, and those who support her find happiness" (ibid. v. 18).

Yes, wealth can bring a modicum of happiness, but it is of brief duration. It may be compared to the euphoria of a person who uses a chemical that brings on a superb sensation of well-being, but as soon as that sensation is dissipated, the discontent is profound, resulting in the pursuit of more chemical euphoriants.

Zebulun can rejoice in his commerce only when his wealth is directed to the support of the Torah scholar. The satisfaction of having enabled Torah scholarship is never lost.

זֹאת הָאָרֶץ אֲשֶׁר נִשְׁבַּעְתִּי לְאַבְרָהָם לְיִצְחָק וּלְיַעֲקֹב ...
הֶרְאִיתִיךָ בְעֵינֶיךָ וְשָׁמָּה לֹא תַעֲבֹר
וַיָּמָת שָׁם מֹשֶׁה עֶבֶד־ה׳ בְּאֶרֶץ מוֹאָב עַל־פִּי ה׳ ...
וְלֹא־קָם נָבִיא עוֹד בְּיִשְׂרָאֵל כְּמֹשֶׁה

*"This is the Land which I promised to Abraham,
to Isaac and to Jacob ... I have let you see it with your own eyes,
but you shall not cross over to there." So Moses, servant of God,
died there in the Land of Moab, by the mouth of God ...
Never again has there arisen in Israel a prophet like Moses* (34:4-10)

The Death of Moses

The Talmud asks, "Inasmuch as the entire Torah was written by Moses, how could he truthfully write 'Moses died?'" The Talmud answers that God dictated the words, and Moses wrote them tearfully (*Bava Basra* 15a).

How does that answer the question? Because to God there is no past, present and future. Tenses are a measure of time, and time is finite. There is no way to measure infinity. To God, everything is an eternal present. When God said "Moses died," it was the truth before God.

Some commentaries explain that Moses wept because he had to write about himself, "Never again has there arisen in Israel a prophet like Moses." Being "the most humble person on earth" (*Numbers* 12:3), it gave him great pain to write such adulation about himself.

The Midrashic accounts of Moses' death are heartrending.

"When Moses heard that his death was decreed, he drew a circle around himself and said, 'Master of the universe! I will not budge from this circle until you revoke the decree.' Moses wore sackcloth and covered himself with earth and pleaded before God: 'Master of the universe! You know how much effort I put forth and how much I suffered to have the Israelites believe in You, How much agony I went through to implant Torah and mitzvos among them. I thought that just as I agonized with them, I will see their moment of glory when they enter the Promised Land. And now You say to me, 'You shall not cross over to there!' In Your Torah You say that a laborer must be paid his wage before the end of the day (*Deuteronomy* 24:15). Are You making the words of the Torah meaningless? Is this the wage I receive for my forty years of labor in making the Israelites into a trustworthy and holy nation?'

"God responded, 'It is My decree.'

"Moses entreated and wept, 'Where can I turn to for mercy? Master of the universe! These legs that ascended to heaven, the face that received the Divine countenance, the hands that received the Torah—these shall lie in the dust?'

"God responded, 'That is My will. This is the way the world is conducted. Each generation has its leader. Until now it was your turn to serve Me, and now it is the turn for your disciple, Joshua, to serve Me.'

"God called to Moses' soul, 'My daughter, I had assigned you to be within the body of Moses for 120 years. Now the time has come for you to leave it.'

"At that moment, God kissed Moses (So Moses, servant of God, died there in the Land of Moab, *by the mouth of God*), and with the kiss, Moses' soul joined God."

Other faiths may glorify a miraculous birth. Moses was born of a normal relationship, "A man of the tribe of Levi married a daughter of Levi," but he died as a man of God.

וּלְכֹל הַיָּד הַחֲזָקָה וּלְכֹל הַמּוֹרָא הַגָּדוֹל אֲשֶׁר עָשָׂה מֹשֶׁה לְעֵינֵי כָּל־יִשְׂרָאֵל . . . בְּרֵאשִׁית בָּרָא אֱלֹקִים אֵת הַשָּׁמַיִם וְאֵת הָאָרֶץ

"And by all the strong hand and awesome power that Moses performed before the eyes of all Israel" (34:12)
"In the beginning of God's creating the heavens and the earth" (Genesis 1:1)

The Infinity and Omnipresence of Torah

On Simchas Torah we conclude the cycle of the annual reading of the Torah and promptly read the first portion of Genesis, initiating the cycle for the coming year. There is no break in Torah. Torah is like a circle, without beginning and without end.

Torah is the wisdom of God. Rambam states that in contrast to man, whose wisdom is acquired, God's wisdom is one with God Himself (*Hilchos Teshuvah* 5:5). Just as God is infinite, with no beginning and no end, so is Torah without beginning or end.

The uninterrupted continuity of Torah also means that there can be no part of life that is separated from Torah. We observe Torah not only when we study Torah and perform mitzvos, but also when we eat, sleep, engage in commerce or in any other activity. Not only are there guidelines in Torah for every facet of human behavior, but everything we do should be directed toward the goal of observance of Torah.

Torah is the heart of a Jew and is the heart of Judaism. There is no Jewish life without Torah.

The last letter in the Torah is *lamed*. The first letter of the Torah is *beis*. The continuity of Torah juxtaposes these two letters, *lamed* and *beis*, to form the word *lev* (heart). The continuity of Torah teaches us that Torah is our heart, individually and collectively.

Not only is the heart indispensable to life, but the heart also distributes nourishment to the entire body. Torah provides the spiritual nourishment that enables us to be spiritual beings rather than simply *homo sapiens*, hominoids with some intellect. It is the Torah that gives us the distinction and the dignity of being human.

Inasmuch as the Torah is a reflection of God, when one absorbs Torah, one introjects, as it were, God. Moses, whose entire existence was Torah, earned the title "the man of God" (*Deuteronomy* 33:1). When Rambam says that "every person can be like Moses," he means that every person can become Godly to the extent that one absorbs Torah.

In the blessing for the reading of the Torah, we say, "He implanted eternal life within us." We have the capacity to be eternal with Torah.